MW00559155

The War against Trucks
Aerial Interdiction in Southern Laos
1968-1972

For sale by the Superintendent of Documents, U.S. Government Printing Office
Internet: bookstore.gpo.gov   Phone: toll free (866) 512-1800;   DC area (202) 512-1800
Fax: (202) 512-2250 Mail: Stop SSOP, Washington, DC 20402-0001

ISBN 0-16-072494-5

The War against Trucks
Aerial Interdiction in Southern Laos
1968-1972

Bernard C. Nalty

Air Force History and Museums Program
United States Air Force
Washington, D.C. 2005

Library of Congress Cataloging-in Publication Data

Nalty, Bernard C.
  The war against trucks : aerial interdiction in southern Laos, 1968-1972 /
  Bernard C. Nalty.   p. cm.
  Includes bibliographical references and index.
    1. Vietnamese Conflict, 1961-1975--Aerial operations, American. 2. United
States. Air Force--History--Vietnamese Conflict, 1961-1975. 3. Vietnamese
Conflict, 1961-1975--Campaigns--Laos. 4. Ho Chi Minh Trail. I. Title.

  DS558.8.N37 2005
  959.704'348'09594--dc22   2004026960

Foreword

The Air Force History and Museums Program has prepared accounts of the United States Air Force and the war in Southeast Asia according to a design that reflects the compartmentalized nature of the conflict itself. Besides the special studies like the illustrated history (*The United States Air Force in Southeast Asia, 1961–1973: An Illustrated Account*) and the monographs, some of them quite lengthy, on topics like rescue or tactical airlift, the Air Force history program has published volumes on the air wars over South Vietnam and Cambodia, North Vietnam, and Laos. This book is the last of three recounting operations in Laos, one of them dealing with the war in the northern part of that kingdom and the other two with aerial interdiction in the south.

This history covers the critical years from 1968 through 1972, when the Air Force carried out the Commando Hunt series of aerial interdiction campaigns against the Ho Chi Minh Trail in southern Laos, trying, in conjunction with ground actions, to use air power and electronics to impede the movement of men and supplies from North Vietnam to the battlefields of South Vietnam. Conducted during the time the United States was withdrawing ground forces and turning the war over to the greatly strengthened armed forces of South Vietnam, Commando Hunt sought to prevent a North Vietnamese offensive that would take advantage of the declining U. S. presence. That attack did not come until March 1972 and not only stopped short of overrunning South Vietnam, but also was a setback for the Hanoi government and a cease-fire agreement. The invasion, however, signaled the end of Commando Hunt, for the South Vietnamese did not take over the electronic surveillance network—with its computer, sensors, and communications equipment—that made the series of aerial interdiction operations possible.

"The real war," said Walt Whitman, "will never get in the books." Yet, even though they cannot conjure up the realities of death and suffering, heroism and sacrifice, books like this have a purpose, offering the counsel of the past to help today's policy makers. What useful principle can they derive from an account of the events of a few years in a unique part of the world? Stripped of all that links it to a particular time, place, and strategy, this narrative warns them that a determined enemy may be able to use geography, climate, and ingenuity to blunt the cutting edge of technology. Against such a foe, what seems flawless in theory or has succeeded brilliantly in tests may fail in actual combat, but what fails on one battlefield may succeed years later on another. In the last analysis, military genius does not reside in compiling lists of lessons learned, but in analyzing the past and applying its distilled wisdom in new, perhaps unique, circumstances.

Preface

This history recounts an ambitious attempt by the Air Force to interdict traffic on the Ho Chi Minh Trail of southern Laos, as part of a plan to support the war in South Vietnam by impeding the flow of North Vietnamese troops and military supplies into South Vietnam. Secretary of Defense Robert S. McNamara intended initially to establish a manned barrier guarding the demilitarized zone between the two Vietnams, while using electronic sensors and computers to detect and analyze movement on the Ho Chi Minh Trail so that aircraft could attack the troops and cargo bound for the battlefields of South Vietnam. Only the electronic portion went into service, and the Ho Chi Minh Trail became the object of seven successive Commando Hunt operations, beginning in the fall of 1968 and lasting until the spring of 1972, when a North Vietnamese invasion of the South changed the nature of the war. Although aircraft of the other services participated in this extended campaign of aerial interdiction, the Air Force assumed the greatest responsibility for both equipment and execution.

The book begins by summarizing Secretary McNamara's reasons for substituting an interdiction campaign for the bombing of North Vietnam and then describes the early efforts at aerial interdiction, which were delayed by the need to shift resources for the defense of the Marine Corps outpost at Khe Sanh in northwestern South Vietnam, just south of the demilitarized zone. Because technology held the key to attacking the Ho Chi Minh Trail, the aircraft and other equipment used in the Commando Hunt series receive extensive treatment early in the narrative. Next come the air campaigns themselves, supplemented by ground operations from Laos and South Vietnam, that over the years, with varying success, engaged every component of the Ho Chi Minh Trail through southern Laos and in Cambodia—roads and trails, bivouacs and storage areas, waterways and pipelines, truck traffic, and for a brief time, troop movements. In addition to discussing this activity, the narrative addresses the unsuccessful attempt to Vietnamize interdiction without transferring the entire array of special equipment created or modified for that purpose. The volume also deals with the application of the technology that maintained surveillance over the trail and covers the problem of locating North Vietnamese artillery after the invasion of South Vietnam in 1972. A final chapter evaluates the effectiveness of the air-supported electronic barrier and concludes that the concealment readily afforded by the jungle, the resilience of the North Vietnamese and their control of the tempo of military operations, the limitations of the available technology, and the lack of adequate information about the trail complex combined to prevent the Commando Hunt operations from doing more than inconveniencing the enemy.

In writing this second of two volumes dealing with aerial interdiction in southern Laos, my research benefited from the assistance of several individuals. Mr. Jacob Van Staaveren, the author of the companion volume on southern Laos, suggested the use of certain records collections with which he was already familiar. Lt. Col. Richard R. Sexton, USAF, and Maj. Victor B. Anthony, USAF, the coauthors of a volume dealing with the air war in northern Laos, provided helpful guidance. (Military ranks listed, incidentally, are the highest held by individuals while serving in the Office of Air Force History and its successors.) Capt. William A. Buckingham, Jr., USAF, an intelligence specialist in Southeast Asia during the Vietnam War, unearthed a number of hard-to-locate reports of prisoner of war interrogations; and Capt. Ashby D. Elmore, USAF, assembled a series of maps showing the known North Vietnamese infiltration routes that composed the Ho Chi Minh Trail.

Research for the book required extensive use of material not found in Air Force collections, and I am grateful to all who helped me obtain access to sources of this kind. I owe special thanks to Dr. Jeanne Mintz, Lt. Col. Robert W. Oliver, USMC (Ret.), and Ms. Mary C. Remmy, all of whom served in the Office of Director of Defense Research and Engineering; to Mr. Frank Tapparo and Mr. Charles Pugh, members of what was then the Directorate of Planning and Evaluation in the Office of Secretary of Defense; and to Mr. S. A. Tucker, then the Deputy Historian, Office of Secretary of Defense, who succeeded in explaining why an outsider like me should have access to files maintained in that organization. Dr. Oscar P. Fitzgerald arranged for the loan of Navy records, Mr. Vincent Demma made Army materials available, and Dr. Robert J. Watson cooperated fully, both as a member of the Historical Division, Joint Chiefs of Staff, and as its head. Dr. Watson's successor in charge of the Historical Division, Mr. Willard J. Webb, proved equally helpful, and Dr. Ronald H. Cole, a member of Mr. Webb's staff, provided perceptive comments and useful suggestions. Much of the assistance rendered by these individuals resulted directly or indirectly from the extensive contacts among military historians cultivated by Mr. Max Rosenberg, the senior historian at that time in the Office of Air Force History.

Along with Mr. Rosenberg, almost the entire staff of the Office of Air Force History and its successors contributed in one way or another to the completion of this volume, including Maj. Gen. John W. Huston, USAFR, Dr. Richard H. Kohn, Col. David A. Tretler, USAF, Dr. Richard P. Hallion, Dr. Stanley L. Falk, Mr. Warren Trest, Mr. Herman Wolk, Mr. Jacob Neufeld, Col. Ray L. Bowers, USAF, Col. John Schlight, USAF, Lt. Col. Drue L. DeBerry, USAF, Dr. B. Franklin Cooling, III, Dr. Alfred M. Beck, Lieutenant Colonel Sexton, Lt. Col. Vance O. Mitchell, USAF, Major Anthony, Capt. Earl H. Tilford, Jr., USAF, Captain Buckingham, Mr. Carl Berger, Mr. Van Staaveren, Dr. Wayne W. Thompson, Dr. Elizabeth H. Hartsook, Mr. Lawrence J. Paszek, Mr. Eugene P.

Sagstetter, Mr. David Schoem, Mrs. Gail Guido, Mr. William C. Heimdahl, MSgt James R. Cason, Dr. George M. Watson, Jr., Mr. Samuel Duncan Miller, Mrs. I. Jewell Newman, Mrs. Ann Caudle, and SrA Terry Nance.

Although these, and probably others I have inadvertently slighted, share in whatever strengths the book may have, I am solely responsible for its weaknesses of fact or interpretation.

Bernard C. Nalty

The Author

Before retiring in 1994, Bernard C. Nalty was a senior historian in the Office of Air Force History. He earned a B.A. from Creighton University and an M.A. from Catholic University and served as an officer in the U.S. Army from 1953 to 1955. He was chief editor and coauthor of *Winged Sword, Winged Shield* (1997), the Air Force's two-volume 50th-anniversary history, and has written *Air War over South Vietnam, 1968–1975* (2000); *Air Power and the Fight for Khe Sanh* (1973), an Air Force monograph on the Vietnam War; *Tigers over Asia* (1978), an account of the Flying Tigers during World War II; *Strength for the Fight: A History of Black Americans in the Military* (1986); and two pamphlets dealing with the Marine Corps in World War II — *Cape Gloucester: The Green Inferno* (1994) and *The Right to Fight: African American Marines in World War II* (1995). He is coauthor with Henry I. Shaw, Jr., and Edwin T. Turnbladh of *Central Pacific Drive* (1996), a history of Marine Corps operations in World War II. With Morris J. MacGregor, Jr., he edited the thirteen-volume *Blacks in the United States Armed Forces: Basic Documents* and its single volume abridgement *Blacks in the Military: Essential Documents* (1981).

Contents

Illustrations

Maps

Photographs

CHINA

NORTH VIETNAM

★ HANOI

BURMA

LAOS

Gulf of Tonkin

VIENTIANE
★

UdornS

Nakhon
Phanom S

THAILAND

S Takhli

S Korat

Ubon
S

S Phu Bai

S Da Nang

Chu Lai S

SOUTH

S Don Muang
★ BANGKOK

U-Tapao
S

Pleiku
Phu Cat
S

Qui Nhon S

CAMBODIA

Tuy Hoa S

VIETNAM

Nha Trang S

Cam Ranh Bay S

Phan Rang S

Gulf of Thailand

PHNOM
PENH ★

Tan Son
Nhut S Bien Hoa
★ SAIGON

S
Binh
Thuy

South China Sea

Southeast Asia

★ National Capital

S Principal U.S. Air Base

The War against Trucks
Aerial Interdiction in Southern Laos
1968-1972

Introduction

The Coming of a Surveillance System

In 1968, the air war in southern Laos intensified, as the United States embarked on a new aerial strategy, limiting (and then ending) the bombing of North Vietnam. Instead, attacks increased in Laos on the routes of supply and reinforcement that sustained the North Vietnamese campaign to conquer South Vietnam and unify under communist rule what had once been French Indochina. Following World War II, Ho Chi Minh, a communist revolutionary and Vietnamese nationalist, led an uprising that toppled the French. However, the Geneva Conference of 1954, in which the great powers, East and West, sought to resolve the major issues in the Orient, set up two Vietnams, North and South, separated by a demilitarized zone along the 17th parallel, North latitude. What began as a temporary expedient, pending unification by means of elections, rapidly evolved into a permanent boundary. The United States provided most of the economic and military support needed by South Vietnam, while the communist North relied for assistance on the Soviet Union, China, and the Soviet-dominated nations of eastern Europe. An uneasy truce prevailed for a time between the two Vietnams, as Ho Chi Minh in the North and Ngo Dinh Diem in the South consolidated control over their respective nations.[1]

In the late 1950s, North Vietnam, with Ho Chi Minh and the communist party firmly in control, embarked on a campaign to take over the South by force. The Central Military Committee at Hanoi, the North Vietnamese capital, at first had visions of a largely self-sustaining revolution ignited by a cadre of five hundred to seven hundred South Vietnamese, who had come to the North when the two Vietnams separated. Plans called for this small force to return south and recruit and train perhaps seven hundred self-defense platoons, which would form the cutting edge of the army of liberation, arming them with some seven thousand weapons captured from the French. The revolutionaries (whom the South Vietnamese government soon begin calling Viet Cong, short for Vietnamese communists) could not, in fact, sustain themselves and required routes of communication and supply.

Brig. Gen. Vo Bam assumed the burden of establishing these links between North and South. He initially thought, he later acknowledged, of merely setting up supply points in southernmost North Vietnam, near the demilitarized zone, where carrying parties from the South could pick up cargo destined for the battlefield. As the leaders chosen to conquer South Vietnam pointed out, such a plan was doomed to fail, for the Viet Cong would not have the manpower to fight a war and at the same time smuggle supplies past South Vietnamese patrols. The solution, Vo Bam realized, lay in using North Vietnamese, rather than Viet Cong, to build, maintain, and operate a route carved through the formidable Truong Son mountains, where the terrain discouraged patrolling.

The North Vietnamese organization that undertook the task of supplying the war in the South was the 559th Transportation Group, its numerical designation reflecting its activation in May, the fifth month, of 1959. The unit went to work enlarging the narrow trails, some of them used by communist troops during the war against the French, that wound through ravines and valleys among the mountains that vary from eighteen hundred to three thousand feet in height and define the boundary between the Vietnams and Laos. The engineers faced a sobering challenge, for a variety of dangers lurked in this wilderness. Ahead lay swiftly moving streams that over the centuries had attacked the porous limestone ridges, gouging out caves and creating pillar-like karst formations. Jungle blanketed the mountains, with dense thickets of bamboo flourishing at lower elevations beneath a thick canopy of trees, while above twenty-four hundred feet, towering evergreens replaced the other growth. Wild animals, including tigers and elephants, prowled the forest, but the region's human inhabitants posed no real threat, for they were primitive tribesmen who hunted and practiced a crude form of agriculture, setting fires in areas of sparse natural growth to clear land for crops. Since the region's subsistence farming could produce little additional food for the North Vietnamese, a portion of the cargo traveling this route would have to feed the men of the 559th Transportation Group. Also, the prevalence of disease, especially malaria, forced the planners at Hanoi to provide medicine and medical care.

The climate of southern Laos further impeded the efforts of the transportation group in its struggle to tame the mountains. Each year between May and September, high atmospheric pressure over the Indian Ocean sends the moisture-laden southwest monsoon blowing over Laos, bringing torrential rain that turns trails to mud and sends rivers and creeks rampaging from their banks to flood low-lying areas. Only during the northeast monsoon, which originates over the mainland of Asia and normally brings dry weather from November through April, could North Vietnamese engineers, and those Laotians serving as laborers, engage in extensive construction.

As initially laid out, the route between North and South, which came to be called the Ho Chi Minh Trail, followed the eastern slope of the Truong Son range, crossing South Vietnamese Route 9 on a fairly open plateau just south of the demilitarized zone. The first shipment of supplies reached the Viet Cong in August 1959, but the route had to be changed early in 1960 after South Vietnamese troops, patrolling Route 9, discovered weapons that had been dropped by careless porters. The government at Saigon, the capital of South Vietnam, immediately tightened security along the highway. The 559th Transportation Group reacted to the more vigorous patrolling of northwestern South Vietnam by shifting the main infiltration effort west of the Laotian border to the vicinity of Tchepone, a village that soon became an important way station on the relocated Ho Chi Minh Trail.[2]

This move marked the first in a succession of changes as the North Vietnamese modified the trail complex to sustain an expanding war. An extensive enlargement of the Ho Chi Minh Trail began in the summer of 1964, during a period of political chaos in Saigon following the overthrow and murder of Ngo Dinh Diem, when South Vietnam seemed ripe for the plucking. Col. Bui Tinh of the People's Army of Vietnam has recounted how he trudged southward over the trail during the dry season of 1963–1964 and returned with a report that helped confirm the government's belief that the prompt introduction of North Vietnamese troops would win the war. Since thousands of troops and hundreds of tons of cargo, instead of hundreds of men and tens of tons of supplies, would begin traveling the trail, the 559th Transportation Group had to improve roads to accommodate large numbers of trucks, establish supply dumps, and prepare hospitals, living quarters, and stocks of food and medicine not only for the group itself but also for the infiltrating soldiers.[3]

During 1965, the United States intervened with air and ground forces to prevent a South Vietnamese collapse, the government at Hanoi countered with more troops of its own, and a war of attrition ensued in which the United States tried, by means of mobility and firepower, to inflict losses so severe that the enemy would abandon his effort to conquer South Vietnam.[4] As the ground war intensified, the Ho Chi Minh Trail kept pace. According to Maj. Gen. Dinh Duc Thieu, who headed North Vietnam's General Logistics Department, heavier truck traffic began rumbling over the improved infiltration route in 1965, and within seven years the network totaled some four thousand miles of roads, rivers, and trails, some of them paralleling one another and providing a bypass if an attack should block a major artery in the system. In the broadest sense, infiltration began where supplies entered North Vietnam, at the border with China or at Haiphong and the other North Vietnamese ports. Men and material usually entered the Ho Chi Minh Trail at Mu Gia or Ban Karai Pass and exited in the Provinces of Pleiku, Dar Lac, and Kontum in South Vietnam. An extension through Cambodia channeled men and cargo into Tay Ninh Province northwest of Saigon.

To operate, maintain, and defend the logistics network, all the while improving and expanding it as necessary, required a vast number of North Vietnamese soldiers and Laotian auxiliaries. North Vietnam's General Thieu, who was responsible for sustaining the war in the South, placed the total at thirty thousand, but U.S. estimates exceeded thirty thousand, including truck drivers, porters, engineers, laborers, antiaircraft gunners, and medical technicians. The unceasing efforts of those who toiled in southern Laos enabled what one North Vietnamese general described as "a river of revolutionary forces" to move southward, bringing the troops and supplies needed for combat and for the operation of the trail. In the beginning, when a few tons of cargo traveled the Ho Chi Minh Trail on bicycles and the backs of porters or on pack animals, the 559th Transportation Group established about a hundred way stations, roughly one-day's journey apart, and assigned each a small contingent to move supplies from that station to the next. In the dry season, the troops could sometimes double the usual pace and complete two trips in a single day. Certain of the way stations had elaborate living quarters, facilities for cooking, medical dispensaries, and large storage bunkers, where cargo could be kept for distribution during the rainy season. The practice of dividing the trail into operating segments continued after the introduction of trucks; a group of drivers assumed responsibility for moving supplies from one station to the next, much as the porters, handlers of pack trains, and bicyclists had done. Besides the roads and trails, supplemented by streams, that carried cargo, U.S. intelligence believed that a separate network, a component of the Ho Chi Minh Trail, but having its own way stations and operating cadre, existed for the exclusive use of troops infiltrating through Laos to fight in South Vietnam.[5]

In short, the North Vietnamese campaign to overthrow the government at Saigon and establish a unified, communist Vietnam ruled from Hanoi depended on the Ho Chi Minh Trail. Gen. William C. Westmoreland—who became Commander, U.S. Military Assistance Command, Vietnam, during 1964, before the United States assumed control of the ground war—realized the importance of the trail and hoped to establish a blocking position athwart it. He did not, however, have enough combat battalions to sever the infiltration routes in southern Laos while at the same time hunting down the enemy throughout South Vietnam. The war of attrition, on which he embarked in 1965, took precedence, and a lodgment in Laos, which would have required Presidential approval for extending the ground war there, remained only a concept, as Westmoreland tried to bleed the North Vietnamese until they abandoned their designs on South Vietnam.[6]

Instead of attempting to influence the battle in South Vietnam by blocking the Ho Chi Minh Trail in Laos, the United States tried to produce that result by attacking North Vietnam directly. In February 1965, before the arrival of U.S. ground forces and the launching of a war of attrition, Air Force and Navy aircraft struck the North, at first in retaliation for North Vietnamese attacks within the South and afterward in Operation Rolling Thunder, a succession of bombing "programs" that lasted three and one-half years. Initially, Rolling Thunder attacked the will of the communist leadership in Hanoi. Robert S. McNamara, President Lyndon B. Johnson's Secretary of Defense, believed that gradual intensification of the bombing would convince Ho Chi Minh that he risked the destruction of his nation if he persisted in waging war against the South. McNamara and Johnson reasoned that the communist leader, rather than face the loss of everything his people had struggled to build, would pull back, either unilaterally or by means of negotiations providing for the survival of an independent South Vietnam. In using the bombing to test the enemy's will, McNamara sought to avoid destroying at the outset the things that he believed the Hanoi government most wanted to save—a steel mill, for instance, or a modern electrical generating plant—lest he, in effect, kill the hostage and deprive North Vietnam of an incentive to call off the war.

Ho Chi Minh did not react as the U.S. leadership had expected. Viet Cong forces, aided by an increasing number of North Vietnamese troops, kept up the pressure on South Vietnam. Rolling Thunder continued, but instead of persisting in attacks on the enemy's resolve, the operation sought to weaken him militarily by bombing various classes of targets, the destruction of which seemed likely hamper the communist forces in the South. Although now directed against structures like bridges and buildings, rather than at an intangible like a leader's determination, the bombing remained subject to certain constraints. The Johnson administration, which tended to think in terms of a communist bloc, remembered how China had intervened during 1950 to save North Korea from destruction and was concerned that, if the United States forced North Vietnam to the brink of collapse, the Chinese might again come to the rescue. Moreover, the President and his principal civilian advisers, in attempting to coerce North Vietnam into calling off its aggression against the South, tried consciously to avoid unleashing the kind of violence that would alienate the allies of the United States. From time to time Rolling Thunder came to a halt to give Ho Chi Minh a chance to call off the war in the South or at least offer to engage in negotiation, but the pauses served only to grant North Vietnam a respite in which to recover from the aerial attacks.

Once the purpose of the bombing shifted from breaking the enemy's will to weakening his ability to fight, the military officers who planned the Rolling Thunder strikes began searching for a decisive category of targets; within the restraints adopted by the administration, they sought to cut the single thread that, when broken, would cause North Vietnamese military power to unravel, much as German might had done after the destruction of the oil industry in 1944 and 1945. By mid-1966, the North Vietnamese transportation net had come under attack, but without appreciable effect on the war in South Vietnam, and the air campaign then embraced oil storage. Attacks on the tank farms at Hanoi and Haiphong produced raging fires and towering columns of smoke and seemed to have dealt North Vietnam a staggering blow in terms of the oil destroyed. Analysts reported the destruction of 80 percent of the storage facilities at Haiphong, while flames consumed an estimated thirty-four thousand metric tons stored at Hanoi.[7]

The loss of oil did not result, however, in negotiations or the cessation of hostilities, for the status of North Vietnam's petroleum reserves proved less precarious than first believed. The tank farms specialized in short-term storage, as fuel moved swiftly from these sites to small, scattered, and carefully camouflaged dumps, which rapidly multiplied, and from them to the using units. Once again the bombing had no immediate impact on the fighting in the South. As the weeks passed, it became apparent that the enemy would have oil enough to continue the war. The difficulty of locating all the small fuel dumps strewn throughout the North, and President Johnson's unwillingness to attack those located in villages where air attacks might maim or kill noncombatants, prevented the oil campaign from being pursued further.[8]

Before the bombing shifted from transportation and the interdiction within North Vietnam of supplies destined for the Ho Chi Minh Trail and ultimately the battlefields of South Vietnam to the destruction of North Vietnamese oil reserves, a group of civilian consultants offered to assess for Secretary McNamara overall progress in the war. During the spring of 1966, four distinguished scientists— George B. Kistiakowsky and Karl Kaysen of Harvard and Jerome Wiesner and Jerrold Zacharias of the Massachusetts Institute of Technology—approached the Department of Defense about arranging a "summer study" of "technical possibilities relating to our military operations in Vietnam." The department readily accepted the offer, since all four possessed impressive credentials: Kistiakowsky had worked on the atomic bomb during World War II and later served as science adviser to President Dwight D. Eisenhower; Wiesner had advised President John F. Kennedy; Zacharias had contributed to the development of atomic weapons after World War II; and Kaysen, an economist, had recently assisted McNamara in the Office of Secretary of Defense. The Institute for Defense Analyses, a "think tank," arranged funding for the study through the organization's Jason Division, which handled short-term projects by outside scholars. After the scientists had chosen the key members of a staff that peaked at sixty-seven members, the Jason Summer Study met for the first time at Wellesley, Massachusetts, on June 13, 1966, for ten days of briefings by officials of the Department of Defense. Afterward the membership divided into four working groups, and in September the summer study produced four reports that, taken together, concluded that Rolling Thunder was having no real effect on the fighting in South Vietnam. Instead of pursuing further the bombing of North Vietnam, the scientists recommended the creation of an air-supported barrier to reduce the flow of supplies into the South by concentrating on vulnerable choke points outside the North.

The idea of such a barrier against infiltration did not originate with the Jason Summer Study; indeed, McNamara asked specifically that the group evaluate such a plan. The basic concept had emerged in January 1966, when Roger Fisher, a professor at the Harvard Law School, suggested it in a memorandum to John T. McNaughton, the Assistant Secretary of Defense (International Security Affairs). Fisher, who from time to time served as an adviser to McNaughton, became convinced that Rolling Thunder had failed and offered as an alternative a line of barbed wire and mines designed to impede infiltration and generate targets for aerial attack. McNaughton passed the proposal to Secretary McNamara and sounded out the Joint Chiefs of Staff. The Joint Chiefs, in turn, solicited the comments of the Commander in Chief, Pacific, Adm. U. S. Grant Sharp, who recommended against such an undertaking, condemning the barrier as a wasted effort that would require too many troops, take too long to build, and have little likelihood of succeeding. Despite the objections of Admiral Sharp, whose views reflected General Westmoreland's commitment to the use of firepower and mobility to wear down the enemy, the Secretary of Defense remained so fascinated with the idea that he gave the Army the money to begin research and development on the weapons and techniques needed for systematically attacking traffic on the Ho Chi Minh Trail.

The ten-day briefing at the outset of the Jason Summer Study may well have included a summary of the progress the Army had made on the barrier proposal. In

8

any event, by the beginning of the study, McNamara had made up his mind to test the concept, and research and development began before the reports of the scientists reached his desk. The participants in the study knew so much about the progress in devising electronic equipment and techniques for its use that they went beyond merely endorsing the barrier and explained in some detail just how it would work. Kistiakowsky, Wiesner, Kaysen, Zacharias, and their colleagues described an "air supported barrier" against infiltration by truck or on foot through the demilitarized zone or along the Ho Chi Minh Trail in southern Laos. They called for placing acoustic sensors, modified versions of a type used in antisubmarine warfare, at carefully plotted locations where the devices would listen for targets that air power could attack. Aircraft would scatter thousands of aspirin-sized "gravel" mines along infiltration routes believed used by troops or trucks; these munitions did not inflict casualties, but when detonated by tires or boots they emitted a noise that the sensors would broadcast to relay aircraft overhead for retransmission to a control center. Since the center had charted the precise location of the sensors, analysts there could determine just where the movement had occurred and dispatch aircraft to attack.

The Jason Summer Study warned, however, that the effectiveness of the barrier would not become immediately apparent, since men and supplies already en route when the mines and sensors were emplaced would enable the North Vietnamese, at least for a time, to sustain the war in the South at the existing level of violence. Moreover, the enemy could devise countermeasures—tricking the sensors, sweeping the mines, building shelters against air attack, setting up antiaircraft batteries, and even finding new routes through areas not yet under electronic surveillance. The attempt to impede traffic on the Ho Chi Minh Trail would therefore require patience in the search for results, perseverance in the detailed photographic coverage of southern Laos, and ingenuity in the development of the weapons and tactics necessary to retain the advantage over an alert and resourceful enemy.

The scientists realized that interdiction of the trail would require a substantial effort, costing perhaps eight hundred million dollars exclusive of aircraft, but they considered the undertaking worthwhile. Whatever the cost and attendant difficulties, the barrier should produce better results than Rolling Thunder was achieving. Disappointment over the effects of the air war against the North, along with the mounting losses in crews and aircraft, had caused Secretary McNamara to embrace the notion of a barrier against infiltration. In short, he had anticipated the findings of the participants in the summer study that bombing could neither shatter North Vietnamese resolve nor destroy the war-making potential of an essentially agricultural nation that imported the materials of war from factories and refineries immune to air attack. The findings of the panel reports reaffirmed McNamara's decision to go ahead with the barrier project, which he now entrusted to Lt. Gen. Alfred E. Starbird of the Army, who would operate under the guidance of the Director of Defense Research and Engineering in the Office of Secretary of Defense. Although Admiral Sharp, who was responsible for air operations against the North, continued to oppose the projected barrier, the Joint Chiefs of Staff endorsed the undertaking, provided that the necessary money was not diverted from other, possibly more important, military projects.[9]

Convinced that Rolling Thunder had failed at its current level of intensity, Secretary McNamara believed that to step up the attacks could only increase U.S. losses without inflicting proportionate damage on the enemy. Isolating one aspect of the air war, the attacks on the logistics network inside North Vietnam that supported the war in the South, the Secretary of Defense conceded that this one aspect of Rolling Thunder had forced the Hanoi government to employ some three hundred thousand men to operate, defend, and repair the logistics system; but that was not enough. Supplies and reinforcements continued to move, despite a sortie rate, a compilation of flights by individual aircraft, that reached twelve thousand per month. An examination of past losses convinced McNamara that the price of intensifying the air war would be four aircraft, their crews, and $20 million for every thousand additional sorties flown each month. This sacrifice, moreover, would have only a marginal impact on the North Vietnamese, who, in his opinion, could improve their defenses and repair the additional damage with a comparatively minor increase in manpower and expenditures.

Besides being concerned about the cost of an escalating air war in comparison to the likely results, Secretary McNamara believed that Rolling Thunder had become self-defeating; instead of forcing North Vietnam to abandon its attempt to overwhelm the South, the air war seemed to him to present an obstacle to a negotiated settlement that would preserve South Vietnamese independence. Instead of more bombing of the North, he wanted less or none at all. Thus far, the leadership at Hanoi had responded neither to the bombing nor to temporary suspensions of the aerial attacks, and McNamara concluded that Ho Chi Minh would not negotiate until he could claim that the bombing had been halted unconditionally. For this reason, the Secretary of Defense favored stopping the bombing, or at least shifting the focus of the air war away from heavily populated Hanoi and Haiphong. If North Vietnam did not respond as he expected, the air war could resume or expand.

The idea of halting or reducing the Rolling Thunder attacks to encourage the beginning of negotiations toward a settlement reflected McNamara's view of the bombing as a limited and carefully controlled operation designed to change the policy of North Vietnam rather than to destroy the nation itself. The United States could "bomb the North sufficiently to make a radical impact on Hanoi's political, economic, and social structure," he readily acknowledged; but to do so "would not be stomached either by our own people or by world opinion, and it would involve a serious risk of drawing us into an open war with China." He thus endorsed the conclusion of the Jason Summer Study that there was no feasible level of the bombing that could force Hanoi to call off the war.

In October 1966, McNamara incorporated his views on Rolling Thunder and the anti-infiltration barrier in the draft of a memorandum for the President, which he circulated for comment to the Joint Chiefs of Staff and other interested agencies. Although he outlined his proposal to trade an end to the bombing campaign for the beginning of negotiations with the North, he offered the idea as a possibility for the future rather than an immediate alternative to continued air attacks. Indeed, he made just three basic recommendations: that Rolling Thunder remain at the existing level, even though the Joint Chiefs of Staff wanted it intensified; that General Westmoreland receive only modest increase in his forces, instead of the large increment he was seeking; and that the anti-infiltration system become operational.

Although they did not advocate all-out bombing, not even with conventional weapons, the Joint Chiefs of Staff believed that only the use of increased force could achieve the ultimate goal of a secure and independent South Vietnam. Rather than merely commenting on Secretary McNamara's draft, they prepared their own memorandum, also intended for President Johnson, that recommended stepping up Rolling Thunder to include attacks on ports, powerplants, irrigation dams, and the nation's only steel mill. In the opinion of the Joint Chiefs, to stop or cut back on the air war would amount to giving away "one of the . . . trump cards in the hands of the President." The United States, they maintained, should cut back or suspend the bombing of North Vietnam only in response to some conciliatory action by the Hanoi government; Rolling Thunder should never be offered "as a carrot to induce negotiations."

Of McNamara's three recommendations—holding the line on the bombing of North Vietnam, giving Westmoreland a minimum of reinforcements, and building the barrier against infiltration—only the barrier survived pretty much intact. Debate continued on the level of the air war. For the present, Rolling Thunder would go ahead, essentially unchanged, but the basic issue remained unresolved. For now the President refused to risk cutting back; McNamara would try to convince him of the need for restraint, while the uniformed leadership argued for an expanded list of targets. General Westmoreland got additional men, fewer than he sought, though more than the Secretary of Defense would have liked.[10]

This one success, the commitment to try to interdict infiltration into South Vietnam, had its roots in Secretary McNamara's disenchantment with Rolling Thunder. Ironically, during August of 1967 he found himself called on to defend that very air campaign, in which he had lost confidence, before a group of Senators who were concerned that he had hobbled the nation's airmen by interfering in the conduct of the bombing. Headed by John C. Stennis, a Democrat from Mississippi, the Preparedness Investigating Subcommittee of the Senate Committee on Armed Services quickly confirmed that a sharp divergence of opinion separated the civilian and the military leadership of the Department of Defense. Whereas the Secretary of Defense, who hoped to freeze the bombing at existing levels before ultimately reducing or ending it, insisted that casualties in South Vietnam had no direct relation to the intensity of the air war in the North, officers like Admiral Sharp and Gen. John P. McConnell, the Chief of Staff of the Air Force, maintained that heavier bombing meant fewer U.S. soldiers killed or maimed. Similarly, McNamara denied that bombing in the North could prevent the military leaders in Hanoi from delivering enough supplies to sustain the war in the South, although his military subordinates argued that sealing the port of Haiphong and severing the rail line to China would appreciably reduce the amount of cargo reaching the communist forces on the battlefield. Understandably, in view of their opinions, the uniformed witnesses urged an extension of the bombing and the closing of the ports of North Vietnam, recommendations that the subcommittee endorsed. Indeed, Senator Stennis and his colleagues made it clear that they had lost confidence in the Secretary of Defense. The senators branded as a failure his policy of limited and carefully controlled attacks, and although neither the subcommittee nor the officers that testified before it advocated indiscriminate bombing, the panel's report concluded that it was "high time . . . to allow the military voice to be heard in connection with the tactical details of military operations."[11] The hearings resulted in some relaxation of the restrictions on targets, but President Johnson remained wary that China might intervene if the United States planted mines in the waters off Haiphong.[12]

In December 1967, some three months after the subcommittee's hearings, with McNamara in effect a lame duck—Clark M. Clifford, an attorney and adviser to Democratic Presidents since Harry S. Truman, would replace him on March 1—the electronic barrier that McNamara advocated faced its operational test. The concept for the anti-infiltration system called for two components. One was a line of conventional manned strongpoints, barbed wire, and minefields across the comparatively open expanse of Quang Tri Province south of the demilitarized zone; the other extended the barrier across the roads and trails of southern Laos, using mines and electronic sensors, for the most part planted by air, to locate trucks and troops for attack by U.S. aircraft.

The conventional segment of the barrier employed sensors planted by hand, but otherwise represented no advances in technology that might require extensive testing. Construction began in the spring of 1967, but gathering the building material and the trucks to haul it proceeded slowly. Improving the road net to survive the pounding of heavily laden trucks cost additional time. The delays enabled the North Vietnamese to prepare a violent welcome for the troops engaged in the work, and artillery fire thoroughly disrupted the project, which ground to a stop early in 1968. Instead of the mutually supporting bunkers and the minefields, barbed wire, and sensors that protected them, this portion of the barrier ultimately consisted of no more than four major bases—Khe Sanh in the west, Camp Carroll, Con Thien, and Gio Linh—from which the military assistance command intended to conduct mobile operations to intercept North Vietnamese infiltrators.[13]

The complicated electronic surveillance network designed to monitor the Ho Chi Minh Trail in southern Laos presented a far greater technological challenge than the obstacles in the demilitarized zone. As the pace of operational testing of the air-supported barrier increased, Navy-supplied Lockheed OP–2E patrol bombers and Air Force helicopters planted two types of sensors along the suspected trace of the Ho Chi Minh Trail. The parachute of the acoustic model was supposed to become entangled in the jungle growth so that the sensor would hang unobserved, picking up sounds, including the detonation of gravel mines scattered by Air Force pilots from Douglas A–1E attack craft and set off by troops or trucks. The second kind, a seismic sensor, fell through the trees and buried its snout in the soil in order to monitor vibrations in the earth, such as those caused by vehicles passing nearby. The sensors operated either continuously or at fixed intervals, listening for signs of movement and sending signals, by way of a Air Force Lockheed EC–121 relay aircraft, to the Infiltration Surveillance Center at Nakhon Phanom Air Base in Thailand. Task Force Alpha, commanded by Maj. Gen. William P. McBride of the Air Force, assumed responsibility for operating the surveillance center. A computer at Nakhon Phanom stored the data the sensors reported; target analysts called up that information, evaluated it, and when they found what appeared to be a worthwhile target, alerted an airborne battlefield command and control center, a modified Lockheed C–130 transport. An Air Force controller inside the flying command post then called in an air strike.

The test of the electronic portion of the barrier consisted of two phases, one to evaluate effectiveness of Task Force Alpha against trucks and the other to determine its usefulness in locating infiltrating troops. Each part had its own separate site and time, so that analysts could more easily identify and interpret the results. Since truck traffic seemed to funnel through the valleys south of Mu Gia Pass and west of the demilitarized zone, an area there, nicknamed Mud River, served as the testing ground for the vehicular surveillance system. The sensors seeking to detect foot traffic kept watch over the trails that crisscrossed Dump Truck, a crescent-shaped region north and west of the intersection of the demilitarized zone with the Laotian border. Operations in Mud River began early in December and by the end of the month had demonstrated that Task Force Alpha could determine the location of truck convoys precisely enough to permit successful aerial attacks. The scene shifted to Dump Truck, but operations there had barely begun when the enemy surrounded the marines at Khe Sanh, who now needed the sensors for the ultimately successful defense of that base.[14]

While attention focused on Khe Sanh, units of the Viet Cong and the People's Army of North Vietnam moved into position to attack the cities of South Vietnam during a cease-fire for Tet, the celebration of the lunar new year. The U.S. Military Assistance Command had evidence that the enemy was preparing for some kind of attack, but the threat to Khe Sanh seemed much more dangerous; after all, the Marine outpost was being compared publicly to Dien Bien Phu, the isolated French bastion that communist troops had overrun in 1954, in effect forcing France to call off the war. Moreover, border strongpoints other than Khe Sanh had experienced fierce, though unsuccessful, attacks. Despite these diversions, which focused attention away from the major cities, the Tet offensive got off to a bad start; some units failed to get word of a last-minute postponement and struck on the night of January 29–30, thus giving warning of the main effort 24 hours later. Nevertheless, the scope and fury of the operation proved startling, as fighting erupted from Hue in northern South Vietnam, to Saigon itself, to the villages of the Cau Mau peninsula in the southernmost part of the country. The ancient citadel in the heart of Hue, where

The War against Trucks

Vietnamese kings had once held court, remained in enemy hands for some three weeks, but elsewhere the enemy soon fell back after sustaining grievous losses. So severe were these casualties that the Viet Cong all but ceased to exist as a fighting force, leaving the conduct of the war in the South to elements of the North Vietnamese army. Moreover, Khe Sanh held out; the climactic assault never came, and a column of Army air cavalry linked up with marines from the base on April 6, after encountering resistance that was described as "stiff."[15]

The Tet offensive ended in a tactical defeat for the enemy, who lost tens of thousands killed and wounded, but neither gained ground permanently nor toppled the government of South Vietnam. The effects on that government were mixed: atrocities committed by communist forces when they controlled Hue angered the very people the killings were supposed to have coerced, aligning them with the Saigon regime; but the fighting created perhaps another million refugees nationwide, who turned for help to leaders ill-prepared to feed or house them. Unfortunately, the refugees tended to become dependents rather than supporters of the government of South Vietnam.[16]

The sudden onslaught against the South Vietnamese cities had its greatest impact in the United States, where dissatisfaction with the war was deepening. A portion of the populace agreed with the findings of the recent hearings by the Stennis subcommittee, blamed McNamara for using military force ineffectually, and urged that the air war be intensified. Another, more vocal segment had turned against the war. Those in both groups acted from a variety of motives. Some of those who sought to step up the aerial attacks believed that the expansion of communism in Southeast Asia had to be stopped and that bombing could help do this, others argued that McNamara's restrictions should be abandoned because they needlessly increased the danger to airmen, and still others felt that the United States should fight to win, or get out. Another argument in favor of increased attacks on the North pointed out that the United States had promised to preserve the independence of South Vietnam and should bomb as necessary to redeem that pledge.

Similarly, foes of the war objected on various grounds. They might, for example, consider all wars immoral or oppose just this one because a mighty nation, in Operation Rolling Thunder, was bombing an obviously weaker one, because an outsider was interfering in what was perceived as a struggle among Vietnamese, or because the United States appeared to be squandering on distant battlefields the resources and energies needed to improve life at home. Personal considerations also played a part in turning people against the war; some surely objected to the conflict because they or their sons might be called on to risk their lives in a war that seemed no closer to a resolution, despite two years of heightened U.S. involvement, than it had in 1965. Inspired by such varied motives, an antiwar movement gathered strength and influence until, by the end of 1967, it had organized demonstrations that attracted tens of thousands of protesters.[17]

Although the strength of the antiwar movement could easily be overestimated because of its ability to assemble crowds and capture the headlines, the popular consensus that supported the war was beginning to erode. On the one hand, Americans questioned the wisdom or morality of fighting the war; on the other, they objected to the way in which it was being fought. Actually, support for the Vietnam conflict, as measured by the response by a sampling of the public to the question whether the nation's involvement was right or a mistake, peaked late in 1965 and began a decline that slowed from time to time or briefly reversed. On an average throughout 1967, roughly half of those questioned said that the United States had been right in going to war in Southeast Asia.[18]

Late in 1967 President Johnson took steps to restore the slowly fading support for his policy in Southeast Asia. In order to buoy the spirit of the people, he turned to General Westmoreland, who presented an optimistic view of progress during a brief visit to the United States. For example, in a speech before Congress, the general said that the enemy, though not yet beaten, had been badly hurt, and he suggested that the war might be won in two years. Granted that Westmoreland did mention the possibility of enemy counterattacks and further hard fighting, the thrust of his message remained overwhelmingly confident, and his optimism proved contagious, heightening the shock of the Tet offensive.

Looking beyond the immediate future, and the role of Westmoreland in shoring up support for the war, the President called on a panel of senior advisers, who met whenever requested, and asked their advice how to unite the nation behind the war. This group, nicknamed the "Wise Men," included former Secretary of State Dean G. Acheson, retired Generals Matthew B. Ridgway and Maxwell D. Taylor, and former Secretary of the Treasury C. Douglas Dillon. Meeting well before the Tet offensive, the Wise Men expressed general approval of the President's policies, although they warned at the time that the seemingly "endless inconclusive fighting" in Southeast Asia had become "the most serious single cause of domestic disquiet." The advisers therefore suggested a new approach to the war, less costly in lives, that would return to the South Vietnamese increasing responsibility for combat operations. In effect, the U.S. had taken over the war, beginning in 1965. Not yet convinced of a need to change strategies, the President nevertheless indicated that in the near future he would review the conduct of the war.

Such a review took place after the Tet offensive. Although shaken by the attacks, the President's first impulse had been to fight back, sending Westmoreland whatever troops he needed. The Chairman of the Joint Chiefs of Staff, Gen. Earle G. Wheeler of the Army, hoped to capitalize on this attitude to reestablish the sorely depleted strategic manpower reserve. Wheeler arranged for Westmoreland to ask for 206,000 men, which would require a large-scale mobilization of reservists, as well as increased draft calls. The President decided that this number was far greater than Westmoreland could use, as indeed was true since Wheeler and Westmoreland intended to restore the reservoir of manpower available to meet emergencies throughout the world. The administration chose to send only token reinforcements to South Vietnam and to call up a small number of reservists, whose mobilization was in part justified by North Korea's seizure of the intelligence ship *Pueblo* as it patrolled in international waters off the Korean coast. In effect, the Johnson administration imposed a ceiling on U.S. involvement in the war in Vietnam.

The ceiling was already in place when news of Westmoreland's request for 206,000 men surfaced in the press. The accounts did not disclose that the majority of these troops would reconstitute the strategic reserve in the United States or that the President had decided to do far less. Meanwhile, reporting from South Vietnam continued to stress the audacity of the enemy and the confusion he had sown. In these circumstances, the massive increase, believed by the public to be destined for Westmoreland, looked like proof that Ho Chi Minh had surprised an overconfident Johnson administration and inflicted a bad beating on U.S. forces. No wonder that voters in New Hampshire rallied behind the antiwar write-in candidate, Senator Eugene J. McCarthy of Minnesota, who stole the headlines from the President by receiving more than 40 percent of the vote in the Democratic Presidential primary.

Amid these chaotic circumstances, the administration reviewed its policies as the Wise Men had suggested back in November, and this group participated in the latest review, which produced a strategy aimed at bringing about a negotiated settlement while turning the war over to the South Vietnamese. Indicative of the new relationship developing between the United States and South Vietnam, President Johnson sent only 13,500 reinforcements to Westmoreland's command, whereas the South Vietnamese President, Nguyen Van Thieu, added 135,000 men to his army. In an attempt to encourage negotiations, Johnson announced during a televised address on March 31, 1968, that he was suspending the bombing of North Vietnam except in the panhandle region stretching northward from the demilitarized zone. Although the strategy had changed, the objective remained the same; President Johnson continued to believe the United States could somehow persuade Hanoi to agree to a settlement that would ensure the survival of an independent South Vietnam. He left that task to another President, however, for he used the same speech to declare that he would not seek reelection in November.[19]

Thus ended the escalation of U.S. efforts that began in 1965. For the United States, the war had reached its peak intensity, at least in terms of its own involvement. As the Wise Men had suggested, U.S. participation in the fighting would decrease, following the absorption of these last reinforcements, as the South Vietnamese assumed greater responsibility for fighting the war. The shield to protect this change would not be the bombing of the North—already scaled back, it came to an end on November 1, 1968—but aerial interdiction of the Ho Chi Minh Trail, as envisioned by the Jason Summer Study.

Chapter One

A Time of Transition

The testing of Task Force Alpha's Infiltration Surveillance Center at Nakhon Phanom in Thailand signaled a transition in the air war in southern Laos. Armed reconnaissance—the use of fighter-bombers or attack aircraft to patrol known or suspected segments of the Ho Chi Minh Trail and strike targets of opportunity— gave way to strikes against truck convoys and far less frequently, troops detected by electronic sensors. Aerial photography, forward air controllers, and reconnaissance or ambush teams that penetrated short distances into the maze of roads and trails had produced general knowledge of the Ho Chi Minh Trail and the traffic it carried; the sensors themselves would provide further, more specific information. The operational tests during late 1967 and early 1968 against vehicular traffic in the Mud River area and infiltrating troops in Dump Truck proved encouraging, though not entirely conclusive. The sensor strings reporting to the analysts at Nakhon Phanom clearly demonstrated an ability to detect truck traffic in Mud River, but because Task Force Alpha had to curtail the tests in Dump Truck and divert the sensors to the defense of Khe Sanh, the Surveillance Center could not determine how accurately the equipment would locate soldiers traveling the trail network. At Khe Sanh, the information from sensors detected patterns of movement by enemy forces and thus generated targets for artillery and aircraft, but the North Vietnamese were massed boldly there against a compact objective, the Marine outpost, rather than moving cautiously along a concealed route toward a distant battlefield.

Before Task Force Alpha could function as planned, the United States and South Vietnam had to win the fight for Khe Sanh and together with their South Korean allies, crush the Tet offensive. Although of far greater magnitude in both geographic scope and impact on U.S. policy, the Tet battles had less effect on the aerial interdiction campaign in southern Laos than did the battle for Khe Sanh, which continued through the month of March. Indeed, the Tet offensive proved comparatively brief, considering its intensity; the worst of the fighting ended by mid-February 1968, and on the 24th, South Vietnamese troops recaptured the citadel at Hue, a victory that signaled the failure of any plan for a general uprising to topple the Saigon regime.[1]

The Tet offensive and encirclement of Khe Sanh resulted in a shifting of the aerial resources used in Operation Rolling Thunder away from North Vietnam to targets in the South. This change of focus in the air war coincided with wretched flying weather over the North that would have impeded Rolling Thunder regardless of events in South Vietnam. Indeed, during February, according to Pacific Air Forces statisticians, airmen attacking the North encountered the worst weather "that we have faced . . . in the last three years." Bad weather and the increased demand for air support in the South caused the number of sorties by Navy and Air Force squadrons against the North to decline to an "all-time low" in February, some 62 percent below the monthly average for 1967.[2]

Although the diversion of aircraft from Rolling Thunder made sorties available for other operations, the fight for Khe Sanh had a special impact on aerial interdiction in nearby southern Laos. The Marine Corps combat base lay just a short distance from the Ho Chi Minh Trail, and the North Vietnamese troops, apparently massing for an assault, presented targets suited to the same aircraft, ranging from modern jet fighter-bombers to reconditioned Douglas A–26 light bombers and modified North American T–28 trainers, that otherwise would have attacked the infiltration network. Largely because of the fight for Khe Sanh, the total number of sorties flown by tactical aircraft against targets in Laos declined by some 25 percent in February, as fighters and attack bombers aided the surrounded marines, temporarily abandoning armed reconnaissance of the trail and strikes set up by ground reconnaissance teams. Although more than six thousand attack sorties took place in Laos during February, almost one thousand of them went after targets in the northern region, far from the Ho Chi Minh Trail. The effort in northern Laos represented an increase of roughly 25 percent over January and reflected a flurry of hostile activity there. During March, as the threat to Khe Sanh diminished, the number of tactical sorties against infiltration in southern Laos increased from five thousand to more than six thousand despite the waning of the dry season and the appearance of thunderstorms brooding over the trail. The number of sorties elsewhere in Laos remained higher than usual since the enemy continued to be active in northern Laos, near the border with North Vietnam.[3]

The defense of Khe Sanh had an even more pronounced effect on B–52 operations. During February and March, all B–52 strikes in Laos battered the region just west of the base and provided direct support for the embattled marines. In March, for example, the bombers flew 1,463 sorties in defense of Khe Sanh, 184 of them against the enemy massing in nearby Laos, and only 200 against targets elsewhere in South Vietnam not related to the survival of the Marine base. General Westmoreland, the Commander, U.S. Military Assistance Command, Vietnam, concentrated his B–52 sorties in the area around Khe Sanh because he believed the bombers provided the most effective instrument for killing and demoralizing the hostile troops poised there. The failure of the enemy to storm the base convinced him he was right; after the relief of Khe Sanh during the first week of April, he told the crews of these aircraft that "the thing that broke their back was basically the fire of the B–52s."[4]

The successful defense of the Khe Sanh combat base, besides absorbing air strikes that might otherwise have hit the Ho Chi Minh Trail, focused interest on the value of sensors. For instance, the marines directing Khe Sanh's defense credited sensor data for an artillery barrage that frustrated a night attack on one of the bastion's hilltop outposts. As if to demonstrate the importance of sensors, a portion of this particular assault force apparently branched off after the devices had reported the movement, advanced over ground not under electronic surveillance, and stormed a different objective. The defenders beat back the second attack, but only after savage fighting; in contrast, artillery fire based on sensor data easily blunted the other thrust. During the encirclement of Khe Sanh, sensors monitored enemy troop movements, sometimes reporting directly to a Marine Corps fire support coordination center equipped with portable monitoring gear, but usually indirectly by way of the Task Force Alpha Infiltration Surveillance Center at Nakhon Phanom. Once the pattern of sensor activations revealed the scheme of maneuver, the defenders reacted with air power or artillery to engage the hostile units.

Col. David E. Lownds, the Marine commander at Khe Sanh, praised the sensor as "a valuable tool in the effective coordination of exceptionally responsive and particularly flexible firepower," though not a "panacea" for all the problems of static defense. The new technology could not replace "courage, sacrifice, professional skill and dedication," but in his opinion, it enhanced these traditional military virtues. The sensor strings planted around the combat base had enabled the alert and highly trained defenders "to quickly locate enemy assembly areas and destroy or render ineffective the main force" before it could launch a decisive attack. Of greatest importance to Lownds, that the sensors did the work of manned outposts, saving lives even as the devices helped to kill North Vietnamese; the electronic sentinel was expendable, "which is something that your son and my son are not."[5] While the marines prevailed at Khe Sanh, the Defense Communications Planning Group, responsible for developing the electronic components of the air-supported monitoring system known as Igloo White, took steps to safeguard surveillance technology and make sure that the sensor remained the valuable tactical tool that had so impressed Lownds. To discourage the North Vietnamese from removing electronic sensors or disassembling them for study and the possible development of countermeasures, ordnance technicians loaded some with explosive charges. The boobytrapped version, which looked exactly like the normal seismic intrusion detector, entered service in May 1968, as the year's southwest monsoon rains were falling.[6]

Before the fate of Khe Sanh had been decided, while Lownds was acquiring the experience on which he based his favorable evaluation of the sensor, officials began descending on Nakhon Phanom to observe the Surveillance Center in action. An example of technology in all its complexity, the center proved a magnet for distinguished visitors. As the fight for the Marine stronghold entered its final phase, Seymour J. Deitchman, a member of the Advanced Research Projects Agency of the Department of Defense and a participant in the Jason Summer Study, arrived at the Thai air base. He reported receiving assurances that "the antipersonnel part of the system," as employed at Khe Sanh, "was working well beyond expectations." Where the sensors were in place, they consistently enabled artillery to fire on groups of men whose "order of magnitude" could be determined to the nearest hundred, but the electronic devices could not calculate the effects of artillery or air strikes on the units they located. Although successful in acquiring targets around Khe Sanh, if not in assessing the death and destruction visited on them, the Surveillance Center had not, in Deitchman's opinion, contributed at all to the interdiction of enemy supplies and reinforcements destined for South Vietnam. "It strikes me," he told the Director of Defense Research and Engineering, Dr. John S. Foster, Jr., "that with the tight encirclement of Khe Sanh and the concentration of the barrier systems on its approaches, North Vietnamese troops are still free to bypass the area."[7]

Deitchman further concluded that the antipersonnel element of the electronic barrier would not "perform its originally designed mission, helping to block the Ho Chi Minh Trail,"[8] an estimate that proved accurate even after the diversion of sensors to Khe Sanh had ended. Except around a strongpoint like the Marine base, where avenues of movement were comparatively few, locating troops promised to be infinitely more difficult than detecting vehicles. Brig. Gen. George J. Keegan, Jr., chief of intelligence for the Seventh Air Force, feared that success at Khe Sanh might place exaggerated emphasis on the value of sensors in finding troops. He accurately predicted that years might pass before the antipersonnel network could function effectively and at an acceptable cost.[9]

The likely inability of the infiltration barrier to detect the passage of troops resulted in part from the gravel mines then in use. These weapons, designed to detonate when stepped on and trigger nearby sensors, proved useless, as did a slightly larger and more powerful type of mine capable of inflicting wounds as it alerted the sensors. The fault lay in the rain and high humidity of southern Laos, which quickly neutralized the explosive charge in both. To demonstrate the failings of the mines, Col. Roland K. McCoskrie, commander of the 56th Air Commando Wing at Nakhon Phanom, drove a staff car over gravel that had been exposed to the elements and failed to cause even one explosion.[10] Even if the mines had worked to perfection, the detection of infiltrating troops would still have remained largely a matter of luck. Task Force Alpha knew so little about the trails used by North Vietnamese soldiers that planners could not design sensor fields effective against foot traffic. Not until late 1971 would the Surveillance Center acquire enough data to plan a systematic attack against the web of trails spun beneath the jungle canopy.[11]

Although more successful than the antipersonnel measures, the effort to disrupt truck traffic did not proceed during the early months of 1968 as the authors of the Project Jason report had hoped. "We were told at Nakhon Phanom," Deitchman advised Dr. Foster in early March, "that about 15 percent of the [sensor] detections are followed by air strikes and that the numbers of strikes are controlled by Seventh Air Force in Saigon, rather than by the barrier system command [Task Force Alpha]." Deitchman feared that the Surveillance Center had become "simply a sophisticated target detection system for air strikes that are mounted in the same way as previous . . . strikes, rather than an integrated recce-strike [reconnaissance-strike] system as was originally conceived."[12]

Meanwhile, Gen. William W. Momyer, commander of the Seventh Air Force , which waged the air war in South Vietnam and southern Laos, opposed the course of action advocated by Deitchman and his colleagues in the Jason Summer Study. To some extent, doctrinal considerations influenced the Air Force officer. Westmoreland, late in the battle for Khe Sanh, agreed to place the 1st Marine Aircraft Wing under Momyer's operational control, a concession to the Air Force doctrine calling for centralized control over tactical aviation within a combat theater. Determined to retain control over its own squadrons, the Marine Corps had vigorously but unsuccessfully opposed Westmoreland's decision, carrying the argument up the chain of command and attracting the attention of President Johnson. Even though he acknowledged the "paradox" that the Surveillance Center lacked control over aircraft to attack targets discovered by its sensors, General Momyer pointed out that, "as single manager of USAF [United States Air Force] and, more recently, Marine air resources, I am faced with the task of supporting the total war with its innumerable individual tasks." To place a specific force under Task Force Alpha, he told Air Force Secretary Harold Brown, would undermine his control of "limited air resources," all of which he needed to "meet the demands of the overall campaign and future contingencies like Khe Sanh, NEUTRALIZE [the heavy bombing around Con Thien, South Vietnam, late in 1967], and the Tet offensive ." By directing operations through his own command and control mechanism, Momyer believed he could ensure that "All necessary air, and not just a dedicated force, can then be quickly switched via ABCCC [airborne battlefield command and control center] to exploit lucrative targets developed by the Infiltration Center, FACs [forward air controllers] or any other collection source." His concern for centralized control, however, reflected the possibility that dividing the recently unified aerial resources between Seventh Air Force and Task Force Alpha might well encourage the Marine Corps to revive its campaign to regain operational control of its own aircraft.[13]

As General Momyer presented his case, Secretary Brown was already acting on a suggestion by Dr. Foster that Task Force Alpha begin performing an operational role, a proposal that was adopted in time for Commando Hunt, the 1968–69 dry season interdiction effort. (This operation got under way in the autumn of 1968, after the Seventh Air Force, by this time under the command of Gen. George S. Brown, had begun placing blocks of sorties by Marine Corps aircraft at the disposal of Marine commanders, thus easing tensions over the issue of centralized control.) The new arrangement, however, did not assign a specific force to the exclusive use of Task Force Alpha. Instead, aircraft that the Seventh Air Force dispatched to operate over certain segments of the trail took their orders from the Surveillance Center.[14]

Late in May 1968, Dr. Foster's Special Assistant for Southeast Asia Matters, Leonard Sullivan, Jr., visited Nakhon Phanom. An aeronautical engineer by profession and a marine during World War II, Sullivan was impressed by the Surveillance Center, which he termed "the Mecca of U.S. R&D quick reaction in this war." Quick reaction described it perfectly, since less than two years elapsed between Professor Roger Fisher's memorandum launching the project and the beginning of operational testing. When Sullivan arrived at the base in Thailand, he entertained doubts about the "utility and relative importance" of the undertaking, but he had to admit that "the Air Force is managing a superlative operation," that was "virtually fully automated with direct evaluated print-out available to the Tactical Analysis Officers every five minutes, untouched by human hands from its origin in the implanted sensor." In addition, he told Dr. Foster, "I had the opportunity to listen to active acoubuoys, overhearing conversations and activity in a suspected truck park." Having observed the Surveillance Center in action, Sullivan acknowledged that "just as it is almost impossible to be an agnostic in the Cathedral of Notre Dame, so it is difficult to keep from being swept up in the beauty and majesty of the Task Force Alpha temple."

Yet, Sullivan did resist, at least to the extent that a tour of the Surveillance Center failed to dispel his every doubt. He remained concerned that emphasis within the task force seemed to be shifting from "people finding," proposed for Dump Truck and carried out at Khe Sanh, to "truck detections and strategic intelligence gathering on potentially lucrative truck parks and supply depots." The enemy's only known reaction thus far to the monitoring of truck routes had been to increase antiaircraft protection against aircraft dropping sensors or delivering strikes. The apparent lack of urgency on the part of the North Vietnamese caused Sullivan to wonder if the campaign against trucks actually impeded the flow of supplies. Perhaps, he suggested, an "equivalent effort" to employ sensors in South Vietnam, especially along the demilitarized zone, might prove more valuable.[15]

Sullivan also warned of problems to come. He seemed especially concerned that competition would arise between Task Force Alpha and ground units requiring sensors. General McBride, he believed, was "going to work too hard to keep it an out-country asset at the expense of exploiting its capabilities in-country."[16] As Sullivan predicted, interdiction in southern Laos did eclipse projects in South Vietnam, so that during the latter months of 1968, when sensor production lagged behind demand, many requests by tactical units went unheeded. The shortage proved temporary, however, and soon the Army, Navy, and Marine Corps (and eventually the South Vietnamese armed forces) were deploying and monitoring sensor fields scattered from the demilitarized zone to the Mekong Delta.[17]

Despite the impressive automation at the Surveillance Center, results often proved disappointing during the operational tests. A sequence of sensor activations did not necessarily mean either that one or more vehicles had actually triggered the string or that a successful air strike would be forthcoming. Of 4,665 possible targets nominated by the between December 1, 1967, and March 31, 1968, roughly half escaped aerial reconnaissance and possible attack because of bad weather, lack of available aircraft, or higher priority operations to help defend Khe Sanh or crush the Tet offensive. Indeed, air crews succeeded in verifying only 12 percent of the total nominations (547 targets) and attacked slightly more than half of these. Sometimes a forward air controller had already launched a strike when an unneeded second aircraft arrived on the scene, but many airmen either could find no trucks, possibly because of false alarms, or lost sight of the convoy due to fog, cloud cover, or jungle growth. A total of 569 aircraft, responding to electronic signals processed by the Surveillance Center, conducted 282 attacks and claimed 384 trucks destroyed.[18]

These initial contributions of Task Force Alpha seemed inconsequential. As early as November and December 1967, with the enemy massing for the impending Tet offensive, streams of trucks, headlights shining, clogged the roads of southern Laos. Forward air controllers sighted five to ten times as many vehicles as were spotted in the same weeks of the previous year, sometimes reporting 150 to 250 trucks in a single night, far too many for the available aircraft to attack. According to an evaluation conducted at General Westmoreland's headquarters, the actual number of vehicles detected through electronic surveillance and attacked did not matter at this time, as long as the surveillance system worked as planned, "the sensor field was successfully deployed, the sensors *did* respond to passing trucks (among other things), the EC–121s *did* pick up the sensor signals and relay them to the ISC [Infiltration Surveillance Center], and the computer-assisted ISC analysts *did* derive usable movement reports."

With traffic choking the roads and visual sightings almost routine, the quality of sensor data took precedence over quantity. By the end of the 1967–68 dry season, according to Westmoreland's headquarters, "the emphasis changed from nominating a maximum number of new target candidates to a broader intelligence role of naming only the most lucrative targets, such as large convoys." In keeping with this change of orientation, Task Force Alpha devoted greater energy to monitoring road cuts and reporting whenever large numbers of vehicles halted behind landslides or bomb craters.[19]

The ability of the center to gather intelligence impressed even those who worried that Task Force Alpha might become too deeply involved in directing air attacks. Colonel McCoskrie hailed the electronic sensor as "a soldier with infinite courage" who will "stay out there forever and tell you everything he knows." As the commander of a combat organization assigned to attack the trail, the colonel appreciated the "computer models and programs" that helped sensor technicians "actually track those trucks down the road ." Despite being impressed by the work of Task Force Alpha, he considered the data emanating from Nakhon Phanom to be only one of many tools that commanders, from the level of squadron and wing commanders all the way to General Momyer, could use against the trail. Unlike those civilians who envisioned placing strike and reconnaissance aircraft under the control of Task Force Alpha, McCoskrie still believed that the center should limit its activity to "just gathering the intelligence," making "rapid analysis," and forwarding the results to "the operators" like himself, letting "the operators . . . order the strikes ."

Unaware that Dr. Foster and other defense officials had endorsed an operational role for Task Force Alpha, McCoskrie attributed the impending Alpha involvement in operations to two factors. One was the commander's personal commitment: "General McBride was sent out here to make the thing work and he was an extremely dedicated guy." The second, according to the colonel, was the natural tendency toward growth demonstrated by almost every organization. In McCoskrie's view, the

The War against Trucks

Task Force Alpha staff could not resist the temptation to acquire the means of acting on the intelligence it had collected: " like so many others, when they found they had all this information in their hands, [they said] wouldn't it be wonderful if we had control of a dozen airplanes so we could go out and take some action on our own ."[20]

Colonel McCoskrie was correct in one regard: General McBride was determined to succeed. The colonel may not have realized, however, that the task force commander opposed doing violence to the principle of unified control over tactical aviation that Westmoreland had recently approved. Indeed, McBride told General Momyer that "the logical place in the command network" for the application of sensor technology "is within the U.S. Air Force Tactical Air Control System." To allow Task Force Alpha too much autonomy, McBride feared, might offer an opening for the Army or Navy to pry the interdiction mission away from the Air Force. A successful task force, operating independently of the Seventh Air Force, might set a precedent under which one of the other services might take over the Surveillance Center and direct the interdiction of the Ho Chi Minh Trail.[21]

As the mission of Task Force Alpha took shape, Secretary of Defense Clark M. Clifford had difficulty determining how well the new organization performed. Leonard Sullivan conceded that no one in Southeast Asia believed "that any meaningful experiment can be run to definitely establish its potential capability."[22] As a result, the Department of Defense formed a panel of scientists and military men, headed by Adm. James S. Russell, USN (Ret.), to do what could not be done on the scene and evaluate the actual and potential contribution of sensors to the war effort throughout Southeast Asia.[23]

When asked to state his views for the evaluation committee, Leonard Sullivan proposed closer integration of intelligence and operations, in effect using Task Force Alpha's sensors to locate targets "in those areas where forward air controllers cannot go." He maintained that the surveillance network could "still come into its own," at least as a weapon against vehicles, "once a strike capability is available." Sullivan thus seemed to be losing, temporarily as events would prove, his enthusiasm for "people finding," since he acknowledged that sensors, though able to locate trucks, had "not done well with people," partly because of the failure of the gravel mines to activate the monitoring devices.[24]

After conducting its evaluation of the sensor program, the Russell Committee endorsed Task Force Alpha's attempt to impede truck traffic, but warned that existing munitions were poorly suited to the task. The group offered little hope of successful strikes against troops infiltrating southward, at least for the present. Two deficiencies conspired against the antipersonnel aspects of the barrier scheme: the lack of "wide-area" antipersonnel bombs to drop on units in bivouac or on the road and the inability of existing sensors to locate troops, unless someone stepped on gravel, the mines actually exploded, and the transmitter in the sensor broadcast the sound. An operational test against infiltrators, the Russell Committee suggested, might someday prove feasible, if Task Force Alpha had improved munitions, more sensitive monitoring devices, and greater accuracy in planting the new sensors.

For now, reported Admiral Russell and his colleagues, attacks against truck traffic afforded greater prospects for success than did strikes on infiltration groups. As a result, the committee recommended that interdiction of the road net receive top priority, eclipsing even the tactical sensor projects set up within South Vietnam. Once the Surveillance Center had covered the supply routes through southern Laos, the monitoring efforts in the South would receive additional sensors, with Task Force Alpha in some instances relaying or processing signals from these fields.

The tactical projects, to which the committee referred, began in 1967 as part of the never-to-be-completed line of mutually supporting strongpoints designed to impede infiltration across the demilitarized zone. The electronic array, called Duel Blade, that went into place in connection with the beginning of work on the manned barrier against infiltration was complemented in mid-1968 by Duffel Bag, which tried to provide elsewhere in South Vietnam the kind of sensor-derived information on enemy movement that had proved so valuable at Khe Sanh. On occasion, Duffel Bag produced spectacular results, as in February and March 1969, when sensor activations revealed groups of North Vietnamese troops, enabling attacking marines to kill 250 during a 15-day operation in westernmost Quang Tri Province. As the scientists of the Jason Summer Study had predicted, however, the enemy improvised countermeasures. Occasionally, when expecting electronic surveillance of an attack route, the North Vietnamese drove domesticated water buffaloes toward U.S. positions to activate the Duffel Bag sensors; the resulting electronic signals drew fire that sometimes revealed gaps in the defenses. Another sensor project, Tight Jaw, which began in 1969, sought to train the South Vietnamese to use the devices for both border surveillance and tactical operations.

The Russell Committee understood the diplomatic overtones of the war in southern Laos, recommending closer cooperation between the U.S. ambassador at Vientiane, William H. Sullivan (not to be confused with Leonard Sullivan, Jr., the Deputy Director of Defense Research and Engineering for Southeast Asia Matters), and the military commanders at Saigon. Ambassador Sullivan sought to maintain in power the government of Laos, headed by Prince Souvanna Phouma, which was under attack by domestic communist forces, the Pathet Lao (translated as "Land of the Lao"), supplied by North Vietnam and reinforced to some extent by soldiers of the North Vietnamese army. In this precarious situation, with William Sullivan's help, Souvanna tried to preserve the independence of his kingdom by resisting the Pathet Lao, while avoiding the kind of military action that would either cause casualties among his noncombatant supporters, and thus make converts to the enemy, or compel the North Vietnamese to intervene in force. Both the United States and North Vietnam viewed the war as primarily a struggle for the future of South Vietnam; Laos was a subsidiary battlefield that influenced the course of events in the south. Although the fighting in northern Laos did divert North Vietnamese men and resources from the main effort, the Johnson administration considered it less important than interdiction of the Ho Chi Minh Trail, which fed men and material to the battlefields of South Vietnam. Consequently, the Russell Committee suggested that "strike approval authority" for attacks on the trail, "be pre-delegated by the U.S. Ambassador." While this proposal took shape, Ambassador Sullivan and General Brown, the recently appointed Seventh Air Force commander, were laying the groundwork for future collaboration between the embassy and Brown's headquarters, an effort that bore fruit during the 1968–69 dry season.[25]

As the Russell report neared completion, the interdiction technique had already begun changing. The ideas of Professor Fisher and the Jason Summer Study converted aerial interdiction from a comparatively simple undertaking, armed reconnaissance, to a highly complex effort incorporating new developments in electronics. The air war in southern Laos became a battle that pitted advanced technology, typified by the electronic sensor and automated Surveillance Center, against a carefully camouflaged and well organized transportation net, defended at this time by antiaircraft weapons of World War II vintage. The increasing reliance by the Air Force on this new technology resulted in an enlargement of Task Force Alpha's responsibilities, the launching in November 1968 of the first in the Commando Hunt series of systematic year-round interdiction campaigns, and the termination or reorientation of a number of earlier programs that had harassed supply lines in southern Laos.[26]

On November 15, 1968, for example, at the outset of the first Commando Hunt operation, Task Force Alpha officially took over the old Steel Tiger program, a joint undertaking of the Air Force and Navy that had been harassing the trail since April 1965. The same fate, absorption in Commando Hunt, befell Tiger Hound, in which Air Force, Army, Navy, and Marine Corps airmen had been flying interdiction missions since December 1965. Diverted to the defense of Khe Sanh early in 1968, Tiger Hound continued to attack road and river traffic, sometimes dropping sensors, until the summer of 1969, when publication of the Commando Hunt III plan for the 1969–70 northeast monsoon season deprived the group of its separate identity. With the appearance of this plan, almost every aspect of aerial interdiction became part of the recurring Commando Hunt operations.[27]

Commando Hunt also superseded the SLAM (Seek, Locate, Annihilate, Monitor) program, in which so-called Prairie Fire teams, led by U.S. soldiers and dispatched by the Military Assistance Command, Vietnam, entered southern Laos to help locate targets for air attack, usually by B–52s. However, only one SLAM B–52 attack took place during all of 1968, an attack triggered by a Prairie Fire ground reconnaissance team against a base area some thirty miles northeast of Attopeu. Beginning late in November and continuing into December, the Prairie Fire unit called down a total of 152 strikes by helicopter gunships and tactical aircraft, but none by B–52s. Aircrews and members of the reconnaissance team reported almost four hundred secondary explosions and sixty-four large fires, but could offer no concrete information about the kind of material being destroyed. Following the last SLAM, a variant of the nickname reappeared in Operation Grand Slam, a series of photographic missions conducted over the demilitarized zone during the spring of 1969.[28]

Closely related to SLAM, the Shock program of aerial attacks obtained targeting information from a number of sources, including the reconnaissance teams sent into southern Laos by the Central Intelligence Agency or the military assistance command. Unlike a typical SLAM (and the last in that series was an exception), Shock relied solely on Air Force tactical aircraft, excluding B–52s, Army helicopter gunships, and Navy or Marine Corps squadrons. A total of five Shock operations took place, four in 1967 and the last in February 1968. Although the usual targets during 1967 lay along Route 110 near the Cambodian border, Shock III, conducted from June 30 to July 4, 1967, focused on traffic on the Kong River east of Saravane. The final Shock air strikes, Shock V in February 1968, differed from the 1967 operations in purpose as well as location. Although the attack contributed to interdiction by hitting lines of communication and storage areas in the Mahaxay region amid the Route 12 complex, planners further intended that it help restore morale in a Lao army recently defeated at Ban Nam Bac in northern Laos. Whatever their effect on morale, the strikes produced fewer explosions and fires than anticipated, but the undertaking nevertheless appeared successful because traffic around Mahaxay seemed to decline for the remainder of the dry season.[29]

As Task Force Alpha's role in aerial interdiction expanded, the Navy OP–2Es that had planted the first sensors departed from southern Laos. Fitted with a Norden bomb sight dating from World War II, plus the latest in long-range navigation equipment, the converted Lockheed patrol craft dropped sensors accurately, provided that the pilot maintained a straight and level course at an air speed of one hundred fifty to two hundred knots and an altitude of fifteen hundred feet. When employing these tactics, the one hundred–foot wing span of these airplanes filled the sights of the 23-mm and 37-mm guns that the North Vietnamese had begun setting up in southern Laos. Hostile fire forced the OP–2Es to fly higher, but to achieve the necessary accuracy they could not exceed three thousand feet, still within range of the enemy weapons, which downed two of the aircraft. As a result, the survivors restricted their flights to lightly defended areas identified by Seventh Air Force intelligence officers. To maintain a separate squadron exclusively for use in permissive areas seemed wasteful indeed, and the OP–2Es dropped their last sensors on June 25, 1968, after some seven months on the job. Although officers of the Navy squadron complained that the Seventh Air Force had sometimes mistakenly sent the lumbering aircraft against supposedly ill-defended areas that actually bristled with guns, General Momyer's headquarters insisted that the fault lay in assigning an airplane originally designed for patrolling the oceans to a region where antiaircraft batteries were increasing in number and continually changing location.

Until North Vietnamese antiaircraft fire became too dangerous, Sikorsky CH–3 helicopters helped plant the sensors. Using maps or aerial photos, the pilot flew a designated course, hovered over each site, and used the intercom or a hand signal to tell the flight engineer when to drop a sensor out the cargo door. In undefended areas, when the weather was good enough to permit accurate navigation, a skilled crew could plant each device within a few yards of the desired impact point.

The War against Trucks

Not until February 1969, when the less vulnerable F–4Ds replaced them, did the CH–3s abandon this mission entirely.[30]

Plans called for installation of the newest loran navigation gear, the type carried by the OP–2E, in those McDonnell Douglas F–4 Phantoms assigned to take over the mission of dropping sensors, and this modification delayed the arrival in Thailand of the squadron selected for the task. In the meantime, other loran-equipped F–4Ds already based at Ubon took over the assignment; six of them began dropping seismic detectors as early as February 1968. By the end of March the CH–3s and OP–2Es were leaving defended regions to the Phantoms that, when using loran, could plant a sensor with acceptable accuracy from altitudes of five hundred to fifteen hundred feet at five hundred fifty knots. The combination of low altitude and great speed made tracking difficult with the optical antiaircraft sights then in use, or even with fire-control radar.[31]

Loran, the name a contraction of the term long-range aid to navigation, required transmitting stations on the ground, a suitably equipped aircraft, and a crew trained to use the system. To determine its location, an aircraft received precisely timed radio pulses broadcast from two widely separated stations, one of which sent its signal slightly later than the other. Since the interval between transmission from the two sites was known, the difference in arrival time revealed proportionate distance from each site (twice as far from one as from the other, for instance). A signal from a third source, like the second having a known relationship to the first station, pinpointed the aircraft by triangulation. A computer in the aircraft made the calculations necessary to fix the position of the fighter-bomber and, also based on the difference in the time of arrival of radio signals, the location of an initial point for the bombing run and of the target itself. As the campaign against the Ho Chi Minh Trail gathered momentum, and the air war both intensified in northern Laos and extended into Cambodia, the loran network covering the region had to change. Besides the equipment operating more or less permanently from Ubon, Mukdahen, and Nakhon Phanom in Thailand, loran transmitters broadcast at various times from two other sites in that country. A station functioned at the airport at Phnom Penh, Cambodia, once the war spread to that nation, and two or three operated from Laos, the exact number and the locations depending on the progress of the ground war, as the loran transmitters moved to keep out of the hands of the enemy. The Air Force Communications Service and Air America, an airline owned and operated by the Central Intelligence Agency, shared responsibility for the loran stations in Thailand, Laos, and Cambodia.[32]

Besides forcing adoption of the loran-equipped Phantoms for planting sensors, enemy gunners settled for good the controversy over whether older-model, propeller-driven aircraft or more modern jets were deadlier against truck traffic along the Ho Chi Minh Trail. Early in 1968, hostile antiaircraft fire combined with structural fatigue and engine failure to persuade the Seventh Air Force to find a less demanding job than interdiction of the trail for the T–28D, a converted trainer. This propeller aircraft flew its last armed reconnaissance over the enemy road net during

June of that year, its place being taken by the Douglas A–1 Skyraider, also propeller-driven but faster and more rugged. Unfortunately, the A–1 soon revealed its own vulnerability to the increasingly deadly defenses of the trail.[33]

The 56th Special operations Wing at Nakhon Phanom, which had flown the T–28, acknowledged in September 1969 that "Geographical area restrictions evolved from experience [with the T–28] have been applied to A–1 and A–26 operations." Only at night or during the rainy season could these propeller aircraft venture near Mu Gia Pass, Tchepone, Ban Laboy Ford, or other heavily defended areas.[34] Within a few weeks, as the 1969–70 dry season began, the Air Force removed the A–26 from combat; despite its reputation as a truck killer, this twin-engine light bomber could no longer survive strengthened defenses to attack the roads where traffic was heaviest. Of the three propeller-driven attack aircraft in action during early 1968, only the Skyraider still flew combat missions for the Air Force when the interdiction effort ended about four and one-half years later. Instead of attacking the Ho Chi Minh Trail, however, the A–1 served in auxiliary roles like supporting Lao units operating outside the trail network or escorting the helicopters that rescued downed airmen or landed and retrieved reconnaissance teams. The interdiction burden gradually shifted to the swift F–4, supplemented to some degree by other jet aircraft, notably the Martin B–57.[35]

Even as the T–28 and A–26 entered the autumn of their operational lives, the Seventh Air Force attempted to reduce the time required to react to sightings of truck convoys by the Central Intelligence Agency's roadwatch teams posted along the Ho Chi Minh Trail.[36] The solution seemed to lie in establishing direct radio contact between the teams and the forward air controllers responsible for a particular area, but results during 1968 proved disappointing. Between March 6 and September 25, a period that included the rainy months when aerial observation was difficult, the teams radioed sightings of 11,712 trucks, but could confirm the destruction of only 101, or 0.86 percent. The agency's station chief at Vientiane, the administrative capital of Laos, concluded that the project had not produced results worth the cost of the radios and proposed returning to normal intelligence reporting channels, unless the Air Force would pay for continuing the project. This the Air Force refused to do. As the Task Force Alpha staff pointed out, the lack of forward air controllers and shortage of suitable munitions prevented attacks on all of the targets generated by sensors, let alone those reported by observers on the ground. Moreover, Air Force analysts considered roadwatch teams less credible than either forward air controllers or electronic monitors, and therefore used reports from the teams mainly to substantiate information from other sources. The Seventh Air Force saw no need to put roadwatch elements in direct radio contact with the forward air controllers.[37]

In January 1969, Air Force Lt. Gen. John D. Lavelle paid a visit to Nakhon Phanom after taking over from General Starbird as Director of the Defense Communications Planning Group, responsible for developing the electronic equipment used in the fight against infiltration. Possibly as a consequence of Lavelle's tour of the facility, Task Force Alpha showed a renewed interest in direct radio reporting by roadwatch teams. The command proposed that the signal from team radios (that transmitted each time the operator saw a vehicle and pushed a button), be relayed via EC–121 aircraft directly to the Surveillance Center and processed with the sensor data. For essentially the same reasons as before, the Seventh Air Force rejected this latest attempt to tie the roadwatch teams into the tactical air control system.[38]

Although direct radio reporting by roadwatch teams came to an end late in 1968, the Central Intelligence Agency continued to send these probes into southern Laos. Some Seventh Air Force officers, however, condemned the presence of the teams along heavily traveled roads and streams as more hindrance than help. To avoid accidentally bombing the teams, the Seventh Air Force had to coordinate, through the air attaché at Vientiane, with Ambassador Sullivan and the Central Intelligence Agency station chief and take special precautions whenever a roadwatch team was observing traffic on the trail. As a result, a convoy or a group of parked trucks might escape air attack because of the need to protect the surveillance unit.

In September 1968, while meeting with representatives of the Seventh Air Force on the problem of coordination, Ambassador Sullivan insisted that he retain close control over air strikes in places where roadwatch teams or guerrilla forces operated. He expressed special concern about Route 23 and its feeder roads. This road complex, connecting Pakse, Paksong, and Ban Thateng, then heading northward toward Muong Phine, carried "traffic . . . from North Vietnam to support the Pathet Lao and North Vietnamese forces . . . targeted against Laos, rather than something that's going on down south." Therefore, the ambassador continued, "no matter what arrangement we can make about pulling roadwatch teams out of other areas, we are going to keep them in this area to screen for our own forces"—that is, the Laotian army, the mountain tribesmen defending northern Laos, and the various guerrilla groups.[39]

Guerrilla forces supported by the Central Intelligence Agency rarely probed the Route 23 net as far as Muong Phine, site of important supply depots for the Ho Chi Minh Trail, leaving that target to air strikes. Although this stretch of highway could be attacked more readily by air than on the ground, roadwatch teams continued to operate there, preventing air strikes as they gathered intelligence useful to the forces loyal to Souvanna Phouma. Well into 1970, Seventh Air Force staff agencies still complained that the presence of these units along Route 23 and the resulting need to check with authorities in Vientiane impeded strikes against a main supply route.[40]

Whenever the roadwatch teams proved too great a nuisance to the enemy, he strengthened security and denied access to the roads that he considered vital. As the grip on the road net tightened, retrieving the roadwatch teams became increasingly difficult, according to Lt. Col. Howard K. Hartley, a member of the staff of the air attaché in Laos. Air Force or Central Intelligence helicopters usually succeeded in picking an isolated spot to land the men, who then approached the objective on foot, but as they drew nearer discovery became more likely. All too often the patrol vanished, or the helicopter crew found the enemy waiting when it returned for the pickup. "The difficult thing about roadwatch teams," Colonel Hartley observed, "was trying to recruit, because the mortality rate was so high."[41]

On occasion, the North Vietnamese tried using roadwatch teams as bait to trap U.S. helicopters. In March 1970 Lt. Col. Homer J. Carlile was leading three aircraft to a rendezvous where three teams had gathered to await recovery. As Carlile made his approach, the interpreter—known only as Mr. Sun—who was riding in a different helicopter, spotted hostile troops hiding below. Thanks to Mr. Sun's alertness, the trap failed; the helicopters pulled up, and the roadwatch units took to the jungle, escaping to an alternate site where recovery helicopters could safely meet them.[42]

In addition to the Central Intelligence Agency's roadwatch teams, Prairie Fire units sent by the military assistance command continued to penetrate the jungle that concealed the many roads, byways, and streams of the Ho Chi Minh Trail. During 1968, the military assistance command's Studies and Observations Group launched 327 incursions into Laos. Twelve-man reconnaissance teams, each led by three members of the U.S. Army Special Forces, carried out 271 of these probes. More heavily armed combat patrols, each consisting of 41 South Vietnamese soldiers and the usual command element of three U.S. soldiers, conducted the remainder of the operations. Besides gathering information and occasionally staging raids, Prairie Fire units sought out targets for aerial attack within an assigned area adjacent to the South Vietnamese border. Throughout the year, tactical aircraft and helicopter gunships hit camps and supply caches found by the teams. Air attacks struck the greatest concentration of these Prairie Fire targets during the final SLAM operation, which ended in December 1968. This action generated about 18 percent of the 635 "air exploitation sorties" flown by A–1s or other tactical aircraft in support of that year's Prairie Fire activity, along with 15 percent of the year's helicopter gunship sorties. The last operation in the SLAM series produced more than half the reported fires and explosions triggered during 1968 by aerial attacks on Prairie Fire targets.[43]

Like the Central Intelligence Agency's roadwatch teams, Prairie Fire units normally entered and left southern Laos by helicopter. Two or more helicopter gunships, either Army or Air Force, and at least two Skyraiders flown by Air Force crews, escorted the Army, Air Force, or Central Intelligence Agency troop carriers. An Air Force forward air controller, usually in a Cessna O–2A, stood by to direct A–1 strikes, and an Army plane like the de Havilland Otter served as a relay station for the Prairie Fire radio operator, generally an American.

Because Prairie Fire teams enjoyed the kind of "pre-delegation" that the Russell committee recommended for air strikes generated by Igloo White sensors, detailed coordination with the Vientiane embassy was not necessary before launching a probe into a precisely designated area. The military assistance command merely provided advance notice to the Commander in Chief, Pacific, observed certain rules governing the number and type of units patrolling at the same time, and made sure the team did not stray from the assigned operating area.[44]

Most roadwatch teams destined for the main roads leading from North Vietnam into southern Laos took off by helicopter from Nakhon Phanom, staging if necessary through auxiliary airfields in Laos. Some Prairie Fire units followed the same general route after U.S. forces abandoned the Khe Sanh combat base in June 1968, and it could no longer serve to launch probes of southern Laos. Flying a roadwatch or Prairie Fire team from Nakhon Phanom to a landing site such as the hills around Ban Karai Pass required crossing almost the entire width of the Ho Chi Minh Trail. As the number of antiaircraft guns guarding the communist transportation net increased, these flights grew more dangerous. By January 1970, with more than seven hundred 23-mm and 37-mm weapons believed guarding the trail, CH–3s from Nakhon Phanom could find only one undefended crossing point, located in rugged terrain that required them to climb to high altitude, thus increasing fuel consumption. Consequently, these helicopters frequently had to proceed to an airstrip in South Vietnam, stop there for fuel, and run the risk that bad weather might keep them grounded for days. The problem persisted until the appearance, later in 1970, of the larger, longer range Sikorsky CH–53, which could cruise at eleven thousand feet and avoid fire from the 23-mm and 37-mm weapons.[45]

Like the antiaircraft defenses, weather presented an obstacle to the helicopters infiltrating Prairie Fire or roadwatch teams, and to fighter-bombers, as well. In March 1970, for example, intense antiaircraft fire kept Central Intelligence Agency transports from parachuting supplies to a roadwatch unit near Ban Karai Pass, causing the station chief to request Air Force helicopters retrieve the men. Each day for five consecutive days, three CH–3s struggled over the Laotian mountains and approached the landing zone only to encounter a solid layer of cloud. Luckily for the team members, the weather improved enough for a rescue on the sixth attempt.[46]

To obtain timely weather forecasts for attacking the Ho Chi Minh Trail, the Air Weather Service sent special teams to train members of roadwatch units to take and transmit meteorological observations. The first attempt, in April 1966, lasted only until November when the radio equipment gave out. The effort resumed in March 1967, when Frank W. West, an Air Force sergeant, began teaching classes in a Lao dialect. Within four months, five posts in the central panhandle of Laos, all west of Route 23, were using Central Intelligence Agency radio channels to make two reports each day. The weather reporting network expanded or contracted whenever ground changed hands, as in 1969, when the enemy overran a guerrilla camp near Muong Phalane that doubled as a weather station. Lao T–28s promptly obliterated the captured site with bombs and napalm.[47] By 1968, however, with Seventh Air Force planners thinking in terms of year-round interdiction, other aids to weather forecasting were needed, such as weather photographs transmitted from orbiting space satellites. Using these pictures, forecasters could predict holes in the cloud cover that prevailed over the Ho Chi Minh Trail throughout the southwest monsoon season, so that aircraft could take advantage of the fleeting gaps.[48]

Whether obtained from crude stations in Laos or sophisticated satellites, meteorological information went to the Southeast Asia Joint Operations Weather Center located at Tan Son Nhut Air Base in Saigon, adjacent to Seventh Air Force headquarters. On the basis of the center's forecasts, senior Air Force officers might cancel or divert scheduled missions. At least every six hours, the center revised the detailed prediction that included the Ho Chi Minh Trail.[49]

Besides forecasting, the Air Force continued its attempts at weather modification, flying rain-making missions during six southwest monsoon seasons before the project ended on July 5, 1972. Aircraft dropped photoflash cartridges inside certain clouds, relying on the release of silver iodide or lead iodide in the updraft to trigger the release of moisture. The annual cost of the effort was roughly $3.6 million, including the operation and maintenance of three Lockheed WC–130s and two McDonnell Douglas RF–4Cs, purchase of seeding materials, and pay for the people involved. It proved impossible, however, to determine the amount of additional rainfall caused by cloud-seeding and thus justify the recurring outlay. The Defense Intelligence Agency estimated that seeding increased rainfall "in limited areas up to 30 percent above that predicted for the existing conditions," but this figure admittedly was the result of "empirical and theoretical techniques based on units expended and the physical properties of the air mass seeded"—in short, a scientific guess. Sensor data showed only that the enemy consistently experienced difficulty keeping traffic moving through the monsoon rains, a normal problem for that time of year.[50]

From time to time, especially during 1971, tropical storms either intensified the downpour associated with the southwest monsoon or extended the rainy season beyond its anticipated close. Atmospheric conditions over either the Indian Ocean or the South China Sea, rather than cloud seeding over southern Laos, spawned these typhoons. Ironically, typhoon-induced rains interfered with cloud seeding, cooling the earth and preventing the updrafts of heated air that were essential to the project.[51]

Rainmaking sometimes complemented defoliation, another attempt at environment modification. Originally defoliation sought to deprive the enemy of concealment, with destruction of crops later an objective. In southern Laos, however, another effect loomed larger than these: once stripped of their jungle cover and exposed to the heavy rains of the southwest monsoon season, the roads would become quagmires. During 1968 and 1969, the Ambassador and his successor, G. McMurtrie Godley, authorized several attempts to kill the vegetation that shielded parts of the Ho Chi Minh Trail. These efforts represented a continuation of a program to defoliate segments of the trail begun in December 1965. The first such mission during 1968 sent Fairchild UC–123 spray planes to destroy the foliage that concealed enemy activity along Route 110 southeast of Muong May. Later, in January 1969, these aircraft defoliated some twenty square miles along a secondary road west of Tchepone in order to permit armed reconnaissance by fighter-bombers. In March of the same year, in their final a herbicide mission against the trail, UC–123s sprayed a four-square-mile area on a recently discovered road leading from Ban Karai Pass.[52]

The ponderous converted transports seemed certain to provide a feast for the increasing number of antiaircraft gunners guarding the Ho Chi Minh Trail; a less vulnerable spray plane would have to take over if operations there were to continue. The F–4 looked like the best substitute, and a mission against the Ho Chi Minh Trail in January 1969 tested a jury-rigged herbicide dispenser for this versatile fighter-bomber. The device, actually a modified 370-gallon auxiliary fuel tank, tended to collapse because the herbicide was heavier than jet fuel. After another mission in

March, during which ground fire downed one of the F–4s and a dispenser broke loose from another plane, this development project came to an end.[53]

Besides flying their last defoliation missions over the trail, the spray-equipped UC–123s tried to destroy some enemy-cultivated rice fields and sought to strip the concealment from certain weakly defended roads that were not components of the Ho Chi Minh complex. In the case of herbicide missions, whether defoliation or crop destruction, the U.S. embassy at Vientiane had no fixed policy concerning consultation with the Lao government. Sometimes the ambassador obtained formal clearance; at other times he approved the mission on the assumption that no objection would arise. In September 1968, however, Ambassador Sullivan chose to call off the defoliation of a road north of Vientiane, a project endorsed by Souvanna's government, when friendly villagers complained.[54]

Although antiaircraft fire put an end in 1969 to low-altitude defoliation missions against the Ho Chi Minh Trail, higher flying Air Force planes continued showering as many as twenty million propaganda leaflets per month on this network of roads, rivers, and footpaths. The product of psychological warfare specialists at the Military Assistance Command, Vietnam, this material urged North Vietnamese infiltrators to escape the disease and hardship of the trail by surrendering to the South Vietnamese. Ambassador Godley was enthusiastic about the concept, extending coverage to other parts of Laos where he believed psychological warfare might exploit apparent friction between North Vietnamese and Pathet Lao or otherwise erode enemy morale.[55] The impact of these efforts defied measurement, for many factors might prod an individual into surrendering. As one unit historian pointed out, "it was virtually impossible to assess the results of a single mission or even a series of missions, because enemy soldiers often would retain the message . . . for weeks before they had an opportunity to escape ."[56]

Until the Northeast Monsoons returned in the fall and Commando Hunt began, 1968 was a time of transition for both the war itself and the campaign against the infiltration of men and supplies on the Ho Chi Minh Trail. The nature of the war changed when President Johnson decided to pursue the goal of an independent, noncommunist South Vietnam by means of negotiations, cutting back on (and later ending) the bombing of North Vietnam in the hope of persuading the Hanoi government to enter into discussions. As the Rolling Thunder air campaign drew to a close, the barrier against infiltration joined the U.S. ground forces still fighting in the country to form a shield behind which the South Vietnamese could begin preparing to assume greater responsibility for the conduct of the war. At the heart of the barrier lay Task Force Alpha's Surveillance Center at Nakhon Phanom in Thailand, where computers processed and stored the information gathered by the Igloo White sensors. While the analysts there learned the strengths and limitations of electronic surveillance, the task force passed from operational testing, through limited operation, to eventual year-round activity in what became the Commando Hunt series.

Chapter Two

Codifying the Rules of Engagement

While preparing for the Commando Hunt operation, scheduled for the dry northeast monsoon season of 1968, the Seventh Air Force not only maintained pressure on the Ho Chi Minh Trail, but also participated in a clarification of the rules of engagement governing operations in Laos. The changes in the rules sought to improve relations between the Seventh Air Force, which carried out air operations against the Ho Chi Minh Trail, and the U.S. ambassador at Vientiane, Laos, who functioned, in effect, as the head of a country team, coordinating military activity with the other aspects of national policy. Closer cooperation would enable air power to respond to sensor data more quickly and with deadlier effect, as President Johnson's decision to limit, and then halt, the Rolling Thunder attacks on North Vietnam increased the importance of aerial interdiction in southern Laos.

The approach of Commando Hunt caused no change in the overall command arrangements for Air Force units conducting interdiction missions. The commander of the Seventh Air Force exercised operational control over the squadrons based in Thailand, as well as those located in South Vietnam. The Deputy Commander, Seventh/Thirteenth Air Force, continued to function as a deputy to the commander of the Seventh Air Force, retaining responsibility for the operational readiness of the units flying from Thailand, but he also remained responsible to the commander of the Thirteenth Air Force, located in the Philippines, for carrying out certain administrative and support functions. From his headquarters at Udorn Air Base, Thailand, the Deputy Commander, Seventh/Thirteenth Air Force, also rendered "operational assistance and air advice" to the U.S. embassies at Bangkok, Thailand, and Vientiane, as well as to the Air Force section of the joint military advisory group in Thailand.[1]

Although the Air Force command structure within Southeast Asia stayed the same, the nature of the war changed. On March 31, 1968, President Lyndon B. Johnson announced that the bombing of North Vietnam would be restricted to the panhandle region, a move designed to encourage Hanoi's leadership to negotiate a peace that would preserve the independence of South Vietnam. The North promptly agreed to preliminary discussions, but adopted a policy of fighting while talking that delayed the onset of formal negotiations and stymied progress once they began. The United States sought a tactical advantage by attacking the North Vietnamese bases in Cambodia during 1970 and tried to break the diplomatic impasse by engaging in secret talks with officials from Hanoi. North Vietnam lost patience, however, and in 1972 launched an invasion of South Vietnam that bogged down when U.S. air power intervened on the battlefield and resumed systematic bombing of the North. After dragging on more than four years, negotiations at last produced a cease-fire that took effect in January 1973. Despite the fighting and conferences that lay ahead, the President's 1968 restrictions on bombing changed the course of the conflict: militarily, his decision reoriented the air war toward the interdiction of enemy supply lines in southern North Vietnam and southern Laos; politically, it started the United States on the long road toward disengagement from Southeast Asia.[2]

Before President Johnson confined the bombing in North Vietnam to the panhandle, the Seventh Air Force staff began working on Cobra, a plan proposed by General Momyer to combine Rolling Thunder strikes against the heartland of North Vietnam with the creation of "interdiction belts" in the southern part of the country. The Air Force general intended that his own squadrons spearhead the attacks in the Hanoi-Haiphong region, while Navy units conduct the interdiction campaign to the south, concentrating on the network of streams and canals around the North Vietnamese towns of Bai Thuong and Thanh Hoa, along with the Ca River at Vinh.[3] President Johnson's decision to stop the bombing north of the 19th parallel North latitude put an end to the Cobra plan. Seventh Air Force could not attack the rail line leading to China or the port and storage facilities around Hanoi and Haiphong, nor could naval aviators hit the other targets, among them the Thanh Hoa and Bai Thuong waterways, that lay outside the panhandle and were therefore exempt from bombing. Because the focus of the air war had thus narrowed, sorties formerly directed against targets north of the 19th parallel became available for strikes in southern North Vietnam and for rainy season attacks in southern Laos. Those elements of Cobra calling for interdiction inside North Vietnam now merged with a southwest monsoon campaign plan for southern Laos, the latter based on the operational test of Task Force Alpha during the dry season just ended, to form an aerial interdiction program covering parts of both countries.[4]

Reflecting the increasing importance of Task Force Alpha in the southwest monsoon campaign plan, electronic sensors focused on the known avenues for the shipment of supplies to South Vietnam. When the rainy season began, Igloo White sensor fields monitored the old Dump Truck and Mud River areas in Laos (where the surveillance net had initially been tested), parts of the demilitarized zone that had been covered electronically during the fight for Khe Sanh, the approaches to the A Shau Valley, base areas inside or adjacent to northernmost South Vietnam, and routes in the panhandle of North Vietnam. Not until the approach of the northeast monsoon season in the autumn of 1968 did Task Force Alpha concentrate on those fields reporting on traffic through southern Laos that could be incorporated into Commando Hunt, allowing other sensors to expire, like those around the abandoned base at Khe Sanh.[5]

Throughout the 1968 southwest monsoon season, road-monitoring sensors helped find targets for the aircraft freed from operations in the northern reaches of

North Vietnam. Even though the Surveillance Center did not yet have the new equipment that would enable it to exercise direct control over this windfall of sorties, the electronic sensors produced intelligence used by the Seventh Air Force in planning or diverting air strikes to disrupt the truck traffic that continued in some parts of southern Laos even after the rains started falling. Intelligence reports disclosed that, despite cloud seeding, "for the first time in recent years, a significant portion of the Ho Chi Minh Trail was open to vehicles" during the southwest monsoon. Weather, in fact, caused only brief interruptions in the movement of truck convoys between Mu Gia Pass and the A Shau Valley. Farther south, however, torrential rain caused the North Vietnamese to postpone road maintenance as well as travel until the skies began clearing in September.[6]

Task Force Alpha used sensor data and other intelligence to produce new studies designed to aid in interdiction during both the 1968 southwest monsoon season, lasting from May to September, and the dry months, beginning in November, when the automated Surveillance Center should fulfill its planned potential. Much of the data that General McBride's organization produced merely confirmed existing information on the operation of the trail. For example, these early analyses demonstrated that trucks, known to be supplied by the Soviet Union, China, and the East European communist states, did indeed shuttle mainly by night among cargo transshipment points, pausing when necessary at intermediate refueling or repair points. Access roads, extending some five hundred yards from the principal supply arteries, led to storage depots for cargo, to parking and repair facilities for trucks, and to camps for the laborers engaged in construction or repair. U.S. intelligence concluded that as many as forty-three thousand North Vietnamese and Lao, using pick and shovel along with a few bulldozers and some other heavy equipment, were engaged during 1968 in operating, improving, and expanding the road net and its satellite installations.

Those who operated the trail relied on simple signals to communicate. For example, gunshots or blasts on a whistle, repeated by sentinels posted along the trail, could spread the word of an imminent air attack quickly and surely. In contrast, the mountains often interfered with radio contact, and truck traffic or bombing sometimes tore up telephone wire.[7]

As knowledge of the trail increased, the selection of targets became more ambitious. In mid-April, Task Force Alpha received a request from the Seventh Air Force to help the military assistance command select profitable targets for rainy season attacks by B–52s. Col. Howard P. Smith and the other Air Force targeting specialists at Seventh Air Force headquarters on Tan Son Nhut Air Base near Saigon, objected to lavishing the overwhelming weight of B–52 bombardment on battlefield targets in South Vietnam instead of battering supply lines in southern Laos. Better, they insisted, to conduct interdiction as far as possible from the battlefield, instead of waiting to intervene after the fighting had begun. The Air Force officers argued their case before General Westmoreland and persuaded him to send more of his authorized sorties against the Ho Chi Minh Trail, provided that Task Force Alpha could locate worthwhile targets and that the diversion of the bombers to targets in southern Laos did not jeopardize troops engaging the enemy in South Vietnam.

Besides interpreting signals from specially planted sensor strings, analysts at Nakhon Phanom examined aerial photographs, studied reports from roadwatch teams and forward air controllers, and went over the data stored in computers at the Surveillance Center. Out of this mass of evidence came a basic list of fifty-four proposed targets, soon enlarged to 70, that encompassed the key installations identified along the road net. Designated simply as "truck parks," these locations included transshipment points, fuel depots, repair shops, and any other places where vehicles stopped while shuttling cargo southward. The Seventh Air Force planners accepted fifty-three of the targets on the revised list, rejecting the others because evidence of enemy activity seemed weak or because they clearly lay within restricted areas established by the U.S. embassy at Vientiane.[8]

The need to coordinate with Ambassador Sullivan before B–52s could attack a specific target diminished the responsiveness of the huge bombers in the interdiction campaign. According to Colonel Smith, "we initially started off with a problem because many of our recommended Arc Light boxes [target areas for B–52s] had not yet been validated by Vientiane." As a result, while the embassy staff pored over certain of the more important requests, the B–52s had to deliver their first strikes along less heavily traveled routes passing through regions that the ambassador did not consider sensitive. From five to eight days elapsed before bombs began falling on what the colonel considered "the most lucrative targets." Delays might also arise because General Westmoreland chose to send the bombers against troop concentrations or enemy bases in South Vietnam, for these targets continued to enjoy a higher priority than the Ho Chi Minh Trail.[9]

The B–52 raids recommended by Colonel Smith formed a part of Operation Turnpike, an intensive aerial interdiction effort lasting from April 19 to June 24, 1968, in which tactical aircraft joined the bombers in pounding the roads leading from Mu Gia Pass. When the enemy diverted his convoys through Ban Karai Pass to the south, the operation shifted to routes in that area. By the time Turnpike ended, enemy activity near the two passes seemed to have declined to a level that tactical aircraft could handle, at least for the present, with less frequent help from the B–52s.[10]

The damage inflicted by B–52 raids during the 1968 southwest monsoon season proved difficult to assess. The jungle canopy that concealed the truck parks frustrated the aerial cameras, which rarely recorded more than gaps torn in the forest or, if explosions had ripped away enough cover, bomb craters in the jungle floor. Once again Seventh Air Force intelligence officers called on Task Force Alpha for sensor counts of trucks moving on nearby roads as a clue to the effect of the raids on supply movements.[11] At best, however, sensor activations afforded arguable proof of bombing effectiveness, since a number of factors—from rainy weather and muddy roads to the enemy's plans—might reduce the volume of traffic.

The tactical aircraft that joined the B–52s in attacking the Ho Chi Minh Trail during the southwest monsoon season had various means of locating the target.

Sometimes the crews searched visually for the enemy, conducting armed reconnaissance, or responded to instructions from forward air controllers, but they also might rely on loran data, radar bombing equipment in the aircraft, or the Combat Skyspot ground-based radar that B–52s used so effectively against targets concealed by darkness or jungle canopy. Fighter-bombers attacked truck parks, supply dumps, fords or other choke points, and convoys moving despite the rainy weather.[12]

The F–4D Phantoms operating over southern Laos could take advantage of their on-board radar bombing equipment even though an image of the target itself did not appear on the scope. The weapon system officer on board the Phantom could use any of fifteen previously chosen terrain features, each offering a sharply defined radar return, as an offset aiming point, and rely on a computer in the fighter-bomber to perform the necessary calculations that would place the bombs on the target. This technique permitted attacks anywhere within a square measuring ten thousand feet on a side and centered on each of the aiming points. Though less accurate than visual bombing, airborne radar provided a means of attacking through clouds and darkness, affording considerably more flexibility in the planning of missions.[13]

The results obtained with airborne radar depended on the skill of the crew in using the equipment. For this reason, the Seventh Air Force exercised caution when dispatching radar strikes, whether an aircraft attacked alone or served as a pathfinder, doing the aiming for other tactical fighters. In pathfinder attacks, a second crew, previously qualified on any offset aiming point being used, normally employed its radar bombing equipment to verify that the leader had either acquired the target itself or chosen the right aiming point and located the target in relation to it. Attacks by single aircraft using on-board radar were forbidden in all but free-strike zones. When a lone aircraft used its radar to bomb in an approved area, the crew checked its radar position against the tactical air navigation system or tacan, which consisted essentially of a beacon, at a known location on the ground, which broadcast a signal that triggered a transponder in the airplane. Tacan automatically calculated the distance from the beacon and displayed that information on the instrument panel of the aircraft.[14]

Besides dropping bombs—visually, by loran, or by radar—Phantom tactical fighters enabled forward air controllers to patrol, by day and night, the most heavily defended portions of the Ho Chi Minh Trail, areas where the light aircraft ordinarily used for this mission could not survive. As an aircraft for controlling strikes, the F–4D had its disadvantages, including a comparatively large turning radius and air intakes for the two jet engines that interfered with downward vision from the rear seat. Moreover, the engines themselves trailed a distinctive plume of black smoke that served in daylight to alert enemy gunners. Nevertheless, this model of the Phantom proved less vulnerable than the slower and older F–100F that it supplemented and then supplanted. Later, the F–4E, which generated somewhat less smoke, took part in directing strikes against the Ho Chi Minh Trail. On some daylight missions, an RF–4C, the reconnaissance version of the Phantom accompanied the forward air controller's F–4, photographing potential targets the moment they appeared.[15]

Forward air controllers in less dangerous skies did not need fast jets like the F–4. Two converted light planes, the Cessna O–1, which undertook missions elsewhere as the defenses of the Ho Chi Minh Trail grew deadlier, and the newer and more powerful Cessna O–2A, continued to see action. The O–2A had two engines, mounted tractor-pusher fashion fore and aft of the crew compartment, and two booms extending backward from the wing to support the tail surfaces. In the autumn of 1968 the North American Rockwell OV–10 Bronco—a two-place, twin-boom, twin-turboprop aircraft especially designed for counterinsurgency—joined forces with the O–2As and remaining O–1s.

During night operations against North Vietnamese supply lines in southern Laos, crews of the O–2A, who responded to the radio call sign of Nail, used a starlight scope light intensification device to spot the target initially and then dropped flares and slow-burning incendiary "logs" to mark it for other aircraft. As enemy defenses grew still stronger, these craft proved vulnerable to antiaircraft weapons. In May 1971, Seventh Air Force headquarters prohibited "slow moving FACs" like the O–2A from conducting visual reconnaissance of areas defended by surface-to-air missiles except when "fast moving FACs" were not available.[16] As if to demonstrate the danger from these missiles, an O–2A tried to avoid a thunderstorm and strayed over North Vietnam within range of a surface-to-air missile battery that launched one of its weapons. Flying at seventy-five hundred feet, the forward air controller saw the approaching missile just in time to make a diving turn to the left, avoiding it by a mere three hundred feet.[17]

The OV–10 Bronco, a replacement for the O–2A, had the speed and armor protection that enabled it to probe defended areas and earn the respect of North Vietnamese troops infiltrating through southern Laos. One defector, whose unit had carelessly revealed its presence and then undergone an attack by F–4s directed from an OV–10, confessed that the men had marveled at the accuracy with which the forward air controller could direct such devastating firepower. "After this strike, he said, "they were afraid of OV–10s," a fear that inspired them to pay strict attention to camouflage and concealment.[18]

By the time the 1968 southwest monsoon season rolled around, the OV–10 was undergoing combat tests, and the O–2A was replacing the O–1 Bird Dog on most missions over southern Laos, although one group of forward air controllers flying in the kingdom of Laos continued to operate the Bird Dog until the 1971–72 dry season. These men, who used the call sign Raven, normally supported both guerrilla forces and Lao regulars fighting in the region west of the most heavily defended segments of the Ho Chi Minh Trail. Until October 1970, when the U.S. embassy at Vientiane acknowledged their actual status, the Ravens carried papers identifying them as employees of the U.S. Agency for International Development. If shot down and captured, they were to say that they had been flying rescue missions out of Thailand. The number of Raven forward air controllers peaked at twenty-seven in

1971, but by this time so few O–1s were available that some of the pilots had to fly T–28s. The Air Force ended the Raven project shortly after a training program for Lao forward air controllers, launched in November 1971, began turning out graduates.[19]

Air Force gunships also controlled strikes over the Ho Chi Minh Trail. In those areas where the rules of engagement permitted armed reconnaissance, a qualified crew in one of these sensor-laden aircraft could, in effect, act as its own forward air controller, finding and validating targets. The variety of sensors on board the different kinds of gunships might include infrared devices, laser target designators, low-light-level television with a telescopic lens, and Black Crow detectors, which picked up the electronic emissions from the ignition systems of gasoline-powered vehicles. This array of equipment enabled the gunships to locate and engage targets without the aid of flares or a forward air controller.[20]

Indeed, experienced gunship crews began in 1968 to direct attacks by other aircraft, taking the place of forward air controllers and even flareships, the specially equipped transports used to illuminate the trail for fighter-bombers. During that year's southwest monsoon campaign, the usefulness of flareships had not yet ended, and two types saw action—the Fairchild C–123 Candlestick and the Lockheed C–130 Blindbat. To locate a target, the Candlestick relied on the starlight scope, a device for intensifying available light, and the Blindbat used a flexibly mounted night observation device, actually an improved starlight scope, and eventually a laser target designator and a Black Crow sensor. After spotting a truck convoy or other target, the aircraft provided illumination by dropping incendiary "logs" and flares. Blindbat had greater endurance and flare capacity than Candlestick, and both had greater success by night than the Nail O–2A dropping flares. As the defenses guarding the Ho Chi Minh Trail became more formidable, first Candlestick and then Blindbat had to shift operations to other areas. By the end of 1969, antiaircraft fire over the trail had proved too dangerous for the converted C–123, and six months later, in June 1970, the modified C–130 also moved on to operations elsewhere. The job these flareships could no longer do devolved on Martin B–57G jet-powered light bombers, fitted out with television cameras and other sensors, and on AC–130 gunships.[21]

What had the 1968 southwest monsoon season campaign accomplished, as it sent almost every type of aircraft from B–52s, through flareships, to light observation craft against the Ho Chi Minh Trail? General Keegan, in charge of intelligence for the Seventh Air Force, declared that the operation had "established beyond doubt that by heavy concentration of effort against nonbypassable chokepoints, the enemy's traffic flow can not only be interdicted effectively, but it can be done without unacceptable attrition from the enemy's concentration of antiaircraft defenses." As proof, the general described a series of "daily radar bombing attacks by fighter-bombers" against Ban Laboy Ford during July and August. Although cloud cover frustrated aerial observation, sensor signals indicated that "the enemy was having great difficulty moving his trucks across the ford," apparently because of seasonal flooding. At one time in mid-August, General Keegan recalled, a total of twenty-two southbound convoys appeared to have unloaded at a transshipment point north of the ford, but the evidence suggested that only four convoys from the south had crossed the stream to load for the next leg of the shuttle. As a result, an estimated eight thousand tons of food and war material choked local supply depots. Logic called for B–52 attacks, but because a U.S. pilot who later escaped from the Pathet Lao had once been confined in this area, Ambassador Sullivan, before agreeing to the strikes, demanded proof that the enemy no longer held prisoners at the camp where the flier had been detained. Evidence that the site was no longer used as a prison proved convincing, and the bombers struck the storage areas on September 18. The total of seventy-three secondary explosions, though gratifying, provided no real measurement of the damage done.

Whatever the destruction inflicted on the enemy, the Ban Laboy attack did not provide a typical example of aerial interdiction in southern Laos during the 1968 rainy season. The region, General Keegan acknowledged, afforded "few good non-bypassable road segments" such as the ford. In fact, most of the disruption of enemy road traffic had taken place in comparatively open areas of North Vietnam, south of the 19th parallel, on highways that either hugged the coastline or funneled into Ban Karai and Mu Gia Passes. "Only the availability of a large commitment of fighters, B–52s, and improved munitions," he warned, "can possibly compensate for the disadvantages of the Laotian terrain."

Could increased numbers of aircraft and deadlier munitions bring results, as General Keegan implied? Five years of aerial interdiction would fail to establish a direct link, principally because neither electronics, nor photography, nor visual observation could precisely determine what was happening on the disadvantageous terrain below. Analysts tended to measure effort, mainly sorties and bombs dropped, along with the fires and secondary explosions attributable to the bombs and other weapons. The jungle hid the exact results — persons killed or maimed and supplies destroyed. The enemy's plans also remained concealed, so that inaction might reflect a strategic decision rather than disruption of the Ho Chi Minh Trail.[22]

Dr. Robert T. N. Schwartz, chief of the Office of Operations Analysis at Seventh Air Force headquarters, sounded a note of caution when he advised against attributing the changes in enemy traffic patterns during the summer of 1968 solely to aerial interdiction. The weather, he suggested, might have done more than aerial attacks to reduce the volume of road traffic during the southwest monsoon season. Although trucks kept moving in parts of southern Laos during the rainy season, the numbers never approached dry-season levels, and it seemed safe to conclude that such would have been the case even if there had been no attempt at aerial interdiction. Moreover, during the southwest monsoon period just ended, two tropical storms had deluged southern North Vietnam and further impeded a pattern of travel already affected by the normal rainfall in southern Laos.[23]

Although a taint of uncertainty thus clung to assessments of the results of the 1968 southwest monsoon campaign, planners looked ahead to what they could do in the approaching dry season. Delays caused by the need to coordinate with the embassy at Vientiane raised doubts among airmen that the forthcoming Commando Hunt operation could fulfill its potential unless an accommodation could be found between military efficiency and diplomatic constraints. The rules enforced by the ambassador already seemed to deprive Task Force Alpha of much of the technological advantage provided by its computerized Surveillance Center and the net of electronic listening posts placed across portions of the Ho Chi Minh Trail. Not only did proposed strikes undergo review, General McBride's command also had to submit through the Seventh Air Force a request for approval by the U.S. embassy at Vientiane before planting or replenishing the strings of sensors. The delay between a request by the task force to drop sensors and an ambassadorial decision usually amounted to three or four days, and for an area that Ambassador Sullivan considered sensitive, a week or more of deliberation might be required.[24]

Following the interdiction campaign during the 1968 southwest monsoon season, Ambassador Sullivan yielded his veto power over the sensor field. He agreed to allow Task Force Alpha greater freedom in maintaining sensor coverage of the Ho Chi Minh Trail itself, provided he retained control farther west, where a scattering of friendly villages served as bases for patrols and roadwatch teams. Consequently, the Placement Planning Committee at Nakhon Phanom—staffed by representatives of the Task Force Alpha's directorates of intelligence, operations, and technical operations—assumed exclusive responsibility for laying out the sensor fields that monitored movement on the trail. This group evaluated each proposed string, sending its recommendations to Seventh Air Force headquarters for a decision. After receiving approval from Tan Son Nhut, task force intelligence specialists prepared maps and loran data for the squadron that would drop the sensors.[25]

The ambassador's early interest in sensor placement reflected his continuing desire to focus the air war on the Ho Chi Minh Trail itself and keep the sensors, and the bombing they would surely trigger, away from areas where Lao civilians or troops loyal to Souvanna might suffer death or injury. This concern stemmed, in turn, from his responsibility to support the regime the prince headed. Besides trying to prevent bombing incidents, which might set the people against the government at Vientiane, Ambassador Sullivan sought to forestall publicity that would reveal cooperation between the supposedly neutral kingdom of Laos and the U.S. military and thus expose the already fragile nation to revenge by the North Vietnamese.[26]

The ambassador's authority over the use of air power in Laos had, by 1968, resulted in a division of the southern part of the kingdom into Steel Tiger Zones I through IV, each with its own rules of engagement. The resulting jigsaw puzzle caused confusion, and to establish order, the Seventh Air Force in the summer of 1968 proposed combining some of these sectors and simplifying clearance procedures for air strikes. This suggestion led to a discussion of the rules of engagement for air operations throughout all of Laos. On September 9, 1968, Ambassador Sullivan and his aides conferred at Udorn, Thailand, with General Brown, who had taken over from General Momyer in August, and members of the Seventh Air Force staff.[27]

The War against Trucks

The one-day meeting began with an outline of the Commando Hunt plan by Brig. Gen. Robert J. Holbury, General Brown's Director of Combat Operations. Ambassador Sullivan responded by suggesting that "some of the rules of engagement are not too well understood," as indicated by the fact that rules adopted by the Seventh Air Force sometimes proved stricter than his own. For example, Sullivan's policy declared that Steel Tiger Zone I, which hugged the border of South Vietnam, was "to all intents and purposes" a free-fire zone, except in the immediate vicinity of suspected prisoner of war camps, but General Momyer had nevertheless insisted on using forward air controllers in the northern part of that zone. Actually Momyer had imposed controls within a free-fire area to prevent accidental bombing in adjacent territory where the embassy's restrictions were in force; in short, the patchwork of free-fire zones and restricted areas set up by the embassy, along with the characteristics of the strike aircraft, had forced him to impose the seemingly arbitrary restrictions. In applying the ambassador's rules, Seventh Air Force leaders had to take into account the speed and turning radius of aircraft and visibility from the cockpit. "Pilots," said General Brown, "are not able to see neat lines on the ground."

Despite this somewhat contentious start, the conferees at the Udorn meeting soon turned from blame for the past to cooperation in the future, and the session not only resolved a basic misunderstanding, but also opened the way for further clarification of the rules of engagement. Ambassador Sullivan's main contribution to the Udorn talks consisted of correcting the impression, which colored Holbury's introductory remarks, that aircraft on armed reconnaissance could not, under any circumstances, attack truck parks or transshipment points located farther than two hundred yards from a known road. This, the ambassador declared, was simply not true. As he explained it: "If the truck got from a motorable road to a truck park . . . ,you can assume it got there by a motorable road or trail." In other words, truck parks, supply depots, and similar installations were fair game, on the Ho Chi Minh Trail at least, if not throughout all of Laos. The meeting on September 9 could not, of course, resolve every issue as neatly as this one, but the session did create a spirit of cooperation that persisted in subsequent discussions between airmen and diplomats.[28]

The embassy's insistence on approving B–52 strikes led to further talks. Experience during the southwest monsoon campaign of 1968 convinced Seventh Air Force planners that the need to obtain embassy clearance for these attacks had become an obstacle to military efficiency. On the other hand, since Ambassador Sullivan had to make sure the bombers did not undermine Souvanna Phouma by causing civilian casualties and stirring up resentment against the government of Laos, he could not simply unleash the bombers to attack at will throughout the kingdom. Realizing this, representatives of General Brown proposed that the embassy make its evaluation well beforehand and, insofar as possible, "locate 'free strike zones' around the planned Commando Hunt interdiction points." These zones would embrace truck parks and storage areas and permit targeting specialists to shift or establish target boxes within the zones, as dictated by current intelligence. Such a policy, its advocates believed, would enable the B–52s to react promptly to sensor activations, avoiding the delays characteristic of the southwest monsoon campaign.[29]

A survey of Seventh Air Force records relating to Operation Turnpike disclosed that when the headquarters selected a target for the first time, an average of 5.8 days elapsed from submission to the Military Assistance Command until receipt of a decision from the embassy in Vientiane. If a second request proved necessary, either because the target remained active or the first nomination had been rejected, the aggregate delay averaged 14.5 days. Review within the embassy seemed to account for most of the lost time, an average of 4.4 days for initial requests and 9.9 days for renominations. Embassy officials protested these figures, insisting they could reach a decision within a day or two unless the presence of roadwatch teams, or possibly prisoners of war, forced them to exercise greater caution. Like their Seventh Air Force counterparts at Tan Son Nhut, members of the ambassador's staff searched the files at Vientiane for evidence to support the embassy's position, and the battle lines seemed to have formed. Fortunately, both the civilians at Vientiane and the airmen at Tan Son Nhut recognized that bombing might endanger friendly forces or inhabited villages and prove self-defeating; they therefore could avoid a defensive chip-on-the-shoulder attitude and concentrate on the real issue—minimizing the delay when the B–52s posed no threat to Souvanna's troops, to the civilian populace of his kingdom, or to prisoners held by the enemy.

Once the representatives of the Seventh Air Force and the embassy had focused on the key point, a compromise emerged. During a meeting at Udorn on September 24, one of Ambassador Sullivan's delegates suggested that the Seventh Air Force request advance approval for areas encompassing important B–52 target boxes. If the proposed area lay farther than one kilometer from a road that was part of the Ho Chi Minh Trail, aerial photos should accompany the request so the ambassador could determine quickly whether occupied villages, roadwatch sites, or prison camps might preclude or limit an attack. Once the embassy approved a special Arc Light operating area, a name decided on by the conferees, B–52s might hit any of the boxes within it during a period of thirty days or more, provided that the Seventh Air Force, through the Military Assistance Command, notified the U.S. Ambassador to Laos 24 hours in advance of a strike. The requirement enabled the Central Intelligence Agency's station chief at Vientiane to make a last-minute check on the position of guerrilla forces or roadwatch teams. Within a year, the embassy gained direct access to photo interpreters at Seventh Air Force headquarters for aid in handling requests for attacks by the B–52s; on just three hours' notice, the embassy could shift an Arc Light strike from one approved operating area to another.[30] Looking back on the results of the September 24 conference, Colonel Howard Smith, the Seventh Air Force targeting specialist, declared that "the most significant improvement in [B–52 target] validation was the development of Special Arc Light Operating Areas ."[31]

Important though it was, this latest coordinating technique could not satisfy everyone. General Keegan continued to complain, with some justification, that vehicles still might escape from a truck park or bypass a blocked road before B–52s could attack them. Delays, in fact, did occur from time to time when a possible prisoner of war camp had to be investigated or because a roadwatch team posted near the special Arc Light operating area broke contact with headquarters, became lost, or embarked on a special mission.[32]

The September 1968 discussions between the Vientiane embassy and the Seventh Air Force foreshadowed a more general relaxation of operating restrictions in Laos, but as this trend evolved, attention again shifted to North Vietnam. In the United States, the Presidential campaign approached its climax. On the Democratic side, President Johnson had announced on March 31, 1968, that he would not seek reelection and halted the bombing of North Vietnam, north of the 19th parallel, in the hope of inducing the Hanoi government to negotiate a settlement that would ensure the independence of South Vietnam. The talks began at Paris, France, but the differences between the United States and North Vietnam proved irreconcilable, as the U.S. negotiators insisted that the North withdraw its troops from South Vietnam and the North Vietnamese demanded that the communists participate in a coalition government to be established at Saigon. The war thus remained a dominant issue in the election, even though the antiwar faction of the Democratic Party had lost its leaders. By winning the California primary, Robert F. Kennedy, the late President John F. Kennedy's brother and attorney general, now a senator from New York, put an end to the candidacy of Senator Eugene J. McCarthy of Minnesota, who had challenged Johnson in the New Hampshire primary. Then, on the very evening of Robert Kennedy's victory, an assassin shot him to death.

At Chicago, where the Democrats held their nominating convention, the police tried to prevent an antiwar crowd from marching on the hall where the party was meeting. The ensuing violence, which has been described as a "police riot," produced televised scenes of police using clubs and tear gas against demonstrators, some of them waving the Viet Cong flag, who responded with rocks and bottles. Amid this turmoil, the delegates nominated Hubert H. Humphrey, who, as Johnson's vice president, found himself saddled with the unpopular war in Southeast Asia. His opponents were Richard M. Nixon, a Republican, who had served as Vice President to Dwight D. Eisenhower and lost the presidential election to John Kennedy in 1960, and George C. Wallace, a former governor of Alabama, running as a third-party candidate.

Whereas Wallace and his vice presidential candidate, retired Gen. Curtis E. LeMay, a former Chief of Staff of the Air Force, stood for a more vigorous prosecution of the war, Nixon profited when a reporter misinterpreted a routine speech, delivered in New Hampshire in March 1968, and filed a story to the effect that the candidate had a "secret plan" to end the war. In late September, Humphrey revealed his own program for dealing with the war—an end to all bombing of the North as a further means of encouraging negotiations and pursuit of the policy, suggested earlier by the Johnson administration, of turning the war over to the South Vietnamese. These actions, the Democratic candidate declared, constituted an "acceptable risk" for peace. President Johnson apparently agreed, for on October 31 he announced that all bombing of North Vietnam would end on the following day. If the President hoped that his action would win the election for Humphrey, he was disappointed, for on November 5, the Republican ticket won by a narrow margin; nor did the bombing halt gain any concessions from the North Vietnamese, as the stalemate continued at Paris.[33]

President Johnson's ban on bombing the North imposed new burdens on the Seventh Air Force. To avoid accidental violations of North Vietnamese territory, the command exercised radar control over aircraft attacking or patrolling near the border of North Vietnam. Despite the concern that pilots might inadvertently stray into North Vietnamese air space, deliberate incursions were permissible in certain circumstances. The Johnson and Nixon administrations insisted that the Hanoi government had tacitly agreed to permit unarmed reconnaissance craft to fly surveillance missions over the nation, something that the North Vietnamese publicly denied. If the enemy should enforce this denial by firing against the reconnaissance missions, or if weapons in North Vietnam should engage aircraft over South Vietnam or southern Laos, the United States felt free to retaliate against the offending antiaircraft or missile batteries.

Before long, further changes occurred in the rules of engagement relating to North Vietnam. During 1970, the Joint Chiefs of Staff obtained an easing of existing policy to permit attacks on fire control or surface-to-air missile radars that posed an imminent threat to aircraft over Laos. Indeed, as a form of reconnaissance, fighter-bombers carrying radar-homing missiles received permission to fly over North Vietnamese soil, placing themselves between B–52s bombing in Laos and known radar sites in the North, and even "trolling," offering themselves as targets, so that enemy radar would begin transmitting and thus expose itself to attack. Similarly, the Joint Chiefs of Staff directed that aircraft using laser beams to designate targets along the border might intrude into North Vietnamese airspace to keep the laser accurately focused; any fighter pulling away after releasing a laser-guided bomb also could cross the border to complete the maneuver.[34]

By the time the new rules of engagement for North Vietnam began taking effect, the equivalent of free-fire zones existed on most major truck routes of the Ho Chi Minh Trail along the eastern border of Laos. Beginning in the 1968–69 dry season, U.S. airmen had permission to jettison any ordnance, including napalm, in the special Arc Light operating areas, provided only that an airborne battlefield command and control center gave clearance. Also, when visibility was good, crews could drop any type of munitions, "armed or safe," except napalm, on any "motorable trail, road, ford, or bridge in . . . Zone I and II" and along Route 110 in the vicinity of Attopeu. Jettisoning bombs within five hundred yards of a village remained forbidden.[35]

Napalm caused Ambassador Sullivan special concern, even though a number of less spectacular munitions, among them some of the antipersonnel bomblets, could prove equally as deadly. The billowing flames generated by napalm evoked a special horror, however, and accidents involving this weapon, as the embassy real-ized, might cause worldwide revulsion. Nevertheless, napalm came into more gen-eral use beginning with the 1968–69 dry season, for as the North Vietnamese tight-ened their control over the trail, U.S. intelligence concluded that very few genuine noncombatants remained in the area. In Zones I and II, therefore, aircraft directed by forward air controllers could drop napalm on vehicles or other targets within two hundred yards of a road. Throughout Zone I, airmen could respond with napalm if fired on by antiaircraft guns, and in Zone II they could use it against a battery that had not yet opened fire. In Zone III, with its pockets of noncombatants whose vil-lages might play unwilling host to enemy gunners, the rules forbade the use of napalm against antiaircraft sites. Under no circumstances could air crews drop napalm on inhabited villages anywhere in southern Laos.

Even as he eased the restrictions on napalm, the ambassador also relaxed the requirement that forward air controllers direct strikes throughout most of southern Laos. By the end of the 1968–69 dry season, the old policy no longer applied over many of the main supply routes of the Ho Chi Minh Trail. Within a swath extending two hundred yards on either side of most of the heavily traveled roads in Zone I, such as Route 110, and along the Route 8 complex in Zone III, aircraft on armed reconnaissance could now attack without benefit of a forward air controller.

Strikes by F–4s fitted out for radar bombing at first required embassy valida-tion, but such attacks became generally permissible in Zones I and II as early as December 1968. The following March, the ambassador agreed to these radar-direct-ed strikes throughout Laos, except for specified areas, principally Zone IV, that he and his staff continued to examine on a target-by-target basis as requests arrived. By the spring of 1969, moreover, loran began serving as an acceptable substitute for either airborne radar or Combat Skyspot in attacks at night or during bad weather.[36]

Somewhat greater caution was required of the Navy and Marine Corps Grumman A–6s that used airborne radar with a moving target indicator to track vehicles on the ground. During the 1968–69 northeast monsoon season, these air-craft probed darkness and cloud cover to attack trucks on segments of highway near Ban Karai Pass and at the western edge of the demilitarized zone. Although vehicles appeared on the radar scope mounted in the A–6, small villages frequently did not. As a result, in granting permission for the Grumman attack bombers to conduct nighttime armed reconnaissance of roads, or carry out strikes in special Arc Light operating areas, the ambassador insisted that they avoid inhabited villages (few of which still existed on major supply lines) by five hundred yards plus the average bombing error with this type of airborne radar.[37]

In general, Ambassador Sullivan's relaxation of the rules of engagement for Zones I and II and parts of Zone III enabled U.S. aircraft to respond more rapidly to information obtained from electronic sensors planted there. He did not, however, loosen the controls over aerial activity in those portions of Laos where, in his opin-ion, misdirected bombs might cause tragedy and weaken Souvanna Phouma's hold on the kingdom. The Ambassador remained especially concerned about possible attacks on roadwatch teams, or other units dispatched into southeastern Laos, or on Lao villagers who aided these groups.[38]

Because of the danger of adverse publicity, which made no distinction between tear gas and lethal types, the ambassador resisted General Westmoreland's efforts to use tear gas as a standard means of harassing North Vietnamese engineers repairing bomb damage along the Ho Chi Minh Trail. Nevertheless, nonlethal chemical agents could always be used against enemy troops who tried to prevent the rescue of downed airmen. Similarly, both Ambassador Sullivan and his successor, G. McMurtrie Godley, usually agreed to the use of gas in extricating patrols from hostile territory.[39]

Determined to avoid tragic and unnecessary loss of life, Ambassador Sullivan not only refused to approve B–52 strikes that might conceivably endanger prisoners of war held at known locations in southern Laos, but also insisted that forward air controllers direct all attacks near suspected sites of prison compounds. Yet, as the ambassador had promised during the September 1968 Udorn conference, he remained "always willing to consider any evidence . . . , any photographs or other intelligence, that would indicate these [prison camps] are no longer active."[40]

In spite of this pledge to be open-minded, both Adm. Ulysses S. Sharp, Jr., and his successor as Commander in Chief, Pacific, Adm. John S. McCain, Jr., considered the embassy officials overly scrupulous, rejecting proposed strikes that had scarcely a remote possibility of harming prisoners. The fact remained that deciding whether a camp was occupied continued to be a responsibility of the ambassador, usually acting on evidence provided by ground reconnaissance teams or Air Force aerial photographs. Under Sullivan's rules and those enforced by Ambassador Godley, U.S. fliers had to exercise caution near all prison sites judged active by the embassy. Aircraft could not conduct visual strikes within five hundred fifty yards of a confirmed prisoner of war compound or closer than three thousand yards (finally changed to one thousand yards) using all-weather bombing equipment.[41]

The succession of piecemeal changes made to the rules of engagement during late 1968 and early 1969 cried out for codification; and in April, after Ambassador Sullivan had left Vientiane for a new assignment, representatives of the Seventh Air Force, the Military Assistance Command, Vietnam, and the embassy met at Vientiane. Since Ambassador Godley had not yet arrived, Edward E. Archer, the Political Officer, represented the diplomatic staff. Although Archer impressed one Air Force officer as having "a closed mind on various subjects,"[42] another member of the Seventh Air Force delegation felt that the embassy official "came around" once he realized that the meeting was not an "Air Force trick."[43] Despite the initial misgivings on both sides, the session proved singularly productive.

Basically, Archer and his fellow conferees drew a line down the middle of the Laotian panhandle, dividing the region into eastern and western sectors called Steel Tiger East and Steel Tiger West. Included in the eastern part were Zones I and II and a part of III, plus the special operating area along Route 110, while the west embraced the remainder of Zone III and all of IV. Rules of engagement in Steel

The War against Trucks

Tiger East resembled those for the former Zone II, while the directives for Steel Tiger West followed the pattern for Zone IV, the most restrictive of the old sectors. As a result, in Steel Tiger East the free-fire zones established during the recent dry season remained in effect, as did the practice of not insisting on a forward air controller when attacking most main roads. In contrast, throughout Steel Tiger West, radar bombing and the use of napalm required embassy consent. As in the old Zone IV, aircraft could not fly armed reconnaissance in the western sector, nor could they return ground fire unless recovering downed airmen or retrieving roadwatch teams.[44]

Revision of the rules of engagement continued after Godley arrived at Vientiane in June 1969. Extensive fighting in northern Laos, along with the "rapid turnover of personnel in SEA [Southeast Asia]," prompted the convening in August of another meeting to consolidate and simplify the rules governing the air war in the kingdom.[45] Most of the conference's decisions, which went into effect in September, dealt with northern Laos, although the delegates did shift slightly westward the boundary separating the two segments of Steel Tiger. Compared to aircraft operating in the western sector, those in Steel Tiger East continued to have greater freedom in selecting both targets and ordnance. In the east, for example, aircraft could drop napalm on trucks or occupied antiaircraft emplacements, attack villages that fired on them, or, if fitted with all-weather bombing equipment, hit any worthwhile target regardless of its proximity to a road.[46] Normally, forward air controllers had to handle all strikes in the western zone, including those in response to antiaircraft fire, but in the more permissive Steel Tiger East, only those directed against targets more than two hundred yards from a road. In the west, like the east, loran or radar could take the place of an airborne controller.[47]

As a consequence of the August 1969 conference, Godley took action against the increasing movement of supplies from southern Laos, through Cambodia, into South Vietnam. To disrupt this activity, he created three special operating areas at the southern extremity of the Ho Chi Minh Trail where tactical fighters could attack without forward air controllers. One of them he established in Steel Tiger East and the others just west of the boundary between two sectors. Within each of these areas, air strikes were "authorized against all forms of military activity," including antiaircraft fire from villages.[48]

In another change, effective October 1, Godley authorized the assistant air attaché at Savannakhet to validate strikes on targets "fleeting in nature" but "visible to someone," against which "air has not been scheduled or requested." Authorization to attack these "targets of opportunity" remained in effect for seventy-two hours and could be extended for an additional twenty-four hours. Once validation by the assistant air attaché expired, Vientiane had to approve further attacks.[49]

Meanwhile, Raven forward air controllers assumed greater responsibility for initiating attacks. Operating mainly on the fringes of the Ho Chi Minh Trail when they directed strikes in southern Laos, Ravens had formerly obtained approval from a Lao observer, either in the aircraft or with troops on the ground, before engaging a target. By the fall of 1969, they no longer needed such permission, for in most instances (the use of napalm would be an exception) the airborne controllers could now check in with a Laotian officer at the operations center and obtain the necessary clearance before taking off.[50]

The changes in the rules of engagement during 1968 and 1969, although they failed to give military commanders all the authority they desired, did result in greater freedom to wage war in southern Laos. One senior officer who expressed general acceptance of, if not enthusiasm for, the evolving arrangement was Lt. Gen. David C. Jones, Deputy Chief of Staff for Operations, later Vice Commander, Seventh Air Force, and still later Air Force Chief of Staff. He concluded that coordination with the embassy at Vientiane during the dry season of 1968–69 had proved cumbersome, but not crippling. Despite Ambassador Sullivan's concern for the survival of Souvanna Phouma's government, General Jones believed that U.S. officials, not Lao, made the basic operational decisions. Although the general acknowledged that the need to coordinate with Vientiane could cause annoying delays, he seemed satisfied that military realities received consideration in drafting the self-imposed rules governing U.S. actions in southern Laos. "It was pretty much what the United States said," Jones observed, "whether we would bomb a certain point or operate under a certain restriction." On the other hand, he pointed out, a more efficient course of action from a purely military point of view might have been to consider the supply and infiltration routes through Laos as part of the battleground in South Vietnam, assigning responsibility for both to the same military commander and eliminating the U.S. ambassador at Vientiane from the command structure.[51]

The process of amending the rules of engagement did not end in 1969, however. After the combined U.S. and South Vietnamese invasion of Cambodia in the spring of 1970, Ambassador Godley tried to use air power against roads and waterways leading into that country, where the communist Khmer Rouge sought to overcome an American-sponsored regime. Besides retaining the three special operating areas that covered land routes to Cambodia, he assigned Raven forward air controllers to patrol the Mekong River, another supply artery for the communist insurgents.[52]

Even though U.S. ground forces pulled out of Cambodia by midsummer, South Vietnamese troops continued fighting there, and southwestern Laos increased in importance as a supply corridor for the Khmer Rouge opposing them. Consequently, American-assisted forces probed this corner of Laos, triggering counterthrusts by the North Vietnamese and Pathet Lao. In this sort of fighting, the battlefield itself and nearby enemy-held routes of supply and reinforcement became, in effect, special operating areas or free-fire zones. When intense combat erupted during the 1970 southwest monsoon season, Ambassador Godley gave the assistant air attaché at Pakse authority to approve the use of napalm in support of Lao troops in contact with the enemy in southern Steel Tiger West. Either a trained Lao controller on the ground or a U.S. forward air controller with a Lao observer on board had to direct the actual delivery of the incendiary canisters.[53]

The War against Trucks

The enemy in Steel Tiger West did not exert the firm control that he maintained over the eastern region. Towns, roads, and terrain features in the west frequently changed hands, increasing the danger of accidentally bombing friendly outposts or inhabited settlements. Only in the special operating areas could aircraft attack villages that had fired on them, although the ambassador permitted automatic retaliation of this sort in Steel Tiger East. Finally, during the 1971–72 dry season, as attempts to disrupt traffic on the Ho Chi Minh Trail were coming to an end after the North Vietnamese invasion of the South, the ambassador at Vientiane amended the rules for Steel Tiger West to permit instant retaliation against villages from which 14.5-mm or larger antiaircraft weapons had opened fire. The altitude at which an aircraft drew fire apparently indicated the caliber of weapon.[54]

Rules of engagement, however detailed, could not prevent occasional bombing accidents, although these were less frequent in southern Laos than in the northern part of the kingdom or in South Vietnam. Few inhabited villages survived near the Ho Chi Minh Trail to fall victim to accidental attack, and the precautions taken to protect roadwatch teams and other reconnaissance units apparently succeeded. The most serious mishap occurred in July 1971, when an AC–130 incorrectly reported its position as being over a free-fire zone in Cambodia and received permission for an attack that killed nine Lao fishermen and wounded seven.[55]

An ever-evolving set of rules of engagement governed the air war in southern Laos. The greatest change took place between the summer of 1968 and the autumn of 1969 and coincided with the start of systematic year-round interdiction on the Ho Chi Minh Trail, an undertaking that depended on sensors, aircraft, and other equipment designed or modified for that purpose. In general, the rules for southern Laos were stricter in the west, where there existed a greater danger of accidentally bombing friendly troops or villagers, and more permissive in the east, along the border with South Vietnam. There the electronic sensors maintained their vigil, the volume of North Vietnamese infiltration was heaviest, friendly casualties less likely than in the west, and rapid reaction more important. Unless proposed attacks endangered roadwatch teams or prisoners of the enemy, the planners of Commando Hunt and the subsequent interdiction operations would enjoy almost a free hand.

Chapter Three

Weapons for Interdiction

Although the Infiltration Surveillance Center operated by Task Force Alpha, the automated nerve center that responded to impulses from the sensor fields, served as the showpiece of U.S. research and development for the Vietnam War, other examples of advanced technology aided the attacks on the Ho Chi Minh Trail. The Commando Hunt series of operations, lasting from the dry season of 1968–69 until the spring of 1972, attempted year-round interdiction of the trail and depended on a variety of technological innovations other than the sensors planted along infiltration routes and the computers and display terminals at Nakhon Phanom that processed their electronic signals. Indeed, in the summer of 1968, when planning got under way for the first operation of the Commando Hunt series, the Air Force Systems Command, especially its Aeronautical Systems Division, was working on roughly one hundred items intended for use in Southeast Asia. Most of these were grouped in Project Shed Light, an attempt to improve the ability of the Air Force to fight at night. Because of its purpose, Shed Light had an impact on the interdiction campaign in southern Laos, where the enemy took full advantage of darkness. In general, Air Force-developed equipment useful for impeding enemy movement through southern Laos fell into two broad categories: strike aircraft and aids to intelligence or targeting. Strike aircraft included gunships and the so-called self-contained night attack types, fitted with radar and infrared sensors, some employing laser-guided bombs. Aids to intelligence or targeting included aircraft for relaying sensor signals to the Surveillance Center, reconnaissance techniques and equipment, and beacons for accurate bombing. The Air Force did not monopolize research and development, however. Among other agencies, the Defense Communications Planning Group played a dominant role in developing sensors for electronic surveillance of the trail, and both the Army and Navy contributed to the interdiction effort, for example, in the use of radar and infrared equipment for general surveillance and target tracking.[1]

In the category of strike aircraft, the Air Force's fixed-wing gunship (a name that distinguished it from the helicopter gunship, used so extensively in Southeast Asia) seemed to provide a devastating weapon for night attack. By the end of December 1965, the Douglas AC–47 had demonstrated the potential value of this kind of aircraft for interdicting the Ho Chi Minh Trail. After locating a truck convoy or other target, the pilot circled to his left, using a sight, which might be as simple as a mark on the window next to him, to adjust the angle of bank and keep the automatic weapons firing downward from the side of the airplane trained on the enemy below. Unfortunately, this particular gunship, based on the obsolete C–47 transport, mounted just three multibarrel machine guns, and the crew had to rely on flares to locate targets by night. The lack of speed and armor protection, along with the short range of its weapons, left the AC–47 so vulnerable to antiaircraft fire (four of the gunships were shot down in one six-month period, three over Laos) that it had to withdraw to the safer areas of South Vietnam in mid-1966.

The search for a successor to the AC–47 produced Gunship II, the AC–130A, based on the successful Lockheed C–130A transport. Together, the four Allison turboprop engines that powered the new gunship developed roughly seven times the combined horsepower of the two Pratt and Whitney radials on the older airplane. In addition to four multibarrel 7.62-mm machine guns, the kind used in the AC–47, four heavier 20-mm multibarrel cannon also fired downward from the left-hand side of Gunship II's fuselage. A night observation device, essentially a telescope that captured and intensified the light of the moon and stars, enabled the new gunship to make minimal use of flares, which served to alert enemy gunners and could silhouette the aircraft, if an overcast reflected their light. The prototype of the AC–130A also boasted an array of radars for navigating, detecting vehicles, and locating reflectors or transponders set out to mark positions held by friendly troops. A searchlight fitted with interchangeable filters to project ultraviolet, infrared, or ordinary light further reduced the dependence on flares to illuminate targets below. An infrared detection unit, located in the lower left side of the fuselage, searched ahead for heat from internal combustion engines or campfires or scanned areas on which the searchlight operator had focused the infrared beam.[2]

From late September through November 1967, Gunship II went to war, bursting on the scene with deadly effect. In one night over the Ho Chi Minh Trail, it demolished eight trucks in a single convoy, and during its operational test, the new gunship received credit for destroying thirty-eight of the ninety-four trucks detected by its sensors. All of these kills occurred on armed reconnaissance missions carried out before the Mud River sensor field began reporting to Nakhon Phanom on the flow of truck traffic along the trail, and the Infiltration Surveillance Center, once it began functioning as designed, promised to enhance the effectiveness of the AC–130A. Since the sensors did not yet report on traffic along the trail, finding, attacking, and destroying trucks depended on the skills of a crew that included Maj. Roland W. Terry, the pilot, who had helped develop both the AC–47 and the vastly improved Gunship II; Maj. James R. Krause, the navigator and an expert in the development and use of infrared equipment; and Maj. James R. Wolverton, who worked out the tactics used during the operational evaluation. Besides flying interdiction missions, Gunship II conducted test firings to prove that the 20-mm shell could actually penetrate the jungle canopy, went to the aid of outposts under attack, and tried unsuccessfully to intercept North Vietnamese helicopters believed to be operating near the demilitarized zone.

Following the operational evaluation in South Vietnam and Laos, Gunship II returned to the United States for refurbishment, but was back in action over the Ho Chi Minh Trail by the end of February 1968. During the preliminary testing in the United States and the operational evaluation in Southeast Asia, the infrared sensor and the night observation device proved more reliable than radar in detecting trucks. Once the sensors had discovered their prey, they fed information into an analog computer that compared the line of sight between the gunship and the target with the cones of fire from the 7.62-mm machine guns and 20-mm cannon that poked their snouts from the aircraft. A visual display enabled the pilot to superimpose an image that outlined the impact area of his weapons on another image representing the target; having done this, he unleashed a torrent of fire on the trucks, troops, or enemy installation in the darkness below.[3]

Although on the basis of shaky evidence, the Aeronautical Systems Division declared the Gunship II prototype a spectacular success in terms of cost effectiveness. Relying almost exclusively on what the crew members reported seeing during the various attacks, the division's operations analysts tried to add up every "major event" attributable to this aircraft. These included such diverse and difficult to verify elements as trucks or boats destroyed, fires and explosions, antiaircraft guns destroyed, and even enemy troops reported killed when Gunship II went to the aid of friendly outposts. (In this last category, every five victims reported by the defenders counted as one major event.) The analysts then calculated all the costs associated with the project from the airframe, excluding depreciation, to each bullet fired and flare dropped. Out of this jumble of figures emerged a cost per event of slightly less than five thousand dollars, making the unescorted AC–130A, by this imprecise and arbitrary standard, one of the most efficient interdiction weapons in the entire Air Force.[4]

The apparent success of the Gunship II prototype aroused enthusiasm for additional AC–130As. Although Secretary of the Air Force Harold Brown initially favored installing Gunship II equipment in the obsolescent Fairchild C–119 cargo plane, he soon agreed to the conversion of seven of the first-line Lockheed transports, so that by the end of December 1968, four AC–130As had begun flying combat missions over Laos. Along with the sensors tested in Gunship II, the AC–130As mounted the Black Crow ignition detector, which reacted to the electromagnetic emissions from an operating gasoline engine. Because signals from ground-based radars tended to interfere with Black Crow, pilots tried, insofar as possible, to shield the sensor head, on the left side of the airplane, using the fuselage to block transmissions from any nearby radar site.

By the time the four AC–130As, nicknamed Spectres, went into action, President Johnson had already stopped all aerial attacks on North Vietnam, shifting the air war to the Ho Chi Minh Trail, where airborne sensors probed for an enemy concealed by haze, cloud, jungle, camouflage, and cover of darkness. Because of its ability to locate and destroy cargo-laden trucks, the AC–130A received a starring role in the continuing drama of aerial interdiction. Various officials, including Gen. George Brown, the Seventh Air Force commander, and Ambassador Sullivan at

The War against Trucks

Vientiane, warned late in 1968 of a second Tet offensive on the anniversary of the first, and their words brought to mind the columns of trucks, too numerous to be attacked effectively by the available aircraft, that streamed headlights-on through the Laotian night in preparation for the previous Tet attack. In massing for a second great offensive to coincide with the 1969 holiday, the North Vietnamese would not be so foolhardy as to drive with their lights on, as they had done with near impunity in late 1967. Because U.S. air power had grown so much stronger, concealment would be the watchword, as the trucks moved in darkness and took advantage of the jungle canopy. In the belief that properly equipped aircraft, alerted by monitoring devices on the ground, could find and batter the road convoys, Secretary Harold Brown and the uniformed leadership of the Air Force decided to acquire sensor-laden, single-purpose gunships instead of the more versatile jet fighter-bombers they would otherwise have preferred.[5]

While Gunship II, based on the C–130A, took shape, Secretary Brown persisted in his plan to convert the older and slower C–119 into a gunship. The question of modifying the Fairchild transport for this purpose first surfaced in June 1967, at about the time the Gunship II was undergoing its initial testing at Eglin Air Force Base, Florida. General Momyer, then in command of the Seventh Air Force, immediately objected to the introduction into Southeast Asia of yet an another aircraft, like the different variants of the C–47, that he considered obsolete. Acquisition of the elderly C–119, he believed, would further complicate the already difficult problems of maintenance and logistics that his organization faced. At the time, Secretary Brown insisted on the development of an AC–119, for he opposed the diversion of additional C–130s from transport duty, a position he clung to until Gunship II demonstrated its worth in Southeast Asia. Prior to the successful combat test of the AC–130A, he intended to use the C–119G, powered by two piston engines, as the basis for a gunship to replace the AC–47, even though the lumbering AC–119G, like the earlier gunship, could not to survive over defended portions of the Ho Chi Minh Trail. To attack the logistics complex, he proposed a faster, higher-flying gunship, based on the C–119K, which had two auxiliary jet engines mounted in pods beneath the wing to improve performance. As a result of Secretary Brown's views, a mixed force of gunships took shape. The AC–119G Shadow replaced the AC–47, which was earmarked for the South Vietnamese air arm, and the AC–119K Stinger joined the AC–130 Spectre in attacking road traffic through southern Laos.[6]

Intended for interdiction, though with a secondary mission of supporting ground troops, the Stinger carried heavier armament than the Shadow, a pair of multibarrel 20-mm guns and four multibarrel 7.62-mm machine guns, whereas the AC–119G mounted only the machine guns. Both aircraft used the standard night observation device, but the K model could also search out targets with infrared equipment. A beacon-tracking radar helped the AC–119K pinpoint friendly troops, who had the necessary transponder; this feature helped the Stinger interpose a curtain of fire to protect besieged outposts, for example, but served no purpose on interdiction missions. In their fire control systems, both the AC–119G and the K version used the same kind of analog computer as had been tested in Gunship II. Basically, the computer lacked flexibility, since it could be programmed for only a limited range of airspeeds, bank angles, and altitudes. If a shift from one sensor to another, or enemy fire, dictated a marked change in altitude, the crew might have to reprogram the computer to continue the mission. The inability of the automatic pilot to hold the gunship in a steeply banked turn further complicated the task of fire control with the Shadow and Stinger.[7]

Although the AC–119K Stinger performed adequately during a combat evaluation lasting from November 1969 through February 1970, the sixteen aircraft of this type assigned to Southeast Asia soon revealed other weaknesses, as well as certain strengths, in missions against the trail. Experience in combat demonstrated that the 20-mm shell was too light to destroy trucks, and the rapid-fire weapon often jammed. Although the two auxiliary jet engines improved performance, they increased the operating ceiling to only about fifty-five hundred feet above ground level, beyond reach of machine guns, but well within range of the 23-mm, 37-mm, and 57-mm antiaircraft guns that were becoming more numerous along the trail. On the other hand, the auxiliary jets also enabled the flight engineer to reduce the power setting and richness of the fuel mixture for the piston engines, adjustments that curtailed the exhaust plumes and made optical tracking difficult for the gunners below.[8] Moreover, if the gun crews should knock out an engine or inflict other severe damage, the auxiliary powerplants gave the Stinger a chance to survive, provided the crew reacted promptly and skillfully.

On the night of May 8, 1970 near the ruins of the abandoned village of Ban Ban in Laos, enemy fire ripped a fourteen-foot piece, including the aileron, from the right wing of a Stinger piloted by Capt. Alan D. Milacek. The plane fell about a thousand feet, but Milacek leveled off by applying full left rudder and aileron while forcing maximum power from the right-hand engines, piston and jet, both of which trailed fiery plumes almost a yard long. Luckily the exhaust did not attract the further attention of North Vietnamese gunners. The crew then stripped the interior, lightening the craft so that it could cross a range of mountains, and the captain managed to land at Udorn, Thailand, using the entire runway after touching down, without flaps, at 150 knots, 33 knots faster than normal landing speed.[9]

The ordeal of Milacek and his crew demonstrated the vulnerability of the AC–119K to antiaircraft fire, which became deadlier as the enemy deployed an increasing number of weapons that could reach the Stinger's normal operating altitude. Unable to climb out of range of the antiaircraft guns, the AC–119K also lacked the maneuverability to avoid the strings of tracers rising from the ground, for the added thrust of the jet engines could not fully compensate for the additional weight of guns, fire control system, and sensors, leaving the aircraft likely to stall if the pilot banked too steeply or pulled up too sharply. Because of this vulnerability, pilots tried to avoid "any AAA [antiaircraft artillery] environment of larger than 57-mm weapons," although even the 57-mm weapon could be effective, without radar control, at altitudes of nine thousand to eleven thousand feet.[10] By February 1971, the

The War against Trucks

AC–119K gunships no longer attacked traffic in the vicinity of Mu Gia, Ban Karai, and Ban Raving Passes; Tchepone; and Ban Laboy Ford, though the planes continued to serve elsewhere in Laos.[11]

As General Momyer had feared, maintenance problems dogged the Fairchild gunships throughout their service in Southeast Asia. The G models in particular proved to be a mechanic's nightmare, though the Ks had troubles enough. Beginning in December 1971, 20-mm fire from the Stingers unaccountably kept missing targets. The problem appeared to lie in the computerized fire control system, which somehow misinterpreted the sensor data it was translating into instructions for the pilot. Accuracy had not improved by the end of March 1972, when North Vietnam invaded the South, and emphasis shifted from interdiction of the Ho Chi Minh Trail to the support of South Vietnamese troops.[12]

Although better performing, easier to maintain, and more reliable than the AC–119K Stingers, the AC–130A Spectre gunships also revealed increasing vulnerability to North Vietnamese antiaircraft batteries as the first of the Commando Hunt operations progressed. During March 1969 enemy gunners scored their first hit on one of the Spectres, and on May 24 another of the aircraft sustained mortal damage. On board the doomed gunship, SSgt. Jack W. Troglen, who peered into the night from the partially open cargo ramp in order to spot strings of tracers, warned the pilot, Lt. Col. William J. Schwehm, that antiaircraft fire was climbing toward them, but before the pilot could dodge the shells, two 37-mm rounds struck the fuselage, fatally wounding Sergeant Troglen and severing the hydraulic lines that operated the rudder, elevator trim, and automatic pilot. The sergeant died while Schwehm struggled to fly the plane to Ubon Air Base, Thailand, where most of the surviving crew members parachuted into the darkness. Remaining on board to help with the emergency landing were the copilot, Maj. Gerald H. Piehl; one of the sensor operators; and SSgt. Cecil F. Taylor, the flight engineer, who had to crank down the flaps as the plane descended toward the runway. Flaps extended, the Spectre settled onto the pavement with its main landing gear, but the nose dropped suddenly, causing the gunship to bounce out of control, collide with a hut, and burst into flame. Sergeant Taylor died in the crash, but the pilot, copilot, and sensor operator escaped with their lives, as did those who had parachuted. The loss of this AC–130A reduced the number in Southeast Asia to just three, but three others arrived almost immediately from the United States, so that six were available for the dry-season interdiction operation, Commando Hunt III, which began in the fall of 1969.[13]

An escort of F–4s had orbited above Schwehm's AC–130A to discourage antiaircraft fire by attacking any battery bold enough to engage the gunship, but in this instance the enemy gunners got off ten rounds, scoring hits with two, before the fighter-bombers could react. Since antiaircraft fire destroyed the aircraft and killed two crewmen while Secretary of the Air Force Robert C. Seamans, Jr., recently appointed by President Richard M. Nixon, was visiting Southeast Asia, the service secretary took a particular interest in reducing the vulnerability of AC–130 gunships by pushing ahead with modifications already under consideration by the Aeronautical Systems Division. The division's plan called for improved sensors plus longer range and harder hitting weapons; taken together, the modifications would enable the gunship to attack while out of range of all but the heaviest of the enemy's antiaircraft weapons.[14]

The determination of Secretary Seamans to improve the AC–130 reflected the importance of aerial interdiction of the Ho Chi Minh Trail to a new administration that had inherited its predecessor's policies toward the war. President Johnson shifted the focus of the air war from North Vietnam to southern Laos, called for greater participation by the South Vietnamese in fighting the war, and pursued negotiations with the North Vietnamese that were intended to end the war and ensure the survival of South Vietnam.

Unfortunately, the negotiations had gone nowhere, and on January 21, 1969, the day after his inauguration, President Nixon asked the Chairman of the Joint Chiefs of Staff, Gen. Earle G. Wheeler of the Army, for some means to increase the pressure on the enemy, thus prodding North Vietnam into making concessions in the Paris talks. The Presidential request generated a number of suggestions ranging from attacks on North Vietnamese depots and bases in Cambodia to guerrilla warfare in North Vietnam. Although the President began the secret bombing of the bases in Cambodia during March 1969, and attacked them with ground forces in April of the following year, he concentrated for the moment on actions inside South Vietnam, and all that could be done there was to strengthen the nation's government and armed forces.

Even as the new Chief Executive searched for ways to intensify pressure on North Vietnam, signs multiplied that the enemy intended to attack the cities of South Vietnam either at Tet, as in the previous year, or at some later date as part of a spring offensive. The Nixon administration believed that the government at Hanoi, in return for President Johnson's halting the bombing of the North, had, among other concessions, tacitly agreed to refrain from attacking the cities of the South. Since an offensive against the population centers seemed to be in the making, Nixon intended to retaliate, but the question immediately arose how he should do so. Too violent a response could touch off new demonstrations by the antiwar movement, but too weak a reaction might permit the enemy to regain the territory and aura of invincibility lost, along with the lives of thousands of his soldiers, as a result of the Tet offensive in 1968. The Joint Chiefs of Staff recommended that warships and aircraft respond by bombarding, for at least forty-eight hours, carefully selected military, industrial, and communications targets in North Vietnam, south of the 19th parallel, North latitude. Dr. Henry A. Kissinger, the President's adviser for national security, asked what would happen if the communist attacks proved less savage than anticipated. General McConnell, Chief of Staff of the Air Force and the acting Chairman of the Joint Chiefs of Staff in the temporary absence of General Wheeler, replied that the violence and duration of the bombardment could be adjusted accordingly.

The President had adopted this basic plan of retaliation when the enemy on February 23 launched his offensive, which proved feeble in comparison to the previous year's violence. Resuming the attacks on North Vietnam, for forty-eight hours or even less, seemed out of proportion to the provocation, and overreaction might conceivably fan the flames of antiwar dissent in the United States and cause North Vietnam to break off the negotiations in Paris. Consequently, Nixon decided not to strike back.

During the Nixon administration's first months in office, the opportunity for dramatic and forceful retaliation failed to materialize, and the new President found no better way to exert pressure on North Vietnam than by strengthening South Vietnam. Nixon contented himself with a strategy that represented a continuation, clarification, and acceleration of the Johnson administration's basic policies. The objective continued to be an independent South Vietnam, and like his predecessor, President Nixon intended to achieve this goal through negotiations. U.S. air power—attacking the trail in southern Laos, bombing secretly in Cambodia, and intervening on the battlefields of South Vietnam—would form a barrier behind which the South Vietnamese armed forces could take over the task of pressuring North Vietnam into making concessions at the talks in Paris. The war would undergo what Nixon and his advisers called Vietnamization; while the South Vietnamese made use of training and equipment supplied by the United States and expanded their share of the fighting, the U.S. forces would pull out, beginning with the ground forces, which were manned for the most part through the Selective Service System. The order established for the withdrawals, ground forces departing first, reflected the fact that sending young men drafted into the armed forces to fight in Southeast Asia had become an increasingly emotional issue among the populace as the casualty lists grew longer. When the number fighting in South Vietnam declined, so too would casualties; and airmen, who were professionals or volunteers rather than draftees, would to an increasing extent suffer the losses that did occur. President Nixon sought, through Vietnamization, to satisfy antiwar sentiment by reducing direct U.S. involvement, especially in the ground war where both draftees and casualties were most numerous, while at the same time maintaining military pressure on the North Vietnamese to reach a satisfactory agreement ending the war.[15]

As a key component of the aerial shield for Vietnamization, the interdiction of the Ho Chi Minh Trail loomed large in the Nixon strategy, and the AC–130 seemed essential to this effort. With the enthusiastic backing of Secretary Seamans, the Aeronautical Systems Division proposed a series of modifications, called the Surprise Package, to reduce the vulnerability of this aircraft. So that the gunship could attack from a greater and therefore safer range, the package substituted a pair of 40-mm Bofors antiaircraft guns for two of the Spectre's four multibarrel 20-mm cannon. The sensor array consisted of an ignition detector to locate gasoline-powered vehicles, an improved infrared sensor, a radar with a moving target indicator to track convoys, and low-light-level television. The modification package also featured a laser target designator, so that the gunship, after using its sensors to locate a truck or other object, could point it out for aircraft carrying the laser-guided bombs already in use in Southeast Asia. In addition, a new inertial navigation system stored the target coordinates, which the gunship crew could retrieve and relay to strike air-craft. To enable the crew members to make rapid and effective use of the weapons and sensors at their disposal, a digital computer replaced the analog device and the fire control system responded instantly to changes in altitude or in the angle of bank.[16]

From December 12, 1969, through January 18, 1970, a prototype carrying Surprise Package equipment underwent a successful evaluation over southern Laos. Of the new items on board, only the laser target designator and an experimental helmet gunsight failed to live up to expectation, while an attachment for taping what the television camera saw seemed to afford a sorely needed means of verifying damage claims. All in all, "performance of the weapon system as a whole was very satisfactory," for the improved C–130A "demonstrated a capability to detect trucks and destroy truck-size targets at eighty-five hundred to nine thousand feet altitude." Even though the laser had failed, the result of either poor maintenance or faulty installation, the Tactical Air Command declared the Surprise Package gunship "the single most effective truck killer in SEA [Southeast Asia]" at the time.[17]

Despite the successful operational test, General Momyer, who had taken charge of the Tactical Air Command in August 1968 when General Brown assumed command of the Seventh Air Force, objected to surrendering additional C–130 transports for Surprise Package modification. "I can appreciate Seventh Air Force's position on the need to increase the truck kill rate while increasing the survivability of AC–130s," Momyer acknowledged, but at the same time he warned that this kind of aircraft "will only have survivability as long as the enemy doesn't choose to employ the full arsenal of his weapons." The introduction of "a liberal number of 85-mm guns" would, Momyer predicted, sound the knell for the Surprise Package gunship and its 40-mm weapons.[18]

The peculiar needs of the Vietnam War prevailed, however, regardless of General Momyer's reluctance to convert more C–130 transports to gunships. The Air Force embarked on a project, nicknamed Pave Pronto, to fit out enough of the transports with 40-mm guns and most of the other Surprise Package equipment, so that a dozen AC–130As could fly interdiction missions over southern Laos. To save time in getting the aircraft into combat, the Pave Pronto modification omitted the digital computer and the inertial navigation system, but included the use of flame retardant foam in the fuel tanks and the fitting of additional armor to the aircraft. In November 1970, the first of five AC–130As that had survived combat in southern Laos completed its refurbishment and returned to action. (The number of AC–130s operating against the trail declined to five in April of that year when a 37-mm battery near Saravane downed one of the gunships; only one member of the eleven-man aircrew survived.) By the end of January 1971, six other Pave Pronto gunships joined the first five in Southeast Asia. Since the original Surprise Package aircraft had also returned to combat, a total of twelve improved AC–130As were attacking the Ho Chi Minh Trail, while three others served as training craft in the United States.[19]

The War against Trucks

In the meantime, planning began for the conversion of newer C–130Es into gunships in a program called Pave Spectre. The E models could carry a greater weight of fuel and ammunition than the A version and patrol the trail for a longer time each night. Six AC–130Es, also known as Spectre gunships, joined the AC–130As at the beginning of the 1971–72 dry season. The AC–130Es carried the basic Surprise Package armament and equipment: two 20-mm and two 40-mm guns; a Black Crow ignition detector; low-light-level television; the latest in infrared equipment; and the digital fire control computer. Two other C–130Es became Pave Aegis gunships, each armed with a 105-mm howitzer in place of one of the 40-mm weapons. All the gunships attacking the trail, whether AC–130As or Es, now carried radar jamming pods for protection against surface-to-air-missiles, which had appeared in southern Laos in the spring of 1971, but failed to score hits on the AC–130A gunships.

As the AC–130E Spectres began arriving in Thailand in the fall of 1971, the Surprise Package AC–130A received two new pieces of experimental equipment. One, the gated laser night television, consisted of a pulsed laser beam operating on a wave length designed to cut through haze and even foliage to illuminate solid objects, like trucks or shelters. Because the unaided camera could not penetrate this sort of screen, the laser-television combination did succeed in locating targets that might otherwise have escaped detection. Certain other objects, among them optical gunsights and the reflectors mounted on the back of trucks to help drivers keep their distance in convoys, also reflected the beam of the gated laser and became visible to a crewman using the night observation device. The operator of the scope picked up the reflection best when he watched at an angle, from a second aircraft. Looking through the device directly down a gated laser beam emanating from the gunship produced a fiery image that tended to blind the observer.

Further to improve the original Surprise Package aircraft, technicians installed a modified laser target designator that permitted the operator to project a visible beam of green light to mark targets for fighter-bombers. This marking beam was intended to replace the Navy-developed Misch munitions, 40-mm rounds lined with a flint-like material that shattered on detonation and caused sparks when the shards struck a hard surface. From high altitude, the sparks proved difficult to see, although the rounds sometimes ignited fuel tanks and set fire to the target the gunship was trying to mark for some other aircraft. Unfortunately, the modified laser, nicknamed the "green weenie," did not work out as planned. Not only did the green light blend with the color of the jungle, the visible beam aided enemy gunners by pointing like a finger to the gunship where it originated.[20]

Beginning in February 1972, gunships from the Pave Pronto, Pave Spectre, and Pave Aegis programs patrolled the Ho Chi Minh Trail in southern Laos. Indeed, the designation "Pave"—that indicated that the Aeronautical Systems Division bore responsibility for the development project—had become so common that gunship crews selected it for Pave Pig, a weapon in an improvised psychological campaign against enemy gunners. Some members of the gunship crews bought a pig, had a flight suit made for the animal and a parachute for its cage, then dropped the beast into the darkness along with a note—in French, Cambodian, and Vietnamese—explaining that the animal was a reward from the United States for wretched marksmanship.[21]

Since the loss of Colonel Schwehm's gunship in 1969, North Vietnamese gunnery had improved to the point where Pave Pig took on overtones of gallows humor. The deadly effect of enemy batteries could be judged from the brief career of the prototype of the newest and most formidable of gunships, Pave Aegis. This aircraft carried a standard U.S. Army 105-mm howitzer, which took the place of one of the 40-mm weapons, for a total armament of one 105-mm weapon, one 40-mm gun, and two multibarrel 20-mm cannon. A deflector mounted on the barrel of the howitzer prevented muzzle blast from damaging the left wing, and a recoil mechanism, capable of absorbing the shock as the gun leaped back some four feet when fired, replaced the side-looking radar. The beacon acquisition radar remained in place, however, and added to the effectiveness of the 105-mm weapon in support of troops equipped with the necessary transponder. The sensor array included an infrared detector, radar with moving target indicator, television, and an ignition detector.

The Pave Aegis prototype began its combat evaluation in February 1972 and quickly demonstrated the increased destructiveness of the 5.6 pound explosive warhead of the 105-mm shell, nine times as powerful as the 40-mm type. Experience had shown that a truckload of bagged rice would smother the force of the lighter round, but a howitzer shell not only burst the bags and scattered the rice, but also demolished the vehicle. A 40-mm round had to hit the cab or engine to kill a truck; a near miss from the 105-mm shell could reduce the vehicle to junk. Also, Pave Aegis seemed to have a better change of survival than the earlier gunships because it could engage targets from altitudes as high as ten thousand five hundred feet, depending on haze and cloud cover, roughly twice the usual operating height of the original Gunship II with its 20-mm weapons.

The increase in altitude did not, however, prevent a 57-mm shell from scoring a direct hit on the first Pave Aegis gunship during the night of March 15, 1972. Luckily, the crew escaped injury, and the howitzer sustained no damage, but the explosion sidelined the airplane. Technicians therefore removed the 105-mm weapon and installed it in another gunship. The replacement continued flying interdiction missions until the night of March 30, when 57-mm fire shot it down. All the crewmen parachuted safely, and a Spectre gunship managed to locate the survivors with low-light-level television, contact them on the radios in their survival gear, and direct them to a hiding place where they stayed until picked up by helicopter on the next day.

A second howitzer had by now reached Thailand for installation in still another AC–130E. This aircraft carried on alone until another newly modified Pave Aegis joined it on May 1, but aerial interdiction in southern Laos had by that time yielded precedence to operations designed to help stop the North Vietnamese forces that had invaded the South. Diverted to assist South Vietnamese troops, the two Pave Aegis gunships destroyed fortified buildings and even tanks, far sturdier targets than the trucks they had formerly attacked.[22]

Unlike the howitzer shell fired by Pave Aegis gunships, other munitions, including the 20-mm and 40-mm projectiles, did not always do the intended job. Mines proved especially unreliable. When the Commando Hunt series began late in 1968, the Air Force had no mine that could be relied on to disrupt truck traffic. Gravel mines—pebble-sized pressure-activated explosive devices intended merely to activate sensors—proved at most an annoyance to road repair crews and posed no impediment to vehicles. The magnetically detonated Mk 36, also used against river traffic, contained enough explosive to demolish a truck, but the North Vietnamese had little trouble detecting, removing, or harmlessly exploding the device. During its first six months of use, which ended in April 1968, the Mk 36 "showed no evidence of deterring or stopping traffic, other than for short periods of time and, in some instances, not at all."[23]

Other types of mines soon saw action. One was the dragontooth, weighing 0.71 ounces and capable, under ideal conditions, of puncturing a tire. More effective than the dragontooth, the casualty-causing wide-area antipersonnel mine reached Southeast Asia in the fall of 1968. When this spherical weapon, 2.38 inches in diameter and weighing one pound, hit the ground, the shock released spring-loaded trip wires that extended as far as twenty-five feet. Merely touching a wire caused the mine to detonate. F–4s and F–100s scattered wide-area antipersonnel mines from specially designed dispensers.[24]

The coming of the dragontooth and wide-area antipersonnel mines coincided with improvements in gravel that permitted its delivery from jet aircraft, enhanced its explosive effect, and lengthened its useful life in a hot and humid climate. By the summer of 1969, with the new gravel arriving, the Seventh Air Force had on hand some twenty thousand canisters of the old kind, containing perhaps twenty-four million of the tiny weapons. Headquarters drafted plans to have propeller-driven A–1 Skyraiders scatter as much of the old gravel as possible before the explosive deteriorated or improving antiaircraft defenses barred the A–1s from worthwhile targets. The piston-engine aircraft showered almost all the canisters of the old gravel on thirty-six different locations just west of the demilitarized zone in an attempt to harass the enemy on the Ho Chi Minh Trail, but the actual effect remained unknown.[25]

Because no one type of mine could seriously impede traffic, Seventh Air Force planners devised the munitions package, combining the best features of the different antivehicular and antipersonnel weapons, sometimes reinforced by five hundred pound bombs with delayed-action fuzes. The munitions package sought to cause delay and inflict casualties as the enemy tried to repair roads cut by high-explosive bombs. The Mk 36 Destructor, powerful enough to cripple a bulldozer, formed the centerpiece of such a package, protected by antipersonnel mines that discouraged the enemy from taking advantage of the magnetic fuze by dragging chains or other metal within detonating distance. The wide-area antipersonnel mine killed or wounded those who approached carelessly, and the new and more powerful gravel could cause painful injury if stepped on.[26]

While the munitions packages thus complicated the task of repairing road cuts, various kinds of bomblets blasted the transportation network and the antiaircraft batteries that protected it. Scattered hundreds at a time from dispensers, the individual weapons had a spherical shape and usually weighed less than two pounds. Except for the Rockeye bomblet, which contained a shaped charge capable of blasting through armor, they tended to have frangible casings, sometimes in the form of pellets embedded in plastic, that scattered on detonation. The fragmentation weapons might stop a truck by killing or wounding the driver or by punching holes in the radiator, tires, or fuel tank, but they rarely could demolish a vehicle.[27]

In attacking trucks, incendiary bombs seemed more destructive than the fragmentation type, for they could start fires that consumed the cargo even though the vehicle might still be salvaged. The favorite incendiary was the M36 "funny bomb," which scattered its 182 thermite bomblets over an area the size of a football field, four to five times the space that a container of napalm could envelop in flame. Col. Frank L. Gailer, Jr., commander of a tactical fighter wing during the first Commando Hunt operation, declared that: "when the M36 was available our truck kills were five times higher that the kills obtained after the supply . . . was exhausted."[28]

Tests at Eglin Air Force Base, Florida, revealed that the funny bomb could not do all that Gailer believed. During September 1969, a B–57 carrying six M36s made three passes at fifty trucks, parked ten to a row. Each vehicle had a full gas tank and also carried two 55-gallon drums of fuel. According to Col. Howard M. Sloan, present as an observer for the Department of Defense, only one of the forty-six trucks within the aggregate impact area of the six bombs sustained damage that defied repair. The funny bomb created an illusion of effectiveness that simply did not reflect reality.[29]

Despite this test in Florida, an evaluation by the Pacific Air Forces concluded that the funny bomb was "the most effective (based on bomb damage) truck killing munition available, whether used alone or in combination with other munitions." Napalm, the report continued, also proved effective if used in conjunction with fragmentation weapons. Shards from the exploding bomblets punctured fuel tanks and the petroleum drums carried as cargo, providing pools of gasoline for the napalm to ignite.[30] At most, the funny bomb may have outdone napalm, itself a truck killer only in conjunction with fragmentation bombs.

Because of the limitations that these other kinds of munitions revealed, only the guided bomb rivaled the howitzer shell fired from a Pave Aegis gunship as a one-shot killer of trucks. The Air Force used two kinds of guided bombs in southern Laos, one of them laser-directed and the other electro-optical. The laser-guided weapon contained a mechanism that homed on the reflection caused when a laser beam focused on an object. When an F–4, for instance, released this bomb within a specific cone, or "basket," the sensing device automatically manipulated the weapon's controls to bring the bomb squarely onto target. The other type, the electro-optically guided bomb, depended on contrasts in reflected light, as a self-contained television camera enabled the guidance mechanism to lock onto the target, provided that object had a clearly defined "edge," like a factory building or tunnel.[31]

In aerial interdiction of traffic on the Ho Chi Minh Trail, the electro-optical weapon had few targets suitable for its pinpoint accuracy. Out of thirty-five launches during a combat evaluation, twenty-nine of the bombs guided properly, and twenty scored direct hits on such targets as ferry landings, bridges, roads, and caves. The twenty-nine bombs that locked onto their targets missed by an average distance of just six and one-half feet at ranges between eleven thousand and twenty-four thousand feet, but these results depended on daylight. At night, when so many interdiction targets appeared, electro-optical guidance became blind and useless. During 1970, a television guidance kit, when added to a two thousand pound bomb costing $685, increased the price by $17,000, compared to $4,200 to fit laser guidance onto the same kind of bomb. Cost presented an irrefutable argument against using the electro-optical bomb on any target that a laser-guided weapon could destroy. Indeed, by the summer of 1972, Task Force Alpha characterized electro-optical guidance as too costly for the kind of targets found in southern Laos.[32]

Unlike the electro-optically guided bomb, which came in just a two thousand pound size, laser guidance mechanisms could at the outset fit either the seven hundred fifty pound or two thousand pound bomb. Combat evaluation of both laser weapons took place in the summer of 1968, during Operation Turnpike, and they entered the Southeast Asia arsenal immediately afterward. Of the two sizes, the two thousand pound bomb appeared better suited for aerial interdiction. Besides containing more explosive, it demonstrated greater accuracy because the control surfaces were located near the nose instead of at the tail, an arrangement that caused the larger weapon to respond more quickly to movements of these fins. Success with the first laser-guided weapons resulted in the development of a three thousand pound bomb that made its debut in October 1969. During 1970, the seven hundred fifty pound model gave way to a five hundred pound version; because of the accuracy of laser guidance, the slight reduction in weight had little effect on destructive power, and the smaller size enabled an aircraft to carry additional bombs.[33]

The two thousand pound laser-guided bomb gained a reputation as a relentless truck killer in southern Laos after technicians installed a laser target designator in the Blindbat C–130 that normally dispensed flares over the Ho Chi Minh Trail. A night observation scope mounted coaxially with the laser enabled the operator in the flareship to keep the beam trained on target and to determine whether the fighter-bomber releasing the weapon had scored a hit, but he could not, unfortunately, assess the damage from a near miss. Four of the first eight trucks illuminated in this fashion vanished in a cloud of flame when the two thousand pound bomb struck home. The average circular error for the two thousand pound and seven hundred fifty pound types declined from thirty feet during the August 1968 evaluation to seventeen feet a year later. The three thousand pound bomb achieved an average error of twenty-three feet, compared to the hoped-for thirty feet. This exceptional accuracy depended to some degree on the absence of antiaircraft fire during most of the early missions, which permitted the laser operator to make a leisurely search for vehicles, keep the beam precisely focused, and coach the bomb-carrying F–4s onto the target.[34]

Normally, in using laser-guided weapons, one aircraft illuminated the target with a laser beam, while another maneuvered into the guidance cone and released the bomb. At night, especially, this kind of hunter-killer attack required precise coordination and flying skill. Even gunships, with their formidable array of sensors, could have difficulty locating a target, for the enemy set fires to blind infrared equipment and a camouflaged truck, blending into the jungle, might escape detection by a night observation device or television camera. Once the hunter had found the target, both the laser operator and the attacking pilot had to be sure they were looking at the same thing, and even when they did, haze or smoke could interfere with the reflected laser beam, thus frustrating the guidance mechanism.[35]

Until antiaircraft fire forced the C–130 flareships to give up the mission of laser designator in the spring of 1970, the navigator on board the transport calculated the geographic coordinates of the target illuminated by the laser beam, and radioed the information to the fighter making the attack. The weapon systems officer in the killer aircraft converted the data into a loran release point from which the bomb homed on the target. Thanks to the use of loran coordinates, the attacking crew did not have to see the intended point of impact; the pilot could fly straight and level, remaining beyond the reach of antiaircraft guns, and the guidance system steered the weapon, provided only that release occurred within the basket and the laser operator on board the C–130 kept the beam on target.[36]

When the flareships stopped patrolling the trail network, gunships took over as laser designators. Although the AC–130A had quickly gained a reputation for spotting and destroying trucks, using sensors and comparatively short-range weapons, this aircraft became vulnerable to the antiaircraft guns appearing in increasing numbers along the Ho Chi Minh Trail. The laser enabled gunships that had located enemy batteries to remain out of range of enemy weapons and rely on the beam instead of flares, or bursts of gunfire using Misch rounds, to point out targets for other aircraft. The laser target designator proved especially effective in conjunction with an advanced kind of loran tested in the Surprise Package gunship, a set so precise that it eventually became standard for all AC–130s. Indeed, it demonstrated an accuracy measurable in tens of yards. Thanks to the navigation equipment, a gunship could provide bomb-carrying F–4s with loran rather than geographic coordinates, thus eliminating one step in the basic hunter-killer tactics developed when flareship teamed with fighter-bomber.[37]

As the defenses of the Ho Chi Minh Trail grew more dangerous, faster aircraft had to take over the task of designating targets. The choice fell initially on the workhorse of the air war, the F–4 fighter-bomber. A laser mounted on this aircraft transmitted its energy from the left side of the rear cockpit, as the fighter-bomber flew an elliptical path at a constant altitude, keeping the beam focused on target. Smoke, haze, or cloud cover could scatter the laser beam, preventing the guidance mechanism from locking onto the reflected energy, even though the crew had located the target using only a night observation device, a challenging task in heavily forested portions of the trail. The pilot, moreover, needed a steady hand on the controls, for at a range of twenty thousand feet a one-degree variance while banking would shift the laser beam 350 feet from the aiming point. While the laser carrying Phantom illuminated the truck, roadway, or gun position, a second F–4 dived into the acquisition basket and released a guided bomb.[38]

Delivered by any of the hunter-killer teams, the laser-guided bomb could shatter trucks, cut roads, and silence, though not necessarily destroy, antiaircraft guns. In February 1969, Leonard Sullivan, Jr., the Deputy Director of Defense Research and Engineering for Southeast Asia Matters, credited the two thousand pound laser-guided bomb, usually delivered by a pair of F–4s, with reducing by 80 percent the number of sorties required to cut a given segment of highway. Summing up activity during the first two months of 1970, analysts at Pacific Air Forces headquarters in Hawaii reported that laser-guided bombs had destroyed three 57-mm guns and sixty-one weapons of smaller caliber. In short, the analysts claimed that the bombs had destroyed not quite 10 percent of the total number of guns believed to be defending the Ho Chi Minh Trail, an estimate that defied verification. Some of the weapons listed as destroyed may well have survived and returned to action at different sites, when new gunners replaced those killed or wounded.[39]

In theory, at least, the combination of a Surprise Package gunship and loran-equipped F–4s carrying laser-guided bombs provided a formidable means of destroying trucks. Analysts at Pacific Command proposed sending one AC–130A, fitted out with the Surprise Package equipment, as a hunter, accompanied by three F–4s that would kill trucks with five hundred pound laser-guided bombs. The mathematicians who inspired these tactics predicted that improved accuracy would enable such a team to destroy a truck for just six thousand dollars compared to currently accepted estimates of fifty-two thousand dollars per truck for an F–4 on armed reconnaissance or sixteen to twenty thousand dollars for an AC–130A escorted by one or more Phantoms. A further reduction in cost seemed likely if an aircraft such as the North American Rockwell OV–10, which cost only about 30 percent as much to operate, replaced the gunship as laser designator.[40]

In actual practice, however, the laser-guided bomb added little to the effectiveness of the AC–130 against individual trucks, although it did enable the gunship to continue operating over roads strongly defended by antiaircraft batteries. After detecting a convoy, the Spectre usually attacked with its own 20-mm or 40-mm cannon, challenging the North Vietnamese antiaircraft batteries, which could match the range of the gunship's weapons. If the gunners on the ground opened fire, the laser target designator came into play, as the operator on board the Spectre used it to direct the escorting Phantoms against the hostile guns.

A new device for use in laser-directed attacks entered service on a few of the Phantoms during January 1971 and simplified the task of protecting gunships against the increasing danger from antiaircraft fire. This item was a receiver that picked up the reflected energy when the laser beam from an AC–130 focused on target, enabling the attacking pilot to see his aiming point. After focusing the laser beam on the enemy battery, the gunship would open fire with tracer and Misch ammunition to show the escorting pilot where to look; on seeing the illuminated target in his receiver, he began a dive, usually from about twenty thousand feet, plummeting through the darkness until, at about twelve thousand feet, he entered the basket for releasing the laser-guided bomb.[41]

While this passive sensing device made its debut in southern Laos, work went ahead to adapt a cheaper aircraft than the F–4 or the gunship to the role of target designator. The obvious choice was the two-place, twin-turboprop OV–10 Bronco—reasonably fast, adequately armored, and economical to operate. Fitted with a night observation device, a pod-mounted laser projector, and a radar transponder to help strike aircraft locate it as it circled the target, the modified OV–10 saw its first action in the summer of 1971. The laser in this aircraft, besides pointing out the target, doubled as a range finder. A viewer in the cockpit displayed the distance to the target, and the same information passed automatically into a computer tied to the loran navigation system, which determined the coordinates for use by the attacking fighter-bombers.

Early combat tests achieved spectacular results, as Phantoms, dropping two thousand pound laser-guided bombs on targets designated by OV–10s, "destroyed nearly every bridge in Cambodia held by the enemy."[42] Afterward the OV–10s moved to southern Laos, where they pinpointed fords, road interdiction points, and occasionally individual trucks. On August 29, 1971, for example, an F–4D scored two direct hits on trucks designated by a laser-carrying OV–10, not only destroying the vehicles, but also opening yawning craters in the roadway.[43]

Unfortunately, when the roads dried in the fall of that year and traffic began picking up, the OV–10s experienced frequent equipment failure, causing the contractor responsible for the laser pod and its controls to send additional technicians to Nakhon Phanom where the airplanes were based. Another problem, besides difficulties with the laser projector, that affected performance resulted from the tendency of fog and haze to scatter the reflected laser beam, a handicap encountered by every aircraft that employed the device for designating targets. Weather conditions ill-suited to the use of the laser prevailed throughout much of southern Laos during February 1972, a time of heavy traffic on the trail, but, despite poor visibility and problems with equipment, this latest of the hunter aircraft seemed a success.[44]

Besides contributing to the effectiveness of hunter-killer attacks, the laser target designator enjoyed further success in the self-contained night attack aircraft that the Air Force had been trying to develop since 1966. Work on this weapon began with Project Tropic Moon I, which produced four two-place Douglas A–1E propeller-driven attack planes, modified to carry low-light-level television. Two cameras acquired targets for the Tropic Moon I crew, one of them taking wide-angle pictures, while the second produced a magnified image of a small area within the larger scene. The pilot could select either camera, usually shifting to narrow focus after seeing a worthwhile target with the wide lens, and use the television image as an optical gunsight.

Meanwhile, low-light-level television was also being installed in three Martin B–57B jet-powered light bombers, along with a laser ranging device and a weapons delivery computer. When the single zoom-lens camera mounted on these twin-engine Tropic Moon II prototypes acquired a target, the television operator used the laser to determine range. He then fed this data into the computer, which was programmed for a certain altitude, air speed, and type of ordnance. The pilot made sure the bomber maintained the selected speed and height, and the computer determined the precise moment of release that would cause the bombs to detonate on target.

Both varieties of Tropic Moon underwent combat evaluation in Southeast Asia. The B–57Bs saw their first action in the Mekong Delta of South Vietnam during December 1967. After one of the bombers accidentally attacked a police post, the Tropic Moon II test moved across the border into areas of southern Laos firmly in enemy hands. The television-equipped A–1E began its evaluation after the first of the year, flying sorties near Muong Phine and Tchepone in Laos, where enemy fire forced it too high for the camera to penetrate the nighttime ground haze. Like the modified B–57B, Tropic Moon I proved ill-suited to armed reconnaissance along the roads of southern Laos. The television simply could not pick up a target at a distance that would permit pilots to attack without turning and trying to reacquire the picture, a dangerous practice in heavily defended regions. Despite these early disappointments, the Air Force pushed ahead with the Tropic Moon project, adding new sensors and weapons to the B–57.[45]

While the Air Force experimented with laser ranging and television cameras in its Tropic Moon I and II self-contained attack aircraft, the Navy introduced an airplane with a similar purpose, the fruit of that service's Trail-Road Interdiction Multisensor project (an apparent case of the acronym, TRIM, determining the title). The TRIM aircraft carried a formidable array of sensors, all of which saw duty in Air Force gunships—an infrared detector, low-light-level television, radar, the night observation device, and an ignition detector. The Navy chose to test this gear, much of it handcrafted, in an obsolete aircraft, the Lockheed AP–2H, a variant of the OP–2E, which had already proved unacceptably vulnerable to antiaircraft fire during an abbreviated sensor-dropping career. Even though enemy gunners soon drove the AP–2H from the skies over southern Laos, the Navy profited from the experiment, fitting out an interdiction version of the Grumman A–6C Intruder that combined infrared equipment, a radar capable of tracking vehicles, and low-light-level television. The first of the modified Grumman jets began flying armed reconnaissance over the Ho Chi Minh Trail during the southwest monsoon season of 1970, joining other A–6s already in action.[46]

The Air Force experimented with another self-contained night attack craft, the NC–123K Black Spot, redesignated the AC–123K. Twin jet engines slung in pods beneath the wing supplemented the original pair of piston engines and improved the performance of this Fairchild tactical transport, which had entered service in 1955.

The two Black Spot prototypes featured equipment that came to be more or less standard for night interdiction—television, a laser range-finder, an infrared sensor, a radar that searched ahead of the plane to track moving vehicles, and in one of the aircraft, a Black Crow ignition detector. As in the Tropic Moon II B–57Bs, a computer determined bomb release, but in Black Spot all the sensors automatically fed data into this device. The cargo compartment contained a dispensing unit, originally designed for possible installation in the bomb bay of a B–47 or B–52 strategic bomber, which held 72 canisters, each one packed with either 74 or 177 bomblets, depending on weight and shape of the individual weapons. The canisters dropped through the dispenser's twelve vertical chutes to burst open and scatter the bomblets, either a fifteen-ounce cylindrical type or a spherical variety that weighed twenty-six ounces. Both kinds scattered fragments on exploding, inflicting damage on trucks and other equipment and also causing casualties.[47]

An emergency in Korea delayed the arrival in Southeast Asia of the two Black Spot aircraft. During the tense months following North Korea's capture of the U.S. intelligence ship *Pueblo* in January 1968, North Korean infiltrators began landing from small boats, bypassing the demilitarized zone that separated South Korea from the communist North. The two AC–123Ks arrived in Korea during August, remained there about three months, trying to intercept gasoline-powered motor boats, and only then flew to Southeast Asia for their evaluation. From November 15, 1968, until January 9, 1969, the Black Spot aircraft attacked trucks in Laos, showing enough promise to cause the Commander in Chief, Pacific Command, Admiral McCain, to retain them until the end of the 1968–69 dry season and use them again when the rains ended in the fall of 1969.[48]

Although Black Spot received credit for destroying 1,128 trucks during roughly fourteen months of action, the kinds of munitions dropped by the converted transports lacked the punch to cause such havoc. Intelligence analysts may not have realized at the time that the bomblets generally did only superficial damage to vehicles, puncturing tires, gas tanks, and radiators. The fragments might wound or kill drivers, but seldom did the weapons start a fire that consumed a truck and its cargo.

The Black Spot aircraft, moreover, proved vulnerable to antiaircraft fire. The best of the sensors, the infrared detector that scanned ahead of the aircraft, could not locate targets from altitudes above five thousand feet. This limitation doomed the project, for during 1969 antiaircraft guns capable of reaching this altitude already were appearing along the major roads of southern Laos. "I have concluded," declared General Brown, the Seventh Air Force Commander, in June 1970, "that despite past accomplishment and our need for sensor equipped first-pass-capable truck killers, the AC–123's reduced effectiveness due to vulnerability dictates . . . removal from SEA."[49]

A subsequent attempt to restrict Black Spot to lightly defended routes, relying on the Black Crow sensor to spot trucks through the jungle canopy, ended in failure, for the ignition detector in the AC–123 indicated only the general presence of gaso-

The War against Trucks

line engines; it could not pinpoint individual vehicles. Black Spot had outlived its usefulness; in June 1970, the combat careers of the two prototypes came to a close. The 8th Tactical Fighter Wing, which had flown them, recommended canceling the project and preserving one of the aircraft in the Air Force Museum at Wright-Patterson Air Force Base, near Dayton, Ohio.[50]

Like the A–1Es and B–57s of Tropic Moon I and II, the Black Spot AC–123s represented a partial and temporary solution to the problem of night attack. While these airplanes were undergoing evaluation, work progressed on a more ambitious project, Tropic Moon III. In the summer of 1968, Westinghouse Aerospace Division of Baltimore, Maryland, received a contract to convert sixteen B–57s to G models, intended to be the ultimate self-contained night attack aircraft for interdiction of the Ho Chi Minh Trail. Among other special devices, Westinghouse installed a laser for target designation, an infrared scanner to search the ground ahead of the aircraft, and low-light-level television. A radar set with a moving target indicator could, under ideal conditions, locate and follow a vehicle the size of a jeep, traveling at normal convoy speed, acquiring this target at a distance of eight miles.[51]

From mid-October 1970 until January 17, 1971, the 13th Bomb Squadron, Tactical, conducted a combat evaluation of eleven B–57Gs. During this introduction to the air war in Laos, the squadron paid particular attention to communications security, a problem common to all air operations in Southeast Asia. Tropic Moon III crews relied on secure radio transmissions, whenever possible, or used manual cryptological devices. Uncoded radio conversation remained at a minimum. Concerned that the North Vietnamese had "a special interest in shooting down a B–57G and recovering equipment for technical exploitation," the officers responsible for communications security applauded such efforts, while warning of dangers over which the squadron itself had no control. In fact, an analysis of radio procedures revealed some uncoded traffic between airborne command and control centers and command agencies on the ground contained the results of missions just flown, along with the call signs and mission numbers for subsequent flights. Moreover, copies of the daily operations order were widely distributed and might easily be seen by enemy agents.[52]

In spite of the concern for communications security, North Vietnamese gunners succeeded in shooting down a B–57G near Tchepone on the night of December 12–13, 1970. The two crew members—Lt. Col. Paul R. Pitt, the pilot, and his sensor operator, Lt. Col. Edwin A. Buschette—had to make several passes to mark a convoy for F–4s, repeatedly coming within range of the enemy, and ultimately the anti-aircraft gunners scored a disabling hit. Both officers parachuted safely and were rescued after daybreak. Air strikes promptly blasted the wreckage so that enemy technicians could not examine the equipment on board. North Vietnamese gunners claimed only this B–57G during the evaluation, although an engine fire put another one out of action temporarily.[53]

In attacks on the Ho Chi Minh Trail, Tropic Moon III equipment operators faced several problems not encountered during tests in the United States. Westinghouse engineers had intended that the radar, with its ability to track moving vehicles,

72

would serve as principal "cuing sensor," telling the crew when to switch on the laser, but this method of target acquisition proved a total failure. Since the radar got the clearest return from an altitude of three thousand feet, and antiaircraft fire forced the B–57G above five thousand feet, this sensor could not pick up targets for the laser to illuminate. As a result, crews used the infrared detector as cuing sensor, closed to within television range, locked onto the victim with the laser beam, and released a laser-guided bomb. Reliance on infrared and television, both of which had difficulty penetrating the haze that clung to the trail during the dry season, so reduced the acquisition distance that about 60 percent of the time the pilot had to make a dangerous second pass before the laser could focus on the target.

Without the aid of radar, the ideal attack began at a slant range of roughly thirty thousand feet. The weapon systems operator in the rear seat of the B–57G kept the appropriate sensor locked on target, and a computer automatically tracked the victim. After shifting from infrared to television, the "back-seater" aimed the laser beam. As the cuing sensors had done, the laser responded to signals from the computer as the pilot entered the guidance basket. At an altitude of six thousand to eight thousand feet, with an indicated air speed of two hundred fifty to three hundred knots, the pilot pulled up, then nosed over to release the five hundred pound weapon. The computer was supposed to keep the beam locked onto the target until the bomb actually detonated, but the laser had only a limited rotation, and the pilot had to avoid the kind of maneuver that would wrench the laser beam away from the target, causing the bomb to go astray. At the same time the systems officer shut down the television to prevent the flash of the exploding bomb from permanently damaging the camera.

To compensate for the failure of the radar and its moving target indicator, crews of the B–57Gs tried to work with forward air controllers. The improvised tactics failed, however, largely because the infrared sensor and low-light-level television carried by the bomber proved overly sensitive to the flares and incendiary logs dropped by the controllers. The illumination that helped the human eye pick out a truck or gun emplacement utterly blinded these devices. The controllers tried to compensate for the loss of the electronic aids by coaching the bombers onto the target, perhaps using rockets as markers, but this took time, and the B–57G, which lacked the equipment to refuel from aerial tankers, had no more than forty minutes to spend over the Ho Chi Minh Trail.

A direct hit from one of the five hundred pound laser-guided bombs dropped by the B–57G could destroy truck and cargo, killing the driver and any passengers on board. The explosive power of the weapon, combined with the accuracy of laser guidance, led to claims of 363 trucks destroyed out of 759 sighted and 565 attacked. In most cases, however, no wreckage littered the road to verify the reported kill, and the bomber had no way of videotaping its success, since fires and explosions blinded the television camera. An attempt was made to use the AC–130 to photograph the results of strikes by the B–57Gs, but to do so required the jet bomber, boring through the darkness, to maneuver in close proximity to the slower aircraft. Since the gunship might have to turn suddenly to avoid antiaircraft fire, the danger of midair collision seemed too great to permit this practice.[54]

Although the B–57G appeared at first glance to be a thoroughly modernized truck killer, its basic design had been around for some twenty years. The extensively modified airplane consequently lacked the speed of newer jets and had greater vulnerability to optically controlled antiaircraft fire. Also, the Tropic Moon III version normally carried just four laser-guided weapons. At most, the B–57G demonstrated that the Air Force still needed a true "self-contained laser delivery system" capable of refueling in flight and venturing into heavily defended areas either to attack targets or designate them for other aircraft carrying laser-guided weapons.

The answer to this need lay in the versatile F–4D with a so-called Pave Knife laser projector installed in a pod beneath the fuselage, instead of being aimed out the left side of the rear cockpit as in the earlier laser-carrying F–4s assigned to hunter-killer flights. In the newest version of the laser-equipped Phantom, the weapon systems officer located the truck or other target on low-light-level television, then kept the gyrostabilized laser beam focused while the pilot dived to attack. During combat tests in the spring of 1971, an F–4D fitted with Pave Knife equipment scored direct hits in 61 percent of its single-aircraft attacks; when designating a target for another Phantom, the ratio of direct hits increased slightly to 65 percent. Following this impressive debut, the Pave Knife F–4s overshadowed the B–57Gs during the 1971–72 dry season, dropping 1,317 laser-guided bombs against trucks, antiaircraft batteries, choke points, and logistical facilities, compared to 184 for Tropic Moon III.[55]

Pave Knife displayed no major disabilities during its service in Southeast Asia. The few problems that surfaced early in the evaluation stemmed from the television camera, which explosions, smoke, or fog sometimes blinded. By flare light, however, the television screen inside the cockpit provided a sharper picture than could be obtained with the naked eye. Once North Vietnam invaded the South and the Commando Hunt series ended, the modified F–4s sometimes operated in driving rain. The bad weather revealed flaws in the seals around access doors in the pod containing the laser. Water tended to leak into this equipment whether the plane was parked in a downpour or flying through rain. To remedy the problem, ground crews placed waterproof covers improvised by local craftsmen over the pods whenever one of the planes was parked; during flight, tape covered the access ports to keep moisture out. These measures preserved the effectiveness of one of the most promising of the night attack weapons spawned by Project Shed Light.[56]

These aircraft—gunships, flareships, the Tropic Moon series, the OV–10, and the redoubtable F–4—formed the armada that attacked traffic on the Ho Chi Minh Trail. To locate specific targets, pilots and crews depended on a variety of airborne sensors: a target designator for use with laser-guided bombs, low-light-level television, an ignition detector, various types of radar, and the widely used night observation device. None of the aircraft that harried movement on the trail was specifically designed for the purpose. Even the designers of the OV–10 Bronco, a recent addition to the Air

Force inventory, originally thought in terms of counterinsurgency operations in general rather than day-and-night, year-round interdiction of a well defended logistics network.

Although awesome indeed, the thunderous detonation of hundreds of bombs dropped from a B–52 invisible in the daylight sky or the shriek of jet fighters attacking by the light of swaying flares formed but one element in the interdiction campaign. The war against trucks could succeed only if Task Force Alpha, using the Igloo White sensor field and other sources of intelligence, managed to define the route structure over which the enemy traveled and along which he stockpiled his supplies. Neither flares nor lasers would have much effect if patient and repetitive analysis failed to work out the infiltration pattern and locate its weaknesses. Finding the enemy and discovering his methods of supply and reinforcement depended on advanced technology different from that which produced the specialized aircraft swarming over the trail.

Tet 1968. A convoy of trucks headed for South Vietnam just before the Tet attacks (top); the hard-hit Cholon area of Saigon (center); the Imperial Palace in Hue, damaged during the 1968 Tet attacks (bottom).

Khe Sanh combat base.
The craters at the top of
the picture came from
bombs dropped by B–52s
(top). During the fiercest
part of the siege, transport
aircraft didn't land, but
dropped cargo on the run-
way (center). Smoke rises
from a fuel dump hit by
mortars during the siege
(bottom).

77

Sensors. A seismic sensor is attached to a pylon on a Navy OP–2E (top), an OP–2E releases a sensor (center), and a CH–3 releases a seismic sensor (bottom).

Acoustic sensors are loaded into a CH-3 (top), seismic sensors mounted on a pylon under an Air Force F–4 (center), an acoustic sensor hanging in brush (above left), and a seismic sensor embedded in the ground (above right).

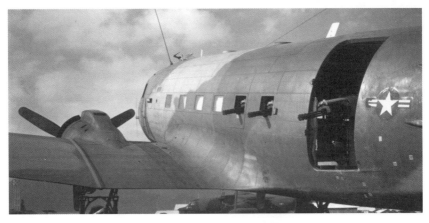

Gunships. Gunship I, an AC–47 (top), carried three 7.62-mm miniguns; the Gunship II prototype, an AC–130A (center), had four 7.62-mm miniguns and four 20-mm guns; the AC–119G, Gunship III, (bottom), had four 7.62-mm miniguns.

80

The second model of Gunship III, the AC–119K (top), had a jet engine under each wing and added two 20-mm guns. Later versions of the AC–130 carried two 40-mm Bofors guns(center) and a 40-mm Bofors and a 105-mm howitzer (bottom). Each improved gunship also had advances in numbers and types of on-board sensors.

Task Force Alpha. The Infiltration Surveillance Center (top), Nakhon Phanom Air Base (center), with the Surveillance Center at the middle left, and the EC–121 relay aircraft (bottom).

Chapter Four

Finding the Enemy

Efforts to improve techniques for locating the enemy paralleled the development of new weapons like the Pave Knife F–4, the Spectre gunships, and the B–57G with its laser-guided bombs. For example, the new Phase II electronic monitoring devices that entered service beginning in October 1968 proved more efficient than the Phase I equipment they replaced. Whereas the Phase I sensors remained on the air for as long as the batteries functioned, broadcasting continuously and tying up the assigned reporting channels, the newer ones transmitted in response to commands from Nakhon Phanom. Instead of listening passively, monitors at the Surveillance Center could direct the new commandable sensors to perform any of three functions: to report what was happening at the moment, transmitting noises or earth tremors; to keep silent, but count the number of impulses and respond with the total when queried; or to remain active for an extended time and function like the older Phase I devices. Also, as the projected useful life of a Phase II sensor neared its end, technicians could deactivate the transmitter by remote control and reassign its reporting channel. Because the Phase II sensor need not draw continuously on its batteries, planners could anticipate that the newer type would last about fifteen days longer than the Phase I counterpart.

To state that a particular sensor had a life span of, for example, forty-five or sixty days did not mean that the shock of landing, a defect in manufacture, enemy tampering, or simply a bad battery might not silence it well ahead of schedule. In practice, usefulness did not depend on how long each individual sensor might last, but on the adequacy of coverage by a particular string of several sensors. A string, after all, produced nothing of value if too many of its sensors missed the mark, even though all of them survived the shock of landing and broadcast as designed. Conversely, an accurately placed string might do an acceptable job even though some of its sensors failed.[1]

The Phase II devices included the Acoubuoy II and Spikebuoy II, the Fighter Air-Delivered Seismic Intrusion Detector (Fadsid), and the Acoustic Seismic Intrusion Detector (Acousid). Acoubuoy II, dropped by parachute, hung suspended by the shroud lines from the jungle canopy, but Spikebuoy II plummeted downward and buried its snout in the earth. Except for the added ability to report on command, both acoustic devices resembled their Phase I counterparts and performed satisfactorily. The Fadsid, however, proved too fragile, tending to break up on impact, so that its predecessor, Air-Delivered Seismic Intrusion Detector, or Adsid, remained in use. Considered the most versatile of the Phase II sensors, the Acousid combined the functions of seismic and acoustic surveillance; this single instrument could do the work that, with Phase I equipment, would have required two different sensors, one to detect motion in the ground and the second to transmit the noise made by whatever was causing the vibrations. The Acousid enabled monitors at Nakhon Phanom to investigate reported seismic activity by simply turning on the microphone and listening for the sounds of trucks driving past or troops moving about in a bivouac area.

Although the second generation of sensors represented an improvement over the first, getting useful information still involved human skill. The commandable feature conserved batteries, but required that Task Force Alpha query particular strings during the likeliest times for enemy activity. The knack of timely activation depended on careful study of sensor locations and patterns of enemy behavior; otherwise the technicians had to switch on the sensors frequently and for long periods of time, thus cutting into battery life and forfeiting a major advantage of the commandable devices. Phase II acoustic sensors, like all others of the acoustic type, posed a special challenge to the person trying to interpret their signals, for they reported sounds from every direction and at distances up to one kilometer. Consequently, the analyst might fail to locate the source of the activity being reported unless he knew the terrain and the road net and had access to intelligence from other sources.[2]

The second generation of sensors yielded, in turn, to Phase III equipment that began appearing late in 1969. Like their immediate precursors, the latest transmitters responded to commands from either the Surveillance Center or orbiting Lockheed EC–121R sensor relay aircraft, but the newer devices had a greater number of available channels and permitted the seeding of a larger sensor field without fear of signal interference. The most frequently planted of the Phase III types were Adsid III and Acousid III, although two others, a commandable microphone and an ignition detector, saw increasing service as interdiction continued.[3]

Dropped by parachute to dangle from the treetops, the commandable microphone transmitted sounds on command from surveillance monitors. After tests early in the 1970–71 dry season, this Phase III sensor demonstrated its usefulness for a variety of purposes. Besides verifying enemy activity reported by seismic sensors or other sources of intelligence, the commandable microphone could pick up the sound of voices, which might indicate the presence of foot paths or bivouac areas, two kinds of targets that thus far had proved extremely difficult to locate.[4]

The engine detector, designed like the Black Crow airborne sensor to respond to electromagnetic signals from the unshielded ignition systems of gasoline engines, underwent an operational test between March 27 and June 3, 1971. To determine the instrument's sensitivity to passing trucks, Task Force Alpha had forty-four engine detectors parachuted into locations covered by other monitoring devices. When checked against the activation record of the other sensors, the ignition detectors agreed with the acoustic or seismic equipment about 80 percent of the time. The engine detector had certain failings, however; aside from its inability to detect diesel powered vehicles, it tended to confuse lightning with ignition emissions and respond with a false alarm. Nevertheless, when used in conjunction with commandable microphones, engine detectors helped locate truck parks and cargo transshipment points. Alerted by signals from the engine detector that gasoline engines were operating nearby, a ground surveillance monitor at Nakhon Phanom could use the commandable microphone to listen for sounds associated with repair facilities, for instance, or supply dumps.[5]

The cost of sensors varied according to type. The Adsid, made up of parts interchangeable with various other models, cost the least, $619 in the spring of 1972. An Acousid, with its greater versatility and complexity, cost $1,452, and the engine detector carried a price tag of $2,997.[6]

Relay aircraft linked the various kinds of sensors to the Surveillance Center, but systematic electronic surveillance of the Ho Chi Minh Trail had barely begun when the Tactical Air Command became concerned about the age and vulnerability of the EC–121R Bat Cats that flew the sensor relay mission. After almost two decades of service, the much-modified aircraft required frequent overhaul; and parts, especially for the turbo-boosted piston engines, had become scarce. Air Force planners, however, worried more about the human investment in the Bat Cat program than about the maintenance difficulties. The enemy, by shooting down one EC–121, might kill from fifteen to twenty-two crewmen and surveillance specialists. To protect these highly trained individuals from radar-guided surface-to-air missiles, the EC–121Rs kept well clear of known launch sites and also carried radar jamming gear for use in an emergency. Careful planning of relay orbits, along with surveillance by ground-based or airborne radar, afforded protection from fighters.[7]

Since the EC–121R seemed such a temptation to the North Vietnamese, the Tactical Air Command suggested early in 1968 that a remotely controlled pilotless drone, carrying automatic relay equipment, replace the Bat Cat, at least in especially dangerous areas. The Beech Debonair, a low-wing cabin monoplane, normally powered by a single 225-horsepower Continental piston engine, seemed adaptable for conversion into a radio controlled relay platform. The Air Force therefore modified this business aircraft with a turbosupercharged 390-horsepower Continental engine, additional fuel capacity, plus sensor relay and remote control equipment. In March 1969 five specially equipped Debonairs, designated YQU–22As, began operating from Nakhon Phanom to test the soundness of the drone concept.[8]

For six months the 553d Reconnaissance Wing substituted the Beechcraft for the Bat Cat on normal relay missions. To avoid risking the loss of the aircraft should the radio link fail, while at the same time providing practice for the controllers on the ground, a pilot took off and flew to the assigned orbit, where the radio controller took over, directing the craft through a succession of elliptical turns until the mission ended and the pilot returned the airplane to Nakhon Phanom. In the event of equipment failure or interference between the control signal and other transmissions, the pilot could take over and either complete the mission or terminate the orbit, depending on the seriousness of the emergency.[9]

Maj. Richard M. Atchison, a navigator flying out of Nakhon Phanom late in the war, has described the typical QU–22 pilot "coming out with his blanket, a gallon of coffee, and *War and Peace*" to fly the long, cold, boring, and sometimes dangerous mission. In climbing to orbit height, the aviator had to avoid defended areas, for altitude alone protected the A models and their successors from antiaircraft fire. One evening Atchison saw a QU–22, the strobe light retained from the Debonair flashing rhythmically as the plane flew off course over the batteries protecting Ban Karai Pass. Every ten seconds or so an 85-mm shell exploded behind the Beechcraft, but its pilot, apparently unaware of the danger, continued steadily on until out of range of the North Vietnamese gunfire.[10]

The telltale strobe light, however, proved to be the least of a pilot's worries. Three times during training or on combat missions, the YQU–22As suffered sudden engine failure, and once, near Nakhon Phanom, the pilot had to parachute to safety when the engine refused to start again. The absence of deicing equipment for the wings or propeller proved almost as dangerous as the balky powerplant. Since the Beechcraft flew above twenty thousand feet, where the air temperature hovered at twenty-two degrees below zero, Fahrenheit, the airman had to avoid towering, moisture-laden clouds prevalent in the southwest monsoon season, or a sudden coating of ice might tip the plane into a fatal spin. Other less deadly failings included a cramped, poorly heated cabin that lacked pressurization.[11]

From the men who flew it, the A model received a rating of only "marginally effective,"[12] but despite their lack of enthusiasm, the idea of a relay drone remained alive, for a fleet of remotely controlled light aircraft could do the work of the Bat Cats at one-fifth the cost and with one-fourth the manpower.[13] Saving money by substituting automated drones for the EC–121Rs formed just one aspect of a program of economizing that affected every element of government. President Nixon, who had promised during his successful campaign for office to cut federal spending, proposed to shave $4 billion from the aggregate budget of $195.3 billion for fiscal 1969 that President Johnson had submitted to Congress before leaving office. The Department of Defense faced the loss of $1.1 billion from a Johnson budget that had totaled $79 billion, excluding funds for nuclear weapons and for administering the Selective Service System.

Budget cuts within the Department of Defense had an immediate impact on the war in Vietnam. Presented with what they interpreted as a choice between a decrease in monthly B–52 sorties and the withdrawal of tactical fighter units, the Joint Chiefs of Staff accepted fewer Arc Light strikes, reasoning that in an emergency, it would be easier to increase the tempo of B–52 attacks than to deploy fighter squadrons across the Pacific. The Nixon administration, however, did not choose one or the other but a combination of both, for the authorized number of B–52 sorties declined from eighteen hundred per month to sixteen hundred and then to fourteen hundred, even as two tactical fighter squadrons redeployed from Southeast Asia. In addition, one aircraft carrier steamed out of the Gulf of Tonkin, reducing from five to four the number on station there, and other warships also withdrew to conserve funds. The pressure to save money persisted into fiscal year 1970, which began on July 1, 1969, and resulted not only in restrictions on sorties by tactical aircraft and on naval gunfire, but also in the earlier departure of some ground units.[14]

Even though the Air Force reduced the number of sorties available to attack infiltration routes and supply depots outside South Vietnam and enemy forces within the country, air power continued to protect Vietnamization and the ongoing withdrawal of ground forces. The reductions in U.S. participation in the ground war did not, however, mollify antiwar sentiment in the United States. Indeed, when Secretary of the Army Stanley R. Resor welcomed the first battalion to return from South Vietnam to the United States, protesters in the crowd at McChord Air Force Base, Washington, interrupted his speech with shouted demands that all the troops come home. Moreover, individual senators and representatives introduced resolutions designed to put an end to U.S. involvement in the conflict, actions that reflected the mood of a large segment of the public, as demonstrated on October 15, 1969, when the antiwar movement staged peaceful protests throughout the nation. In some cities, notably in the Northeast, as many as one hundred thousand persons gathered to call for an end to the fighting; counterdemonstrations in support of administration policy attracted fewer participants and less coverage by newspapers and television.[15] Looking back on the events of 1969, Dr. Kissinger recalled warning, in his function as national security adviser to the President, that troop withdrawals "would become like 'salted peanuts' to the public; the more troops we withdrew, the more would be expected." Kissinger's prediction was coming true even before the year had ended.[16]

Air power continued to protect stepped-up Vietnamization and accelerated withdrawal, but, because of pressures on the budget and the declining public support for the war, increasingly fewer aircraft interdicted traffic on the Ho Chi Minh Trail or intervened on battlefields elsewhere in Southeast Asia. As military appropriations declined, the lure of savings, even in something as comparatively inexpensive as the radio relay portion of the electronic surveillance of the trail, proved so attractive that the Air Force refused to give up on the use of drones as less expensive substitutes for the EC–121Rs. Five QU–22Bs replaced the earlier A models. The latest version featured deicers and a modified Continental engine, but still lacked a pressurized cabin.[17]

In spite of the improvements, the B models soon began having engine trouble. The first instance of power failure resulted from a defective fuel valve and the second from a loose connection in the radio control unit—scarcely grounds for concern about the engine itself. Complaints of rough running became more frequent, however, culminating in two failures that occurred less than a week apart in December 1970. The first victim, Maj. Matthew H. Peach, parachuted to safety when sparks erupted from the cowling as he attempted to restart the engine. Next, Capt. Theodore R. Diltz, Jr., lost power as he climbed past seventeen thousand five hundred feet following a normal takeoff, but he managed to limp to a landing at Savannakhet.[18]

No clear pattern of engine failure had emerged, so the Air Force went ahead with plans to replace the EC–121Rs, sending an additional dozen QU–22Bs to Nakhon Phanom for that purpose. Besides being cheaper to operate, the latest version of the Beechcraft could orbit some seven thousand feet higher than the Lockheed. The additional altitude enabled the relay equipment to avoid terrain masking to the extent that coverage increased by an estimated 30 percent on a typical mission.[19]

Since a pilot sat in the cockpit, ready to take over the controls in an emergency and carry out the mission, the remote control equipment seemed wasted, especially since its operation and maintenance required some forty-six individuals at an annual cost of $463,000. Although Gen. Lucius D. Clay, Jr., the Seventh Air Force commander, advocated scrapping radio control, which he considered unreliable, the men who flew the QU–22B wanted to retain this feature. To the individual flier circling for several hours at an altitude where oxygen failure could result in death, remote control remained a desirable safety feature, for the man on the ground could bring the aircraft safely home if a pilot blacked out and could not respond to periodic radio checks. The argument that remote control promoted safety carried little weight, however, for money had to be saved, and radio guidance equipment had twice failed during the evaluation of the B model. As a result, on March 8, 1971, Gen. Joseph J. Nazzaro, the Commander in Chief, Pacific Air Forces, authorized General Clay to cancel this aspect of the project.[20]

By the time that Nazzaro approved the deletion of radio control, a team of technicians had come to Nakhon Phanom to investigate complaints about the powerplant in the QU–22Bs. After examining the airplane and talking with pilots, representatives of Continental Motors and the Aeronautical Systems Division proposed a series of modifications designed to make the QU–22B a reliable piece of equipment. The Seventh Air Force staff remained skeptical, however, pointing out that "there is no guarantee that the problems will be solved . . . . or that future problems will not arise." The difficulties experienced by the Beechcraft, the staff officers believed, resulted from flying it "in an environment and on a schedule considerably more demanding than that for which the basic aircraft was designed."[21]

Events soon confirmed the doubts expressed at Seventh Air Force headquarters. Hope lingered for a time that carefully maintained QU–22Bs could begin replacing the Bat Cats in September 1971, but recurring engine failures caused Task Force Alpha to request that the Seventh Air Force test the C–130E airborne battlefield command and control center as the new sensor relay craft. Although this airplane could do the job, serving as a flying command post enjoyed a higher priority, causing the Seventh Air Force to install relay equipment in older C–130B transports, which had less endurance than the C–130Es. Despite this shortcoming, modified C–130Bs took over from the EC–121Rs, the last of which left Thailand in December 1971.[22]

Meanwhile, the QU–22B, rejected as a replacement for the Bat Cat, performed limited duty, supplementing the work of the modified C–130Bs by relaying signals from sensors planted along the borders of South Vietnam. On August 26, 1972, after the North Vietnamese invasion of the South had rendered these sensor fields largely superfluous, evidence of corrosion in the wing structure forced the grounding of the Beechcrafts. As the drone program limped toward termination, a "Blue Ribbon Team" from the Aeronautical Systems Division conducted a review and suggested several reasons for failure, none of them new. According to this group, the QU–22 lacked the power for the intended mission, and the engine, although soundly designed, did not run smoothly at high altitudes, despite installation of a turbosupercharger. In short, it was the wrong airplane for the job. Poor maintenance, the study continued, had complicated the problem, for mechanics not only lacked training and proper tools, but also found key engine components to be almost inaccessible because a larger powerplant occupied the space intended for a nonsupercharged 225-horsepower engine.[23]

While the relay aircraft, and the sensors whose signals they retransmitted, maintained surveillance over the trail, the Air Force used other equipment and a variety of different techniques to ferret out the enemy's infiltration routes in Southeast Asia. Indeed, the greatest volume of data did not come from advanced technology, but from visual observation, principally by forward air controllers and the crews of aircraft flying armed reconnaissance, although roadwatch teams also reported sightings of enemy activity.

Quality took precedence over sheer volume, however, and aerial photography, when conducted over the same territory for a long period, enabled intelligence specialists to make comparisons and discover subtle signs not easily discernible to an aerial observer, even on frequently repeated missions. Consequently, routine and "quick reaction" photography, with regular or infrared film, covered the road network during both wet season and dry. Since the heaviest truck traffic occurred in dry weather, routine coverage intensified at this time, and targets requiring special missions appeared more frequently. For example, during April 1971, as the dry months came to a close, Air Force and Navy reconnaissance planes routinely flew daily missions over two of the main entry routes into southern Laos, Mu Gia and Ban Karai Passes, and also over the Tchepone area, abounding in hidden storage dumps and transshipment points. Photo missions covered most major north-south roads once each week, and twice a week the camera scanned the exits leading into South Vietnam and Cambodia, such as the routes passing through the A Shau Valley or extending southward from Attopeu. The less heavily traveled roads, like those lying west and south of Pakse, received monthly visits from photo reconnaissance aircraft.[24]

Besides looking for targets, the aerial camera sought evidence of damage done to the enemy transportation network. During the 1969–70 dry season, a pair of RF–4C reconnaissance craft flew early morning photo missions over selected road segments where trucks had been reported destroyed or damaged, trying to arrive before the enemy had time to drag wrecked vehicles from the highway and hide them in the jungle. During the first six weeks of this coverage, however, the camera confirmed just 7 of 103 reported truck kills. A number of factors could explain the failure of the project: grid coordinates reported by the crews of strike aircraft may not always have been accurate, for instance, so that the reconnaissance craft found only empty trail, and weather sometimes delayed photo missions for twenty-four hours or longer, enabling the enemy to conceal any wreckage. As a result, the lack of confirmation did not cause a downward revision of the total number of vehicles listed as damaged or destroyed.[25]

This "first light" aerial reconnaissance continued; and a related effort, begun in March 1970 to verify the results of gunship attacks on truck convoys, soon complemented it. Since gunships had already earned a reputation as the deadliest of truck killers, their activity deserved special attention. As many as four RF–4Cs, on airborne or ground alert, took infrared or photoflash pictures when summoned by gunship commanders after apparently successful attacks. This attempt to verify the damage done by the gunships persisted into the 1971–72 dry season, but, as in the case of the photographic missions flown at dawn, results proved inconclusive.[26]

The difficulty in determining accurate coordinates, an obvious handicap to attempts at using RF–4Cs for early morning photography of damage to traffic on the trail, presented a recurring problem in poorly mapped southern Laos. Photo interpreters discovered errors of several thousand meters on the standard charts. To overcome these inaccuracies, the Air Force tried, beginning in 1970, to introduce loran-controlled aerial photography into Southeast Asia. Basically this corrective technique involved using loran, which determined aircraft position by automatically comparing the elapsed time of radio signals from precisely surveyed ground stations, to pinpoint a terrain feature over which the airplane was flying. The crudest and least successful form of loran correction consisted in having F–4s carrying this navigation aid take as many as twenty fixes on a previously photographed point, like a road junction or mountain peak, to determine an average set of coordinates. A more complex and far more accurate method of using loran to correct maps began with high-altitude photographs of large sectors of Southeast Asia that cartographic specialists divided into blocks ten miles on a side. Loran-equipped RF–4Cs took detailed photographs of each segment, and technicians at the Aeronautical Charting and Information Center at St. Louis, Missouri, transferred the loran coordinates of selected control points from the recently photographed blocks to the original photo maps. The center's data automation specialists then used the control points to calculate the precise coordinates of various natural features, incorporating all the information in a computer program made available by mid-1971 to the 12th Reconnaissance Intelligence Technical Squadron at Tan Son Nhut Air Base near Saigon. When queried about a particular location, members of the unit consulted the data base to find a mountain, or perhaps the confluence of two streams, with a known loran fix. From the location of such features, technicians could extrapolate the loran coordinates of a suspected truck park or antiaircraft site. The process of using the data base to determine the coordinates of a specific point took no more than forty-five minutes. By the time interdiction ended, the specialists at Tan Son Nhut could apply loran control to all photographs of the trail taken by the RF–4Cs of the 432d Tactical Reconnaissance Wing.[27]

The loran data base also enabled photo interpreters to help the forward air controller calculate loran positions within his zone of responsibility. Each controller received loran-controlled photographs of his sector with an arbitrary grid superimposed. After spotting a target, he determined the grid coordinates and radioed them to Tan Son Nhut. There technicians consulted the data base, found the loran position that corresponded to the grid coordinates, and made the information available to strike aircraft equipped to use it. The officers manning the airborne battlefield command and control center used the same basic technique of calling on the specialists to convert grid coordinates to a loran position.[28]

Weather and darkness hampered aerial reconnaissance, but interdiction continued year-round, wet season and dry. The greatest enemy activity often occurred between dusk and dawn, and photographic surveillance had to keep pace. To conduct night photography with a minimum of risk from antiaircraft fire, the Air Force tested a laser illuminator. Unlike the usual string of bursting photoflash cartridges, the laser did not disclose to enemy gunners the heading of the reconnaissance craft. Unfortunately, the beam could not penetrate ground haze or fog, and the camera took a very grainy picture with this form of illumination, causing the Air Force to put aside the project for future development.[29]

Although more successful than the laser-camera combination, infrared imagery also suffered from the vagaries of weather, for rain, fog, and even mist affected the amount of heat available for the film to record. Under ideal conditions, infrared photography could detect the heat from engines and exhaust systems, thus pinpointing truck parks; and early in 1971, the 432d Tactical Reconnaissance Wing tested the technique to obtain loran coordinates for facilities of this kind. During a combat evaluation, an RF–4C returned with exposed infrared film that disclosed a large volume of engine heat concentrated in a small area near Tchepone. Sensor signals confirmed the presence of vehicles at the location, and an apparently successful attack ensued. Unfortunately, the technique seldom worked so well, for it sometimes overlooked truck parks discovered later by other means. As the rainy season approached, with its cloud cover and fog, and the volume of traffic diminished, infrared imaging declined in usefulness as a means of finding truck parks.[30]

The rain-drenched southwest monsoon period always proved an especially dangerous time for aerial reconnaissance. Cloud cover forced the aircraft to fly as low as forty-five hundred feet above the ground, well within range of almost every weapon the North Vietnamese had deployed in southern Laos. Since the continuing deluge interfered with infrared photography and persistent cloud cover hid the roads from conventional film, photographic coverage provided less information at this time of year as risks outweighed results.[31]

Along with visual reconnaissance and aerial photography, U.S. forces conducted various kinds of electronic surveillance to locate the enemy. For instance, the

The War against Trucks

Army's twin-engine Grumman OV–1 Mohawks patrolled the South Vietnamese border, using radar or infrared sensors to detect truck traffic through the A Shau Valley and other exit gates. In addition, Air Force, Navy, and Marine Corps airmen flew missions to pick up signals from radars that the enemy might have set up in southern Laos to control either antiaircraft batteries or surface-to-air missiles guarding the Ho Chi Minh Trail.[32]

Another form of electronic reconnaissance, airborne radio direction finding, produced targets for B–52s and tactical aircraft, but antiaircraft fire imposed limits on the usefulness of the variants of the old C–47 transport that flew such missions. Enemy gunners quickly demonstrated their ability to hit the slow-moving EC–47D, which, when damaged, revealed great structural strength. Early in April 1968, as Maj. Edward B. Sheldon was patrolling at an altitude of ninety-five hundred feet some six to eight miles west of Tchepone, a 37-mm antiaircraft shell tore a two-by-four-foot hole in the left horizontal stabilizer, damaging the left elevator, severing control cables for the elevator and trim tab on that side, and punching holes in the vertical stabilizer and rearmost portion of the fuselage. Sheldon nevertheless brought his airplane safely back to its base, but the incident showed that the EC–47, rugged though it was, could not coexist with antiaircraft batteries.[33]

By avoiding the most dangerous areas like Tchepone, EC–47s continued their mission of locating radio transmitters in southern Laos. Early in 1970, for instance, these aircraft obtained a series of fixes on radio broadcasts from what appeared to be a headquarters of the 559th Transportation Group near Saravane. Because this organization operated the Ho Chi Minh Trail, the target seemed worth attacking, and a B–52 strike caused a reported eighty-seven secondary explosions, silencing the station.[34]

During the summer of 1970, the 460th Tactical Reconnaissance Wing tried to mesh the operations of two of its aircraft: the EC–47 and McDonnell RF–101 reconnaissance jet. After locating a transmitter, the EC–47 summoned an RF–101, which had been orbiting nearby, to photograph the area. Analysis of this type of coverage failed, however, to disclose any information that the direction-finding equipment alone could not obtain, so the wing abandoned the project.[35]

Intercepted radio traffic might also provide clues to North Vietnamese plans, morale, and levels of manpower and supplies. Consequently, forms of signal intelligence other than radio direction finding flourished as the war progressed. At the peak of the interdiction effort during 1971, when disrupting the flow of enemy supplies protected the continued withdrawal of U.S. troops, three airborne collection projects recorded various kinds of electronic signals from southern Laos. About twenty times each month, Boeing RC–135Ms, specially modified versions of the Air Force aerial tanker, monitored enemy communications. To supplement this collection effort, modified Lockheed C–130B transports made as many as seventy ten-hour reconnaissance flights each month from Cam Ranh Bay, South Vietnam, participating in two separate programs and spending between five and seven hours per sortie recording enemy signals.

As early as December 1970, the Department of Defense became concerned about the vulnerability of the C–130Bs when intercepting electronic transmissions in certain regions, for the destruction of one of these aircraft would claim the lives of highly skilled electronics specialists. Once again the remotely controlled Beechcraft QU–22B, this time fitted with automatic recording equipment, seemed a solution. Unfortunately, the same engine problem that prevented the Beechcraft from taking over the sensor relay mission also frustrated plans to use it for communications monitoring. The first QU–22B modified for intelligence work flew in July 1971, but mechanical shortcomings prevented the Seventh Air Force from mustering enough airworthy craft for an operational evaluation. Meanwhile, one of the two C–130B collection programs neared the planned termination date of November 1, when its aircraft would undertake a new assignment. Since the Beechcraft program had bogged down, Gen. John D. Ryan, the Air Force Chief of Staff, temporarily increased RC–135M coverage until December when newly modified C–130 transports began filling the gap caused by failure of the QU–22B and the reassignment of the C–130Bs used earlier.[36]

Along with electronic eavesdropping and related techniques, improved optical aids helped locate targets for aerial interdiction in southern Laos. These devices included a camouflage detector, intended for daylight use, that saw limited service over the Ho Chi Minh Trail. Under development since 1966, the detector incorporated two filters attached to viewing binoculars, one keyed to the reflective properties of leaves, tropical growth, and soil; and the other sensitive to reflections from cloth and some kinds of camouflage paint. When an observer scanned an area with the filters in place, the natural background seemed stable, while cloth-covered weapons and some painted objects appeared to pulsate.[37]

Preliminary tests in Southeast Asia during December 1967 and January 1968 proved so successful that the Air Force purchased five of the battery-powered camouflage detectors for a more demanding evaluation. During tests in Panama, operators succeeded, under ideal conditions, in locating a man-sized cloth target from an altitude of ten thousand feet at a range of fourteen thousand feet. Results of this sort were possible from about one hour after sunrise until roughly an hour before sunset, provided that visibility exceeded three miles. In rough air the instrument proved worthless, since the viewer could not keep contact with the eyepiece as the airplane bounced around in the turbulent sky.[38]

Maj. Richard E. Pierson and 1st Lt. James N. Hutchinson, assigned to the Tactical Air Warfare Center at Eglin Air Force Base, Florida, brought the five camouflage detectors to South Vietnam and supervised the installation of four sets in Cessna O–2A observation planes based at Da Nang. The equipment proved successful in both South Vietnam and southern Laos, locating guns concealed by fresh foliage placed in cloth nets and even zeroing in on the uniforms worn by individual North Vietnamese soldiers. After the formal evaluation ended in May 1971, the detectors remained in Southeast Asia, operating mainly in southern Laos. From November of that year until the March 1972 invasion of South Vietnam, mainte-

The War against Trucks

nance men trained by Major Pierson and Lieutenant Hutchinson cannibalized some of the sets for spare parts so that the others could remain in action to help pinpoint bivouac areas and supply points on the troop infiltration routes leading from North Vietnam into South Vietnam and Cambodia. Cannibalization became necessary when the manufacturer sold out to another firm, which abandoned the project. The camouflage detector declined in usefulness after the North Vietnamese invasion of the South brought the war into the open. Over the Ho Chi Minh Trail, the device performed almost exactly as planned, but too few saw service to affect the course of the war.[39]

Another optical device, a television camera with a telescopic lens, also underwent testing in the skies over southern Laos. The Air Force Systems Command fitted two F–4Es with gyrostabilized television cameras, each having two telescopic lenses that could be changed during flight to permit either wide-angle search or narrow focus. The magnified image picked up by the camera appeared on screens in the front and rear cockpits, enabling the crew, at least in theory, to detect an approaching interceptor before it could attack, or to locate targets on the ground while remaining beyond reach of antiaircraft guns. Test missions flown over Laos between February 12 and March 10, 1972, revealed that neither of the telescopic lenses swiveled quickly enough to permit the search of the roads that twisted through southern Laos, nor could the camera's eye penetrate vegetation or camouflage. As a result, daylight television proved an effective reconnaissance tool only on long stretches of comparatively straight roadway in the open areas of northern Laos. Since the two F–4Es made no contact with enemy fighters, the crews could not determine how well the equipment could acquire fast approaching aircraft.[40]

To hit targets located by sensors or other means, but shrouded by cloud cover, fog, or darkness, the Seventh Air Force in 1969 began evaluating both radar transponders and light beacons as nighttime aiming points for interdiction missions. Designed to be dropped near a target and serve as point of reference, the transponders began transmitting when prompted by radar signals from an approaching aircraft. The first such instrument to undergo evaluation, Rabet I (an acronym for radar beacon transponder I), emitted too weak a signal for accurate plotting, an average output of just five watts. The basic idea, however, appeared sound enough to justify further experiments with the more powerful Rabet II, capable of generating a maximum of four hundred watts. Members of the fighter unit that had tested the beacon enjoyed spectacular success, picking up a return signal fifteen out of nineteen times at an average distance of thirty-five miles and an average altitude of ten thousand feet. Never again would the results be so encouraging. Another squadron made thirty-two attempts to trigger a beacon, but succeeded only once.[41] The abrupt decline in effectiveness undermined the confidence that the first tests had generated. "Judging from the information available," said a Seventh Air Force status report in July 1970, "it appears that Rabet units will have limited usefulness . . . . They can be used only in clear areas and even then they will be useful only for general target acquisition." Maj. Gen. John H. Buckner, Seventh Air Force Deputy Chief of Staff for Operations, summed up the status of the beacon when he wrote across a summary of the report, "Looks like a loser."[42] Further tests on the Ho Chi Minh Trail underscored this judgment, for the evidence soon disclosed that the radar pulse emitted by the F–4E was not strong enough to be certain of triggering Rabet II. Finally, in December 1970, the Defense Communications Planning Group canceled the project.[43]

Another effort to improve F–4 bombing accuracy also ended in failure. Involved in this project was a different type of beacon, a strobe light that could be dropped from the air and turned on or off on command from the cockpit of a Phantom. During a combat evaluation lasting from January 29 through February 10, 1970, fighter-bombers planted seven of these bombing aids in southern Laos, but only two responded to control signals. Neither of the pair that actually worked provided a suitable aiming point, and one of them inadvertently helped the defenders, since the flashing light, combined with the roar of the approaching jet engines, warned antiaircraft gunners to open fire.[44]

Yet a third variation on beacon bombing appeared early in 1971 when the Strategic Air Command suggested that a gunship might ferret out appropriate targets using infrared and other sensors, drop a radar transponder to mark the area, and summon a B–52, which had been orbiting in the vicinity, to trigger the device and use it for offset aiming in dropping bombs. The lone bomber would make as many passes as necessary, each time dropping a single general purpose weapon, until the gunship's sensors had confirmed the bombardier's aim, then salvo the remaining explosives. Tests in the United States had indicated that three "single releases" usually confirmed the aiming point. The Strategic Air Command therefore proposed a combat evaluation using one B–52 sortie per day for as many as twenty-five days in some "non-threat" portion of southeastern Laos.[45]

Although General Ryan, Air Force Chief of Staff, initially liked the idea, arguments mustered by two of his key commanders, General Momyer of the Tactical Air Command and General Nazzaro of the Pacific Air Forces, caused him to reconsider. The plan, as Momyer pointed out, would in effect convert the gunship into a "ten million dollar FAC," a job usually done by a light, twin-engine craft like the OV–10 or O–2, or by an F–4 in heavily defended areas.[46] Nazzaro warned that the "nonavailability of excess AC–130 sorties and lack of suitable targets" made the evaluation seem "questionable."[47] Momyer scotched the plan when he warned that these tactics endangered the F–4s protecting the gunship from antiaircraft batteries, since "a Mk 82 [five hundred pound bomb] time-to-fall from thirty-four thousand feet . . . is slightly less than one minute, during which the F–4 escort travels about 5–7 miles . . . [and] could fly through the attack axis during bomb travel even though not in the radar field of view at the time of bomb release."[48]

Although beacon bombing and some of the other techniques and equipment failed when tested against the Ho Chi Minh Trail, the Air Force nevertheless acquired hardware and devised tactics that seemed suitable for finding targets on the infiltration network and attacking them by day and by night. The sources of infor-

The War against Trucks

mation varied from visual observation to aerial photography, from acoustic and seismic sensors planted along the trail to enemy radio traffic intercepted by airborne monitors. In making use of this intelligence, gunships worked almost exclusively during darkness, patrolling the roads when traffic seemed heaviest, but most attacks on truck parks and storage areas occurred during the day, and F–4s cut roads and dropped munitions packages in daylight to establish interdiction points. Most of the aerial photography took place in daylight, as did the armed reconnaissance sorties designed to force the enemy to operate his truck convoys at night, when darkness impeded the drivers and the gunships were their deadliest. During a typical northeast monsoon campaign, when dry weather permitted a heavier volume of traffic, daylight sorties outnumbered those flown at night, but the vast majority of actual attacks on road traffic took place between sunset and dawn. Without technological innovations such as the airborne and ground surveillance sensors, the gunship, or the laser-guided bomb, air power could scarcely have contested the movement of supplies through southern Laos—a critical element in preventing the enemy from mounting a major offensive as President Nixon withdrew ground forces from South Vietnam.[49]

Chapter Five

Launching the Truck War

The attempt to impede the passage of men and supplies over the Ho Chi Minh Trail encountered natural obstacles, active and passive defenses put in place by the North Vietnamese, and uncertainties that stemmed from the very composition of the logistics network itself. Throughout the year, nature complicated the task of aerial interdiction in southern Laos. When the southwest monsoon was blowing, rain and a thick overcast hampered aerial attack; and even during the dry season, clouds might obscure an important area, such as Ban Karai Pass, although the sky remained clear just a few miles away. Fog often blanketed the twisting valleys during the dry months, combining with dust from road traffic and smoke caused when Montagnards burned away the undergrowth to clear land for farming. The resulting veil could frustrate aerial observation throughout the morning; and after the fog had lifted, the enemy still enjoyed the concealment afforded by layered rain forest, limestone caves, dense underbrush, and finally, by dark of night.

The defenders of the trail used nature to their advantage, operating whenever possible beneath the jungle canopy and when necessary, improving this concealment by the use of trellis work that suspended vines and freshly cut branches over the roads, trails, supply dumps, and other elements of the Ho Chi Minh Trail. Hidden from the naked eye, the aerial camera, and many of the new airborne sensors, the enemy built additional roads and cutoffs when and where he needed them, repaired or improved the existing routes, and set up a dispersed web of repair facilities, storage areas, and encampments. Even as he concealed his true activity, the enemy became increasingly skillful at deception, ultimately building entire dummy truck parks, with wooden or canvas vehicles that were visible from the air, but not so obvious as to arouse immediate suspicion. Sometimes the defenders of the trail placed cans of fuel in truck carcasses; when gunfire from attacking aircraft ignited the fuel, the resulting fire blinded infrared sensors and created the illusion that a truck had been destroyed.[1]

As if nature and the enemy's use of his natural surroundings did not cause difficulty enough, airmen attacking the Ho Chi Minh Trail had to face an expanding array of antiaircraft guns. In the summer of 1968, during the planning of the northeast monsoon season interdiction campaign that became Commando Hunt, fairly weak antiaircraft defenses guarded the trail, a condition that began changing on the very eve of the operation. President Johnson's decision to suspend the bombing of North Vietnam, effective November 1, 1968, upset the existing balance between offense and defense in southern Laos. The change in policy immediately enabled the United States to hurl an additional 480 aircraft against the transportation complex each day, raising the daily sortie average to 620. So important had the trail become, that in June 1969, for instance, Air Force, Navy, and Marine Corps squadrons flew five times as many sorties against southern Laos as they had in June of the previous year. The enemy, freed from the threat of raids against his homeland, countered this increased activity by moving guns across the border into Laos, strengthening his defenses there from an estimated 166 weapons at the end of November 1968 to a reported 621 at the end of April 1969.[2]

The defenses of southern Laos remained crude, however, compared to the radar-directed combination of guns, missiles, and interceptors that guarded North Vietnam. Seventh Air Force intelligence believed that, throughout the dry season of 1968–69, optically aimed 37-mm weapons, effective against aircraft flying below eighty-two hundred feet, accounted for more than half the guns protecting the Ho Chi Minh Trail. Fighter-bombers or gunships might encounter these anywhere along known highways, with the heaviest concentrations east and west of Tchepone and on the roads leading from Mu Gia and Ban Karai Passes. Twin-mounted 23-mm types, accurate below five thousand feet, provided much of the remaining firepower and helped guard many of the same targets protected by the 37-mm pieces. Pilots and photo interpreters reported a few 57-mm guns, effective up to twelve thousand five hundred feet, near Tchepone and west of Ban Karai Pass, along with one 85-mm gun, capable of hurling a shell to thirty-nine thousand feet, defending a ford carrying traffic from Ban Karai Pass across the Nam Tale River. Large numbers of machine guns supplemented the antiaircraft batteries and proved deadly up to forty-five hundred feet.[3]

Electronic reconnaissance did not detect fire-control radar for any of these guns. The possibility existed, however, that early warning sites located inside North Vietnam telephoned the antiaircraft batteries in nearby Laos whenever formations of U.S. aircraft approached. On sections of the trail beyond the range of North Vietnamese radar, warning probably depended on observers, posted on hilltops or in trees, who watched with binoculars, listened, and then used field telephones, flags, lights, or rifle shots to alert gun crews to imminent air attacks.

Camouflage and mobility contributed to the deadliness of the defenses of the Ho Chi Minh Trail. Dummy antiaircraft emplacements, for example, might serve as bait for flak traps, luring the fighter-bombers into the killing zone of real weapons hidden nearby. In addition, the enemy invested a great deal of time and energy in building and concealing alternate positions, to be occupied when the primary site came under attack. When air strikes dictated a move to an alternate site, a light truck usually towed the mobile 37-mm gun from one place to another, hooking up and vacating a gun pit within five minutes; ten minutes after reaching the new location, the weapon could be firing again. As nearly as U.S. intelligence could discover, the crews of both the 23-mm guns and the machine guns broke down their weapons and carried them to the alternate site themselves, although they might use pack animals if the intensity of aerial attack permitted.[4]

Braving these defenses to attack an enemy concealed by cloud, fog, forest, and darkness, airmen sought to disrupt the flow of supplies to South Vietnam by concentrating on truck transport. Later, a campaign against pipelines and waterways would flourish for a time, and eventually air power attacked infiltrating troops; but as the 1968–69 dry season approached, roads, trucks, and related installations seemed both vulnerable and comparatively easy to locate. Unfortunately, knowledge of the road net, and the fleet of trucks that traveled it, proved incomplete, at best. Analysts at Task Force Alpha, after examining sensor data and other intelligence, concluded that a maximum of 872 trucks had been operating in southern Laos during the 1968 southwest monsoon season. This figure for the rainy summer months represented an increase of 169 over the total believed active during the preceding dry season, when the Tet offensive generated heavy traffic; but on the eve of that attack, sensor coverage had barely begun. In announcing this estimate, Task Force Alpha cautioned that "the size of the North Vietnamese truck fleet is difficult to determine," a warning clearly worth heeding.[5]

In spite of the promised difficulty, U.S. intelligence sought for a time to keep a careful tally of trucks imported into North Vietnam, subtract the number destroyed by aerial attack, and thus arrive at an estimate of the inventory available to sustain the fighting in South Vietnam. By the early autumn of 1968 and the end of the rainy season in southern Laos, Air Force analysts took heart from reports of successful interdiction in southern North Vietnam, where the bombing had not yet ended, and indications that the Hanoi government was attempting to buy trucks in Japan and France. Shortly afterward, as the first Commando Hunt operation drew near, the realization dawned that the productive capacity of the various communist states—an estimated fifty thousand trucks each month in the Soviet Union and eastern Europe, and still others in China—could more than make good North Vietnam's losses. Consequently, the war on trucks became an open-ended campaign, a matter of destroying as many of them as possible. During 1969, for instance, Air Force analysts tended to compare trucks killed to the number sighted, rather than to an estimated inventory, even though they had detailed figures on North Vietnamese imports.[6]

Even as uncertainty veiled the size of the truck fleet, weather and natural or artificial concealment complicated efforts to plot the road net these vehicles used to shuttle cargo from the mountain passes leading out of North Vietnam, through southern Laos, and into South Vietnam. The Ho Chi Minh Trail, moreover, was continually changing, as an estimated 19,450 North Vietnamese and Pathet Lao engineers and laborers struggled to keep the trucks rolling. Each year, for as long as weather permitted, these men braved aerial attack and not only repaired bomb damage, but also built new roads, truck parks, and storage areas, while maintaining the old ones. Thanks to their activity, truck transport offered an ever-evolving target within the logistics network.[7]

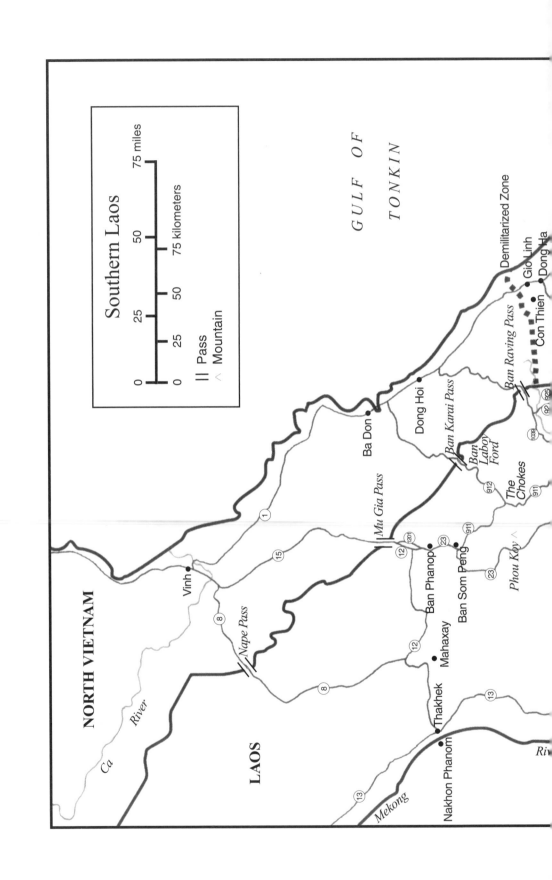

Southern Laos

0   25   50   75 miles
0   25   50   75 kilometers

|| Pass
∧ Mountain

GULF OF TONKIN

NORTH VIETNAM

LAOS

Ca River

Mekong

Riv

Vinh

Ba Don

Dong Hoi

Demilitarized Zone

Gio Linh

Con Thien

Dong Ha

Ban Raving Pass

Ban Karai Pass

Ban Laboy Ford

The Chokes

Mu Gia Pass

Nape Pass

Ban Phanop

Ban Som Peng

Phou Koy ∧

Mahaxay

Thakhek

Nakhon Phanom

1

15

8

8

12

201

12

23

23

911

911

912

92

925

1039

13

13

8

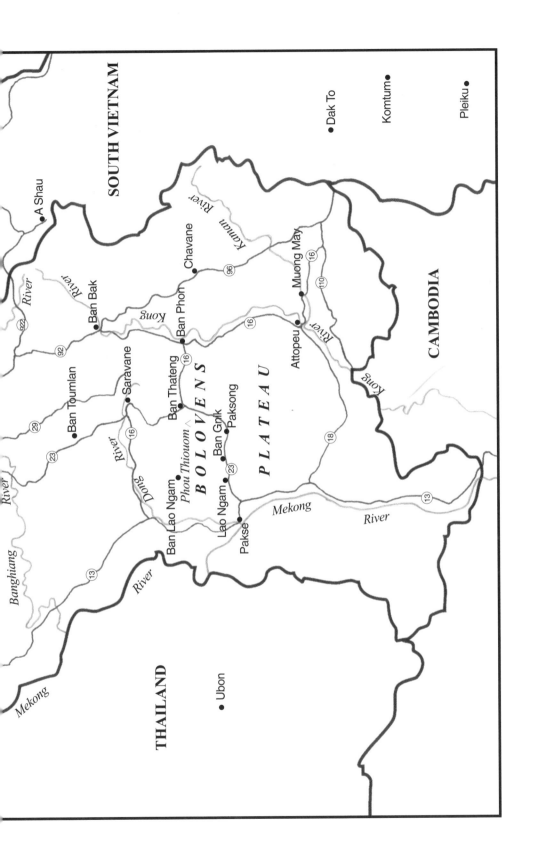

The War against Trucks

To the commander in Saigon, General Westmoreland, disrupting traffic over the Ho Chi Minh Trail in southern Laos presented the most important goal to be attained anywhere in the kingdom, for the interdiction of supplies and reinforcements directly affected the fighting in South Vietnam. On the other hand, from his office in Vientiane, Ambassador Sullivan pointed out that "the people of Laos are more concerned about U.S. air support of 'their war,' namely the one in the north [of Laos] which directly concerns them." Sullivan worried that Prince Souvanna Phouma, preoccupied with keeping the Pathet Lao away from the Plain of Jars, the royal capital at Luang Prabang, and the administrative capital of Vientiane, might feel that the United States was "receiving carte blanche for activities in the south" of his kingdom, while giving the Laotian people nothing in return. However Souvanna interpreted it, the decision to conduct Commando Hunt confirmed that interdiction of the Ho Chi Minh Trail enjoyed an infinitely higher priority than operations elsewhere in Laos.[8]

Planning began in the summer of 1968 for Commando Hunt, the aerial interdiction campaign that would last throughout the coming northeast monsoon season, from November until April. The Seventh Air Force staff joined Task Force Alpha in trying to merge new technology with proven aerial tactics to prevent repetition of the Tet offensive that had burst on South Vietnam earlier in the year. The operating area for this first Commando Hunt campaign formed a dogleg extending an average of twenty-nine miles westward from the Laotian border, including the highways entering the kingdom through Nape, Mu Gia, and Ban Karai Passes, along with the transportation hub that had grown up around Tchepone. The Commando Hunt area formed a part of a larger interdiction zone that embraced southern Laos, but subsequent Commando Hunt campaigns would expand until the Surveillance Center traced the progress of supplies all the way to the Cambodian border.[9]

Operation Commando Hunt sought "to reduce the flow of enemy resources into South Vietnam" by destroying "trucks and caches of military supplies along routes leading south," while tying down "substantial forces and resources supporting and defending the infiltration route structure."[10] In impeding the flow of supplies, first priority went to disrupting truck traffic by establishing interdiction points where roads converged or seemed especially vulnerable to bombing, in other words, at choke points. Each interdiction point—at this time called a traffic control point—consisted of a road cut surrounded by antipersonnel and antivehicular mines. When traffic halted and the enemy tried to clear the mines and close the cut, he became vulnerable to air attack. Strikes by B–52s and tactical aircraft on transshipment points and similar installations enjoyed second priority. Sensor-assisted attacks on moving convoys received third priority, and silencing antiaircraft guns ranked fourth, even though these weapons claimed most of the fifty-six aircraft the Air Force lost during Commando Hunt.[11]

The Jason Summer Study had envisioned a barrier command, Task Force Alpha, that directed air strikes on the basis of the intelligence it gathered. Once the crisis at Khe Sanh seemed past, emphasis shifted to the Ho Chi Minh Trail, and Dr.

John S. Foster, Jr., Director of Defense Research and Engineering, suggested "the possibility of increasing the kill effectiveness of the [interdiction] system at the point where timely intelligence is being developed; that is, at Task Force Alpha." Secretary of the Air Force Harold Brown endorsed the idea, passing it along to General McConnell, the Air Force Chief of Staff. Ultimately, Commando Hunt planners incorporated Dr. Foster's suggestion in their concept, assigning the operation a secondary mission "to exploit the effectiveness of the Igloo White System as a participant in the truck killing effort."[12] To increase the "kill effectiveness" as Dr. Foster desired, Task Force Alpha received direct control over certain aircraft as they arrived over the Commando Hunt operating area. Previously, if sensor activations disclosed a blacked out convoy groping through the night, a target assessment officer—subsequently rechristened a ground surveillance monitor—advised the Surveillance Center duty officer, who reported the potential target to an airborne battlefield command and control center that had the authority to commit any available aircraft. During Commando Hunt, however, controllers sitting near the target assessment officer could call down an air strike without recourse to the airborne battlefield command and control center.[13]

The earlier concern that giving Task Force Alpha control over aircraft might undermine the single manager concept no longer prevailed. Not only had the marines failed to overturn Westmoreland's decision to give the Seventh Air Force "mission direction" over Marine Corps tactical aircraft, the policy itself had undergone a reinterpretation that promoted interservice harmony. In effect, the Seventh Air Force agreed to set aside a specific number of sorties for Marine Corps commanders to use as they saw fit, a concession that reassured the marines and helped them meet their needs for air support.[14]

Task Force Alpha's operational mission required the construction of a $130,000 combat operations center in a glass-enclosed balcony overlooking the Surveillance Center's plot room with its electronic display of sensor locations and activations. About six weeks of work remained, however, when Commando Hunt got underway on November 15, 1968. As expected, the two IBM 360/65 computers that Task Force Alpha had already leased as replacements for the original IBM 360/40s met the basic demands of the interdiction effort, even though the old display consoles and related equipment had to be used because the new ones were not yet functioning. Installed at a cost of $610,000, exclusive of rental costs and service fees, the new computers could accept and store more data, and retrieve it faster, than the older models.[15]

Although Task Force Alpha had used computers and therefore adjusted quickly to the improved models, the organization lacked experience in directing air strikes. Gen. George Brown's Seventh Air Force, which exercised operational control over Task Force Alpha, set aside a shakedown period, lasting from October 22 until the launching of Commando Hunt on November 15, during which veterans of the airborne battlefield command and control centers showed the recently chosen Task Force Alpha controllers how to bring air power to bear against a specific target. A group of trained tactical air controllers also participated in this indoctrination; they used the call sign Invert and served as the conduit through which the Nakhon Phanom operations center, called Sycamore, passed orders to the aircraft under its control.[16]

The 621st Tactical Control Squadron, which had been exercising radar control of aerial refueling over the border between Laos and Thailand, initially sent a dozen experienced controllers to handle the Invert operation and provide the essential link between Sycamore and the aircraft it controlled. Operating from Nakhon Phanom, the detachment kept Task Force Alpha apprised of all aircraft over the Commando Hunt operating area, whether the airplanes took orders from Nakhon Phanom or flew missions assigned by the Seventh Air Force. The hard-pressed Invert controllers, who ultimately numbered 25, took over at any of eight entry points, where another control center—Da Nang in South Vietnam, for example, or Udorn, Thailand—handed over the flight, and the detachment maintained surveillance as long as the aircraft remained within Commando Hunt airspace.[17]

Unfortunately, the new control arrangement got off to a bad start; on only the third day of the shakedown period, the volume of air traffic overwhelmed the tactical control detachment. Several factors combined to cause this "saturation of the control capability." During the morning, large numbers of aircraft passed through Commando Hunt airspace en route to targets elsewhere; and not all crews, whether transients or actually assigned to Commando Hunt, checked in at the appropriate entry points, which were designated by their loran coordinates. Unused at first to the new role, Task Force Alpha tended to allow its assigned fighters to mill about before directing them against specific targets, a failing that experience corrected. Finally, the Seventh Air Force found it hard to break habits acquired during Rolling Thunder, the air offensive against North Vietnam that ended on November 1, and launched "major waves" instead of spreading out the planned arrivals over a longer time.[18] The Seventh Air Force learned, however, to adjust its scheduling so that aircraft reached the Commando Hunt area "in a steady flow rather than the two-wave-a-day pattern that had characterized the campaign against NVN [North Vietnam]."

Sycamore control meanwhile became so proficient that the instructors borrowed from the airborne battlefield command and control centers returned to their jobs almost a week earlier than planned. As a result of the November bombing halt, the volume of air traffic grew even heavier, testing the newly acquired skills of those who directed strikes from Nakhon Phanom.[19] On the day after the ban against attacks on the North went into effect, the number of sorties directed into the Commando Hunt area doubled, setting the pace for the period that followed. A power failure on November 12 lasted almost two hours, blacking out the radar scopes used by the Invert detachment. Although the Seventh Air Force instructors had already gone, Sycamore controllers met the emergency, establishing direct radio contact with forward air controllers until standard procedures resumed. The normal methods had become obsolete, however, for the power failure demonstrated that Sycamore could talk directly with the aircraft assigned to Task Force Alpha, bypassing Invert and causing its elimination.[20]

104

Not every sortie within the Commando Hunt region came under Task Force Alpha control, but even those aircraft assigned targets by the Seventh Air Force benefited from the work of the Surveillance Center. Besides directing immediate strikes by aircraft under orders from Task Force Alpha, a target intelligence officer at Nakhon Phanom might recommend "long-range" targets that did not have to be hit immediately. If the data in the computers at the Surveillance Center, which included not only sensor activations, but also reports from roadwatch teams and other sources, convinced him that a target was worth striking in the near future, he forwarded a request to Seventh Air Force headquarters, which, if it approved, obtained any necessary clearance from the embassy at Vientiane and included the mission in one of the daily operations orders. When the aircraft arrived in the Commando Hunt zone, the pilot checked in with the controllers at Nakhon Phanom, but he could attack only the primary target or a previously assigned alternate; Sycamore could not divert him elsewhere.[21]

Besides forwarding intelligence, based at least in part on sensor surveillance, to Seventh Air Force headquarters, Task Force Alpha also advised the appropriate airborne battlefield command and control center of possible targets south of 16 degrees, 30 minutes, North latitude, at this time the southern boundary of Commando Hunt. Whenever a target assessment officer at Nakhon Phanom received promising sensor data relating to this region, he passed it to a target intelligence officer for transmittal to the intelligence section in the crowded command capsule within the converted C–130. There a specialist evaluated the information and if satisfied of its importance, passed it to a controller seated nearby, who, in turn, relayed it to a forward air controller or gunship commander.[22]

Just as the southern boundary of the Commando Hunt zone might at times blur, the three phases into which planners had arbitrarily divided the operation tended to overlap and lacked sharp definition in time or geography. Precise delineation proved impossible because the Commando Hunt interdiction campaign sought to keep pace with the movement of cargo toward South Vietnam, and the timing and progress of the truck convoys depended on the enemy's tactical plans, the amount of supplies in the depots along the trail and immediately available for forwarding, and the damage done to the roads by flooding during the rainy season. In general, the three phases of interdiction began at the mountain passes leading from North Vietnam and followed the trucks southward as the trail dried out and heavy traffic resumed.

During the first phase of Commando Hunt, the emphasis rested on traffic control points (later called interdiction points) located at choke points where two or more roads converged and the construction of bypasses seemed difficult. The most frequently attacked choke points lay along roads leading from Mu Gia Pass through the Ban Phanop area or southward from Ban Karai Pass by way of Ban Laboy Ford. Sensor reports from strings near the traffic control points told Task Force Alpha's analysts whether bomb damage to the roadway and minefields planted by air actually closed the road and delayed repairs. If the traffic control point seemed to be in place, but monitoring devices planted beyond it reported trucks driving past, intelligence specialists knew that the enemy had built a bypass. Reconnaissance aircraft then photographed the area around the choke point, and photo interpreters tried to penetrate the natural concealment, possibly enhanced with camouflage, and find the new road.[23]

Besides helping locate roads, sensors of every type afforded valuable clues to the location of truck parks. The sudden activation of certain strings of seismic devices immediately after sunset indicated that a convoy had left a truck park and turned onto a highway. This evidence—possibly confirmed by intercepted radio traffic, aerial photos, or visual observation—frequently led to the planting of acoustic sensors or commandable microphones, which could pick up the sound of motors or even the voices of North Vietnamese soldiers, or to the use of engine detectors. Acoustic signals, although they frequently helped the Seventh Air Force find and attack truck parks, could prove deceptive. Col. Lee A. Burcham, chief of targeting for Task Force Alpha during the early weeks of Commando Hunt, recalled hearing tape-recorded sounds "presumably from a sensor . . . , and these voices might be from people on the flight line at Udorn or the Saigon police—in other words, it represented radio interference—so the tape had to be interpreted to be sure you were hearing North Vietnamese or Lao voices before attacking."[24]

The second phase of Commando Hunt saw a shift in emphasis from the Phase I choke points, as U.S. air power tried to exert pressure against enemy logistic activity wherever it occurred. Task Force Alpha planned new traffic control points on major roads and recently discovered bypasses, while the Seventh Air Force sent more of its fighter-bombers against the antiaircraft batteries that were increasing in number since the bombing of North Vietnam had ended. Truck parks and storage areas located within special Arc Light operating areas came under B–52 attack, and at this point, as part of a relaxation of the rules of engagement, the embassy at Vientiane designated certain road segments as free-fire zones for tactical fighters, so that fewer of these aircraft would return to base with ordnance still on board.[25]

Two subsidiary operations, Road Rip and Search, took place during Phase II of Commando Hunt. Road Rip, the earlier undertaking, began in January 1969 with late afternoon attacks against sections of highway where sensor signals, visual sightings, or other intelligence indicated heavy nighttime traffic. First, fighter-bombers dropped so-called "high-drag" munitions, bombs fitted with braking devices to slow their descent and improve accuracy. Once these weapons had blasted several craters along about a mile of road, other aircraft dropped several delayed action bombs to wound or kill engineers trying to reopen the route to traffic. After nightfall, flareships assisted tactical fighters and gunships in destroying trucks halted by the craters.[26]

Whereas sensor data figured prominently in Road Rip, Operation Search, begun on February 1, depended on a combination of visual sightings and photo reconnaissance. Forward air controllers in two-place F–100Fs looked for areas where the enemy seemed especially active; and on the basis of their reports, camera-equipped RF–4Cs carried out intensive reconnaissance. The Phantoms flew morning and afternoon photographic missions, the results of which reached tactical units within a few hours. This effort produced attacks on seventy targets, among them a base area not far from Muong Nong, just south of the Commando Hunt operating area.[27]

Task Force Alpha tried to perfect its techniques during the second phase of Commando Hunt, which included Operations Road Rip and Search. To improve the timeliness of its information on convoys, the Surveillance Center laid out special sensor zones along known or suspected truck routes. In each zone, three strings planted parallel to the flow of traffic reported the size, direction, and speed of convoys, enabling analysts to predict a point where aircraft under Sycamore control could intercept the vehicles. At the same time, the task force set up a computerized traffic analysis and prediction program, also designed to reveal more about the enemy's use of trucks in southern Laos. Technicians at Nakhon Phanom divided Commando Hunt into compact sectors and on the basis of sensor activations and truck sightings, tried to determine the volume of traffic in each. By comparing the movement in contiguous sectors, intelligence officers sought to discover traffic patterns, locate bypasses, and by determining where a particular convoy disappeared from surveillance, identify transshipment points and storage areas. The activations in each sector during a night might also provide an insight into the number of trucks on the trail; by subtracting from this figure the number reported destroyed, and multiplying the survivors by an average load, analysts could make a rough estimate of the amount of cargo transiting the Ho Chi Minh Trail.[28]

A number of important technical or tactical innovations surfaced during Commando Hunt's second phase. In January 1969, for instance, four of the new AC–130A gunships received credit for 28 percent of the trucks reported destroyed during the month. The Black Spot AC–123 began flying interdiction missions in Southeast Asia during February, scattering bomblets on the convoys it discovered. The Navy, meanwhile, introduced so-called "pouncer" tactics whereby a Grumman A–6 Intruder, equipped with a moving target indicator for its radar, tracked enemy vehicles and then dropped flares so that other naval aircraft that were following behind, either Phantom fighter-bombers or Ling-Temco-Vought A–7 Corsair IIs, could pounce on the convoy.[29]

Phase III, conducted in March and April 1969, combined intensification of air attacks inside the Commando Hunt area with a southward extension of the sensor field to monitor the increasing road traffic south of Tchepone, an adjustment that required creation of a new EC–121 relay orbit. During this last of the three arbitrary phases of Operation Commando Hunt, planners tried to devise a standard munitions package for establishing traffic control points. Such a package consisted at this time of a laser-guided bomb, if available, to cut the road, antipersonnel mines to kill or injure members of repair crews, and magnetically fuzed antivehicular mines to disable any heavy equipment that the enemy might use. According to sensor reports, one munitions package tied up traffic for four nights, and scarcely had North Vietnamese engineers closed the cut when Air Force and Navy planes created a second interdiction point not far beyond the first.

The War against Trucks

The final phase of Operation Commando Hunt also featured a refinement in use of sensor strike zones. In Phase II, analysts at the Infiltration Surveillance Center had used them to predict a point of interception, based on the route and speed of a convoy as revealed by sensor activations, and then alerted aircraft to search for and attack the trucks. Now, after predicting a point and time of interception for a particular convoy, Task Force Alpha contacted an airborne battlefield command and control center, which converted the grid coordinates into a loran position and radioed this information to F–4s fitted with this navigation aid. Two or more Phantoms, flying in single file, reached the predicted point at the specified time and saturated the area with baseball-sized bomblets. This use of loran coordinates in conjunction with sensors foreshadowed the Commando Bolt strike technique, in which fighter-bombers reacted to the activation of certain sensors by bombing loran coordinates based on the position of that particular string.[30]

While Commando Hunt moved toward completion, a new administration took over at Washington, D.C. President Nixon, who would soon emerge as the architect of Vietnamization, called for a systematic review of military policy and activity in Southeast Asia. Dr. Kissinger, the national security adviser to the new President, directed the review, asking twenty-nine questions about the conduct of the war, including the effect of aerial interdiction in southern Laos. How successful was the attempt to impede infiltration along the Ho Chi Minh Trail? On this point, which would become vital when the administration embraced a policy of Vietnamizing the war and withdrawing U.S. forces, Kissinger found a lack of agreement among the military and civilian officials that he consulted. In general, the Central Intelligence Agency, Office of the Secretary of Defense, and Department of State offered a pessimistic assessment, whereas the Joint Chiefs of Staff, Pacific Command, the Military Assistance Command, Vietnam, and the Saigon embassy presented a more encouraging view.[31]

The pessimists argued that aerial interdiction, though it disturbed the flow of supplies, did not affect the ability of the North Vietnamese to wage war in the South; the disruption simply was "not severe enough to prevent significant increase in the rate of infiltration."[32] The absence of any decisive impact, they said, resulted from the small volume of supplies, only ten to fifteen truckloads per day, that were believed necessary to sustain operations in South Vietnam. Since the North Vietnamese dispatched their convoys over an ever-expanding road net, screened by camouflage and natural concealment and protected by an increasing number of antiaircraft guns, this amount seemed certain to survive aerial attack and reach its destination.[33]

In contrast, the optimists insisted that aerial interdiction imposed definite, though hard to define, limits on enemy activity in South Vietnam. Gen. David Jones, Deputy Chief of Staff, Operations, and Vice Commander, Seventh Air Force, later expounded this point of view when he looked back on Commando Hunt and declared that a shortage of food and ammunition, "a lot of it . . . the result of the interdiction campaign," had prevented the North Vietnamese from launching another massive Tet offensive in 1969. Air attacks against the trail, "along with the Army's finding caches in South Vietnam," had, he believed, frustrated Hanoi's plans.[34]

Indeed, some grounds for optimism did exist, at least for the immediate future, though not necessarily for the ultimate survival of South Vietnam. The year 1969, in which President Nixon embarked on his policy of Vietnamization, proved a time of shortages and suffering for the communist forces in South Vietnam. In the region south of Da Nang, according to the recollections of an officer who served there, "The situation was terrible. The whole district was a no man's land . . . . We were hungry. There was nothing to eat." Four Viet Cong, who believed they were the only survivors of a once-powerful band of guerrillas, toyed briefly with the notion of surrender, but they kept on fighting, encouraged by the realization that they did not have to defeat the United States, but needed only to hold out during the withdrawal, so that afterward they could confront the Vietnamized forces of the Saigon government.[35] The shortages that crippled the Viet Cong at this time and in this particular region may not have been widespread. Nor did they result exclusively from interdiction in southern Laos, for casualties suffered and supplies consumed in the previous year's Tet offensive undoubtedly contributed to the enemy's weakness.

The unusual nature of the Southeast Asia war allowed optimism and pessimism to coexist. The measures of success from World War II no longer applied: advancing forces did not capture cities or islands and destroy hostile armies; nor did air power cripple clearly defined elements of vital industries. In the absence of such indicators, those responsible for waging war had to devise other standards for measuring progress. Columns of numbers took the place of captured banners. General Westmoreland acknowledged that the statistics generated to help manage the conflict were "an imperfect gauge of progress," but, as he also pointed out, many of the goals established by civilian authority were "essentially statistical," such as increasing the percentage of the rural populace under control of the South Vietnamese government.[36]

Given a choice between optimism and pessimism, Dr. Kissinger chose the former, accepting the views of the senior military commanders—officers like Admiral McCain, Gen. Creighton W. Abrams, who had replaced Westmoreland at Saigon, and Gen. George Brown—a collective judgment that dovetailed with the administration's plans for liquidating the Vietnam war through a process of Vietnamization and withdrawal. In June 1969, Mr. Nixon announced that 25,000 U.S. troops would leave South Vietnam, the first step in the withdrawal of more than 60,000 during the year, which would reduce U.S. strength in South Vietnam to 474,400. The departures continued, so that by March 1971 the administration was committed to withdrawing an average of 3,000 men each week until only a small contingent of advisers and support units remained. To prevent the enemy from gathering supplies for a major offensive before the South Vietnamese were fully prepared, the administration continued the systematic aerial attacks on the Ho Chi Minh Trail, as one Commando Hunt operation followed another, wet season and dry, until the spring of 1972 when the North Vietnamese invasion of the South signaled an end to Commando Hunt VII.[37]

The War against Trucks

The administration's endorsement of aerial interdiction in southern Laos did not end the discussion of the value of such operations. Intelligence organizations continued to disagree, Air Force intelligence and the Defense Intelligence Agency claiming success and the Central Intelligence Agency questioning their findings. The methods of evaluation used by the various analysts accounted in large measure for this irreconcilable difference. The Air Force reached its optimistic conclusion on the basis of statistics from Tan Son Nhut and Nakhon Phanom. Its analysts in Southeast Asia counted various types of "events," from burning trucks to secondary explosions touched off by bombs, assigning a value to each in terms of cargo destroyed, multiplying the values by the number of events, and subtracting the total from the amount of cargo believed to have entered the Ho Chi Minh Trail from North Vietnam. During the first Commando Hunt operation, each truck destroyed, whether reported by an observer or located on an aerial photograph, represented the loss of 2.09 tons of supplies, with 0.52 tons counted as lost if the truck were only damaged. Analysts also assigned a value in cargo destroyed to each fire or secondary explosion reported during attacks on supply dumps of transshipment points. On the basis of these various events, the Seventh Air Force concluded that during January 1969 the enemy in South Vietnam received fewer than the 43 tons per day its analysts considered necessary for normal military activity. Although the estimated volume of cargo that survived air attacks in southern Laos increased to 66 tons per day during February, Seventh Air Force intelligence officers concluded that much of this amount went to replenish stockpiles, a task not finished until April. If these calculations were correct, only 18 percent of the cargo that entered southern Laos during Commando Hunt reached the battlefields of South Vietnam; the remainder either perished in air strikes, went into storage depots for future distribution, or sustained units operating the supply complex.

Throughout Operation Commando Hunt, Seventh Air Force analysts tried in like fashion to tally the number of North Vietnamese troops and Lao auxiliaries who died as a result of air attack. Since friendly patrols could not roam the Ho Chi Minh Trail counting bodies, a formula had to take the place of eyewitness reporting. This method of calculation accepted the estimate that 5 percent of the infiltrators entering southern Laos—in this instance 4,295 of 85,900 men—died because of air strikes that either inflicted fatal injury or destroyed vital medicines and food. Statisticians added to that number the men assigned to operate the transportation net who perished in strikes on trucks, antiaircraft batteries, and transshipment points or other installations. To arrive at the second figure, analysts calculated the number of persons required to operate a truck, man a gun position, or handle cargo at a supply dump. Next they determined the number and type of bombs dropped on these targets, together with the bursting characteristics, and thus arrived at a rough estimate of casualties that a specific kind of bomb directed against a particular category of target could inflict. The number of dead represented the total of bombs dropped multiplied by the likely deaths that each had caused, a process based on so many assumptions that the end product represented an exercise in metaphysics rather than mathematics. By this method, however flawed, Gen. George Brown's Seventh Air Force headquarters concluded that air strikes killed 20,723 persons during Commando Hunt, almost 15 percent of the total number believed traveling on, operating, or defending the Ho Chi Minh Trail.[38]

The statistics prepared by the Seventh Air Force on Commando Hunt depended on the accuracy of the bombing itself, precise reports of damage done, and thorough knowledge of enemy and his supply complex. Unfortunately, the very agency that prepared these figures acknowledged that southern Laos was a "sea of trees"[39] beneath which bombs exploded and the enemy moved. Seventh Air Force headquarters, with the encouragement of the Defense Intelligence Agency, nevertheless persisted in counting individual events, assigning each an amount of cargo destroyed, and calculating a total tonnage of supplies claimed by air attack. Although this practice survived, the attempt to estimate casualties fell into disuse, presumably because of the even weaker foundation on which the method rested.[40]

In contrast to the Seventh Air Force and the Defense Intelligence Agency, the Central Intelligence Agency rebelled against what it later termed a "numbers game," declaring that hostile activity in South Vietnam provided the only standard for measuring the effectiveness of interdiction. If, as "highly reliable sources" indicated, enough supplies were reaching North Vietnamese forces in South Vietnam to enable them to retain the initiative, fighting when they chose, aerial interdiction, at most, inconvenienced the enemy. The Central Intelligence Agency conceded that the scarcity of supplies might sometimes frustrate enemy plans, but these shortages seemed to be the result of events inside the Republic of Vietnam, rather than the product of bombing the Ho Chi Minh Trail. "Allied spoiling operations (ground interdiction), inadequate numbers of transport laborers, poorly disciplined troops, and improper battlefield preparation" appeared to cause scattered, short-lived problems.[41] Whatever questions the Central Intelligence Agency might raise, true debate proved impossible; aerial interdiction would have to provide a major part of the shield for Vietnamization and withdrawal. Whatever the obstacles and uncertainties, the Commando Hunt series had to work.

As the discussion of effectiveness continued, the first Commando Hunt operation revealed problems acquiring information and controlling aircraft. In trying to make aerial interdiction work, Task Force Alpha and the Seventh Air Force had trouble with the Central Intelligence Agency's roadwatch teams. These units no longer maintained direct radio contact with airborne controllers, reporting instead to a headquarters at Savannakhet, which passed the information to Task Force Alpha via secure radio. A target assessment officer at Nakhon Phanom, after evaluating such a report, might call for a strike within the Commando Hunt area by an aircraft under Sycamore control, advise the proper airborne battlefield command and control center if the target lay outside Commando Hunt, or merely have a target intelligence officer relay the information to the Seventh Air Force for further action. Most reports from roadwatch teams apparently went to the Seventh Air Force where, according to Gen. David Jones, they helped "in the long-term analysis," even though "the information coming in was slow and we questioned its reliability." Too often, he complained, "we didn't get information as to which way trucks were moving, or you'd just get a spot report that trucks had passed this point."[42]

In the opinion of General Jones, the roadwatch program, besides producing reports that were tardy and of dubious value, had another grave disadvantage, for the presence of one of the teams in an area required the suspension of air strikes. Central Intelligence Agency field planners and Seventh Air Force headquarters usually cooperated closely, the general acknowledged, but "every once in a while we'd have a roadwatch team all of a sudden arrive at some place . . . , when we had planned to put in [munitions] packages at a critical point, and it took lots of negotiations to get them out." He therefore preferred electronic surveillance, since "you didn't have the tremendous zones you couldn't bomb in as a result of having sensors down there." True, roadwatch teams did prove helpful in areas where monitoring strings had not been planted, but he did not consider the Central Intelligence Agency program "critical to our operations."[43]

Although the roadwatch teams were an inconvenience, and sometimes a handicap, for Air Force planners at higher headquarters, at the operating level roadwatch reports seemed more useful, and Air Force operational units cooperated more enthusiastically with officials of the Central Intelligence Agency. Each week two or three representatives of the agency's stations at Savannakhet, Laos, or Udorn, Thailand, journeyed to Nakhon Phanom to talk with the helicopter crews of the 56th Special Operations Wing, who landed and picked up the roadwatch teams. Capt. Ron F. Myers, a briefing officer at wing headquarters, expressed the "unsubstantiated opinion" that the spirit of cooperation evaporated somewhere between Nakhon Phanom and Seventh Air Force headquarters at Tan Son Nhut. "Basically," Myers said, "we felt that these . . . people with their roadwatch teams and other sources of information were coming up with some real good targets," so good that his unit would arrange for forward air controllers to take pictures that were annotated and sent to the Seventh Air Force in support of target recommendations. "We never had any luck on this at all," he admitted, almost certainly because higher headquarters preferred sensor data or sightings by pilots to roadwatch reports in allocating sorties.[44]

After Commando Hunt ended, the Seventh Air Force tried to discover just how the sensors had helped the operation destroy an estimated 4,356 trucks, damage another 1,653, kill almost twenty-one thousand of the enemy, and create a deficiency of as much as 82 percent between the volume of supplies that entered the trail and the amount that exited into South Vietnam. Analysts tabulated information from 159 responses to a questionnaire designed to measure the value of sensor data in aerial interdiction. Those who replied included members of AC–130A gunship crews, forward air controllers, and officers assigned to Seventh Air Force headquarters, Task Force Alpha, and the airborne battlefield command and control centers. When asked to identify the primary influence on their own mission planning, 27 percent listed the electronic surveillance net, compared to 56 percent for visual reconnaissance and none for roadwatch team reports. A total of 73 percent described as "valuable" or "highly valuable" Task Force Alpha's contribution to planning and executing the recent aerial interdiction campaign. As for the soundness of the intelligence derived from sensors, 35 percent described the products of the Infiltration Surveillance Center as entirely accurate, and just 4 percent complained that the analysts at Task Force Alpha had proved wrong as much as half the time.[45]

As these responses imply, during Commando Hunt, Task Force Alpha enjoyed its greatest success in gathering and forwarding intelligence, rather than in directing operations. Indeed, during the closing weeks of the dry-season interdiction campaign, the Seventh Air Force arranged for Sycamore control to issue instructions through an airborne battlefield command and control center instead of continuing to make direct contact with assigned aircraft. The reasons for the change included Sycamore's difficulty in maintaining radio contact with aircrews in the region south of Tchepone, where aerial activity increased in the final phase of Commando Hunt. The airborne controllers in the modified C–130 did not encounter the problem of fading radio signals, for they flew high enough to avoid terrain masking and were nearer the targets being attacked. The reintroduction of this layer of command caused annoyance at Nakhon Phanom, where the chief of targets, Colonel Burcham, complained that "one of the great bottlenecks in the air campaign in Laos has been the ABCCC [airborne battlefield command and control center]"; in his opinion, "the ABCCC in no way represents the kind of capability that existed with Sycamore control."[46]

On the other hand, the earlier division of responsibility for aircraft operating over southern Laos proved awkward and argued for the reliance on some agency other than Task Force Alpha. A gunship, for instance, might have to report to a succession of controllers as it flew over the Ho Chi Minh Trail, and a crew intent on detecting the enemy below might easily neglect to check in at an assigned point. Pilots, moreover, preferred to work with the airborne battlefield command and control center, where they normally dealt with other fliers who might well have first-hand knowledge of the characteristics of the strike aircraft. The changed status of Task Force Alpha probably resulted, however, from the belief, later expressed by General Jones, that the "sensor business" was "trying to run the show." The Surveillance Center, the general suggested, had overemphasized data from electronic sensors at the expense of reports from forward air controllers, two sources of intelligence that he considered almost equally valuable.[47]

Although Task Force Alpha no longer directed air strikes, electronic surveillance had demonstrated that it could provide up-to-the-minute intelligence on truck traffic, at least on those roads that had been plotted accurately enough for the effective planting of sensors. Moreover, the Spectre gunship, with its own array of airborne sensors, showed an ability to take advantage of the intelligence from the Surveillance Center and attack large numbers of trucks. Whether sensor coverage could encompass more of the road net, whether electronic surveillance could detect infiltrating troops along with trucks, and whether the AC–130 gunship would fulfill its promise as a truck killer were questions that could not be answered until the next dry season and Commando Hunt III. For the present, Task Force Alpha and the Seventh Air Force faced the problem of maintaining interdiction throughout the approaching rainy season, as they executed the southwest monsoon campaign plan for 1969, Commando Hunt II.

Chapter Six

Interdiction During the 1969 Southwest Monsoon Season

Before Commando Hunt ended in the spring of 1969, the Seventh Air Force convened a staff planning group to determine how best to maintain pressure on enemy supply routes during the coming southwest monsoon (wet) season. The deliberations of this Southwest Monsoon Planning Group contributed to an operation plan that covered all of southern Laos and used Task Force Alpha in an advisory rather than an operational capacity. The document retained the basic arrangement in effect when Commando Hunt ended: instead of controlling aircraft directly, as it had when Commando Hunt began, Task Force Alpha supplied information that the Seventh Air Force used in conducting operations. According to the procedures adopted for the rainy season of 1969, a target assessment officer at Nakhon Phanom, after detecting a moving convoy, normally contacted the appropriate airborne battlefield command and control center rather than a strike aircraft. The Task Force Alpha Surveillance Center dealt directly with fighter-bombers or gunships only if the activation pattern lay within a sensor strike zone, permitting an immediate attack based on loran data. Otherwise, the airborne battlefield command and control center calculated the loran position of the target and forwarded a recommendation to the Seventh Air Force control center, proposing both a location and time for the strike, and the Seventh Air Force approved or rejected the proposal. When recommending the creation or replenishment of interdiction points, or requesting strikes against truck parks or other "non-perishable" targets, Task Force Alpha submitted its nominations directly to Seventh Air Force headquarters, instead of contacting the airborne battlefield command and control center.[1]

The 1969 southwest monsoon campaign began in mid-May and lasted through September. Fighter-bombers flew armed reconnaissance, weather permitting, over the roads leading from Mu Gia and Ban Karai Passes and established interdiction points near Ban Phanop and the ford at Ban Laboy. The AC–130 gunships braved the elements to attack nighttime traffic, as did Navy and Marine Corps A–6s with their airborne moving target indicators. The diminished volume of rainy season truck traffic thus came under attack, as did the movement of supplies on the rivers, where the rains resulted in higher water and a swifter current, which in turn accommodated heavily laden boats and a large volume of floating containers. Navy aircraft dropped mines in the rain-swollen Kong and Banghiang Rivers, which were known elements in a system of waterways as yet imperfectly charted, but boats and watertight barrels and boxes rarely contained enough metal to detonate the magnetically fuzed weapons.[2]

Looking back on the southwest monsoon season, Task Force Alpha concluded that "for all practical purposes the Ho Chi Minh Trail was quite effectively interdicted from June through September," principally because of the weather. Possibly augmented by cloud seeding, the monsoon rains of 1969 ranked among the heaviest ever recorded in southern Laos, with forty-eight inches falling in July alone. Reports from roadwatch teams and guerrilla units tended to confirm the sensor data, and aerial photos at times revealed an absence of traffic on some important highways.[3]

Interdiction may have seemed more effective than it actually was, however, for the weather impeded observation from the air at least as much as it did traffic on the ground. Indeed, during the worst of the July downpour, roadwatch teams discovered that Route 914 southeast of Tchepone carried moderate traffic, with freshly emplaced logs providing a corduroy surface over low spots. Reconnaissance probes reported that Routes 12 and 1201 leading from Mu Gia Pass carried a number of 25-truck convoys at night beginning early in September, even though aerial photography failed to confirm the reopening of either road until dry weather returned in October. Within these active sectors, trucks may have been positioning cargo so that supplies could be moved southward as soon as the rains ended and the waterlogged segments of highways reopened. Also, some of the wet-season convoys may have carried material for repairing flood-damaged roads.[4]

Again during the southwest monsoon season, roadwatch teams proved a mixed blessing, sending reports of enemy activity that sometimes could not be detected, or confirmed, by any other means, but occasionally delaying by their very presence an aerial response. Three times the Seventh Air Force sought to establish special Arc Light operating areas along routes east of Muong Nong and northeast of Muong May, but the Vientiane embassy refused approval because of roadwatch teams in or near the desired target boxes. Each time that General Brown's staff made the request, it had to resubmit all the supporting evidence, a time-consuming process. To speed its processing of requests from the Seventh Air Force, the embassy agreed to modify its treatment of previously investigated Arc Light operating areas already cleared for attack except for the possible presence of friendly patrols. When the Seventh Air Force sought clearance to attack this kind of target, it could now send just the basic request, without the documentation already in the hands of the embassy. Since the embassy's files contained the location of prisoner of war camps and friendly villages, the ambassador need only check on the current location of the guerrillas or roadwatch teams before making a decision. In June 1969, Ambassador Godley approved and B–52s attacked three such targets, called "partially validated" Arc Light operating areas because they required only a last-minute determination that the bombing would not endanger friendly forces.[5]

Although roadwatch teams did complicate targeting, they occasionally produced spectacular results. In August 1969, one of these units, en route to meet the recovery helicopters at a pickup point, came across a camouflaged truck park containing fifty-two vehicles in storage for the coming dry season. After returning to their headquarters, however, the team members could not pinpoint the target on the standard charts used for air strikes. The Central Intelligence Agency officials in charge of roadwatch operations reinforced the team, equipped it for demolition work, and sent it back into the jungle. After disembarking from its helicopters, the force quickly found the parked trucks, and planted a hundred explosive charges among them. Air Force A–1s, which had escorted the helicopters, used the exploding trucks as aiming points for attacks of their own on the surrounding bunkers; in all, tactical aircraft flew fifty-seven sorties against the site.[6]

A similar reconnaissance in May 1969, some fifteen miles north of Muong Phine, produced poorer results. After roadwatch teams and photo interpreters located a North Vietnamese headquarters surrounded by truck parks and storage sites, eighteen B–52s and ninety tactical aircraft attacked. Enemy fire downed one of the fighter-bombers, an F–100C; when the pilot's parachute opened, hopes of a rescue soared, only to end tragically when the ensuing search, which forced a suspension of the planned strikes, recovered his body. A subsequent probe of the area by a guerrilla patrol revealed that most of the headquarters staff had fled between the time the roadwatch team found the target and the attack began.[7]

While roadwatch elements probed the enemy transportation network, both guerrillas and Lao regulars fought a series of skirmishes west of the main routes making up the Ho Chi Minh Trail. In a typical year, according to Colonel Hartley, an assistant air attaché in Laos, fighting in this area tended to be inconclusive, since the enemy "only occasionally would make forays . . . , perhaps seizing small towns and villages and holding them for various lengths of time," while "the Lao army, not wanting to make waves or anger the North Vietnamese, generally made no incursion against them, no aggressive moves."[8] In the rainy season of 1969, however, the normal pattern did not prevail, for that period saw aggressive activity on the part of government troops throughout the region west of the Ho Chi Minh Trail. Lao forces, strengthened by Thai mercenaries, launched a series of thrusts, designed mainly to restrict, if only temporarily, the movement of supplies to South Vietnam, and to improve local security in southwestern Laos. In no instance did the forces loyal to Souvanna Phouma try to conquer territory where the Pathet Lao or North Vietnamese were strongly entrenched, although the government did attempt to occupy and hold lightly defended areas. During the southwest monsoon season, scattered fighting ranged from Ban Thateng to Muong Phine, eighty miles to the northwest.

The War against Trucks

At the beginning of April 1969, with the approach of the wet weather, North Vietnamese and Pathet Lao troops, after advancing throughout the dry months, held Muong Phine, threatened Saravane and Attopeu, and massed before Ban Thateng. Distracted to some extent by the Meo guerrillas far to the north, the communists chose not to commit the manpower necessary to storm either Saravane or Attopeu, but at Ban Thateng the mere threat of an attack proved enough, for the Lao army garrison abandoned its prepared defenses and allowed the town to fall to the enemy. Air Force helicopters helped ferry in government reinforcements, both regulars and more aggressive and better disciplined guerrillas, who dug in on the high ground overlooking the broad valley that embraced both enemy-held Ban Thateng and the junction of Routes 23 and 16. Of the two roads, Route 23 had the greater value, since, as Ambassador Sullivan had pointed out, it not only carried supplies destined for the enemy in Laos, but also passed among villages whose inhabitants fed and sheltered roadwatch teams. The fresh troops held, so that by the end of the southwest monsoon season, a stalemate emerged; Lao forces clung to the high ground, although unable to disrupt enemy movement on the two highways in the valley east and north of Ban Thateng.[9]

As the stalemate developed at Ban Thateng, representatives of the Central Intelligence Agency in Laos proposed a thrust into the southeastern part of the kingdom. The attack would have three main purposes: to cut Route 110 for at least three days, disrupting the road net linking Cambodia, Laos, and South Vietnam; to locate targets for air strikes; and to relieve the hostile pressure on Attopeu. The operation, called Left Jab, began on June 21 when Air Force and Air America helicopters landed some 350 troops southwest of Attopeu. A combination of Lao irregulars, units of Souvanna's army, and Thai mercenaries seized a portion of Route 110, planted mines, and reduced the threat to Attopeu at least temporarily. Left Jab produced only one profitable target for aircraft, however, when fighter-bombers scattered a force of about 180 men approaching a road block.[10]

Once the immediate threat to Attopeu eased, Lao troops could take steps to relieve the pressure on Saravane. This undertaking, Operation Diamond Arrow, commenced on September 20 as four Lao army and three guerrilla companies pushed from Saravane toward Ban Toumlan while simultaneously maneuvering against enemy forces to the east of Route 23, the main road between the two towns. Overcoming sporadic resistance, elements of the Diamond Arrow force reached Ban Toumlan on October 8, and then continued northward to link up with troops falling back after an even more ambitious venture, a thrust to Muong Phine on the western edge of the Ho Chi Minh Trail.[11]

Compared to simpler operations like Left Jab or Diamond Arrow, the advance on Muong Phine, planned mainly by members of the Central Intelligence Agency, required extensive support from the U.S. and Royal Laotian Air Forces. It called for some nine hundred Lao guerrillas to isolate Muong Phine by blocking Routes 9 and 23, then seize the village. Capturing the objective would sever a route that carried cargo to enemy forces in either Laos or South Vietnam.[12]

Operation Junction City, Junior, the advance on Muong Phine, began on September 1, 1969, supported by Air Force helicopters, Raven and Nail forward air controllers, flareships, and A–1 Skyraiders, along with aircraft of the Royal Laotian Air Force. The helicopters shuttled troops among several landing zones during the advance, and on one occasion the troop carriers mistakenly tried to land reinforcements on fiercely contested ground. Fortunately, Maj. William R. Knapp saw from his helicopter what was happening below and pulled the flight out of small-arms range until a forward air controller could direct strikes that silenced the hostile fire.[13]

A dozen A–1 sorties and two Nail forward air controllers supported Junction City, Junior, each day, along with one flareship at night. Raven forward air controllers and Lao T–28s also participated, as did U.S. aircraft diverted to help when clouds hid their primary targets elsewhere in Laos or in South Vietnam. The A–1s proved especially deadly in battering enemy fortifications; on a single day, for example, two Skyraider pilots received credit for destroying or damaging forty-five "enemy structures." By mining the roads leading to Muong Phine from enemy base areas, the A–1s also helped other tactical aircraft isolate the objective.[14]

After brushing aside a Pathet Lao battalion, the main force entered Muong Phine on September 7, and for the first time in seven years the royal flag flew over the ruined village. With the objective captured, principally through the efforts of Thai mercenaries and their supporting aircraft, Lao army officers proposed flying in regular troops to occupy the place for an indefinite time and set up a military government, which would symbolize the return of royal authority to an area long in the hands of the communist faction.[15]

Optimism sired boldness; talk circulated at Savannakhet, a regional headquarters, that Muong Phine might serve as a springboard for an advance to Tchepone, a principal storage area for supplies trucked through the mountain passes into southern Laos, and at least one Lao officer suggested the possibility of seizing the enemy stronghold at Mahaxay. The introduction of Lao army troops to defend war-ravaged Muong Phine became a key element in an expanded Operation Junction City, Junior, which now included a raid on Tchepone. While regulars loyal to Souvanna dug in at Muong Phine, guerrillas would probe as far as Tchepone, try to cut Route 9 east of that town, and destroy supply bunkers and other structures. During the advance beyond Muong Phine, two Nail forward air controllers would continue to assist the Ravens, a dozen A–1s would provide daytime support for the ground troops, and a Candlestick, with a Lao observer on board, would stand by at Nakhon Phanom should its flares be needed at night. As before, the Seventh Air Force could divert aircraft into the area and dispatch missions to cut roads the enemy might use to meet this thrust.[16]

The decision to hold Muong Phine afforded the royal government an opportunity to evacuate local farmers to refugee centers farther west and deprive the enemy of the mountain rice grown in the region. The acting commander in chief

119

of the Lao army and his chief of staff at first favored the idea of a U.S. Air Force herbicide mission against the rice paddies, once the farm families had left; and the two men apparently persuaded Ambassador Godley to endorse the proposal. The ambassador, although he did not raise the subject during talks with Souvanna Phouma, concluded that the premier had heard about the plan from a son, an officer in the Lao air arm, who served as his father's aide. Godley interpreted the fact that the prince "did not bring the subject up though we discussed military operations in the Muong Phine-Tchepone area" as tacit approval of the proposed defoliation.[17]

Unlike the ambassador, others closer to the scene objected to the use of herbicides. At the Savannakhet headquarters, officials of the Agency for International Development and some officers on the staff of the air attaché opposed the scheme, pointing out that it would do worse injury to potentially friendly rice growers than to the enemy. Most of the families that had agreed to leave hoped to return and harvest their crops if the royal government maintained its grip on the area, and consequently they planned to leave someone behind to look after the land and prevent the theft of buffalo and other property. The family members standing guard and subjected to the spraying might suffer harm, even though the Air Force had adopted a chemical believed less toxic to humans than the agent formerly used.[18]

Despite the misgivings at Savannakhet, the evacuation got off to a rapid start. The 21st Special Operations Squadron, which flew the Air Force helicopters engaged in the task, carried almost thirteen hundred people and their personal belongings from Muong Phine to Muong Phalane.[19] The U.S. Embassy in Vientiane arranged for permission from the Thai government to operate the UC–123 spray planes from that country. The schedule called for the herbicide operation to start on September 24, but by that time the plan had begun breaking down.[20]

The very Lao officers whose enthusiasm so impressed Ambassador Godley now had second thoughts. When higher headquarters refused to issue specific instructions for crop destruction, one of the lower ranking officers responsible for the defense of Muong Phine wondered aloud if he would be made the scapegoat for what he considered a bad idea. To destroy the rice crop, he told a U.S. Air Force officer, would "admit to the enemy our basically weak position," for Muong Phine could scarcely serve as a permanent seat of government if the occupying forces killed off the local food supply.[21]

The orders finally arriving at Muong Phine spared the food supply, not because the government intended to stay, but because the royal army worried that crop warfare might prod the enemy into a counterattack that Lao troops could not contain. The final plan exempted about 90 percent of the crop from defoliation, a grave error in the opinion of those who supported the idea. The assistant air attaché at Savannakhet complained that the decision "effectively emasculated the . . . operation," but a question immediately arose as to whether even this much spraying was feasible.[22]

During the discussion of crop destruction in the vicinity of Muong Phine, the enemy began moving automatic weapons into the hills surrounding the village. As a result, Seventh Air Force planners realized that they could not commit the vulnerable UC–123s without both preparatory bombing and a flak suppression escort. Before the modified transports could plod over the fields releasing their chemicals, fighter-bombers would have to attack gun positions with five hundred pound, seven hundred fifty pound, and even three thousand pound bombs. During the actual spraying, F–4s and A–1s carrying antipersonnel bombs would orbit nearby, ready to silence any weapons that opened fire.[23] Because of the "staggering cost" of such an undertaking, the "notoriety" that "might accrue" because of "curious journalists," and the potential danger to "friendlies" remaining in the area, Ambassador Godley withdrew his support, signalling the collapse of the defoliation plan.[24]

As the ambassador made his decision, "unorthodox friendly maneuvers"—a euphemism for panic—"threatened to sabotage Operation Junction City, Junior." Fearing an imminent attack in overwhelming numbers, Souvanna's commander at Muong Phine fled with his troops, and an adjacent unit of mercenaries, finding itself isolated, also fell back.[25] Reinforcements reoccupied the abandoned positions, however, enabling patrols to advance toward Tchepone against stiffening resistance that soon endangered the entire force at Muong Phine and beyond. The North Vietnamese easily contained the advance toward Tchepone, outflanked Muong Phine, and recaptured the village of Ban Tang Vai, near which Operation Junction City, Junior, had begun. Threatened from the rear, the Muong Phine salient, which had sustained itself for almost two months, rapidly withered. The troops retreating from Muong Phine met the Diamond Arrow force as it advanced beyond Saravane, and together they stabilized the tactical situation.[26]

The military impact of Junction City, Junior, proved difficult to gauge. In the area around Muong Phine, Lao guerrillas overran supply dumps, destroyed abandoned bivouac sites, and searched unsuccessfully for prisoner of war camps. Although government forces did reap some benefit from the operation by disrupting the enemy's logistic network, they did not hold Muong Phine long enough to convert it into a symbol of royal strength around which the peasants of the region might rally. The slow reaction by the North Vietnamese and Pathet Lao indicated that they were either inconvenienced rather than hurt or, perhaps, preoccupied with operations elsewhere. The counterattack, when it came, hit the lightly held base of the salient rather than the advance elements, settling for regaining ground rather than destroying the government column. In spite of the enemy's measured response, the capture of Muong Phine did force a westward deployment of North Vietnamese troops who otherwise might have helped operate and defend the Ho Chi Minh Trail. Besides attracting enemy forces and compelling the enemy to divert food and ammunition to supply them, Operation Junction City, Junior, interfered with the local rice harvest and displaced a number of farmers, at least temporarily, to areas where their crops could not help the communists.[27]

The War against Trucks

Even as the Lao regulars and their guerrilla auxiliaries pulled back from Muong Phine, the seasons were changing. Within days the northeast monsoons would arrive, drying the roads and trails that made up the Ho Chi Minh Trail. From southwestern Laos the action shifted eastward to the highway transportation net carrying supplies into Vietnam. There the United States would again call on modern technology to disrupt enemy supply lines in another of the recurring interdiction campaigns that bore the designation Commando Hunt. The Seventh Air Force designated the southwest monsoon campaign just ending as Commando Hunt II, and assigned even numbers—Commando Hunt II, IV, and VI—to the rainy season and odd numbers—Commando Hunt III, V, and ultimately VII—to the dry period of the northeast monsoons.

Chapter Seven

The Truck War Continues

The airborne battlefield command and control center, the specially equipped version of the C–130 that began supplanting Task Force Alpha as principal strike control agency during the final weeks of the first Commando Hunt operation, seemed destined to play an even larger role as planners of the 1969–70 dry season interdiction effort, Commando Hunt III, sought to apply lessons learned during the earlier campaigns. Commando Hunt and Commando Hunt II had, for example, demonstrated the "hazards associated with large numbers of aircraft at night in Steel Tiger East," the comparatively small interdiction zone, so the Seventh Air Force, at the time commanded by Gen. George Brown, solicited suggestions from operating units on how best to reduce the danger. General Brown's staff completed a study in time to formulate new traffic control procedures that went into effect in February 1970, roughly midway through Commando Hunt III.

To promote safety and efficiency in handling air traffic, the Seventh Air Force divided Steel Tiger East into fifteen sectors, two of which contained subsectors. Within each of these, an airborne battlefield command and control center designated a single traffic control agency, either a qualified gunship crew, a forward air controller, or Task Force Alpha. No aircraft could descend below fourteen thousand feet without obtaining clearance from the appropriate agency; above that altitude, the airborne battlefield command and control center retained authority over all air traffic. To facilitate control, each sector had its own letter of the phonetic alphabet (for subsectors, a number accompanied the letter), its assigned radio frequency, and a holding point keyed to the tactical air navigation system and located some distance from the Ho Chi Minh Trail. If a gunship or other aircraft had to track targets through two or more sectors, the airborne battlefield command and control center designated a traffic controller in one of the sectors to take charge. Besides serving as an aerial traffic cop, the airborne battlefield command and control center used its radar, its computer that stored and spewed out target information, and its communications circuits to ensure that suitably armed aircraft attacked appropriate targets.[1]

Despite the emphasis on the airborne battlefield command and control center, the modified C–130 had the disadvantage of being badly crowded, which contributed to fatigue on the part of the controllers. Gen. John D. Ryan, the Air Force Chief of Staff during Commando Hunt III, conceded that the capsule installed in the cargo bay of this aircraft was "a pretty confined place," when "six, eight, ten" people were working there. He believed, however, that the airborne battlefield command and control center performed an essential role, regardless of the crowding and discomfort, for it could maintain radio contact from its operating altitude with aircraft that could not be reached from Nakhon Phanom.[2]

Gen. David Jones, assigned to Seventh Air Force headquarters during the first Commando Hunt operation, knew the weaknesses of the airborne battlefield command and control center and compared them to its strengths. He maintained that controllers, as a rule, should operate from an installation on the ground, using facilities less expensive to operate than the airborne battlefield command and control center and less vulnerable to accident or hostile action. Indeed, he believed that considerations of cost and danger may have influenced Secretary of the Air Force Harold Brown to assign an operational role to Task Force Alpha at the outset of the interdiction campaign in late 1968. Having stated his preference for a command center on the ground, Jones addressed the problems unique to Task Force Alpha, pointing out, as Ryan had, that controllers at Nakhon Phanom needed radio relay links to reach the southern limits of the Commando Hunt operating area and to keep in contact with low-flying aircraft masked by the mountains around such routine targets as Ban Laboy Ford or the exit from Mu Gia Pass. As a result of his analysis, Jones endorsed General Brown's decision, as commander of the Seventh Air Force, to modify the concept underlying the original Commando Hunt operation and shift Task Force Alpha from directing strikes to gathering, analyzing, and disseminating sensor-based intelligence.[3]

Eclipsed throughout Commando Hunt II by the airborne battlefield command and control center, Task Force Alpha no longer directed assigned strike aircraft, as the Sycamore controllers had done throughout most of the previous dry season. Although Nakhon Phanom might contact an airborne control center to advise of fleeting targets, most of the information derived from the sensors usually passed from Nakhon Phanom to Tan Son Nhut Air Base where Seventh Air Force headquarters issued the orders for which the airborne battlefield command and control center served as coordinating agency. Commando Bolt, a loran strike technique based on the sensor strike zone, provided the sole exception to the general rule that Task Force Alpha no longer controlled strike aircraft.

The concept behind Commando Bolt dated from the first Commando Hunt operation when the Infiltration Surveillance Center interpreted sensor activations to calculate the speed of a truck convoy and advised pilots where they might intercept and attack the vehicles. Throughout Commando Hunt III, which lasted from November 1, 1969, to April 30, 1970, the Commando Bolt program marked Task Force Alpha's only direct involvement in strike control. From the old combat operations center, which had been replaced by a better equipped facility in the early weeks of initial Commando Hunt interdiction campaign, so-called Sparky FAC (forward air controller) teams monitored strings of Commando Bolt sensors precisely planted along routes leading into Laos from Mu Gia and Ban Karai Passes. Such a team consisted of a strike nominator, a strike controller, and a strike technician. The strike

124

nominator, an intelligence officer, kept watch over a computer console, interpreting activations from Commando Bolt strings to determine the speed, size, and direction of truck convoys. Nearby sat the strike controller, usually an experienced fighter pilot, who maintained radio contact with the assigned aircraft and directed them against one of the previously designated impact points over which the vehicles would pass. The other team member, the strike technician, was an enlisted man who listened in on radio transmissions involving the Commando Bolt areas, kept the airborne battlefield command and control centers informed of Commando Bolt strikes, maintained a log, and in general helped the strike controller.[4]

An array of sensor strings called a strike module constituted the heart of Commando Bolt. During Commando Hunt III, a module consisted of as many as four strings, each having three to six sensors spaced about 660 feet apart, with a varying interval between strings. Officers at the Infiltration Surveillance Center chose heavily traveled roads, had aircraft plant the modules as accurately as possible, and calculated designated mean points of impact—in effect, aiming points for loran bombing—for each module. If the strike nominator, after calling up the electronic display for one of the modules, saw traffic entering the area it monitored, he estimated the speed and size of the convoy and used the computer to determine when the trucks would pass one of the planned points of impact. The strike controller radioed this information in code to a loran-equipped aircraft, and the crew fed the data into a small computer that told them the course, altitude, and speed necessary to detonate bombs on the point of impact just as the trucks rumbled over it.

Usually, Air Force F–4s or Navy or Marine Corps A–6s responded to the Sparky FAC, with two or more fighter-bombers or attack aircraft in single file; each group constituted a Flasher team. Because Task Force Alpha no longer controlled all aircraft in the Commando Hunt zone, the Sparky FAC had to coordinate the activity of Flasher teams with the airborne battlefield command and control center. At a designated point, on the fringe of each Commando Bolt area, the lead aircraft of the approaching Flasher team checked in with Copperhead (the call sign of the Sparky FAC strike controller), remaining under his direction until the attack was complete. The Flasher team leaders in the A–6s differed from those in the F–4s in that the Navy and Marine Corps crews used their airborne moving target indicator to acquire the convoy on radar, while the Air Force crew, flying a plane that lacked such equipment, relied solely on loran coordinates. The radar in the A–6 so impressed General Jones, the former Deputy Chief of Staff, Operations, and Vice Commander of the Seventh Air Force, that he considered one of these aircraft worth four of the Navy's less sophisticated McDonnell Douglas A–4 attack craft.

Commando Bolt suffered, however, from the lack of a really satisfactory weapon against trucks. Air Force Flasher teams dropped bomblets that saturated the area around the designated point of impact with fragments too light to do much damage except to radiators, tires, and gasoline tanks. The Navy and Marine Corps teams used five hundred pound bombs capable of demolishing a truck, but the compact bursting radius required almost a direct hit.[5]

The War against Trucks

Besides the Flasher teams, Panther teams, which operated without benefit of either computer or airborne radar, also made use of the Commando Bolt modules. A Panther team consisted of a forward air controller, in an OV–10 or O–2, who led a pair of A–1s to a designated point of impact selected by a Sparky FAC at Nakhon Phanom. As the Panthers approached the sensor array, an observer on board the observation craft used a starlight scope to find the convoy, and the pilot marked the target with rockets for the two Skyraiders. If all went well, the pilots of the A–1s scored hits on the convoy the rockets had pointed out; if not, the forward air controller dropped flares. When attacking by artificial light, the A–1s remained above the slowly descending parachute flares lest the aircraft present a silhouette against the light and become an easy target for enemy antiaircraft gunners. As a result, the pilots had to look past a blinding source of illumination to find the trucks. In the event of an overcast, however, reflected artificial light could silhouette the aircraft against the clouds even though the pilot stayed above the flares.[6]

Because Commando Bolt attacks took place at night, when traffic was heaviest, the results proved difficult to assess. Haze and cloud cover affected photographic coverage and might obscure fires and secondary explosions or distort their size; indeed, even on a clear night the crew of a fast-moving aircraft might find it difficult to determine the sequence or judge the comparative size of explosions or fires. Nevertheless, Seventh Air Force analysts credited Panther teams with destroying 164 trucks and triggering 466 secondary explosions in 378 Commando Bolt sorties. Flasher teams received credit for 888 trucks destroyed or damaged and 2,055 secondary explosions in 1,848 attacks.[7]

The Commando Bolt operation, with repeated use of the same sensor modules, gave enemy gunners an opportunity to ambush the Flaher and Panther teams. The threat of antiaircraft fire, coupled with bad weather, prevented the slower Panthers from maintaining steady pressure on the roads nearest Ban Karai Pass. Even the Navy and Marine Corps Flasher teams, led by A–6s, required an escort to deal with antiaircraft defenses. EA–6s, A–6 attack aircraft fitted out with electronic countermeasures gear, aided the Flasher teams by jamming the fire-control radars that had begun to appear in North Vietnam near the mountain passes, while the team's escort of A–7 Corsair IIs or F–4 Phantoms bombed gun positions along the trail.

For the Flasher and Panther teams, the most effective defense against antiaircraft fire proved to be the introduction early in January 1970 of secure voice circuits linking them to the Copperhead controllers, replacing the system of code words formerly used. Those aircraft not equipped to receive scrambled voice transmissions carried manual decoders. No longer could the enemy listen in on conversations, figure out the meaning of frequently repeated code words, and alert his gunners accordingly. Consequently, the threat to Commando Bolt missions from antiaircraft fire declined so abruptly that the Navy and Marine Corps could dispense with both countermeasures and flak suppression escorts after February 20.[8]

To permit quicker target acquisition by Panther teams, Task Force Alpha installed a portable sensor monitor in some OV–10s for experimental strikes against targets detected by specially planted sensor strings patterned after the Commando Bolt modules. Weighing only sixteen pounds, the portable monitor responded to the very high frequency signals from the sensors and provided a simple visual display for the aircrew. During the test, whenever one of the strings indicated truck activity, the crew of the OV–10 checked with Copperhead at Nakhon Phanom to avoid interfering with a Flasher or other Panther team; if the OV–10 had precedence, it could direct the Skyraiders accompanying it to attack the vehicles.

Plans had originally called for testing the monitoring equipment at "Rat Fink Valley," a choke point southwest of Ban Karai Pass, but antiaircraft concentrations seemed too deadly for the A–1s. The modified Panther teams instead went into action near a choke point on a main route leading south from Mu Gia Pass. Between January 22 and 31, 1970, the OV–10s detected over four hundred individual sensor activations, and the navigators operating the equipment isolated thirty-one sequences that indicated truck traffic. The OV–10 pilots obtained permission to proceed to the source of the signals and investigate fourteen of the thirty-one sequences, when the danger of collision with another aircraft seemed minimal or nonexistent. Using the starlight scope, the forward air controllers sighted thirty-one targets, led attacks on thirteen, and received credit for causing the destruction of eleven trucks. On one occasion, an O–2, patrolling independently of the Panther project and relying solely on the night observation device, spotted the trucks and called in fighter-bombers before the specially equipped OV–10 could responded to the sensor signals.[9]

Like the marines, who used similarly equipped OV–10 Broncos, the Air Force found that the portable monitors worked as designed, but nevertheless proved ill-suited in operations against the Ho Chi Minh Trail. True, the portable equipment did enable the OV–10 crews to read sensors in the southern extremity of Commando Hunt, thus eliminating the need for a change in EC–121 orbits to relay to Nakhon Phanom the signals originating there, but shortcomings more than offset this advantage. The portable monitor could handle only a limited number of sensors, and the OV–10 flew at a comparatively low altitude, so that in mountainous southern Laos, terrain masking posed a problem. Also the cost of installing the gear seemed excessive, as did the demands imposed on the navigator, who already had the responsibility for keeping his aircraft on station, finding the proper segment of road, and using a night observation scope to detect the target. Against the trail, the specially equipped OV–10 succeeded only in the narrowest technological sense; tactically it failed completely.[10]

In no sense could airborne sensor monitoring with the OV–10 duplicate Task Force Alpha. When the person monitoring the sensor display console at Nakhon Phanom played a tiny beam of light on the screen, the system responded with current data for all types of sensors in the portion of the field selected. The available information underwent revision every sixty seconds, and each display included a summary of activity during the previous thirty minutes. The sensor monitor could see the location and activation record of both seismic and acoustic sensors and could request the audio operator to trigger any of the acoustic devices to verify the presence of trucks. If a convoy was passing through the area displayed on his screen, the operator had the computer calculate the number of vehicles, direction, and speed. This information might enable Copperhead to call for a Commando Bolt strike or, if there were no sensor modules in this sector, to advise the airborne battlefield command and control center that a profitable target had appeared on a particular stretch of road. The portable airborne monitoring gear did nothing even remotely comparable.[11]

The portable equipment had just one major advantage: its ability to trigger sensors that Task Force Alpha could not contact using the normal relay orbits. During Operation Commando Hunt in the previous dry season, a Lockheed EC–121 had assumed a new orbit to relay to Nakhon Phanom signals from sensors planted south of the area originally under surveillance. Commando Hunt III, however, saw the introduction of an airborne automatic plotting device that enabled a relay aircraft on distant orbit to serve as an adjunct of the Infiltration Surveillance Center, recording and analyzing activations among sensor strings in the area. When fitted with one of these X–T plotters, an EC–121 could monitor a theoretical total of ninety-nine sensors. Each time the machine received a signal lasting more than ten seconds, an electric charge passed through a pin representing that sensor and burned a line on a sheet of paper. Contiguous pins represented a sensor string, with one pin left unassigned to mark the division between strings, a practice that reduced the plotting machine's capacity but made interpretation easier. Although able in this way to differentiate between strings, the operator had no computer to store and retrieve data and no equipment for analyzing the sounds from acoustic signals to determine the kind of activity being reported.

Despite these limitations, the specially equipped Bat Cats could react faster than the Nakhon Phanom Surveillance Center to sensor activations in southernmost Laos, for the airborne analysts focused on just that one area, whereas the Surveillance Center watched over the entire sensor field. Moreover, radio signals that the EC–121 relayed over the mountains proved vulnerable to natural interference, and, even with flawless transmission, processing the reports at Nakhon Phanom took perhaps ten or fifteen minutes. As a result, the airborne battlefield command and control center responsible for the southernmost region agreed that Bat Cats carrying the X–T plotters should pass sensor data directly to forward air controllers or gunship commanders. A 15-day test conducted in May 1970 (after Commando Hunt III had ended) confirmed the wisdom of this decision, revealing that the so-called Ferret III aircraft with the X–T plotting system could establish radio contact with a gunship patrolling the southern tip of Laos before the last vehicle in a five-truck convoy had passed through an average route monitoring string. In contrast, the last truck had cleared the sensor string by an average of thirteen minutes before the airborne battlefield command and control center received a traffic advisory based on information relayed to Task Force Alpha and evaluated there.[12] However, neither the Ferret III EC–121s nor Commando Bolt replaced the forward air controller.

In mid-October 1969, shortly before the northeast monsoon campaign began, forward air controllers in F–4Ds launched a special operation, flying the first of some 244 sorties over choke points near Mu Gia and Ban Karai Passes. By refueling from aerial tankers, the crews, who were thoroughly familiar with the region they covered, managed to remain on station from dark until dawn, using night observation devices to locate targets. The venture, called Nite Owl, lasted four weeks, but produced just four truck kills and only a few secondary explosions. The disappointing results and the cost of Nite Owl, two fighter-bombers shot down, led to the cancellation of this special nightly coverage.[13]

On November 1, at the midpoint of Operation Nite Owl, Commando Hunt III began. Air Force, Marine Corps, and Navy aircraft dropped munitions packages to create or renew interdiction points near Mu Gia and Ban Karai Passes; at "the chokes," where several highways converged southwest of Ban Karai Pass; near Muong Nong, where a main route branched off toward the A Shau Valley; and finally in the vicinity of Chavane. Keeping pace with the movement of supplies, the focus of interdiction passed through three phases, shifting in January from the passes to "the chokes" and moving during February to the Muong Nong region and the main road leading eastward from Chavane.[14] Visual sightings and aerial photographs indicated that the munitions at the interdiction points, besides stalling traffic temporarily, destroyed or damaged fifty-seven bulldozers or other pieces of construction equipment. Clearly, the enemy found the munitions packages enough of an impediment to risk scarce heavy equipment in removing them.[15]

To supplement the interdiction points, U.S. aircraft attacked moving convoys, using sensor data and various airborne detection devices to locate targets. Most truck strikes took place at night, when movement on the roads reached its peak. During January 1970, which saw the heaviest traffic of Commando Hunt III, more than three-fourths of some thirty-eight hundred sorties against truck convoys occurred between dusk and dawn.[16]

Attempts to disrupt road traffic by means of interdiction points and attacks on convoys coincided as before with strikes by B–52s and tactical aircraft on truck parks and storage areas. Seventh Air Force analysts acknowledged that bombing results frequently "were hard to observe because of poor weather, dust, smoke, and foliage over the target," including "tree canopies" that "concealed much of the damage inflicted." Despite these difficulties, which caused 35 percent of all sorties directed against area targets to report unobserved results, Seventh Air Force statisticians recorded a total of 21,552 secondary explosions in storage dumps and parking areas.[17] During Commando Hunt III, prior to March 24, 1970, analysts credited each secondary explosion and fire with destroying seven hundred fifty pounds of supplies. Afterward, until the campaign ended on April 30, the arbitrary standard became one thousand pounds, for intelligence indicated greater quantity of goods stored in dumps and near truck parks than previously believed.[18]

Attacks on truck traffic produced equally encouraging claims, with a total of 6,428 vehicles reported destroyed and 3,604 damaged. The standards adopted for

The War against Trucks

Commando Hunt III counted only those vehicles headed south as carrying cargo, in the amount of one ton; northbound trucks were considered empty. The AC–130s retained the title of deadliest aircraft, with the new Surprise Package version destroying or damaging 822 trucks, while other models claimed 2,562. Nevertheless, General Ryan, the Air Force Chief of Staff, pointed out that however great the toll in vehicles on the trail, trucks parked on the docks at Haiphong or some other North Vietnamese port presented an easier target than those skittering beneath a jungle canopy; interdiction, he believed, should take place as far as possible from the ultimate destination. Yet, if air power had to hunt down vehicles and destroy them individually, the AC–130 did the best job. In 603 sorties, the AC–130s claimed some 1,800 more victims than F–4s reported destroyed or damaged in almost ten times as many sorties.[19]

As with the first operation of the series, the evaluation of Commando Hunt III depended on statistical compilations of trucks and cargo believed destroyed. Gen. George Brown, as his tenure as Seventh Air Force commander came to an end, warned against this tendency to rely on numbers. Truck kills, he said, "are not the only measure of how you're doing, nor are secondaries [secondary explosions]. It's the constant pressure that counts."[20] Gen. David Jones, who had served in Seventh Air Force headquarters, acknowledged before Commando Hunt III began that aerial interdiction "got an image as a truck-killing campaign and that it depended on how many trucks we killed." This interpretation ignored reality, Jones maintained, pointing out that "we could have been 100 percent successful and killed zero trucks . . . ." The true objective, as he defined it was not to destroy trucks but to "keep . . . supplies from coming into South Vietnam" and undermine the ability of the enemy to fight there.[21]

During Commando Hunt III, air strikes got credit for destroying or damaging more than ten thousand trucks and touching off more than twenty thousand secondary explosions. In visiting this destruction on the Ho Chi Minh Trail, aircraft of the Seventh Air Force sustained a slightly higher loss rate to antiaircraft fire than during the first Commando Hunt campaign. The number shot down increased from fifty-six to sixty and the loss rate per thousand sorties from .63 to .74, with almost twice as many planes sustaining some degree of flak damage as were shot down. Not unexpectedly, the widely used 37-mm gun claimed the most victims, downing at least twenty-one planes.[22] The increase in losses and battle damage reflected better gunnery and more antiaircraft guns, a maximum of 743 weapons of all types, which exceeded by more than a hundred the largest number in action during the previous dry season. Enemy crews, better trained and more experienced, opened fire about twice as frequently as in the first Commando Hunt operation. Moreover, antiaircraft concentrations now appeared all along the road net, from Mu Gia, Ban Karai, and Ban Raving Passes through Tchepone to the A Shau Valley, the Chavane exits, and those east of Attopeu. In addition to the 23-mm, 37-mm, and 57-mm weapons along the trail itself, surface-to-air missiles and 100-mm guns located east of Mu Gia and Ban Karai Passes engaged U.S. planes attacking just west of these entry gates.[23]

Improved defenses resulted in greater emphasis on flak suppression. All fighter-bombers and attack aircraft carried munitions for hitting antiaircraft sites, and some had the specific assignment of escorting gunships or other types in heavily defended areas and suppressing enemy fire. The usual flak suppression weapons were antipersonnel bomblets, dispensed by the hundreds to saturate an area with deadly fragments, and general purpose high-explosive bombs with fuze extenders to prevent the blast and fragmentation from being absorbed in the earth. Rockeye, a five hundred pound cluster bomb that opened to scatter 247 individual bomblets, saw limited service, but seemed especially effective because the shaped charge within each bomblet could penetrate up to eight and one-half inches of steel. The most accurate flak suppression weapon of all was the laser-guided two thousand or three thousand pound bomb, for analysts concluded, largely on the basis of reports by pilots and crewmen, that one out of four launchings against antiaircraft sites resulted in the destruction of the target. Estimates by the Seventh Air Force claimed that aerial attack destroyed or damaged 750 antiaircraft weapons, in effect forcing the enemy "to replace essentially his entire Steel Tiger [southern Laos] active gun inventory during the campaign." If this assessment were correct, which in retrospect seems unlikely, the enemy succeeded in deploying so many guns that the number believed to be in action at the end of April 1970 exceeded the November 1969 total by about 150.[24]

In spite of the improvements in enemy defenses, the achievements of Commando Hunt III seemed to greatly outweigh the losses and make the effort and investment in technology appear worthwhile. According to the evaluation provided by the Seventh Air Force, the recent campaign, like the first of the Commando Hunt series, had "resulted in a marked decline in enemy activity during March and April." To support even this reduced level of combat, the North Vietnamese had to "shift to the southern input gates"—Ban Raving Pass and the western edge of the demilitarized zone, instead of Mu Gia and Ban Karai Passes—remaining for as long as possible within North Vietnam, where the bombing had ended in November 1968, so as "to minimize the time that supplies were exposed to air attack."[25]

Truck sightings, sensor data, reports by aircrews of vehicles destroyed, and counts of secondary explosions and fires formed the basis for the official Seventh Air Force estimate that the enemy had started 66,196 tons of supplies southward, lost 31,954 tons, or almost half, to air attack, and consumed 15,266 tons en route. Only 18,976 tons reached Viet Cong and North Vietnamese units fighting in South Vietnam, a total that represented just 28.6 percent of the cargo that started southward on the Ho Chi Minh Trail during the 1969–70 dry season. To remain combat effective, the analysts believed, the enemy withdrew an additional 11,919 tons from stockpiles in Laos.[26]

At least one senior Air Force officer did not share the optimism reflected in the Seventh Air Force statistics. Within ninety days of publication of the Commando Hunt III report, Brig. Gen. Chester J. Butcher, commander of Task Force Alpha during the operation, questioned both the overall impact of aerial interdiction in southern Laos and the value of sensors to that undertaking. Although Butcher agreed that

131

aerial interdiction had made North Vietnam pay a high price to supply its forces by means of the Ho Chi Minh Trail, he maintained that the amount of material destroyed had not seriously curtailed enemy activity within South Vietnam. Air power, he believed, could not do greater harm without bombing docks and supply dumps around Hanoi and Haiphong.

As for the importance of sensors in the recent dry season campaign, the general believed that the Seventh Air Force had overestimated the contribution of Task Force Alpha. He doubted that Commando Bolt had been as effective as claimed or that electronic surveillance did anything that forward air controllers could not do. After all, he argued, during a typical northeast monsoon season, when the sensor field was largest, forward air controllers normally found more targets than the available aircraft could attack. Electronic monitoring, he insisted, "merely confirms what we already know," duplicating the work of aerial observers and photo interpreters.[27]

General Ryan tended to endorse Butcher's contention that finding targets had never been a serious problem. "There were really more targets than we could handle with air assets," said the Chief of Staff, but he also believed that the technology embodied in Task Force Alpha benefited the aerial interdiction campaign. "The sensors . . . ," said Ryan, " certainly have proven of great value out there as an intelligence gathering device and really now give us an area in which we can put out gunships to look for traffic." He wondered, nevertheless, "whether or not we should have put that much money into the . . . [sensor] project," a decision he considered "debatable."[28]

In spite of the reservations of Butcher and Ryan concerning the importance of sensors, these devices, able to function in weather that frustrated visual observation or aerial photography, continued to maintain surveillance in future Commando Hunt operations. Moreover, aircraft could respond more quickly to sensor data thanks to improved coordination with the embassy. In effect, the ambassador to Laos agreed to apply to all strikes that required embassy approval the same basic concept of partial validation used for Arc Light bombing. Since the embassy staff already had the basic information on most areas embracing potential targets, the Seventh Air Force need not supply a complete justification in every instance. As in the case of attacks by B–52s, approval depended on the location of guerrillas or roadwatch teams, information the ambassador could easily obtain. During Commando Hunt III, Task Force Alpha assigned an enlisted man to temporary duty with the assistant air attaché at Savannakhet, where he had access to a secure telephone. When Task Force Alpha called to nominate a new target, he passed the coordinates to the assistant attaché and usually within an hour, obtained either outright approval, rejection, or a statement of any conditions, like the use of a forward air controller, that the embassy wanted.[29]

Although the embassy staff at Vientiane felt confident enough of the results of aerial interdiction to accelerate its response to requests for strikes, the overall effect of the Commando Hunt series remained a topic of some debate. Did the arbitrary statistical yardsticks employed by the Seventh Air Force actually mirror reality or merely result in what the Central Intelligence Agency denounced as a "numbers game"? In deciding that Commando Hunt III claimed almost thirty-two thousand tons of cargo and destroyed or damaged more than ten thousand trucks, Seventh Air Force analysts used the same basic technique employed for the first of the operations, but shortly after the latest report appeared in the spring of 1970, an interagency task force, meeting at Washington, D.C., questioned the assumptions on which the analysis rested. Within the task force, representatives of the Department of Defense, Central Intelligence Agency, and Department of State—the pessimists—objected to the Seventh Air Force decision, endorsed by the Defense Intelligence Agency, to "count large numbers of discrete items, aggregate them, and convert to tonnages." The objection arose from a belief that, "both the counting and conversion processes are subject to large error."

In illustrating why they had no faith in this method, the dissenters focused on the Seventh Air Force's preliminary estimates of cargo entering southern Laos during Commando Hunt III. The early discovery of new pipeline construction in southern Laos and realization that key sensor strings near Mu Gia Pass had failed well ahead of schedule convinced General Brown's analysts that they initially had underestimated by 38 percent the tonnage of supplies starting down the Ho Chi Minh Trail. "Adjustments of this magnitude," the interagency report declared, "bring into question the basic validity of the estimating system."[30] The fact remained, however, that the Seventh Air Force had caught the error and made an effort to correct it in the final report.

In spite of interagency criticism, the Seventh Air Force continued to use essentially the same methodology in assessing the effect of interdiction during future Commando Hunt campaigns. Commenting in 1974 on the analysis effort, General Keegan, a former Seventh Air Force Deputy Chief of Staff for Intelligence, declared that

> We integrated communications intelligence . . . exploited captured documents . . . [and] took everything the Army could give us on the character of enemy movement. Then we used the sensors and the computers to discipline our knowledge of how the enemy moved. We computerized our new data base and developed a significant logistics input-throughput-output model of enemy logistics. We undertook to measure every pound of supplies the enemy put into his net. A reporting system was developed to determine consumption for road repair, feeding, active defense, and the like.
>
> We were thus able to determine net input into South Vietnam . . . . We were then able to determine the real impact of interdiction.[31]

In short, what the interagency committee considered dangerously imprecise seemed carefully thought out and accurate at the headquarters of the Seventh Air Force.

Besides challenging the methods described by General Keegan, members of the interagency group questioned the conclusion of Seventh Air Force analysts that "emphasis on trucks . . . had substantially increased the cost to North Vietnam of maintaining an adequate number of vehicles in Laos."[32] According to the task force, the Soviet Union, the East European satellites, and China—not North Vietnam itself—bore the expense of replacing the trucks that the Commando Hunt series killed. Moreover, the cost to the United States of establishing and maintaining the electronic barrier far exceeded what North Vietnam's allies paid to replace the vehicles destroyed. Nor did aerial interdiction exact a severe penalty in terms of manpower, if the interagency body were correct in its estimate that operating, servicing, and defending the Ho Chi Minh Trail required no more than 10 percent of North Vietnam's armed forces or 3 percent of the able-bodied males between fifteen and thirty-four years of age.[33] Only by killing North Vietnamese could the Commando Hunt operations force the enemy to pay a direct price for continuing the war, a consideration that would revive interest in aerial attacks on the troops infiltrating through southern Laos. For the present, however, the logistic network remained the objective, with trucks killed and secondary explosions the usual means of measuring success, and the interdiction campaign for the southwest monsoon season of 1970, Commando Hunt IV, would follow the established pattern.

Chapter Eight

Cambodia, Commando Hunt IV, and Southwestern Laos

Commando Hunt IV, the southwest monsoon season interdiction campaign conducted between April and October 1970, formed but one of three interdiction efforts undertaken outside South Vietnam at that time. While air power attacked the Ho Chi Minh Trail, Laotian forces, as they had during the previous rainy season, exerted pressure on the western fringes of the logistics complex, and U.S. and South Vietnamese troops, supported by aircraft, advanced into eastern Cambodia, attacking the base areas that B–52s had secretly been bombing since March 1969. Of the three undertakings launched in the spring of 1970, the invasion of Cambodia, a large-scale raid rather than a permanent lodgment, offered the greatest promise and the gravest peril. Even as the attack struck another blow against North Vietnamese logistics and reduced the likelihood of a major offensive as U.S. forces withdrew from Vietnam, it rekindled opposition to the war in the United States and committed the nation to the support of a weak Cambodian government.

In the spring of 1970, however, the benefits of destroying the enemy's stockpiles in Cambodia stockpiles seemed to outweigh any disadvantages, and when the opportunity appeared, the Nixon administration seized it. This chance to forestall any North Vietnamese attempt to disrupt Vietnamization and impede the U.S. withdrawal stemmed from the overthrow during March of Prince Norodom Sihanouk, the ruler of Cambodia. His successor, Lon Nol, declared the nation a republic, closed the port of Sihanoukville to cargo destined to support the war against South Vietnam, and ordered the North Vietnamese to leave the country, something they would not willingly do, since it meant the abandonment of bivouacs and supply dumps adjacent to South Vietnam and the loss of increasingly valuable supply lines passing through Cambodia. Consequently, the North Vietnamese and the Cambodian communists, the Khmer Rouge, attacked Lon Nol's ill-prepared forces.

The Central Intelligence Agency, which had at first been wary of the evidence linking Cambodia to the North Vietnamese logistics network, concluded on the basis of information obtained after Sihanouk was overthrown that, at least since 1966, the Prince had allowed weapons, ammunition, and other supplies to pass through Cambodia to the communist troops fighting in South Vietnam. Most of the cargo arrived at Sihanoukville in Chinese ships and crossed the country in trucks bound for the border area, though a smaller quantity came down the Ho Chi Minh Trail, made a detour through northeastern Cambodia, and eventually entered South Vietnam. Once Lon Nol seized power, Cambodian officers formerly involved in the movement of supplies inland from the seacoast provided bills of lading and other documents that revealed that some twenty-nine thousand tons of cargo—including more than four thousand tons of food, clothing, and medical supplies—passed through Sihanoukville between December 1966 and April 1969 destined for the camps and depots along the border. Analysts could not determine the tonnage that entered the country by way of the Ho Chi Minh Trail en route ultimately to South Vietnam, but the available evidence indicated that from December 1966 to the spring of 1968, the total included from one hundred to three hundred tons of ammunition. Although a lesser volume of supplies passed through Cambodia into South Vietnam than arrived there by way of southern Laos, North Vietnam refused to give up the route from Sihanoukville, safe for much of its length from aerial or ground attack. Without the Cambodian seaport and the all-weather highways leading inland, the enemy had to rely exclusively on routes through southern Laos, thereby increasing his vulnerability to Commando Hunt operations.[1]

While Sihanoukville still served as a port of entry for cargo destined for the enemy in South Vietnam, the Studies and Observations Group, U.S. Military Assistance Command, Vietnam, had dispatched reconnaissance units, at first known as Daniel Boone teams and later as Salem House teams, across the Cambodian border into areas where the North Vietnamese maintained bases to support operations in the South. Normally composed of three members of the Army Special Forces and nine South Vietnamese, the teams located roads, trails, bivouac sites, and supply caches, observed enemy movement, found and sometimes tapped telephone lines, and took an occasional prisoner. Prior to the spring of 1970 and the advance into Cambodia, Salem House teams tried to avoid combat, though fighting often erupted when hostile security forces discovered one of the units. During 454 missions in 1969, for instance, the teams reported killing between 613 and 1,167 of the enemy—a vagueness reflecting hurried reports of confused action often resulting from an ambush—at a cost of ten U.S. and eleven South Vietnamese personnel killed. In addition, forty-seven Americans and forty-four Vietnamese suffered wounds, and three Americans and one South Vietnamese failed to return and were listed as missing in action.[2]

The incursion into Cambodia, lasting from April 29 through June 30, 1970, and the subsequent U.S. air strikes to help Lon Nol stave off the communist forces changed both the role and composition of the Salem House teams. Not only did the operating area expand, but the Studies and Observations Group now sent exploitation teams with forty-four men across the border expressly to inflict casualties on the enemy. Moreover, the reconnaissance units continued to locate or verify targets for tactical fighter strikes throughout an aerial interdiction zone that encompassed northeastern Cambodia. Salem House soon underwent Vietnamization, however, in keeping with Nixon's pledge that U.S. ground troops would withdraw from Cambodia at the end of June 1970. When the ground forces pulled back into South Vietnam, as the President had promised, the Joint Chiefs of Staff prohibited U.S. servicemen from leading or accompanying either reconnaissance or exploitation groups, although tactical aircraft and helicopter gunships could still support the Salem House mission.[3]

Like the Salem House probes, B–52 missions against targets in Cambodia occurred before the invasion. These strikes were called Menu bombings because the areas that served as targets bore nicknames like Lunch, Breakfast, or Snack. Cloaked in secrecy, the Menu raids struck enemy bases and supply depots just west of the South Vietnamese border, especially those in the "Fishhook" region south and east of Mimot and Snoul that was one of the objectives of the 1970 incursion.[4]

During the secret bombing of Cambodia, from March 18, 1969, through May 26, 1970, B–52s five miles in the sky released a deluge of high explosives against the North Vietnamese bases hidden in the jungle below. Truong Nha T'ang, a member of the Central Office for South Vietnam, the Cambodia-based political and military headquarters that directed operations in the South, recalled returning to a jungle bivouac to discover that "there was nothing left," for a vast field of craters had swallowed up lean-to huts and underground shelters alike. "It was," he said, "as if an enormous scythe had swept through the jungle, felling the giant . . . trees like grass in its way, shredding them into scattered splinters." This frightful demonstration of explosive power, he boasted, had not killed even one member of the central office, which he correctly assumed to be one of the targets of the Menu bombing.

The secret of survival lay in timely warning. According to Truong, Soviet trawlers fitted out to gather intelligence waited for the B–52s taking off from Guam, then tracked those aircraft until North Vietnamese radar could take over. Similarly, a combination of ground observers and radar sites kept watch on the bombers based at U-Tapao, the airfield in Thailand used by the B–52s. This warning network advised the central office of the course of the approaching bombers, which provided a clue as to the target area so that those troops believed to be in danger could flee or at least take cover. After receiving this kind of advance notice, which, in effect, eliminated the least likely targets, the central office normally had to choose among a number of possibilities and sometimes guessed wrong, with results that could shatter the spirit as well the bodies of persons caught among the exploding bombs. Provided they received sufficient warning, those who manned the headquarters, operated the bases, or camped in the bivouac areas could move; but the supplies, although stored in sturdily built bunkers, remained immobile and vulnerable to the Menu bombing.

To a greater degree than any of the Menu attacks, the invasion of Cambodia in April 1970 caught the Central Office for South Vietnam unprepared, but North Vietnamese troops fought desperately and slowed the onslaught enough for the headquarters contingent to escape encirclement and death or capture.[5] Many of the soldiers and their leaders managed to survive and resume the fight, but huge caches of supplies imported through Sihanoukville or transported painfully and slowly by truck down the Ho Chi Minh Trail fell into the hands of the advancing force. The spoils included some twenty thousand weapons and almost seven thousand tons of rice — enough, said Dr. Kissinger, to equip seventy-four infantry battalions with small arms and feed all the North Vietnamese combat troops in the South for four months — plus roughly sixty tons of medical supplies and fifteen million rounds of ammunition.[6]

The closing of Sihanoukville, which Lon Nol renamed Kompong Som so that it no longer commemorated the former ruler, came at an awkward time for the North Vietnamese and Viet Cong. General Abrams, Commander, U.S. Military Assistance Command, Vietnam, had launched a campaign to ferret out enemy supplies hidden in South Vietnam. Reports from Saigon claimed the capture or destruction of twenty-five hundred caches containing 6,831 tons of supplies, more than twice what the Central Intelligence Agency, to cite one of the estimates under discussion in the summer of 1970, believed necessary to sustain enemy activity for a month. Secretary of Defense Melvin R. Laird seemed delighted with these results, declaring that it was far cheaper and more effective to capture supplies in South Vietnam than to spend one and one-half billion dollars per year attacking the Ho Chi Minh Trail in southern Laos,[7] but aerial interdiction and this search for hidden supplies actually complemented each other, so that he could not choose between them. Discovering caches in South Vietnam had the same basic effect as shutting down the supply route through Sihanoukville; both increased the impact of aerial interdiction by making the enemy more dependent on goods shipped through southern Laos.

Regardless of the publicity surrounding the hoped-for destruction of the Central Office for South Vietnam, the United States invaded Cambodia primarily because special circumstances: the coup by Lon Nol and the anti-North Vietnamese actions that ensued afforded an opportunity to enhance the impact of the Commando Hunt series and reinforce the shield for Vietnamization and withdrawal. Looking at events from the viewpoint of the Viet Cong, Truong interpreted the attack on the ground as evidence that air power alone could not protect the declining number of U.S. troops in South Vietnam, but aerial interdiction remained critical to the success of the Nixon policy. By advancing into Cambodia, an operation officially described as an incursion rather than an invasion, the President took chances that the Commando Hunt series avoided. He gambled that U.S. forces could carry out their mission and swiftly disengage; that the South Vietnamese could afterward neutralize the border region; that Lon Nol's army could, with largely material assistance, hold the Khmer Rouge in check; and that the people of the United States, already weary of the conflict, would accept the increased casualties suffered in a quick thrust designed specifically to facilitate the withdrawal of troops from South Vietnam.

Operation Rock Crusher, as the U.S. assault was called (the South Vietnamese thrust carried the name *Toan Thang* or Total Victory), forced a postponement of any large-scale offensive that the enemy might have planned for South Vietnam in 1970. Otherwise, the gamble failed on most every count. The South Vietnamese could not maintain a grip on easternmost Cambodia, nor could Lon Nol contain the Khmer Rouge, even though U.S. air power remained active in the country after President Nixon had withdrawn the ground forces. Moreover, the Nixon administration miscalculated the willingness of the antiwar movement in the United States to tolerate even a brief intensification of the fighting.[8]

President Nixon and his advisers might well have assumed that the antiwar movement had peaked in the demonstrations of October 1969. Resistance to the draft persisted, but the President had already begun to treat that source of irritation. In March 1969, he appointed a commission to study the feasibility of relying exclusively on volunteers for the armed forces, and in May, before the panel reported, he asked Congress to amend the Selective Service System by establishing a lottery, whereby eligible men, excluding students, might be called up at any time during a one-year period of vulnerability in a sequence based on the month and day of birth. While awaiting action by Congress, and with the nationwide antiwar demonstrations planned for October looming on the horizon, Nixon announced the cancellation of the draft calls for November and December and spread the October quota over the last three months of the year. In November, after the demonstrations, Congress approved the lottery that the President had proposed, and in December, a drawing established the order of precedence for the coming year. Finally, in January, the President's commission recommended the creation of an all-volunteer force, with the Selective Service becoming a standby source of manpower available in time of emergency. The draft, however, threatened to emerge once again as an issue after the President in April 1970, on the eve of the incursion into Cambodia, asked Congress for authority to put an end to future student deferments, excluding men already enrolled in college. His proposal may have been a gesture of solidarity with what he described as the "silent majority," a constituency made up largely of blue-collar workers who supported the war and tended to resent the special treatment given students.

Although Nixon probably enjoyed the active support of comparatively few college students, he nevertheless had addressed their concerns when he established a lottery intended to ease the disruptive influence of Selective Service on young men about to embark on a career. By compressing into a single year the period of vulnerability, which previously might have lasted from the age of eighteen years to thirty-five, and by drafting the youngest of the eligibles first rather than the oldest, the administration simplified and made more predictable the complicated and often arbitrary rules that governed the draft. Moreover, the President's proposal to scrap student deferments had not yet gone beyond the talking stage and even if enacted, would have exempted those young men currently enrolled in classes. Finally, even if student deferments should end, U.S. involvement in Vietnam was abating and the day approaching when volunteers would man the armed forces, except in time of some future national emergency.[9]

The invasion of Cambodia, however, seemed to signal an expansion of the war, an increase in casualties, and a reversal of the policy of Vietnamization and withdrawal that had contributed to fewer losses, reduced draft calls, reforms of the Selective Service System, and serious discussions of shelving it as the normal source of manpower. An abiding distrust of the President by a generation reluctant to believe in anyone over 30, genuine moral outrage at the extension of the fighting into Cambodia, and alarm that personal plans, indeed life itself, might again be placed in jeopardy because of military service coalesced to produce student protests that erupted spontaneously on campuses across the nation. During one such demonstration at Kent State University in Ohio, National Guardsmen fired into a group of students, killing four and wounding nine.[10]

The shootings at Kent State further divided the country and inflamed the opponents of the war. Another massive rally against the war took place on May 9, 1970, when seventy-five thousand to one hundred thousand protesters gathered at Washington, D.C. The voices of opposition rang out on the campuses and in the streets, and also in the halls of Congress. The legislators considered, but rejected, proposals to limit or cut off funds for the war, but Senators John Sherman Cooper, a Republican from Kentucky, and Frank Church, a Democrat from Idaho, proposed, in the form of an amendment to an appropriation bill, a deadline for the withdrawal of U.S. troops from Cambodia. Events overtook the original Cooper-Church amendment, for in eight weeks the invasion force pulled out. The two senators, however, introduced a revised version attached to other legislation that, in its final form, forbade the introduction of U.S. ground forces into Laos or Thailand.[11]

In a symbolic gesture, the Congress also repealed the Tonkin Gulf resolution. In 1964, after North Vietnamese patrol boats attacked U.S. destroyers in the Tonkin Gulf off the coast of North Vietnam, President Johnson had asked Congress for authority to take "all necessary steps, including the use of armed forces" to prevent aggression in Southeast Asia. A resolution to this effect passed with just two dissenting votes in the Senate and none at all in the House of Representatives. As he increased U.S. involvement in the war, Johnson had often cited the resolution as the legal basis for his action, and now Congress, by rescinding the Tonkin Gulf resolution, expressed its displeasure with the conduct of the war, including the most recent escalation, Nixon's invasion of Cambodia.[12]

Despite the Cooper-Church amendment and the nullification of the Tonkin Gulf resolution, Congress refused to take responsibility for pulling the plug on the Vietnam War and thus accepting undisguised defeat. Moreover, the antiwar movement remained divided internally, and from other elements of society, by considerations of age, education, wealth, and race, united only in its opposition to the conflict. Some of those disenchanted with the war balked at taking to the streets or hoped to avoid conceding victory to the North Vietnamese. The possibility of a defeat troubled the silent majority, already declining in strength, which tended to see the antiwar activity as an attack on lawful authority and traditional values led by a class of college students who seemed irresponsible, spoiled, and deserving of contempt. Hardcore support, along with the divisions among those troubled by his conduct of the war, enabled President Nixon to survive the domestic turmoil

140

caused by the thrust into Cambodia and continue to pursue his policy of Vietnamization and withdrawal.[13]

Even as they turned the war over to the South Vietnamese, the armed forces of the United States suffered a decline in morale and discipline. The contributing factors included the nature of the war, the lack of popular support for the conflict, racial strife that erupted throughout the country, and the availability in Southeast Asia of drugs and alcohol. The Vietnam War began in what could be called a spirit of naive optimism, as the United States sought to help South Vietnam resist communism and remain independent. When the Saigon government and its armed forces, for various reasons, failed to make effective use of the assistance, the United States took over the war and tried unsuccessfully to wear down the enemy and force him to expend men and material at a rate he could not sustain. When attrition failed, the administration turned to Vietnamization— training and equipping the South Vietnamese to fight the war and survive afterward—and, as South Vietnamese strength and competence increased, the withdrawal of U.S. forces.[14]

By 1970, the war presented a tangle of inconsistencies; the United States fought to disengage rather than to win, and rules of engagement imposed strict limits on the use of force for that purpose. No wonder that one squadron commander complained of spending "an inordinate amount of time either defending our involvement in the war or trying to explain away the political restrictions on the use of air power." He did not consider the young airmen and junior officers who took up his time "dissidents in the accepted sense of the word"; instead, he found them "highly intelligent and keenly inquisitive" but "confused by the lack of credibility between stated policy and the application of policy as reported in the news media."[15]

As the commander's reference to the media would indicate, some officers, at least, had grown wary of those who reported on the war, accusing them of sacrificing accuracy for melodrama and of being just plain careless with the facts. Without resorting to censorship, which would have been difficult because reporters could file their stories from a number of nearby countries linked to South Vietnam by commercial airlines, the military assistance command tried to put the best possible interpretation on events, as did the Johnson and Nixon administrations. When journalists found that official accounts did not reflect reality, they emphasized the errors, inconsistencies, and deceptions, thus encouraging the distrust of authority so prevalent among young people at the time. Inconsequential issues sometimes captured the interest of the reporters, who themselves proved fallible and made errors of their own in fact, judgment, or interpretation.[16]

Well might the airman in Southeast Asia believe himself forgotten, if not despised, by his fellow citizens in the United States. Coverage of the war by the press and television aroused little public encouragement or appreciation for those men waging a war that the nation was trying to liquidate. Huge crowds gathered at times in cities like New York, San Francisco, or Washington, D.C., to demand an end to the fighting. Nor had the nation's leaders remained united behind the war effort, as demonstrated when Congress rescinded the nearly unanimous Tonkin Gulf resolution and imposed restrictions on the use of U.S. troops. Congressional opposition to the war provoked an Air Force colonel, the commander of an air base in Southeast Asia, to complain, "The single most destructive element that delayed and undermined our objective in Vietnam and contributed to the disciplinary and morale problems of the younger troops was the fact that public figures, under the guise of freedom of speech, maligned the administration for an honorable withdrawal from Vietnam that would also ensure a reasonable opportunity for the survival of a free Vietnam."[17]

The officer or airman serving in Southeast Asia—although he may well have felt this sort of an alienation from life in the United States, its freedoms, and its politics—could not isolate himself from the issues that divided U.S. society, among them racial animosity. Catch phrases like black power and white backlash summarized the attitudes that culminated, following the murder in April 1968 of Rev. Martin Luther King, Jr., the Nobel laureate and civil rights leader, in rioting that gutted portions of several large cities. The underlying hostility that contributed to the urban violence followed individuals into the armed forces and erupted in fights or demonstrations at bases throughout the world. Beginning in 1971, the Department of Defense established a training course to turn out instructors who could teach others to work together in racial harmony, and the Air Force used graduates of this course, when they became available, to provide indoctrination in race relations at all its installations. Meanwhile, local commanders anticipated many of the techniques employed in the formal program of instruction and sought to promote racial understanding through discipline, discussion, consultation with interracial councils, and, in general, commonsense efforts to anticipate and ease friction between whites and blacks. By the time the Commando Hunt operations ended in 1972, every major unit in Southeast Asia had a social actions office, usually headed by a trained specialist, that not only sought to resolve racial friction, but also attacked two other deep-rooted problems: the illegal use of drugs and the abuse of alcohol.[18]

The use of marijuana, heroin, and a variety of other illegal or dangerous substances captured headlines in the United States, but in Southeast Asia, the danger proved even more acute, for, as the commander of one of the bases pointed out, "Every type of pill, marijuana, and heroin is readily available locally."[19] Initially, the threat of punishment provided the only available weapon against drug abuse, but the Air Force soon found it necessary to establish a program of detection, treatment, and rehabilitation to complement the military justice system. The campaign against the illegal use of drugs seemed to be making headway by the time the air war over southern Laos came to an end.[20]

Since it was both legal to use and formed a part of the macho image cultivated by many young men, alcohol proved harder to deal with than drugs. As late as the summer of 1972, the commander of a civil engineering squadron in South Vietnam acknowledged, "The number one problem is still the excessive use of alcohol."[21] Not until operations against the Ho Chi Minh Trail had ended did the Air Force launch a campaign against alcoholism comparable in intensity to the efforts to eradicate drug abuse or promote racial harmony. Ultimately, however, a treatment program began functioning, and the Air Force encouraged the formation of chapters of Alcoholics Anonymous at major bases.[22]

As the war spilled over into Cambodia, as race relations deteriorated and problems of drug and alcohol abuse demanded solutions, the Seventh Air Force continued to attack traffic on the Ho Chi Minh Trail in Commando Hunt IV, carried out during the rainy months of 1970. As had happened throughout the previous year's southwest monsoon season, the downpour impeded traffic and construction, but neither halted the trucks entirely nor prevented repairs to existing roads and the building of new ones. The enemy rarely used Mu Gia Pass during the late spring and early summer, probably because of the rain, and Task Force Alpha responded by increasing sensor coverage at the other entry points, adding new Commando Bolt strings near Ban Raving and Ban Karai Passes and maintaining closer surveillance over the routes leading westward from the demilitarized zone. Traffic monitoring detected North Vietnamese engineer units that remained in southern Laos throughout the southwest monsoon period to perform extensive work on the road net. Moreover, attacks on the trail encountered antiaircraft batteries that, according to U.S. intelligence, had spent the rainy season of 1969 in North Vietnam, in case the bombing resumed there.[23]

Vietnamization proceeded throughout Commando Hunt IV, as the United States reduced its strength while simultaneously building up South Vietnamese forces. The Nakhon Phanom Surveillance Center seemed a logical candidate for cost cutting and manpower reductions, since it operated mostly at night, when the heaviest traffic used the roads, and no longer exercised control over strike aircraft except in the Commando Bolt operation. Reflecting these limitations on its activity, the command reduced the strength of its operations directorate by 155 persons and got rid of one of the two 360/65 computers leased from IBM. From late afternoon until dawn, the remaining computer processed current sensor reports and other perishable intelligence, leaving the daylight hours for maintenance and the retrieval of data for use in routine reporting.[24]

Until Lon Nol seized power in Cambodia during March 1970, the fighting in southwestern Laos tended to follow a pattern of advance and retreat. Despite some unusually vigorous campaigning by Laotian government forces in the summer and fall of 1969, territory changed hands temporarily. Neither government nor communist forces chose to make the effort necessary to seize ground and hold it, and during the 1969–70 northeast monsoon season, both sides resumed their maneuvering. Guerrillas loyal to Prince Souvanna reacted to a communist threat to Muong Phalane by reoccupying the airstrip at Ban Tang Vai, springboard for the thrust to Muong Phine earlier in 1969, and North Vietnamese and Pathet Lao forces again closed in on Saravane, Paksong, and Attopeu.[25]

Combat during the spring and summer of 1970 might have been a repetition of the indecisive action of the previous year, had it not been for Lon Nol's coup in Cambodia. The emergence of a U.S. supported ruler in that nation closed, at least temporarily, the communist supply line through Sihanoukville, forcing the North Vietnamese to float supplies down the Kong River, which flowed southward past the town of Attopeu into Cambodia. A Laotian army garrison held Attopeu against the danger that arose and subsided almost annually as the North Vietnamese and Pathet Laos menaced the town, but stopped short of delivering a decisive blow when resistance stiffened. After Lon Nol seized power in March 1970, North Vietnamese troops once again surrounded the town, this time offering the garrison a choice between abandoning its fortifications or dying in them. As a combined U.S.-South Vietnamese force advanced into Cambodia some two hundred miles to the south, four hundred Lao soldiers laid down their weapons and filed out of Attopeu over an escape route the attackers had deliberately left open.[26]

Air units again saw action in southwestern Laos throughout the southwest monsoon season, bombing, for example, a regional headquarters north of Muong Phine, along with a transshipment point and its satellite supply dumps at the western edge of the Ho Chi Minh Trail. In addition, A–1 crews from the 56th Special Operations Wing at Nakhon Phanom claimed to have caused twenty-five secondary fires and killed or wounded more than one hundred fifty defenders when attacking in support of a guerrilla raid on the site of an abandoned airstrip near Tchepone.[27] The most extensive fighting, however, did not begin until September, as the rainy season yielded to drier weather.

Plans called for Operation Gauntlet, "a large scale offensive against the North Vietnamese route structure and enemy support elements in south Laos," to kick off on September 1. The basic concept, which originated with Central Intelligence Agency officials in Laos, received "the endorsement of top level Washington policy makers" and support from the Military Assistance Command, Vietnam, which agreed to dispatch a Prairie Fire company westward from South Vietnam in cooperation with the eastward advance of the guerrillas. (General Abrams could send his soldiers across the border because the modified Cooper-Church amendment had not yet become law.[28]) An unusually complicated endeavor, Gauntlet required extensive preliminaries, including the capture and improvement of airstrips and an advance on Chavane, before some fifteen hundred troops could make the final thrust toward Muong Phine and Tchepone.[29] Irregular forces of one variety or another would be maneuvering in four areas: in the vicinity of Ban Toumlan, along the Banghiang River, from Saravane toward Chavane, and from Muong Phalane eastward to Tchepone, creating a widespread and rapidly changing battlefield and imposing severe demands on Laotian air units and the Air Force squadrons based at Nakhon Phanom to support the scattered battalions, especially at night. As a result, the Seventh Air Force agreed to place an AC–119K gunship on ground alert at Da Nang, South Vietnam, to help Laotian AC–47s protect the ground forces during darkness.[30]

On September 8, 1970, after postponements because of bad weather, Lt. Col. Roy L. Maddox led four CH–3s over the eastern fringe of the Bolovens Plateau to land the first contingent in Operation Gauntlet's initial phase, the guerrilla sweep toward Chavane. Three days later, the huge new CH–53 made its combat debut, outperforming the older helicopter—now dubbed the "nitnoy," a Thai word for small— so thoroughly that, according to those who flew both types, "it was somewhat comic." On the 13th, while flying in reinforcements for this part of the operation, the CH–53 came under fire for the first time, but sustained no damage, though an auto- matic weapon concealed in a tree line near the landing zone scored three hits on one of the five CH–3s taking part in the mission.[31]

The Military Assistance Command, Vietnam, aided this phase of Gauntlet by launching, on September 11, Operation Tailwind, a Prairie Fire raid some 20 miles southeast of Chavane. Besides diverting enemy security units from the larger force advancing toward that town from the west, the Prairie Fire company overcame determined resistance to destroy several huts containing material that ranged from 23-mm ammunition, to bicycle parts, to eight tons of rice. Daylight air support for Tailwind, and for Gauntlet as well, consisted of A–1s from Nakhon Phanom and F–4s from Phu Cat, while AC–130s came to the aid of the Prairie Fire unit after dark. Strikes by these aircraft claimed the lives of an estimated 288 Pathet Lao and North Vietnamese, twice the number reported killed by troops on the ground. Although the enemy apparently suffered badly, Lt. Col. Paul D. Thompson, a Seventh Air Force staff officer, concluded that air support had not prevented the Tailwind force from getting "bloody noses a couple of times." Indeed, during the two days before they withdrew, South Vietnamese members of the Prairie Fire com- pany suffered three killed and thirty-three wounded, with sixteen U.S. soldiers wounded.[32]

After some Thai guerrilla units, in collaboration with Prairie Fire troops, had probed toward Chavane, other irregulars advanced on Muong Phine, about 110 miles to the northwest. Since this second phase of Gauntlet appeared to be going well, the royal army again tried to exploit the gains made by the guerrillas. In what came to be called Gauntlet II, helicopters landed three government battalions west of Muong Phine and three others between that village and Tchepone. Beginning on October 31, while irregulars patrolled to the north and west, these units destroyed supply dumps and mined roads, but made no attempt to seize either enemy strong- hold.[33]

Looking back on the combination of Gauntlet, Tailwind, and Gauntlet II, the Seventh Air Force staff declared that, taken together, they formed "the most success- ful of all irregular operations against the Ho Chi Minh Trail." By the time the six Lao army battalions broke off the action on November 13 and withdrew, they had for a time held the junction of Routes 9 and 914 between Muong Phine and Tchepone, planted mines to disrupt traffic on both roads, and called down air strikes on enemy troops and installations. In a single skirmish fought northwest of Tchepone, for instance, a guerrilla battalion reported killing two hundred North Vietnamese or Pathet Lao at a cost of forty killed.[34]

The enemy, in the meantime, had not remained on the defensive. Whereas the Lao and Thai troops followed the old tactical pattern, raiding and then falling back, the enemy came to stay. Besides overrunning Attopeu, he seized Saravane, although government forces continued to occupy the heights nearby. Communist forces now controlled the eastern part of the Bolovens Plateau and stood ready to extend their authority during the northeast monsoon season.[35]

The return of dry weather to the Ho Chi Minh Trail permitted the truck war to resume in earnest; Commando Hunt V, in fact, started while Gauntlet II was still in progress. Aerial interdiction throughout the length of the trail loomed larger in U.S. plans than ground operations from its western edge, as demonstrated by the hundreds of Commando Hunt sorties each day, even in the rainy season, compared to the dozens supporting guerrilla units or elements of the Laotian army. In September 1970, for example, thirty-two sorties during a single day represented a strong effort in support of Gauntlet, but this amounted to less than 3 percent of the average of 1,210 daylight sorties launched each day throughout southern Laos. The eastern part of southern Laos, which contained the main trunk of the Ho Chi Minh Trail, received almost 75 percent of the daylight sorties flown in southern part of the kingdom and 97 percent of those dispatched at night, with the remainder assisting ground operations against the trail's western branches.[36] Interdiction absorbed a lion's share of the U.S. aerial effort in the southern Laos, and Commando Hunt V, the campaign scheduled for the northeast monsoon season of 1970–71, promised impressive results.

Chapter Nine

Commando Hunt V
The Best up to this Time

Later characterized by General Momyer, a former commander of the Seventh Air Force, as "the best of the interdiction campaigns up to this time,"[1] Commando Hunt V lasted from October 10, 1970, until April 30 of the following year. Once again the northeast monsoon season campaign focused on truck transportation, including roads, transshipment points, parking and repair facilities, supply dumps, and the moving convoys. Task Force Alpha remained a key element in the operation, despite the reservations voiced by a recent commander, General Butcher, who had described the organization as "nice to have" though not really essential.[2] Regardless of his evaluation, the increased size of the sensor field testified to the continuing importance of the task force and its electronic surveillance devices. From a maximum of about seven hundred acoustic and seismic sensors during the previous dry season, the array for Commando Hunt V had expanded to more than eight hundred of these types, plus the commandable microphones used mainly to search out truck parks and storage areas.[3]

Although Task Force Alpha remained a key instrument of the interdiction effort, it underwent some fine tuning as planners at Nakhon Phanom and at Seventh Air Force headquarters tried to take advantage of its unique ability to find targets. For example, the Martin B–57G, undergoing combat evaluation during Commando Hunt V, received special target advisories from Nakhon Phanom, and the AC–130 gunships, the deadliest of truck killers, now patrolled areas covered by Commando Bolt modules and, like the B–57Gs, responded to coded instructions radioed from the Surveillance Center. Because of the danger of midair collision, Flasher teams could not attack where the AC–130s were prowling, so Task Force Alpha began providing the team leaders with the loran coordinates of fixed targets, such as supply dumps or truck parks, instead of impact points on major roadways now covered by gunships.

Since Commando Bolt generated information for advisories from Task Force Alpha to the gunships and B–57Gs and, to a lesser extent, the Flasher and Pouncer teams, the Infiltration Surveillance Center tried, by lengthening the strike modules, to improve their usefulness in determining the speed of trucks and, insofar as possible, in locating bypasses. The modules now consisted of two or three strings of eight sensors each, instead of six, though a single 18-sensor string might sometimes be used. The longer module monitored a convoy over a greater distance, providing a more accurate average speed, and also reported the disappearance of trucks turning onto an uncharted cutoff anywhere along the segment of road covered by the sensors.

The Infiltration Surveillance Center, although receiving transmissions from a larger number of sensors than before, no longer used relay aircraft as surrogate monitors for distant portions of the sensor field. The Ferret III EC–121s had no assignment in Commando Hunt V because planners expected the ill-starred QU–22B drones, which could not accommodate the X–T plotters, to take over the relay mission sometime during the operation. Task Force Alpha used the Ferret III plotting equipment removed from the Bat Cats when the computer at Nakhon Phanom underwent maintenance or when a particular part of the sensor field required close surveillance.[4]

As the X–T plotters assumed this auxiliary role, the basic alignment of the sensor field underwent adjustment in preparation for Commando Hunt V. Until the fall of 1970, Task Force Alpha had laid out route monitoring strings parallel to the flow of traffic, concentrating on each individual route more or less in isolation from all others, but the speed with which North Vietnamese engineers could build cutoffs frequently enabled drivers to bypass some of these linear strings. For that reason, and to facilitate the division of the operation into the usual three phases as the heaviest traffic moved southward from the passes, the Commando Hunt V plan called for grouping the various parallel strings to form what amounted to bands of sensors placed perpendicular to the direction of movement. To establish such a band, planners chose natural bottlenecks, where traffic converged, and seeded the sensors not only along known roads that passed parallel to each other but also along adjacent valleys or watercourses where the North Vietnamese might readily build alternate routes.[5]

Modifications to the sensor field, especially to the Commando Bolt strings, along with the increased use of Task Force Alpha to issue advisories to aircraft, apparently paid dividends. As Commando Hunt V approached peak intensity, Gen. William P. McBride, a former commander of Task Force Alpha, informally inspected the Nakhon Phanom facility. After watching the Surveillance Center gather information and issue advisories during typical periods of the evening and early morning, he concluded that "the equipment is really locating and tracking vehicular traffic in as near real time as we are going to achieve in the next ten years, short of eyeball observation . . . , i.e. less than five minutes." He found Commando Bolt so impressive that he wanted to make greater use of the sensor modules in directing strikes. Consequently, he warned Maj. Gen. Joseph G. Wilson, the Seventh Air Force Deputy Chief of Staff for Operations, that at Nakhon Phanom "there was entirely too much of an intelligence influence as opposed to an operational one." Since Commando Hunt V was under way, no immediate adjustment of the balance between intelligence and operations seemed wise, but by the time the next dry season arrived, Task Force Alpha might play a more dominant role in operations.[6]

Commando Hunt V: The Best Up to this Time

During the period of the northeast monsoon in 1970–71, Commando Hunt V made up just one of three major efforts, supplemented by Prairie Fire probes, to impede the movement of men and supplies down the Ho Chi Minh Trail to South Vietnam and Cambodia. While air power continued attacking the trail, Thai and Lao troops loyal to Souvanna Phouma harassed its western flank, and as the dry season neared an end, South Vietnamese forces thrust westward from Khe Sanh toward Tchepone. Taken together, these actions formed the most ambitious attempt at interdiction yet mounted against the roads and trails of southern Laos.

To a greater extent than in any previous northeast monsoon season, ground operations in late 1970 and early 1971 affected the aerial interdiction effort, sometimes reinforcing its impact, but at other times feeding on its resources. From the east, for example, Prairie Fire units still harassed the enemy forces operating the logistic system, but these attacks constituted an annoyance only, a mere pinprick rather than a rapier's thrust. The North Vietnamese responded quickly and decisively to Prairie Fire, as when they fell on one of the teams with such fury that A–1s had to deliver napalm on a smoke canister that a forward air controller had dropped just five meters from the troops; with flames billowing "right at their feet," the patrol managed to break contact and escape.[7]

On the opposite flank of the Ho Chi Minh Trail, attacks by Lao and Thai units represented a potentially greater danger to the enemy, but could not prove really decisive as long as the assault forces withdrew after each offensive. One such raid in southwestern Laos, Gauntlet II, began during the recent rainy season, continued beyond the beginning of Commando Hunt V, and ended in mid-November just sixty days before the beginning of another, Silver Buckle, which U.S. observers described as the best planned Lao guerrilla action to date from the standpoint of air support. Instead of relying as before on "last minute notification,"[8] which previously had seemed necessary to preserve security, representatives of the Central Intelligence Agency arranged well in advance for what the Seventh Air Force considered "a sizable package" of supporting aircraft for Silver Buckle.[9]

On January 12, 1971, a dozen Air Force helicopters shuttled almost twelve hundred soldiers of the Silver Buckle force into a landing zone forty-three miles southwest of Tchepone. After setting up outposts, these units and their reinforcements probed the region around Muong Nong, attacking work parties, destroying supplies and construction equipment, mining roads, and trying to find a reported prisoner of war camp and release the men held captive there. Resistance, scattered at first, rapidly coalesced, checking the advance short of the supposed site of the prison compound and containing the threat to the transportation net. Silver Buckle came to an end on February 11 when the Lao force retreated as planned. The tactics of the previous rainy months thus prevailed into the dry season, for Souvanna's units remained content to probe and withdraw, rather than seize and hold, as the North Vietnamese and Pathet Lao had begun to do.[10]

Silver Buckle, which lasted for one month, received more air support than normal for such a raid. Besides the transport helicopters, their A–1 escorts, and four

The War against Trucks

Nail forward air controllers, Seventh Air Force assigned eighteen tactical sorties per day to the enterprise. As the battle developed, four F–4Ds served as a quick reaction force to respond to calls for assistance, and other aircraft were at times diverted to targets around Muong Nong. After dark, two Candlestick C–123s joined the gunships that already patrolled the area and helped the Laotian troops defend themselves. All these aircraft accomplished very little, however, for thunderstorms not only forced cancellation of several strikes, but also combined with haze and natural concealment, frustrating efforts to locate targets or assess the effect of bombing. Weather thus prevented the Silver Buckle troops from taking full advantage of the air power available to them.[11]

As Silver Buckle ended, four battalions of Lao irregulars advanced toward Muong Phine, a frequent objective of the fighting in southwestern Laos. In carrying out Operation Desert Rat, as this raid was called, a force of twelve hundred men harassed traffic on the western fringe of the road complex, in case the South Vietnamese attack from Khe Sanh to Tchepone, Operation Lam Son 719, should force the North Vietnamese to reroute truck convoys in that direction. Desert Rat received slightly less U.S. air support than either Gauntlet II or Silver Buckle, initially just sixteen scheduled sorties each day by fighter-bombers, plus the necessary flights by troop-carrying helicopters, their escorts, and forward air controllers. Despite additional sorties late in the operation, Desert Rat had a negligible impact on Commando Hunt V in terms of diverting resources or reinforcing results.

On February 16, 1971, a dozen U.S. helicopters shuttled the Desert Rat irregulars into the landing zones from which the troops would advance toward the junction of Routes 9 and 23. Under orders to raid rather than seize and occupy, the force had the assignment of mining the two highways, pinpointing enemy installations and troop concentrations for tactical air strikes, and generally disrupting logistic activity around Muong Phine. In spite of encouraging progress at the outset, the Desert Rat battalions did not accomplish much, killing an estimated 121 North Vietnamese in 110 skirmishes, capturing two and one-half tons of ammunition, and planting some fifteen hundred mines before beginning their withdrawal two weeks ahead of schedule. Desert Rat ended early because the South Vietnamese attack toward Tchepone had encountered fierce opposition. In Desert Rat, air power had no more impact than the ground units, with crews reporting just thirty-nine trucks destroyed, some craters blasted in both highways, and 221 secondary explosions or fires.

Much of the aerial activity during Desert Rat took place at the beginning of the operation or as the troops fell back toward Muong Phalane in mid-March. For example, on March 15 and 16, AC–130s patrolled Route 23 because nighttime traffic on that highway had suddenly increased. Also, between the 16th and 20th, the Seventh Air Force assigned an additional dozen sorties each day to suppress antiaircraft fire along the same road so that Laotian T–28s could attack during daylight.[12]

Desert Rat and its immediate precursor, Silver Buckle, produced an unwelcome result, for they contributed to the enemy's decision to secure the western flank of the Ho Chi Minh Trail against future probes of this sort. By the end of May 1971,

North Vietnamese and Pathet Lao garrisons occupied Muong Phalane, Ban Houei Sai, and Paksong, as well as Attopeu, Saravane, and Ban Thateng. For the time being, at least, the communists held the government's usual jumping-off places for attacks toward Muong Phine and could use Route 13 to supply insurgents in Cambodia without fear of ground attack.[13]

Desert Rat had as its ultimate goal the disruption of truck traffic forced westward by Lam Son 719, which was a far more ambitious operation launched against the eastern flank of the Ho Chi Minh Trail. Named for the village of Lam Son, the birthplace of Le Loi, the legendary Vietnamese hero who had defeated the Chinese in the fifteenth century, the plan called for South Vietnamese troops, supported by U.S. aircraft and long-range artillery fire, to attack westward from Khe Sanh along Route 9, seize the storage depots around Tchepone, destroy the supplies stockpiled there, and then withdraw into South Vietnam. Because of the recent Cooper-Church amendment, U.S. advisers could not accompany the assault forces beyond the border with Laos in an operation that President Nixon looked on as an opportunity to gain time for further Vietnamization and the withdrawal of additional U.S. troops. In discussing his goals with his principal military advisers, the President declared that "our overall objective during the months of February, March, and April is to take the heat and take the risks, and when the heat is at the highest level we will announce additional [troop] withdrawals . . . if warranted." Once the public had received renewed assurance that the South Vietnamese were taking over the war, he proposed to devote the rest of the year to creating "an enduring Vietnam . . . one that can stand up in the future." As Lam Son 719 tried to buy time for the President, it also would reveal how successful he had been in Vietnamizing the conflict.[14]

Intelligence indicated that a drive to Tchepone could hurt the enemy not only in South Vietnam, but in Cambodia as well, where fighting continued between Lon Nol's government and the communist Khmer Rouge. Vast amounts of supplies should have filled to overflowing the storage bunkers around Tchepone, for the loss of Sihanoukville as a port of entry had cut one North Vietnamese supply line and resulted in what the Defense Intelligence Agency termed a "considerable buildup" of cargo along the surviving infiltration routes through southern Laos.[15] At least one prisoner of war, captured in South Vietnam, reported that Viet Cong units at the end of a long and badly clogged logistic pipeline had become desperate enough to try buying weapons and ammunition from South Vietnamese troops.[16]

Lam Son 719 began on February 8, 1971, when the South Vietnamese task force crossed the border into Laos. Because the one highway from Khe Sanh to Tchepone wound through rugged terrain and could easily be cut, U.S. Army helicopters landed South Vietnamese troops at various hilltops along the axis of advance to establish outposts for the protection of the tanks and other road-bound elements of the spearhead. The North Vietnamese reacted quickly, but tactical fighters, despite the handicap of cloud cover and thundershowers, joined B–52s in successfully keeping the enemy at bay. General Abrams and other senior officers urged the South Vietnamese to exploit the early momentum, commit additional troops, and fight a major battle; never again, they argued, would the South Vietnam have so much air power at its disposal, for the U.S. withdrawal would inevitably continue. In contrast, President Thieu of South Vietnam worried about the impact on the morale of the army and the nation, should Lam Son 719 end in disaster. He chose, therefore, not to press the attack after South Vietnamese casualties reached a limit that he intuitively believed his countrymen could accept without becoming demoralized. Early in March, as losses approached that number, he halted his troops and as a condition for renewing the offensive, demanded that U.S. ground forces join in the attack, clearly an impossibility in view of the Cooper-Church amendment. Lam Son 719 therefore ground to a halt, and preparations began for a withdrawal.

Instead of pushing vigorously onward and seizing Tchepone, as Abrams wanted, Thieu's generals settled for a symbolic hit-and-run raid. A small force landed from helicopters on March 6, destroyed some stockpiled supplies and withdrew. Meanwhile, the main force remained strung out along the highway or scattered among the outposts that provided flank security. Unsure of themselves and inferior to the enemy in firepower, without U.S. advisers at their elbow, the South Vietnamese commanders reacted indecisively when the enemy at mid-month launched a savage counterattack, eliminating the hilltop strongpoints and sending the task force reeling in disarray toward the border. On March 22, Air Force fighters destroyed a number of tanks closing in on the tail of the retreating column, and on the following morning, the survivors crossed into South Vietnam, the road behind them littered with abandoned equipment. Except for token raids on two supply dumps just inside Laos, in which helicopters landed, then retrieved, the assault troops, Lam Son 719 had ended.[17]

General Abrams promptly claimed success, declaring on March 21, with the South Vietnamese in headlong retreat, that Lam Son 719 had reached Tchepone, disrupted the southward movement of men and supplies, and inflicted heavy casualties on the defenders of the Ho Chi Minh Trail. The enemy, he reported, had shifted westward one entire station on the main supply line, with its living quarters, troops, and stored supplies. Moreover, some thirty-five hundred "well trained experienced rear service personnel" were either killed, wounded, or diverted to moving cargo to safer areas. He also maintained that the North Vietnamese had rerouted trucks to alternate highways, overcrowding these routes and presenting easy targets to marauding aircraft. Although available intelligence indicated that the volume of supplies entering South Vietnam through Laos during March 1971 remained approximately the same as in March of the previous year, Abrams argued that, since the enemy sought more ambitious goals for 1971, this tonnage actually represented "a degradation due to air interdiction."[18]

Shortly after the chaotic retreat from Laos ended, Abrams again pronounced Lam Son 719 a success, although conceding that the operation had disclosed certain weaknesses in the South Vietnamese military forces. "The RVNAF [Republic of Vietnam Armed Forces]," he acknowledged, "cannot sustain large-scale major cross-border operations without external support." In his opinion, South Vietnam's survival depended largely on U.S. bombing, and the United States should continue to provide each month as many as one thousand sorties by B–52s and eight to ten thousand by tactical aircraft. Indeed, during the fighting on the road to Tchepone, air power, including Army helicopters, had offset a deadly North Vietnamese advantage in armor and field artillery and given the South Vietnamese whatever mobility they enjoyed. Despite South Vietnam's dependence on U.S. air support, Abrams nevertheless believed that Vietnamization, plus the "confidence gained . . . during operations in Cambodia and Laos," would bring about continued improvement in the South Vietnamese forces as U.S. troops were withdrawing.[19] Although aware that "total effects . . . on the enemy may not be evaluated for some time," his headquarters insisted that the battle had "dramatically changed" enemy plans, forced the diversion of troops en route southward through Laos, destroyed "thousands of tons" of supplies, and compelled the North Vietnamese, at least for the present, to cease stockpiling supplies around Tchepone.[20]

President Nixon and his advisers knew by the end of February that the plan was breaking down, a failure that he ultimately blamed on Abrams, but the Chief Executive, committed to successful Vietnamization, had no choice but to emphasize the most optimistic evaluations of Lam Son 719, repeating them in a televised interview broadcast on March 22. He told newsman Howard K. Smith that the operation had reduced road traffic south of Tchepone not by 20 percent as General Abrams' headquarters claimed, or by 50 percent as the President had at first believed, but by "perhaps 75 percent." After choking off traffic to this extent, the South Vietnamese were returning from Laos, "the great majority of them with higher confidence, with greater morale, despite the fact that they have taken some very severe losses." In addition, Nixon declared, the attacking force had "chewed up great amounts of ammunition, great amounts of materiel that otherwise would have gone South and would have been used, incidentally, against many Americans fighting in South Vietnam." The President insisted that Lam Son 719 would facilitate the U.S. withdrawal and South Vietnam's assumption of increasing responsibility for the conduct of the war.[21]

As Nixon admitted, the South Vietnamese had suffered gravely in bloody fighting. Some 45 percent of the seventeen thousand–man invasion force were killed, wounded, or missing in action, while North Vietnamese casualties totaled an estimated thirteen thousand. In so ferocious a struggle, the South Vietnamese soldiers deserved better leadership than they received, for their commanders, without the prompting of U.S. advisers, neither reacted swiftly enough to a rapidly developing threat nor, when retreat became necessary, fell back in an orderly manner along the single available escape route, a highway vulnerable to attack along its entire length. The vast amount of equipment left behind—including 96 artillery pieces and 141 tanks or armored personnel carriers—gave mute testimony to the loss of unit cohesiveness, although the retreating soldiers did manage to disable some items to prevent their use by the enemy.[22]

Whatever its temporary effect on North Vietnamese supply lines, Lam Son 719 did little permanent damage. As the dry season ended, the Seventh Air Force acknowledged that "the restriction of . . . logistic flow did not equal expectations held prior to the operation," because the enemy succeeded in rerouting traffic west of the battle area, in spite of Operation Desert Rat. After the South Vietnamese withdrew from Laos, sensors detected slightly more southbound traffic on the Ho Chi Minh Trail than when the invasion began, but some of the trucks surely carried cargo needed to replace what had been consumed in the recent fighting.[23]

Although launched with a minimum of news coverage to preserve secrecy, Lam Son 719 ended under the scrutiny of the press and television. The U.S. public saw scenes that appeared to contradict the optimistic statements emanating from Saigon and Washington. For example, South Vietnamese soldiers, their weapons discarded, wandered listlessly down a road, and wounded men, their fresh bandages contrasting sharply with their dirty uniforms, lay in the open on stretchers or peered from inside rescue helicopters. In one filmed sequence, South Vietnamese soldiers clung to the landing skids of U.S. helicopters in the hope of reaching safety.[24] President Nixon complained that the pictures told "basically an inaccurate story" because they reflected the ordeal of the comparatively few battalions caught in an ambush, while ignoring those units that retreated in good order.[25] To the public, however, these battle scenes offered powerful evidence refuting the President's interpretation of the results.

The enemy could indeed view the operation as a military and psychological triumph, even though South Vietnamese troops had reached Tchepone. When its account of the campaign appeared later in the year, the Hanoi government boasted that the South Vietnamese offensive had "ended in complete fiasco, with the rout of the invading forces." The North Vietnamese ignored the hit-and-run raid on Tchepone and charged that in a "big trial of strength," provoked by South Vietnam, the "aggressor achieved none of his strategic objectives."[26]

The military assistance command had claimed that Lam Son 719, besides the physical damage it inflicted, had caused a "high degree of turbulence in the political, social, and economic life of NVN [North Vietnamese] civilians . . . ."[27] In fact, it was in South Vietnam rather than in the North that civilians, shaken by the bloodletting, began protesting the way their government waged war. Charging that the United States proposed to fight to the last South Vietnamese, students protested the lengthening casualty lists, and the anger spread to the ordinary citizens, who now tended to react violently to any incident, such as a traffic accident, that might somehow be the result of U.S. callousness or carelessness.[28]

Signs of war weariness in South Vietnam coincided with a renewal of antiwar demonstrations in the United States during the spring of 1971, although these protests represented a continuation of earlier activity and did not result directly from the South Vietnamese attack into Laos. Vietnam veterans opposed to the war converged on Washington in April; their representatives testified before various congressional committees, and some seven hundred of them left their medals and campaign ribbons in a heap on the capitol grounds. Antiwar veterans of the Vietnam fighting staged a similar protest in Boston and its suburbs. Other major antiwar rallies took place during April at Washington, where some two hundred thousand persons engaged in an orderly protest, and in San Francisco, where a splinter group, intent on involving the antiwar movement in broader social issues, disrupted a smaller demonstration.

A violent outburst against the Vietnam War shook the District of Columbia between May 3 and 5, when demonstrators tried to set up roadblocks, immobilize traffic, and paralyze the federal government. Police expelled an estimated thirty thousand persons from their encampment in one of the city's parks. Arrests during the three days totaled twelve thousand, but only two hundred persons were actually convicted of criminal acts. These antiwar riots not only failed to cripple the government, but may well have alienated those citizens who opposed the war, yet respected law and order. Whatever the reason, and lower draft quotas together with the continuing withdrawal of forces from South Vietnam clearly played a role, antiwar activity ebbed throughout the remainder of the year.[29]

Besides having a psychological impact in South Vietnam, if not in the United States, Lam Son 719 affected the conduct of Operation Commando Hunt V. Once the South Vietnamese divisions came under attack on the road to Tchepone, their predicament attracted aircraft that otherwise would have been flying interdiction missions against the Ho Chi Minh Trail. Prior to the South Vietnamese advance into Laos and the North Vietnamese counterattack, no more than 10 percent of the strike sorties in southern Laos supported ground units (usually Lao irregulars or Prairie Fire teams); the overwhelming share of the aerial effort pounded enemy supply lines. During the thrust to Tchepone, however, more than half the combat sorties flown in southern Laos attacked the North Vietnamese on or near the battlefield, while only 20 percent struck typical Commando Hunt targets.[30]

The advance westward from Khe Sanh also influenced sensor coverage, preventing the reseeding of certain route monitoring strings southwest of the demilitarized zone. Air Force F–4s succeeded, nevertheless, in maintaining existing strings north of the battlefield and also planted new ones in this area to detect the approach of armor, artillery, or truck-borne reinforcements. On the basis of data from these strings, Task Force Alpha issued target advisories to forward air controllers or gunships patrolling the South Vietnamese salient. East of the border, in northwestern South Vietnam, both the Army and Marine Corps set out sensor fields of their own to provide local security for major bases like recently reoccupied Khe Sanh and to locate targets for artillery. An Air Force deployable automatic relay terminal at Quang Tri monitored the Army strings, along with some of those set out by Task Force Alpha, passing the information thus acquired to an Army corps headquarters for further dissemination.[31]

Like Lam Son 719 and, to a lesser degree, Operations Silver Buckle and Desert Rat, the fighting in northern Laos, far from the Ho Chi Minh Trail, caused a diversion of aircraft that might otherwise have participated in Commando Hunt V. Late in February, Ambassador Godley urged that the Seventh Air Force utilize AC–119Ks to assist in the defense of Long Tien, where Gen. Vang Pao's mountain tribesmen faced defeat by the North Vietnamese. "I realize that under normal circumstances it would be wiser to use the AC–119s as truck killers," Godley told General Clay, the commander of the Seventh Air Force, "but during this emergency period I believe we must strike the python's teeth rather than his less dangerous parts." Despite the ambassador's lack of knowledge about snakes, the python being a constrictor, he correctly assessed the value of the AC–119s, which helped Vang Pao survive the threat and retain his hold on Long Tien.[32]

However much the AC–119K impressed the ambassador as a killer of trucks, it had never caused the kind of destruction attributed to the latest AC–130s, which had a more versatile array of sensors to find targets for their heavier 40-mm guns. As many as possible of the AC–130s patrolled the trail each night, but the squadrons flying the Spectres could not ignore routine maintenance, and from time to time an overhaul proved necessary. To prevent maintenance and repair from cutting into the most productive time for truck-killing—nights during the dry season—mechanics in the squadrons worked by day to ready the aircraft for patrols after dark, and depot maintenance, which required a flight to Clark Air Base in the Philippines and a stay of about seventy-five days, took place during the rainy months. Insofar as possible, half the AC–130s underwent inspection and repair at Clark Air Base during the southwest monsoon, so the other half would be available for the rainy season and the force would be at full strength when the roads dried and traffic intensified.[33]

Along with the AC–130, the Martin B–57G, radically modified for attacking trucks at night, saw extensive action during Commando Hunt V. A squadron of B–57Gs got credit for destroying not quite one truck for every hour spent patrolling the Ho Chi Minh Trail during the operation, or a total of 2,103 vehicles. Despite the impressive claims, the aircraft revealed deficiencies in both basic design and truck-killing equipment. Since this U.S. version of the British Canberra light bomber dated from the mid-1950s and the onset of the jet revolution, it used the inefficient engines of that time; in the hot and humid climate of Southeast Asia, which reduced lift, a fully loaded B–57G required a takeoff roll of eight thousand feet on runways nine thousand feet long. Moreover, the radar installed for tracking convoys did not have adequate range, and when the dry season ended, technicians removed the sets from the aircraft for shipment back to the United States, where Texas Instruments modified them.[34]

Any success achieved by the B–57G resulted mostly from its use of laser-guided bombs, weapons that also increased the deadliness of F–4 fighter-bombers against antiaircraft guns. Because laser designators were in comparatively short supply, Col. Larry M. Killpack, the commander of the 8th Tactical Fighter Wing, began sending laser-equipped F–4s, without bombs, on so-called White Lightning missions to patrol segments of the trail and illuminate targets for other F–4s, each carrying four of the guided bombs. As many as four of the bomb-laden Phantoms trailed the aircraft carrying the laser operator, who thus had up to sixteen guided bombs at his disposal.[35]

Besides attacking with laser-guided weapons, Killpack's wing planted the sensor strings for the Infiltration Surveillance Center. Dropping the electronic devices was becoming increasingly dangerous, for the mission required the pilot to fly straight and level at low altitude over areas protected by concentrations of antiaircraft guns. After two F–4s were shot down while delivering sensors for Commando Hunt V, forward air controllers stopped marking the center of each string with smoke; the crews of the F–4s delivering the sensors kept their radio chatter to a minimum and relied exclusively on loran, which did the work of the target marker and permitted operations even at night or in bad weather. These measures deprived enemy gunners of clues that had alerted them to imminent sensor drops. Nevertheless, during February the threat from antiaircraft batteries compelled the Seventh Air Force to suspend temporarily the planting of sensors within three and one-half miles of Ban Karai Pass, within eight miles of Mu Gia Pass, and in the vicinity of Tchepone. Moreover, the Seventh Air Force began insisting, as a general rule, that teams of two F–4s conduct sensor drops in the more dangerous areas; while one of the loran-equipped Phantoms planted the sensors, its escort "rode shotgun" in the event enemy gunners opened fire.[36]

Had it not been for Lam Son 719, the antiaircraft defenses guarding the trail might have been even more formidable in the closing months of the dry season. When the North Vietnamese realized how much the advance into Laos depended on aircraft for mobility, supply, and combat support, they shifted to the battlefield an estimated nineteen antiaircraft units, totaling perhaps 150 guns of various calibers. Much of this concentration came from segments of the Ho Chi Minh Trail elsewhere in southern Laos. Because of the transfer of weapons to defend the eastern approach to Tchepone over which the South Vietnamese were advancing, some 650 guns of all calibers guarded the Ho Chi Minh Trail when Commando Hunt V ended, roughly a hundred fewer than when Commando Hunt III came to a close a year earlier. Lam Son 719 attracted U.S. sorties as well as enemy guns and to some extent shifted the focus of the air battle; partly as a result of this reorientation—though aggressive flak suppression must also have made a contribution—antiaircraft fire downed only eleven aircraft over the trail, compared to sixty in the previous dry season.[37]

During Commando Hunt V, gunners and missile crews in North Vietnam fired on U.S. aircraft over southern Laos or on unarmed reconnaissance missions over the North. In such instances, the rules of engagement permitted air strikes to punish those who had actually fired and to discourage similar actions in the future. On November 21, 1970, after 23-mm fire downed an unarmed reconnaissance plane flying over Route 15 in southern North Vietnam, retaliatory air strikes hit missile sites, antiaircraft batteries, and oil storage tanks in the area, along with choke points on roads leading westward toward the mountain passes. Because of bad weather, which also hampered damage assessment, only about half the 431 planned sorties actually attacked their assigned targets.

Throughout December, the second month of Commando Hunt V, the enemy deployed surface-to-air missiles on the North Vietnamese side of the Laotian border. Three times during the month, missile crews fired unsuccessfully at aircraft flying just west of Mu Gia and Ban Karai Passes, and on January 1 a volley of three missiles missed a cell of B–52s dropping bombs in southeastern Laos. The Seventh Air Force responded with intensified aerial reconnaissance, as RF–4s and their armed escorts sought out the missile sites, but adverse weather interfered. Not until February 20, 21, and 28 did the Seventh Air Force retaliate against the missile sites in the southwestern corner of North Vietnam. Even then the weather proved bad and results poor; a total of sixty-seven attack sorties produced claims of five missiles destroyed, along with fifteen missile transporters, and fourteen miscellaneous vehicles.

North Vietnam's response to Lam Son 719 led to the final protective reaction raids launched against the North during Commando Hunt V. Missile batteries inside North Vietnam engaged aircraft supporting the South Vietnamese attack westward from Khe Sanh, shooting down an Australian Canberra bomber near the western edge of the demilitarized zone, damaging an F–4 near Tchepone, and missing a cell of three B–52s west of Ban Raving Pass. On March 21 and 22, as the battered South Vietnamese task force finally extricated itself from Laos, 264 retaliatory sorties hit a variety of targets in southwestern North Vietnam. Considering the larger number of sorties, this last effort at retaliation during the northeast monsoon season produced results no better than those achieved by the February raids—eight missiles reported destroyed, along with two missile transporters, one radar, six support vans, sixty-four buildings, and forty-five trucks.[38]

Despite the retaliatory attacks, surface-to-air missiles continued to pose a threat in the vicinity of the passes. On the night of April 27, at the very end of Commando Hunt V, 1st Lt. Gregory A. Miller was piloting his O–2A at an altitude of seven thousand feet over the heavily traveled roads just south of Mu Gia Pass, when his observer saw what looked like flares low in the sky behind them. Miller changed direction to investigate, for no other forward air controller should have been dropping flares in this sector at the time, and discovered that the bright lights were not flares but burning propellant from a pair of missiles launched somewhere east of the pass and streaking toward the airplane. The pilot broke sharply to the left and almost got away, but at least one of the warheads exploded, driving a hail of fragments into the rear of the O–2 and flipping it upside down.

Miller righted the plane and turned to his observer, whom he found to be unconscious and bleeding from a facial cut. Indeed, both men might have been killed instantly if the pusher engine had not stopped most of the missile fragments that would otherwise have torn into the cabin. The aircraft sustained crippling damage—besides knocking out the rear engine, the explosion damaged the two booms that supported the tail and ripped away a piece of the wing—but the tractor engine still worked, though it could not keep the plane in the air for long. Luckily, the observer regained consciousness as Miller headed west, away from the heavily defended road net and both men managed to parachute into the darkness. The observer landed in a tree on a limestone outcropping that rose some 250 feet above a grassy plateau, Miller came down near the base of the same karst formation and found cover in a nearby ravine. After daybreak a rescue team from the 56th Special Operations Wing picked up both crew members. The observer experienced some uneasy moments when downwash from the main rotor of a hovering helicopter blew him out of the tree onto a narrow ledge, but this merely caused a momentary delay in his rescue.[39]

Besides sharpening his defenses, including the deployment of surface-to-air missiles like those that shot down Miller and his observer, the enemy also expanded his road system. Photographs taken in the vicinity of Muong May, for instance, disclosed a new bypass leading from the junction of Routes 96 and 110 west-southwest toward the Cambodian border. Finding this cutoff led to the discovery of other road building activity in the area along the Kaman River, a tributary of the Kong.[40] Elsewhere the pattern of sensor activation indicated possible construction along the road net carrying traffic generally southward from Mu Gia Pass, and forward air controllers patrolling in daylight spotted a heavily traveled bypass along Route 237, though much of the new road remained hidden by the jungle canopy.[41] In addition, the North Vietnamese 95th Engineer Battalion was building a new highway in South Vietnam to ease congestion in storage areas west of the A Shau Valley. The continuing expansion of the logistic complex, by now a matter of routine, included a new spur of the Ho Chi Minh Trail to channel men and material into northeastern Cambodia.[42]

When Commando Hunt V ended, intelligence analysts at Task Force Alpha, using sensor data and other information, estimated that the transportation net in southern Laos consisted at any given time of fifteen sectors operating a total of about 3,375 trucks. Each night between 50 and 60 percent of these vehicles took to the road. With the approach of daylight, however, traffic came almost to a standstill, as the trucks took cover, a few at a time, among an estimated five thousand truck parks, storage areas, and transshipment points scattered throughout the web of highways.[43]

Along the length of the Ho Chi Minh Trail, or so the evidence indicated, the truck route for cargo functioned independently of a system of trails and waterways used for troop infiltration. Indeed, one defector reported that his group of about three hundred men marched and traveled by boat from the vicinity of Attopeu, down the Mekong, and deep into Cambodia without once seeing a tire track, let alone a truck. Although Seventh Air Force planners as yet knew little about the routes followed by the infiltrating troops, they could safely assume that the web of trails underwent continuous improvement and expansion, just like the roads.[44]

In spite of new road construction, improved defenses, and the diversion of aircraft caused by Lam Son 719, Commando Hunt V appeared to be a singularly successful campaign. General Momyer, when reviewing the results of the campaign a few years later, expressed the judgment that, during the northeast monsoon months of 1970–71, "only about a quarter" of what entered the Ho Chi Minh Trail "found its way to the troops in South Vietnam." He also pointed to the absence of hostile activity in South Vietnam throughout the spring of 1971, which he considered conclusive proof that aerial interdiction had succeeded. "The measure of the effectiveness of the . . . campaign," he declared, "is reflected in the lack of a concentrated enemy assault at a time when we were most vulnerable, with the withdrawal of U.S. troops and the transition to complete responsibility for the ground war by the ARVN [Army of the Republic of Vietnam]."[45]

General Momyer's estimate that roughly 25 percent of the supplies entering Laos actually reached the battlefield contradicted the assessments made immediately after Commando Hunt V. Initially, the Seventh Air Force had reported that some seventy-seven thousand combat and reconnaissance sorties by all types of aircraft from the Air Force, Navy, and Marine Corps had destroyed, or forced the enemy to expend, all but 11.7 percent of the 60,158 tons of cargo that entered Laos during the northeast monsoon season that began in the fall of 1970.[46] Momyer, with the benefit of hindsight, also rejected the claim, advanced in 1971 by the Seventh Air Force, that air power had destroyed or damaged 20,926 trucks in the course of Commando Hunt V.[47] It was "very difficult," said the general, "to reach a good basis for assessment of damage to the enemy truck inventory, especially when claims were exceeding the total truck inventory by a factor of two at times."[48]

As though anticipating Momyer, who looked in retrospect at the problem of verifying truck kills, the Seventh Air Force staff had addressed this question during Commando Hunt V. Clearly, the operations analysts needed some means of checking claims, for even then the suspicion existed that, in the words of the commander of a special operations unit, "The FACs are telling commanders what they want to hear, not what actually is happening."[49] In order to document at least some claims of trucks destroyed, AC–130 crews tried to make videotapes of the pictures acquired by either the low-light-level television or the infrared sensor. Since this type of aircraft received credit for 12,741 vehicles destroyed or damaged, evidence of this sort would by inference have provided a clear insight into the entire campaign. Unfortunately, fires and exploding ordnance tended to blind both television cameras and infrared equipment, so that photo interpreters examining the tapes could verify no more than half the reported hits on trucks, and a hit need not result in the vehicle's destruction.[50]

Despite the nagging question of verification, the emphasis on destroying vehicles and the cargo they carried persisted from late 1968, when systematic aerial interdiction got under way in southern Laos, through Commando Hunt V in the spring of 1971. In the opinion of Lt. Col. Vaughn H. Gallacher, who served in the tactical air control center of the Seventh/Thirteenth Air Force, the soaring toll of trucks destroyed meant nothing. Looking back on the early months of 1971, when claims of trucks killed approached ten thousand, with a similar number damaged, he characterized the numbers as "impossible to prove" and "highly suspect."[51] In sharp contrast to Gallacher, Col. William H. Fairbrother, who commanded a special operations wing, accepted the truck kills at face value. "You know," he conceded, "people have said, 'I don't believe they could kill that many trucks,'" but regardless of what they might say, he insisted that he could "tell you for sure that the ones we claimed were in fact destroyed, because . . . if the thing didn't blow or burn, . . . it wasn't a kill."[52] Thus did the claims that aroused skepticism in one officer seem thoroughly believable to another.

Like the Air Force, the Office of Secretary of Defense tried to evaluate the effect of aerial interdiction, which had become a war on trucks. A Department of Defense review group, however, could conclude only that since 1965 interdiction had succeeded in destroying supplies and delaying deliveries. The exact amounts destroyed and the length of the delays defied accurate measurement, as did the effect of all this on the enemy. On the one hand, a chronic shortage of supplies could have forced the North Vietnamese to husband their resources and after the Tet offensive of 1968, avoid decisive combat in South Vietnam. On the other hand, they might have amassed adequate stockpiles, but deliberately postponed the next offensive, maintaining pressure as the United States departed, but awaiting completion of the withdrawal and the opportunity to overwhelm the Vietnamized defenders. Although unable to produce definitive answers to these basic questions, the panel nevertheless concluded that aerial interdiction of the Ho Chi Minh Trail should continue, with the South Vietnamese, at some appropriate time in the future, relieving the United States of responsibility.[53]

The architects of the Commando Hunt series deferred action on using Task Force Alpha and its sensors to impede troop infiltration, as the Jason Summer Study had proposed it its original study of the barrier concept. Attacks on infiltrating personnel would have to await improved monitoring devices and more precise knowledge of the routes the enemy soldiers followed. Although the standard seismic sensors could pick up vibrations caused by men walking, the effective range under ideal conditions did not exceed 165 feet, a distance reduced by as much as 40 percent in the rain forest. The commandable microphone, however, gave promise of being able to maintain surveillance, provided that intelligence could somehow pinpoint the trails followed by the enemy.[54] While preparations went ahead for a campaign against infiltrators, to be fought in conjunction with the war on trucks, another element of the Ho Chi Minh Trail came under attack, the waterways and pipelines of southern Laos, targets that had proved almost as difficult to find and hit as the troop infiltration routes.

Leaders. Lyndon Johnson (top left), President, 1963–1968; Robert McNamara (top right), Secretary of Defense, 1961–1967; Richard Nixon (center left), President, 1969–1975; Melvin Laird (center right), Secretary of Defense, 1969–1973; Henry Kissinger (opposite), National Security Adviser, 1969–1973, Secretary of State, 1973–1977.

162

Souvanna Phouma (top left), Prime
Minister of Laos, 1962–1975; Ho Chi
Minh (top right), President of North
Vietnam, 1954–1969; Ngo Dinh Diem
(center left), Prime Minister of South
Vietnam, 1954–1955, President of
South Vietnam, 1955–1963; Nguyen
Van Thieu (center right), Chief of
State of South Vietnam, 1965–1967,
President of South Vietnam,
1967–1975; Norodom Sihanouk
(opposite), Head of State of
Cambodia, 1960–1970.

Seventh Air Force Commanders.
William H. Momyer (top left), July 1,
1966–July 31, 1968; George S. Brown
(top right), August 1, 1968–August 31,
1970 (Air Force Chief of Staff, August 1,
1973–June 30, 1974); Lucius D. Clay, Jr.
(center left), September 1, 1970–July 31,
1971; John D. Lavelle (center right),
August 1, 1971–April 6, 1972; John W.
Vogt, Jr. (opposite), April 7, 1972–
September 30, 1973.

Cambodian Incursion. Bags of rice (top) and crates of ammunition (center) captured in Cambodia. Lon Nol speaks with Cambodian troops in the field (left).

Below. A Soviet trawler viewed from a U.S. ship in the Tonkin Gulf.

Lam Son 719. A U.S. Army helicopter lands at Khe Sanh, South Vietnam, March 5, 1971 (top); South Vietnamese soldiers walk on a trail in Laos (center); a South Vietnamese column on the Ho Chi Minh Trail in Laos (bottom).

166

Chapter Ten

Waterways and Pipelines

When shipping supplies through southern Laos, the North Vietnamese did not depend exclusively on roads. Although truck routes carried most of the cargo and received the greatest share of the U.S. firepower unleashed in Laos, the enemy had other means to help sustain his forces in South Vietnam and the Khmer Rouge in Cambodia. Waterways provided a more primitive alternative; petroleum pipelines, which snaked through the mountain passes leading from North Vietnam into Laos, afforded one that was more advanced. Waterways and pipelines proved almost invulnerable to air attack, since both river traffic and the pipelines themselves were inherently difficult targets to find and bomb or strafe in a mountainous, jungle-covered region bristling with antiaircraft guns. Indeed, in late November 1970, Col. Charles M. Morrison, chief of the fighter division of the Seventh Air Force staff, described the road-pipeline-river complex northeast of Tchepone as "the most heavily defended area in Laos."[1]

The North Vietnamese already used rivers to supplement roads when the Commando Hunt series began in 1968. Two years earlier, Ambassador Sullivan allowed the Tiger Hound task force to attack barges and other cargo-carrying river craft, provided that a forward air controller directed the strike. Evidence of further reliance on river transportation came in February 1967, when aerial photographs disclosed fuel drums bobbing down the Kong south of Ban Bak, following a channel created by a combination of stone dikes that hugged the shore generally parallel to the current and jetties that extended diagonally into the stream. This early experience on the rivers of southern Laos, plus similar experiments along the Ou River, far to the north, taught the enemy how to channel the flow of streams and use them to supplement the road net of the Ho Chi Minh Trail for the transportation of cargo.[2]

Systematic use of newly channeled waterways in southern Laos began on the Kong River in late 1967, and within three years, streams tamed by dikes and jetties—both structures loosely described as channeling dams—carried a large volume of cargo during the southwest monsoon season, thus ensuring the year-round delivery of supplies and to some extent easing the burden on overworked road-maintenance crews who could now schedule some of their projects in the dry season. As the waterways carried more cargo, dry-season highway traffic declined somewhat in importance, enabling the engineers to close a road briefly, even though the northeast monsoon continued to blow. Construction crews might, for example, use the time to corduroy a flood-prone roadway, placing logs lengthwise across the right of way so the section could carry traffic well into the rainy months. Despite the flexibility that use of the rivers provided by permitting the delivery of supplies throughout the year, the operators of the Ho Chi Minh Trail tended to schedule major construction for the rainy months, when the waterways operated at peak efficiency and the downpour interfered with highway traffic.[3]

Applying lessons learned during 1966 and 1967 on the Ou and the Kong, the 559th Transportation Group came to rely on the Banghiang River to carry much of the waterborne cargo entering southern Laos. The stream's tributaries crossed the demilitarized zone, and the river itself flowed southwest past the supply depots near Tchepone and Muong Phine before eventually reaching the Mekong. Between the demilitarized zone and Tchepone, a straight-line distance of roughly thirty miles, the river threaded its way through a maze of roads and bypasses, offering an alternate route through a heavily bombed region.

As the North Vietnamese learned progressively more about shipping cargo by river, they incorporated certain refinements into Waterway VII, their name for this stretch of the Banghiang. For example, instead of relying exclusively on stone dikes or jetties to direct the current, the North Vietnamese sometimes drove bamboo poles into the water to form walls that served the purpose, and the comparatively smooth bamboo did not damage barrels or other containers as it kept the floating cargo in deep water. Depending on the velocity of the current, the firmness of the banks, and the availability of materials, engineers might use either bamboo, stone, or ballasted metal drums for the structures that helped direct the current, prevent erosion, and maintain deep water in the main channel. Channeling dams of various materials also appeared on the larger creeks that fed the Banghiang, so that the 559th Transportation Group could launch supplies from dumps hidden some distance from the river itself. By opening bamboo watergates or breaching temporary earthen dams on these tributaries, the North Vietnamese could release the water behind the barriers and temporarily increase the depth and current of streams throughout the drainage basin.[4]

After being launched, perhaps by the opening of a floodgate on some nameless and uncharted creek, the drums and watertight bags had to reach a specific destination for transfer to trucks, pack animals, or porters. To control river traffic, the transportation group scattered monitoring stations an average of one-half mile apart all along the waterway. At some of these posts, a river watcher merely reported on the flow of cargo, but at most of them, the monitor could pole his way out on a raft, break up any jams that might stop traffic, and thus remove a potential target for patrolling aircraft.[5] To supplement the work of the monitoring stations in controlling the passage of supplies, the enemy sometimes sent along an innocent-looking boat to guide the containers past obstacles. Of course, he avoided using a motorboat, rare in southern Laos and certain to attract bombs or gunfire. The operators of the waterway also could keep barrels and bundles from drifting out of the channel by attaching a piece of cloth, resembling a miniature parachute, that caught the current and pulled the container along.[6]

At an average interval of two miles, the enemy built transshipment points to move cargo from the river to some other form of transportation, taking advantage of existing inlets or digging new ones, sometimes using nets or booms to divert containers from the channel. A short distance inland of the bank, he built bunkers capable of storing as much as thirty tons of cargo. If the forest proved too thin, lattice-work camouflage reinforced nature in hiding the inlet and the storage area.[7]

The use of Waterway VII increased during 1969 until it became a key element in the transportation system, supplementing the road net. The local defenses reflected the importance of the Banghiang and the highway complex—Routes 103, 91, and 92—through which it passed. By the summer of 1970, some twenty-five to thirty 37-mm guns, eight to twelve 23-mm sites, and both heavy and light machine guns defended the river and roads. Throughout 1971 and for as long as aerial interdiction continued in 1972, weapons like these fired at aircraft attacking almost anywhere along the Banghiang, from the demilitarized zone to Tchepone, and also helped protect the main roads in the region.[8]

The guns mounted around Waterway VII proved so formidable that U.S. planners groped for an alternative to aerial interdiction that would not expose aircraft and their crews to hostile fire. The discussions generated some unusual suggestions, among them a scheme for pouring into the river chemicals that would corrode fuel drums and eat away plastic bags. The idea perished in the planning stage, however, once hasty calculations revealed the impossibility of hauling so vast a quantity of corrosives to the river bank and dumping it in. Another proposal involved duplicating the barrels used by the enemy, then filling them with either explosives to inflict casualties or contaminated fuel to ruin truck motors, but before these phony containers could be built, a sample of the real thing had to be captured.[9]

Because of the strong defenses guarding overland approaches to the waterway, General Abrams decided against sending a patrol to seize one of the drums, but examples came into U.S. hands quite by accident. Some friendly villagers fished a barrel from the Banghiang and gave it to a Central Intelligence Agency reconnaissance team that brought it to Vientiane. Meanwhile, the Military Assistance Command acquired thirty-three of the containers, probably released from an enemy junk to drift ashore near Chu Lai in northern South Vietnam.[10] Even though actual drums could now serve as models, two flaws doomed the plan to build and launch the imitations: first, only a massive amount of contaminated fuel or high explosive could disrupt the logistic system; and second, patrols burdened by the required number of barrels could never penetrate North Vietnamese security and reach the waterway to float their loads downstream.[11]

After these proposals for clandestine action had faded away, General Abrams turned to a more direct kind of activity, aerial bombardment. Both tactical aircraft and B–52s attacked the stoutly defended waterway complex. Crews, even of low-flying fighter-bombers, had little success in detecting objects that floated almost flush with the river's surface, but with the help of aerial photographs, they could locate and bomb the jetties that projected into the Banghiang. Consequently, beginning in July 1970, tactical fighters concentrated on these structures, which proved difficult to destroy because of their small size and simple construction. U.S. pilots kept trying, however, dropping five hundred pound or two thousand pound bombs, some of them with delayed action fuzes. During the summer of 1970, air crews reported the destruction of 54 of the 140 channeling dams built between the demilitarized zone and Tchepone, but reconnaissance disclosed that the enemy had repaired all of them before the dry season began in November.[12] Damage to the jetties temporarily enhanced the effectiveness of cluster bomb units against river traffic, for as the current slowed and the water level declined, the containers tended to run aground. Whenever a pilot saw the stationary barrels or boxes, he could drop cluster bombs with deadly effect, since fragments from the individual bomblets easily shredded the watertight containers.[13]

Unfortunately, the effectiveness of fragmentation bomblets, which weighed less than a pound, but were scattered hundreds at a time, depended on two factors: sluggish and shallow water, which was caused by damage to channeling dams, structures that the enemy easily repaired, and the absence of overhead foliage that concealed the containers and could prematurely detonate at least some of the bomblets. Where the current ran swift and deep or jungle concealed the watercourse, fighter-bombers tried dropping five hundred pound mines that lay on the river bed, exploding when a floating metal object disturbed the magnetic-influence fuze. Although deadly against the few metal-hulled boats used in southern Laos, the fuze did not react to the small quantity of steel in a drum. Indeed, clusters of metal containers, drifting slowly downstream, might sometimes pass over a mine without triggering an explosion. Enough of the mines detonated, however, to compel the enemy to meet the threat by wrapping chains around logs floated ahead of the supply containers. The chains rarely failed to trigger the magnetic fuze, and the procedure was far safer than trying to clear the mines with either explosives or electrical current.[14]

The presence of villages and prisoner-of-war camps, which prevented the bombing of the surrounding areas, impeded the campaign against Waterway VII. B–52s, for example, could not simply saturate the waterways with high explosives, although these aircraft had permission to attack certain previously cleared target boxes that included segments of the Banghiang, as well as storage areas and transshipment points for both road and river cargo. From the beginning of February until the end of August 1970, the big bombers conducted 566 sorties against logistic targets directly or indirectly related to Waterway VII, while tactical aircraft and gunships flew more than 5,000 missions of the same kind. Crew members involved in the sustained attacks reported 2,796 secondary explosions and 1,882 secondary fires. Seventh Air Force intelligence analysts credited the strikes with destroying almost one thousand drums of fuel, plus other supplies, and reducing the estimated volume of river traffic below the normal forty tons per day.[15]

Although the damage claims lacked verification, Waterway VII and its related storage and cargo handling areas did receive a severe aerial battering during the wet season of 1970. Throughout September and October, as the rains tapered off, the 559th Transportation Group, using North Vietnamese engineers and locally recruited laborers, repaired or built roads and fords, storage facilities, and cargo transfer points and thus increased the volume of river traffic despite the approach of the dry season. As the rains came to an end, the new construction resulted in a smooth transition from rivers supplemented by roads to roads supplemented by rivers. Once drier weather enabled the trucks to resume their preeminence, the enemy prepared for the next rainy season along the Banghiang and its tributaries by replacing or installing watergates, dikes and jetties, and the cables or nets used to retrieve supplies.[16]

For the remainder of the war, Waterway VII continued to be a valuable link in the transportation complex that supplied and reinforced units fighting in South Vietnam or Cambodia. As Colonel Morrison, the Seventh Air Force staff officer, pointed out, the Banghiang provided one of several alternate means of moving supplies, but he found this fact "a hard thing to get across to people, they are so truck oriented." If bombing blocked one road, the enemy used another, shifted to porters or pack trains, or increased river traffic; if air attacks impeded the waterway, he routed the cargo by land.[17]

In the meantime, the North Vietnamese converted the Kong River, used to distribute cargo since 1967, into a second major waterway in southern Laos, this one flowing from the South Vietnamese border generally southward past the burgeoning transportation center of Ban Bak into Cambodia. Near Ban Bak, just a short distance from the Kong, the main highway through Ban Raving Pass intersected with roads and trails that led directly to the A Shau Valley of South Vietnam, to other road junctions near Chavane and Muong May in Laos, or to northern Cambodia and west-central South Vietnam. The increasing use of the Kong River, and the existence of highways nearby, caused the North Vietnamese to strengthen the antiaircraft defenses as they had done along the other waterway. Development of the second stream and its tributaries as a supply thoroughfare coincided with the refurbishment of the Banghiang after the 1970 rainy season, so that by December of that year both were important arteries. To handle the heavy volume of river traffic on them, the 559th Transportation Group built new storage and transshipment facilities, sometimes using rafts to shuttle cargo among them.

The growing traffic on the Kong River enhanced the value of Ban Bak in routing and transferring cargo and persuaded the enemy to set up more antiaircraft batteries in the area and to construct underground storage bunkers. This activity caught the eye of Air Force photo interpreters, with the result that fighter-bombers pounded a cluster of new bunkers northwest of Ban Bak. During a sustained attack, which lasted from December 19, 1970, until January 15, 1971, crewmen reported seeing an astonishing ten thousand secondary explosions and fires, despite clouds and bursting antiaircraft shells. This count, of course, lacked verification, and even if reliable, the nature and quantity of the supplies destroyed remained unknown.[18] Despite apparently damaging attacks like these, the enemy made extensive use of both waterways until April 1971, when the 1970–71 dry season entered its final weeks and water levels fell too low to permit the passage of floating containers. Along the Kong River, the North Vietnamese at times defied aircraft patrolling the night skies and used lights to speed the handling of supplies.[19]

The basic structure of the Banghiang and Kong waterways changed very little during roughly three years of systematic operation. Troops from the 559th Transportation Group gathered sealed containers behind a temporary earthen dam or watergate on some tributary of either river, breached the dam or opened the gate, and launched the cargo on a freshet that carried it into the larger stream. Supplies usually began their journey at dusk and floated an average of about ten miles every twenty-four hours, drifting past dikes, jetties, and the usual monitoring stations until caught in nets or diverted by cables at a particular transshipment point or storage area.

Although the mechanics of waterborne supply stayed much the same, responsiveness of the waterways to the needs of troops in the field improved markedly. At first, the transportation group planned its deliveries on the basis of the estimated requirements of combat and support units and launched the volume and variety of cargo that group headquarters believed necessary. Downstream, the intended recipients retrieved the containers, storing the material for subsequent distribution as actually needed to sustain combat. By mid-1971, however, the network of river monitors and cargo handlers had become skilled enough to fill requisitions. Units in the field could request that the transportation group float specific items and amounts to a particular destination, where a team plucked the cargo from the water, transferred it as necessary to trucks, pack animals, or porters, and sent it directly to the organization that had asked for it.[20]

Despite thunderous explosions reported at various times by aircrews, mainly during attacks on supply dumps, the waterways themselves proved almost indestructible. Air Force gunships, for instance, had no sensors expressly for detecting floating containers, and cargo drifting with the current did not cause sound or seismic vibrations to trigger Igloo White surveillance devices. As a result, planners shifted from bombing river traffic to attacking storage areas, which seemed far more vulnerable on the basis of reported results. Targeting became a matter of choosing appropriate interdiction boxes, which served primarily to impede truck traffic along the Ho Chi Minh Trail, but also included the waterways and their satellite facilities. When the dry season began in the summer of 1971, Seventh Air Force target planners incorporated most cargo transfer and storage areas along both waterways, except for those too close to prisoner-of-war camps or villages, into the category of "logistic area targets," which also embraced truck parks and other components of the nearby road net.[21]

Improvement of the waterways in southern Laos coincided with the construction of fuel pipelines. Although President Johnson suspended bombing north of the

19th parallel effective April 1, 1968, the North Vietnamese decided to reduce the volume of petroleum products imported through Haiphong, now exempt from air attack, and began bringing fuel and lubricants through Vinh, a port city in the panhandle of North Vietnam that afforded more direct access to the Ho Chi Minh Trail in Laos. U.S. aircraft could attack the port facilities at Vinh, but not the foreign ships using them. Tankers drawing as much as fourteen feet moored at Vinh's docks, while larger ships anchored at the mouth of the Ca River, which flowed past the town, and pumped their cargo into small craft that ferried the fuel ashore. The North Vietnamese also expanded the nearby petroleum storage area, building new tanks, some of them underground.[22]

Aerial photographs taken in July 1968 revealed construction crews at work on a pair of pipelines that extended westward from the enlarged Vinh tank farm, passed on either side of the town's citadel, and met a north-south line being built along Route 15 in the direction of Mu Gia Pass. Air attacks hampered the project until November 1, when President Johnson halted the bombing throughout all of North Vietnam. Aerial reconnaissance continued, however, and revealed that work leapt forward once the threat of air strikes had ended.[23]

The pipeline from Vinh along the Route 15 corridor entered Laos early in 1969, but came to a halt just fifteen and one-half miles beyond Mu Gia Pass. Photo interpreters spotted this extension because the enemy had dug long trenches to accommodate sections of pipe, thus disturbing natural ground contours and vegetation patterns. During the summer, intelligence analysts, and the forward air controllers who directed attacks in this part of Laos, detected evidence of pipeline construction, including trucks loaded with lengths of pipe, as far south as Muong Nong in Laos and along the Laotian approaches to the A Shau Valley. In September 1969, aircraft of the 460th Tactical Reconnaissance Group photographed a petroleum storage area near Ban Na, twenty-two miles northwest of Tchepone, where laborers assigned to the 559th Transportation Group were filling fifty-five-gallon drums for further distribution in Laos and South Vietnam.[24]

Roadwatch teams of the Central Intelligence Agency helped gather information on pipeline construction in Laos. These units took photographs of unguarded sections of the line near the terminus of the first segment to enter Laos, not far from Mu Gia Pass, and even managed to cut out a piece where two lengths of tubing met within a bolted sleeve. The men who cut the pipe could not estimate the capacity of the line, although they reported that a lot of gasoline spilled onto the ground. The sample of pipe, which originated in the Soviet Union, revealed that the conduit itself was made of lightweight plastic four inches in diameter with walls one-eighth inch thick. From this information analysts could calculate the capacity of the line, but not the times of use and the actual volume and kinds of liquids it carried.

Reconnaissance patrols made several subsequent visits to the pipeline, charting portions that could not be photographed from the air and examining the pumps that kept the petroleum flowing. As additional information became available, U.S. intelligence concluded that North Vietnamese engineers were using two kinds of plastic tubing. Besides the usual rigid type, they employed a flexible variety to go over or around limestone outcroppings or similar obstacles. To frustrate aerial cameras, they crossed streams by snaking flexible pipe along the river bottom instead of mounting the rigid kind on piers above the surface of the water.[25] Like the pipe and the fittings, the pumps came from the Soviet Union. The interval between pumping stations depended on the terrain over which the fuel had to travel. Where the ground was generally level, pumps operated about half a mile apart, compared to as little as 165 feet in rugged terrain. The Soviet Union also supplied the valves that regulated the rate of flow and diverted petroleum from one line to another.[26]

The evidence indicated that motor oil, diesel fuel, gasoline, and kerosene flowed through the same pipe. To prevent contamination, operators cleansed the conduit whenever they shifted from one petroleum product to another. The crew at one pumping station shut down, then inserted thirty to thirty-five linear feet of water, sometimes mixed with detergent, and alerted another station down the line. Technicians at this second location watched for the water, which they dumped on the ground; after the pipe had thus been cleansed, the next consignment of fuel began its journey.[27]

The number of pipelines entering Laos increased to six during 1970. By the end of the year, three lines pumped fuel through Mu Gia Pass, serving all truck parks and other installations centered around Ban Phanop. Ban Raving Pass carried a fourth pipeline that paralleled the Banghiang waterway, terminating at a distribution point northeast of Tchepone. From this installation, branches extended beyond the town, apparently leading to a fifth line that linked the Ban Som Peng area of Laos with Lao Bao Pass on the South Vietnamese border. Still another pipeline, the sixth, led southwestward from Ban Karai Pass, apparently tying into a branch of the Ban Som Peng–Lao Bao Pass line that approached the A Shau Valley. Because of dense jungle, aerial photographs could pinpoint only short segments of the pipeline complex, and from these fragments intelligence specialists tried to piece together the entire network.[28]

In addition to collecting information on the pipeline, Central Intelligence Agency teams sometimes blew up pumps or slashed the pipe. On one occasion in the spring of 1969, a team member dove to the bottom of a stream and cut the flexible plastic tube part way through. No sudden loss of pressure alerted the pipeline operators, who reacted slowly, allowing gasoline to leak into the river, while water contaminated the fuel that traveled beyond the break.[29]

The idea of contaminating, on a large scale, the fuel coursing through the pipelines seemed worth pursuing, until the proposal underwent detailed evaluation. Intelligence specialists concluded that to foul the engines of trucks using the fuel would require six thousand pounds of contaminant, such as sugar or molasses, for every fifty thousand gallons of gasoline or diesel oil. For such an undertaking, declared Capt. Daniel A. Adair, an Air Force intelligence officer serving in Thailand, "you would have to transport about two chopper [helicopter] loads of contaminant, plus troops to make the insertion into the pipe, plus troops to protect them . . . ." A helicopter armada of this sort could not help but alert the enemy. Adair therefore believed that "continued interdiction of the pipeline by ground teams, by air strikes, by smart bombs, by some overt military activity rather than by clandestine contamination would continue to be the answer."[30]

Air attacks on the various components of the pipeline complex began in 1969 and continued into 1972, though with little success. Experience soon taught that a single strike by tactical aircraft or even B–52s could not cut the line for longer than eighteen hours. Sustained bombing proved more effective, of course, but weather and the need to hit other targets prevented unceasing air attacks, and when a respite came, the engineers who maintained the line could repair even the worst damage in no more than three weeks.[31]

Simply to harass the enemy, rather than to disable the pipeline, the Seventh Air Force directed forward air controllers to instruct any aircraft, about to return to base after attacking targets in the vicinity, to exhaust its remaining ammunition strafing sections of pipe visible from the air. Whether firing off leftover 20-mm shells or dropping bombs, airmen faced a problem summarized by Colonel Morrison, the chief of the fighter division at Seventh Air Force headquarters, who pointed out that the line itself was "usually overgrown," and then asked: "Even if you could see it, how do you hit a four-inch pipe?"[32] Because the pipe itself proved so difficult to cut from the air, planners tried dispatching tactical aircraft against the pumping stations and fuel dumps and also using B–52s to hit target boxes that embraced these installations. Unfortunately, the petroleum stockpiles, often hidden in limestone caves, and the carefully camouflaged pumps proved almost as hard to locate and destroy as the pipeline itself.[33]

In attacking fuel pipelines or river traffic, Colonel Morrison believed that the United States was using "over-sophisticated methods" against "elemental systems." He preferred that infiltrating ground teams sever the pipeline. If enemy patrols prevented ground probes, he advocated the use of B–52s to bomb target boxes superimposed on known fuel dumps, on other segments of the fuel distribution network, and on the waterways complex. Since precision strikes had proved all but impossible, saturation bombing seemed the only answer.[34]

In spite of the difficulties in bombing accurately, attacking aircraft sometimes achieved spectacular results. In September 1969, for instance, a forward air controller thought he spotted a pumping station and called on a pair of A–1s, one of them piloted by Lt. Col. John M. Cargo, to attack the site. The bombs touched off a series of explosions that sent smoke towering some five thousand feet into the air, evidence that the North Vietnamese had stored petroleum there.[35]

Although seldom this successful, attacks on pipelines and pumping stations did force the enemy to take countermeasures. At river crossings, where low water might expose the pipe to an aerial camera, he built alternate lines some distance apart to carry the petroleum should the main segment come under attack. Throughout the entire pipeline complex, he anticipated breaks by installing valves to divert oil into storage dumps hidden not far from the lines. His troops, many of them from the

592d Pipelaying Regiment, became adept at building storage facilities and alternate lines, replacing damaged pumps, repairing broken tubing, and camouflaging their handiwork. The pipeline operators also obtained Soviet-built portable pumps, which could be moved by truck from a damaged line to an alternate.[36]

In June 1972, after the last Commando Hunt operation had ended, Admiral McCain, Commander in Chief, Pacific, acknowledged that "previous . . . experience with the North Vietnamese pipeline system in Laos has shown it to be a very difficult interdiction target." The pipe could be cut, but repairs were "made quickly with the minimum loss of POL [petroleum, oil and lubricants] and pumping time." As was true of the waterways, storage facilities formed the most vulnerable component of the petroleum distribution network.[37]

Indeed, the vulnerability of fuel dumps—in comparison, at least, to the pipelines themselves—convinced the planners of Commando Hunt VII to incorporate these installations into "logistic area targets," as they were doing with the supply dumps and transhipment points along the waterways. This category of target embraced all known storage, transfer, and support facilities, whether part of the road, river, or pipeline networks. Data from Igloo White sensors, aerial photographs, visual observation, radio intercepts, and other forms of intelligence helped locate the targets. By November 1971, the aerial campaign against pipelines and waterways had lost its separate identity and had merged with Commando Hunt.[38]

Chapter Eleven

The 1971 Southwest Monsoon Season

The merging of the attack on waterways and pipelines into Commando Hunt, foreshadowed during the dry season interdiction campaign of 1970–71, took place during Commando Hunt VI, the southwest monsoon campaign that lasted from May 15 through October 31, 1971. The Seventh Air Force planned to launch an integrated attack during the rainy months, "when activity is indicated by intelligence sources," targeting not only the road network of southern Laos, but also the waterways.[1] As expected, the coming of heavy rains slowed truck traffic, and the streams again became essential conduits for the movement of supplies. Throughout the 1971 rainy-season interdiction campaign, aerial photographs of Waterway VII, the Banghiang, revealed less activity than normal, whereas forward air controllers and reconnaissance teams reported extensive movement along the Kaman River, recently developed as a waterway, and the Kong. The diversion of river traffic away from the Banghiang seemed to indicate that most of the cargo shipped by water during this period went to southwestern Laos or Cambodia, rather than South Vietnam.[2]

Although roads carried fewer supplies in the rainy season than in dry weather, the comparatively small number of trucks presented lucrative targets, as did the supply dumps, transshipment points, and other installations serving the highway system. Throughout much of the 1971 southwest monsoon season, targets like these existed on and along the roads, at times in greater numbers than usual for this time of year, but finding them proved as difficult as ever. Persistent clouds and recurring thunderstorms appeared each day, as they had in the original southwest monsoon season campaign of 1969 and in Commando Hunt IV during the summer of 1970. Commenting on Commando Hunt II and IV, one squadron commander said, "The most inefficient use of air power was night interdiction during the wet season." Often clouds hovered so thickly over an area that forward air controllers could not see the truck traffic, if, indeed, any vehicles were driving through the murky dampness; the typical fighter pilot, he recalled, "took off in bad weather, flew three or four hours in bad weather, and returned to base with a full load [of munitions] to land in bad weather."[3] Another flier complained that, during the wet season, crews "hardly see anything except clouds."[4] Whatever the prospects for success, U.S. airmen defied the weather to attack trucks and the facilities they used, bomb natural choke points, and cut the highways over which the vehicles traveled.

The War against Trucks

During the period of heaviest rains, road cuts not only caused traffic congestion behind the interdiction points, thus creating targets for aircraft, but also helped the downpour undermine the roadbeds.

In carrying out strikes on the various elements of the transportation system, forward air controllers faced the demanding task of locating targets despite cloud cover that might conceal a limestone pillar or mountaintop as effectively as it hid a highway. Despite the difficulty and the danger, these pilots often succeeded. After spotting a target, if no fighter-bomber orbited nearby, the forward air controller summoned aircraft on alert at an airfield; unfortunately, the weather might deteriorate before a strike aircraft actually checked in. Within minutes, the clouds might not only hide the target once again, but also drop a curtain between the approaching jets and the slower aircraft that summoned them, thus increasing the danger of a midair collision.[5]

The reliance on forward air controllers to acquire targets visually, insofar as weather permitted, meant that aircraft responding to strike requests continually checked in and out of the controlled airspace sectors over southeastern Laos. Prior to Commando Hunt V, the Seventh Air Force had adjusted the boundaries of the fifteen sectors and two subsectors established for control purposes during the previous northeast monsoon campaign. By the time Commando Hunt VI began, these seventeen areas were compressed into fourteen, each with an appropriate control agency to handle traffic by day and night.[6] Effective on July 1, about midway through the operation, a further consolidation took place, reducing the total to nine, so that a gunship or fighter-bomber would have to change controllers even fewer times during a mission.[7]

For the 1971 southwest monsoon campaign, Task Force Alpha both provided intelligence and directed operations. The Surveillance Center interpreted sensor data, especially from the Commando Bolt modules, to fashion advisories that enabled forward air controllers, gunships, and Flasher teams to engage either moving or static targets. In addition, the computer at Nakhon Phanom digested signals from the entire sensor field and spewed out statistics for traffic predictions, which had three purposes: helping planners allocate strikes among different areas and various kinds of targets; giving them clues to the location of bypasses, truck parks, storage areas, or transshipment points; and showing them likely sites for interdiction points.[8]

The size of the sensor field that reported to the Surveillance Center changed from time to time during Commando Hunt VI to reflect the actual volume of truck traffic. With the coming of monsoon rains to the Ho Chi Minh Trail, truck traffic inevitably declined, and Task Force Alpha did not replenish those sensor strings reporting progressively fewer activations. From a high of 113 in May, the number of route monitoring strings dropped to a low of 60, enough to serve as an electronic "trip wire" to warn of any sudden increase in logistic activity.

Since some convoys continued to roll throughout the southwest monsoon season, a few Commando Bolt modules remained active, and Task Force Alpha exper-

178

imented with extending them by placing a supplementary monitoring string at each end, so that fifty or more sensors might cover a given stretch of road. Theoretically, the extensions should have alerted the Surveillance Center well before the trucks approached the designated point of impact within a strike module, revealed the speed and number of those that survived a Commando Bolt attack, and indicated if any had turned off the main route in an attempt to escape. In actual practice, however, the extra sensors merely increased the possibility of terrain masking or errors in sensor placement and gave the drivers additional space in which to find an uncharted bypass or hidden parking area. The longer Commando Bolt strike modules introduced in Commando Hunt V did not benefit at all from further lengthening with the kind of supplementary monitoring strings added for Commando Hunt VI. Although the modified Commando Bolt strings used during the 1971 southwest monsoon season permitted foul-weather attacks on traffic moving through Mu Gia and Ban Karai Passes, where trucks remained active throughout the rainy months, the fifty-sensor arrangement proved no more effective than a module with eighteen to twenty-four of the devices. Away from the mountain passes, other sensors helped aircraft find worthwhile targets along Route 922, leading eastward from Muong Nong toward South Vietnam, and on the roads that served the Bolovens Plateau, where renewed fighting had erupted.[9]

The deployable automatic relay terminal at Quang Tri, which had been monitoring sensor strings along South Vietnam's northwestern borders, closed down on July 5 as part of the program of Vietnamization and withdrawal. A C–130 flew the van and its equipment to Nakhon Phanom, where the terminal resumed operation on August 1, as part of Task Force Alpha's electronic array. Two months later, the X–T plotting equipment housed in the van took up a more permanent location inside the Surveillance Center. At Nakhon Phanom, technicians used the terminal's monitoring gear to observe sensor activations in and just west of the demilitarized zone, and Task Force Alpha strike coordinators used the information to wage an interdiction campaign against the road complex there, providing the Seventh Air Force with advisories that singled out both truck convoys and repair parties for possible air attack. Within an hour of receiving an advisory, Seventh Air Force headquarters at Tan Son Nhut could dispatch all or part of a quick reaction force of F–4s kept in readiness on the ground.[10]

Besides hitting moving targets like trucks and river traffic, Commando Hunt VI went after storage areas, construction sites, and transshipment points. Using the combined intelligence stored in the computer at the Surveillance Center, analysts tried to pinpoint these fixed targets for B–52s, gunships, B–57Gs, and Flasher teams.[11] As demonstrated in earlier aerial interdiction operations, fixed targets sometimes produced spectacular results in terms of fires and secondary explosions, but during Commando Hunt VI, fighter-bombers, rather than B–52s, received credit for the "most lucrative" strikes. Acting on information provided by Task Force Alpha, the air attaché at Vientiane arranged for the planting of Commando Bolt sensor modules along Route 917 as it passed through a validated Arc

Light target box due west of Tchepone. Instead of dropping their bombs to catch a convoy as it crossed an designated impact point on the road, the loran-equipped fighters used the coordinates as an offset aiming point to bomb suspected storage areas some three thousand feet on either side of the highway. One such strike, conducted in late September as the wet season was ending, reportedly ignited four hundred secondary fires and touched off over one thousand secondary explosions.[12].

Devastating though the fireworks along Route 917 may have been, Commando Hunt VI achieved mixed results. Throughout the operation, U.S. air power had to shift from the Ho Chi Minh Trail and its integral waterways to engage the enemy not only in southwestern Laos, where such diversions had become routine, but also in South Vietnam and Cambodia. In South Vietnam, as the rainy season interdiction effort got started, aircraft that otherwise might have attacked the Ho Chi Minh Trail had to fly more than four thousand sorties in support of a South Vietnamese probe of the A Shau Valley. Scarcely had the action ended there, when the Seventh Air Force undertook an aerial offensive, consisting of almost one thousand sorties, against the supply lines of the Khmer Rouge in Cambodia. Finally, in September as the seasons were changing, the North Vietnamese mounted local offensives against South Vietnamese troops in eastern Cambodia and nearby South Vietnam, forcing the United States to carry out some two thousand air strikes in helping the defenders to blunt the attacks.[13]

This diversion of aircraft from possible use against the Ho Chi Minh Trail occurred at a time when Air Force units were withdrawing from Southeast Asia. Indeed, the total number of Air Force aircraft of all types based in South Vietnam and Thailand, which totaled 1,777 when the Commando Hunt series began, declined during the course of Commando Hunt VI from 1,199 to 953.[14] In anticipation of the dwindling numbers and the seasonal bad weather over southern Laos, the Seventh Air Force established a quick reaction force, standing by armed and fueled on the ground, that could take advantage of sudden breaks in the cloud cover through which forward air controllers might discover profitable targets. Planners would have preferred to launch a daily schedule of strikes with the available aircraft, diverting some of them to meet emergencies, but circumstances made this impossible. The fleeting nature of the targets, the likelihood of cloud cover, and the rapid formation and movement of thunderstorms prevented the headquarters from drawing up a full slate of operations even a day ahead of time. Consequently, the quick reaction force, responding to actual sightings through breaks in the clouds, provided a better chance of a successful strike, even though it immobilized a number of airplanes on the ground. Operations analysts from the Pacific Air Forces described the quick reaction force, under the existing conditions, as "a useful management tool for effective allocation of air resources."

The North Vietnamese continued to improve the logistic network and its defenses during Commando Hunt VI. Much of the work, however, took place outside southern Laos. In North Vietnam, for example, the enemy positioned surface-to-air missiles to cover Mu Gia and Ban Karai Passes and nearby segments of the trail. At the northwestern corner of South Vietnam, construction went ahead, until stopped by a combination of weather and bombing, on another access route to the A Shau Valley.

Throughout the summer of 1971, construction, repair, and travel on the Ho Chi Minh Trail had to surmount both aerial attack and weather. Of the two, weather proved the more formidable, by far. Throughout May and a part of June, the cumulative effect of the seasonal rains washed away road surfaces, and traffic turned the infrastructure into goo. A brief and unexpected spell of dry weather provided a respite, during which road repair crews and truck convoys engaged in frenzied activity. Then, in July, two typhoons and a tropical storm lashed the area within just three weeks, inflicting severe damage on roads and waterways and reducing highway traffic to about a third of the volume normal for this period of the rainy season.

In assessing the impact of Commando Hunt VI, analysts for the Pacific Air Forces tried to compare enemy activity in two successive southwest monsoon seasons. During 1970, Commando Hunt IV got credit for impeding traffic to such an extent that only 18 percent of the 13,287 tons of cargo dispatched from North Vietnam actually arrived in South Vietnam or at storage areas along the border. Estimates for 1971 indicated that a greater proportion of cargo, 30 percent, slipped through despite Commando Hunt VI, but that a smaller volume, fewer than 5,000 tons, started down the trail. If the figures for 1971 were correct, the decline in tonnage entering the logistic complex could have reflected the damage and disruption caused by the storms of July. Because cargo entering the Ho Chi Minh Trail late in the rainy months would be the first to reach South Vietnam or Cambodia when the roads dried, the analysts concluded that Commando Hunt VI "did succeed in impeding enemy preparations for the initial surge of logistic traffic in the following dry season."[15]

While U.S. airmen braved the southwest monsoon weather to attack the trail and hamper the movement of supplies, Lao government forces again challenged the enemy on the Bolovens Plateau. The previous dry season ended in April with North Vietnamese and Pathet Lao forces holding sway over the region, but the government promptly launched a counteroffensive. Both Prince Souvanna Phouma and Ambassador Godley were determined to recapture the plateau, for control of the territory and its populace would strengthen the government's hand if peace negotiations should begin. Instead of resuming the usual cycle of advance and retreat, Lao army units and irregular forces attacked in July to expel the enemy from the area and establish strongpoints from which royal forces could defeat the counterattack expected when dry weather returned in November.

Once again, helicopters provided by the Central Intelligence Agency and the Air Force assured the regular and guerrilla battalions of mobility. The Royal Lao Air force, using T–28s by day and AC–47s at night, supported the advance, while U.S. tactical fighters conducted daylight strikes against antiaircraft batteries, defensive positions, and targets of opportunity, such as troops moving on the roads or newly discovered storage sites. After dark, the Seventh Air Force could, as necessary, divert AC–119K or AC–130 gunships to assist the Lao AC–47s.

The advance onto the Bolovens Plateau began on July 28 with a sudden helicopter descent on Saravane, which proved to be undefended. One day later, Lao forces launched a series of attacks designed to clear the enemy from Routes 16, 23, and 16/23 in the vicinity of the reoccupied town, destroy the supplies stored along the Dong River, and recapture Paksong. One contingent landed by helicopter at Ban Lao Ngam, some twenty-five miles north of Paksong and advanced toward that objective. Another group pushed eastward along Route 23 from Lao Ngam (easily confused with Ban Lao Ngam to the northeast) to Ban Gnik, where the North Vietnamese checked the thrust until fresh government units arrived by helicopter and regained the initiative. Abandoning Ban Gnik, the enemy maneuvered to repulse the force moving southward from Ban Lao Ngam, driving the Lao irregulars back to their advance base. When reinforcements promised by the royal government failed to appear, the force that had fallen back to Ban Lao Ngam melted away. A Lao army battalion hurriedly deployed there, but four companies could not do the work originally assigned to four battalions and momentum flagged. Although the North Vietnamese and Pathet Lao contained one element of the attacking force at Ban Lao Ngam, other irregular and army units captured Paksong, raising the royal flag on September 15. When the Bolovens operation ended on October 31, the government clung to three islands—Paksong, Saravane, and Ban Lao Ngam—in a hostile sea. The enemy retained control of the roads in the area, and his supply dumps along the Dong River remained largely untouched.[16]

Despite the government's feeble hold on the Bolovens, the recovery of two important towns, Saravane and Paksong, inspired a dry-season attack on Ban Thateng, held by the enemy since April 1969. Saravane served as jumping-off point for the operation, which commenced on November 21 when helicopters landed a force of one thousand that established a temporary advance base at Ban Phon, some twenty-two miles west of Ban Thateng. On the same day, other helicopters landed a second government force, armed with 75-mm pack howitzers and charged with seizing Phou Thiouom, an enemy-held peak just two miles southwest of the main objective. At Phou Thiouom, communist infantry resisted almost from the moment that the government soldiers disembarked from the helicopters, and air strikes proved necessary to dislodge some of the defenders from positions near the base of the peak. Cloud cover prevented accurate bombing, however, so that some thirty North Vietnamese soldiers survived and made their way to the nearby landing zone where they planted electrically detonated mines and waited for the chance to use them. On November 23, after two Central Intelligence Agency helicopters had touched down, the ambush party closed the firing circuits, triggering explosions that destroyed both aircraft and wounded three crewmen. In spite of this setback, Lao troops managed to capture the mountain.[17]

While the first government force was establishing a fire base atop Phou Thiouom, another column marched south from Saravane and occupied Ban Thateng on the 25th. Three days later, the soldiers who had landed at Ban Phon a week earlier broke camp and started westward along Route 16 toward Ban Thateng, attempting to clear the enemy from along the highway. On the night of December 9, as the column from Ban Phon advanced westward, enemy tanks spearheaded a counterattack on the 150 Lao troops holding Ban Thateng. The North Vietnamese and Pathet Lao emplaced 12.7-mm machine guns that kept the AC–47s of the Royal Lao Air Force from intervening, as the armored vehicles and accompanying infantry routed the defenders. Undaunted by being driven out of Ban Thateng, the government soldiers regrouped on the following afternoon and reentered the town, but the enemy beat them back. When the fighting at Ban Thateng ended on December 16, royal forces held roughly the same position they had after the North Vietnamese captured the town thirty-two months earlier. Souvanna's men once again clung to outposts near Ban Thateng, while the North Vietnamese and Pathet Lao occupied the town and controlled Routes 16, 23, and 16/23. The principal benefits from this latest offensive had been the capture of a North Vietnamese hospital by troops advancing from Saravane and the destruction of "substantial" amounts of supplies and a few trucks during the sweep from Ban Phon toward Ban Thateng.[18]

Four days before North Vietnamese tanks led the assault on Ban Thateng, the enemy moved against Saravane, occupied by government forces earlier in the year to serve as staging area for the dry-season offensive. On the night of December 5, the North Vietnamese began probing Saravane's defenses. Shortly before dawn on the following day, three battalions hit the royal army garrison in simultaneous attacks, and by dusk the Lao troops were in full retreat over an escape route the enemy had left open.[19]

Events on the Bolovens Plateau during the southwest monsoon season of 1971 and the early weeks of the subsequent dry season confirmed the enemy's ability to protect the western flank of the Ho Chi Minh Trail. The North Vietnamese expanded their control of this region throughout the remainder of the northeast monsoon period, erasing the earlier gains made by government forces and threatening Pakse. After the North Vietnam invaded the South at the end of March 1972, the security of the western reaches of the Ho Chi Minh Trail no longer mattered, and Hanoi withdrew units from southwestern Laos to fight possibly decisive battles in northern and western South Vietnam. This reordering of priorities enabled the government of Laos to extend its authority, at least temporarily, for without the help of North Vietnamese troops, the Pathet Lao fought at a grave disadvantage. By the end of June 1972, the balance shifted in favor of Souvanna Phouma, as royal troops joined guerrillas in spectacular advances that resulted in the temporary recapture of Saravane and even Muong Phalane. Unfortunately, progress in Laos had no effect on the fighting in South Vietnam.[20]

During Commando Hunt VI and the faltering initial phase of Souvanna's attempt to regain the Bolovens Plateau, planning moved ahead for aerial interdic-

The War against Trucks

tion during the approaching dry season, which would begin in November 1971. Besides absorbing the campaign against waterways and pipelines into Commando Hunt VII, the next operation in the series, the Seventh Air Force staff, with the urging and assistance of officials on the Department of Defense, sought to locate and attack troop infiltration routes throughout southern Laos. If all went well, air attacks during the coming northeast monsoon season would destroy trucks and war materials provided by foreign sources and also exact from North Vietnam a price in human life for continuing the war in the South.[21]

Chapter Twelve

Hitting Them Hard Enough to Hurt

The Jason Summer Study of 1966, which inspired the use of electronic sensors in conducting aerial interdiction of the Ho Chi Minh Trail, called for attacking North Vietnamese troops as they infiltrated through southern Laos, but the Seventh Air Force and Task Force Alpha made only sporadic and generally ineffectual efforts to do so until Commando Hunt VII began in the late fall of 1971. The earliest effective use of electronic sensors against troops occurred during the successful defense of Khe Sanh in the spring of 1968. The ability of sensors at Khe Sanh to locate enemy units maneuvering beyond the hills north and northwest of the base, and to generate targets for air strikes and artillery fire, kindled enthusiasm for using the electronic devices to find columns of troops moving beneath the jungle canopy of southern Laos. Many of the enthusiasts failed to realize, however, that the hostile divisions surrounding Khe Sanh had to follow a limited number of natural corridors that served as avenues of approach to the base or its outposts. Conditions differed markedly on the Ho Chi Minh Trail, where enemy soldiers moved over a labyrinth of trails concealed by clouds, fog, haze, and jungle growth. Nor did it seem in the late 1960s that sensor data on truck routes would be of any help, for U.S. intelligence analysts had concluded that infiltrating North Vietnamese troops followed a web of trails separate from the highway network. Aware of the difficulty in pinpointing these trails and planting sensors accurately, General Keegan, the chief of intelligence for the Seventh Air Force, warned in the summer of 1968 that "it may be years before this antipersonnel capability is developed to a point that it will be useful without being extravagantly expensive."[1]

In November, some seven weeks after the general expressed this judgment, a group headed by Adm. James S. Russell, which had met at Washington, D.C., to evaluate the effectiveness of sensor operations in Southeast Asia, submitted its findings to Dr. John S. Foster, Jr., the Director of Defense Research and Engineering. The Russell Committee endorsed the current emphasis on killing trucks, rather than North Vietnamese infiltrators, along the Ho Chi Minh Trail, but it also recommended a test, when conditions permitted, of the effectiveness of sensors against the North Vietnamese units that moved almost unopposed through Laos to South Vietnam.[2]

The War against Trucks

Until tests demonstrated that sensors actually did pinpoint foot traffic, air power could inflict only accidental harm on enemy infiltration groups as they followed a route that generally paralleled, but did not coincide with, the road net. Since the available intelligence on troop infiltration did not permit Task Force Alpha to conduct the kind of experiment proposed by the Russell Committee, let alone mount a systematic attack on the trails, the enemy retained, throughout 1968 and for almost three years afterward, an unimpaired ability to adjust the flow of reinforcements and replacements to sustain whatever level of combat he desired.

Although air power focused on trucks rather than troops, North Vietnamese soldiers faced disheartening natural obstacles during a grueling march lasting from thirty to ninety days over rugged mountains and through dense jungle, an ordeal made even worse by seasonal rains, by tropical diseases ranging from skin infections to malaria, and occasionally by bombs aimed at the logistic network.[3] A notebook kept by one of the infiltrators told of traveling 620 miles in thirty-eight days. From his unit's cantonment area in North Vietnam, the soldier rode by truck to the Laotian border, arriving there late in the dry season of 1967–68. For a month the four hundred to four hundred fifty men in his group walked from one bivouac site to another until they entered South Vietnam through the A Shau Valley and turned eastward into Thua Thien Province. According to the diary, only fifteen men failed to complete the trek because of disease, injury, or exhaustion, a remarkable achievement since by 1968 the primitive hospitals in southern Laos had already run short of medicine, especially for the treatment of malaria.[4]

The succession of well-trained infiltration groups traveling one after another down the Ho Chi Minh Trail kept watch for both ambush and air strikes, even though neither posed a serious threat to troops passing through southern Laos in late 1968 or early 1969. To guard against ambush by patrols dispatched from South Vietnam, a security unit scouted ahead of each column, looking for trampled undergrowth, broken branches, fresh marks on the trail surface that might indicate the presence of antipersonnel mines, or other evidence of hostile activity. As the infiltrators marched south, they passed from one sector to another, each responsible for a particular segment of the trail and able to provide guides thoroughly familiar with the area and fully alert to signs of danger.

The jungle itself afforded the best defense against air attack. In places, towering rain forest concealed the narrow paths, scarcely more than shoulder width, so completely that a column could ignore the sound of aircraft and continue moving. When marching beneath a thinner natural canopy, the troops took cover from aircraft overhead and refrained from using their weapons, since small-arms fire would give them away and invite aerial attack. The active air defense of the entire transportation network—roads, trails, and waterways—rested in the hands of trained gunners firing weapons ranging from heavy machine guns to 57-mm and even 100-mm cannon.[5]

A forward air controller, Capt. David L. Shields, described the difficulty of locating the enemy from the air, except "in the inhabited areas, fairly open." Over jungle, he found that visual reconnaissance was "of very little value" and required "a lot of looking with very few results." On one occasion, just inside the borders of South Vietnam, Captain Shields did spot the footprints of hundreds of troops who had waded a shallow river to escape a B–52 strike. Unfortunately for these men, the area where they sought refuge was bounded on three sides by a horseshoe bend in the stream and on the fourth by a cliff. Shields called in fighter-bombers that saturated the finger of land with antipersonnel bombs and apparently killed a large number of North Vietnamese.[6] Success like this remained elusive, however, for as another forward air controller pointed out, "a man could stand motionless under a tree in full view of the aircraft and go unseen" by the pilot of a light plane flying at only fifteen hundred feet.[7]

Whether on the march or in bivouac, infiltration groups sometimes came under air attack, due to their own lack of discipline—careless use of radio, open cooking fires, or giving way to panic and firing at U.S. planes—or simply as a result of bad luck, such as being in the way of bombs directed at another target. Accidental or not, a B–52 strike—usually by a cell of three bombers, each aircraft carrying as many as twenty-seven tons of high explosives—could cause slaughter among infiltrating troops, and the North Vietnamese seemed to fear the high flying bombers more than any other type. For example, a member of one unlucky infiltration group reported a hundred of his comrades killed in April 1968 when a deluge of five hundred pound bombs caught his column as it entered a bivouac area.[8]

Seldom did B–52s or other Air Force aircraft exact so gruesome a toll among the infiltrating units. A sampling of statements by North Vietnamese soldiers who had surrendered or been captured in 1967, before the Commando Hunt series began, disclosed that only one man in ten had so much as seen an air strike during the march through Laos. Aerial ordnance probably killed no more than 2 percent of that year's infiltrators, though air power might have contributed to the death of perhaps three times that number, men who perished because bombing of the supply route prevented them from receiving proper food and essential medicine.[9]

Infiltrating personnel remained reasonably safe from air attack throughout 1968, provided they took routine precautions, for the Seventh Air Force knew so little about the troop routes that it had no choice but to emphasize killing trucks rather than killing soldiers. Neither air strikes nor ambushes seriously disturbed the movement of men through the maze of footpaths believed to lie somewhere west of the main north-south truck routes, nor did U.S. intelligence arrive at a precise estimate of the number of infiltrators. The Military Assistance Command maintained that during 1968 some two hundred forty thousand North Vietnamese infiltrated into the South, roughly one hundred thousand more than operations analysts in the Office of Secretary of Defense accepted. The lower figure reflected a belief that during the first three months of 1968, the height of the dry season, an estimated sixty thousand men entered South Vietnam to launch or exploit the Tet offensive and an additional fifty-one thousand arrived in the country before the end of June and the coming of the monsoon rains to southern Laos after marching south principally to replace casualties suffered during the Tet fighting. Bad weather reduced infiltration to an estimated twenty-nine thousand from July through September, and the probable number remained low, some nine thousand for the final quarter, even though the rains abated. The Washington-based operations analysts did not link U.S. pressure against the Ho Chi Minh Trail to the enemy's failure to capitalize on the improving weather; they believed instead that North Vietnam, for reasons of its own, had decided to avoid for the near future combat on the scale of the 1968 Tet offensive.[10]

Although the analysts on the scene agreed with those in the Pentagon that infiltration slowed late in 1968, the Tet fighting had generated an immediate need for replacements and reinforcements, as North Vietnamese troops took over the war from the savagely battered Viet Cong. Since the rush of troops down the Ho Chi Minh Trail from May through June dramatized the importance of infiltration, the Joint Chiefs of Staff, after reviewing the Russell Committee report, endorsed the group's recommendation to evaluate the use of sensors against infiltrators. General Lavelle, the Director, Defense Communications Planning Group, went even further, urging that the Seventh Air Force take the lead in organizing such a test. At Seventh Air Force headquarters, however, General Brown, the organization's new commander, proved reluctant to become involved with the experiment.[11]

Before Brown left Washington to take command at Tan Son Nhut, George B. Kistiakowsky, a scientific adviser to the Department of Defense, had reminded him of the investment already made in an antipersonnel system—mainly data processing equipment, mines, and acoustic sensors—and emphasized the importance of a combat test. Although the scientist's words kindled no great enthusiasm or confidence, the general prepared for the test, whatever his reservations about its outcome. "While I hold very little conviction that the system will prevent personnel infiltration," Brown declared, "it may be possible, but that is really of secondary importance." He believed that the "basic purpose for doing anything with the proposed antipersonnel system is to avoid a charge by the scientific community that their concept was never exploited, even though considerable funds were spent in the development of hardware and munitions." Although "interested in evaluating the system," he did not want "to pay an unreasonable price to do so."[12]

The price might well be high, especially in terms of the diversion of resources from the apparently successful war against trucks. In early 1969, Task Force Alpha's Infiltration Surveillance Center had 25 radio channels that could handle transmissions from 562 sensors, though its capacity could easily expand to accommodate an additional 68. Plans for the 1969–70 dry season called for 474 sensors in the Commando Hunt truck-killing operation and another 120 to detect vehicles approaching the A Shau Valley, but according to officers assigned to the task force, the kind of test suggested by the Russell Committee required roughly 200 sensors. Some compromise would be necessary if Nakhon Phanom undertook all three efforts— Commando Hunt III, surveillance of the A Shau Valley, and the antipersonnel test— at the same time.[13]

The proposed antipersonnel sensor field, Seventh Air Force planners agreed, represented the likeliest area for compromise. Consequently, they cut in half the number of sensors assigned to it, proportionally reducing the need for radio channels and tone codes. With careful scheduling, the Surveillance Center could operate the new total of 694 sensors. Despite the reduction in the coverage of suspected troop infiltration routes, the planned operating technique for the test remained unchanged. First, antipersonnel minefields sown from the air channeled foot traffic into areas covered by seismic and acoustic devices. Then, explosions caused when an unwary North Vietnamese stepped on a mine, detonations that occurred during attempts to clear the fields, and the normal sounds and ground vibrations of troops on the march triggered the sensors, which reported the activity to Nakhon Phanom. Once the electronic equipment had pinpointed a column, F–4 fighter-bombers, guided by loran or a Combat Skyspot radar controller on the ground, would shower the infiltrators with antipersonnel bomblets. After the strike, the monitors at Nakhon Phanom turned to the acoustic sensors for evidence of its effectiveness, for example, the screams of the wounded or the shouted instructions of medical teams.[14]

Unfortunately, the computers at Nakhon Phanom had in their memories almost no reliable information about patterns of troop infiltration, so that guesswork rather than logical deduction would have to determine where to plant the sensors and scatter the mines. As a result, finding a suitable location for the test proved far more difficult than setting aside the necessary reporting channels and tone codes. General Brown's staff at Tan Son Nhut Air Base nominated a possible test site, asking the Task Force to supply "as soon as possible any data available . . . on Laotian trail networks in a strip . . . approximately twenty kilometers in width extending along the RVN [Republic of Vietnam] border from the Cambodian border north to Route 92A," a highway located above Tchepone along the far bank of the Banghiang River. In making this request, Seventh Air Force planners revealed their misgivings when they expressed the "subjective judgment . . . that the trail network may be so comprehensive and complex as to preclude a meaningful test with a realistic investment of resources."[15]

Within twenty-four hours, the task force at Nakhon Phanom replied that it had no information on the precise location of the trails in this region; its intelligence holdings on personnel infiltration dealt with techniques employed rather than the specific routes followed.[16] Most of what Task Force Alpha knew about the subject came from reports it had received of interrogations of individual North Vietnamese defectors or prisoners of war who told what they personally had experienced during the trek to South Vietnam. Although they talked freely about the size of infiltration groups, travel time, and accommodations en route, they seldom knew the trail network in any detail, were unfamiliar with U.S. military maps, and therefore could not pinpoint the route they had followed. Moreover, U.S. intelligence had not exploited them to the fullest as a source of information on troop infiltration; not even one prisoner or defector out of ten underwent questioning about the journey south or other matters not directly related to the tactical situation in the immediate area where he surrendered.[17]

The War against Trucks

Instead of responding with information on the proposed site for the test, Task Force Alpha could only promise to use its sensors against enemy infiltrators, provided it could somehow remedy the existing "intelligence deficiencies." As this meaningless commitment indicated, the leadership at Nakhon Phanom had as little enthusiasm for the project as it had solid information. A test undertaken in dry weather seemed certain to interfere with the Commando Hunt campaigns against road traffic, credited with killing more trucks in each successive northeast monsoon season; whereas during the rainy season, flooding reduced the volume of infiltration, whether of cargo or troops, and low-hanging clouds would prevent F–4s from planting sensors accurately enough to detect the few troops that might be moving along the labyrinthine route, should intelligence analysts manage to find it.[18] In June 1969, after some five months of study, the Seventh Air Force abandoned the idea of a test that would pit the Infiltration Surveillance Center, its computers and its sensors, against the North Vietnamese columns moving through southern Laos. Factors contributing to this decision included a lack of knowledge about the trail net, which raised doubts that sensors could be planted accurately enough to do the job, and a reluctance to divert resources from Commando Hunt operations.[19]

Unlike intelligence, munitions did not pose a serious problem for those who sought to attack infiltrating troops. If Task Force Alpha found the trails and fighter-bombers planted sensors precisely, the Air Force had a variety of weapons for attacking the infiltrators, including high-explosive, antipersonnel, and fire bombs and antipersonnel mines. The Mk 82, a five hundred pound weapon designed by the Navy after the Korean War, seemed the likeliest high-explosive bomb for attacking troops, since it had the best fragmentation pattern, but no such general-purpose bomb killed or wounded troops as efficiently as the antipersonnel types.[20] Specially designed antipersonnel bomblets like the 1.6 pound BLU–24 or BLU–66 bomb live units, scattered from dispensers carried by aircraft, had the best chance of claiming victims among people screened by the jungle canopy. The principal advantage of these spherical weapons in the rain forest stemmed from their stabilizing fins, reduced in size and enclosed with a circular band to prevent the bomblet from becoming entangled in the treetops and exploding harmlessly or not at all.[21] The Air Force arsenal of weapons for use against infiltration groups included incendiaries like the funny bomb, which at the time seemed so damaging to truck convoys, and napalm, deadly against troops in the open. Neither, however, proved nearly as destructive as the antipersonnel bomblets against enemy soldiers hidden beneath a thick jungle canopy. Different kinds of antipersonnel mines would also see service, including pebble-sized gravel, employed mainly to channel foot traffic and trigger sensors. Also available were the larger dragontooth mine, capable of puncturing truck tires and inflicting injury, and the wide-area antipersonnel mine, widely used against road repair crews.[22]

The idea of attacking infiltration groups from the air surfaced again during May 1970, though in a slightly different form. This revised scheme, which got only perfunctory consideration, involved fitting out Air Force gunships to receive and plot signals from sensors covering the routes used by North Vietnamese soldiers. The suggested solution, however, addressed the wrong problem, for it focused on quick reaction to sensor activations rather than on planting the sensors where they could actually locate troops. If Task Force Alpha succeeded in finding the main troop infiltration routes, the normal interdiction procedures would work: F–4s could drop sensors with acceptable accuracy, although either helicopters or ground patrols would be more precise, assuming they penetrated the defenses now guarding certain segments of the Ho Chi Minh Trail; and the Infiltration Surveillance Center could convert the sensor activations into actual targets. Moreover, the portable receivers proposed for the gunships had gone out of production and were becoming scarce in Southeast Asia.[23]

Even though the kind of test recommended by the Russell Committee in 1968 underwent a succession of postponements before being shelved indefinitely, U.S. intelligence gradually learned more about the trail network, but not enough, as of mid-1970, to permit the kind of systematic war that was being waged against truck traffic. Interrogations of prisoners disclosed that disease, rather than ambush or bombing, remained the worst danger facing the infiltrators. After reviewing these statements and reports by crewmen who had hit targets in Laos, Department of Defense systems analysts questioned whether air power had killed or wounded more than 1 percent of the troops infiltrating over the Ho Chi Minh Trail.[24]

Although aircraft might have inflicted fewer than twenty-five hundred casualties during all of 1968 (fewer than fifteen hundred based on the annual infiltration suggested by these same Department of Defense analysts), assuming this pessimistic assessment of effectiveness reflected reality, North Vietnamese troops marching through Laos nevertheless respected the destructive power of the B–52 and the threat posed by the much smaller, two-place North American Rockwell OV–10, used to direct attacks by F–4 or F–105 fighter-bombers. One battalion infiltrating southward during 1970 had the misfortune to undergo two air attacks. On the first occasion, while the men rested at a bivouac near one of the way stations en route, the earth all around them began erupting from the detonation of bombs dropped by B–52s invisible in the skies above. The troops did not even have time to run to the shelters prepared for them and could only hug the ground. The attack, which reportedly killed 90 and wounded 40, sought to destroy some nearby component of the truck route, but the bombing pattern encompassed the troops camped in the vicinity.

Bad luck surely contributed to the first bombing, but the behavior of the troops invited the second. While camped near another way station farther along the infiltration route, some of the soldiers left a camouflaged bivouac area to wash their clothes and bathe in a nearby stream. An OV–10 happened overhead, and the North Vietnamese realized they had been spotted when the plane fired rockets to mark their location. Within three minutes, fighter-bombers attacked with napalm and delayed-action bombs. Most of the group had by this time taken cover, but the strike killed three of those along the river bank and wounded five.

The War against Trucks

Four other times while camped along the trail, this same battalion received warning of imminent attack by B–52s. Each time the North Vietnamese quickly packed up and marched to a new site. Once the unit took refuge too close to the original bivouac, and an errant bomb killed one man. Another time the entire group got safely away and listened in awe to hundreds of explosions that rocked the area they had just left. Twice when the battalion moved, the bombers failed to appear.[25]

As early as 1966, North Vietnamese forces in South Vietnam began receiving warnings of air attacks by B–52s, and the alert network soon extended to southern Laos. U.S. intelligence gradually learned of the warning net, at first from prisoners like the captured North Vietnamese who insisted that the Soviets or Chinese had to be responsible, since his own country's primitive intelligence service could not possibly collect and disseminate this sort of information. Actually, Soviet and North Vietnamese intelligence collaborated. Soviet trawlers off Guam, the site of a B–52 base, served as the trip wire that alerted the radars in North Vietnam to acquire and track the Guam-based bombers. For Arc Light strikes originating at U-Tapao in Thailand, agents watching the airfield sounded the first alarm that alerted the North Vietnamese radar screen. Additional information came from local residents, sympathetic to the North Vietnamese cause, who found jobs on the base that gave them access to bulletin boards, waste baskets, and living quarters. The intelligence obtained in this fashion included the infrequently changed radio call signs, which identified an aircraft as taking off from U-Tapao, and the place of origin might provide a clue to the likely target.[26]

Radar formed a key element in the warning net, as did the scraps of paper found at U-Tapao, but the enemy also monitored electronic signals in attempting to predict likely targets of the B–52s. A study made late in the war showed that radio call signs used by the bombers and by escorting aircraft, together with the type of radar, if any, that the bombers were trying to jam electronically, provided additional clues to the area that the B–52s would attack. Once the North Vietnamese narrowed the threat to a general area, they could decide which sectors of the transportation network within this zone presented the most important targets and warn the sector headquarters accordingly. Infiltration groups then abandoned any bivouac that seemed in danger, either because U.S. aircraft might have detected their presence, as sometimes happened, or because they had camped too near a supply dump or truck park that B–52s were likely to bomb. As element of risk remained, however, for the B–52s might not attack as expected and the group, in fleeing a bombing that never came, might blunder into a strike delivered elsewhere in the same sector. Infiltrating troops benefited most from these warnings because they could move immediately, whereas cargo and trucks remained tied to storage sites or other fixed installations. There the cadre members might take cover, but to attempt to move parked trucks or stacked supplies took too long and invited fighter-bomber attack.[27]

Although Task Force Alpha had not yet tried to plant sensors along the trails, infiltration groups frequently encountered sensors from strings intended to monitor truck traffic or locate supply installations. One veteran of the passage through Laos reported that whenever his group's guides spotted a sensor, they "pointed it out by gesture and each man in the battalion therefore saw it." The troops then picked up the pace, maintaining strict silence as they hurried past. Responsibility for removing or destroying the sensor, which might be booby-trapped, rested with the sector headquarters that operated the particular segment of the trail.[28]

During 1970, the enemy strengthened the defenses protecting the expanding web of roads and trails in southern Laos and, after the U.S. invasion of Cambodia in April, increased his pressure against Lon Nol's forces there. Assuming the validity of the Military Assistance Command's estimate for 1968, the trail network could accommodate two hundred forty thousand infiltrators in a single year, though the total for 1969 represented two-thirds of capacity, and infiltration for 1970 apparently did not exceed fifty-five thousand. Most of those who traveled the trail in 1969 and 1970 fought in South Vietnam, but some remained in southern Laos or entered Cambodia. Ellsworth Bunker, U.S. Ambassador to South Vietnam, predicted that the enemy would not change his strategy in 1971. Infiltration, he believed, might surge, but the additional men would either fight in Cambodia or defend and further improve the Ho Chi Minh Trail complex; they would not launch a major offensive in the South.[29]

Before the April 1970 incursion into Cambodia, North Vietnamese infiltrators had passed through that country en route from southern Laos to South Vietnam. U.S. intelligence believed that the 26th Battalion, for example, entered Cambodia early in February of that year and reorganized there for future operations across the South Vietnamese border. The evidence indicated that the 559th Transportation Group directed the unit's journey from the mountain passes linking North Vietnam and Laos southward into Mondol Kiri and Kratie Provinces of northeastern Cambodia.[30]

Following the invasion, data collected during 1970 and 1971 revealed that the enemy reacted to Cambodian fighting by establishing a branch of the Ho Chi Minh Trail to channel men and supplies to the new battlefields. This extension, sometimes called the Liberation Route to distinguish it from the tangle of roads and footpaths that made up the original trail, turned westward near the village of Muong May in southernmost Laos then paralleled the Kong River into Cambodia. Gradually this supply and infiltration route extended past Siem Prang, Cambodia, reached the Mekong River near Stung Treng, and then followed the highway just west of that stream.[31]

Once Cambodia became a battleground, the enemy created a transportation group, the 470th, whose designation referred to April 1970, to operate the new extension of the Ho Chi Minh Trail and direct the movement of men and supplies into that country. The boundary between the 470th and 559th Transportation Groups lay somewhere in the vicinity of Saravane. Like the older organization, the 470th controlled movement by means of a series of sector headquarters responsible for roads and trails in a specific area. Each sector had the number of combat troops and engineers believed necessary to protect the infiltration and supply routes, maintain and improve them, and keep the men and trucks moving according to plan. The Cambodian sectors, however, did not need the powerful antiaircraft batteries or the strong infantry units that defended the Ho Chi Minh Trail in southern Laos against air or ground attack.[32]

U.S. intelligence concluded that the 559th and 470th Transportation Groups operated almost identically as they channeled troops through their areas of responsibility. Within each sector of the infiltration route were several way stations, varying in size and function and situated about a day's march from each other. Two or three men operated the smallest stations and served mainly as guides, meeting an approaching infiltration group, showing it to its overnight camp, and then leading it at least halfway to the next station. The larger installations, manned by a cadre of as many as twenty persons, rendered other services, such as issuing food, conducting training, and providing medical care. Depending on the denseness of the surrounding vegetation, the stations lay from six to six hundred feet from the trail. The available concealment also determined the layout of the larger facilities, where gaps of sixty to one thousand feet separated the various components—supply caches, dispensaries, and bivouac areas. The operating technique of the 470th and the 559th differed in only one respect. Guides in Cambodia accompanied a column roughly halfway to the next destination, where a team from the new station met the replacements and finished the day's journey; in southern Laos the guides led a group from one station all the way to the next.[33]

While tracing the extension of the Ho Chi Minh complex into Cambodia, the Military Assistance Command reexamined the relationship of the trail net to the road system. Reports from prisoner of war interrogations and statements by defectors now tended to suggest that the supply and infiltration routes might intersect at two or more points within each sector. Near the intersection, the North Vietnamese established a subordinate headquarters, called an interstation, through which the sector commander exercised control over both foot and truck traffic. Since the interstations apparently included facilities for road convoys as well as for the infiltration groups, they seemed to present profitable targets, if the intelligence analysts could locate them.[34]

Determined to take advantage of the discovery of the interstations, Leonard Sullivan, still serving in May 1971 as Deputy Director of Defense Research and Engineering for Southeast Asia Matters, resurrected the idea of attacking the North Vietnamese troops infiltrating through southern Laos. He recommended these attacks first because they would hurt North Vietnam directly and second because South Vietnamese forces could continue them after the United States had withdrawn. He did not, however, favor abandoning the truck war, for he believed that Commando Hunt was "exacting a substantial price in supplies destroyed and consumed," while tying down "engineering, communications, antiaircraft, and infantry manpower that could be used in more offensive roles." Sullivan endorsed the intelligence estimate that "over seventy-five thousand men, women, and children are . . . devoted to getting the supplies through."

Thus far, Sullivan admitted, the enemy seemed able to pay the price in cargo destroyed and manpower immobilized, for he continued to ship "enough supplies and ammunition to enable him to maintain a level of activity of his own choosing." Except for casualties among infiltrators, truck drivers, or soldiers employed along the roads and trails, the direct loss was sustained "primarily by the Communist block nations (in trucks and materiel) and not by the North Vietnamese." Nor did air attacks on the supply lines seem to exact much of a penalty from these suppliers. Indeed, he predicted that Commando Hunt VII, planned for the 1971–72 dry season, would destroy only about 1 percent of the combined annual truck production of China and the Soviet Union.

Unlike the Russell Committee of three years earlier, Sullivan sought to avoid reliance on sensor-guided aircraft to attack the maze of hidden trails. Instead he favored dispatching small numbers of South Vietnamese troops, more mobile and self-reliant than the task force that had recently been ambushed during Lam Son 719. In what amounted to a rehearsal for interdiction of the trail without U.S. assistance, the South Vietnamese units, equipped exclusively with the kind of armament they would have after the U.S. withdrawal, would probe the jungle wilderness, ambushing North Vietnamese columns and planting antipersonnel mines along the infiltration route. He predicted that such a campaign could inflict "a 50 percent to 75 percent attrition against walking personnel over a four hundred–mile trail system."[35]

The idea of enabling South Vietnam to attack North Vietnamese infiltrators and thus exact direct retribution for North Vietnam's continued prosecution of the war also appealed to Secretary of Defense Melvin Laird. On May 17, 1971, he asked the Joint Chiefs of Staff to comment on the "feasibility, desirability, and possible concepts for RVNAF [Republic of Vietnam Armed Forces] targeting of the personnel infiltration system by either ground or air operations, employing currently planned force levels." Secretary Laird showed special interest in "harassing, terror, and other unconventional warfare tactics" that would depend for success on locating and filling "intelligence gaps."[36]

When the Joint Chiefs asked the various commanders to respond to Laird's request for comments, the Seventh Air Force suggested, as Sullivan already had done, that patrolling on the ground afforded the South Vietnamese their best chance of locating the trails and harassing foot traffic. Experience, said the air force headquarters, had already shown that aerial photography seldom detected narrow paths winding through dense forests, a strong argument for reconnaissance on the ground. South Vietnam, moreover, had only rudimentary equipment for intercepting radio traffic among infiltration control points, pinpointing the location of transmitters, and gaining some insight into conditions on the Ho Chi Minh Trail. A Vietnamized radio monitoring unit already taking shape likely would be unable to penetrate strong antiaircraft defenses and zero in on transmitters broadcasting in southern Laos, since it would fly slow and vulnerable EC–47Ds. Patrols probing southern Laos on foot, perhaps after helicopters had inserted them into the region, would have to supplant aerial reconnaissance as a source of information, taking prisoners for interrogation, tapping telephone lines, and reporting activity beneath the jungle canopy. Seventh Air Force headquarters concluded that the principal role of South Vietnamese aviation in future interdiction would be to respond to strike requests from ground units probing the trail complex.[37]

In his response to the Joint Chiefs of Staff, Admiral McCain, the Commander in Chief, Pacific, sounded a pessimistic note about future interdiction in southern Laos, declaring that the United States had no "intelligence system which can be provided the RVNAF that will consistently and reliably locate infiltrating personnel." He conceded that "aggressive ground patrolling, agent operations, and increased employment of all forms of aerial surveillance" could help the South Vietnamese gather the essential intelligence, but he warned that the enemy, if pressure became really severe, could carve out new trails beyond reach of ground probes.[38]

The Joint Chiefs of Staff proved to be more optimistic than McCain, concluding that it was "feasible and desirable to increase effort on targeting the personnel infiltration system," as Sullivan and Laird proposed. Although intelligence about the trails seemed sketchy at this time, the Joint Chiefs believed that knowledge of the trails would increase before the war became totally Vietnamized. The integration of existing data, they suggested, would improve the probability of pinpointing interstations and other installations.[39]

As the Joint Chiefs observed, useful data already existed, awaiting systematic exploitation. For example, representatives of the National Security Agency reported locating about one-third of the larger stations through which the infiltration groups passed, but most of those they had found lay along the least vulnerable portion of the trail in southern Laos. "Unfortunately," as Leonard Sullivan observed, "the data go from good to crude below Chavane in Laos and become nonexistent in the permissive areas of northern Cambodia, which might be the easiest to attack." Knowledge of the more vulnerable regions would increase, he believed, when South Vietnamese ground patrols became more active.[40]

As a "personal favor" to Sullivan, officials of both the National Security Agency and Central Intelligence Agency reexamined their holdings on troop infiltration through Laos. "In general," the Department of Defense official discovered, "they surprised themselves with the amount of data they had which they had not really collated 'because no one ever asked for it.'" Although admitting that the intelligence specialists did not believe the trails could be "made to stand out like varicose veins," Sullivan agreed with them that "more effort in both collection and analysis" would yield worthwhile results. The door to attacking the troop infiltration network seemed ajar, if not yet fully open.[41]

The preliminary views of the intelligence specialists on disrupting the movement of troops seemed so encouraging that Secretary Laird called for a test to determine the feasibility of an interdiction campaign against infiltrators. He directed the Joint Chiefs of Staff to consult the commanders who would be involved, review the latest available intelligence, and prepare an overall interdiction plan for the fiscal year ending in June 1972, which would involve the South Vietnamese in actual air and ground operations. Laird told the Joint Chiefs to "consider," when drafting the plan, the preparation of a "data base" that would, "at an appropriate time" permit an evaluation of the attacks against the troop infiltration route.[42]

Admiral McCain's headquarters assumed responsibility for preparing a master plan for interdiction, called Island Tree, that featured regional cooperation among Thai, Cambodian, and South Vietnamese forces in disrupting movement on the Ho Chi Minh Trail. A task group at the headquarters of the Military Assistance Command, Vietnam, drafted its own Island Tree plan, essentially a test of the capability to attack troop infiltration through southern Laos as an element of the multinational interdiction concept. Two closely related activities thus carried the same name, Island Tree. To prevent confusion between them, Operation Island Tree usually referred to the master plan drawn up by McCain's Pacific Command and Project Island Tree to the attack on infiltrators devised for General Abrams. Because Task Force Alpha had "perhaps the most responsive display of intelligence" concerning enemy supply lines and infiltration routes, the Infiltration Surveillance Center at Nakhon Phanom became the centralized targeting facility for Project Island Tree.[43]

For a time, it seemed that Task Force Alpha would benefit from an especially promising source of intelligence, a North Vietnamese lieutenant captured in Cambodia. When questioned at Saigon by intelligence specialists from the Seventh Air Force, he revealed interesting details about troop infiltration such as the typical layout of the way stations where the groups rested and the security measures at these stations, including camouflage. The lieutenant did not, however, know the precise route he had followed and the exact places he had stopped between North Vietnam and Cambodia.[44]

Although this source of information failed to pan out, the analysts at Nakhon Phanom could nonetheless combine data from Army and National Security Agency sources with their own holdings and request aerial reconnaissance of those areas in Laos, ultimately numbering 29, that seemed to merit closer attention. During September they managed in this fashion to isolate three trail segments and fix, to their satisfaction, the location of the way stations along these portions of the troop infiltration route.[45] To check the accuracy of its analysis, Task Force Alpha recommended planting strings of five remotely actuated sensors within listening distance of suspected bivouac sites near the stations. If the first string in a given area reported nothing when triggered from Nakhon Phanom, F–4s would plant a parallel string one and one-fourth miles distant, for the evidence indicated that these facilities usually lay within a two and one-half mile radius of the station. By switching on the microphones several times each day, the task force hoped to locate the camps accurately enough for B–52s to bomb them and also to determine the hours that troops usually occupied them, so that the attacks would kill North Vietnamese rather than merely tear up the jungle.

On October 10, 1971, Seventh Air Force approved this plan for reconnaissance by sensor, but early results proved discouraging. For instance, Task Force Alpha concluded that one of the way stations on the troop infiltration route lay just beyond the Laotian end of Ban Karai Pass and arranged for F–4s to drop a string of sensors there. Unfortunately, a surprisingly strong wind caught the parachutes and blew the sensors away from the intended location; they came to rest alongside a road, where the noise and vibration from trucks masked any sounds that might have been made by troops. A second string went into place a week later, but it, too, produced no information of value. Despite this thoroughly frustrating experience, the Deputy Chief of Staff, Intelligence, at Seventh Air Force headquarters, Brig. Gen. Ernest F. John, insisted that "until reliable ground reconnaissance is routinely employed, air-dropped sensors will prove the most effective means of establishing target location and lucrativity." Because of the ground defenses in place during the dry season of 1971–72, patrols did not have even the slimmest chance of systematically penetrating the area around Ban Karai or the other passes. The dropping of sensors would therefore continue.[46]

While the initial efforts to ferret out the infiltration routes brought only frustration, Leonard Sullivan kept close watch from Washington over the effort to locate and bomb the troops moving down the Ho Chi Minh Trail, conferring with intelligence specialists and encouraging those who worked on the data bank for Project Island Tree. As he confided to General Lavelle, now in command of the Seventh Air Force, Sullivan worried that the B–52s would hit the infiltration route "just hard enough to move it but not hard enough to hurt it for the whole year."[47] He intended to give the South Vietnamese, who "can't kill trucks like we have," the ability "to go after the one purely North Vietnamese commodity for which the NVN pays—their troops." Specifically, he hoped to kill, wound, or neutralize half the troops infiltrating through southern Laos. Some estimates maintained that the North Vietnamese were already losing some 10 percent, mainly to disease and desertion; systematic attack should kill or wound 30 percent and force another 10 percent to desert, thus achieving the attrition rate that Sullivan sought.[48]

To increase North Vietnamese casualties, Sullivan hoped to locate twelve stations, 20 percent of the estimated sixty stations where the average group bound for South Vietnam might pause during its journey through Laos. According to his interpretation of data based mainly on the interrogation of prisoners and defectors, 15 percent used just twenty of them to enter the northern provinces of South Vietnam, another 10 percent of the infiltrators passed through thirty-five of the stations en route to the A Shau region, and the remaining 75 percent, while marching farther south, might utilize all the sixty stations, (seventy stations if following the new spur to Cambodia). He believed that as many as five hundred men passed each of the sixty points every day during the height of the dry season.

Once Task Force Alpha had pinpointed the dozen stations, Sullivan proposed sending B–52s against half of them every night. These strikes, he claimed, would kill or wound 75 North Vietnamese per day; other air attacks, plus ambushes and raids by ground forces, ought to account for another 150, so that the toll of dead and wounded would reach 225 each day during the peak infiltration season, with disease and increased desertion accounting for 25 or more. Every day, his campaign would cost the enemy the equivalent of at least half of the estimated 500 men bivouacked at any one of the stations along the route through Laos.[49]

Sullivan's contacts at the Central Intelligence Agency tried to come up with data that would help convert this idea into reality. They turned to the computer tapes on which Admiral McCain's analysts had recorded information on troop infiltration over the last six months of 1970, but the data proved too general. For example, the agency's computer specialists could not determine whether an infiltration group merely passed through a station, paused only briefly, or rested there for a few days.[50]

Undeterred by this setback, Sullivan had one of his assistants, Everett A. Pyatt, chart the progress of several infiltration groups, using National Security Agency reports on file at the Pentagon. Although the earlier computer analysis had failed, Pyatt succeeded, at least to Sullivan's satisfaction, but in doing so he destroyed an assumption underlying the interdiction scheme. Pyatt found that the rate of infiltration did not remain constant, as Sullivan had believed. The evidence revealed that five hundred soldiers did not pass through every station every day; instead, the number occupying a particular bivouac area fluctuated unpredictably. As many as eight days might separate the infiltration groups, according to Pyatt, but up to four groups might bivouac simultaneously at different sites clustered around one of the larger way stations. Pyatt's study offered two general conclusions, one somewhat promising, the other discouraging. On the positive side, a station might have enough satellite bivouac areas to accommodate two thousand men, four times the number usually suggested, and this could improve the chances of detection and attack. On the negative, the North Vietnamese had foreseen the possibility of attacks on the trails their troops used, and they therefore dispatched the infiltration groups at random, avoiding a predictable schedule. Sullivan believed that the greater numbers offset the effect of random scheduling, and he remained optimistic about locating and attacking the infiltration groups.

The analysts at Nakhon Phanom shared Sullivan's confidence. Despite the discouraging start, Task Force Alpha believed it had found some of the stations. Carefully planted acoustic sensors, commandable microphones, infrared photography, and other detection devices would indicate, with acceptable certainty, when North Vietnamese soldiers bivouacked at the sites.[51] Consequently, the analysts at Nakhon Phanom felt certain enough to obtain the approval of the Seventh Air Force for a combat test using the Project Island Tree data bank. Based on the premise that sensors, together with other means of collecting intelligence, could detect worthwhile targets along the infiltration route, the test sought to discover how the enemy would react to air strikes directed specifically against personnel. If the individual stations on the troop route proved small, as initially believed, the North Vietnamese could easily abandon them and shift the entire route westward to avoid further attack. If they were larger and to some degree enmeshed with the road net, as recent intelligence seemed to indicate, the enemy might have to continue using them and endure the resulting punishment.[52]

The War against Trucks

The test began on November 29, 1971, when F–4s dropped commandable sensors around a way station, where troops seemed likely to arrive in a few days, so as to pinpoint the actual bivouac sites. When triggered from the Surveillance Center, these microphones transmitted both human voices and the sound of trucks, evidence that this was an interstation where the routes used by trucks and troops converged. B–52s pounded the location on December 6, and sensors activated after the attack picked up shouts and screams, as well as the revving of truck motors and detonations characteristic of exploding storage dumps.[53]

Secondary explosions of the kind heard on December 6 posed a problem to technicians trying to interpret sensor transmissions, for the delayed-action bombs, which disrupted attempts to fight fires or otherwise deal with the damage, could be exploding, along with drums of fuel and burning ammunition. Tests with recordings made after earlier B–52 strikes proved, however, that each type of detonation had its own distinctive sound. The baseball-sized cluster bomb unit, for instance, exploded with a higher pitch than a secondary explosion, whereas the secondary was louder and lasted longer.[54] Despite this yardstick for helping determine bomb damage, Task Force Alpha relied on a standard technique for polling sensors instead of comparing the acoustic signature of detonations. After testing the microphones shortly before the planned attack, the operators issued no further commands until twenty to forty minutes after the strike, so that all delayed-action bombs would have detonated, ensuring that the microphones picked up only genuine secondary explosions. As a result of the delay, however, the Surveillance Center missed the earliest of the secondaries.[55]

Despite the adoption of this cautious sensor technique and the apparent success of the first Island Tree strikes, certain questions remained unanswered. Did the sound of trucks indicate a common link on the road and trail nets, or simply a large transshipment point or truck park on the highway network? Why did the microphones pick up so many explosions when the infiltration groups carried only small-arms ammunition? Were the screams actually from wounded infiltrators or from injured members of the cadre that operated the station? Those asking such questions included Leonard Sullivan, who wondered if the B–52s had really killed any of the infiltrators. "I am reminded," he wrote Georges Duval, science adviser to the Military Assistance Command at Saigon

> of my plea to Jack Lavelle to "hit 'em hard enough to hurt 'em not just enough to move 'em." I'm not sure he even hit 'em. It raises some interesting questions about early warnings of impending B–52 strikes. It surely doesn't look as though it's worth maintaining B–52 strikes against anything that can move.[56]

Although officials like Sullivan might have doubts, Task Force Alpha plunged ahead with the Island Tree project. On December 13, intelligence specialists assigned to the Military Assistance Command reported that elements of the 320th North Vietnamese Army Division were moving down the Ho Chi Minh Trail through southern Laos. Once again F–4s dropped commandable sensors in likely bivouac areas, and the microphones almost immediately reported truck activity. Although lacking any evidence confirming the presence of troops, the task force insisted on a B–52 strike against the most active site. Finally, on December 22, just three and one-half hours before the scheduled attack, the sensors detected human voices. The bombers struck as planned, touching off secondary explosions that thundered continuously for an hour. Indeed, two hours after the last bomb fell, instruments at Nakhon Phanom were still recording screams and an occasional explosion when the operators activated the microphones.[57]

Attacks of this severity continued into March 1972. From December through February, Task Force Alpha nominated 355 targets for B–52 attack, and the bombers struck 186 of them with a mixture of high explosive and antipersonnel munitions. The number of secondary explosions counted at Nakhon Phanom exceeded ten thousand before March 1. The sixty-three strikes conducted during February got credit for preventing an offensive expected that month, but in spite of the bombing, the enemy invaded South Vietnam at the end of March, a further indication of the difficulty of assessing the effect of Project Island Tree. The available evidence— mainly from commandable microphones, since the camera could not penetrate the jungle cover nor patrols the enemy's ground defenses—showed only that the raids caused explosions, which apparently destroyed ammunition and supplies stockpiled in dumps either associated with the existing truck route or established specifically to support some future offensive in South Vietnam or Cambodia. The number of infiltrators killed remained unknown, as did the impact of these deaths on North Vietnamese plans.[58]

The experience of a North Vietnamese soldier actually caught in an Island Tree strike underlined the difficulty of relying on secondary explosions to calculate the results. One night late in January, as the infiltrator and his comrades slept in hammocks slung between trees in a jungle bivouac, bombs began exploding among them. Taken by surprise, the men scrambled for cover, but not quickly enough. Weeks later, after his surrender, this soldier told an interrogation team that after the attack he had seen five bodies and five or six wounded men. Except for some bombs apparently fitted with delayed-action fuzes, he remembered no explosions after the strike. His group, moreover, carried nothing that would cause secondary explosions, and the only postattack fires burned in trees set ablaze during the bombing.[59]

This prisoner's story suggests that fires and secondary explosions did not necessarily prove that bombing killed North Vietnamese infiltrators. The particular B–52 strike that caught his infiltration group killed or wounded at least ten men, probably more, without touching off the kind of secondaries that Task Force Alpha's microphones regularly reported. Yet, the Surveillance Center at Nakhon Phanom kept citing secondary explosions as proof of Project Island Tree's success, insisting that the detonations occurred because the enemy was storing munitions and other supplies near the bivouac sites.[60]

Although the number of secondary explosions escalated, evidence of casualties among infiltrating units became increasingly scarce, despite an occasional bit of encouragement like the report from a prisoner-of-war that bombs had killed his reg-imental commander.[61] Enemy activity at previously identified stations declined after January 28 and did not revive for a month, a lull that the Military Assistance Command attributed to the deadly effect of Project Island Tree.[62] Intelligence reports later suggested, however, that the enemy had adopted a policy of abandoning any station on the troop infiltration route that came under air attack, whatever the results of the strike, and constructing a new station two or three miles away.[63] The establishment of new way stations and their satellite bivouac areas could have caused U.S. intelligence temporarily to lose contact with the North Vietnamese infiltration routes, and during such a period the troops moving south would have remained safe from Island Tree strikes.

A sudden resumption of activity around previously located way stations result-ed in Operation Orgy, a raid conducted on March 6 by thirty-six B–52s against a bivouac site where troops appeared to have returned. At the time of the bombing, an airborne relay aircraft experienced an equipment failure, preventing the Surveil-lance Center from receiving sensor transmissions and making the usual damage assessment. Bomber crews, however, reported seeing forty-six secondary explo-sions, most of them concentrated in two target boxes.[64]

After North Vietnam invaded the South on March 30, 1972, the number of Island Tree strikes declined abruptly as emphasis shifted from southern Laos to the battlefields of South Vietnam, and on May 9 the project officially ended. Since late November of the previous year, sixty-seven specially planted sensor strings had monitored twenty-nine carefully chosen areas, providing or confirming information that helped Task Force Alpha nominate more than 350 potential targets, 197 of which the B–52s actually bombed. The strikes produced 15,192 secondary explo-sions and inspired intelligence officers at Task Force Alpha to hail Project Island Tree as "one of the most important and successful operations" of what proved to be the last Commando Hunt campaign. In retrospect, however, the tribute seems wild-ly exaggerated.[65]

What had Project Island Tree accomplished? Before the attacks on the infiltra-tion route officially ended, Admiral McCain acknowledged that the actual impact on troop movements would almost certainly remain a matter of conjecture. Neither aerial photography, intercepted radio messages, nor even prisoner-of-war interroga-tions could verify what was happening when bombs exploded beneath the jungle canopy. In his opinion, only ground patrols might ferret out the truth, and these could not penetrate the strengthened enemy defenses to gather the evidence. Maj. Gen. Alton D. Slay, Deputy Chief of Staff, Operations, of the Seventh Air Force, shared the admiral's doubts. The Air Force officer conceded that aerial photography of Island Tree targets revealed scars on the jungle canopy, but he pointed out that bombs exploding in the treetops could have caused these as readily as secondary explosions on the ground below. No matter how much faith the specialists at Nakhon Phanom might place in their sensor polling technique or their interpretation of the signals, Slay remained unconvinced that the microphones were picking up secondary explosions rather than delayed-action bombs. Neither Admiral McCain nor General Slay accepted the claims made for Project Island Tree.[66]

Explosions rocked the jungle in the aftermath of the B–52 strikes; that much no one could deny. Assuming that Slay's skepticism had no foundation and that secondary explosions actually produced the sounds reported by the sensors, the impressive total did not prove that the Island Tree data base had achieved its "principal object" that, from the viewpoint of Task Force Alpha, was "to pinpoint infiltrating enemy troops, thus making them vulnerable to bombing, harassment, ambush, etc."[67] Secondary explosions indicated the presence of supplies, particularly ammunition, rather than troops, and supply dumps served the truck route rather than the troop infiltration network. If roads and trails, storage areas and bivouacs, proved dangerously close together, the North Vietnamese could easily separate them by a safe distance. The way stations for troops, unlike the supply depots, possessed an inherent mobility, so that the enemy, perhaps after being stung by the first few strikes, could have neutralized Project Island Tree by moving the bivouac sites as the bombing progressed. Leonard Sullivan may well have been right when he suggested that the B–52 strikes on the troops infiltration route might force the enemy to move, without really hurting him.

Propeller Aircraft. The A–26 (top) was one of the earliest aircraft attacking the Ho Chi Minh Trail in Laos. The T–28 (center), shown here with Laotian Air Force insignia, served in the air forces of several countries. The A–1 (bottom) filled many roles, here escorting an HH–53 rescue helicopter.

Jet Aircraft. The B–57 (top), B–52 (center), and an F–4 refueling from a KC–135, an aircraft that extended the range and flight time for many aircraft (bottom).

Navy Aircraft. An A–6 attack aircraft (top); the carrier USS *Coral Sea* (center) with F–4s, A–7s, and A–6s on the bow; and an EA–3B electronic reconnaissance aircraft (bottom).

Controller Aircraft. Both the O–1 (top), which dated from World War II, and the twin-engine O–2 (center) were modified commercial products. The twin-turboprop OV–10 (bottom) was designed for visual reconnaissance, was armored, and had hard points for armament. This one has a laser designator pod on the fuselage under the cockpit.

Reconnaissance Aircraft. An EC–47 (top), an RC–135M (center), and an RF–4 (bottom), with technicians removing the film.

Two Versatile Aircraft. The Airborne Command and Control Center module is loaded into a C–130 (top), and a C–130 carries a 20,000-pound bomb that will create a helicopter landing area (center left). An F–4 is armed with Sparrow and Sidewinder missiles for the air-intercept mission (center right), and an F–4 releasing a laser-guided bomb has a Loran antenna on top of the fuselage, enabling it to accurately drop sensors (bottom).

Air Force Experiments. The AC–123K Black Spot (top), the B–57G (center), and the QU–22 (bottom).

210

Chapter Thirteen

Interdiction Comes to an End

Late in Commando Hunt V, the 1970–71 dry-season interdiction campaign, President Nixon consulted with his advisers at his San Clemente, California, estate and decided on an interagency review of U.S. policy toward Laos, including operations against the Ho Chi Minh Trail. Maj. Gen. Frank B. Clay of the Army, the Deputy Director of the Joint Staff for National Security Council Affairs, served as chairman of a panel that included representatives of the Department of Defense, the Department of State, the Central Intelligence Agency, and the National Security Council. The group's report, issued in April 1971, reaffirmed the importance of interdicting the passage of supplies and reinforcements from North Vietnam through southern Laos as a means of protecting Vietnamization and the ongoing U.S. withdrawal from South Vietnam. The Commando Hunt series, supplemented later in the year by Island Tree strikes, would continue, as would the operations elsewhere in Laos designed to sustain the pro-United States government of Prince Souvanna Phouma.[1]

Project Island Tree tested the ability of sensors and aircraft to find and hit North Vietnamese troop infiltration routes through southern Laos. Essentially experimental, the project had its greatest success against stockpiled supplies rather than infiltrating troops, its intended victims. In contrast, by the fall of 1971, the Commando Hunt operations had amassed a record of apparent successes stretching back to the dry season of 1968–69. The planners of Commando Hunt VII expected it to equal or surpass its predecessors in killing trucks, its natural prey.

The signs at first indicated that Commando Hunt VII would not lack for targets. Indeed, the volume of truck traffic began picking up as soon as southern Laos recovered from the severe flooding that had taken place in July, when tropical storms struck during the height of the rainy season, and seemed likely to approach peak levels for the dry season in October, one month earlier than usual. The enemy's logistic system came to life like someone awakening from a nap; the entire Ho Chi Minh Trail stirred, and cargo, the life blood of the war, began circulating simultaneously throughout the transportation system. Near the southern terminus, depots filled before the seasonal rains and maintained by river traffic throughout the period of the southwest monsoon, began releasing material for combat units in South Vietnam and Cambodia, even as trucks brought fresh supplies from depots farther

The War against Trucks

north in southern Laos and North Vietnam. As in any northeast monsoon season, the volume of cargo reaching the forward units rapidly increased as the rains abated and a new tide of supplies rolled southward, passing from one sector to another, and by season's end, filling the depots in each sector to sustain operations during the coming rainy months.[2]

The northeast monsoon season did not, however, get off to a normal start in the fall of 1971. Scarcely had trucks started moving throughout the road net when nature intervened; tropical storms deluged the region on October 1 and again on the 9th. Enemy convoys returned to the highways on the 13th, but ten days later, a typhoon struck Chu Lai on the coast of South Vietnam, triggering three to four inches of rain in the mountains of Laos and halting traffic on the trail until November 1, when the weather at last became stable.[3]

By washing out the dams essential for continued use of the waterways and flooding the roads, the storms disrupted the flow of cargo and deprived the aerial interdiction campaign of targets, in effect, postponing Commando Hunt VII. The delay enabled U.S. airmen to continue aiding the embattled Laotian forces on the Plain of Jars in the northern part of the kingdom, where the North Vietnamese and Pathet Lao inflicted a succession of defeats on the troops loyal to Souvanna Phouma. The intensified air campaign began in northern Laos during July 1971, after road traffic had decreased in volume throughout southern Laos because of the seasonal rains triggered by the southwest monsoon. Lacking suitable targets on the Ho Chi Minh Trail, AC–130 gunships patrolled the night skies over the Plain of Jars in search of enemy motor convoys. At first, the gunships responded to truck sightings by Army Grumman OV–1 Mohawks, fitted with radar and infrared equipment, but experience soon showed that the AC–130s could detect trucks just as well using their own sensors, without help from the OV–1s. As a result of the flooding in southern Laos, the gunships remained in action in northern Laos for much of October, flying armed reconnaissance, and Souvanna's forces on the Plain of Jars, still clinging to a defensive line, thus benefited from the weather that postponed the annual surge of truck traffic in southern Laos. The North Vietnamese and Pathet Lao, superior in numbers and firepower, advanced relentlessly throughout the northeast monsoon season, as air power focused on the Ho Chi Minh Trail, but the invasion of South Vietnam, at the end of March 1972, caused the enemy to yield ground on the Plain of Jars in northern Laos (and also further south on the Bolovens Plateau), while shifting men and weapons to new battlefields in Quang Tri Province, at Kontum, or at An Loc.[4]

Despite the bad weather that delayed its start, Commando Hunt VII promised to be the most devastating of the dry-season interdiction campaigns, eclipsing even Commando Hunt V. Everything needed for success seemed now at hand: AC–130 gunships armed with 40-mm cannon, plus a 105-mm howitzer on a few; laser-guided bombs in greater numbers than before; low-light-level television and other sensors; and the experience of three other northeast monsoon seasons in detecting, predicting, and disrupting traffic on the Ho Chi Minh Trail. The advantages in aircraft,

212

weapons, and sensors—and the claims of past success—concealed a number of weaknesses, however. For example, the Commando Hunt series had produced many officers familiar with various aspects of the interdiction campaign, but few who had truly mastered the complex undertaking. The dilution of experience resulted from an Air Force policy that restricted the normal period of service in Southeast Asia to one year, except for high-ranking officers in certain assignments, and tried to avoid requiring involuntary second tours of duty there. The Strategic Air Command faced a further complication, the need to remain prepared for nuclear war while fighting conventionally in Southeast Asia; to avoid removing highly trained units from the retaliatory force for long periods, it chose to rotate B–52 crews as often as necessary on short tours, 179 days of temporary duty, rather than a single assignment of a year's duration.

Besides facing the consequences of diluted experience, the planners of Commando Hunt VII had fewer aircraft available than during previous northeast monsoon season campaigns. When the original Commando Hunt operation began in the fall of 1968, 105 B–52s stood ready in the western Pacific, and the 1,700-odd aircraft in South Vietnam and Thailand included 621 fighter-bombers and light bombers. The totals in the two most important categories declined to 89 B–52s and 545 fighter-bombers and light bombers for Commando Hunt III, 54 and 309 for Commando Hunt V, and 54 and 226 for Commando Hunt VII. An increase in the number of AC–130 gunships from 6 at the beginning of Commando Hunt V to a total of 18 a year later provided an exception that dramatized the shrinkage of the overall force.[5] The reduction in resources did not affect just the Air Force. The Marine Corps had withdrawn its expeditionary forces earlier in 1971, including the attack aircraft and fighter-bombers available for previous Commando Hunt operations. The Navy now maintained just two aircraft carriers in the Gulf of Tonkin and for five days in December 1971 had only one on station. Although U.S. aerial strength steadily declined, Vietnamization had not yet produced a South Vietnamese Air Force that could share the burden of interdiction in southern Laos.[6]

The prediction of heavier traffic than in any previous dry season seemed accurate when the skies began to clear, but the unexpected rains in October hampered both the North Vietnamese, who could make little or no use of their roads and waterways, and the airmen whose aircraft could not locate the targets that did exist. When large numbers of trucks finally began moving during November, recurring cloud cover concealed the traffic and made even more dangerous the difficult task of attacking convoys on the heavily defended roads that twisted among jungle-covered hills. Dense clouds screened the trucks throughout most of December 1971, with clear skies favoring the attacker only 2 percent of the time. Airmen usually found thick cloud cover below twelve thousand feet and visibility less than three miles. February 1972 afforded the best weather of Commando Hunt VII, with aircraft operating under favorable conditions some 48 percent of the time. In short, North Vietnamese cargo handlers, drivers, and repair crews generally benefited throughout the operation from cloud cover without the handicap of torrential rain.[7]

The War against Trucks

Beneath the persistent clouds, a fleet of trucks, reconstituted since Commando Hunt V, drove over a more extensive highway net than ever before. An estimated thirty-three hundred miles of roadway served the North Vietnamese in southern Laos, with construction and repair continuing year around. As in previous years, the return of dry weather and the increase in truck traffic resulted in the detection of newly completed bypasses and hitherto unknown segments of road. During Commando Hunt VII, intelligence specialists detected some three hundred miles of additional highway, though, in some cases, photo interpreters may have discovered old roads hidden for years beneath jungle canopy or lattice-work camouflage.

Route 29 represented the most ambitious road-building project that surfaced in the 1971–72 northeast monsoon season. Even though the oldest sections may have existed as early as 1968, it accounted for 20 to 25 percent of the construction detected during Commando Hunt VII. Part of the so-called "core route structure," Route 29 originated along Route 91A northeast of Muong Phine. From this important storage area, it headed southeast, finally disappearing in a maze of roads and trails east of Saravane. In addition to this main supply route, North Vietnamese engineers cut a short north-south road through the jungle about sixteen miles west of Khe Sanh. Designated Route 1033, it paralleled an older highway and afforded an alternate passage between Routes 925 and 9. Other new construction included a road to speed traffic southwest from Ban Karai Pass, plus several routes in southernmost Laos that led into either South Vietnam or Cambodia.[8]

Although supplemented by waterways, pipelines, and even porters, the ever-changing road net carried most of the supplies that passed through southern Laos en route to South Vietnam and Cambodia. The flexibility inherent in the motor transport system enabled the North Vietnamese to succeed in moving cargo by truck, despite unrelenting air attack. Aerial operations seldom cut roads or closed passes long enough to create the kind of traffic tie-ups that provided profitable targets for bombing. Blocking tactics usually achieved no more than partial success because of the proliferation of alternate routes and the speed with which North Vietnamese engineers and Lao laborers could bypass or repair cuts in the roadway. Monitors posted every few kilometers, and linked by telephone, directed traffic on vulnerable sections of roadway, dispersing trucks to avoid bunching up behind a cut and then rerouting them on still-hidden alternate roads until construction crews completed a bypass or closed the cut.[9]

Besides expanding and repairing the network of roads, the leadership at Hanoi maintained adequate inventories of trucks and fuel. It increased fuel storage capacity in southernmost North Vietnam by 15 to 20 percent during 1971, until a reserve of some seven and one-half million gallons was on hand, enough to operate twenty-nine hundred trucks over the roads of southern Laos for an entire dry season. Besides stockpiling fuel, North Vietnam replenished its fleet of trucks, placing orders in 1971 for some fifty-six hundred vehicles, almost 90 percent of them types normally used on the Ho Chi Minh Trail. Since the Commando Hunt series began in the northeast monsoon season of 1968–69, the government had obtained about this number of trucks each year, but the latest order specified delivery of twenty-two hundred vehicles by July 1972, about three times the number received in the first half of 1971. In addition, imports by rail and sea increased during 1971, and military aid from the Soviet Union tripled compared to 1970. According to a Pacific Air Forces' assessment, the influx of trucks and other war material could indicate that Hanoi was doing more than merely making good the losses suffered during Commando Hunt V and might point to a massive resupply effort over the Ho Chi Minh Trail, perhaps as early as 1972 and possibly in support of a major offensive.[10]

Some of the new trucks had diesel engines, which do not use electrical ignition systems and were therefore undetectable by the Black Crow ignition detectors mounted in the latest gunships. Although Black Crow rarely pinpointed a truck, it could find areas where gasoline-powered trucks operated, cuing other sensors, like the combination of infrared and television, that zeroed in on individual trucks. Defectors and prisoners of war told interrogators that the North Vietnamese not only knew about Black Crow and its ability to pick up electromagnetic impulses from gasoline engines, but had also tried to shield ignition systems with metal foil and contain the telltale emanations. Diesel power, however, without electrical ignition, completely thwarted Black Crow.[11]

Strengthening the already powerful antiaircraft defenses of the Ho Chi Minh Trail proved the best countermeasure of all against airborne sensors or aerial attack, for the increased firepower forced the marauding aircraft to fly higher, use their sensors at extreme range, and take evasive action when diving into the envelope of gunfire. The aircrews who conducted Commando Hunt VII faced heavier antiaircraft fire than in previous campaigns against the Ho Chi Minh Trail. The estimated number of guns more than doubled between April 1971 and November of that year, increasing from about seven hundred to perhaps fifteen hundred. Until the 1970–71 dry season, 37-mm guns predominated, but within a year, 57-mm weapons surpassed them in numbers. By February 1972, forward air controllers were reporting twin 37-mm and 57-mm guns, probably single weapons paired in jury-rigged mounts to increase the volume of fire. In the course of Commando Hunt VII, 85-mm guns, tentatively identified as seeing action during the previous dry season, definitely joined the handful of 100-mm types that protected the trail. As usual, the enemy concentrated his antiaircraft batteries around supply dumps, truck parks, and other immobile targets, generally encircling his 85-mm or 100–mm weapons with 23-mm or 37-mm guns.[12]

As the number of guns increased, antiaircraft crews proved more aggressive. Previously, the enemy avoided firing on forward air controllers to prevent them from pinpointing the muzzle flash and calling down an air strike, but he now blasted away at these aircraft. Gunships too became prime targets. Prisoners reported the existence of an incentive program that offered food and cigarettes to gun crews engaging or downing U.S. planes, with the biggest award reserved for the destruction of an AC–130. A 57-mm crew claimed this top prize, bringing down one of the gunships on March 30, 1972.[13]

The War against Trucks

The threat to the AC–130 gunships increased the tension felt by all crew members, especially by the two scanners most responsible for telling the gunship pilot how to maneuver to avoid fire from the ground. One scanner kept watch in comparative comfort from behind a starboard window, while the other leaned halfway out of the cargo compartment into the cold and darkness. Before moving to his perch at the rear of the airplane, the airman donned winter flying clothes and put on a parachute harness attached to a lifeline. He then crawled along the cargo ramp, locked in a roughly horizontal position, and hung over the rear edge so that his upper body and arms projected into the slipstream. To lessen his discomfort during the night-long missions, he sometimes jammed wooden flare boxes into a metal lip at the edge of the ramp and used these makeshift supports as arm rests. According to Lt. Col. Kenneth D. Negus, Jr., who flew the AC–130, the rear lookout, "bouncing around in the wind, . . . was to scan inside the orbit, and outside the orbit, and forward as far as he could see under the nose of the airplane." Whenever he spotted a muzzle flash, he looked for the stream of tracers, estimated "based on the length and direction of the tail . . . whether or not the tracer would be a threat to the aircraft," then reported over the interphone. Lieutenant Colonel Negus recalled, "This guy would judge the stuff," giving the direction from which it was coming. "Then you'd generally get some kind of clue from him, like 'It's a threat,' or 'No threat.' Or you might hear him say 'Jesssus Chriiist!' Then you knew it was going to be pretty close." As soon as danger appeared, the lookout told the pilot how to avoid it, whether to break right or left or to roll out of the banked turn from which gunships did their firing.[14]

Because of the danger from antiaircraft fire, F–4s, some of them carrying laser-guided weapons, escorted the gunships. After sighting a stream of tracers piercing the darkness, the fighter pilot coordinated with the gunship, which might use its laser to designate the gun position if the F–4 carried a laser-guided bomb, and then rolled in on the point where the hostile fire originated. In the words of Lieutenant Colonel Negus, who had seen many such attacks, "He hurtles toward the ground in the pitch black night with very few outside references, jinking most of the way to avoid enemy AAA [antiaircraft artillery], with a general knowledge of the antiaircraft gun's location and only a rough idea of the . . . elevation" (whether on a hillside or the floor of a valley). Because of these difficult circumstances, Negus believed that half the bombs directed at antiaircraft batteries landed one thousand feet or more from the target and had no observable effect, unless they accidentally hit something that exploded. No more than 10 percent struck close enough to damage the weapon or kill or wound the crew, but fully 40 percent detonated within two hundred fifty to one thousand feet of the target, discouraging the gunners, disturbing their aim, or perhaps sending them diving for cover.[15]

To solve the problem of hitting a compact target, sometimes glimpsed only briefly in the dark, the Seventh Air Force tried a bigger bomb. Where antiaircraft guns formed dense clusters, as around the mountain passes, the larger the blast, the greater the likelihood of destroying some of the weapons, or so the reasoning ran. To create a massive detonation, C–130 transports dropped a device used for leveling trees and heavy undergrowth to create helicopter landing zones—fifteen thousand pounds of explosives lashed to a pallet and parachuted onto the target. Planners at Seventh Air Force headquarters tried to pinpoint the antiaircraft concentrations on their maps and sent the coordinates to Combat Skyspot radar operators who directed the bomb-carrying C–130 to a release point. Despite spectacular explosions, results proved mixed. Sometimes antiaircraft fire diminished; and other times the bomb missed its mark by thousands of feet, shaking up the gunners, but failing to silence their weapons. The fault for the misses lay not in the radar, but in reliance on maps of southern Laos not yet corrected by loran-controlled photography.[16]

Except for the few aircraft mounting the 105-mm howitzer that saw action in Commando Hunt VII, the AC–130 gunships lacked weapons with sufficient range to duel successfully with the larger of the North Vietnamese antiaircraft guns. As a result, the gunships used their sensors to guide F–4s against the batteries that protected the Ho Chi Minh Trail. The laser designator, boresighted with the low-light-level television camera, proved especially effective. While the sensor operator kept the camera and laser locked on the gun position below, a pilot dived his F–4 into the guidance basket, released a laser-guided weapon, and pulled up. This technique, tested during the previous dry-season interdiction campaign, saw service during Commando Hunt VII.[17]

Fire from the ground posed so great a danger to AC–130s and other aircraft that the Seventh Air Force launched a daytime "recce [reconnaissance] gun kill program" against the antiaircraft batteries. Beginning on January 17, 1972, RF–4Cs photographed the probable locations of these guns. Forward air controllers met with the reconnaissance crews and photo interpreters, reviewed the film, and within twelve hours after the photographic mission received prints showing actual or suspected weapon positions. After coordinating with the crews of Phantoms carrying laser-guided bombs, the forward air controllers took off in their laser-equipped OV–10s (that bore the name Pave Nail) to rendezvous with the F–4s and direct strikes on the designated sites. Guided by the up-to-date photographs, the crews of the OV–10s used binoculars and the starlight scope, which functioned in daylight as a simple magnifying device, to find the actual gun positions, a difficult task since the scope and the binoculars had different powers of magnification. To shift from binoculars to the other device involved, in the words of someone who had done so, "one hell of a transfer problem." The combination of RF–4C, laser-equipped OV–10, and F–4 with laser-guided bomb claimed the destruction of 30 antiaircraft guns of the aggregate of 252 listed as destroyed during Commando Hunt VII. The small number of weapons reported destroyed cast doubt on the value of the recce gun kill program, especially since new weapons almost immediately replaced those that air attack had eliminated. Intelligence analysts could not, however, determine how many casualties the program had inflicted on trained gun crews, though the killing of gunners must have hurt the enemy as much or more than the destruction of weapons. Even with the aid of fresh photographs and use of the laser, the most skilled and boldest of airmen did not destroy many enemy weapons, but they did kill or discourage some of the gunners, at times force batteries to shift position, and thus make life easier and longer for the crews of the slow-moving gunships.

Whereas antiaircraft fire became gradually more deadly as one dry-season interdiction campaign succeeded another, surface-to-air missiles, only faintly fore-shadowed in the 1970–71 interdiction effort, had a dramatic impact on Commando Hunt VII. The storm-delayed first phase of Commando Hunt VII, the interdiction of the access routes from North Vietnam into southern Laos, which finally began on November 1, called for a total of twenty-seven Arc Light strikes per day, divided unevenly among Mu Gia, Ban Karai, and Ban Raving Passes and the maze of roads and trails at the western edge of the demilitarized zone. The appearance of surface-to-air missiles disrupted the planned Arc Light strikes, even though the weapons did not destroy or damage even one of the bombers. The North Vietnamese launched the first missiles of the campaign on November 2, when two of the weapons roared aloft from a site in North Vietnam and streaked past a Navy aircraft near Mu Gia Pass. Missile launchers next appeared within range of Ban Karai Pass. Because of the increased danger there, B–52 operations halted on November 9, resumed on the 18th when missile activity abated, and stopped for good just three weeks later after a battery tried unsuccessfully to down two naval aircraft. In December, near Mu Gia Pass, missiles claimed their first victims of the campaign. On the 10th, a battery in North Vietnam destroyed an F–105G Wild Weasel equipped to detect missile-control radars and attack them with missiles that homed on the transmissions, and a week later a missile forced an F–4 to maneuver so violently that the pilot lost control of the aircraft and had to eject, along with his weapon systems officer. As a result, Mu Gia Pass joined Ban Karai on a proscribed list for B–52s. By the end of December 1971, launchers in North Vietnamese territory had fired twenty-two missiles, compared to just three in the final two months of 1970.

In December 1971, reconnaissance crews spotted the first missile site set up in southern Laos since the close of Commando Hunt V; on Christmas Day batteries began occupying four partially complete firing locations, and others became operational during the new year. On January 10, 1972, an F–4 successfully dodged missiles fired from Laotian soil. Between January 11 and 17, hunter-killer aircraft teams tried to deal with the threat, but in spite of their efforts, a strip of southern Laos, extending westward some thirty miles from the South Vietnamese border and stretching from Mu Gia Pass to the vicinity of the A Shau Valley, became a danger zone. Since surface-to-air missiles could now engage targets as far west as Muong Nong and Tchepone, their presence forced the AC–130s to pull back, even as truck traffic increased in the region. During February, the enemy launched fifty-one missiles, all but one of them from North Vietnamese soil, but destroyed only one aircraft, an F–4E hit over the western edge of the demilitarized zone. On March 28, however, a missile crew in Laos scored a direct hit on an AC–130 southwest of Tchepone, killing everyone on board.[18]

Surface-to-air missiles claimed ten victims and antiaircraft fire thirteen during Commando Hunt VII, but the improving defenses throughout the transportation network had far greater effect than the twenty-three losses would indicate. Missiles forced the B–52s to avoid, at various times, important target boxes near Mu Gia and Ban Karai Passes, Tchepone, and Muong Nong and imposed similar limits on the gunships. During one eight-day period in January, an estimated 240 vehicles escaped attack because gunships could not patrol segments of road defended by surface-to-air missiles. To obtain some degree of protection from these weapons, all AC–130s began carrying jamming equipment to disrupt the radar guiding the missiles. Efforts by the Seventh Air Force to locate and destroy missile sites caused the diversion of both reconnaissance sorties and fighter strikes from the war against trucks. In March 1972 alone, 182 reconnaissance sorties, an average of almost six per day, searched for missile launchers covering the core route structure.[19]

While surface-to-air missiles and antiaircraft guns disrupted the interdiction of the Ho Chi Minh Trail, in the process downing several aircraft, MiG interceptors intervened over Laos, normally by daylight. Radar controllers based at Ba Don airfield near Dong Hoi, assisted by others at Cam Quang south of Vinh and Moc Chau in northwestern North Vietnam, maintained surveillance over most of southern Laos and the Plain of Jars to the northwest and could direct the MiGs in radar-controlled passes at U.S. aircraft throughout the region. When North Vietnamese fighters crossed into Laos, policy dictated that U.S. aircraft get clear of the area east of the Mekong River. Thus, the enemy, by investing in an hour's flying time by a MiG, could force pilots to withdraw and return, depriving them of as much as three hours of operating time over Laos. Commando Hunt VII had been under way less than two weeks, when the first MiG of the campaign ventured over southern Laos, probing the skies near Mu Gia Pass. Eight days later, on November 20, two MiGs entered Laotian airspace, one of them ineffectually firing a missile at a B–52. By the end of January, when the threat from surface-to-air missiles had already forced the B–52s farther south, seventy-six MiG–21s and four MiG–19s had made fifty-eight separate incursions in the vicinity of the Commando Hunt area of operations in southern Laos. Meanwhile, North Vietnamese fighters conducted sixty-five penetrations over northern Laos, each time disrupting air support for troops loyal to Prince Souvanna Phouma.[20]

As the Seventh Air Force staff drew up plans to overcome whatever defenses the enemy might employ and execute for Commando Hunt VII, questions arose about the validity of the precise and impressive statistics generated by the earlier campaigns. The planners of Commando Hunt VII added up the claims for the last four aerial interdiction campaigns—from the beginning of Commando Hunt III through the final stages of Commando Hunt VI—and found that aerial interdiction received credit for destroying 99,494 tons of supplies, even as the enemy consumed another 53,304 tons operating and defending the trail. The cargo believed to have entered southern Laos during these four aerial interdiction operations totaled only 135,360 tons, however, about 17,000 tons less than the amount listed as destroyed and consumed. Further to complicate the tally, analysis indicated that 13,522 tons reached South Vietnam and 1,768 tons arrived in Cambodia. Unless the enemy had squirreled away some 32,000 tons along the Ho Chi Minh Trail before Commando Hunt III began, the numbers made no sense.

After reexamining the total, Seventh Air Force headquarters accepted the input and exit figures—135,360 tons in and 15,290 out—for they reflected the aggregate of the typical loads of the trucks counted by the sensor fields covering the entrances and exits of the Ho Chi Minh Trail. The volume of supplies consumed seemed slightly less certain, since it reflected the estimated cargo, varying from rice to gasoline, needed by the probable number of antiaircraft gunners, laborers, and drivers operating, defending, or using the roads, bivouacs, depots, trails, and waterways. The category of supplies destroyed, because it incorporated the most assumptions, received the closest scrutiny as a possible source of error. To calculate the amount of destruction, planners assigned an arbitrary weight of cargo destroyed to such events as a truck kill, a secondary fire, or a secondary explosion and then totaled the number of events and the values assigned to each to arrive at an aggregate number. During 1970, analysts reduced the amount of cargo counted as destroyed in each kind of incident, but apparently not by enough, for the total did not reflect the existence of stockpiles along the trail that had to be replenished constantly if the North Vietnamese were to keep at least a trickle of cargo moving to the battle front year-round, wet season and dry. Staff officers of the Seventh Air Force therefore reduced by more than a third the total weight of supplies destroyed to arrive at a number that reflected the existence of this reserve.

"It is obvious," the planners acknowledged, "that the last element, supplies destroyed, is questionable and deserves detailed attention." Although "a positive relationship" existed between tonnage actually destroyed, "whatever that may be," and the "observed effects of air strikes—secondary fires, explosions, and numbers of trucks destroyed and damaged," the "absolute tonnage values" previously assigned to these effects "could not equate to the true weight of supplies destroyed because all effects are not observed." As a result, the planners cautioned that tonnage values obtained in this fashion "must be regarded as an index of effects rather than as an absolute value."

Although questioning the validity of statistics as an absolute measure of progress, Seventh Air Force headquarters still hoped to interpret general trends in terms of tonnage. The search for an accurate index led to Task Force Alpha, which used a slightly different method of counting. The Infiltration Surveillance Center divided the Ho Chi Minh Trail into six zones and relied on its sensors to count the number of trucks entering and leaving each one. Analysts concluded that every vehicle that did not continue southward to the next sector had either unloaded its cargo or been destroyed. By subtracting the number of trucks reported destroyed in each sector from the number that did not resume the journey, and then multiplying the remainder by the weight of cargo believed carried by the average truck, Task Force Alpha calculated the amount of cargo deposited in each sector. The aggregate left in all the sectors represented the amount on hand for local consumption and the reserve for future distribution.

When the Seventh Air Force shaved more than a third from the estimate of cargo destroyed, its new total closely approximated the figure produced at Nakhon Phanom. On the basis of these two generally consistent estimates, the planners of Commando Hunt VII concluded that stockpiles remained essentially the same in the fall of 1971 as they had been a year earlier, at the onset of Commando Hunt V, and could support only about a month of sustained combat. In a burst of optimism, they assumed that the volume of supplies delivered over the Ho Chi Minh Trail would remain unchanged from one dry season to the other and that "the enemy could not markedly increase the level of activity by main force units in the Republic [of Vietnam] and Cambodia during the period of U.S. withdrawal regardless of how attractive that option might be."[21]

Even as Air Force officers at Tan Son Nhut questioned the statistical approach and with help from Task Force Alpha, answered those questions to their own satisfaction, the Deputy Director of Defense Research and Engineering for Southeast Asia Matters, Leonard Sullivan, expressed reservations about the tally of vehicles destroyed or damaged, which analysts used to help determine the amount of war material denied to the enemy. "Skepticism over the accuracy of the Air Force's claimed truck kills in Laos," he wrote, "ranks second only to disbelief of the Army's 'body count' numbers as the longest standing argument over U.S. effectiveness in SEA." He raised the question on the eve of Commando Hunt VII because of "fresh intelligence estimates that, for the umpteenth time, have indicated that the North Vietnamese are importing fewer trucks than we claim 'killed,' while giving no indication of running out of trucks."

Sullivan's "personal feelings" persuaded him that Air Force claims of trucks killed were exaggerated. He doubted that 20-mm and 40-mm cannon, carried by most gunships, could destroy a truck even with a direct hit. These vehicles, after all, could survive startling damage, for, as he pointed out, articles in Hanoi newspapers "attest to how 'beat up' an operational truck can be and still work." He also felt that analysts underestimated the enemy's ability to make repairs on these worn and battered vehicles, but, in his opinion, the major weakness in Air Force estimates was the absence of "photographic evidence to support the vast wreckage that should have accumulated on the Laotian landscape (at least ten carcasses per mile of road and trail)." His final argument against the claims of trucks destroyed rested on the construction of petroleum pipelines in southern Laos; if the convoys could not get through, North Vietnam certainly would not have invested manpower and materials in a project to bring them fuel.[22]

Part of the problem that troubled Sullivan, the obvious discrepancy between results claimed and results verified, stemmed from the use of arbitrary standards, which varied over the years, to determine the severity of damage inflicted on a truck. At times a gunship victim, for example, need not burn to be listed as destroyed; the criteria for the earliest Commando Hunt operation stated that an immobilizing hit with even a 20-mm shell killed a truck, a dubious proposition at best. Other weapons were governed by different rules, so that a truck overturned by a bomb blast was considered damaged rather than destroyed, in most cases an accurate assessment, since repair was probable. By November 1971 and the beginning of Commando Hunt VII, a vehicle had to explode or catch fire to be counted as destroyed.[23]

Sullivan did not overestimate the enemy's ability to keep trucks in action. A gunship pilot who had attacked numerous convoys agreed that the North Vietnamese operating the road network had "some of the finest mechanics and ingenious young country boys that know how the hell to make a truck work that you'll ever find." Their job was to fix trucks in a hurry, as shown by an aerial photograph he had seen in which someone was already changing the punctured tires of a damaged vehicle less than one hour after an air attack had disabled it. To divert attention from damaged trucks that could be repaired, the North Vietnamese left charred hulks near the roadside and built dummies from rocks and logs; moreover, they set fires to blind infrared equipment that otherwise might have revealed the absence of heat from the hood of a dummy vehicle or, in conjunction with the television camera, shown mechanics actually at work.[24]

Although Sullivan questioned the number of actual truck kills, he remained convinced that the Commando Hunt series hurt the enemy. He sought to improve damage assessment rather than to challenge the value of the truck war. After all, he insisted, "it is relatively easy to *disable* a flammable, gasoline driven, water-cooled truck, which runs on pneumatic tires." As a result, he placed "high confidence" in Air Force claims of "damaged/destroyed," provided that "D/D stands for 'disabled' and therefore out of action for some time." Disabled trucks, he further argued, imposed more of a burden on the enemy than did vehicles actually destroyed, for the cripples required "additional assets to compensate for their 'down time,'" forcing the North Vietnamese to maintain a reserve of trucks and make frequent adjustments to convoy schedules.

After redefining trucks damaged or destroyed as trucks disabled, Sullivan declared that the air campaign in southern Laos did not, in the final analysis, seek to destroy or even disable vehicles, but tried to prevent their cargoes from arriving as planned. Commando Hunt accomplished this goal in several ways, he maintained. Air strikes not only destroyed supplies carried on trucks or stored near the highways, but also had the indirect effect of forcing the enemy to deploy antiaircraft and road repair units that consumed food and material that otherwise would have sustained the war in South Vietnam or Cambodia. In short, he did not quarrel with the belief that aerial interdiction had proved effective, but with the emphasis on trucks killed rather than trucks crippled.[25]

Sullivan simply did not believe that the effort and technology invested in the Commando Hunt operations could fail, and the view from the cockpit reinforced the judgment that the enemy must be suffering. For instance, many crew members must have agreed with Lieutenant Colonel Negus, an AC–130 pilot, that these gunships, at least, were hurting the North Vietnamese. "We'd have fires going all the time," he said. "I mean you just don't make those big monster bonfires out of rock piles and log things." Despite his confidence, Negus had to admit that the next day's reconnaissance flight usually would show "nothing there, not a thing," though he attributed the lack of verifiable results to the ability of the enemy to make emergency repairs on damaged trucks and clear wreckage from the trail.[26]

Sullivan shared the opinion that the war against truck transportation hurt the enemy, and he expected Commando Hunt VII to "hardpress the NVA [North Vietnamese Army] to get enough supplies to seriously threaten the GVN [Government of Vietnam]."[27] Maintaining this degree of pressure would not be easy, however. Because of the continuing U.S. withdrawal, the number of sorties available throughout Southeast Asia during the 1971–72 dry season had declined sharply. Instead of the fourteen thousand tactical aircraft and one thousand gunship sorties allocated each month during Commando Hunt V, planners could now rely on just ten thousand sorties by tactical aircraft and seven hundred by gunships. Nor could B–52s take up the slack, for the monthly sorties by these bombers would remain one thousand for all of Southeast Asia. In conducting Commando Hunt VII, laser-guided bombs, improved gunships, and control of aircraft by Task Force Alpha would have to compensate for the reduction in authorized sorties, but enemy defenses had improved, raising questions about the damage this reduced effort could inflict.[28]

To help make the most of the available sorties, the Seventh Air Force gave Task Force Alpha control over strike aircraft in the sectors nearest the mountain passes, authority the facility at Nakhon Phanom had exercised over the entire operating area during the first of the Commando Hunt series. The Surveillance Center underwent modification during Commando Hunt VI that permitted exercise of this responsibility when dry weather returned. After June 10, for example, a new computer program enabled technicians there to convert grid coordinates into loran data for aircraft equipped with this navigation aid, principally AC–130s and F–4Ds.[29]

During Commando Hunt VII, two new operating cells within the Surveillance Center, each responsible for handling assigned aircraft over a specified portion of southern Laos, made use of loran conversion. Plans originally called for three cells, but the task force did not have enough technicians to man them, for during each working shift, a cell required six persons to interpret sensor data, select targets, and contact the assigned aircraft. Of the two cells actually organized, one controlled aircraft in Visual Reconnaissance Sectors 1 through 3 in southeastern Laos—including Nape, Mu Gia, and Ban Karai Passes—while the other kept watch over Sectors 4 through 9, encompassing Ban Raving Pass, Tchepone, and Chavane, then extending to the Cambodian border. Each cell had its own computer terminal and radio equipment, plus large-scale charts of the visual reconnaissance sectors for which it was responsible. The new cells sought to avoid the inflexibility of Commando Bolt, with its dedicated sensors and designated points of impact, by directing aircraft against loran coordinates determined on the basis of activations anywhere in the sensor field.

Within both functioning cells, members known as ground surveillance monitors (or sometimes as surveillance technicians) determined which sensors had detected traffic and passed this information through the computer to the team's target analysts, who examined all the stored data derived from the particular strings and decided whether the signals represented a worthwhile moving target. In the case of fixed targets, a person called a targeteer, rather than a target analyst, weighed sensor data against intelligence from other sources to determine whether an attack would be profitable. Both target analysts and targeteers gave their nominations to controllers who radioed an advisory or a directive to the assigned aircraft.[30]

The remodeled combat control center at Nakhon Phanom went into limited service on November 10, 1971, with only one of the two recently organized cells making full use of its equipment. This cell, called Headshed, controlled aircraft in the three northern visual reconnaissance sectors. The other, known at first as Headshed II, issued target advisories throughout the rest of southern Laos, but did not exercise direct control, thus following the practice in effect during Commando Hunt V. Headshed functioned so well, however, that on November 23, Headshed II, renamed Termite to avoid confusion, started directing strikes by assigned fighters in Sectors 4 and 5, which included Tchepone, Muong Nong, and the approaches to the A Shau Valley. In the sectors farther south, Termite continued to furnish target advisories, working through an airborne battlefield command and control center.[31]

The southernmost sectors posed a serious problem for Termite because Nakhon Phanom could not, at so great a distance, maintain reliable radio contact with low flying aircraft sometimes masked by mountains or ridge lines. Despite the communications problem, gunship pilots like Lt. Col. Loyd J. King found the advisories helpful; he reported that, on the average, he received one or two good targets each night, and on one occasion he was told to look for ten trucks in a ten-mile stretch of road, found them and, unless his sensors deceived him, destroyed them all. To the north, where the Infiltration Surveillance Center controlled aircraft and issued directives rather than advisories, the Seventh Air Force normally assigned Task Force Alpha perhaps ten or fifteen sorties each night, supplementing them by diverting aircraft from other targets. In the northern sectors, pilots complained that the Surveillance Center needed radar to keep track of the aircraft it controlled; because fighters and gunships moved continuously, as did the trucks they were stalking, positions plotted manually became instantly out of date. The lack of radar, along with poor long-distance communications, handicapped Task Force Alpha as a control agency.[32]

Besides manning the Headshed and Termite cells, Task Force Alpha continued to operate Commando Bolt, which Col. Thomas J. Mathews, one of the center's last commanders, saw as a research and development project rather than a functioning system. After reviewing the various factors that affected its performance—ranging from the need for accuracy in the placement of sensors to the requirement for unvarying speed on the part of the trucks—Mathews concluded that "the probability of placing bombs within a lethal radius of the target was extremely small."[33]

For Commando Hunt VII, the Surveillance Center supervised the planting of new Commando Bolt sensors and the replacement of those that had fallen silent during the monsoon rains. On October 1, a month before the dry-season operation finally began, fifteen strike modules remained in place from Commando Hunt VI, five of them "marginally effective" and the others mute, but F–4s planted, replaced, or replenished the ten modules planned for the initial phase of Commando Hunt VII. Characteristically, the sensors began to fail from the moment of their first transmissions, so that by the end of the year, only four modules were operating at peak efficiency, while three were marginal and the remaining three required reseeding. As the tide of war material rolled southward, North Vietnamese engineers built new roads that bypassed many of the original Commando Bolt strings, forcing the Surveillance Center to arrange for new ones. By the time Commando Hunt VII ended with the North Vietnamese invasion of South Vietnam in March 1972, Commando Bolt strings covered twenty-seven road segments, an increase of seventeen from the number in phase one, though not all the sensor arrays remained active.[34] The sensor modules for Commando Hunt VII differed from those used earlier in the series of operations. To conserve sensors, planners reduced from twenty-four to twelve the total in each module, relying on three four-sensor strings to generate targets for prowling A–6s and F–4s.[35]

During the 1971–72 dry season, Commando Bolt controllers, who used the call sign Copperhead, faced the sort of problems encountered whenever Task Force Alpha directed operations. Like Termite, and to a lesser extent Headshed, Copperhead's worst difficulties had to do with communications. When traffic on the roads attracted a number of aircraft to a particular visual reconnaissance sector, Copperhead sometimes had to get clearance before its F–4 Phantoms or A–6 Intruders could respond to Commando Bolt sensor activations. If gunships and fighter-bombers already were swarming nearby when a module became active, Copperhead might not be able to make contact with the appropriate control agency—the airborne battlefield command and control center, Headshed, or Termite—in time for an attack on the moving convoy. Radio failure could complicate the task of obtaining prompt clearance, for even the latest model set might fall victim to terrain masking at a crucial moment.[36]

In March 1972, as the wet season approached, Task Force Alpha became involved in Project KISS, an acronym for "kill in selective strings," an attempt to destroy trucks at the risk of knocking out sensors, which seemed a fair trade in the final weeks of Commando Hunt VII when the period of heaviest truck traffic neared an end. The project required that Phantoms loaded with canisters of fragmentation bomblets orbit within five minutes of the road monitoring strings likeliest to detect the movement of vehicles. When these sensors began transmitting, the Surveillance Center alerted a nearby F–4, which dumped at least part of its bomb load on the string. Because most of the road under electronic surveillance lay within the fragmentation pattern of bombs dropped on the sensors, prospects seemed excellent for inflicting damage on passing trucks. "The technique," Task Force Alpha reported, "has been found to be successful on several occasions."[37]

During Commando Hunt VII, controllers at Task Force Alpha and patrolling gunships worked closely together. Formerly, the gunship commander, once he obtained permission from the airborne battlefield command and control center to enter a sector, had relied on the sensors carried by his aircraft and if he chose, ignored the advisories radioed from Task Force Alpha. During Commando Hunt VII, however, the Surveillance Center exercised control over gunships in the area from Muong Nong northward. Serving as traffic cop, the airborne battlefield command and control center still gave permission for the gunship to enter a sector, but the Surveillance Center assigned "a specific location to go and work," as one pilot phrased it. Once the aircraft had attacked targets on this segment of roadway, the crew contacted Nakhon Phanom to "sort of get cleared and work another area." This procedure enabled Task Force Alpha to determine if its directives were being followed, assuming that radio contact remained unbroken. Unfortunately, the radio link with patrolling gunships often failed, forcing Task Force Alpha to call on the airborne battlefield command control center to assume responsibility for passing along target information to gunships. To compensate for loss of contact with the gunships, analysts at the Surveillance Center sometimes estimated the route and speed of a convoy for Headshed or Termite, who would set up a "strike box" on the road the trucks followed. After receiving the coordinates from the appropriate cell at Nakhon Phanom, the airborne battlefield command and control center forwarded the information to the gunship, which used its own sensors to search out trucks within the box and attack them.

The increased use of directives or advisories radioed from Nakhon Phanom troubled some gunship pilots, who believed that the enemy listened to these messages and carefully tracked the AC–130s. During the previous dry season, North Vietnamese drivers seemed to respond to advisories almost as quickly as U.S. aircrews had. One gunship commander pointed out that "people have to realize that when you get an advisory over the air in the clear, if you aren't pretty well on top of the place, five or ten minutes is all the enemy needs to . . . drive under a tree . . . somewhere and hide." The apparent ability of the North Vietnamese to react to U.S. radio traffic undermined the confidence of some aircraft commanders in the instructions sent from Nakhon Phanom, though others tried to take advantage of any monitoring the enemy might do, waiting perhaps twenty minutes before responding, in hope of catching the convoy as it returned to the road.[38]

Listening in on radio transmissions formed the most complex part of what one gunship pilot called "a very rudimentary and [yet] sophisticated system of countermeasures." Traffic monitors posted along the roads strained to hear the distinctive sound of a turboprop AC–130 as it responded to an advisory. If one of these men heard the aircraft, he reported its heading by telephone to the sector command post. An alert went out to antiaircraft batteries in the gunship's probable path, telling them to fire a single round if they spotted the airplane, thus warning nearby convoys to scatter and take cover. "I'm convinced," an AC–130 veteran declared, "that they kept track of us this way on boards at command centers and watched our operation. If they once knew where we were, they could pretty well guess where we would be five minutes from now."[39]

Of all the countermeasures used by the North Vietnamese during Commando Hunt VII, one of the most effective was to reschedule the heaviest road traffic from late night to late afternoon and early evening. Previously, the movement of trucks reached a peak after 8:00 p.m., when it was fully dark and the gunships could make the deadliest use of their sensors and firepower. As these aircraft demonstrated their effectiveness, the operators of the Ho Chi Minh Trail dispatched fewer trucks at this most dangerous time, instead sending them out at dusk or, to a lesser degree, near dawn. At these times, antiaircraft gunners, who did not have fire-control radar, could easily silhouette the black-painted AC–130s against the pale sky, while on board the gunship, the infrared sensor and the low-light-level television performed poorly, if at all, in the partial light. General Slay, the Deputy Chief of Staff, Operations, at Seventh Air Force headquarters, tried to use the gunships at dawn and dusk by having them patrol at about 12,500 feet, beyond the reach of the lighter antiaircraft guns. The enemy, however, now had enough 57-mm guns to challenge the AC–130s, driving them even higher, and as altitude increased, the sensors became less useful. By the end of January 1972, Slay gave up on dawn and dusk patrols.

As the dry season progressed, more and more trucks moved by daylight, especially on the densely forested western fringe of the Ho Chi Minh Trail. By the time Commando Hunt VII ended, almost one-fourth of all sensor activations occurred in the daytime, most of them on the western routes, but jungle canopy protected the traffic. The Air Force had no sensor that could penetrate the foliage and pinpoint trucks or roads. At times, forward air controllers circled a stretch of jungle and failed to see the enemy even though sensors hanging among the trees signaled his presence. Occasionally a B–52 strike or a fifteen thousand pound bomb might blow a hole in the canopy and expose a segment of road, but North Vietnamese engineers and Laotian laborers quickly bypassed the potential interdiction point.[40]

Although truck killing remained the dominant objective throughout Commando Hunt VII, Task Force Alpha did not devote all its electronic resources to attacks on traffic, for sensors also contributed to strikes on transshipment points and other support installations. To locate this sort of fixed target, the Surveillance Center set up an acoustic targeting area, a concept tested inconclusively during Commando Hunt VI. An acoustic targeting area consisted of several strings of two or three acoustic sensors dropped near possibly lucrative targets. The array transmitted the sound of any activity to Task Force Alpha, which could call for a strike without awaiting further verification. Before the adoption of this targeting method, planners had relied on detailed aerial reconnaissance to select areas where strings of acoustic sensors might produce indications of enemy activity and, if the sensors reported a hostile presence, insisted on photographic or visual confirmation before approving an air attack. The change attempted to correct serious failings in the earlier method of area monitoring; formerly, the reconnaissance conducted before planting sensors and again before an air strike tended either to reveal the enemy's presence, rendering the sensor strings unnecessary, or to alert the North Vietnamese that they faced imminent discovery and attack.[41]

The War against Trucks

Besides handling the Commando Bolt operation, directing other operations, and issuing advisories to fighter-bombers and gunships, Task Force Alpha collected and analyzed data on the road network. To accomplish this, the organization spun a web of monitoring strings that reported on the volume and pattern of traffic. Roadwatch teams dispatched by the Central Intelligence Agency also gathered this kind of information, but by this time, they concentrated mainly on the roads exiting from Mu Gia Pass, where the antiaircraft defenses enabled the North Vietnamese to run longer convoys at more frequent intervals than was possible in the core route structure. In terms of area covered and type of traffic observed, the road monitoring strings proved essential for determining the flow of traffic and locating the stops that might represent sector boundaries, transshipment points, or storage areas.

To monitor traffic throughout Commando Hunt VII, Task Force Alpha again plotted air-delivered sensor bands across selected choke points from the vicinity of Mu Gia Pass southward to the exit routes into South Vietnam or Cambodia. Although the sensor bands, first employed in Commando Hunt V, afforded better prospects of detecting traffic patterns than the linear strings previously used, the concept had at least one defect. An analysis conducted prior to Commando Hunt VII demonstrated that the series of sensor bands produced a consistently high count of total traffic. The assumption that every truck failing to exit promptly from a sector either unloaded or was killed, though convenient for keeping track of tonnage, did not provide an accurate record of traffic. Some trucks paused within a sector not just for fuel or a change of drivers, but also for emergency repairs, or to pick up as well as drop off cargo, and in doing so broke contact with the sensor field, only to trigger a monitoring string on resuming the journey. Each time the vehicle vanished and reappeared, the Surveillance Center counted it anew. Capt. Eugene A. Taylor, on four nights during March 1971, extracted from the task force computer all the applicable data on transshipment points, convoy speeds, sector boundaries, and road conditions. By interpreting the sensor sequences in the light of this information, he concluded that no more than 59.5 percent of any night's activations signaled the passage of a truck not already counted that same evening. At least 40 percent of the time, sensor bands counted a vehicle twice or more.[42]

Once the intelligence analysts at Nakhon Phanom were aware of the likelihood of "multiple counting," they could compensate for it in their calculations. They found it more difficult, however, to estimate how much traffic they missed entirely because the vehicles traveled on undiscovered or poorly monitored roads. During Commando Hunt VII, officers at the Surveillance Center saw their traffic counts diminish in accuracy, as the North Vietnamese shifted trucks to recently built alternate routes. Hastily implanted strings, sown as new roads were discovered, did detect some of the diverted traffic, but the lack of up-to-date photographs, attributable at least in part to the bad weather prevailing throughout the campaign, prevented thorough coverage of the expanding pattern of roads.[43]

The need to replenish and adjust the basic sensor field taxed the ingenuity of Task Force Alpha. Commando Hunt VII began with the largest field deployed thus far—160 route monitoring strings of five sensors each, ten twelve-sensor Commando Bolt modules, plus thirty-three acoustic targeting areas with varying numbers of three-sensor strings. During the operation, changing traffic routes required not only seventeen additional Commando Bolt modules, but 63 new road monitoring strings and another acoustic targeting area, this one located near the juncture of the borders of Laos, Cambodia, and South Vietnam. In addition, Project Island Tree, the attempt to locate and bomb troop infiltration routes, required a dozen strings of commandable microphones.[44] While extending coverage to newly reported segments of the road net, Task Force Alpha tried to maintain the useful parts of the original field, for example, by replacing 156 of the original 160 route monitoring strings at least once during the campaign. As a result, the total number of reporting strings approached the capacity of the IBM 360/65 computer at Nakhon Phanom. Before replenishing an old string or planting a new one, planners had to determine whether the computer could absorb and act on the additional data.[45]

The Commando Hunt VII sensor field reported to the Surveillance Center through the Green, White, and Blue relay orbits flown by QU–22Bs—when those disappointing airplanes actually functioned—or by the more dependable C–130s. The aircraft on Green orbit retransmitted signals from sensors covering Mu Gia and Ban Karai Passes, while the Blue and White orbits combined to cover strings planted near Ban Raving Pass, around Tchepone, and along roads leading to the south. When this final dry season interdiction campaign started, the Green orbit lay near Muong Phalane, Laos; the White orbit was west of Pakse, also in Laos; and the Blue orbit was near the Laos-South Vietnam border about midway between Quang Tri City, South Vietnam, and the A Shau Valley.

As events unfolded, the orbits changed in response to either enemy pressure or the need to monitor newly planted sensors. The C–130 on White orbit, for instance, shifted at times to an alternate position farther south to relay signals from Island Tree sensors along suspected infiltration trails leading toward the Kontum region of South Vietnam. More serious was the decision to move Green orbit eighteen miles to the west, a reaction to the threat from both surface-to-air missiles and interceptors. After the Green orbit changed on March 29, one day before the invasion of South Vietnam, the mountains of southern Laos masked key sensor strings near Ban Karai Pass and along roads leading from it. This was the first of five adjustments to the Green orbit, but none of the subsequent changes could restore the lost coverage. Similarly, Blue orbit underwent seven moves because of increasing danger from missiles and antiaircraft fire. Once again, the shifts resulted in diminished coverage because of terrain masking, reducing the flow of intelligence from parts of southern Laos, the demilitarized zone, and the northernmost reaches of South Vietnam.[46]

Commando Hunt VII evolved in three phases, as planned, with the weight of effort falling first on the routes entering southern Laos. This initial phase lasted from November 1 through 22, as Air Force and Navy planes attacked "logistical area targets"—such as fords, waterways, truck parks, and supply dumps—throughout designated interdiction areas located near Mu Gia and Ban Raving Passes and along the border between Laos and the demilitarized zone. An average of eleven B–52 target boxes, plus numerous interdiction points, impeded movement on major road and river arteries within each interdiction area. Tactical aircraft concentrated on the interdiction points, dropping bombs and planting mines, and the big bombers, flying in three-aircraft cells, scattered explosives throughout an area measuring either one by three kilometers or one kilometer square, depending on the target.

Transition to the second phase of Commando Hunt VII began on November 23, when Air Force and Navy planes again collaborated in creating blocking belts where main roads paralleled each other and the construction of bypasses seemed difficult. Three such choke points—near Tchepone, Ban Bak, and Chavane—afforded suitable locations, and aircraft established blocking belts at each. Planners realized that the belts would not stop a resourceful enemy, but the obstacles could disrupt and delay road movement, inflicting casualties while doing so.

A blocking belt consisted of from two to six blocking points, enough to place munitions packages across every known road passing through the belt. To set up one of the blocking points, which resembled the interdiction points of the earlier phase, required six sorties by Air Force or Navy Phantom jets and eight by Navy A–7 Corsair IIs. Such an operation normally took place in the afternoon, when it was light enough to deliver accurately all the various bombs and mines. First a pair of F–4s cut the road, dropping four two thousand pound laser-guided bombs. Immediately afterward, two additional F–4s scattered some twenty-three thousand gravel mines around the cut, seeding an area measuring two-tenths by five-tenths of a mile. Another pair of Phantoms then saturated the same area with a total of 4,320 wide area antipersonnel mines packed in eight dispensers. This weapons delivery sequence kept falling gravel from striking the wire triggers extending from the wide area antipersonnel mines and detonating them; better to lose gravel to accidental detonations than the far deadlier mines. Next, eight Corsair II attack aircraft dropped eighty Mk 36 mines capable of disabling bulldozers or other construction equipment. Obviously, the Mk 36s would on impact detonate some gravel and antipersonnel mines, but the "fratricide" rate seemed acceptable. If all went according to plan, when truck traffic picked up at nightfall, the cut and its surrounding minefield would disrupt movement and inflict casualties on road repair crews.

Nearby sensors, elements of traffic monitoring strings, reported North Vietnamese efforts to reopen the road. Before filling the cut and restoring the road to service, the repair crew had to deal with the minefield. Soldiers, lying prone to avoid fragments, threw rocks tied to long cords into the danger zone and slowly retrieved them, detonating both gravel and wide area antipersonnel mines. Once they had cleared the lanes, engineers removed the antivehicular mines so that bulldozers could close the cut, but delayed action high-explosive bombs, dropped along with the Mk 36 mines, might increase the danger. When surveillance monitors at Nakhon Phanom decided that the reported activity presented a good target, they could summon an air strike, after which the minefield might be replenished. To deal with attacks on work crews or attempts to sow more mines, the North Vietnamese sometimes set up antiaircraft guns and converted the blocking point into a flak trap.[47] The enemy's dogged efforts to remove mines and restore the road surface kept traffic moving through the natural choke points, but in the final analysis, according to General Slay, the sheer size and complexity of the road net provided the key to North Vietnamese success in keeping the trucks rolling. There were, he said, "just too many routes and too many bypasses, a large number of which were not even known to us."[48]

Phantoms and Corsair IIs set up the first blocking belt of the second phase near Tchepone in December, but road convoys slipped past, apparently by making a time-consuming detour to the west. Later that month, when sensor activation patterns disclosed increasing traffic beyond the first belt, the effort shifted to Ban Bak, almost sixty miles to the south, where blocking points troubled the enemy until February. Once traffic moved beyond Ban Bak, a new blocking belt went into place at Chavane, as planned, only to be abandoned after one month for lack of results, presumably because the enemy had bypassed it.

The third phase, interdiction of the "exit areas" from southern Laos, began in November, lasted through March, and required the establishment of interdiction boxes across each of the seven main exits leading from southern Laos into South Vietnam and Cambodia. As in the second phase, Air Force and Navy planes created blocking points on roads passing through the boxes. The action began west of Khe Sanh, then moved progressively southward past the A Shau Valley, the Chavane exits, and the tri-border area, finally reaching the highway from Attopeu into Cambodia.

Such was the skeleton of Commando Hunt VII. To flesh out the operation, gunships, B–57Gs, and tactical fighters flew armed reconnaissance over heavily traveled stretches of road. Gunships and forward air controllers in Pave Nail OV–10s used laser illuminators to pinpoint targets for Phantoms carrying laser-guided bombs. Besides attacking target boxes in the entry areas, B–52s joined in battering truck parks, supply dumps, and other installations throughout the core route structure.[49]

Once again, airborne radio direction finding played a role during the campaign. In tests conducted before the 1971–72 dry season, a modified EC–47D, after locating an enemy transmitter, determined the map coordinates and using secure radio circuits passed the location to a forward air controller, who proceeded to the place where the enemy broadcasts seemed to originate and called in fighter-bombers if he spotted a worthwhile target. On December 20 an EC–47D nicknamed Brown Beaver began flying this mission, operating out of Nakhon Phanom to locate potential targets for forward air controllers in southern Laos. At the outset, radio intercepts by the modified transport resulted in the destruction of several bunkers and gun positions, but as the tempo of the interdiction effort increased, the forward air controllers usually proved too busy developing other more easily located targets to respond to Brown Beaver's calls.

The five EC–47Ds normally based at Nakhon Phanom, a contingent that included Brown Beaver, formed but a minor element of the reconnaissance effort against the truck routes. Broadly defined, reconnaissance in southern Laos included visual observation, photography with conventional or infrared film, and the interception and analysis of radio or radar signals. In March 1972, for example, Air Force RF–4Cs flew 330 photo missions and Navy reconnaissance craft 97. In addition, target drones modified to take pictures occasionally penetrated heavily defended areas near the mountain passes. Air Force EB–66Cs flew most of missions to locate radars, though some EA–3Bs, a Navy version of the same airplane, also took part. During the early months of Commando Hunt VII, when surface-to-air missile batteries were extending their coverage deeper into Laos, EB–66Cs provided up to twelve hours of surveillance each day. As the campaign progressed, however, strike aircraft competed with the EB–66Cs for the available aerial tankers, and the hours of electronic monitoring declined. Meanwhile, Air Force RC–135s and modified C–130s were acquiring data on communications traffic, information that helped locate surface-to-air missiles and provided a sharper insight into convoy movements and enemy supply levels.[50]

Photographic reconnaissance also helped count truck kills. When Commando Hunt VII began, many AC–130s again carried videotape equipment to record the damage they inflicted. Unfortunately, the taping system frequently broke down, complicating the task of assessing the results of the operation. To verify gunship effectiveness, the 432d Tactical Reconnaissance Wing dispatched an RF–4C that orbited near the Ho Chi Minh Trail, ready to proceed to loran coordinates reported by the AC–130 and photograph the results of an attack. Based on a combination of aerial photographs, videotape, and crew reports, the AC–130s received credit for destroying or damaging 7,335 vehicles, an average of 4.55 trucks per sortie and a lion's share of the 10,689 trucks claimed, though not necessarily verified, as victims of air attack between November 1, 1971, and the conclusion of Commando Hunt VII on March 31, 1972.[51]

The planners of Commando Hunt VII believed that during the dry season the enemy would "maintain the level of military activity followed in Commando Hunt V, [and] seize the initiative wherever possible by shifting tactics, to offset allied strength, and exploit allied weaknesses as U.S. forces withdrew."[52] After visiting South Vietnam in October 1971, Leonard Sullivan agreed that the level of activity would stay about the same as during the previous dry season. "Neither the GVN [Government of Vietnam] nor NVN [North Vietnam]," he concluded, "is capable of decisive military victory without a dramatic change in their current strategies." For the North Vietnamese, he believed, such a change would require them "to 'surge' down the trails or across the DMZ [Demilitarized Zone] . . . ," actions that seemed unlikely at the time.[53]

Signs of just such a surge soon appeared, however. Not only did North Vietnam order the bulk of its new trucks delivered early in 1972, it stockpiled a larger than usual amount of supplies at depots in the southern part of the country near the demilitarized zone and the passes leading to the Ho Chi Minh Trail. As the dry season at last began, traffic intensified in southern Laos, MiG interceptors appeared at North

Vietnamese airfields, and surface-to-air missile sites proliferated along the border and in southern Laos, further indications that this would be no ordinary year. The Nixon administration decided that the principle of protective reaction applied to this buildup, and Secretary of Defense Laird approved a request by the Joint Chiefs of Staff to conduct a series of attacks designed to disrupt any North Vietnamese attempt to take advantage of diminishing U.S. numbers by launching a major offensive.

Concerned that any indiscriminate bombing might fuel the fires of opposition to an already unpopular war, General Abrams insisted that Seventh Air Force planners take precautions to spare noncombatants. In *Vietnam at War*, his history of the conflict, retired Maj. Gen. Phillip B. Davidson, an Army officer who served both Westmoreland and Abrams as an intelligence specialist, suggests that similar considerations prompted President Nixon to approve the strikes for Christmas vacation, when few students would remain on college campuses to engage in protests. Whatever the precautions, some civilians obviously would die because some military targets, like airfields and fuel dumps, lay near towns and villages, and cloud cover seemed almost certain to cover the panhandle of North Vietnam during the winter months. Because of the weather, U.S. pilots might well have difficulty finding targets, let alone preventing stray bombs from falling among nearby noncombatants.

The Commander in Chief, Pacific, Adm. John S. McCain, Jr., combined two existing contingency plans, Fracture Deep and Proud Bunch, into Proud Deep Alpha, a blueprint for destroying MiG fighters on the ground at Bai Thuong and Quang Lan airfields and damaging the logistic underpinning for a possible thrust into South Vietnam. In keeping with the concern voiced by General Abrams, the plan specified visual bombing insofar as possible, although the highly accurate loran system could serve as a backup. After planning ended on the last day of November 1971, Proud Deep Alpha waited until the day after Christmas, when cloud cover thickened as the aircraft approached their targets so that only a few crews succeeded in attacking.

Since the weather proved uncooperative, the Air Force and Navy airmen turned to loran, supplemented by airborne radar in some naval aircraft, and conducted four days of bombing. Whereas a mere twenty-nine aircraft could bomb visually on December 26, 240 sorties attacked on the following day using instruments, 207 on December 28, 242 on the 29th, and 217 on the 30th. In addition, the forces assigned to Proud Deep Alpha flew twenty-nine armed reconnaissance sorties and 102 to suppress surface-to-air missiles, using radar warning equipment and missiles that homed on the source of radar emissions. Besides forcing the attackers to rely mainly on loran, the bad weather interfered with the aerial photography needed to verify the effects of the bombing.

The results proved mixed: politically, Proud Deep Alpha achieved success in that the four full days of bombing aroused no outcry in the United States; militarily it accomplished much less. As nearly as could be determined, the attacks blasted nineteen craters in runways, superficial damage at most. North Vietnamese oil storage and distribution sustained the greatest damage, as bombs severed pipelines at fourteen points and destroyed or damaged eighty-eight storage tanks and a pumping station. The overall impact on petroleum supplies remained uncertain, however; the Combined Intelligence Center, operated by the United States and South Vietnam, declared that flames had consumed 870,000 gallons of fuel, but analysts at Pacific Air Forces, after viewing the same evidence, cut the total to 194,000 gallons. On balance, the results proved disappointing, especially since the operation resulted in the loss of two Navy and three Air Force aircraft and death of one Navy and six Air Force crewmen.[54]

By the end of January, despite the Proud Deep Alpha attacks, a shift in enemy strategy seemed imminent. Abrams advised McCain that "indicators show a willingness by Hanoi to commit four of the five reserve divisions held in NVN, a commitment which has previously occurred only during Tet 1968 and during Lam Son 719 in March and April 1971." The surge of movement down the Ho Chi Minh Trail, which Leonard Sullivan had described as an essential preliminary to a North Vietnamese offensive, now began in earnest, as General Abrams received evidence of "a very high level of infiltration of personnel and units from NVN into RVN and Cambodia, far in excess of that for a like period last year."[55]

The gathering storm broke on March 30, 1972, when North Vietnamese divisions thrust southward across the demilitarized zone. Within a few days, other columns, spearheaded by tanks that had traveled the Ho Chi Minh Trail, advanced from base areas along the Laotian and Cambodian borders toward the towns of Kontum and An Loc. During the weeks immediately following the invasion, the sensor field continued reporting on truck movement throughout southern Laos, even though U.S. air power, now concentrated over the battlefield, had abandoned interdiction operations. According to admittedly spotty data compiled at the Surveillance Center from sensor reports, 50 percent of the supply tonnage entering Laos in April reached its destination by the end of the month, compared to estimates averaging 16 percent from November through March and 10 to 25 percent in any one month during previous dry seasons. Because of the transfer of aircraft from interdiction to close air support, the enemy enjoyed uncontested movement on the Ho Chi Minh Trail.[56]

The invasion not only cut short Commando Hunt VII, but also forced abandonment of Commando Hunt VIII, the rainy-season interdiction campaign scheduled to follow. Early in April, General Clay, now the Commander in Chief, Pacific Air Forces, contacted Lt. Gen. Marvin L. McNickle, in command of Thirteenth Air Force, which had administrative responsibility for the Thailand-based squadrons assigned to the Deputy Commander, Seventh/Thirteenth Air Force. Clay explained that, after consulting with his Pacific Air Forces staff, he had decided that "we can no longer afford to work on the Mu Gia/Ban Karai input problem or continue to concentrate on the Laos core structure." Emphasis, "for the foreseeable future," would have to rest on the battlefield in South Vietnam and on the exit routes carrying supplies and reinforcements to the advancing enemy.[57]

As the air war shifted away from southern Laos, Task Force Alpha became involved in new projects, such as locating North Vietnamese 130-mm artillery pieces. This change in orientation and Clay's policy of concentrating on battlefield interdiction halted rainy-season surveillance shortly after it began. Phantoms planted only thirty-nine Commando Hunt VIII sensor strings in all of southern Laos. Gaps in coverage and the lack of aircraft for attacks in response to sensor signals deprived the Surveillance Center of an operational role, effective June 20, although it continued to gather a limited amount of information on enemy movements. One week later White orbit came to an end, leaving Blue and Green to relay data from northern South Vietnam and the exit routes from southern Laos. By mid-September only eleven sensor strings still reported on road traffic; Task Force Alpha had lost the war against trucks.[58]

What had Commando Hunt VII accomplished? The last of the aerial interdiction campaigns had not prevented the enemy from invading South Vietnam, attacking from southern Laos as well as across the demilitarized zone. The supplies sent southward during this operation might have sustained an offensive launched with supplies stockpiled earlier. If so, interdiction of the trail had already failed, for the filling of these supply dumps would indicate that neither Lam Son 719, the South Vietnamese raid into southern Laos early in 1971, nor Commando Hunt V did more than inconvenience a determined enemy. General Slay of the Seventh Air Force staff believed that the offensive had shallower roots, with the buildup of supplies for the invasion taking place mostly during the northeast monsoon season of 1971–72. In his opinion, " . . . it was obvious at the start of the North Vietnamese offensive that in spite of . . . Commando Hunt VII the enemy had amassed huge quantities of supplies to support his forces." He refused to brand the operation a failure, however, arguing that aerial interdiction preceding the attack had increased the cost to North Vietnam in lives and cargo. "It is reasonable to assume," he insisted, "that, without the Commando Hunt VII interdiction effort, the enemy could have mounted a much better campaign."[59]

The planners of Commando Hunt VII had expected that aerial interdiction would prevent North Vietnam from taking advantage of the U.S. withdrawal by launching a major attack,[60] but the enemy struck a more savage blow than the Tet offensive of 1968. In summing up, General Slay could say only that the last of the interdiction campaigns made things somewhat harder for the enemy. Why had Commando Hunt VII failed to live up to expectations? According to Slay, the disappointing results reflected the interplay of U.S. and North Vietnamese tactics and strategy.

At the root of the failure lay the system of priorities in which reducing U.S. participation and casualties in the war took precedence over preparing the South Vietnamese to take over the fighting. Consequently, in the dry season of 1971–72, when the Air Force and Navy had cut back the number of aircraft for interdiction, the South Vietnamese air arm could not make up the difference. Nor was the United States willing to risk either gunships, the deadliest of truck killers, or B–52s against surface-to-air missiles. Taking advantage of this reluctance to incur losses, the enemy extended his missile coverage deeper into southern Laos, forcing the gunships and big bombers from important segments of the Ho Chi Minh Trail.

General Slay believed that equipment shared the blame with policy. In his opinion, only the AC–130 "played an impressive role" in the interdiction campaign. The AC–119K was "not very effective" because of its limited ceiling, firepower, and speed. He considered the B–57G, hampered by inadequate sensors and voracious fuel consumption, to be "a disaster." Fighters, he concluded, demonstrated limited value against trucks, even when dropping laser-guided bombs, but the difficulty lay in finding the target initially and not in locking onto it with a laser. The laser-equipped OV–10 proved especially disappointing, for it had only a night observation device to spot trucks at night; without a better cuing sensor, the crew of the OV–10 could not make effective use of the laser.

Task Force Alpha came under fire for its deficiencies as a control agency, principally the breakdowns in communication that forced it to shift responsibility to the airborne battlefield command and control center. Slay also wondered how the Surveillance Center could have failed to detect the tanks that traveled the Ho Chi Minh Trail before clanking out of the jungle into South Vietnam.[61] An officer more familiar with the functioning of Task Force Alpha, Colonel Mathews, a onetime commander, believed that the expansion of the road net, much of it still undiscovered when Commando Hunt VII ended, enabled the North Vietnamese tanks and many trucks to escape detection. Even though the passes into southern Laos were fairly well covered by sensors, by the time traffic reached the exits "the road system had expanded so greatly that it was virtually impossible to sensorize all output gates."[62] In brief, Commando Hunt VII had pitted a dwindling force, much of its equipment experimental or downright unsatisfactory, against a concealed and aggressively defended road net. The United States, bent on disengagement, faced an enemy determined to fight. In these circumstances, Commando Hunt VII could not succeed.

Chapter Fourteen

Vietnamizing Interdiction:
An Afterthought to the Nixon Program

When the Air Force, as a result of the North Vietnamese invasion of the South in the spring of 1972, shifted its effort from the Ho Chi Minh Trail to the battle-fields of South Vietnam, the South Vietnamese air arm lacked the experience, training, and equipment to take over the interdiction campaign. Indeed, the idea of Vietnamizing interdiction came as an afterthought to the ongoing program of expanding and improving the armed forces of South Vietnam. Since the summer of 1970, President Nixon's Vietnamization program, which traced its roots to the last months of the Johnson administration, emphasized the expansion of the South Vietnamese armed forces to 1.1 million officers and men by July 1, 1973. The growth in manpower of South Vietnam's army, navy, marine corps, and air force proceeded on schedule. Unfortunately, the selection of equipment for this expand-ed military establishment tended, until the North Vietnamese invasion in 1972, to reflect what the United States could spare and what the South Vietnamese could easily master. The U.S. advisers, moreover, expected the Vietnamized armed forces to carry out the same essentially defensive missions as before in trying to maintain the security and territorial integrity of the nation. Air Force planning called for the South Vietnamese air arm to continue to concentrate on the support of ground operations, relying on lightweight fighters designed for export, trainers converted into attack aircraft, and surplus types like the early model gunships. Since Vietnamization did not include aerial interdiction of the Ho Chi Minh Trail, the program failed to provide the deadliest and most complex weapons used for that purpose—the AC–130s that General Slay valued so highly, laser-guided bombs, F–4 fighters, or the B–52s that pummeled area targets like truck parks or troop bivouacs.[1]

When Secretary of the Air Force Robert C. Seamans, Jr., reviewed his impressions after visiting South Vietnam late in 1970, the Vietnamization of inter-diction seemed less a problem than the ability of an expanding South Vietnamese Air Force to manage its resources. The fact that Dr. Seamans, a scientist by train-ing, held an administrative, rather than operational, post in the U.S. defense hier-archy may have affected his outlook. In general, he found the progress of South

The War against Trucks

Vietnam's air arm impressive, even though he foresaw a worsening "middle management and leadership problem," as the nation assumed responsibility for additional air bases handed over by the United States. He believed, however, that the situation would prove "manageable, in view of the high degree of professionalism and determination that had been reflected in program accomplishment to date." His only recommendation at all associated with interdiction called for replacing South Vietnam's Douglas AC–47 gunships with newer and better equipped Fairchild AC–119Ks.[2]

Although slow to surface as a major issue, Vietnamizing interdiction had been under consideration within the Department of Defense at least since December 1969, when Leonard Sullivan, the Deputy Director of Defense Research and Engineering for Southeast Asia Matters, called attention to the need "to develop better border security components to replace the Commando Hunt program, which cannot go on forever."[3] Sullivan and other officials sought to "stimulate thinking" by dusting off a 1966 plan for international control over a neutral zone along Route 9 from Khe Sanh all the way to Savannakhet in western Laos. Intended mainly to promote discussion, the revived proposal reflected the U.S. belief that South Vietnam lacked the technological base to take over the surveillance network used in the Commando Hunt series; according to this concept, an international peacekeeping force would do what the South Vietnamese could not do: choke off the Ho Chi Minh Trail. Critics in the Department of Defense quickly punctured the trial balloon. "Instead of thinking up more realistic things to do," Sullivan complained, "our opponents have just come back and said it was impractical."[4]

Sullivan and his colleagues had hoped to inspire actions that would replace the " 'non-Asianizable' air assets" used in Commando Hunt with "some 'Asianizable' means of countering infiltration down through Laos." Vietnamization could not succeed, he declared, "without doing something" to impede the southward movement of men and supplies. The Defense Communications Planning Group, which had put together the sensor-based anti-infiltration barrier, suggested that South Vietnamese troops create a sensor-supported ground salient extending westward from Khe Sanh toward Tchepone, an idea that generated little enthusiasm at the time.[5]

The armed forces of South Vietnam had to conduct interdiction on the ground since the United States, which felt that its Asian ally could not take advantage of advanced technology, denied the South Vietnamese a chance to learn to operate a Vietnamized Task Force Alpha and direct air strikes against targets located by sensors and validated with the aid of computers. With varying U.S. support, the South Vietnamese launched two large-scale overland attacks on the Ho Chi Minh Trail complex. In April and May 1970, the army of South Vietnam joined U.S. troops in an offensive against the bases and depots near the terminus of the trail in Cambodia. Not quite a year later, a South Vietnamese task force advanced from Khe Sanh toward Tchepone during Operation Lam Son 719. The two attacks revealed flaws in the performance of South Vietnam's army. The thrust into Cambodia demonstrated that the South Vietnamese could fight effectively, provided they had competent leadership and received strong support from U.S. aircraft and artillery. Unfortunately, South Vietnamese leaders all too rarely demonstrated competence, in part a result of a long and bloody war that often killed the best. For example, two generals, whom U.S. advisers listed among South Vietnam's finest, died in helicopter accidents during the fighting in Cambodia. The attack toward Tchepone underscored the need for both U.S. fire-power and skilled South Vietnamese leadership, for the ineptly led force could not defeat a heavily armed and mobile enemy defending familiar ground.[6]

In February 1971, when an aura of optimism still surrounded Lam Son 719, Secretary of Defense Laird moved at last to correct the oversight that had left South Vietnam with no means of interrupting "the southward flow of men and supplies destined to sustain the North Vietnamese Army threat." In raising the subject of Vietnamizing interdiction, he accepted the premise that "we cannot give the government of Vietnam all the capabilities U.S. forces now have," arguing that the "economy of the Republic of Vietnam could not support such a force struc-ture." Laird insisted, however, that the United States could provide its ally with some suitable means of impeding infiltration by land and sea. He cautioned against letting "semantic differences . . . obscure the fact that an interdiction capa-bility can be Vietnamized," as he called for an "optimum interdiction" in which the enemy would "bear the full expense and back-breaking burden" of moving troops and supplies through Laos to the vicinity of the South Vietnamese border, only to see them captured or destroyed. Although the armed forces of the Republic of Vietnam, in attacking the exits from the Ho Chi Minh Trail, might not inflict the kind of destruction the United States could, Secretary Laird maintained that "acceptably effective interdiction can occur very near or even at the destina-tion points."[7]

The Secretary of Defense seemed to suggest that a comparatively minor adjustment of the Vietnamization effort could rapidly provide South Vietnam with the means for disputing the passage of North Vietnamese reinforcements and sup-plies into the country. Not everyone, however, believed that the Vietnamization of interdiction would prove so simple. The dissenters included Maj. Gen. Ernest C. Hardin, Jr., Vice Commander of the Seventh Air Force. After examining the types and amounts of equipment being turned over to the South Vietnamese, he pro-nounced "the current VNAF [South Vietnamese Air Force] program . . . sound and achievable within recognized constraints." These limitations reflected the U.S. objective: the development of a "self-sufficient military capability to counter a progressively decreasing insurgency within the RVN [Republic of Vietnam], pro-vide national stature, and contribute to the maintenance of RVN as a sovereign nation." South Vietnamese interdiction of enemy supply lines through Laos did not figure in the basic U.S. strategy and according to General Hardin, remained "beyond the ability of the RVNAF [Republic of Vietnam armed forces] and, in fact, of the GVN [Government of Vietnam] itself." As a result, the United States would have to reorient the current Vietnamization program to equip and train the South Vietnamese to disrupt enemy traffic through Laos, whether at midpassage or when it debouched into South Vietnam. Laird, the Air Force general suggested, underestimated the difficulty of adding interdiction to the Vietnamization program, but nevertheless did a service in calling attention to the importance of continued attacks on the logistic network. As Hardin observed, "It's hard to resist blabbing the truth, which is: If the North Vietnamese continue to use Laos to resupply their forces in the South, we'd better keep substantial U.S. air nearby."[8]

In mid-April, Leonard Sullivan outlined a concept for Vietnamizing interdiction that captured the spirit of Laird's memorandum and incorporated the experience of Lam Son 719. Disregarding any U.S. and South Vietnamese claims of success along the highway to Tchepone, the Deputy Director of Defense Research and Engineering concluded that the operation had proved it "unlikely" that "the South Vietnamese will ever be able to cut off Laotian infiltration on their own—at least if they try to use the operational tactics of this campaign." Sullivan believed that the attack had been too ambitious. "A U.S. helicopter-supported, three-division RVNAF force was unable to accomplish this thrust with acceptable losses" against an enemy who was "too strong, too determined, and too well prepared to permit a sustained confrontation this close to his source of supply." Nor could Sullivan "extrapolate any variation of Lam Son 719—without U.S. support—that could have lunged all the way to Muong Phine," and remained there long enough to disrupt North Vietnamese supply lines. He did believe, however, that the South Vietnamese could "for shorter duration operations . . . conduct damaging forays with far less U.S. support."[9]

General Abrams, in the aftermath of Lam Son 719, acknowledged that South Vietnam could not "sustain large scale major cross border operations" without U.S. help,[10] and Sullivan looked ahead to the day when such assistance would no longer be available. If deprived of U.S. air power as employed in Commando Hunt and Lam Son 719, South Vietnam, in Sullivan's opinion, had "no demonstrated means of cutting off continued NVA [North Vietnamese army] aggression," but he also believed that the nation's survival depended on its ability, after the United States left, to hack away at the lines of supply and reinforcement that sustained North Vietnamese forces in the South. This line of reasoning led him to propose an "alternative means of interdicting and disrupting Laotian infiltration with RVNAF forces operating alone—for many years to come."[11]

Sullivan's alternative differed radically from the kind of interdiction being conducted in Laos by the U.S. Air Force, which used the computer, sophisticated aircraft, specialized munitions, and a variety of electronic sensors in trying to locate and attack roads, trucks, supply depots, and other components of the logistic network extending from the North Vietnamese border southward through Laos. He proposed that the South Vietnamese use large numbers of less elaborately equipped airplanes to saturate the skies over those areas of Laos nearest

240

South Vietnam's western border. In an oversimplified comparison, he suggested that if the Seventh Air Force used twenty AC–130s to cover some two thousand miles of roadway, each patrolling a hundred miles, the South Vietnamese Air Force could obtain the same coverage with two hundred light aircraft, armed with side-firing 20-mm cannon, each one responsible for just ten miles of the road net. Actually, the South Vietnamese coverage would be even denser because Sullivan planned to restrict the swarming light planes to the region south of the 17th parallel, an area of interdiction that excluded the northern passes, which lay beyond effective range of the miniature gunships. His minigunships would respond to data from electronic sensors, but receive their target information from "simplified airborne read-out" equipment in other "command-and-control configured" light aircraft instead of from "a large centralized read-out facility at Nakhon Phanom."

Although he considered Lam Son 719 a failure, Sullivan included ground operations in his interdiction scheme. The South Vietnamese would avoid major operations, but instead send small raiding parties across the border to attack supply caches and rest areas located with the help of sensors planted from the air. These units would kill North Vietnamese infiltrators, destroy supplies, force the enemy to divert troops to defend the road net, and discover targets for air strikes or additional raids on the ground. Patrol actions of this kind could not apply, in Sullivan's phrase, "the step increase in difficulty to the enemy that could cause him to change his ultimate intentions." A successful Lam Son 719, he believed, might have forced Hanoi to reconsider its objective of conquering the South, but that operation had failed. Another such attack, moreover, seemed to him "beyond our grasp as a Vietnamizable operation," forcing the United States and South Vietnam to "accept a compromise solution" in the form of the less ambitious probes by small units.[12]

Sullivan's endorsement of such a compromise reflected his optimistic evaluation of South Vietnam's limited experience in conducting small-scale incursions into hostile territory. Whereas the mauling of the South Vietnamese task force advancing toward the storage areas around Tchepone discouraged him from advocating such operations in the future, U.S.-led Prairie Fire units, numbering from a dozen to two hundred men, impressed Sullivan with their ability to conduct both raids and reconnaissance patrols in a zone that extended some thirty miles into Laos, from the vicinity of Phou Koy mountain near the demilitarized zone southward to the Cambodian border. He hoped to combine minigunship patrols with raids modeled on Prairie Fire activities to Vietnamize interdiction in southern Laos.

Thus far, Prairie Fire had operated independently of the AC–130 gunships used in the Commando Hunt interdiction campaign, although the patrols, over the years, had found targets for B–52s and tactical aircraft. According to General Abrams' Studies and Observations Group, which directed Prairie Fire activity, a total of 48 combat platoons and 404 reconnaissance units crossed the border during 1969, an increase of more than a hundred over the previous year's total missions. These probes generated a reported 689 helicopter gunship and 1,016 tactical aircraft sorties, destroyed twenty-five supply caches, and killed 454 of the enemy, with another 718 believed slain. In short, the average penetration of Lao territory disclosed targets for roughly four aircraft and killed perhaps three North Vietnamese or Pathet Lao. Although an overwhelming number of the Prairie Fire patrols throughout 1969 had sought information about the enemy, not one returned with a prisoner of war. The cost of the year's operations to U.S. Special Forces totaled 19 killed, 199 wounded, and 9 missing, while the South Vietnamese suffered 56 killed, 270 wounded, and 31 missing.[13]

During 1969, the Military Assistance Command organized a few reconnaissance teams composed exclusively of South Vietnamese, either guerrillas or regular troops, instead of the usual three Americans and nine South Vietnamese. Members of the U.S. Army Special Forces continued, however, to lead the larger combat units. While the Army provided planning and some leadership, South Vietnamese CH–34s joined Air Force UH–1F helicopters in landing, supporting, and recovering most Prairie Fire teams. Air Force forward air controllers and fighter pilots also participated in the operations.[14]

Ground forces other than Prairie Fire units operated in southeastern Laos. In January 1969, the Studies and Observations Group sent the first of that year's twenty Earth Angel patrols, each made up of three or four defectors from the North Vietnamese army, to reconnoiter roads in either the Prairie Fire area or in northeastern Cambodia. Short-term roadwatch and target acquisition teams, which formerly had conducted missions along the western border of North Vietnam, sought information in the Prairie Fire zone, as well as in Cambodia.[15]

In spite of the frequency of the border crossings, the task of penetrating the Prairie Fire operating area grew increasingly dangerous. In fact, the Studies and Observations Group reported at year's end, "Throughout CY [calendar year] 1969 the enemy's increased ability to react swiftly to heliborne operations posed a significant threat to cross border operations." The key to this improved defensive response seemed to be a "chain of observation posts, interconnected and linked with communication circuits."[16]

Prairie Fire activity for 1970 continued at about the previous year's level. Reconnaissance or combat teams advanced across the border 491 times, with 149 of these missions directed against the southernmost part of the operating area where Laos, South Vietnam, and Cambodia converged. The year's efforts produced targets for 1,116 sorties by helicopter gunships and 1,419 by tactical aircraft. The resulting air attacks ignited a reported fifty-seven secondary fires and received credit for killing at least eighty-two of the enemy. The ground probes themselves claimed 485 definitely killed with another 701 possible victims. Even though Prairie Fire killed perhaps a hundred more in 1970 than in 1969, U.S. and South Vietnamese casualties declined from 585 to 330. The U.S. Army suffered 12 killed, 98 wounded, and 4 missing, while the South Vietnamese lost 53 dead, 157 wounded, and 6 missing.[17]

Vietnamizing Interdiction: an Afterthought to the Nixon Program

Some thirty Prairie Fire teams departed from Nakhon Phanom or Ubon, Thailand, during 1970. After August 19, however, the patrols no longer used Ubon, for CH–3s based there had to refuel at Quang Tri City in South Vietnam, thus crossing the most heavily defended portions of the Ho Chi Minh Trail both going and returning. In contrast, the larger CH–53s operating out of Nakhon Phanom, thanks to their greater endurance, could follow a circuitous and less dangerous course, fly nonstop to the landing zone, and return by a different, but also lightly defended route.[18]

In crossing the trail, helicopter pilots tried to avoid following a reciprocal course on the return trip, a practice that sometimes proved unavoidable with the CH–3, particularly if storms had shut down the landing sites in South Vietnam. On March 26, 1970, the weather prevented Lt. Col. Hulbert F. Weitzel, Jr., from choosing an alternate route, and as a result, he inadvertently led his flight into a barrage from antiaircraft guns awaiting his return. Although enemy gunners scored a direct hit on his aircraft, none of the crew suffered injury. As the rotor windmilled and the helicopter sank toward the jungle, Weitzel succeeded in restarting a damaged engine and brought the men safely back to Thailand.[19]

Helicopters based in Thailand, after successfully inserting Prairie Fire Teams, sometimes had to brave enemy fire to retrieve them. On March 24, 1970, three days after a Marine Corps helicopter had been shot down while trying to extricate a unit surrounded by the enemy, a dozen A–1s pinned down three North Vietnamese platoons, enabling four CH–3s, one of them piloted by Weitzel, to rescue the patrol.[20] The members of a reconnaissance team that landed on January 27 ran into trouble, called for helicopters to bring them out, and divided into two groups in the hope of confusing the North Vietnamese. Only one group met the helicopters at a designated pickup point, where the survivors reported that security forces had captured and immediately executed all the others.[21]

Earth Angel units developed during 1970 into "reliable short-term, walk-in, walk-out reconnaissance teams . . . . capable of moving approximately fifteen kilometers to the target and observing for two or three days before overland exfiltration." By year's end, Earth Angel patrols carried out twenty-four area reconnaissance and sixteen roadwatch assignments, losing five killed, four captured, and one who defected to rejoin his former comrades.[22] Until mid-1970, short-term roadwatch and target acquisition teams conducted eighteen missions in Laos, but beginning on July 1, they temporarily restricted their activity to Cambodia.[23]

The year 1970 also saw renewed interest in a proposal under consideration since November 1968, when General Abrams and Admiral McCain had first recommended sending Prairie Fire teams to Nape, Mu Gia, and Ban Karai Passes. After William H. Sullivan, at that time the U.S. Ambassador to Laos, vetoed the idea as compromising the last vestige of Laotian neutrality, the two commanders suggested eliminating Nape, the farthest north of the three, where the danger of detection seemed greatest. Since neither helicopters nor troops on foot seemed likely to penetrate the defenses east of Mu Gia and Ban Karai Passes, the probe would have to originate at Nakhon Phanom, Thailand, rather than in South Vietnam. The experience of the Central Intelligence Agency's roadwatch teams, which approached the passes from the west, indicated that Mu Gia, besides being the nearer of the two to Nakhon Phanom, also had the weaker ground defenses. As a result, the Military Assistance Command suggested a test mission against Mu Gia Pass.[24]

In December 1968, during discussions of a possible mission to Mu Gia Pass, Ambassador Sullivan summarized his objections to any such operation. He told Secretary of Defense Clark M. Clifford that four years as ambassador in Vientiane had convinced him that air attack destroyed only about 15 percent of the supplies destined for the enemy in South Vietnam. Any improvement in interdiction that might result from placing ground patrols near the three passes would not, in his opinion, be worth the political risk, since Prairie Fire already was "being conducted on a clandestine basis contrary to . . . [the] expressed wishes" of Laotian Premier Souvanna Phouma. Neither the value of the proposed operations nor their prospects for success impressed the ambassador. He pointed out that "availability of aircraft, perishability of targets, weather, and other similar factors" had so reduced the effectiveness of Central Intelligence Agency roadwatch teams that air strikes actually destroyed only one percent of the trucks the teams sighted on the roads. "These limitations," Sullivan advised Secretary Clifford, "coupled with the doubtful prospects for team survival in the environment under consideration, are primary causes for my skepticism." Moreover, a "genuine concern that we are sending a great many brave young men to almost certain death in this effort" reinforced his attitude.[25]

In spite of his initial opposition to sending patrols to the mountain passes, Ambassador Sullivan reconsidered the issue and in January 1969 conceded that only an actual mission could determine the usefulness of such a venture. The test mission, he insisted, should "cause no . . . disruption for the time being to the . . . roadwatch effort" of the Central Intelligence Agency, which had two teams in position, one within North Vietnam near Mu Gia Pass and the other covering Ban Karai from a location inside Laos. With the ambassador's reluctant consent, the Military Assistance Command decided on a mission to Mu Gia Pass, Operation Shiloh III. After prolonged planning and delays caused by the weather, the Studies and Observations Group at last scheduled the probe for March 1970, a year after Sullivan left the embassy at Vientiane, but the Departments of State and Defense withheld permission out of concern for Souvanna's nominal neutrality. Further review, followed by more bad weather, delayed the project until the 1970–71 dry season. Meanwhile, the defenses of Mu Gia Pass grew so formidable that Abrams recommended an indefinite postponement, which the Joint Chiefs of Staff approved in October 1970.[26]

With respect to Vietnamizing interdiction, the postponement and eventual demise of Shiloh III paled into insignificance compared to President Nixon's declaration on March 6, 1970, that there were "no American combat troops in Laos."[27] He offered this assurance after one of the recurring invasions of Plain of Jars brought the Pathet Lao and North Vietnamese almost to the threshold of victory, and opponents of the Vietnam War in Congress grew concerned that Nixon might intervene in Laos with U.S. ground forces. The Departments of State and Defense interpreted the President's words as a ban on U.S. participation in Prairie Fire combat patrols, though not the reconnaissance probes, which the South Vietnamese were gradually taking over. Abrams, who intended to increase Prairie Fire combat activity, argued that the operation would collapse without U.S. leadership and technical assistance and obtained approval, despite the President's statement, to continue assigning Americans to combat patrols while the South Vietnamese underwent intensive training.[28]

The organization and training of South Vietnamese units for Prairie Fire raids proceeded so slowly that Abrams had to arrange for incremental extensions of the deadline barring U.S. troops from combat operations. He at last predicted that the South Vietnamese could launch platoon-size attacks as early as February 1971, but doubted that groups this small could survive in heavily defended southern Laos. Until he had trained companies of perhaps three platoons or battalions with two to four companies, which would have a better chance of survival, he proposed that U.S. troops continue indefinitely to take part in both combat and reconnaissance patrols.[29]

General Abrams did not get his wish, though not because his superiors had greater confidence than he in the ability of the South Vietnamese. The Cooper-Church amendment reinforced the President's earlier declaration and barred U.S. ground troops from Laos, where Operation Lam Son 719 was about to begin. On February 5, 1971, the Joint Chiefs of Staff gave Abrams just three days to withdraw all Americans then engaged in Prairie Fire missions, and except for a few who could not return that quickly, they were back in South Vietnam on the 7th. When the Lam Son 719 assault force attacked on February 8 toward Tchepone, Nixon could truthfully say that no U.S. ground forces participated in the fighting in Laos.[30]

In taking over leadership of the Prairie Fire units, South Vietnamese officers and men drew on a variety of tactical experience. Over the years, missions had differed in results and technique, as well as in purpose. A combat patrol might land from South Vietnamese helicopters in a clearing created by a five-ton bomb dropped from a C–130 transport, locate an enemy installation, and direct Douglas A–1Es against it with unknown results.[31] Another might tangle with a larger North Vietnamese unit and escape by helicopter only because the A–1s managed to saturate the enemy position with tear gas.[32] A reconnaissance team might try to land near a road, part of the Ho Chi Minh Trail, and be driven off by enemy fire despite strafing by helicopter gunships,[33] but a similar group could dismount from a truck near the border, walk for a week through enemy-controlled forest, and see no sign of the North Vietnamese.[34]

The War against Trucks

Although U.S. leaders no longer accompanied Prairie Fire teams beyond the border, the U.S. Military Assistance Command, Vietnam, retained its planning role. In January 1971, before the absolute ban on U.S. participation in combat patrols, the command's Studies and Observations Group dispatched units in support of Silver Buckle, the probe by Lao forces of the western fringe of the Ho Chi Minh Trail, and in February, South Vietnamese Prairie Fire teams operated in conjunction with Lam Son 719, the advance on Tchepone. The frequency of incursions declined, however, even though short-term roadwatch and target acquisition teams returned to Laos, conducting two dozen missions by the time Commando Hunt VII ended. Earth Angel teams made forty-one probes into the kingdom between January 1, 1971, and April 1, 1972, one more than during 1970, but Prairie Fire units conducted almost 250 fewer operations in the fifteen-month period than in the preceding year.[35]

At about the time the number of incursions began declining, a newspaper article by Jack Anderson, a syndicated columnist, revealed that the nickname Prairie Fire referred to reconnaissance or combat patrols launched from South Vietnam into Laos. As a result, the Studies and Observations Group chose a new title, the Vietnamese phrase Phu Dung, possibly selected to reflect increased South Vietnamese participation in the operation. Since the operation accomplished less than in earlier years, skeptics suggested that Phu Dung might be an unfortunately accurate choice; the phrase refers to the illusion experienced by opium smokers—that is, a pipe dream.[36]

The reduction in Phu Dung activity resulted from strengthened North Vietnamese security throughout the operating area. The enemy stationed quick-reaction teams on high ground overlooking probable landing sites, and when helicopters appeared, the teams advanced to meet the threat, following instructions radioed or telephoned from observers who remained on the hilltops. In an attempt to counter these tactics, aircraft supporting the insertions dropped five-ton bombs to blast landing zones in the jungle, where the North Vietnamese did not expect helicopters to touch down. In addition, Ambassador G. McMurtrie Godley, William Sullivan's successor at Vientiane, sometimes arranged for Phu Dung landings west of the usual operating area, and on one occasion, an Earth Angel team used a landing zone twenty-seven miles beyond the Phu Dung boundary.[37]

Salem House operations in Cambodia, the equivalent of Prairie Fire in Laos, gave the South Vietnamese some additional experience in ground interdiction, including the planting of mines. The Salem House operating area expanded from a depth of twenty miles in 1968 to thirty miles the following year, and at times, after the 1970 invasion, encompassed almost half the country. Although reconnaissance remained their principal concern, the teams began planting mines during the fall of 1968. At first they relied on plastic antipersonnel types, but by December 1970, they also used antivehicular mines. Neither kind carried U.S. markings, and both could be set to detonate automatically after fifty days.[38]

Vietnamizing Interdiction: an Afterthought to the Nixon Program

Salem House provided experience with electronic sensors, as well as mines. In June 1970, the Military Assistance Command had the teams plant the surveillance devices along certain roads and trails that crossed the border between South Vietnam and Cambodia, but Air Force F–4s took over the delivery task, as soon as the first of the strings expired.[39] Later in 1970, the Seventh Air Force and General Abrams' special operations staff collaborated on a plan for Salem House teams, supplemented if necessary by F–4s, to set up new sensor fields in northeastern Cambodia. When these acoustic devices reported nighttime truck traffic, an airborne battlefield command and control center, not Task Force Alpha, received the signals and summoned an Air Force gunship to attack; Task Force Alpha had no involvement in the project. The sensors, provided by the Army, went into place on December 20, but detected just fourteen trucks during their life span; called on only once, the AC–119G gunship assigned to the operation inflicted no discernible damage.[40]

As in Prairie Fire, the Military Assistance Command tried to train South Vietnamese to replace the U.S. troops who led the Salem House teams. The phase out of U.S. participation, begun in the summer of 1969, faltered at the outset. On August 31, just two weeks after the Joint Chiefs of Staff had approved the Vietnamization of Salem House, the Military Assistance Command had to take over a mission to tap an enemy telephone line in Mondol Kiri Province after three South Vietnamese attempts had failed. A reconnaissance team made up entirely of U.S. troops carried out the assignment.[41]

Despite the false start, South Vietnamese ground forces assumed responsibility for the Salem House project by the summer of 1970. In May of that year, the Chairman of the Joint Chiefs of Staff, Gen. Earle G. Wheeler, U.S. Army, directed that, effective July 1, South Vietnamese helicopters should begin carrying the patrols into Cambodia. U.S. helicopters, however, would continue to provide gunship support. Over the objections of General Abrams and Admiral McCain, the directive went into effect, but the South Vietnamese helicopter unit responsible for Salem House proved inadequate to the task. Although Abrams sought to replace the South Vietnamese with U.S. helicopters, Secretary of Defense Laird at first refused permission, suggesting instead that the United States take over missions in South Vietnam to release other, more highly skilled South Vietnamese helicopter units for Salem House duty. In 1972, however, Laird relented and permitted U.S. helicopters to land South Vietnamese troops and carry out the wounded during patrols into both Cambodia and southern Laos.[42]

The article by Jack Anderson compromised Salem House as well as Prairie Fire. Effective April 8, 1971, Salem House became Operation Thot Not, taking the name of a kind of mangrove commonly found in Cambodia. The frequency of Thot Not patrols, like those in the Phu Dung area of Laos, diminished following Vietnamization. From a peak of 577 during calendar year 1970, the total dropped to 468 for the fifteen months ending on April 1, 1972.[43]

The War against Trucks

Although Prairie Fire/Phu Dung, Salem House/Thot Not, and the lesser operations had given the South Vietnamese some experience in small-scale combat and reconnaissance patrols on the ground in Laos and Cambodia, mighty obstacles stood in the way of their successfully interdicting movement on the Ho Chi Minh Trail. The Vietnamese Air Force, for example, had neither the training nor the equipment for this kind of operation. During the fifteen months ending in February 1971, South Vietnam's fighter-bombers and attack aircraft flew roughly thirteen thousand sorties in South Vietnam and Cambodia, but none at all in southern Laos. The republic's air force had only 137 fighter-bombers on hand at the end of March and just fourteen gunships, all of them AC–47s, suitable mainly for the nighttime defense of outposts.[44]

The experience acquired in conducting interdiction operations clearly did not qualify the South Vietnamese to continue the Commando Hunt series in its existing form; to do so would require new equipment, an intensive training program, and as a concession to Thai political sensitivity, the relocation of the Infiltration Surveillance Center from Thailand to South Vietnam. The United States looked forward to withdrawing the last ground combat troops sometime in 1972 and was economizing in the air war. Consequently, the cost in time and money to train and equip the South Vietnamese for electronic monitoring of the trail ruled out their taking over Commando Hunt. Since Lam Son 719 had shown they could not, on their own, plan and conduct a ground offensive against the trail, small-scale raids seemed the only alternative to complement the proposed fleet of minigunships. Although probes into southern Laos or eastern Cambodia had succeeded for a time, they ultimately prodded the enemy into improving the defenses of the Phu Dung and Thot Not operating areas, so that the number of patrols declined and the results dwindled. In the last-minute effort to Vietnamize interdiction, Secretary Laird hoped to graft a simple form of aerial interdiction onto the continued activity of raiding parties, but the recent experience of South Vietnamese patrols in Cambodia and southern Laos revealed the weakness of the rootstock.

Leonard Sullivan believed that minigunships could provide the aerial component of a Vietnamized interdiction campaign, but he also realized that the light aircraft would prove effective only if they attacked a suitable target. Killing trucks, he warned, should no longer serve as the primary objective, for "without Igloo White . . . and in the face of high air defenses . . . the VNAF could not destroy one thousand trucks in a season—less than 10 percent our present capability." The main target, therefore, had to be troops on the easternmost portions of the Ho Chi Minh Trail, the roads and trails within range of the minigunships. South Vietnam, however, had no bombers to rain high explosives on bivouac areas and other components of the troop infiltration route, as the B–52s sought to do in Project Island Tree. To remedy this failing, Sullivan proposed giving the South Vietnamese not a bomber, but a special bomb, the CBU–55 fuel-air munition, which released a cloud of explosive gas, similar to propane, that clung to the earth, seeping into bunkers and filling foxholes before detonating.[45]

Vietnamizing Interdiction: an Afterthought to the Nixon Program

Although aware of the limited South Vietnamese participation in previous interdiction operations, Secretary Laird persisted throughout the spring of 1971 in trying to Vietnamize this aspect of the war. Henry Kissinger, national security advisor to President Nixon, took an interest in Laird's activity and called for "development of air interdiction options for 1972–73 with associated U.S. and local force programs."[46] The Secretary of Defense promptly replied that his department was reviewing "the interdiction capability of the RVNAF including alternatives to the highly sophisticated air bombardment programs which we have relied upon."[47]

Work went ahead on a plan for the Vietnamization of interdiction that incorporated the ideas Leonard Sullivan had recently advanced. On May 10, 1971, Laird's deputy, David Packard, called on the services and the Defense Special Projects Group, formerly the Defense Communications Planning Group, to find a way to give South Vietnam the means to interdict traffic on the Ho Chi Minh Trail. Since Commando Hunt could not continue indefinitely in its present form and South Vietnam could not take over this "highly sophisticated . . . aerial bombardment capability," Packard called for "reasonably unsophisticated systems . . . within reasonable manpower and dollar limitations." The systems that the Deputy Secretary of Defense mentioned included three that Sullivan had proposed—the minigunships, the CBU–55 bomb, and a simplified means of sensor readout—plus improved equipment for cross-border patrols and more advanced sensors for border surveillance.

In mid-June, Packard began receiving the replies to his memorandum. The Defense Special Projects Group offered recommendations on sensor readout, the Army handled the broader question of border surveillance, and the Air Force dealt with three other subjects—the conversion of short-takeoff-and-landing light aircraft into minigunships, the use of the CBU–55 to give the A–1 attack craft the punch of a heavy bomber, and the equipment that would increase the effectiveness of raiding parties dispatched against the supply and infiltration routes in southern Laos. These responses formed the basis for a Vietnamized interdiction campaign that would undergo combat testing against lightly defended portions of the Ho Chi Minh Trail while Task Force Alpha still functioned and Commando Hunt VII attacked the more formidable core route structure. Even as preparations began for them to take over interdiction of the overland routes, the South Vietnamese also increased their participation in air and naval patrols designed to disrupt infiltration by sea.

Secretary Laird now had a blueprint for a program for Vietnamizing interdiction that demanded a minimum of technological skill from the South Vietnamese and a comparatively modest cash investment by the United States and South Vietnam. He would not attempt to set up a Vietnamized equivalent of the costly and complex operations of Task Force Alpha. The Air Force faced the challenge of developing or modifying the basic tools of Vietnamized aerial interdiction like the minigunship, getting them into the hands of the armed forces of South Vietnam in time for the 1971–72 dry season, and introducing South Vietnamese airmen to the tactics and techniques of attacking the Ho Chi Minh Trail.[48] If the Air Force succeeded, the future would ultimately reveal if the basic concept of cheap and simple aerial interdiction actually worked as Sullivan and other U.S. officials hoped or believed, and if the United States had erred in giving the South Vietnamese only the tools of interdiction they could readily use, instead of supplying whatever equipment might be needed and then teaching them to use it.

Chapter Fifteen

Vietnamizing Interdiction: Equipment, Training, Indoctrination

For better or worse, two principles governed the Vietnamization of aerial interdiction: what the United States could provide at a reasonable cost and what authorities believed the armed forces of South Vietnam could readily use. In addressing the second point, what the South Vietnamese could use, the Joint Chiefs of Staff expressed concern that an ambitious new program like the Vietnamization of interdiction would impose "unmanageable burdens" on the military establishment of South Vietnam. The suggested solution, however, did not call for better training (or better equipment, for that matter), but for a balanced program of Vietnamization during which U.S. air power continued, at least for the immediate future, to attack traffic on the Ho Chi Minh Trail. For example, during a meeting at Saigon of a task force established by Admiral McCain, Commander in Chief, Pacific, to study the Vietnamization of interdiction, General Abrams, Commander, U.S. Military Assistance Command, Vietnam, called attention to the limited ability of the armed forces of South Vietnam to absorb new equipment and warned that adding weapons for aerial interdiction to the agreed program of modernization and expansion might well require subtracting something to reduce complexity and keep the cost under control. Although concerned about the overall program, the Army general also worried that South Vietnamese progress in aerial interdiction might persuade the United States as early as 1972 or 1973, two years that he predicted would be "extremely critical," to furl prematurely the aerial umbrella that had shielded the process of Vietnamization and withdrawal.[1]

From the time he first became committed to the Vietnamization of interdiction, Secretary of Defense Laird looked for inexpensive and comparatively simple equipment he could transfer to the South Vietnamese. He showed an early interest in a portable multibarrel cannon easily installed in any cargo craft, instantly converting it into a crude gunship. The portable gun, nicknamed Pave Cap, seemed at first glance to offer savings in the cost of aircraft acquisition, maintenance, and operation, since the South Vietnamese Air Force could create gunships during periods of peak road traffic and reconvert them to transports when the emergency passed. The same airplane, it seemed, could do double duty. Closer examination revealed, however, that the convertible gunship lacked the firepower of even the AC–47 or AC–119G and required the diversion during the dry season of transports needed throughout the year to carry troops and cargo.[2]

Since the portable multibarrel cannon promised to strain airlift resources rather than ease the burden of Vietnamizing interdiction, attention shifted to the development of a cheap, simple, easily maintained gunship that would not require a diversion of transports from their normal duties. Leonard Sullivan, Deputy Director of Defense Research and Engineering for Southeast Asia Matters, became the most determined advocate of converting light aircraft, rather than large transports, into gunships. Laird liked Sullivan's idea of a heavily armed light plane and soon endorsed it as a possible substitute for the costly AC–130 and its complicated array of sensors in Vietnamizing aerial interdiction.

Sullivan found the aircraft industry already at work, by the spring of 1971, on plans to arm single-engine courier airplanes with side-firing multibarrel cannon. The most promising concept originated with Fairchild Industries, which offered the Air Force an armed version of its Turboporter. With a useful load of 3,385 pounds, the aircraft seemed able to accommodate the gun and ammunition, and it could take off from a primitive airstrip in as little as 305 feet. Helio Aircraft submitted a plan to arm its Stallion, which could carry 3,650 pounds and take off in 320 feet. Both of these short-takeoff-and-landing aircraft were high-wing monoplanes with box-like cabins and elongated cowlings that enclosed a turboprop engine.[3] Secretary Laird promptly decided that the modified Fairchild and Helio airplanes deserved testing and on April 8, 1971, directed Secretary of the Air Force Robert C. Seamans, Jr., to conduct an evaluation in Thailand. At the time, Laird did not see the proposed minigunship as a weapon for attacking the Ho Chi Minh Trail; rather, he considered it to be a "simple, low cost counterinsurgency aircraft for our SEA allies" that could perform cheaply and reliably the missions of the AC–47, like providing fire support for beleaguered outposts or dropping flares.[4]

Sullivan, of course, had a grander vision of perhaps two hundred turboprop light planes, each with a single multibarrel gun, scourging traffic on the roads and trails of southern Laos. The modest cost of the of the armed Turboporter or Stallion made such an airplane especially attractive to Sullivan, who believed that clouds of minigunships could be bought for the price of a few AC–130s and that numbers would compensate for the lack of advanced sensors. The minigunship, and a command and control version of the same aircraft to interpret sensor signals, emerged as the critical element in the U.S. program for Vietnamizing interdiction.[5]

During April, after formally submitting his scheme of aerial interdiction, Sullivan launched a successful campaign for its adoption. He had lunch with Secretary of the Air Force Seamans, already preparing to test the minigunship as a general weapon of counterinsurgency and convinced him of the potential importance of the aircraft in the Vietnamization of interdiction.[6] Sullivan failed, however, to enlist the support of General Lavelle, formerly the director of the Defense

Communications Planning Group, now the Vice Commander, Pacific Air Forces, and soon to assume command of the Seventh Air Force. Although the general conceded that Turboporters or Stallions might perform well enough when planting sensors along the western borders of South Vietnam, he branded as ridiculous the idea of using them as gunships. Neither craft, he warned, had the endurance to patrol the roads and trails of southern Laos, and their lack of speed and armor left them suicidally vulnerable to antiaircraft fire.[7]

The test of the armed light aircraft as a general weapon for counterinsurgency, not specifically for interdiction, took place in Thailand during the early summer of 1971. Since the evaluation did not include extended patrols or exposure to antiaircraft fire, Lavelle's objections remained moot. On the basis of a series of test flights resembling typical counterinsurgency missions, such as conducting armed reconnaissance or strafing guerrilla encampments, the commander of the U.S. Military Assistance Command in Thailand, Air Force Maj. Gen. Louis T. Seith, issued a favorable report. He concluded that both the Helio Stallion and the Fairchild Peacemaker, as the armed Turboporter was now known, could be "used effectively in support of the counterinsurgency operations of the Royal Thai Government." Thailand, however, faced only sporadic violence from lightly armed guerrillas, nothing like the numerous, heavily armed troops dominating southern Laos. Because Seith declared that the "side-firing concept" of the minigunship had "proved to be an extremely valuable configuration for all phases of the operation" in Thailand, though some modification and further testing seemed necessary, Sullivan concluded that it would perform equally well in the far more demanding environment of the Ho Chi Minh Trail.[8]

Meanwhile, planning moved ahead toward giving the South Vietnamese some means of attacking infiltration into their country. An Air Staff study, completed in May 1971, stated that "the continued infiltration of men and supplies, primarily through Laos, is the basic threat to maintaining the viability of South Vietnam." Laos had become critically important because the "fall of Sihanouk and related actions have eliminated the Cambodian sanctuary and placed the VC/NVA [Viet Cong/North Vietnamese Army] on the strategic defensive in South Vietnam and southern Cambodia." Although overly optimistic in its interpretation of the military situation, as events proved, the Air Staff document accurately predicted that the South Vietnamese would have to take over the interdiction campaign in Laos, for "previous assumptions as to continued U.S. . . . efforts," in the form of an open-ended Commando Hunt series, were growing "increasingly untenable." As the withdrawals gathered momentum, the study warned, "public and congressional pressures will increasingly focus on U.S. air activities as U.S. ground forces redeploy." The Air Staff refused. however, to endorse the minigunship as a nighttime truck killer, like the AC–130, because it lacked the necessary sensors and seemed dangerously vulnerable to antiaircraft fire, but despite these failings, the converted courier aircraft might join with ground patrols in attacking infiltration in lightly defended areas along the borders of South Vietnam.[9]

The War against Trucks

The Air Staff planners earned Sullivan's respect, even though they expressed strong reservations about the value of the minigunship as a truck killer against the heavily defended road net in southern Laos. "The Air Force," he declared, "is to be particularly commended for their comprehensive and non-parochial approach to this controversial problem." Besides endorsing the study's premise that the fate of South Vietnam depended ultimately on interdiction of the Ho Chi Minh Trail, he conceded that an armed light aircraft could not do everything an AC–130 could and took heart from apparent willingness of the Air Staff to find suitable work for the minigunship.[10]

Secretary Laird, a sixteen-year veteran of Congressional politics, agreed with Sullivan and the Air Staff that pressure from the public and Congress for a complete U.S. withdrawal foretold the end of the Commando Hunt series. On July 2, 1971, he called for the preparation of plans to increase South Vietnamese "participation in and responsibility for the interdiction effort." Besides aiming at improved border surveillance and the creation of a "primitive" sensor system based on the Army's experience in South Vietnam, the plans would seek to integrate the existing Commando Hunt operations in heavily defended portions of Laos with a South Vietnamese interdiction campaign in less dangerous areas. This integrated effort, which might continue as long as Commando Hunt lasted, employed South Vietnamese resources, which would steadily improve in terms of both equipment and tactics. Looking beyond Commando Hunt, the Secretary of Defense directed the Air Force to participate in the "design of a combat test, to take place during the next dry season [1971–72], of selected equipment and concepts which might allow the RVNAF [Republic of Vietnam Armed Forces] to conduct their own counter-infiltration operations in the future."

This combat test, scheduled to coincide with Commando Hunt VII, featured Sullivan's minigunship scheme, now called Project Credible Chase, which held the key to the Vietnamization of interdiction. Pressure was increasing for a complete U.S. withdrawal from South Vietnam, as evidenced by the nationwide antiwar protests in April 1971 followed by the violence of early May, when a radical group tried unsuccessfully to disrupt the nation's capital and shut down the federal government. Vietnamization, including a South Vietnamese takeover of aerial interdiction, had to proceed swiftly and enable the withdrawals to continue. Because prompt action seemed essential, Secretary Laird turned to Credible Chase as a readily available, if partial, answer to the problem of Vietnamizing interdiction and directed that the concept undergo testing. Speed of implementation now joined cost and ease of use in shaping a program to Vietnamize aerial interdiction.[11]

Secretary of the Air Force Seamans responded to Laird's directive for a test of the minigunship by presenting a general plan for evaluating the ability of the Fairchild and Helio aircraft to conduct interdiction of the Ho Chi Minh Trail. In submitting this outline, Dr. Seamans observed that, even though Air Force "field commanders" questioned the value of the minigunship in this role, he agreed with the Secretary of Defense that only a test could determine its true usefulness. On July 31, the Secretary of Defense approved the "overall concept" forwarded by Seamans and asked the Air Force "to pursue this effort with the priority and aggressiveness now shown in . . . [the] successful AC–130 gunship program."[12]

Preparations for the test involved Air Force headquarters at the Pentagon, the Tactical Air Command, the U.S. Military Assistance Command at Saigon, South Vietnam's Joint General Staff, and the South Vietnamese Air Force. Even the Commander in Chief, Pacific, Admiral McCain, played a part in the preparations, insisting that General Abrams "be fully apprised of the test plan, as conceived in USAF channels, and that the plan be shaped as necessary to meet the realities of the situation in RVN."[13] The Chief of Staff of the South Vietnamese Air Force, Col. Vo Dinh, received a briefing on Credible Chase during a visit to Washington, and the Air Force Advisory Group in Saigon explained the program to the colonel's superiors. At both Washington and Saigon, the South Vietnamese voiced concern lest the minigunships replace equipment already scheduled for delivery. The briefing officers assured them, however, that Credible Chase represented a possible addition to the Vietnamization program rather than a substitution.[14]

At Saigon, the recently formed Combined Interdiction Committee sought to incorporate a test of Credible Chase into an expansion of South Vietnamese participation in aerial interdiction. On October 6, the South Vietnamese Air Force agreed to join in a Credible Chase evaluation by sending crews to Eglin Air Force Base, Florida, for instruction, then conducting a combat test from the airfield at Pleiku, within easy range of exit gates for men and supplies that had traveled the length of the Ho Chi Minh Trail. The South Vietnamese would furnish 50 percent of the air crews and one-third of the mechanics required for the two phases of the evaluation, plus one AC–47 for airborne command and control during combat testing in Southeast Asia.[15]

Scarcely had the South Vietnamese Air Force agreed to the two-phase evaluation when Secretary Laird, early in October 1971, asked the U.S. Air Force and the principal U.S. commanders to make recommendations for incorporating the minigunships into South Vietnam's air arm, assuming a "successful test of the Credible Chase concept." Laird did not, however, confine his interest to the one program, but asked for similar recommendations about other facets of interdiction. He inquired about providing improved sensor fields for ground troops guarding the border, about equipping the air arm to deliver sensors from fighter-bombers and monitor the devices from the air, and about making AC–119K gunships available to the South Vietnamese.[16]

Secretary Seamans elaborated on Laird's request with a memorandum for the Air Force Chief of Staff, General Ryan, on the subject of Credible Chase. "While I appreciate a light armed STOL [short-takeoff-and-landing aircraft] is not an equal substitute for our own capabilities," Seamans wrote, "it can make a significant contribution, directly or indirectly, to accomplishing the objectives enumerated by the Secretary of Defense." He then expressed his own belief that "we must pursue the . . . evaluation vigorously as one means of assuring we have taken all feasible steps to provide the VNAF with the most effective capability possible within the time remaining prior to the withdrawal of combat forces from SEAsia."[17]

Even as Secretary Seamans urged the Air Force to participate wholeheartedly in the forthcoming test, further doubts surfaced about the value of minigunships. The Tactical Air Command, involved in planning the combat evaluation, insisted that the "real world" of Southeast Asia "be allowed to enter the problem." The command warned that aircraft of this type "cannot be employed around the clock in a high threat environment without substantial losses" and suggested that advocates of the Credible Chase program may have intended that the minigunships "fall back until the larger [antiaircraft] guns could be taken out by raiding parties or TAC air."[18] Unfortunately, as Leonard Sullivan discovered on another of his visits to South Vietnam, defenses were improving all along the Ho Chi Minh complex from the northern passes to Kratie in Cambodia and also in western South Vietnam.[19] Consequently, General Abrams' staff suggested in mid-October that the minigunships, if actually provided to the South Vietnamese, should patrol inside the country, freeing A–1s and A–37s for combat in Laos and Cambodia.[20]

Against this backdrop of doubt, Credible Chase moved forward. The Air Force signed contracts for fifteen Stallions and as many Peacemakers for use in the evaluation, selected five segments of the enemy transportation net that seemed vulnerable to minigunship interdiction, and decided that South Vietnam, assuming a successful test, should have one squadron to patrol each of the five. In spite of the initial progress, General Ryan wondered "if a self-sustaining RVNAF capability" could be "achieved by the fall of 1972." He saw many uncertainties looming ahead, among them the actual outcome of the Credible Chase test, cooperation with the South Vietnamese Joint General Staff, success in training programs, and prompt funding by the U.S. Department of Defense.[21]

Secretary Laird, however, remained committed to the minigunship for Vietnamizing aerial interdiction. He apparently believed that Credible Chase represented the best he could do, given the cost, the proficiency of South Vietnamese airmen, and U.S. disenchantment with a long and expensive war. He established, late in November 1971, an objective of five operational minigunship squadrons, a total of two hundred aircraft, in time for the dry season interdiction campaign that would begin in October 1973.[22]

From Saigon, the U.S. Military Assistance Command warned against counting too heavily on an untried weapon. "This headquarters," a message declared, "cannot state a military requirement" for the minigunship until its "suitability in the interdiction role" had been determined by the combat tests scheduled for South Vietnam's western highlands from mid-April to mid-June 1972. Admiral McCain, agreed that "to confirm . . . a military requirement . . . that can be met by the Credible Chase aircraft would be a prejudgment not warranted by the facts in hand."[23] Both Abrams and McCain continued to protest that they could see no military requirement for two hundred of the light-plane gunships. They warned, moreover, of waste in manpower and disruption of training programs if the new weapon should fail after the South

Vietnamese Air Force adopted it on faith alone, without adequate combat testing. Hasty acquisition of armed Peacemakers or Stallions, they declared, could actually weaken South Vietnam's armed forces.[24]

Taking his cue from Abrams and McCain, the Chairman of the Joint Chiefs of Staff, Adm. Thomas H. Moorer, avoided endorsing Credible Chase, though he refused to recommend its rejection. "While unable to confirm that STOL aircraft meet the military requirement for interdiction," he advised Secretary Laird, "the Joint Chiefs of Staff do confirm that there are other military requirements that can be met by STOL aircraft." In other words, such an airplane could play a useful role in Southeast Asia, though not necessarily in conducting aerial interdiction against the Ho Chi Minh Trail. Moorer and the Joint Chiefs, though they stopped short of supporting the minigunship, raised the issue of payment for this last-minute addition to the Vietnamization program, urging that the "undetermined unprogrammed costs" of Credible Chase "not be absorbed in current Service budgets."[25]

In the meantime, events conspired against Credible Chase. President Nixon announced a new reduction in U.S. strength even as plans took shape for testing the minigunship in the Pleiku area of South Vietnam. Adm. Elmo Zumwalt, the Chief of Naval Operations, immediately warned that the decision to withdraw another seventy thousand by April 1972 would prevent the Military Assistance Command from assigning men to the evaluation. Moorer had reached a similar conclusion: the United States could not withdraw these troops and still conduct a variety of activities that included the combat test of the Credible Chase gunship. Compounding the effect of declining U.S. manpower, Fairchild Industries ran late in delivering the required number of Peacemakers, so that, well before the test could begin, enemy troops, massing for the March 1972 invasion, dominated the area near Pleiku chosen for the combat evaluation. The tactical situation in South Vietnam and southern Laos combined with the withdrawal of U.S. manpower to force the transfer of all tests to Eglin Air Force Base. When North Vietnam invaded, the South Vietnamese pilots and mechanics participating in the evaluation found themselves halfway around the world from the battles that might well determine the fate of their country.[26]

The tests conducted at Eglin Air Force Base in the summer of 1972 disclosed basic flaws in both the Stallion and Peacemaker. Frank A. Tapparo, a representative of the Assistant Secretary of Defense (Systems Analysis), filed an especially damning preliminary report based on information he got from the Air Force officers in charge of the evaluation. Tapparo learned that the location of the side-firing gun in relation to the center of gravity made both aircraft tail heavy. In the Peacemaker the condition proved so dangerous that forty pounds of lead had to be inserted under the engine cowling to restore some semblance of equilibrium. To overcome the lack of balance required a heavy hand on the controls and forced the small-framed South Vietnamese to wrestle the stick with both hands in performing basic maneuvers. As if this were not enough, Tapparo found that neither range nor payload lived up to expectation; a minigunship carrying one thousand pounds and flying a distance of one hundred nautical miles could remain on station just thirty minutes before turning back to refuel.[27]

By the time the official test report appeared, the enemy had made inroads into western South Vietnam and further strengthened his defenses in Laos. Even if the minigunships had performed exactly as hoped—and they had not—they could not have carried out interdiction in Laos under the conditions that prevailed in the summer of 1972. To harass enemy movement beyond the border, the Peacemakers and Stallions would have had to fly farther and face stronger defenses than the advocates of minigunships had anticipated.

The Credible Chase program failed to provide South Vietnam with a weapon of aerial interdiction. Both Thailand and Cambodia, however, seemed to need a light aircraft capable of operating from primitive airfields to conduct general counterinsurgency missions. As a result, Cambodia received fourteen Stallions and Thailand thirteen Peacemakers, with one of each type going into storage at Davis-Monthan Air Force Base, Arizona.[28]

Although the minigunship aircraft loomed largest in Secretary Laird's plan for Vietnamizing interdiction, he also sought to give the South Vietnamese AC–119K gunships and CBU–55 bombs. A proposal to arm South Vietnam's air force with laser-guided five hundred pound bombs for night attacks against trucks received consideration, but proved impracticable, since the South Vietnamese forward air controllers, who would use laser beams to spotlight targets, lacked experience in night flying. For aerial interdiction, the South Vietnamese received equipment they already could use, rather than getting whatever they might need and learning to use it.[29]

The principle of giving them what they could easily use also applied in furnishing AC–119K gunships to the South Vietnamese. Rather than begin a series of intensive training programs covering all the equipment carried by these aircraft, the Air Force Advisory Group in South Vietnam proposed removing what seemed unessential before handing over the gunships. "The reason for removal . . . ," explained the advisers, "is that USAF experience indicates that it is not required for the mission (side-looking radar, forward-looking radar, and loran), because the cost of maintenance outweighs its usefulness to the VNAF (radar altimeter and radar homing and warning system) or because the VNAF has no compatible operating equipment (secure voice circuit)."[30] The advisory group, however, recommended retaining the forward-looking infrared equipment, although admitting "its maintenance is considered beyond current VNAF capabilities." Air Force headquarters accepted this recommendation, and the device remained installed in the South Vietnamese AC–119Ks, enabling the crews to detect the heat given off by camp fires at bivouac sites or trucks driving through the night. Maintenance became the responsibility of a U.S. contractor.[31]

Besides lacking electronics technicians to repair and fine tune certain of the AC–119K's sensors, the South Vietnamese Air Force faced a shortage of crews able to fly the aircraft. The transport squadrons operating Douglas C–47s afforded the likeliest source of trained crews, but these men already were doing a vital job. As Admiral McCain pointed out, "Conversion of a C–47 squadron. . . will impact adversely on the limited air transport capability." The March 1972 invasion delayed the beginning of an AC–119K crew training program until December of that year, and the Air Force did not complete the transfer of ten of the gunships until March 1973. By the time the South Vietnamese began flying the AC–119K, its time had passed as a weapon of interdiction; not even the AC–130 could roam at will over an expanded and better defended Ho Chi Minh Trail.[32]

The search for simple, easy-to-use weapons likely to prove deadly against infiltrators led to the CBU–55 fuel-air explosive, a five hundred pound bomb consisting of a delayed-action detonator and three containers of ethylene oxide. Dropped by parachute from a helicopter or slow-moving airplane, the weapon burst on contact with the ground, allowing the contents to escape and form an explosive cloud that seeped into bunkers or collected in foxholes where troops normally took refuge from conventional ordnance. When ignited, the gas killed by concussion.[33] In tests more than a year before, the bomb had proved effective except against targets beneath a dense jungle canopy, when some 13 percent of the weapons failed to detonate, apparently because of the cushioning effect of the treetops. This initial setback did not discourage Leonard Sullivan, who maintained that the CBU–55 "still looks good as a partial B–52 substitute against soft dispersed targets."[34] The weapon fascinated Sullivan, who argued that it gave the South Vietnamese A–1s striking power comparable to the B–52. The light weight of the bomb, he enthused "makes it possible . . . for a VNAF A–1 to carry nine CBU–55s," that, according to his calculations, provided "roughly the equivalent of twenty-seven 750 pounders," more than one-third the weight of ordnance a B–52D might carry.[35]

The bomb, however, failed to justify Sullivan's enthusiasm. Further evaluation in both the United States and South Vietnam showed that its cost, some twenty-five hundred dollars per weapon, was more than it was worth. The explosive gas, though deadly against troops who had taken cover in dugouts, had little effect on aboveground structures or vehicles, both of which might be important targets in a Vietnamized program of interdiction. As a result, the Department of Defense curtailed production, but South Vietnam nevertheless received a number of the weapons in time for the 1972 invasion.[36]

South Vietnamese participation in aerial interdiction depended to a great extent on the vulnerability of the available aircraft —whether Credible Chase gunships, A–1s, A–37s, AC–119Gs, or AC–47s—to enemy antiaircraft guns. When trying to solve this problem, U.S. planners sometimes indulged in wishful thinking. An Air Force study, for example, cited Lam Son 719, an operation characterized by deadly North Vietnamese antiaircraft fire, as evidence that enemy forces "prefer to withdraw these valuable [antiaircraft] assets, in the face of ground operations, to 'safe' areas, rather than expose them to capture/destruction." This misinterpretation of the lessons of Lam Son 719 led to the conclusion that "the VNAF. . . will have the capability to conduct limited aerial interdiction activities in, and around, the input gates to the RVN and Cambodia and in those areas of southern Laos where supported by ground operations."[37]

A similar lack of realism affected the thinking of Leonard Sullivan, who suggested that "the problem of vulnerability of aircraft over Laos is seriously overplayed." He argued that, by remaining south of Tchepone and flying mainly at night, the South Vietnamese would lose fewer than the twenty-five U.S. airplanes downed during Commando Hunt V. The U.S. losses, he said, were "exceptionally low . . . lower by a factor of ten than could be acceptable with cheaper planes (and cheaper pilots)"—minigunships, for instance, flown by South Vietnamese. Although willing to "acknowledge that the increase in total AAA Bns [antiaircraft artillery battalions] in Laos is rising faster than the rate of new road construction," he insisted that "none of these AAA guns are located along the separate personnel infiltration routes," although some of them could protect both road and trail. In his opinion, infiltrating personnel and lightly defended portions of the road network, such as the newer truck routes in Cambodia, would afford suitable targets for the South Vietnamese.[38]

Ground probes figured prominently in any plan for South Vietnamese interdiction in southern Laos. Leonard Sullivan's April 1971 proposal and the Air Staff study produced the following month had called for operations on the ground, and Secretary Laird later requested a study to determine what new equipment could be provided for raiding parties dispatched across the border against truck traffic and infiltrating troops.[39] The use of ground forces, however, raised difficulties that equipment alone could not resolve. After consulting Admiral McCain and General Abrams, Admiral Moorer sketched for Laird a bleak picture of what the South Vietnamese could now do in the Phu Dung zone of southern Laos. South Vietnam's "force structure," the Chairman of the Joint Chiefs of Staff said, "was not designed to provide a significant out-of-country interdiction capability," despite tables of organization that authorized 117 cross-border reconnaissance teams, twenty-seven platoons, and three border security companies. Ground forces encountered a greater enemy threat than ever before in trying to penetrate this region. During the past five years, the patrols in Laos had for the most part gathered intelligence, though they had also harassed the enemy and contributed to interdiction by calling down air strikes against road traffic or supporting installations. These "extensive operations" took place in "generally the same area along the Laotian-RVN border," and for that reason, the enemy had "learned the location of the most suitable landing and drop zones" and had "implanted an alert and highly responsive security system."[40]

Instead of discouraging Laird, Moorer's report caused him to push harder toward his goal of Vietnamizing interdiction. The Secretary of Defense directed the Army, the Air Force, and the Defense Special Projects Group (formerly the Defense Communications Planning Group) "to initiate the design of a combat test" of South Vietnam's current ability to conduct interdiction with available aircraft, raiding parties, and electronic sensors. This evaluation would proceed separately from the test of the minigunships, which, if successful, would take part in future interdiction. "I need not remind you," said the Secretary of Defense, "that the fate of our national Vietnamization policy rests in part on the evolution of a credible RVNAF interdiction capability at the earliest possible time."[41]

Secretary Laird's proposal for testing a skeletal program of Vietnamized interdiction found a place in Operation Island Tree, a combined plan for interdiction during the 1971–72 dry season that included the Project Island Tree attacks on troop infiltration. While naval forces took action against seaborne infiltrators and B–52s tried to bomb the troop routes, Commando Hunt VII would wage war on trucks and introduce the South Vietnamese to the tactics used against the road net in southern Laos. For at least a part of Commando Hunt VII, thanks to Operation Island Tree, South Vietnam's armed forces could help disrupt enemy lines of communication, but the inexperience of the air arm in conducting interdiction forced the South Vietnamese to emphasize operations on the ground. To the extent that North Vietnamese defenses permitted, patrols might ambush truck convoys and attack infiltration groups and support facilities anywhere from Ban Karai Pass to Kompong Som, an operating area that embraced Tchepone and Muong Nong, followed the Kong River from the vicinity of Ban Bak to the confluence with the Mekong, and then cut across Cambodia to the coast. Aerial interdiction would take place on a less ambitious scale; the plan for Operation Island Tree called only for launching all available sorties against transportation routes in those areas of Laos poorly protected by antiaircraft batteries.[42]

Merely assigning the South Vietnamese a broad operating area on the ground and encouraging them to fly some interdiction sorties did not satisfy Secretary Laird, who wanted positive action to ensure that South Vietnam could take over interdiction after a U.S. withdrawal. He feared that too many officials in his department were simply saying that the South Vietnamese could not do the job and assuming that the United States would continue the Commando Hunt series for years to come. This attitude had to change, he warned his subordinates, for the U.S. public would not accept two or three more years of fighting in Southeast Asia, even on a comparatively limited scale.[43]

A directive issued on October 8, 1971, reflected Laird's determination to Vietnamize interdiction. He was pleased, he told Admiral Moorer, that the various interdiction concepts would undergo evaluation during the coming dry season, but he did not want "to have RVNAF interdiction capabilities tied up in lengthy study and test cycles." He was determined that South Vietnamese skills "in this critical functional area" should be "maximized as soon as possible." To accomplish this, he established "the objective of achieving an optimal RVNAF interdiction capability by the fall of 1972 which could, if necessary, be self-sustaining with no more than limited U.S. advisory effort." He seemed to be suggesting, at least obliquely, a change of policy by which U.S. advisers would determine what the South Vietnamese needed, make it available, and then train them to use it, but if he actually envisioned this approach, it did not prevail.[44]

The War against Trucks

Only Operation Island Tree, the plan drafted during the summer of 1971, could serve as the basis for developing this "optimal . . . capability." Although not formally approved by the Joint Chiefs of Staff, the plan included participation by the South Vietnamese and laid a foundation for regional action in impeding the movement of men and supplies through southern Laos and Cambodia.[45] To promote cooperation among Southeast Asian nations, the Military Assistance Command, Vietnam, and the South Vietnamese Joint General Staff in August created the Combined Interdiction Coordinating Committee at Saigon. This group had operated for just a few weeks, however, when Secretary Laird concluded that it did not provide "a fully adequate mechanism for involving the Vietnamese, Thais, and Cambodians in the overall interdiction effort."[46] After visiting Saigon and seeing the committee at work, Leonard Sullivan agreed, "It would appear advisable to increase our emphasis on forging—or forcing if necessary—regional cooperation on a far broader scale."[47]

While efforts to promote international cooperation sputtered along, Generals Abrams and Lavelle tried to help the South Vietnamese prepare for the day when they would take over both ground and air interdiction. Staff officers of the Seventh Air Force, which General Lavelle now commanded, tried to explain to their South Vietnamese counterparts the techniques and purpose of the Commando Hunt series. Whatever its failings as an agency for regional planning, the Combined Interdiction Coordinating Committee enabled the South Vietnamese to become acquainted with the U.S. way of conducting aerial interdiction. Moreover, planning for the Credible Chase test, which continued through the fall and winter of 1971 despite "a certain amount of headshaking," gave the South Vietnamese additional insight into the problems and techniques of waging an aerial campaign against the roadways of the Ho Chi Minh Trail.[48]

According to the Air Force Advisory Group, which sought to modernize and improve the South Vietnamese air arm, the "major problem" in Vietnamizing interdiction was "to convince the RVNAF that the VNAF should be employed in a typical air force role rather than the current diversified Military Region approach." U.S. Air Force doctrine called for "centralizing command and control functions" so there would be "sufficient flexibility to employ VNAF resources in either the interdiction or close support role." The South Vietnamese, however, emphasized close air support and for that reason gave the commanders of the military regions control over aviation as well as ground units. Until the Joint General Staff agreed to change this system, Air Force advisers proposed to make an "interim effort . . . concentrated on training [the] VNAF in planning, coordination, execution, and monitoring of all activities required for their eventual full participation" in aerial interdiction.[49]

While the Air Force Advisory Group tried to nudge the South Vietnamese air arm toward conformity with U.S. Air Force doctrine as a means of ensuring the efficient use of air power against the Ho Chi Minh Trail, the Military Assistance Command attempted to organize and train special commando units to conduct probes on the ground. The plan for Operation Island Tree called for "ten company-size Special Commando operations per month" in areas "contiguous to and across the border" to inflict casualties and locate targets for even larger raids or for air strikes.[50] Meanwhile, Phu Dung ground reconnaissance teams had diminishing success trying to gather intelligence on the transportation network, while South Vietnamese EC–47s sought to pinpoint the source of radio signals from transmitters along the supply and infiltration routes.[51]

The attempt to teach interdiction technique to South Vietnamese airmen began in earnest during November 1971, when the Seventh Air Force put into effect a plan under which South Vietnam's air force would be "centrally scheduled for interdiction targets in RVN and areas adjacent to the RVN border." The South Vietnamese Joint General Staff agreed to set aside a certain number of sorties that a central headquarters, operating under the guidance of Seventh Air Force staff officers, could use exclusively for interdiction missions.[52] First came training in centralized control, which consisted mostly of watching the U.S. airmen. Throughout November, eight South Vietnamese officers underwent indoctrination in command and control, target selection, and intelligence, but the trainees had little to do, since the Seventh Air Force not only provided most of the intelligence data, but also assigned extra advisers to help plan the interdiction missions.

The United States had greater success in teaching South Vietnamese pilots the basic tactics used against enemy supply lines in Laos. By the end of November, enough South Vietnamese crews had flown with an Air Force A–37 detachment to permit a few of them to undertake actual combat missions in their own A–37s or A–1s.[53] From December 1 through 7, 1971, South Vietnamese airmen in A–37s flew forty-nine sorties against transportation targets just inside their nations's western border. After this series of missions, a South Vietnamese operations coordinator, who had completed an appropriate course of instruction, outlined for the participating crews the procedures they would follow in executing a directive of the Joint General Staff authorizing interdiction strikes up to thirty-five miles inside Laos. On December 8, four A–37s from Da Nang bombed a target in Laos, but bad weather forced cancellation of a four-plane mission by A–1s from Pleiku. Throughout the next five days, four Skyraiders and four A–37s carried out orders to hit targets across the border, but operations then came to an abrupt halt because Operation Island Tree had failed to achieve the intended regional cooperation.[54]

Surprised by the South Vietnamese air strikes in the portion of Laos controlled by North Vietnam, Laotian Prime Minister Souvanna Phouma halted the activity. When Ambassador Godley reported his own confusion and Souvanna's anger at learning about the operation from press reports, the Department of State replied that "we were just as surprised as you." Officials at the Department of State had discussed the idea of assigning the South Vietnamese a share in the interdiction campaign, and a consensus emerged that agreements between the governments of South Vietnam and Laos should precede the bombing. No such arrangement yet existed, however, and apparently no one in authority at the Department of State realized that the South Vietnamese strikes in Laos had gone beyond the planning stage and actually begun.[55]

Ambassador Godley predicted that the Prime Minister would reconsider if "VNAF participation in the interdiction effort could be stood down for, let's say, two weeks" to provide "a breathing period vis-a-vis Souvanna" and a "face-saving gimmick."[56] As the ambassador expected, Souvanna proved willing enough to permit the strikes, provided he could avoid acknowledging responsibility for the decision. To reassure the North Vietnamese of his neutrality and forestall punitive action by their troops in Laos, the Prime Minister remained publicly steadfast in his refusal to cooperate in the attacks, but on January 8, 1972, the Minister of Defense, Sisouk na Champassak, agreed privately to a resumption of South Vietnamese air strikes under certain conditions. Godley reported that Sisouk, who claimed that "he understood these matters much better than the Prime Minister," would accept responsibility for the renewed attacks provided there was no "official GVN confirmation" of any "press leaks" about the sorties into Laos.[57] South Vietnamese participation in the aerial interdiction of the trail promptly resumed, and the Air Force Advisory Group in South Vietnam was able to report "VNAF A–37 and A–1 aircraft . . . participating daily in Commando Hunt missions."[58] Until the North Vietnamese invasion forced a shift in air activity from the roads and trails to the battlefield itself, the South Vietnamese Air Force tried to devote 10 percent of its sorties by fighter-bombers or attack aircraft to daylight interdiction missions on either side of the border with Laos.[59]

During Commando Hunt VII, South Vietnamese airmen flew interdiction missions against the exit routes from the Ho Chi Minh Trail in preparation for taking over the interdiction campaign as early as the 1972–73 dry season. Maintaining pressure on the roads and trails through southern Laos seemed essential to the continued existence of South Vietnam and the survival of both Lon Nol's Cambodian government and Souvanna's ostensibly neutral coalition regime in Laos. "If nothing is done," Leonard Sullivan declared, "the NVA can continue to expand their resupply system at will and still release some fifty thousand or so defensive troops for battle in RVN, Cambodia, and Laos." Should the South Vietnamese ignore the Ho Chi Minh Trail and remain on the defensive, content merely with protecting their towns and cities, "we will eventually have to label the Vietnamization program as a failure," he argued, "since the security is bound to drop in the long run."[60]

Because he believed that South Vietnam's survival depended on attacking troops and supplies as they approached or crossed the nation's border, Sullivan objected to a proposal of the Military Assistance Command limiting interdiction to Cambodia and northwestern South Vietnam.[61] Although the suggestion reflected the fact that southern Laos had become too hard a nut for the South Vietnamese to crack by themselves, it marked a retreat from the U.S. practice of conducting interdiction as far from the battlefield as possible, attacking infiltration groups and truck convoys bound for South Vietnam or Cambodia en route to their destination. Sullivan believed that Abrams, in his desire to protect the administrative centers and populated areas, had overlooked the necessity of having the South Vietnamese "project their presence in an interdiction role" as far west as "major north-south routes of the Ho Chi Minh Trail."[62]

Admiral Moorer, who also received a summary of the revised Abrams strategy, raised no objection. He accepted the proposition that maintaining security throughout the populated coastal region took precedence over interdiction in Laos and the corollary that the interdiction effort would have to depend on men and equipment not needed for the primary mission. In fact, the admiral found reasons for optimism about progress toward Vietnamizing interdiction, for he doubted that Abrams' adjustment of priorities would reverse what he perceived as the current trend toward South Vietnamese self-sufficiency. Indeed, Moorer pointed to several signs of progress. The Seventh Air Force, after all, had begun involving South Vietnam's airmen in Commando Hunt operations. The CBU–55, though not yet fully tested against infiltrating troops, seemed to have potential value as a weapon of interdiction. Task Force Alpha had prepared a data base for Project Island Tree, the systematic bombing of the troop infiltration route through southern Laos, which would enable a Vietnamized interdiction campaign to kill North Vietnamese and drive home the cost of continuing the war. South Vietnam would soon receive the first of a projected eighteen AC–119Ks, a gunship that outperformed either the AC–47 or AC–119G. Finally the South Vietnamese air arm would soon learn to plant electronic sensors along infiltration and supply routes and interpret their signals.[63]

As the weeks passed, General Abrams bowed to reality, for the powerful defenses of the Ho Chi Minh Trail shattered hopes that South Vietnam could conduct a simple and inexpensive interdiction campaign combining operations on the ground and in the air. Laird, however, avoided a direct endorsement of Abrams' realistic strategy of subordinating interdiction in Laos to the security of coastal South Vietnam. The Secretary of Defense still urged the military to "move expeditiously in Vietnamizing interdiction operations," but in doing so he emphasized an earlier piece of advice: "we should not limit our thinking simply to the air role or to a mirror image of past U.S. operations—the South Vietnamese should be able to adopt different and perhaps more effective techniques."[64] The retreat from vigorous interdiction of the trail nevertheless continued, and soon he was reminding his principal commanders of his definition, first set forth in February 1971, that "interdiction in the broad sense" consisted of "stopping enemy supplies and troops wherever they may be encountered before they can be used against the South Vietnamese." If the Secretary of Defense had ever hoped to determine what South Vietnam needed to interdict movement on the Ho Chi Minh Trail, provide the necessary equipment, and teach the South Vietnamese how to use it, he had abandoned that goal. In conducting interdiction, the South Vietnamese would have to rely on what they could readily use and the United States could easily spare.[65]

The definition of interdiction as using any available means to impede the movement of North Vietnamese troops and supplies wherever they might be found surfaced again in April 1972, when "higher authority," Secretary Laird himself, "expressed disappointment with the rate of progress in the Vietnamization of interdiction."[66] Enemy forces, however, had already invaded South Vietnam. By the time the South Vietnamese troops and U.S. air power contained the offensive, South Vietnam had no alternative to the strategy that General Abrams advocated: defending the cities and the food-producing coastal region. This task would absorb the overwhelming share of the nation's military resources, leaving nothing for long-range interdiction. No longer would North Vietnam have to divert troops to protect the roads and trails through southern Laos from air attack or ground probes.

Chapter Sixteen

The Sensors Fall Silent

Although Secretary of Defense Melvin R. Laird, in particular, intended somehow to Vietnamize interdiction, U.S. officials had never seriously considered preparing the South Vietnamese to operate the Infiltration Surveillance Center, its computers, and the sensor array that reported movement on the Ho Chi Minh Trail. Gen. Creighton W. Abrams, the Commander, U.S. Military Assistance Command, Vietnam, expressed a commonly held view when he declared in the summer of 1971, "The Igloo White system . . . would offer a significant potential for aiding the RVNAF [Republic of Vietnam Armed Forces] interdiction program . . . but economic constraints limit the scope of operations which can be dedicated to support [the] RVNAF effort."[1] A program with an annual budget approaching two hundred million dollars, including forty million dollars for operation and maintenance, seemed too expensive for South Vietnam.[2] At his headquarters in Fort Shafter, Hawaii, Gen. William B. Rosson, Commander in Chief, U.S. Army, Pacific, also rejected Igloo White as a candidate for Vietnamization, though for a different reason. He pointed out that the system was "ultra sophisticated" and required "massive logistical, technical, communications, and air support," but South Vietnam unfortunately had "neither the technical expertise nor the military hardware to support such a system." Complexity as well as cost barred Igloo White from inclusion in Vietnamization.[3]

Instead of training the South Vietnamese to take over the facility at Nakhon Phanom, Task Force Alpha was to operate through the 1972–73 northeast monsoon season and then disband. The armed forces of South Vietnam inherited the related missions of short-range interdiction, which justified the unsuccessful Credible Chase minigunship program, and sensor-assisted border surveillance. By January 1972, Gen. John D. Lavelle, now in command of the Seventh Air Force, anticipated gradually reducing the use of relay aircraft, as close-in South Vietnamese border security fields increased in number and the more distant traffic monitoring strings diminished. He proposed that Air Force F–4s drop their last Igloo White sensors in mid-February 1973. These devices would continue reporting for at least seventy days, thus covering the last of the dry season, and in May, when the sensors fell silent, Task Force Alpha would cease to exist.[4]

The War against Trucks

With a termination date of May 1973 clearly in mind, the Air Force in the summer of 1972 signed a one-year Igloo White maintenance contract. For a fee of $495,371, Philco-Ford agreed to assume responsibility for the Air Force-owned equipment built, installed, and until this time, serviced by IBM and Radiation, Inc. IBM continued, however, to maintain the Igloo White computer, a 360/50 model that the firm leased to the Air Force. The Air Force and Philco-Ford timed the arrangement to expire as Task Force Alpha closed down, but they could extend it for a second year if plans for the Surveillance Center should change.[5]

Although scheduled to disband, Task Force Alpha undertook new missions during 1972. Early in February, in response to the threat from missile batteries defending the Ho Chi Minh Trail, Secretary of the Air Force Robert C. Seamans, Jr., launched a program, called Pave Onyx, to locate surface-to-air missile sites using "a package of Air Force systems/subsystems that could be deployed to Southeast Asia within the next six months." Pave Onyx tried to use the facilities of the Nakhon Phanom Surveillance Center for locating surface-to-air missile batteries rather than for searching out trucks or infiltrating troops. The antimissile project called for dropping, near suspected launch sites, acoustic sensors modified to respond to the sound of diesel generators, the source of electric power for the radars searching the sky to find and track targets for the missiles.[6]

Navy technicians, using funds transferred by the Air Force, modified the COMMIKE III, the latest commandable microphone, to respond to the noise of diesels. After the technicians had finished, the sensor filtered out all signals except the seventy-five Hertz tone that emanated from a diesel generator operating at fifteen hundred revolutions per minute. Because the modified microphone reacted to any stationary engine with the same harmonics, the Navy specialists sought to avoid false alarms from diesel-powered trucks, idling as they unloaded, by requiring the sensor to listen for seven minutes before accepting the signal as genuine and broadcasting it to Nakhon Phanom. A technician at the Surveillance Center, who acted as monitor, received the signal, recorded it on tape, then processed it on a spectrum analysis scope to confirm that the source actually registered seventy-five Hertz. If the Igloo White facility had temporarily shut down, to perform maintenance for example, and no one was listening, some of the sensors in each string could tally the number of times they received the sound and store the data for retrieval on command from Nakhon Phanom and interpretation by the analysts there.[7]

When the initial sensor reports indicated the presence of a generator, but failed to pinpoint it, aerial photography and radar intercepts helped select an area for Phantom jets to drop additional sensors. If the sensor delivery proved accurate, and the sought-after sound activated three of the devices not in a straight line with the source, the Surveillance Center could locate the generator by means of triangulation. Assuming that noise radiated uniformly from the diesel engine, three activations should enable the analyst to rotate a specially calibrated compass on an overlay showing sensor locations and determine that the generator and the missiles it served stood where the circles overlapped.[8]

An area near Ban Dong, along the Pone River, seemed an excellent place to test the modified microphones. Crews of AC–130 gunships patrolling in this region reported being fired on by surface-to-air missiles, and an aerial photograph disclosed the box-like shape of a parked van, possibly carrying the generator for a missile unit. On March 26, 1972, Task Force Alpha began operating a newly emplaced string of eight modified sensors, three of them capable of storing activation data for retrieval later. A second string of the same composition went into place two days later, planted across the first to form an X.[9] Although diesel noise frequently activated the sensors, triangulation proved impossible until F–4s planted additional strings on April 1 and April 24, increasing the chance that three sensors, not in line with the source, would pick up noise from the same generator. Despite the enlarged sensor array, results remained disappointing. The sensors around Ban Dong reported ninety-one signals from the time the first string went into action until May 1. On three occasions, flights of two to four Phantom jets attacked surface-to-air missile launchers identified by the sensors. The results of two strikes remained hidden beneath clouds, however; the third, delivered on May 9, triggered just two medium-sized secondary explosions.[10]

Despite successful testing at Eglin Air Force Base, Florida. the modified COM-MIKES failed at first to locate diesel generators on the Ho Chi Minh Trail. Those familiar with the tests in Florida blamed the lack of success in southern Laos on sensor placement. "When sensors are placed in strings," declared a message from Air Force headquarters, "the probability of more than one sensor activating is reduced considerably." To have a good probability of "three sensors alarming at the same time," thus ensuring a fix on the generator, "a grid not a string of sensors must be employed."[11]

Until it received the comments from Air Force headquarters, Task Force Alpha had operated on the supposition that even one string, or possibly two arranged in an X, would prove adequate if the technicians at Nakhon Phanom knew the general location of the missile site, as had been the case near Ban Dong. When installing a second field, the task force heeded the advice it had just received and laid out a grid of five strings, completing the job on May 25, too late to evaluate the modified sensor array. By this time, the fate of South Vietnam depended on struggles at An Loc, Kontum, and Quang Tri City, a result of the North Vietnamese invasion on March 30. The air war and sensor surveillance had shifted to battlefields inside South Vietnam. The Ho Chi Minh Trail and the surface-to-air missiles protecting it no longer presented a critical target, and in retrospect the decision to lay out the grid seems puzzling, even though it required comparatively few sensors.[12]

From its inception, the hastily devised attempt to use modified commandable microphones to locate surface-to-air missile launchers stirred little enthusiasm except among its sponsors at the Rome, New York, Air Development Center. Staff members there believed the technique could achieve the same results in Laos that it had in Florida, where it proved accurate to within twelve yards despite "known sensor positional errors up to ten meters."[13] In southern Laos, however, disappointment prevailed. Lt. Col. Earl D. McClintock, a liaison officer from the Tactical Air Warfare Center at Eglin Air Force Base, Florida, which had conducted the preliminary evaluation, visited Task Force Alpha when the first two sensor strings were functioning near Ban Dong. One of them, he said, "had picked up a distant sound which was determined to be a generator"; within minutes, "strike aircraft had made a loran drop resulting in a kill—not of the generator, but of a sensor." The sensor had missed the mark; it had no value as a point of reference and by accident became a target.[14]

As the error noted by McClintock made all too clear, inaccurately placed sensors imposed a severe handicap on technicians at the Surveillance Center. The same conditions—forest, haze, and antiaircraft fire—that made visual detection of surface-to-air missile sites so difficult also affected the F–4s dropping sensors and the RF–4s taking pictures to determine where the strings should go. The twelve-yard accuracy achieved at Eglin Air Force Base proved unattainable in Laos.[15]

Other factors compounded the effects of inaccurate placement. Operators at the Surveillance Center found serious technical shortcomings within the system. For example, the modified sensors reported one specific signal, with all others filtered out. If a monitor turned on the microphone and that sound was not being picked up, he heard nothing and could not determine whether the sensor was functioning. To check the first pair of strings, Task Force Alpha arranged for an AC–130 gunship to fly over the area at a prescribed time in the hope that technicians at the Surveillance Center could hear the bellow of its turboprop engines transmitted by the modified sensors, but the commandable microphones remained mute. Experience also disproved one of the assumptions on which the locating technique rested, the belief that sound radiated uniformly from the diesel motor so that distance alone determined signal strength. Distance proved to be just one factor. As the technicians at Nakhon Phanom discovered, loudness "varies with the azimuth off the exhaust port," requiring "some acoustic factor other than intensity."[16]

Even as the attempt to locate surface-to-air missile launchers ended, the Rome Air Development Center proposed using the same basic technique to ferret out the tanks and heavy guns with which the North Vietnamese invaders battered the defenses of Quang Tri Province. Technicians at the New York installation believed they could identify the clank of armor or roar of artillery, record it as broadcast from a minimum of three sensors, determine the difference in time that the noise reached each of those sensors, then lay out arcs based on the time factor; the intersection of the arcs would pinpoint the enemy weapon. Experience in trying to locate generators had again demonstrated the difficulty of planting sensors accurately from the air, but the development center devised a mathematical averaging technique to compensate for errors in laying out the field. During one computer simulation, the development team had managed to locate the source of sound within three feet even though two of the three reporting sensors had landed 165 feet off the mark.[17]

In mid-May 1972, as the enemy overran Quang Tri City and menaced the northern provinces of South Vietnam, Maj. John V. Kleperis, in charge of the

Aeronautical Systems Division liaison office in South Vietnam, explained the proposed gun-locating theory to Gen. John W. Vogt, Jr., who had succeeded General Lavelle in command of the Seventh Air Force. The major's audience also included Maj. Gen. Alton D. Slay, the Seventh Air Force Deputy Chief of Staff for Operations, and other key Air Force officers. When Kleperis promised to deliver the computer program for a simple gun-locating system to Nakhon Phanom in time to deal with the threat to the city of Hue, General Vogt became interested. The Seventh Air Force commander then discussed the proposal with General Abrams, who was desperate for some means of locating North Vietnamese artillery. When Vogt asked whether Abrams wanted the system deployed, the Army general told him to go ahead, and on May 19, Seventh Air Force submitted a formal request.[18] Because of its experience in using computers to store and interpret sensor data and its brief acquaintance with the scheme to pinpoint surface-to-air missile launchers, Task Force Alpha undertook the gun-locating project. The analysts at Nakhon Phanom would use the computer program described by Kleperis to find the guns and then call on the airborne battlefield command and control center to direct aircraft, or possibly artillery fire, against them.[19]

Air Force Systems Command, parent organization of both the Aeronautical Systems Division and the Rome Air Development Center, felt compelled at this time to sound a note of caution about the system that General Vogt intended to use in Southeast Asia. "It must be pointed out," read a message from the command's headquarters, "that this technique has not been evaluated in an environment containing battlefield noises." The possibility existed that the roar of incoming and outgoing fire might in effect deafen the deployed sensors, depriving them of any clearcut signals to report. As a result, warned Systems Command, "We cannot guarantee success."[20]

Early in June, F–4s began planting the first gun-locating sensor field, laid out in a series of concentric arcs, each with several strings, partially encircling the city of Hue. On the advice of the Office of Director of Defense Research and Engineering, Task Force Alpha established an interval of three miles between arcs. By June 22, 149 individual sensors—68 acoustic-seismic intrusion detectors and 81 commandable microphones—stood in place, and 115 of them had broadcast information to Nakhon Phanom.[21] Task Force Alpha soon discovered, however, that three miles was too far between arcs. Between July 12 and 18, to improve coverage, the Phantom jets planted additional strings that cut the interval to one and one-half miles. Meanwhile Task Force Alpha grew dissatisfied with the arc pattern, so that two other gun-detection fields, planted near Quang Tri City and southwest of Hue, consisted of square grids one and one-fourth miles on a side.[22]

At the Surveillance Center, a trained operator selected a group of six adjacent sensors (three from each of two arcs or lines), determined the appropriate radio channels, turned on a tape recorder, and triggered the microphones. As he replayed the tape, he listened for the noise of cannon firing. When he heard what sounded like a 130-mm gun, he stopped the machine, rewound beyond this point, then played the signal into a device that presented the noise in graphic form and enabled him to determine that one of the artillery pieces had caused it. When three sensors reported the same noise, another specialist, the ground surveillance monitor, determined the time differential among them and used a scale prepared by the Rome Air Development Center to calculate the interval it would take the sound to travel from a common source to the reporting devices. The monitor then fed the locations of the three sensors and the three time intervals into the IBM computer, which solved the problem of triangulation and produced a set of universal transverse Mercator coordinates for the source. No more than twenty minutes usually elapsed between the time the audio equipment operator heard the sound and the computer printed out a location. In another ten minutes or less, technicians adapted the coordinates to the loran navigation system that the strike aircraft used.[23]

However valid the theory, in actual practice these procedures failed to pinpoint North Vietnamese guns. At first the flaw seemed to lie in the scope of the sensor coverage. Since broader coverage might improve results, Task Force Alpha scrounged enough cable and equipment to fit out a second ground surveillance monitoring station at Nakhon Phanom, also capable of triggering a block of six sensors. During the newly christened detection phase, both stations operated simultaneously, querying two sensor blocks at a time in the hope of doubling the chance of detecting a 130-mm gun. If either monitor received an apparently valid signal from even one sensor, he immediately began triggering other adjacent microphones in the hope that two other of these devices would report a subsequent firing and permit an easy solution. To avoid causing confusion during this so-called location phase, the other monitoring station temporarily stopped activating sensors.[24]

Task Force Alpha struggled to make the gun-locating system work, revising polling techniques, setting out denser fields, and even adopting a different pattern for sowing the electronic sensors. In all, the project employed more than seven hundred sensors, planted between June 6 and September 21 at an estimated cost of $5.2 million. Yet, when the batteries at last failed and the microphones fell silent, the task force could not prove that sensor data had led directly to the verified destruction of a single gun. Intelligence from the locator network had resulted in 267 requests for visual reconnaissance, and the combination of electronic reporting and visual observation produced 204 air strikes that generated unsubstantiated claims of seven artillery pieces destroyed or damaged. Sensor data had also contributed to counterbattery fire and shelling by naval guns, but the results remained unproved.

In offering its gun-locating technique, the Rome Air Development Center gambled that an improvised method would work until a system under development by the Navy became available. Because of technical limitations and lack of time for evaluation and experiment, the gamble failed. Hue, however, remained in South Vietnamese hands despite the project's failure, and South Vietnamese troops recaptured Quang Tri City on September 16. Elsewhere, both Kontum and An Loc held out successfully. The crisis in South Vietnam passed before the Navy could deploy its sound ranging equipment that, in any event, shared some of the flaws of the Air Force method and promised no better results.[25]

Long before Task Force Alpha tried its hand at locating surface-to-air missile sites and artillery pieces, while the Surveillance Center still focused its attention on the Ho Chi Minh Trail, the United States began training South Vietnamese to use sensors for battlefield surveillance and border security, though not for the aerial interdiction of traffic on the Ho Chi Minh Trail. The first to offer this instruction were marines stationed just south of the demilitarized zone, along which Secretary of Defense Robert S. McNamara at the time planned to build an anti-infiltration barrier. In the fall of 1968, General Abrams formally acknowledged that mobile forces, able to react quickly to enemy incursions, would substitute for the proposed fixed barrier with its mutually supporting redoubts. Sensors played a critical role in this revised scheme of defense, and on September 14, a combined surveillance team from the 3d Marine Division and the 2d Regiment, Army of the Republic of Vietnam, planted a sensor field between Gio Linh and the demilitarized zone. The marines and their South Vietnamese allies cooperated in sowing additional fields that also reported to monitoring terminals located at bases near the demilitarized zone. Mountains in the rugged western portion of this critical area blocked some sensor transmissions intended for Marine or South Vietnamese terminals, so Task Force Alpha lent a hand. To cover the dead space, Air Force F–4s planted new sensor strings and relay aircraft forwarded the signals over the mountains to the Surveillance Center at Nakhon Phanom, which maintained direct radio contact with Dong Ha, the central processing point for data derived from the fields guarding the northern approaches to South Vietnam.[26]

In March 1969, some six months after the marines began offering training in the use of sensors, the Department of Defense adopted a plan for giving all South Vietnamese army divisions the same basic sensor equipment as their U.S. counterparts. The Military Assistance Command set up a sensor school at Vung Tau in June, and during the following month, the 1st Division, Army of the Republic of Vietnam, received ten days' training from U.S. and South Vietnamese instructors. By the end of January 1970, nine infantry divisions, two separate regiments, and five naval units had completed the course. Emphasis now shifted to the orientation of staff officers, the training of replacements, and the indoctrination of units that had missed the earlier sessions. If all went according to plan, by July 1, 1973 the South Vietnamese would have been able to operate the school without U.S. instructors and also form and dispatch mobile training teams for units in the field.[27]

When it got under way in the summer of 1969, the Vung Tau sensor training project aimed at setting up a combined U.S. and South Vietnamese border surveillance network covering the demilitarized zone, the A Shau Valley, the approaches to Dak To and Pleiku, and vulnerable areas along the Cambodian border. The Army of the Republic of Vietnam, "at an appropriate time," would assume responsibility for "unilateral implementation." After taking over the burden of border security, the South Vietnamese might also have used sensors within the country to help safeguard roads, supply dumps, and villages from Viet Cong guerrillas. Most of the South Vietnamese trained to use sensors served in army or marine corps units. Enough sailors had graduated from the Vung Tau school, however, to permit the U.S. Navy to begin Vietnamizing its sensor program during 1970, enabling the South Vietnamese Navy to take over electronic surveillance of the roads, trails, and waterways in the Mekong delta.[28]

While the Vung Tau school taught soldiers, marines, and sailors, the first class of twenty-two South Vietnamese airmen reported to Pleiku for on-the-job training with the U.S. Air Force technicians operating a deployable automatic relay terminal known as DART II. In an emergency, this monitoring station could pinch-hit for the Nakhon Phanom Surveillance Center, although it lacked the computer that enabled Task Force Alpha's analysts to make instant judgments about fleeting targets. DART operators had to rely on training and experience to interpret data from automatic plotting equipment that charted the status of as many as ninety-nine sensor strings, most of which kept an electronic watch over the borders of South Vietnam.

During the period of instruction at Pleiku, which began on October 31, 1969, the South Vietnamese worked in a portable shelter that housed DART II, learning how to use the equipment and analyze the incoming data. The degree of supervision diminished as the trainees gained experience, until the South Vietnamese operated largely on their own. The biggest class consisted of twenty-seven South Vietnamese airmen—nineteen enlisted men, two of them administrative specialists, and eight officers. Maintenance and other technical support remained the responsibility of the United States, and the South Vietnamese received no instruction in these fields.[29]

Despite the promising beginning at Pleiku, the South Vietnamese air arm did not take over DART II, even though the Defense Communications Planning Group, headed at the time by General Lavelle, suggested that Abrams increase the participation of South Vietnam's airmen in the program of border and battlefield surveillance. The Army general responded by proposing an exclusively South Vietnamese effort, distinct from Igloo White, in which QU–22s operated by the air arm relayed signals from army sensor fields to a DART operated by airmen. Both the Seventh Air Force and the Air Force Advisory Group at Saigon opposed the idea, claiming it would drain away money already committed for more important weapons and give South Vietnam an aircraft, the QU–22, suited to just this one task. General Abrams soon came around to this viewpoint, and in October 1970, almost a year after the first class reported to Pleiku, his headquarters approved a Seventh Air Force recommendation to shut down DART II and give the South Vietnamese a "simple palletized airborne relay package" compatible with the U.S. Army's battlefield area surveillance system, already familiar to the South Vietnamese trained at Vung Tau. The airborne radio link would forward signals to an Army-supplied ground terminal simpler to operate and maintain than DART II.[30]

Neither the phasing out of South Vietnamese training with DART II nor the scheduled termination of Igloo White signaled an end to South Vietnam's sensor program; indeed, expansion—or at least reorientation—still seemed likely. Secretary Laird proposed training the South Vietnamese to use sensors against enemy supply and infiltration routes, even though he shared the belief that Igloo White was too complex and expensive for them. He insisted on somehow including sensors in a Vietnamized program of interdiction, and in April 1971, he launched the effort by instructing Maj. Gen. John R. Deane, Jr., USA, the Director of the Defense Special Projects Group (formerly the Defense Communications Planning Group), to work with the services in evaluating the feasibility of devising an airborne "strategic read-out system" to be used in conjunction with the proposed minigunship fleet. "I believe it will be essential," the Secretary of Defense remarked, "for the South Vietnamese to continue, on their own, to measure enemy inputs into RVN—in a manner roughly equivalent to the present Air Force procedures for measuring input/output through Laos itself." Aware of South Vietnamese limitations, he insisted, "The simplest possible system should be studied, limiting airborne sensor delivery, relay, and output to the minimum."[31]

Air Force headquarters echoed the call for simplicity, and a study conducted by Maj. Gen. Leslie W. Bray, Jr., the Assistant for Vietnamization to the Deputy Chief of Staff, Plans and Operations, concluded that "the interdiction program could be enhanced with an unsophisticated sensor system consisting of air or hand emplaced sensors . . . and (conceptually) an uncomplicated readout capability in the aircraft." According to this scheme, a minigunship crew would know the exact location of each air-dropped or hand-planted sensor in its patrol sector, observing their status on a portable monitor similar to the battery-powered devices used by ground forces. Whenever a light flashed to indicate that a sensor had detected sound or movement, the pilot could "proceed to the location of the sensor, visually acquire the target (using the NOD [night observation device] if necessary), and take the target under fire or request TACAIR [tactical air] as appropriate."[32] This concept conformed to the views of General Deane, who favored a "simplified strategic readout system" costing "between eight hundred thousand and two million dollars" and capable of monitoring " two hundred to four hundred air-delivered sensors."[33]

Throughout June 1971 the principal U.S. commanders in the Pacific and Southeast Asia discussed possible types of sensor equipment for the South Vietnamese. Several points emerged from their exchange of ideas. For example, although these officers agreed with Secretary Laird that Vietnamizing Igloo White was out of the question, they believed that South Vietnam might benefit from certain elements of the system, such as the airborne relay equipment used in the Beechcraft QU–22s, various types of sensors, and possibly DART II, now scheduled to move to Nakhon Phanom since it no longer trained South Vietnamese.[34] Gen. Joseph J. Nazzaro, the Pacific Air Forces commander, suggested that South Vietnam establish two "zones of sensors . . . to extend the surveillance area/distance" of border outposts manned by ground troops. While one zone kept roads and trails under surveillance, the second would provide local security for the bases themselves.[35] General Rosson, who commanded Army forces in the Pacific area, elaborated on the concept, pointing out that ground patrols would bear the heaviest responsibility for border security, harassing the enemy and planting a majority of the sensors, though aircraft could sow the more distant fields.[36]

In October 1971, Secretary Laird decided to proceed with the kind of simplified sensor network that the senior commanders in South Vietnam and the Pacific had discussed during the summer. Specifically, he directed the Defense Special Projects Group to collaborate with the services in providing South Vietnam with "expanded sensor/radar capability for all ground force elements" and "sensor delivery/readout capability" for the air force. The Vietnamized sensor program would take the form described by General Nazzaro—two zones, one for close-in interdiction and the other for border surveillance.[37]

Lack of experience and shortages of equipment impeded progress toward Laird's goal of participation by the South Vietnamese Air Force in the use of sensors. Except for the brief time, not quite a year, spent working with DART II at Pleiku, airmen had never interpreted and used sensor data, and the number of DART II veterans available totaled just 42. Moreover, the air arm had only the vulnerable helicopter to plant the sensors exactly and no aircraft to carry the promised airborne relay equipment that would link the sensors with a ground terminal, not DART II at this stage of planning, but portable equipment the U.S. Army would supply.[38]

For airborne monitoring and signal relay, General Lavelle proposed to start out using the scarce and valuable C–47s, though he hoped soon to settle on some other craft, possibly the QU–22 or even the AC–47. By mid-November, about six weeks after Secretary Laird had decided to include the South Vietnamese Air Force in the sensor program, at least a temporary solution to the airborne relay problem seemed at hand in the form of portable relay equipment suitable for the C–47.[39] Early in 1972, the South Vietnamese received six sets of this relay equipment, mounted on pallets for easy installation and removal, and one ground terminal capable of receiving the relayed signals. The prospect that Vietnamized de Havilland C–7A transports would replace the C–47s encouraged the South Vietnamese to agree to modify as many as twenty of the older aircraft to accept the relay pallets. Plans called for six of the sets to go into action during March, channeling signals from at least part of the forty strings, with 189 reporting devices, that Air Force F–4s were maintaining in northern South Vietnam. A cadre of forty-five South Vietnamese airmen would complete training in the new system at a school that two U.S. technical representatives, sent to South Vietnam by the Defense Special Projects Group, established at Cam Ranh Bay. Besides training operators, the course taught equipment maintenance.[40]

The sensor relay program got off to a discouraging start when the six C–47s chosen for the first missions encountered electrical problems. Among other things, obsolete wiring diagrams frustrated South Vietnamese attempts to install the palletized radio equipment. Luckily, Air Force MSgt. Clarence D. Long had the skill to troubleshoot the wiring without benefit of an up-to-date diagram and see to it that the equipment functioned properly. The struggle to correct the electrical system delayed the first operational flight one month, until April 22, 1972.[41]

The relay gear carried on board the modified C–47Ds could forward signals from as many as 512 sensors, arrayed in 128 strings of four, to a terminal at Da Nang. Like DART II, the portable terminal had no computer, but substituted two automatic plotting devices, each of which at a given time might record the output of 59 strings selected from the total field. Unfortunately, the terminal, which was compatible with the South Vietnamese Army's battlefield surveillance system, and the airborne relay platforms never operated at capacity. In the aftermath of the North Vietnamese invasion on March 30, few F–4s could ignore tactical targets and plant or replenish South Vietnamese sensor arrays, and as a result only five strings were functioning at the end of May. The number increased as battle lines became stabilized, so that during the summer's heavy fighting in Quang Tri Province, South Vietnamese C–47s assumed responsibility for relaying information from thirteen strings that Air Force F–4s had freshly planted in that area.[42]

The South Vietnamese relied on U.S. F–4s to drop sensors because, when the Vietnamized sensor program began, only the helicopter could plant sensors with acceptable accuracy, hovering over a designated spot while the South Vietnamese crew, working from up-to-date aerial photos, pitched the devices out the door. In a defended area, such tactics obviously amounted to suicide. Since a faster aircraft, less vulnerable to fire from the ground, had to take over the job, Lavelle proposed fitting some South Vietnamese A–37s with flare dispensers, modified for releasing sensors and mounted beneath the wings. The general realized, however, that the United States would eventually have to bring the A–37s up to the standard of the F–4s by installing loran equipment to guide crews to the exact release point and cameras to record where the sensor actually fell.[43]

The A–37 project promptly hit a snag when modification of flare dispensers to drop sensors proved more difficult than anticipated. The Tactical Air Warfare Center reported that it had never tested the flare dispenser with either the A–37 or the standard South Vietnamese fighter, the Northrop F–5. As a result, the center lacked the data it needed to calculate ballistic characteristics for the sensors or to work out delivery tactics; flight testing proved necessary, causing a delay. Also, the intervalometer, originally designed to determine the timing for releasing flares, needed rewiring so that it could drop the sensors much farther apart than flares. Technicians, however, did not consider the modification especially difficult, and they were correct. Rewiring the flare dispenser proved simple enough, but the Air Force Advisory Group encountered difficulty finding cameras that South Vietnamese airmen could use to verify accurate emplacement. During this search for cameras, North Vietnam's invasion of the South disrupted the entire sensor project. The South Vietnamese had to use all their F–5s and A–37s to help repel the invaders and could spare none to plant sensors.[44]

Well before the invasion forced the South Vietnamese Air Force to suspend efforts to take over the mission of planting sensors by air, and also disrupted the Commando Hunt interdiction campaign against the Ho Chi Minh Trail, U.S. commanders realized that some kind of communist offensive was in the making and sought to redeploy sensor coverage accordingly. During January 1972, as the enemy prepared for his spring onslaught, General Abrams asked permission to plant sensors in the demilitarized zone north of the provisional military demarcation line. To extend electronic surveillance into this region would, he believed, "greatly enhance the ability to monitor resupply and infiltration activity and permit U.S. and allied forces south of the DMZ to conduct timely counteractions."[45] Adm. John S. McCain, Jr., the Commander in Chief, Pacific, endorsed this request, which he termed "essential," and the Joint Chiefs of Staff approved the aerial seeding of sensors in an area fiercely defended by North Vietnamese antiaircraft weapons.[46]

Despite this northward extension of electronic monitoring, South Vietnamese forces could not stop the enemy's initial thrust across the demilitarized zone in March 1972. Although the Army of the Republic of Vietnam, with the help of devastating bombardment from U.S. aircraft, managed to check the North Vietnamese advance, the invasion shook congressional confidence in the sensor program. Scarcely eighteen months had passed since a Senate subcommittee had marveled at the accomplishments of these devices at Khe Sanh and applauded plans for an electronic battlefield, with Senator Barry M. Goldwater, an Arizona Republican who was a major general in the Air Force Reserve, declaring that sensors were "one of the greatest steps forward in warfare since gunpowder."[47]

Congressional sentiment had changed, however. Stories of sensors in action and schemes for eventually automating the battlefield no longer impressed those who voted the money for such projects. "How can you say we are making progress," asked Representative Joseph P. Addabbo, a New York Democrat, "when you are asking for additional money for sensors and we didn't know the enemy was coming across the DMZ until they were on top of us and we lost millions of dollars of equipment?"[48] Col. Sheridan J. Moran, of Air Force intelligence, replied that sensors had indeed reported unusual traffic just north of the demarcation line and in southern Laos. "We knew all the time what was coming down," he told Representative Addabbo, conceding, however, that knowledge of the size and frequency of truck convoys in these areas had not revealed the change in North Vietnam's tactics, the choice of full-scale invasion over the earlier practice of infiltrating troops for sudden attacks on towns or installations throughout South Vietnam. In the case of a mass attack, when "the enemy chose to pour four divisions across the DMZ," the colonel admitted that "sensors will not help the situation." In short, warning was valuable, but could not of itself prove decisive against overwhelming numbers.[49] Unimpressed with the argument that sensors had done all that could be expected of them, the House Appropriations Committee echoed the opinion of Representative Addabbo. "As we disclosed during our hearings this year," it reported, "the committee has not been favorably impressed with the success of the overall sensor program in past years, and their effectiveness in the recent North Vietnamese invasion of the South has been questionable."[50]

Actually, the changed military situation in Southeast Asia had more impact than the attitude of Congress in altering the future of Igloo White. Prior to March 30 and the Easter invasion, so called because North Vietnam attacked during the Christian Holy Week, plans called for Task Force Alpha to surrender responsibility for sensor fields in the demilitarized zone to the South Vietnamese army, while continuing to monitor the strings in southern Laos through the 1972–73 dry season, after which the Surveillance Center would disband.[51]

By mid-summer, however, the future looked much different. Following the invasion, the Surveillance Center turned its back on southern Laos to focus on northern South Vietnam, searching primarily for 130-mm guns rather than supply convoys. Because resumption of the Commando Hunt series seemed unlikely, Lt. Gen. Marvin L. McNickle, in command of the Thirteenth Air Force, suggested that, "considering [the] changed character and operational locale of the war, coupled with the low take from the sensor fields . . . it might be timely to consider acceleration of the phase down."[52]

General Vogt, the Seventh Air Force commander, agreed to review Task Force Alpha's future, but he wanted to delay the appraisal until a planned South Vietnamese counteroffensive had succeeded in retaking Quang Tri City. At this time, July 1972, hope lingered for the success of the gun-locating project, and he was reluctant to shut down the Surveillance Center, since doing so might undermine the ability of South Vietnamese divisions to neutralize hostile artillery. Once the enemy had been checked and Quang Tri City recaptured, the future of the Surveillance Center rested solely on the increasingly remote possibility of a Commando Hunt IX. Throughout the summer, as prospects for another Commando Hunt operation grew dimmer, sensors failed utterly to locate North Vietnamese artillery, and the importance of Task Force Alpha steadily diminished. By September 25 the Surveillance Center at Nakhon Phanom monitored only three hundred of the roughly twenty-six hundred sensors in service throughout South Vietnam, and all the strings reporting to Task Force Alpha covered areas in the northern provinces. Various portable terminals received signals from the rest.[53]

In the fall of 1972, General Vogt and Lt. Gen. William G. Moore, Jr., General McNickle's successor at the Thirteenth Air Force, discussed the future of Task Force Alpha and proposed shutting it down on the last day of December, five months ahead of schedule. Adm. Noel A. M. Gayler, who on September 1 had taken over the U.S. Pacific Command from Admiral McCain, agreed, suggesting that a computer-equipped sensor reporting post, which could monitor four hundred sensors simultaneously, would afford an acceptable postwar substitute for the more expensive Surveillance Center. Secretary of Defense Laird approved the recommended termination date, and the Joint Chiefs of Staff forwarded his decision to the appropriate commanders, pointing out a possible role for sensors in checking compliance with a cease-fire. Such a surveillance network, the Joint Chiefs observed, might report either to an Army-developed sensor reporting post, as proposed by Admiral Gayler, or to the DART II.[54] The idea of using sensors to police a cease-fire traced its roots at least to September 1968, when William H. Sullivan, then the Ambassador to Laos, had suggested that any international truce supervision group could monitor troop infiltration routes electronically, while maintaining checkpoints to make a visual count of trucks moving through the mountain passes.[55] Now, as plans were taking shape for the phaseout of Task Force Alpha, and cease-fire talks between the United States and North Vietnam seemed to be making progress, serious discussion began about policing the truce that would end the Vietnam War.

In advising Admiral Gayler that Secretary Laird had approved closing down Igloo White at year's end, the Joint Chiefs of Staff acknowledged the "requirement for the surveillance of possible North Vietnamese ground movement . . . in violation of the terms of a ceasefire agreement." To accomplish this they suggested incorporating sensors in "an overall post hostilities surveillance program" that would keep watch over an area "extending from Nape Pass southward along the NVN [North Vietnam]-Laos border to the DMZ, then eastward to the coast." According to this concept, planners should assume that the cease-fire would forbid flights over North Vietnam, though "overflight and implantation of sensors in Laos, Cambodia, and SVN [South Vietnam] will be authorized."[56]

General Clay, the former Seventh Air Force commander now in charge of the Pacific Air Forces, cast the sensors in a subordinate role when he addressed the subject of postwar surveillance. Because charts showing patterns of sensor activations lacked the impact of photos or prisoner-of-war interrogations, he doubted that the electronic devices could provide the kind of "concrete evidence of cease-fire violation" needed to convince the international peacekeeping agency that he expected would enforce the settlement. Clay maintained that "air-delivered sensors . . . are not effective against personnel," thus dismissing the claims of success for the recent Island Tree bombing; nor did he believe that electronic surveillance could "distinguish between friendly, enemy, and neutral traffic that might exist in the cease-fire area." As a result, he wanted to be sure that emphasis rested not on sensors, but on other tools of aerial intelligence—including cameras, infrared devices, and radar—supplemented by communications intercepts and interrogations of North Vietnamese defectors. Although wary of relying on sensors to monitor a truce, Clay believed that the Seventh Air Force and Task Force Alpha could maintain a three hundred–sensor network, in spite of a shortage of acoustic devices caused by the gun-locating project. In offering this projection, however, he again warned that "the lack of demonstrated results and subsequent phaseout of Igloo White do not justify employing sensors as the primary method of surveillance." Without a computer to help interpret its signals, the electronic sensor seemed of dubious value in a situation where all road traffic was not necessarily hostile. Instead of plunging ahead with sensor seeding, the general advised waiting "until the cease-fire monitoring capability of air-delivered sensors has been established."[57]

Gen. Fred C. Weyand, USA, who on July 1, 1972 replaced Abrams as the U.S. commander in Vietnam, approved a joint Task Force Alpha/Seventh Air Force concept for using sensors to determine North Vietnamese compliance with a cease-fire. The postwar electronic array, as endorsed by Weyand in November, would consist of thirty-nine strings, each of them having five air-delivered seismic intrusion detectors and three acoustic-seismic intrusion detectors, for a total of 312 devices. A field of eight strings would stand guard in the demilitarized zone, with four strings in North Vietnam, one in northern South Vietnam, and the rest in southern Laos.[58]

Although Weyand saw no profit in "the emplacement of sensors in North Vietnam other than immediately inside the southern pass and DMZ border areas,"[59] the Joint Chiefs of Staff sought to take advantage of the rules of engagement in effect in the fall of 1972 that permitted air operations, including the seeding of sensors, as far north as the 20th parallel. The F–4s should waste no time in tackling this job, they declared, "as a hedge against the possibility of an early cease-fire agreement that would prohibit overflight of NVN." The Joint Chiefs hoped to collect as much intelligence on southern North Vietnam as possible before a truce went into effect; any benefit in the form of cease-fire surveillance would come as a bonus.[60] Admiral Gayler sided with General Weyand against the Joint Chiefs of Staff, advising them that he considered the "intelligence payoff of immediate sensor implant small compared to the effort and cost." Instead of embarking on a frenzied program of planting sensors, the Commander in Chief, Pacific, wanted to wait for "detailed knowledge of cease-fire agreements." He added, of course, that U.S. forces in Southeast Asia were "prepared to accomplish implants if directed."[61]

The extensive postwar sensor fields never took shape. The Joint Chiefs of Staff, where General Abrams now served as Army Chief of Staff, encountered still another problem, replenishment of the sensor inventory, which lent weight to the objections Gayler and Weyand had raised. Not only had the Commando Hunt series and the various other sensor programs depleted stocks, Congress was withholding production funds. Since a postwar field could not function for long without replenishment, the electronic devices, with their "limited life span," would "provide information only during the early stages of a cease-fire." Rushing sensors into place to gather current intelligence would exhaust the inventory and hamper long-term surveillance of the truce.[62] The shortage of sensors prevented the immediate seeding of North Vietnam's panhandle and caused the Joint Chief of Staff to settle for a variant of the Weyand plan, an array of some three hundred sensors, most of them located along the North Vietnamese border or in southern Laos, that reported by way of C–130 relay aircraft to a DART at Nakhon Phanom. "The concept," the Joint Chiefs told Laird, "is feasible, sufficient resources are available in Southeast Asia to support the concept for approximately six months, and full implementation could begin within a matter of days."[63]

The Secretary of Defense endorsed the views of the Joint Chiefs of Staff, and on December 1, they directed Admiral Gayler and his subordinates to set up the surveillance net with thirty-nine strings. Planting and replenishing fields inside North Vietnam received the highest priority. Since the postwar array would absorb some strings already in place there, the Joint Chiefs of Staff urged that any of the affected sensors that "may have exceeded their estimated half life should now be replaced."[64] Two days later General Weyand reported all thirty-nine strings in place and that the oldest string located in North Vietnam would function until March 1973.[65]

The War against Trucks

In its final form, the truce surveillance project did not include the automatic plotting equipment that had been part of DART II when it saw service as a training device at Pleiku. Since elimination of this feature severely reduced the number of sensors that could simultaneously feed information into the terminal, arguments surfaced for either restoring the automatic plotters or linking DART to the Igloo White computer, which would then remain in service until March 1973 instead of shutting down at the end of December 1972. General Weyand's staff warned that without the automatic plotters, the deployable terminal could barely handle the sensors reporting to it and would have no potential for expansion. Nor would the U.S. government save money by getting rid of the two plotters, since both of them belonged to the military and came under the Igloo White maintenance contract recently signed by Philco-Ford.[66]

While the Military Assistance Command campaigned to keep the plotting equipment, Task Force Alpha and the Seventh Air Force urged retention instead of the Surveillance Center's computer, basing their case on the need for additional sensor monitoring capacity either to permit expanded coverage or to help compensate for the shortage of relay aircraft. By way of comparison, two simultaneous C–130 relay orbits, each reporting directly to an automatic plotter, could cover the entire field, but computerization would provide the same coverage, while permitting double the number of sensors in the field and if the war should resume, enabling DART II to conduct the kind of electronic targeting that Igloo White had performed, though on a lesser scale.[67]

These attempts either to retain the automatic plotters or to tie the deployable terminal into the IBM computer accomplished nothing. General Clay reminded the Seventh Air Force and Task Force Alpha planners that the truce surveillance concept called for random triggering of sensor strings rather than around-the-clock monitoring; automatic plotting equipment, let alone the computer, could make no real contribution in these circumstances. The Air Force, he insisted, had no choice, but to accept the agreed upon surveillance system; otherwise it would be "placed in the position of justifying to joint channels the complete closure of Igloo White on the one hand and then expanding a JCS-directed austere effort on the other." The computer shut down at the end of December; and the postwar sensor network was ready by January 27, 1973, when an agreement formally ended hostilities in North and South Vietnam.[68]

In actual practice, retention of the two automatic plotters or the computer could have made little difference. A sprawling area with comparatively few sensors available to maintain surveillance, mountainous terrain that masked signals, and a lack of suitable relay orbits combined to restrict coverage to southern Laos. The information obtained there apparently proved helpful, however, for analysts using the terminal after the computer had shut down declared that the signals provided "indications of enemy logistic flow and sufficient data to provide samples of trends, area, types, and levels of activity."[69] In anticipation that a cease-fire in Laos would bar U.S. flights over the kingdom, F–4s replenished the strings located there before February

22, 1973, when the Laotian peace agreement went into effect. This final seeding extended postwar surveillance until mid-June. By the time the batteries failed in the last elements of the makeshift post-hostilities monitoring network, the United States had invested some two billion dollars to establish the kind of air-supported electronic barrier proposed in the Project Jason report and then spent at least that amount for its operation.[70]

Trail Traffic. A truck convoy moves south (top), a truck park (center), and a group of walking North Vietnamese (bottom).

Opposite Page. Trucks loaded with crates and boxes (top), a petroleum storage area (center), and an open storage supply dump.

CRATES/BOXES

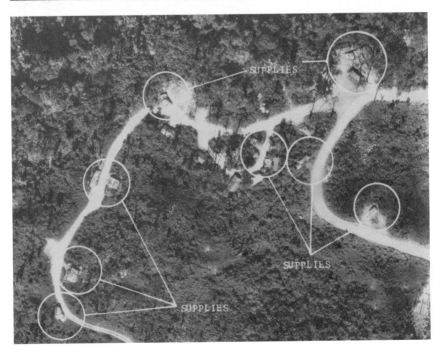

SUPPLIES

SUPPLIES

SUPPLIES

285

Effects. Damaged trucks (top), a destroyed truck forced a detour around it (center), and before-and-after of an attack (bottom).

Opposite page. Downed bridges forced numerous detours and fords (top left), a burning pipeline (top right), and an interdicted road (bottom)

286

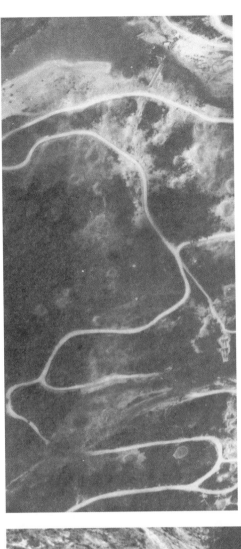

BURNING POL

PIPELINE

287

Enemy Antiaircraft Weapons. North Vietnam used 57-mm (above), 85-mm (right), and 100-mm (below) weapons, as well as surface-to-air missiles (bottom) to combat U.S. aircraft in Laos.

ATS–59 TOWING 100MM AAA

1972 Invasion. North Vietnamese truck convoy approaching the Ban Karai Pass (top), supply trucks pass towed 100-mm guns near Dong Hoi, North Vietnam (center), and two Soviet T–54 tanks (one burning) in An Loc, South Vietnam (bottom).

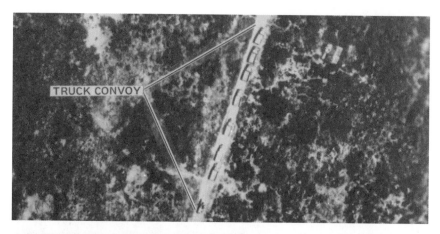

Traffic in 1973. North Vietnam continued to move men and equipment into South Vietnam, even after the cease-fire in 1972: a truck convoy in Laos, February 1973 (top); armored personnel carriers, March 1973 (center); and a truck towing a 122-mm gun in February 1973 (bottom).

290

Chapter Seventeen

The Impact of Aerial Interdiction

When Secretary of Defense Robert S. McNamara concluded in 1966 that the air war against North Vietnam, Operation Rolling Thunder, had failed, he turned to the scientists and engineers of the Jason Summer Study for another means, more effective militarily and less costly in U.S. lives and aircraft, to pressure North Vietnam into calling off the war against the South. Instead of continuing the air offensive against the North, he ratified the study's recommendation—that, indeed, he had inspired—for a campaign of aerial interdiction against the infiltration routes into South Vietnam, at the time less formidably defended than the targets attacked in Rolling Thunder. As adopted by Secretary McNamara, the plan called for two components: one a manned barrier across the routes passing through the demilitarized zone, the other an electronic surveillance system that could monitor traffic on the Ho Chi Minh Trail in southern Laos and detect targets for aerial attack. Unfortunately, his plan relied on advanced technology in a region where weather and geography undermined its effectiveness.[1]

For President Johnson and Secretary McNamara, interdiction proved frustrating from the very outset. Fierce North Vietnamese opposition limited the barrier guarding the demilitarized zone to just four separate strongpoints that did not, as originally planned, form a fully integrated, mutually supporting chain of defensive outposts. A comparatively thin mobile defense, anchored on the four redoubts, took the place of the continuous barrier that McNamara sought.[2]

The electronic surveillance network took shape rapidly enough for an operational test late in 1967, but early the following year, Task Force Alpha, which operated the Surveillance Center that made sensor-assisted aerial interdiction possible, had to divert sensors for the successful defense of the Marine Corps combat base at Khe Sanh. The diversion slowed progress on this part of McNamara's plan, but the surveillance system became operational in time to conduct interdiction during the dry season of 1968. In October of that year, the Seventh Air Force launched Operation Commando Hunt, which lasted until the weather changed in May 1969 and became the first in a series of interdiction efforts bearing the same name.[3] Until the spring of 1972, seven Commando Hunt campaigns followed one another, in the dry season when highway traffic predominated and in the rainy months when the waterways carried much of the cargo, as questions arose about the usefulness of the sensors, the damage that air attacks based on sensor data actually inflicted, the effectiveness of enemy countermeasures against both surveillance and aerial attack, and the deadliness of the various weapons employed.

In the summer of 1972, Maj. Gen. Alton D. Slay, the Seventh Air Force Deputy Chief of Staff for Operations, offered detailed comments on the last point, the effectiveness of munitions, which revealed that he considered few of his organization's weapons truly deadly against targets on the Ho Chi Minh Trail. Four years of Commando Hunt operations had failed, for example, to produce the kind of mines needed for aerial interdiction in southern Laos. Commenting on the three varieties of mines—gravel, the wide-area antipersonnel mine, and the Mk 36 Destructor— that maintained the numerous interdiction points, he gave an unqualified endorsement to just one, the wide-area antipersonnel mine, which had long triggers, resembling the legs of a huge spider, that extended when it landed. He added, however, that during Commando Hunt VII, the last operation in the series, he had only one-quarter the number he would have liked.[4] North Vietnamese Maj. Gen Dinh Duc Thieu disagreed with Slay's evaluation of the wide-area antipersonnel mine, pointing out that hand grenades, thrown rocks, or tree branches dragged across the triggers with ropes could easily clear an area bristling with these weapons.[5] Slay shared the opinion, almost universal in the Air Force, that the pebble-sized gravel mines remained worthless, despite improvements since systematic aerial interdiction began in southern Laos. He believed that the third type, the five hundred pound Mk 36, could be of some value against road traffic, but only if mixed with other mines or delayed-action bombs to prevent the North Vietnamese from using chains or other metal to take advantage of its magnetic fuze and trigger a harmless detonation.

As he had with the mines, Slay found numerous shortcomings in the arsenal of cluster bomb units. For example, the once promising funny bomb, a thermite cluster unit capable of scattering fire over an area the size of a football field, impressed him as better for calling attention to a target than for destroying one. Of the various other cluster bombs, he gave high marks to the CBU–52, which dispensed softball-sized antipersonnel bomblets deadly against antiaircraft guns and trucks, but less effective against tanks. To attack tanks, Slay preferred the older Mk 20 Rockeye, which released bomblets with an armor-piercing shaped charge. The CBU–38 projected its bomb units from a canister that remained attached to the aircraft; according to Slay, releasing the weight of the individual munitions, along with the aerodynamic drag of the empty dispenser, affected the center of gravity of the F–4 and prevented it from refueling in midair. Antipersonnel bomblets from the CBU–24 often failed to detonate and when they did, produced small pellet-like fragments rarely lethal and not especially disabling. As a result, the CBU–49 and CBU–58 replaced the older CBU–24. Both the newer weapons scattered deadlier fragments, but each had its disadvantages: the explosive components of the CBU–58 occasionally misfired; those released by the CBU–49 could create the illusion of fire from the ground, an especially disturbing sight for crewmen on board a slow-moving gunship, because of a fuze that might detonate up to thirty minutes after being armed, causing a succession of random explosions that from the air closely resembled muzzle flashes. Since successful flak suppression with the CBU–49 might nevertheless give the impression of failure, Slay advised against using it to attack antiaircraft guns like those guarding the Ho Chi Minh Trail.

General Slay showed enthusiasm for the principle behind the CBU–55 fuel-air explosive, though not for the model used in Southeast Asia. The Seventh Air Force had to rely on a version that consisted of three canisters of explosive gas weighing a total of five hundred pounds and producing a violent blast confined to a comparatively small area. Moreover, the use of a parachute as a brake prevented aircraft from dropping the bomb in winds exceeding ten miles an hour, for a stronger breeze could fill the parachute and blow the bomb off target. The Air Force, Slay concluded, needed a more powerful model, packing perhaps a thousand pounds of explosive gas, and a mechanical brake instead of a parachute.

The Air Force used two so-called smart bombs, the electro-optically guided and laser-guided types, against targets in southern Laos. The electro-optically guided bomb saw only limited service because it required a marked contrast between the target and its background, a sharp definition rarely found when attacking the Ho Chi Minh Trail, particularly by night. The laser-guided bomb struck with deadly accuracy, provided the laser operator, who might be in a different airplane, could locate the target with infrared, the night observation device, or some other cuing sensor and then keep the laser beam precisely focused. Although antiaircraft fire might force the laser designator to break contact, finding the target often presented the greater challenge, except for the gunship with its versatile array of sensors.

When attacking with laser-guided bombs, the aircraft formation depended on the availability of the weapons and the nature of the defenses. In the absence of surface-to-air missiles, when relying on a laser mounted in a gunship or an OV–10, two or more F–4s might approach the target in trail, flying at an altitude of ten thousand feet and a speed of three hundred knots, and release their bombs in succession. If an F–4 itself mounted a laser, and missiles posed no threat, the fighter illuminated its target and dropped a single laser-guided bomb. Later, as the supply of laser-guided bombs increased, two F–4s concentrated on designating targets for two others, each carrying a pair of the weapons. Against radar-directed guns or surface-to-air missiles, the fighter-bombers maintained a formation designed to provide maximum coverage with the radar-jamming transmitters on board and dropped their bombs simultaneously, trying to place all of them in the invisible cone within which the guidance mechanisms could home on the laser energy reflected from the target below. Accuracy suffered, of course, because of the need to stay in formation; some of the bombs might fail to enter the guidance basket and miss the laser-illuminated target by hundreds of yards.[6]

The inherent failings of some weapons diminished their value, as did problems with related equipment and the need to adjust to evolving defenses. Another factor, predictable tactics, also undermined weapon effectiveness. Indeed, the chief of the Seventh Air Force Tactical Air Control Center during Commando Hunt V, Col.

The War against Trucks

William L. Skliar, questioned whether such basic activities as the establishment of interdiction points had not devolved from carefully considered tactics to meaningless ritual. Every dry season, the Air Force bombed essentially the same choke points until each one "looked like a small section of the surface of the moon, traversed by a road and surrounded by jungle." Truck traffic continued, however, which indicated that the North Vietnamese either reopened the interdiction points almost as rapidly as they appeared, removing mines and closing road cuts, or bypassed the obstacles entirely. To Skliar, bombing the same points at about the same time in successive dry seasons demonstrated "static tactics," a form of "inertia" that enabled the enemy to concentrate work crews where he most needed them and antiaircraft guns where they would take the heaviest toll of U.S. aircraft.[7]

Inertia affected not only the seasonal pattern of warfare, but also day-to-day activity. Operations orders tended to schedule daytime sorties so that the fighter-bombers would return to base late in the afternoon at about the time the ground crews who serviced the aircraft changed shifts. This practice made it easier for the shifts to coordinate their efforts, but opened a gap in the coverage of the Ho Chi Minh Trail between the departure of the aircraft conducting daylight armed reconnaissance and the arrival of those patrolling by night. During Commando Hunt VII in particular, the enemy took advantage of these few hours to run truck convoys with comparative impunity.[8]

Along with the lack of flexibility in scheduling daylight sorties, flaws also appeared in night operations. By the end of the Commando Hunt series, doubts had surfaced about the value of Commando Bolt, the technique of using sensor activations and plotted loran coordinates to attack truck convoys at night. All too often these strikes resulted in bomb flashes amid the darkness, but no real evidence of damage done. "I don't think that anyone can prove," said General Slay, "that we killed a single truck with the Commando Bolt operation."[9]

In spite of special modifications, some of the aircraft that used the various weapons revealed serious shortcomings as they attempted night operations in a rugged, heavily forested area with strong defenses manned by a determined enemy. Hailed originally as fulfilling the need for a self-contained night-attack aircraft, the B–57G did not live up to expectation. Ground haze, prevalent for much of the dry season in southern Laos, dulled the acuity of the sensors, and flares or fires could blind them. Moreover, the engines gulped fuel, and the aircraft lacked the equipment to top off its tanks in midair, so that the time on station over the trail was an hour or less.[10] No wonder that General Slay characterized the airplane as a "disaster."[11]

As the saga of the B–57G demonstrated, finding the target presented the greatest challenge to successful interdiction. For example, as Slay pointed out, the laser target designator and laser-guided bomb could all but guarantee a hit, but someone had to spot the truck or other victim. All too often, that someone relied on the basic night observation device, which successfully captured the available light, but could not penetrate foliage or camouflage. Mounted as an afterthought in the already cramped cockpit, of an F–4 for example, the device focused on a comparatively small area. Only the gunship had a suitable variety of sensors for detecting truck traffic or other exposed targets at night and after the installation of the 105-mm howitzer, a weapon that could unfailingly destroy a vehicle with a single hit.[12]

Although formidable indeed, the AC–130, the best of the gunships, proved vulnerable to antiaircraft weapons, especially the surface-to-air missiles that, during Commando Hunt VII, drove it from heavily traveled portions of the Ho Chi Minh Trail. Moreover, the gunship needed darkness for concealment and for the full use of sensors like infrared, which even the twilight blinded. When within reach of the numerous and dangerous 37-mm and 57-mm guns, the black-painted AC–130s dared not silhouette themselves against the pale sky of late afternoon or early evening. By running truck convoys shortly before the light faded, the North Vietnamese took advantage of the gap between daytime and nighttime coverage of the trail and neutralized the gunships without greatly increasing the risk of attack from fighter-bombers on armed reconnaissance.

To deal with the threat of daylight attack, the operators of the trail relied on concealment, making use of camouflage and avoiding unnecessary activity that might invite aerial attack. The work essential to running the Ho Chi Minh Trail went on beneath canopies festooned with vines, fresh branches, and even potted greenery. By January 1973 and the signing of a cease-fire between the two Vietnams, trucks could drive the length of the trail without emerging from the canopy except to ford streams or cross them on crude bridges built beneath the surface of the water.[13]

Thousands of North Vietnamese soldiers and local laborers kept the Ho Chi Minh Trail open by constructing, camouflaging, and repairing or improving the roads, trails, pipelines, waterways, and storage areas and by clearing or bypassing interdiction points. An umbrella of antiaircraft fire protected this engineering activity, the troops and cargo passing over the trail, and the entire network of infiltration routes, bivouacs, and storage areas. Enemy gunners shot down more than 150 aircraft during four dry-season operations against the logistic network and, in fiercely defended areas, forced aircrews to search for targets from beyond the range of 37-mm and 57-mm guns at altitudes that hampered airborne sensors. Even the fast fighter-bombers had to maneuver radically to avoid fire from the ground as they pounced on their prey. Regardless of the claims of antiaircraft guns destroyed, an estimated five hundred in Commando Hunt VII alone, the volume and effectiveness of hostile fire did not diminish during the course of any dry season and grew more intense as one dry season followed another.[14]

Task Force Alpha trusted in technology to discover what went on among the heavily defended ridges and forests of southern Laos. Two basic kinds of sensors, acoustic and seismic, reported activity on the Ho Chi Minh Trail to the computer-equipped Surveillance Center at Nakhon Phanom Air Base in Thailand. The early model seismic intrusion detectors outshone their contemporary acoustic types in the quality and quantity of information reported. As the Commando Hunt series progressed, both the seismic and acoustic varieties improved, especially the latter. For example, the commandable microphone, which evolved from the basic acoustic model, enabled the analysts at Nakhon Phanom to listen when they chose, thus extending battery life. Initially, the Surveillance Center proved reluctant to take advantage of the on-off switch for fear of missing something, but once a pattern of enemy activity emerged, the feature made it possible to concentrate on the usual periods of peak activity, while sampling the action at other times.[15]

Whatever the advances in sensor technology, the electronic devices produced useful information only if planted accurately in places where they actually could detect and report foot or road traffic. Sensors could monitor traffic on routes already located, but they could not ferret out a concealed transportation network. Knowledge of the web of roads and trails, waterways, and pipelines determined where the sensors would go, but the logistic net proved difficult to chart, as demonstrated anew each dry season when routine surveillance revealed unsuspected portions of a complex that may ultimately have totaled as many as twelve thousand miles of roads and trails and one thousand miles of pipeline. Even if the Air Force had somehow plotted the layout of the Ho Chi Minh Trail, electronic surveillance would still have remained difficult, for an F–4 hurtling over a blurred expanse of heavily defended jungle, even with navigation aids like loran, could scarcely place every sensor exactly at the designated set of coordinates. The North Vietnamese, according to Maj. Gen. Dinh Duc Thieu, believed they could distinguish between sensor missions and bombing or strafing runs; when planting sensors, the aircraft dived at a shallower angle, and the object seemed to fall more slowly. Once the enemy knew the general location, he could search out the individual sensors and destroy them, avoid them, or deceive them, perhaps by simply playing a recording of truck noises.[16]

Despite camouflage, deception, natural concealment, and antiaircraft defenses, Seventh Air Force headquarters claimed an aggregate of forty-six thousand trucks destroyed or damaged in four dry-season interdiction campaigns against the Ho Chi Minh Trail. Commando Hunt V, 1970–71, produced the most impressive statistics, more than nineteen thousand trucks listed as destroyed or damaged, even though second thoughts resulted in new criteria that shaved fifteen hundred victims from that total.[17] Estimates of North Vietnamese truck imports tended to keep pace with the claims of trucks killed and disabled. After acquiring fewer than six thousand trucks per year from 1968 through 1970, the Hanoi government in 1971 ordered as many trucks from the Soviet Union alone as it had from all sources in 1970. At first glance this might seem to indicate that the suppliers—the Soviet Union, the communist nations of eastern Europe, North Korea, and China—were replacing losses sustained in Commando Hunt V, but the offensive planned for early 1972 could just as easily have inspired the increased orders. Since 80 percent of the Soviet-supplied vehicles arrived in North Vietnam at least six weeks before the Easter invasion in March of that year, the deliveries more likely reflected anticipated losses in future operations rather than replacements for trucks destroyed by past aerial interdiction campaigns. Moreover, the total volume of North Vietnamese imports almost tripled in 1971, compared to the previous year, too vast an increase merely to replace supplies and material consumed or destroyed on the Ho Chi Minh Trail.[18]

Regardless of the actual toll of North Vietnamese trucks damaged or destroyed, the Commando Hunt series inflicted savage punishment on the North Vietnamese and Lao who operated the Ho Chi Minh Trail. Whether driving trucks, handling cargo, manning the defenses, repairing or extending the logistic network, or traveling toward the battlefields of South Vietnam, the troops and laborers depended for survival on not being seen, and when the surveillance system found them out and a deluge of high explosives began falling, they entrusted their lives to foxholes and stoutly built bunkers. The nearness of sudden death and the day-to-day hardships of life on the trail could undermine the strongest resolve and cause a soldier to try for a safer assignment or even defect to the South Vietnamese cause.[19] As Tran Van Tra, a North Vietnamese veteran of the trail, sadly observed, "Of course, it was unavoidable that certain backward elements would violate discipline in a cowardly manner . . . but they were a small, insignificant minority."[20] Neither the destruction of war material in the jungles of southern Laos nor the death and suffering there disrupted the functioning of the supply system or dissuaded the North Vietnamese government from pursuing the conquest of the South. Most of the men and women who operated the Ho Chi Minh Trail accepted the punishment and carried on.

U.S. analysts, though they could not chart the Ho Chi Minh Trail complex and had little more than tabulations of explosions to verify the damage done, nevertheless tried to evaluate aerial interdiction on the basis of the information available. Thomas C. Thayer, for three years the chief of the office in the Advanced Research Projects Agency that analyzed the Vietnam War for the Office of Secretary of Defense, stated the obvious: "the more than 1.5 million sorties flown in the out-of-country interdiction campaign did not choke off VC/NVA activity in the South." Commando Hunt did not, however, seek to seal the borders of South Vietnam, but to reduce the flow of men and supplies to an extent that disrupted North Vietnamese plans to conquer the country. In these terms, Thayer said, air strikes "probably did impose a ceiling, but it was pretty high" because the enemy did not need much to sustain the fighting there. As a measure of North Vietnamese ability to fight on despite Commando Hunt, he suggested that only about one-twentieth of the cargo imported into North Vietnam started southward on the Ho Chi Minh Trail and that more than two thirds of this amount reached the battlefield.[21]

Maj. Gen. George J. Keegan, Jr., looking back on his two years (1968–69) as Deputy Chief of Staff, Intelligence, for the Seventh Air Force, insisted, "interdiction worked about as we expected" and denied that he and his colleagues had expected much. Because the enemy had operated "in a hidden mode," taking advantage of weather and jungle to frustrate attempts to locate him, air power "could do no more than impede maybe 10 to 15 percent of the enemy's logistics."[22]

The invasion of South Vietnam in March 1972 triggered an intensive review of aerial interdiction. Charles B. Liddell, Jr., a civilian analyst at Pacific Air Forces headquarters, concluded in his study of the subject that, invasion or none,

The War against Trucks

Commando Hunt had hurt the enemy. He explained away the attack by paying tribute to the determination of the North Vietnamese, who had willingly made the sacrifices necessary to push men and supplies down the trail complex in spite of aerial attack and launch the Easter offensive.[23]

North Vietnam, however, did not pay the entire cost of waging war. Hanoi passed along to its communist suppliers the expense of fitting out its troops and replacing the equipment destroyed by aerial interdiction. True, the nation paid a price in death and suffering to operate the Ho Chi Minh Trail, but the human cost remained acceptable, as long as casualties on the trail did not disrupt its operation or break the national will. The determination of the North Vietnamese survived the loss of Ho Chi Minh, who died in September 1969, but remained a revered symbol of national identity. Commando Hunt failed to inflict the necessary damage or anguish, in part because the communist leadership did what it could to avoid sacrificing lives to no purpose; truck drivers, for example, abandoned their vehicles when necessary, so the supply operation could continue to benefit from their driving skill and knowledge of the trail. Soldiers and cargo kept moving through southern Laos, and the men who marched into the trail complex, never to be heard from again, seemed martyrs to a cause rather than victims of folly. In addition, aerial interdiction attacked the wrong targets to rend the fabric of North Vietnamese society. Only for a brief time at the end of the interdiction campaign did the killing of infiltrating troops, which hurt the North directly, receive emphasis comparable to that given to the destruction of trucks and their cargo, which affected North Vietnam's suppliers. Moreover, when manpower at last became an objective, the campaign against infiltrators produced ambiguous results, mainly secondary explosions.[24]

Gen. William W. Momyer, who commanded the Seventh Air Force from mid-1966 to mid-1968 and then took over the Tactical Air Command, believed that the Commando Hunt series imposed a ceiling on hostilities in South Vietnam by limiting, through the destruction of supplies in transit, the number of troops the North Vietnamese could support there. He conceded, however, that aerial interdiction "had failed to break the enemy's will." Despite this disappointing reality, he believed the outcome could have been different. Had the United States sealed North Vietnam's ports and severed its rail line to China, as was done after Commando Hunt VII, aerial interdiction might "have changed the enemy's will to fight."[25] Of course, the United States in 1972 mined the harbors in response to a grave emergency, the North Vietnamese invasion, and took advantage of a Soviet-Chinese rivalry that earlier in the war it either failed to recognize or did not exploit.

In an analysis that appeared five years after Commando Hunt VII ended, Col. Herman L. Gilster, during the war an operations analyst for Seventh Air Force and later for the Pacific Air Forces, argued that the volume of cargo successfully transiting the Ho Chi Minh Trail peaked during Commando Hunt III, as a result of what he termed a "supply offensive," but declined sharply during Commando Hunt V and VII. The North Vietnamese might have invaded in March 1972, he suggested, because interdiction had been so successful that the dwindling stockpiles in the South soon would fall too low to sustain military operations. Moreover, having chosen to attack, the North Vietnamese may have discovered that Commando Hunt had crippled the distribution system so that vital supplies did not arrive at decisive points in adequate quantities. Gilster pointed out, however, that even if supplies ran short and distribution broke down, North Vietnam, because it controlled the tempo of the fighting in the South, could make effective use of whatever cargo emerged from the Ho Chi Minh Trail. In the absence of relentless South Vietnamese and U.S. pressure on the battlefield, a small amount of supplies could go a long way.

Colonel Gilster also speculated that the United States in its determination "to make the North Vietnamese pay an increasingly greater cost for aggression in the South" may have underestimated the price of maintaining electronic surveillance and conducting aerial interdiction. Launched with an investment of billions of dollars, the surveillance network required hundreds of millions each year to remain operational. In his opinion, the financial burden of employing advanced technology, plus the loss of life in Southeast Asia, contributed "in part at least" to a policy of accelerated Vietnamization and withdrawal.[26]

The price paid by the United States in attempting to interdict traffic on the Ho Chi Minh Trail took the form of diminishing support for the nation's objectives in Vietnam, as well as the continuing expenditure of aircraft, money, and lives, though the human toll rapidly declined after 1969. When Secretary McNamara accepted the report of the Jason Summer Study in 1966, he was aware of flagging enthusiasm for the war, although dissent did not yet endanger national policy. This early erosion of the national will, traceable mainly to casualties in the ground war in South Vietnam and the lack of measurable progress there, also reflected uneasiness about the Rolling Thunder attacks on populated areas of North Vietnam and the likelihood of civilian casualties. Commando Hunt and the halt to Rolling Thunder shifted the air war from the cities to the remote jungle, but, ironically, the most demonstrably effective example of interdiction in distant areas, the incursion into Cambodia in the spring of 1970, not only produced a hoard of captured material, but also aroused a more determined protest than the bombing of the North ever had. Although the attack deprived the enemy of hundreds of thousands of rounds of ammunition, tens of thousands of weapons, and thousands of tons of rice, it triggered demonstrations that temporarily closed colleges campuses throughout the United States and further undercut popular support for the war.[27]

As for the cost in aircraft, the Air Force fared much better against the Ho Chi Minh Trail than it had over North Vietnam, losing less than a third as many aircraft in the dry-season Commando Hunt operations as the 541 downed during the Rolling Thunder offensive.[28] For pilots and crew members shot down in the two campaigns, the prospects for rescue depended on where they parachuted. Rescue attempts rarely succeeded in heavily defended regions like the heartland of North Vietnam or the spine of the Ho Chi Minh Trail of southern Laos. Those whom the Aerospace Rescue and Recovery Service picked up during Rolling Thunder came down either off the coast or far from the cities, while in Laos the prospects for retrieval improved the farther an airman landed from the trail complex.[29]

The financial burden of setting up an air-supported electronic barrier across the Ho Chi Minh Trail proved heavy indeed, requiring the investment of $1.68 billion in defense appropriations for surveillance equipment, such as sensors and computers. Laser-guided bombs and modifications to aircraft added another $450 million to the cost. The price, slightly in excess of two billion dollars, did not include recurring operating expenses of about two hundred million dollars annually.[30]

After pointing out that Commando Hunt raised the cost to both sides—the United States installed and operated the barrier and North Vietnam suffered its effects—Colonel Gilster concluded that the series of interdiction operations inflicted pain on North Vietnam, but not the kind of agony the people and their leaders could not endure. Hanoi retained the initiative and fought in South Vietnam or avoided combat as supply levels dictated. The leaders at Hanoi saw no need to hurry; they exercised patience, husbanding supplies and manpower to attack at the decisive moment, which they determined to be March 30, 1972. The Hanoi government intended that the Easter offensive would, at the very least, seize enough territory to assure eventual victory or, at best, overwhelm South Vietnamese resistance and end the war immediately. In response to the attack, aerial interdiction shifted from the jungle-covered Ho Chi Minh Trail, where flying weather was rapidly deteriorating as the seasons changed, to the ports of North Vietnam and the roads and railway lines that funneled men and supplies to the battlefields. After invading South Vietnam across the demilitarized zone and from bases along the Ho Chi Minh Trail, the North committed itself to a succession of savage battles that consumed large quantities of supplies and vast numbers of its soldiers. By involving itself in sustained combat, a bloody cycle of attack and counterattack, Hanoi forfeited the ability to regulate the level of combat, when necessary breaking off the action to replace tomorrow what air power destroyed today. Merciless attrition of men, supplies, and machines on battlefields like An Loc multiplied the effect of bombs directed against supply lines in North Vietnam and the border regions of South Vietnam, rather than against the Ho Chi Minh Trail.

In short, aerial interdiction could not succeed unless the enemy suffered attrition on the ground. The Commando Hunt series proved indecisive because air and land forces, while attacking the Ho Chi Minh Trail, did not exert simultaneous pressure against North Vietnamese combat units in South Vietnam and also against the most vulnerable components of the supply system within North Vietnam, the ports and the rail link with China. Under President Nixon, Commando Hunt became one segment of a shield to protect the withdrawal, rather than part of a coordinated attack on the North Vietnamese tiger from tooth to tail. The role of air power did not change until the invasion of March 1972, which caused a diversion of effort away from southern Laos, where men and supplies had already massed for the thrusts at Kontum and An Loc, to the battlefields themselves and to other elements of the logistic structure.[31]

Since air power, aided by an occasional ground probe, had not inflicted unendurable harm on the troops and cargo in transit through southern Laos, the question arose whether ground forces, with aviation relegated to a supporting role, could have done the job. Could multidivision attacks, resulting in the establishment of permanent outposts, have cut the Ho Chi Minh Trail? Looking back on his participation in the war, Gen. William C. Westmoreland, who commanded the effort from mid-1964 to mid-1968, declared that four divisions at most, three U.S. and one South Vietnamese, "would have eliminated the enemy's steady flow of men through the Laotian panhandle and would have materially shortened the war." The force Westmoreland described might have advanced along a single axis westward from Khe Sanh, conducted pincer attacks from southwestern Laos and South Vietnam, or launched a combination of helicopter thrusts and ground offensives, but whatever the route, it would have established a series of permanent strongpoints in southern Laos designed to seal the roads, waterways, and trails and sever the pipelines.

Such a ground operation could have raised the cost to the enemy of continuing the war, but the action would also have had the secondary effect, pointed out by Colonel Gilster, of increasing the cost to the United States. The North Vietnamese, in resisting the initial advance or attacking the redoubts astride the Ho Chi Minh Trail, had the advantages of broken terrain, fog and cloud cover, and jungle concealment, all of which hampered aerial attack. U.S. forces would surely have suffered severe casualties, but by 1968, when the plan received serious consideration, the war had fallen into disfavor with a growing segment of the public as emphasis began to shift toward what came to be called Vietnamization, with its insistence on conserving lives.

When General Westmoreland revealed his plan, he acknowledged that an invasion of Laos would have required changes in national priorities, which, beginning in 1969, emphasized Vietnamization and the withdrawal of U.S. combat forces. The United States could not have persisted in these closely related actions and still provided troops to help cut the trail and simultaneously strengthen the defenses against infiltration through the demilitarized zone. Nor could Westmoreland or his successor, Abrams, have carried out one of the alternatives, a proposal to seize a lodgment on the Bolovens Plateau and attack the trail simultaneously from west and east, unless the U.S. government abandoned its commitment to restrict the level of fighting in Laos. Since the policy toward Laos did not change, the U.S. Ambassador at Vientiane continued to avoid actions that would increase civilian casualties and undermine support for Prince Souvanna. Both Sullivan and Godley remained content to direct a small-scale war throughout most of the kingdom, while the Commando Hunt series hammered away at the southeastern panhandle from which Laotians loyal to Souvanna had presumably fled.[32]

The analysis of the 1972 invasion, the attack that signaled an end to Commando Hunt, cast doubt on the trustworthiness of the electronic sensors trusted to monitor traffic on the Ho Chi Minh Trail. Like other operations analysts throughout the Air Force, C. V. Sturdevant and his colleagues at Pacific Air Forces headquarters investigated the apparent failure of these devices. On May 20, 1972, Sturdevant advised Gen. Lucius D. Clay, Jr., the Pacific Air Forces commander, "Due to the duration, intensity, and geographical extent of the current NVN offensive . . . , everyone now recognizes that our estimates were in error." This failure, he believed, resulted not from the sensors themselves, but from a false assumption that the road net had adequate electronic coverage.

How, asked General Clay, did we miss "so many of the enemy tanks, trucks, and artillery, and very considerable amounts of supplies that obviously got into SVN before the invasion"? Sturdevant answered by suggesting that "much of this [material] may have come, a portion of the way at least, by motorable routes that we don't know about." Although intelligence specialists had located the trace of Route 29 and discovered lesser roads during Commando Hunt VII, they almost certainly had missed many others. Also, traffic on waterways remained difficult to monitor, let alone disrupt, and the intricate pattern of bicycle paths and foot trails had yet to emerge. "We should have recognized," Sturdevant declared, "that our monitoring system covered only a portion of the total available output system, the portion consisting of the known and motorable road system."

Sturdevant then addressed the question of whether any sensor field could detect the kind of buildup that had preceded the 1972 invasion. Sensors could do the job, he believed, if aerial and ground reconnaissance ferreted out most of the roads and trails the attacker had to use, if "many, many, more sensors" than planted in southern Laos covered the known and suspected routes, and if a surveillance center had enough men and equipment to process and act on the increased volume of information. He concluded, however, that in southern Laos the cost of these improvements, in terms of casualties and treasure, would clearly have been prohibitive.[33]

The North Vietnamese invasion did not prove sensors useless, only that they had failed in a particular instance. Where topography and natural cover permitted—in a desert like the Sinai, perhaps—these devices afforded "the only consistent, all-weather, twenty-four–hour, comprehensive source of information on enemy logistic activity" in "hostile and remote areas."[34] Although creation of another automated surveillance center modeled after the one at Nakhon Phanom seemed out of the question, the armed forces might again undertake less elaborate forms of electronic monitoring like the surveillance in 1968 of the approaches to the Khe Sanh combat base.

However valuable they might be elsewhere in other circumstances, sensors failed in southern Laos, where coverage had remained truck oriented despite a last-minute attempt to cover troop infiltration routes. The accuracy of the sensor field in reporting either vehicular traffic or the movement of troops depended in the jungles of southern Laos on thorough knowledge of the route structure, along with accurate placement and timely replenishment of the various strings. Unfortunately, the North Vietnamese not only succeeded in concealing many of their roads, trails, and support installations, but also emplaced antiaircraft guns and missiles that hampered air attacks, aerial photography, and sensor delivery.

Did the seven Commando Hunt operations, despite the absence of the planned barrier to infiltration across the demilitarized zone, do as Secretary McNamara hoped and replace Rolling Thunder in discouraging North Vietnamese aggression in the South? Actually, one campaign did as well, or as poorly, as the other; for neither caused the Hanoi government to back down. The interdiction effort, however, had the advantage of costing less in aircraft and the lives of crewmen than the Rolling Thunder strikes.

Those who have analyzed Commando Hunt tend to agree that sensor-assisted aerial interdiction raised the cost of North Vietnamese infiltration, but not to a degree that undermined the enemy's resolve. The air campaign in southern Laos, along with thrusts by ground forces into the Cambodian bases and as far west as the village of Tchepone in Laos, altered only the timing of the enemy's operations against South Vietnam. North Vietnam retained the initiative and never gave up the struggle to conquer the South, an objective finally accomplished in the spring of 1975, when only a few senior U.S. advisers and some civilian technicians remained to assist the South Vietnamese armed forces. From 1968 through 1972, without precise knowledge of the carefully concealed network of roads and trails, pipelines and streams, the Air Force in Southeast Asia could not direct its weapons, many of them ill-suited for the job at hand, against North Vietnamese troops and supplies in southern Laos or assess accurately the damage that was done. In short, the airmen spent almost five years and billions of dollars trying with courage, determination, and ingenuity to do the impossible.

Notes

Introduction

1. Ronald H. Spector, *The United States Army in Vietnam; Advice and Support: The Early Years, 1941–1960* (Washington, 1983), pp 219– 0; Stanley Karnow, *Vietnam: A History* (New York, paperback, 1983), pp 198– 205, hereafter cited as Karnow, *Vietnam*.

2. Robert Shaplen, *Bitter Victory* (New York, 1986), pp 148–53, hereafter cited as Shaplen, *Bitter Victory*.

3. Karnow, *Vietnam*, pp 330–34.

4. Phillip B. Davidson, *Vietnam at War: The History, 1946–1975* (Novato, California, book club edition, 1988), p 314, hereafter cited as Davidson, *Vietnam at War*; Jeffrey J. Clarke, *The United States Army in Vietnam; Advise and Support: The Final Years* (Washington, 1988), p 108, hereafter cited as Clarke, *The Final Years*.

5. Shaplen, *Bitter Victory*, pp 154–59.

6. William C. Westmoreland, *A Soldier Reports* (Garden City, New York, 1976). p 382, hereafter cited as Westmoreland, *A Soldier Reports*.

7. Mark Clodfelter, *The Limits of Air Power: The American Bombing of North Vietnam* (New York, 1989), pp 58–60, 97–98, hereafter cited as Clodfelter, *Limits of Air Power*.

8. *Ibid.*, p 99; *The Pentagon Papers: The Defense Department History of United States Decision-making on Vietnam; The Senator Gravel Edition* (Boston, nd), IV, pp 109–10, hereafter cited as *The Pentagon Papers: Gravel Edition*.

9. *The Pentagon Papers: Gravel Edition*, IV, pp 115–24.

10. *Ibid.*, pp 124–30.

11. Summary Report by the Preparedness Investigating Subcommittee of the Committee on Armed Services of the Senate, *The Air War against North Vietnam*, 90th Cong, 1st sess (Washington, 1967), pp 3–6, 8–10.

12. Clodfelter, *Limits of Air Power*, p 97; John W. Garver, "China and the Revisionist Thesis," in William Head and Lawrence E. Grinter, eds., *Looking Back on the Vietnam War: A 1990s Perspective on the Decisions, Combat, and Legacies* (Westport, Connecticut, 1993), pp 106–12.

13. Hist, USMACV, 1967, III, pp 1090–1102; 1968, II, pp 911–19.

14. Jacob Van Staaveren, hist, Task Force Alpha, Oct 1, 1967–Apr 30, 1968, pp 3–7, 34–49, hereafter cited as Van Staaveren, hist, Task Force Alpha.

15. George C. Herring, *America's Longest War: The United States and Vietnam, 1950– 1975*, 2d ed (New York: paperback ed, 1986), pp 187–90, hereafter cited as Herring, *America's Longest War*; Davidson, *Vietnam at War*, pp 429–30; John R. Galvin, "The Relief of Khe Sanh," *Military Review* (January 1970), p 92.

16. Herring, *America's Longest War*, pp 190–91.

17. Thomas D. Boettcher, *Vietnam: The Valor and the Sorrow; From the Home Front to the Front Lines in Words and Pictures* (Boston and Toronto, 1985), pp 417–27, hereafter cited as Boettcher, *Vietnam*.

18. William S. Turley, *The Second Indochina War: A Short Political and Military History, 1954– 975* (Boulder, Colorado, and London, 1986), p 111.

19. Herring, *America's Longest War*, pp 192– 211.

Chapter 1

1. Chester L. Cooper, *The Lost Crusade: America in Vietnam* (New York, 1970), pp 387– 89, 516, hereafter cited as Cooper, *The Lost Crusade*.

2. Summary of Air Ops, SEA, Hq PACAF, Feb 68, p 1:1.

3. *Ibid.*, Feb 68, p 2:1; Mar 68, p 2:1.

4. *Ibid.*, Feb 68, p 2:3; Mar 68, pp 3:1–2; Gen William C. Westmoreland, USA, speech to 3d Air Div, Jun 13, 1968.

5. Hearings before the Electronic Battlefield Subcommittee of the Preparedness Investigating Subcommittee of Senate Committee on Armed Ser-

vices, *Investigation into the Electronic Battlefield Program*, Nov 18–19, 24, 1970, 91st Congress 2d sess, pp 86–7, hereafter cited as 91st Cong, 2d sess, *Investigation into Electronic Battlefield Program*.

6. DCPG Documentation, Sep 66–Jan 69, p V:6.

7. Memo, S. J. Deitchman, through Dir/ARPA, to DDR&E, subj: Comments on Vietnamese Counterinfiltration System, Mar 13, 1968.

8. *Ibid.*

9. Minutes of Udorn Special Meeting (afternoon session), Sep 9, 1968.

10. Intvw, Lt Col Robert G. Zimmerman with Col Roland K. McCoskrie, Comdr, 56th ACSq, 1967–68, Jul 14, 1975, p 49, hereafter cited as McCoskrie intvw.

11. Lt Col Alan Gindoff, *et al*, *The North Vietnamese Army Logistic System in Steel Tiger* (TFA, Dir/Intelligence, Analysis Div, Jul 1, 1972), pp 76–8, hereafter cited as Gindoff, *NVA Logistic System*.

12. See note 7.

13. Capt Edward Valentiny, *USAF Operations from Thailand, 1 January to 1 July 1968* (Hq PACAF, Project CHECO, Nov 20, 1968), pp 92–93, hereafter cited as Valentiny, *Thailand Ops*; intvw, Benis Frank, *et al*, with Gen Leonard F. Chapman, Commandant of the Marine Corps, 1968–71, Mar 25, 1979.

14. Memo, DDR&E for SAF, subj: Muscle Shoals Effectiveness, Mar 19, 1968; Maj Philip D. Caine, *Igloo White, July 1968–December 1969* (Hq PACAF, Project CHECO, Jan 10, 1970), pp 9–10, hereafter cited as Caine, *Igloo White, 1968–1969*; atch to memo, Gen William W. Momyer for Gen Westmoreland, subj: Single Manager—Preplanned System Modification Test, May 18, 68; msg, Maj Gen. Kirwin to Gen Westmoreland, Gen Abrams, Gen Momyer, 10346Z May 68, subj: Single Managership.

15. App A to memo, Dep DDR&E (SEAM) for DDR&E, Deps DDR&E, Dir/ARPA, and Members, Senior Provost Steering Gp, subj: Vietnam Trip Rprt, May 26–Jun 11, 1968, Trip no 9, Jun 14, 1968.

16. Memo, Dep DDR&E (SEAM) for DDR&E, subj: Summary of Ninth Trip Rprt, Jun 18, 1968.

17. DCPG Documentation, Sep 66–Jan 69, p V:31; Rprt of the Electronic Battlefield Subcommittee of the Preparedness Investigating Subcommittee of the Senate Committee on Armed Services, Feb 22, 1971, 92d Congress, 1st sess, pp 2–3, 5–10, cited hereafter as 92d Cong, 1st sess, *Rprt of the Electronic Battlefield Subcommittee*.

18. Thomas C. Thayer, ed, *A System Analysis View of the Vietnam War, 1965–1972* (Asst SEC DEF, Programs and Analysis, 1975), vol V, pp 40, 42–4, hereafter cited as Thayer, *Systems Analysis*.

19. DDR&E Summary, Igloo White: MACV Six Month Evaluation Rprt, Jun 30, 1968.

20. McCoskrie intvw, Jul 14, 1975, pp 45–9.

21. Ltr, Brig Gen William P. McBride to Gen William W. Momyer, subj: Future Development and Evaluation of Muscle Shoals, May 27, 1968.

22. Memo, Dep DDR&E (SEAM) for DDR&E, subj: Summary of Ninth Trip Rprt, Jun 18, 1968.

23. Memo, Dep DDR&E (SEAM) for DDR&E, Deps DDR&E, Dir/ARPA, and Members Senior Provost Steering Gp, subj: Vietnam Trip Rprt, May 26–Jun 11, 1968), Trip no 9, Jun 14, 1968.

24. Memo for Record, subj: Mr. Leonard Sullivan's Conference with the Igloo White/Duel Blade Committee, Aug 68, Sep 11 1968.

25. Draft memo, DDR&E for Dep SECDEF, subj: Igloo White/Duel Blade/Duck Blind Evaluation Committee Rprt, with App I, Nov 25, 1968; hist, JCS, *The JCS and the War in Vietnam, 1969–1970* (Hist Div, Jt Secretariat, JCS, Apr 26, 1976), pp 169–72, hereafter cites as hist, JCS, *Vietnam, 1969–1970*.

26. Atch to ltr, Asst DCS/Plans, 7AF, to CINCPAC, PACAF, *et al*, subj: Index of OPlans and OpOrds Published by Hq 7AF, Jan 1, 1970.

27. *Ibid.*; msgs, Tiger Hound to Det 1, 6250th Support Sq (ABCCC), 7AF, *et al*, 061550Z Mar 68, subj: Tiger Hound Final Record of V1; Tiger Hound to AIG 7937, 311200Z May 69, subj: Steel Tiger South DISUM for 31 May; 388th TFWg to 7AF, subj: 388th Tiger DISUM for 21 Jun 69.

28. Maj A. W. Thompson, *Strike Control and Reconnaissance (SCAR) in Southeast Asia* (Hq PACAF, Project CHECO, Jan 22, 1969), p 34, hereafter cited as Thompson, *SCAR*; hist data record, 7AF Dir/Targets, Jan–Mar 69; atch to ltr, Asst DCS/Plans, 7AF, to CINCPAC, PACAF, *et al*, subj: Index of OPlans and OpOrds Published by Hq 7AF, Jan 1, 1970; hist, USMACV, 1968, p F:IV:5–7.

29. Thompson, *SCAR*, p 35; Valentiny, *Thailand Ops*, p 60.

30. Hist, TFA, May–Dec 68, pp 50–51; msg, 7AF to CINCPACAF, 061020Z Mar 68, subj: OP–2E Tactics and Survivability; ltr, Comdr, VO–67, to Comdr, 7AF, TFA, subj: Dump Truck Modules, Protests against, Mar 8, 1968.

31. Intvw, Charles H. Hildreth and Bernard Nalty with Col William L. Walker, Dir/Intelli-

gence, TFA, 1967–68, Jun 8, 1971; hist, TFA, May–Dec 68, pp 52–3.

32. Hq AFCS, USAF Communications and Air Traffic Control in Southeast Asia, 1960– 1973, pp 52–66.

33. Hist, TFA, May–Dec 68, p 55.

34. Msg, 56th SOWg to 7AF, 160346Z Sep 69, subj: Operational Restrictions on A1/A–26 Aircraft.

35. Maj Victor B. Anthony, *Tactics and Techniques of Night Operations, 1961–1970* [*The Air Force in Southeast Asia*] (Washington, 1973), p 110, hereafter cited as Anthony, *Night Operations.*

36. Hist, 56th SOWg, Oct–Dec 69, I, p 155; 7AF Rprt, Commando Hunt VII, Jun 72, p 206, hereafter cited as Commando Hunt VII..

37. Msgs, JCS to CINCPAC, 271626Z Nov 68, subj: Proposed Termination of Hark System; 7AF to TFA, 010001Z Dec 68, subj: Proposed Termination of Hark System, Roadwatch Reporting on Laos; TFA to 7AF, 051123Z Dec 68, subj: Proposed Termination of Hark System, Roadwatch Reporting in Laos.

38. Col Paul W. Ridenour, 7AF Talking Paper, subj: Hark Equipment for Roadwatch Team Reporting, Apr 3, 1969.

39. Minutes of Udorn Special Meeting (afternoon session), Sep 9, 1968.

40. 7AF Rprt, Commando Hunt III, May 70, p 52, hereafter cited as Commando Hunt III.

41. Intvw, Lt Col Robert G. Zimmerman with Lt Col Howard K. Hartley, member of the air attache staff in Laos, 1968–69, Jul 19, 1974, p 35, hereafter cited as Hartley intvw.

42. Hist, 56th SOWg, Jan–Mar 70, I, p 54.

43. Hist, USMACV, 1968, pp F:IV:2, 6–7, F:IV:A:1.

44. *Ibid.*, pp F:IV:1–3.

45. *Ibid.*, p F:IV:2; hists, 56th SOWg, Jan–Mar 70, I, p 52, and Oct–Dec 70, I, p 87.

46. Hist, 56th SOWg, Jan–Mar 70, I, p 55.

47. 10th Weather Sq Status Rprt, Laotian Weather Nets, Jun 67; ltr, 10th Weather Team to 1st Weather Gp, subj: Special Warfare Weather Team Activity Rprt, 15 Oct 69 thru 13 Nov 69, Nov 30, 1969.

48. Rprt, 7AF Southwest Monsoon Planning Gp, Feb 22, 1969.

49. 7AF OPlan 530–69, Southwest Monsoon Campaign Plan, May 1, 1969.

50. Subcommittee on Oceans and International Environment, Senate Committee on Foreign Relations, *Weather Modification*, 93d Cong, 2d sess (Washington, 1974), pp 90–93.

51. *Ibid.*, p 103.

52. Msg, Vientiane to SECDEF, SECSTATE, and COMUSMACV, subj: Herbicide Operations, Vientiane Out 8204, Dec 1, 1969; William A. Buckingham, Jr., *Ranch Hand: The Air Force and Herbicides in Southeast Asia, 1961–1971* (Washington: Office of Air Force History, 1982), pp 116–18.

53. Msg, 366th TFWg to 7AF, 011130Z Feb 69, subj: F–4 Defoliation Capability; ltr, Comdr, 366th TFWg to 7AF, subj: Defoliant Spray, Jan 22, 1970.

54. See note 52.

55. Msgs, COMUSMACV to 7AF, COMNAVFORV, *et al*, [day and time illegible] Oct 69, subj: Leaflet Operations against NVA Infiltrators (Trail Campaign); 7AF to CINCPACAF, 130145Z May 71, subj: Trail Campaign PsyOp Support; description, American Embassy OPlan Fountain Pen, Jun 20, 1969; App VIII to Annex B, PACAF OpOrd 70–5, rev Jan 8, 1970.

56. Hist, 14th SOWg, Jan–Mar 69, p 36.

Chapter 2

1. Atch to ltr, PACAF to 13AF, subj: PACAF Command Relationships in Thailand, Jun 7, 1968.

2. Rprt, Hq PACAF, Truck Destruction in SEA, Nov 68–Jun 69, p 1; Cooper, *The Lost Crusade*, pp 392–95.

3. C. William Thorndale, *Interdiction in Route Package 1, 1968* (Hq PACAF, Project CHECO, Jun 30, 1969), pp 7–9, hereafter cited as Thorndale, *Interdiction.*

4. *Ibid.*, pp 8–10.

5. Memo, Gen Momyer for Gen Westmoreland, subj: Utilization of Muscle Shoals Resources, inwire note for Col Benz from Col Fory, May 6,

1968; ltr, Lt Col Charles M. Pease, Chief, Analysis and Rprts Br, to TOI, TFA, subj: Weekly Activity Rprt (1–7 Jun 68), Jun 11, 1968; ltr, with atchs, Maj John P. Mayovich, Analysis and Rprts Br, to DITA, TFA, subj: Igloo White Weekly Analysis, Oct 8, 1968.

6. Memo, National Photographic Interpretation Center, PI Memo R–125/68, subj: Expansion of the Ho Chi Minh Trail Continues, Nov 68.

7. Working Paper, TFA, Means and Methods of Truck Infiltration, Apr 15, 1968.

8. Rprt, TFA Truck Park Working Gp, Aug 68, pp 20–21; intvw, Capt Richard L. Bauer with Col

Howard P. Smith, Dir/Targets, 7AF, Jun 67–Jun 68, Jul 10, 1970, hereafter cited as Smith intvw.

9. Smith intvw, Jul 10, 1970.

10. Maj James B. Pralle, *Arc Light, June 1967–December 1968* (Hq PACAF, Project CHECO, Aug 15, 1969), pp 32–33, hereafter cited as Pralle, *Arc Light*.

11. *Ibid.*

12. Rprt, TFA Truck Park Working Gp, Aug 68, pp 15, 18–19.

13. Hist, 8th TFWg, Oct–Dec 68, I, 20; 7AF Command Briefing Outline, Jun 30, 1969, p 53.

14. Msgs, 7AF to 7ACC, 7/13AF, *et al*, 040248Z Apr 70, subj: Radar Bombing Operations, 7AF to 8th TFWg, 13th TFWg, *et al*, 280310Z Oct 70, subj: Commando Nail Bombing in Box Scores and SOAs.

15. Lt Col Ralph A. Rowley, *FAC Operations, 1965–1970* [*The Air Force in Southeast Asia*] (Washington, 1975), pp 188–97, hereafter cited as Rowley, *FAC Operations*; 366th TFWg OPlan 10–68, Sep 15, 1968; ltr, Lt Col Walter J. Bacon, Comdr, Commando Sabre, to 7AF Chief of Fighters, subj: Rprt of FAC Training: 37th TFWg and 366th TFWg (IAW ltr, 27 Jul 68), Aug 26, 1968.

16. Msg, 7AF to 19TASSq, 20TASSq, *et al*, 070745Z May 71, subj: FAC Operations in Steel Tiger VR Sectors.

17. Anthony, *Night Operations*, pp 74–9; msg, 56th SOWg to AIG 7937, 310850Z May 71, subj: DISUM from 0001Z to 0600Z, 31 May 71; ltr, Dep DCS/Ops, 7/13AF to 504TASGp, subj: FAC Incidents, Jun 6, 1971; Staff Summary Sheet, 7AF Dir/Command and Control, SAM Firing, Jun 1, 1971.

18. DOD Intelligence Rprt 1–516–0577–71 (5800–05–6), Nov subj: Formation, Training, and Infiltration of the 37th NVA Bn, 320th NVA Div, aka 2189th Infiltration Gp.

19. Rowley, *FAC Operations*, pp 164–66, 170–71.

20. 7AF OpOrd 71–17, Rules of Engagement, Southeast Asia, Dec 6, 1971, p IV:12.

21. Rowley, *FAC Operations*, pp 157, 159; Anthony, *Night Operations*, p 89; Thompson, *SCAR*, p 36.

22. Brig Gen George J. Keegan, Jr., "7AF Summer Interdiction Campaign," nd [ca. Nov 68].

23. Thorndale, *Interdiction*, pp 45–8.

24. Col Jesse C. Gatlin, *Igloo White (Initial Phase)* (Hq PACAF, Project CHECO, Jul 31, 1968), pp 12–13; memo, Dep DDR&E (SEAM)

for DDR&E, subj: Summary of Ninth Trip Rprt, Jun 18, 1968.

25. Hist, CINCPAC, 1968, III, 20; 7AF Rprt, Commando Hunt, May 20, 1969, pp 235–36, hereafter cited as Commando Hunt I; Caine, *Igloo White, 1968–1969*, p 25.

26. Hartley intvw, Jul 19, 1974, p 20.

27. Maj John Schlight, *Rules of Engagement, 1 January 1966–1 November 1969* (Hq PACAF, Project CHECO, Aug 31 [sic] 1969) p 28, hereafter cited as Schlight, *Rules of Engagement*.

28. Minutes of Udorn Special Meeting (afternoon session) Sep 9, 1968.

29. Ltr, 7AF DITT to DIT, subj: Arc Light Validation Procedures Conference, Sep 24, 1968.

30. *Ibid.*; Pralle, *Arc Light*, pp 50–51.

31. Smith intvw, Jul 10, 1970.

32. Pralle, *Arc Light*, p 51; Schlight, *Rules of Engagement*, p 28; 7AF Dir/Intelligence, Detailed Discussion of the Fundamental Defects in the Air Force Intelligence Structure in SEA, nd [ca. Jan 69].

33. Karnow, *Vietnam*, pp 579–82; Boettcher, *Vietnam*, p 429; Thomas M. Coffey, *Iron Eagle: The Turbulent Life of Curtis LeMay* (New York, 1986), pp 444–47.

34. Hist, USMACV, 1970, p TSS:27; ltr, Chief, 7AF Air Ops Div, to Dir/Ops, subj: Chronology of Recent Changes in Rules of Engagement in Steel Tiger That Have Influenced Interdiction in Southern Laos, Apr 19, 1969, hereafter cited as Rules of Engagement Chronology; 7AF OpOrd 71–17, Rules of Engagement, Southeast Asia, Dec 6, 1971, pp IV:10–11.

35. Rules of Engagement Chronology; see also Commando Hunt I, p 69.

36. Rules of Engagement Chronology; Schlight, *Rules of Engagement*, p 31.

37. Msgs, 7/13 AF to Ofc, USAIRA, Vientiane, 170135Z Mar 69, subj: A–6 AMTI Armed Recce, retransmitting 7AF msg 160215Z Mar 69; Ofc, USAIRA, Vientiane, to 7AF, 271059Z Dec 68, subj: Validation of Area Target, 7AF to Ofc, USAIRA, Vientiane, 270330Z Dec 68, subj: Validation of Area Target.

38. Rules of Engagement Chronology.

39. Schlight, *Rules of Engagement*, p 31; Minutes of Udorn Special Meeting (afternoon session), Sep 9, 1968; msg, COMUSMACV to Vientiane, 230957Z Jan 67, subj: Use of Riot Control Agent CS; hist, CINCPAC, 1969, III, 162.

40. Minutes, Udorn Special Meeting (afternoon

session), Sep 9, 1968.

41. Hist, CINCPAC, 1968, III, 201–4; 7AF
OpOrd 71–17, Rules of Engagement, Southeast
Asia, Dec 6, 1971, p IV:12; App IV to Annex EE,
7AF OPlan 512–70, change 1, Oct 13, 1969.

42. Memo, Lt Col William J. Donohue, Jr.,
Chief, Current Ops Br, to Dir/Ops through
DOCO, subj: Trip Rprt, Apr 21, 1969.

43. Transcript of intvw with Lt Col R. W. C.
Blessley, Jr., Jun 24, 1969.

44. Schlight, *Rules of Engagement*, pp 31–32.

45. Msg, Air Attache, Vientiane, to CINCPAC,
COMUSMACV, *et al*, 281846Z Jul 69, subj: ROE
Conference.

46. Schlight, *Rules of Engagement*, pp 34–35;
Rules of Engagement Conference Final Rprt, Aug
14, 1969.

47. Capt Paul W. Elder and Capt Peter J. Melly,
*Rules of Engagement, November 1969–Septem-
ber 1972* (Hq PACAF, Project CHECO, Mar 1,
1973), pp 11–12, hereafter cited as Elder and
Melly, *Rules of Engagement*.

48. Rules of Engagement Conference Final
Report, Aug 14, 1969.

49. Ltr, John J. Garrity, Jr., Chief, Intelligence
Div, Ofc, USAIRA, Vientiane, to Assistance Air

Attache, Savannakhet, Sep 30, 1969.

50. Ltr, Lt Col Raymond G. Lawry, Acting
USAIRA, to all AOCs, subj: Rules of Engagement
and Targets, Sep 23, 1969.

51. Intvw, Maj Samuel E. Riddlebarger with Lt
Gen David C. Jones, DCS/Ops and Vice Comdr,
7AF, Feb 69–Jul 69, Nov 4–6, 1969, hereafter cited
as Jones intvw.

52. Elder and Melly, *Rules of Engagement*, pp
14–15; 7AF OpOrd 71–17, Rules of Engagement,
Southeast Asia, Dec 6, 1971, pp IV:3–5.

53. Msg, Ofc, USAIRA, Vientiane, to Assistant
AIRA, Pakse, and 7AF, 270500Z May 70, subj:
Napalm Authorization in MR IV, Steel Tiger West
Area of Laos.

54. Elder and Melly, *Rules of Engagement*, p 15;
7AF OpOrd 71–17, Rules of Engagement, Southeast Asia, Dec 6, 1971, pt IV.

55. Msgs, Pakse to USAID, Pakse 327, 100635Z
Jul 71, subj: none; ltr, Maj Ronald D. McDonald,
Jr., to 7AF and 7/13AF, subj: Short Round
Preliminary Investigation, Jul 8, 1971; ltr Dep
Comdr, 7/13AF to Gen Lucius D. Clay, Jr., subj:
none, Jul 12, 1971; ltr, 7AF to HQ USAF, CINC-
PACAF, COMUSMACV, subj: Short Round
Investigation, Jul 26, 1971.

Chapter 3

1. Herman S. Wolk, *USAF Plans and Policies:
R&D for Southeast Asia, 1968* (Washington,
1970), pp 35–42.

2. Jack S. Ballard, *The United States Air Force in
Southeast Asia: Development and Employment of
Fixed–Wing Gunships, 1962–1972* (Washington:
Office of Air Force History, 1982), pp 14–17, 45–
47, 82–86, hereafter cited as Ballard, *Gunships*.

3. *Ibid*., pp 86, 89–90; hist, 8th TFWg, Jan–Mar
69, I, pp 37–39; Lt Col Ross E. Hamlin, "Side-Firing Weapon Systems: A New Application of an
Old Concept," *Air University Review* (Jan–Feb
70), pp 79–83.

4. Ballard, *Gunships*, p 92.

5. *Ibid*., pp 96–97; Elizabeth H. Hartsook, *The
Administration Emphasizes Air Power, 1969* [*The
Air Force in Southeast Asia*] (Washington, 1971),
pp 10–12, 28–29, hereafter cited as Hartsook, *The
Administration Emphasizes Air Power*; intvw, Lt
Col V. H, Gallacher and Maj Lynn Officer with Lt
Col William B. Hartman, 16th SOSq, Apr 1971–
Feb 1972, Dec 11, 1972,2 p 19, hereafter cited as
Hartman intvw.

6. Ballard, *Gunships*, pp 90–95.

7. *Ibid*., pp 262–63; Hartman intvw, Dec 11,
1972, pp 11–12, 52–53.

8. Combat King Final Draft Rprt, Combat In-
troduction/Evaluation, AC–119K Gunship III,
[Mar] 70; ltr, Comdr, 14th SOWg to 7AF, subj:
Improving Gunship Effectiveness, Jun 30, 1970;
msgs, 14th SOWg to 7AF, 221015Z Jul 70, subj:
Combat ROC 52–70; 100816Z Jan 71, subj:
Commando Hunt Requirements.

9. Ballard, *Gunships*, pp 216–17.

10. Msg, 14th SOWg to 7AF, 100816Z Jan 71,
subj: Commando Hunt Data Requirements.

11. 7AF Rprt, Commando Hunt V, May 71, p 40,
hereafter cited as Commando Hunt V.

12. Msgs, 7AF to 13AF, 010800Z Jan 72, subj:
Inaccurate Fire Patterns, AC–119K Gunships;
240902Z Mar 72, subj: AC–119K FCS [Fire
Control System].

13. Ballard, *Gunships*, pp 121, 123.

14. *Ibid*., pp 158–59, 167.

15. Hartsook, *The Administration Emphasizes
Air Power*, p 84; hist, JCS, *Vietnam, 1969–1970*,

pp 30–43; Henry Kissinger, *White House Years* (Boston-Toronto, 1979), pp. 271–76, hereafter cited as Kissinger, *White House Years.*

16. Ballard, *Gunships*, pp 127–29, 138–39; Hartman intvw, Dec 11, 1972, pp 53–54.

17. TAC Final Rprt, Combat Introduction/Evaluation (Coronet Surprise), Aug 70.

18. Msg, TAC to CSAF, PACAF, *et al*, 210009Z Jan 70, subj: Surprise Package Improvements.

19. Ballard, *Gunships*, pp 143–47, 162–63; Commando Hunt V, pp 253, 255; End of Tour Rprt, Col Francis A. Humphreys, Comdr, 8th TFWg, 1972–1974, Jan 17, 1974, hereafter cited as Humphreys End of Tour Rprt; PACAF Dir/ Tactical Evaluation, Southeast Asia Operations, Apr 1970, p 27

20. 7AF Rprt, Commando Hunt VII, Jun 72, pp 253–56.

21. Intvw, Lt Col Robert G. Zimmerman with Lt Col Stephen J. Opitz, AC–130 Sensor Operator and Navigator, Jul 71–Jul 72, Jul 18, 1972, pp 52–53.

22. Lt Col Jerald J. Till and Maj James C. Thomas, *Pave Aegis Weapon System* (*AC–130E Gunship*) (Hq PACAF, Project CHECO, Feb 16, 1973), pp 14–20, 46; Commando Hunt VII, pp 256–58; Ballard, *Gunships*, pp 173–74.

23. "Standards for Judging Effectiveness," in Hq 7AF Study Guide, War of Interdiction vs Infiltration, May 1, 1968.

24. Hq PACAF, Project Corona Harvest, In-Country and Out-Country Strike Operations in Southeast Asia, 1 Jan 65–31 Dec 69, Vol II, *Hardware: Munitions*, pp 124–25, hereafter cited as Hq PACAF, Project Corona Harvest, *Hardware: Munitions.*

25. 7AF Background Paper, Lt Col Rose, subj: Commando Scarf, Aug 6, 1969.

26. Hq PACAF, Project Corona Harvest, *Hardware: Munitions*, p 126.

27. *Ibid.*, pp 29–36.

28. End of Tour Rprt, Col. Frank L. Gailer, Jr., Comdr, 35th TFW, Sep 68–Aug 69, Aug 4, 1969, p B:30.

29. Memo, H. M. Sloan for Mr. Sullivan, subj: none, Sep 26, 1969.

30. Hq PACAF, Project Corona Harvest, *Munitions: Hardware*, pp 22, 26.

31. *Ibid.*, pp 92–94.

32. *Ibid.*, pp 102–3 IV:1; memo, 7AF Dir/Tactical Analysis for [Lt] Gen [David C.] Jones, subj: Paveway II Operational Evaluation by 8th TFWg,

Jan 18, 1969; TFA Fact Book, Apr 72, p 160.

33. Hq PACAF, Project Corona Harvest, *Hardware: Munitions*, pp 93–94; Commando Hunt V, pp 187–88.

34. Hq PACAF, Project Corona Harvest, *Hardware: Munitions*, p 97; App to memo, Dep DDR &E (SEAM) to DDR&E, Deps/DDR&E, Dir/ ARPA, and Members, Senior Provost Steering Gp, subj: Vietnam Trip Rprt no 11, 5–15 Feb 69, Feb 24, 1969; hist, Current Ops Div, TFA, Jan–Mar 69, atch to hist, TFA, Jan–Dec 69.

35. Hq PACAF, Project Corona Harvest, *Hardware: Munitions*, pp 98, 101–2.

36. Anthony, *Night Operations*, pp 147–48.

37. Ballard, *Gunships*, pp 127, 134–35, 138; memo, T. A. McCarthy for CO, subj: Visit to Loran Transmitter Station at Lampang, Thailand, Jul 10, 1968.

38. See note 3.

39. App to memo, Dep DDR&E (SEAM) to Deps/DDR&E, Dir ARPA, and Members, Senior Provost Steering Gp, subj: Vietnam Trip Rprt no 11, 5–15 Feb 69, Feb 24, 1969; R. F. Linsenmeyer, C. E. Thompson, R. E. Metcalf, and L. L. Henry, "Interdiction Operations in Southeast Asia," CINCPAC Scientific Advisory Gp Working Paper, no 5–70, May 26, 1970; Commando Hunt III, p 30, hereafter cited as Lisenmeyer, "Interdiction Operations."

40. Lisenmeyer, "Interdiction Operations," p iv.

41. Hist, 8th TFWg, Jan–Mar 71, II, p 69, Apr–Jun 71, I, pp 48, 84–85, 136.

42. Hist, 8th TFWg, Jul–Sep 71, I, p 106.

43. *Ibid.*; Commando Hunt VII, p 240.

44. Commando Hunt VII, p 243; msg, Maj Francis J. Twait, SOF Liaison Officer to Comdr, SOF (TAC), subj: SOFLO Activity Rprt 16–72 (16–29 Feb 72), Feb 29, 1972.

45. Ltr, Gen William W. Momyer to Gen James Ferguson, Comdr, AFSC, Mar 14, 1968; Anthony, *Night Operations*, pp 115–22, 127–28; hist, USMACV, 1968, II, p 754.

46. Hist, USMACV, 1968, II, p 752; App A to memo, Dep DDR&E (SEAM) to Deps/DDR &E, Dir/ARPA, and Members, Senior Provost Steering Gp, subj: Vietnam Trip Rprt, 26 May–11 Jun 68, Trip no 9, Jun 14, 1968; memo, SECDEF to SEC-NAV, subj: Reorientation of Project TRIM, Aug 17, 1968; ltr, Dep DDR&E (SEAM) to Comdr, 7AF, May 7, 1970.

47. Anthony, *Night Operations*, pp 172–74; Hq PACAF, Project Corona Harvest, *Hardware:*

Munitions, pp 31–32.

48. Anthony, *Night Operations*, pp 175–76.

49. Msg, 7AF to CINCPACAF, 061150Z Jun 70, subj: AC–123 Aircraft; ltr, DCS/Plans, 7AF, to Dir/Ops, subj: Non-Concurrence, Evaluation of Black Spot Mission, nd [ca. May 70].

50. Msgs, 8th TFWg to 7AF, 210902Z Jun 70, subj: Assessment of Black Spot-Black Crow; to Dir/AF Museum, 180502Z Jun 70, subj: Black Spot.

51. Lt Col Philip B. Hopkins, Jr., Final Rprt, TAC Test 68–17, TAWC Project 0002, B–57G Combat Evaluation, Feb 71, hereafter cited as B–57G Evaluation.

52. OPSEC Survey, B–57G Operations in SEAsia, 281430W [Hawaii time] Dec 70.

53. B–57G Combat Evaluation; hist, 8th TFWg,

III, atch 11, Oct–Dec 70; hist, Wolf FAC, 8th TFWg, Oct–Dec 70, p 9.

54. B–57G Combat Evaluation; Talking Paper, 7AF Dir/Ops, Employment and Effectiveness of Mk 82 LGB Carried by B–57G, Dec 29, 1970; Dir/Ops, Hq USAF, Trends, Indicators, and Analyses, Feb 71, B–57G Combat Evaluation; End of Tour Rprt, Col Larry M. Killpack, Comdr, 8th TFWg, 1970–71, nd, hereafter cited as Killpack End of Tour Rprt.

55. Final Report, USAF Tactical Air Warfare Center, Pave Knife Combat Evaluation, Aug 71; Commando Hunt VII, p 247; Commando Hunt V, p 60.

56. Pave Knife Combat Evaluation, Aug 71; hist, 8th TFWg, Apr–Jun 71, I, p 41; msg, 13AF to 7AF, 170100Z Jan 72, subj: Pave Knife.

Chapter 4

1. DCPG Concepts and Requirements Plan, Jul 1, 1968, pp 12, 102–3, 110–15, 117–22.

2. *Ibid.*, p 12; Caine, *Igloo White, 1968–1969*, pp 22–23; End of Tour Rprt, 1st Lt W. W. Working, TFA Target Analysis Officer, 1968–69, nd

3. Capt Henry S. Shields, *Igloo White, January 1970–September 1971* (Hq PACAF, Project CHECO, Nov 1, 1971), pp 52–53, hereafter cited as Shields, *Igloo White, 1970–1971*.

4. Atch to ltr, TFA to 7AF, subj: Current TFA Ops, Mar 26, 1972; memo (working paper), Maj Ronald A. Cadieux for Col Reubin L. Kingdon, Jr., subj: Acoustic vs Seismic Sensors for Personnel Detection, Sep 8, 1969; msg, TFA to 7AF, 260255Z Jan 71, subj: Common Module and Commike Reliability.

5. Shields, *Igloo White, 1970–1971*, pp 53–54; msg, CSAF to CINCPACAF, 262106Z Feb 71, subj: SEA Evaluation of EDET Sensor; hist data record, Infiltration Surveillance Div, TFA, Apr–Jun 71, Jul 23, 1971; quarterly hist, Data Base Mgt Ofc, TFA, Apr–Jun 71.

6. Atch to ltr, TFA to 7AF, subj: Current TFA Ops, Mar 26, 1972.

7. Caine, *Igloo White, 1968–1969*, pp 27–30.

8. *Ibid.*, p 30.

9. 553d RWg, Pave Eagle Study, Jun 14, 1969.

10. Intvw, Lt Col Robert G. Zimmerman with Maj Richard M. Atchison, OV–10 Navigator, 1971–72, Jul 16, 1975.

11. 553d RWg, Pave Eagle Study, Jun 15, 1969.

12. *Ibid.*

13. Shields, *Igloo White, 1970–1971*, p 72.

14. Hist, JCS, *Vietnam, 1969–1970*, pp 62–69, 133–39.

15. *Ibid.*, pp 139–48.

16. Kissinger, *White House Years*, p 284.

17. Shields, *Igloo White, 1970–1971*, p 72.

18. 553d RWg, Pave Eagle II Evaluation, Sep 17, 1970; msg, Dir/Materiel Management, Kelly AFB, Tex, to ASD and AFLC, 221600Z Jan 71, retransmitting 56th SOWg to 7AF and 13AF, 210840Z Jan 71, subj: QU–22B Blue Orbit Requirements; hist, 554th RSq, 56th SOWg, Oct–Dec 70, pp 162–63.

19. 553d RWg, Pave Eagle II Evaluation, Sep 17, 1970; msg, CINCPACAF to 7AF, 13AF, *et al*, 011930Z Oct 70, subj: Pave Eagle II (additional); Shields, *Igloo White, 1970–1971*, p 73.

20. Ltr, Gen Lucius D. Clay, Jr., Comdr, 7AF, to DCS/Plans and Ops, subj: Pave Eagle II, Nov 11, 1970; msg, 7AF to CINCPAC, 100201Z Dec 70, subj: Deletion of Pave Eagle II Drone Capability; msg, 56th SOWg to 7AF, 030913Z Jan 71, subj: Retention of Pave Eagle II Drone Capability; Shields, *Igloo White, 1970–1971*, p 73.

21. Msg, 7AF to CINCPACAF, subj: QU–22B/ EC–121 Requirements, Apr 10, 1971.

22. Hist, 56th SOWg, Jul–Sep 71, I, pp vi–vii, 111; Shields, *Igloo White, 1970–1971*, pp 76–77; hist, TFA, Jul–Sep 71, pp 2l–22; hist, Dir/Logistics, 7AF, Jul–Dec 71; msg, 7AF to CINCPACAF, AFLC, *et al*, 190700Z Dec 71, subj: QU–22B Utilization.

23. Hist, Dir/Logistics, 7AF, Jul–Dec 71; msgs, CINCPACAF to CSAF, 010622Z Sep 72, subj: QU–22B Disposition, CINCPACAF to CSAF, 13AF, et al, 161005Z Sep 72, subj: PACAF PAD 73–5, 554th RSq.

24. Commando Hunt V, pp 196–97.

25. Hist, 460th TRWg, Oct–Dec 69, I, p 17.

26. Hist, 432d TRWg, Jan–Mar 70, I, pp 15–16; quarterly hist rprt, Reconnaissance-Electronic Warfare Br, Dir/Ops Plans, 7AF, Jan–Mar 72.

27. Annex A to ACIC Sentinel Suffix/Simplex Loran OPlan, Nov 9, 1970; msg, DCPG to CSAF, 251937Z Sep 70, subj: Request for Accomplishment of JTF 728 Task TM 200A–70–8, Modification of Sentinel Suffix/Simplex; Capt Robert F. Colwell, USAF Tactical Reconnaissance in Southeast Asia, July 1969–June 1971 (Hq PACAF, Project CHECO, Nov 23, 1971), pp 33–36, hereafter cited as Colwell, Reconnaissance.

28. Colwell, Reconnaissance, pp 36–38.

29. Ibid., pp 32–33.

30. Ibid., p 30; hist, 432d TRWg, Jan–Mar 71, I, pp 22–23.

31. Colwell, Reconnaissance, p 29.

32. Ibid.; Staff Summary Sheet, Chief, Reconnaissance/Electronic Warfare Div, 7AF, subj: OV–1 SLAR Coverage of Steel Tiger Exit Routes, Jan 12, 1971.

33. Memo, Col Philip Howell, Jr. to Col Robert J. Holbury, subj: Battle Damage to EC–47, 4315979, Apr 24, 1968.

34. Hist, 460th TRWg, Jan–Mar 70, I, p 29.

35. Colwell, Reconnaissance, pp 47–48.

36. Ltr, Dir/Ops, 7AF, to Chief of Staff and Comdr, 7AF, subj: Compass Flag/Igloo White, Jul 17, 1971; msgs, CSAF to CINCPACAF, 162146Z Mar 71, subj: Compass Flag, CINCPAC to JCS, 262225Z Aug 72, subj: Compass Flag, PSR Wheeler AFB, Hawaii, to Det 1, 6990th Security Gp, Cam Ranh Bay, 110155Z Sep 71, CINC-PACAF to 7AF, 231710Z Feb 71, subj: Pave Eagle II Drone Control Equipment, CINCPACAF to 5AF, 240100Z Sep 71, subj: ACRP Realignment, retransmitting CSAF to CINCPACAF, CINC-

USAFE, et al, 222053Z Sep 71, subj: ACRP Realignment.

37. Maj B. H. Barnette, Jr., "Ink" Development and Employment (Hq PACAF, Project CHECO, Sep 24, 1973), pp 2–5, hereafter cited as Barnette, Ink.

38. Final Rprt, TAWC Project 1039, Coronet Ink (Combat Ink Evaluation), Sep 71.

39. Barnette, Ink, pp 16, 28–34; End of Tour Rprt, Lt Col Fred S. Taylor, III, AFSC Liaison Officer, Tan Son Nhut, 1971, Sep 17, 1971.

40. Commando Hunt VII, pp 249–53.

41. Msgs, 432d TRWg to 7AF, 221445Z Jun 70, subj: Rabet II Activity Rprt as of 22 Jun 70, 388th TFWg to 7AF, 151015Z Jun 70, subj: Korat Beacon, 432d TRWg to 7AF, subj: Rabet II Activity, 22 Jun 70 to 29 Jun 70, nd; ltr, Lt Col Tyler W. Tandler, Dir/Ops, TFA, to Historian, subj: Dir/Ops Hist (1 Jan–31 Mar 70), Apr 15, 1970; Staff Summary Sheet, Dir/Tactics and Combat Systems, 7AF, Status Rprt, Radar Beacon Transponder (Rabet II), Jul 4, 1970.

42. Staff Summary Sheet, Dir/Tactics and Combat Systems, 7AF, Jul 4, 1970.

43. Msgs, 388th TFWg to CINCPACAF, 240345Z Oct 70, subj: Rabet II Combat Evaluation, 388th TFWg to CINCPACAF, 300900Z Nov 70, subj: Rabet II Combat Evaluation, 388th TFWg to 7AF, 231015Z Dec 70, subj: Rabet II Termination.

44. Ltr, Lt Col Tyler W. Tandler, Dir/Ops, TFA, to Historian, subj: Dir/Ops Hist (1 Jan–31 Mar 70), Apr 15, 1970.

45. Msg, SAC to CINCPACAF, TAC, et al, 021942Z Feb 71, subj: Combat Sierra.

46. Msg, TAC to CSAF, 082236Z Feb 71, subj: Combat Sierra.

47. Msg, CINCPACAF to CSAF, 092030Z Feb 71, subj: Combat Sierra.

48. Msg, TAC to CSAF, 192302Z Feb 71, subj: Combat Sierra.

49. Commando Hunt III, pp 43, 81, 96–97; Commando Hunt V, pp 39, 60, 63; Commando Hunt VII, p 76.

Chapter 5

1. Commando Hunt I, pp 2, 6–7; Gindoff, NVA Logistic System, pp 29–31; Lt Col Albert J. Macsata, et al, The North Vietnamese Army Logistic System, Jul 10, 1971, pp 29–30; Dir/Int. TFA, Targeting in Southern Steel Tiger, Jun 1, 1972, pp 4–7.

2. Ibid., p 174; Thayer, Systems Analysis, V, p 301; Thompson, SCAR, p 48.

3. Commando Hunt I, pp 174–82; Hq 7AF, 7AF Operations Handbook: Southeast Asia Interdiction, Apr 1, 1970, p 19.

4. Commando Hunt I, pp 186–88.

5. Rprt, Analysis and Rprts Br, Technical Analysis Div, TFA, Report of Truck Park Working Gp, Aug 15, 1968, pp 39, 41.

6. Dir/Ops, Hq USAF, Trends, Indicators, and Analyses, Aug 1968, p 3:16; Sep 1968, p 3:15; Oct 1968, p 3:15; Jul 1969, p 2:52; End of Tour Rprt, Col D. L. Evans, Dir/Int, TFA, 1971–1972, Jul 6, 1972, hereafter cited as Evans end of tour rprt.

7. *Ibid.*, pp 4–5.

8. Minutes, Udorn Special Meeting (morning session), Sep 9, 1968.

9. Commando Hunt I, p 7; Southeast Asia Interdiction, pp 90–91.

10. 7AF OPlan 544–69, Commando Hunt, Aug 29, 1968, Annex B, p 1.

11. Commando Hunt I, pp 27–28, 189.

12. Memos, DDR&E for SAF, subj: Muscle Shoals Effectiveness, Mar 19, 1968, SAF to CSAF, Mar 22, 1968; 7AF OPlan 544–69, Commando Hunt, Annex B, p 1.

13. Hist, TFA, May–Dec 68, p 21; TFA OPlan 100–69, Tab C, App II, Annex EE.

14. Atch to memo, Gen William W. Momyer to Gen William C. Westmoreland, subj: Single Management—Preplanned System Modification Test, May 18, 1968.

15. Hist, TFA, May–Dec 68, pp 36, 94, 156.

16. Commando Hunt I, pp 27–28.

17. Melvin Porter, *Tactical Control Squadron Operations in SEAsia* (Hq PACAF, Project CHECO, Oct 15, 1969), pp 32–36.

18. Msg, Det 5, 621st TACCONSq to 621st TACCONSq, 241100Z Oct 68, subj: Commando Hunt Operation.

19. Hist, TFA, May–Dec 68, pp 154–55.

20. *Ibid.*, p 155.

21. Commando Hunt I, pp 215–17; TFA OPlan 100–69, Tab B, App II.

22. Commando Hunt I, pp 214–15.

23. *Ibid.*, pp 30–31, 41, 59, 62.

24. Intvw, Capts Roger W. Lewis and Larry L. Benson with Col Lee A. Burcham, Chief of Targets, TFA, 1968–69, Jan 29, 1970, hereafter cited as Burcham intvw.

25. Commando Hunt I, pp 31–41.

26. *Ibid.*, p 49; Hq PACAF, Summary of Air Operations, Southeast Asia, Jan 69, p 2:6.

27. Commando Hunt I, p 43; Hq PACAF, Summary of Air Operations, Southeast Asia, Feb 69, p 2:7.

28. Shields, *Igloo White, 1970–1971*, p 11; Commando Hunt I, pp 44–45.

29. Commando Hunt I, p 49; Col James McGuire, *Development of All-Weather and Night Truck Kill Capability* (ASI, Project Corona Harvest, Jan 70), p 14.

30. Commando Hunt I, pp 66, 69.

31. Hartsook, *The Administration Emphasizes Air Power*, p 10.

32. Thayer, *Systems Analysis*, V, p 60.

33. Hartsook, *The Administration Emphasizes Air Power*, p 11.

34. Jones intvw, Nov 4–6, 1969, pp 28–31.

35. William Broyles, Jr., "The Road to Hill 10: A Veteran's Return to Vietnam," *Atlantic Monthly* (Apr 1985), pp 101–11.

36. Westmoreland, *A Soldier Reports*, p 332.

37. Hartsook, *The Administration Emphasizes Air Power*, pp 27, 29, 31–2; Senate Committee on Foreign Relations, Background Information Relating to Southeast Asia and Vietnam, 93d Cong, 2d sess, Dec 74, (Washington, 1975), pp 72, 90, 138; Stanley Millet, ed, *South Vietnam: U.S.-Communist Confrontation in Southeast Asia, 1969* (New York, 1974), p 102.

38. Commando Hunt I, pp 14, 170, 201, 203–4; "Logistics" in Hq 7AF Study Guide, War of Interdiction vs Infiltration, May 1, 1968.

39. Commando Hunt I, p 2.

40. Interagency Study, "The Effectiveness of U.S. Air Operations in Southern Laos, Jun 12, 1970," pp 29–30, hereafter cited as Interagency Interdiction Study.

41. *Ibid.*, pp 4–7.

42. Jones intvw, Nov 4–6, 1969, pp 18–19; rprt, 7AF/TFA/Invert Committee, Sep 30, 1968, p 6.

43. Jones intvw, Nov 4–6, 1969, pp 19–20.

44. Intvw, Maj Joseph Smith with Capt Ron F. Myers, 56th SOWg Briefing Officer, Feb 69–Feb 70, Jul 15, 1970.

45. Commando Hunt I, pp x, 202–4, 345–59.

46. Burcham intvw, Jan 29, 1970, p 8.

47. Jones intvw, Nov 4–6, 1969, pp 17–18, 33–5.

Chapter 6

1. Ltr, Chief of Staff, 7AF, to Dir/Ops, Dir/Int, *et al*, subj: Establishment of SW Monsoon Planning Gp, Jan 8, 1969; with atch; rprt, 7AF Monsoon Planning Gp, Feb 22, 1969; TFA OPlan 101–69,

Southwest Monsoon Campaign, May 1, 1969, Annex B.

2. Hist, 7AF, Jan–Jun 69, I, pt I, p lxviii; TFA Background Paper on Munitions Available, nd [ca. Nov 70].

3. Hist, TFA, Jan–Dec 69, p 83; CIA Intelligence Information Rprts, CS–311/08171–69 Laos, subj: Road Conditions and Traffic Patterns along Route 110 in Southern Attopeu Province, Sep 16, 1969, CS–311/08172–69 Laos, subj: Condition of and Traffic along Routes 911, 23, and 235 in Khammouane Province, Sep 11, 1969.

4. CIA Intelligence Information Rprts, CS–311/06494–69 Laos, subj: Conditions of and Traffic along Route 914 Southeast of Ban Tchepone in Savannakhet Province, Air Strike Results and Foot Trails in the Area, Jul 16, 1969, CS–311/09526–69 Laos, subj: Conditions and Traffic on Routes 12 and 1201 South of the Mu Gia Pass in Eastern Khammouane Province, Oct 23, 1969.

5. Hist data record, 7AF Dir/Targets, Apr–Jun 69.

6. 7AF Laos Summary, 30 Aug–5 Sep 69, Sep 6, 1969.

7. Hist data record, 7AF Dir/Targets, Apr–Jun 69; Hq PACAF, Summary of Air Operations, Southeast Asia, May 1969, p 5:A:1–2.

8. Hartley intvw, Jul 14, 1974, p 12.

9. 7AF Laos Summaries (5–11 Apr 69), nd [ca. Apr 12, 1969], (12–18 Apr 69), Apr 19, 1969, (26 Apr–2 May 69), nd [ca. May 3, 1969], (31 May–6 Jun 69), Jun 7, 1969, (21–27 Jun 69), Jun 28, 1969, (26 Jul–1 Aug 69), Aug 2, 1969; minutes of Udorn Special Meeting (afternoon session), Sep 9, 1968.

10. Hist data record, 7AF Dir/Targets, Apr–Jun 69; 7AF Laos Summary, 21–27 Jun 69, Jun 28, 1969; msg, 7/13AF to 7AF, 191112Z Jun 69, subj: Operation Left Jab; Hartley intvw, Jul 14, 1974, pp 28–29.

11. Hist, 7/13AF, Jul–Dec 69, I, p 16; 7AF Laos Summaries (13–19 Sep 69), Sep 20, 1969, (4–10 Oct 69), Oct 11, 1969, (11–17 Oct 69), Oct 18, 1969.

12. Hist, 7/13AF, Jul–Dec 69, I, pp 13–14.

13. Hist, 56th SOWg, Jul–Sep 69, I, p 37.

14. Hist data record, 1st SOSq, Sep 69; msg, 7/13AF to Dir/Ops, 7AF, 010755Z Sep 69, subj: Operation Junction City, Jr.; hist, 7/13AF, Jul–Dec 69, I, p 14; msg, Asst USAIRA, Savannakhet, to 56th SOWg, 020400Z Sep 69, subj: Operation Junction City, Jr.

15. Hist, 7/13AF, Jul–Dec 69, I, pp 14–15; 7AF Laos Summary (30 Aug–5 Sep 69), Sep 6, 1969; msg, Asst USAIRA, Intelligence, Savannakhet, to USAIRA, Vientiane, 081215Z Sep 69, subj: Operations in Eastern Savannakhet Province.

16. Msg, Col Robert L. F. Tyrell to 7/13AF and 7AF, 121205Z Sep 69, subj: Operation Junction City, Jr.

17. Msg, Vientiane to Bangkok, Out 6418, Sep 19, 1969, subj: Defoliation Request.

18. Msg, Asst USAIRA, Savannakhet, to USAIRA, Vientiane, 160325Z Sep 69.

19. Hist, 56th SOWg, Jul–Sep 69, I, p 37.

20. Msgs, 7/13AF to 7AF, 171012Z Sep 69, subj: Ranch Hand at Junction City, 7/13AF to Ofc USAIRA, Vientiane, and Asst USAIRA, Savannakhet, [illegible] Sep 69, same subject.

21. Msg, Asst USAIRA, Savannakhet, to USAIRA, Vientiane, 211355Z Sep 69, subj: Muong Phine Rice.

22. Msg, Asst USAIRA, Savannakhet, to USAIRA, Vientiane, 281050Z Sep 69.

23. Msg, 7AF to 7/13AF, 101219Z Oct 69, subj: Ranch Hand Mission.

24. Msg, Vientiane to 7AF, Out 6181, Oct 11, 1969, subj: Ranch Hand Mission.

25. 7AF Laos Summary (4–10 Oct 69), Oct 11, 1969.

26. 7AF Laos Summary (25–31 Oct 69), Nov 1, 1969.

27. *Ibid.*

Chapter 7

1. Msg, 7AF to AIG 8272, 050530Z Feb 70, subj: Air Traffic Control for Night Operations in Steel Tiger East.

2. Intvw, Col John E, Van Duyn with Gen John D. Ryan, CINCSAC, 1964–67, Vice CSAF, 1967–68, CSAF, 1969–71, May 20, 1971, p 15, hereafter cited as Ryan intvw.

3. Jones intvw, Nov 4–6, 1969, pp 43–45.

4. Shields, *Igloo White, 1970–1971*, p 16.

5. TFA Rprt on Commando Bolt Operation (20 Nov 69–30 Apr 70), nd [ca. summer 1970], including App B and C; Jones intvw, Nov 4–6, 1969, pp 49–52.

6. Shields, *Igloo White, 1970–1971*, p 18–19; intvw, Lt Col Vaughn H. Gallacher and Maj Lynn R. Officer with Maj James Costin, 56th SOWg,

1969–70, Feb 6, 1973.

7. Shields, *Igloo White, 1970–1971*, p 20; TFA Rprt on Commando Bolt Operations (20 Nov 69–30 Apr 70), nd [ca. summer 1970].

8. Shields, *Igloo White, 1970–1971*, pp 20–21; Commando Hunt III, pp 172–75.

9. Portatale Evaluation, App F, to TFA Rprt on Commando Bolt Operations (20 Nov 69–30 Apr 70), nd [ca. summer 1970].

10. Shields, *Igloo White, 1970–1971*, pp 61–65.

11. *Ibid.*, pp 24–25.

12. *Ibid.*, pp 26–29.

13. Memo, Dir/Tactical Analysis, 7AF, to Dir/Fighters (Col Jamison), subj: Nite Owl Operations, Nov 23, 1969; ltr, Ops Officer, 497th TFSq to DCO, subj: Operation Nite Owl, Oct 19, 1969.

14. Commando Hunt III, pp 104–7.

15. *Ibid.*, pp 123–24.

16. *Ibid.*, pp 80–81.

17. *Ibid.*, pp 68–69; Ryan intvw, May 20, 1971, pp 13–14.

18. Commando Hunt III, p 142.

19. *Ibid.*, p 86.

20. Brown intvw, Oct 19–20, 1970, p 116.

21. Jones intvw, Nov 4–6, 1969, p 28.

22. Commando Hunt III., pp 125–27; Commando Hunt I, pp 188–89.

23. Commando Hunt I, p 173; Commando Hunt III, pp iii–iv, 30–33.

24. Commando Hunt III, pp 30, 131–36.

25. *Ibid.*, p 150.

26. *Ibid.*, p 148.

27. End of Tour Rprt, Brig Gen Chester J. Butcher, Comdr, TFA, 1969–70, Aug 3, 1970, hereafter cited as Butcher End of Tour Rprt.

28. Ryan intvw, May 20, 1971, pp 11–12.

29. Intvw, Capt Richard Bauer with Capt Mike Maddock, Target Officer, Task Force Alpha, 1969–70, Jul 9, 1970, n.p.

30. Interagency Interdiction Study, pp 5, 29, 31.

31. W. Scott Thompson and Donaldson D. Frizzell, eds, *The Lessons of Vietnam* (New York, 1977), p 142, hereafter cited as Thompson and Frizzell, *Vietnam.*

32. Commando Hunt III, p 145.

33. Interagency Interdiction Study, pp 6–7, 71, 84.

Chapter 8

1. CIA Dir/Intelligence Memos, Communist Deliveries to Cambodia for the VC/NVA Forces in South Vietnam (Dec 66–Apr 69), nd [ca. spring 1970]; New Evidence on Military Deliveries to Cambodia (Dec 66–Apr 69), Sep 70; *CIA Studies in Intelligence*, Special Issue, 1984: Bruce Palmer, "U.S. Intelligence and Vietnam," p 78.

2. Hists, USMACV, 1968, pp F:III:4:11, F:IV: H:1, 1969, p F:III:4:B:1.

3. DOD Rprt on Selected Air and Ground Operations in Laos, Sep 10, 1973; hist, USMACV, 1970, pp B:III:37–40.

4. Elizabeth H. Hartsook, *Shield for Vietnamization and Withdrawal* [*The Air Force in Southeast Asia*] (Washington, 1976), pp 107–9.

5. Truong Nha T'ang, with David Chanoff and Doan Van Toai, *A Vietcong Memoir* (New York, 1985), pp 168, 179–82, hereafter cited as Truong Nha T'ang, *A Vietcong Memoir.*

6. Kissinger, *White House Years*, 506–7; hist, USMACV, 1970, p C:103.

7. Memo for Record, Phil Odeen, Ofc of Asst SecDef (Systems and Analysis), Regional Programs, subj: Vietnamization Meeting with Secretary Laird (17 Mar 70), nd; Interagency Interdiction Study, p 4.

8. Norman B. Hannah, *The Key to Failure: Laos and the Vietnam War* (Lanham, Maryland, New York, and London, 1987), 281–82; Kissinger, *White House Years*, pp 503–8

9. *Public Papers of the Presidents of the United States, Richard Nixon, 1969* (Washington 1971), pp 255–59, 365–69, 970–71; *1970*, (Washington, 1971), p 397; *Rprt of the President's Commission on the All-Volunteer Armed Force* (Washington, 1971); Boettcher, *Vietnam*, pp 448–49.

10. Boettcher, *Vietnam*, pp 451–52.

11. Lester A. Sobol, with Hal Kosut, eds, *South Vietnam: U.S.-Communist Confrontation in Southeast Asia, 1970* (New York, 1973), pp 61–62, 74–75, 119–20.

12. *Ibid.*, pp 55, 75–77, 119; Karnow, *Vietnam,* pp 374–75.

13. Boettcher, *Vietnam*, pp 446–47.

14. *Ibid.*, pp 399–402; Clarke, *The Final Years*, pp 120–24, 346–49.

15. End of Tour Rprt, Col Earl Anderson, Comdr, 25th TFSq, 1970–71, Jun 1971.

16. William M. Hammond, *The U.S. Army in Vietnam; Public Affairs: The Military and the Media, 1962–1968* (Washington, 1988), pp 387–88.

17. End of Tour Rprt, Col Robert M. Slane, Vice

Comdr and Comdr, 553d RWg, 1970–71, and
Comdr, 6251st CSGp, 1971, Nov 15, 1971.

18. End of Tour Rprts, Col Edward J. Walsh, Jr.,
Comdr, 56th SOWg, 1970–71, Jul 15, 1971; Col
Clair G. Thompson, Comdr, 432d CSGp,
1971–72, nd; Alan Osur, "Black–White Relations
in the U.S. Military, 1940–1972," *Air University
Review* (Nov–Dec 81), pp 75–78.

19. End of Tour Rprt, Col Edward J. Walsh, Jr.,
cited above.

20. Richard B. Garver, *Drug Abuse in Southeast
Asia* (Hq PACAF, Project CHECO, Jan 1, 1975),
pp 54–58, 64–69, 71.

21. End of Tour Rprt, Col William J. Poad,
Comdr, 554th CESq, 1971–72, Jun 30, 1972.

22. End of Tour Rprt, Col Francis A. Humphreys, Comdr, 8th TFWg, 1972–74, Jan 17, 1974.

23. Shields, *Igloo White, 1970–1971*, p 30;
Commando Hunt VII, p 5.

24. Shields, *Igloo White, 1970–1971*, p 31.

25. 7AF Laos Summaries (13–19 Dec 69), Dec
20, 1969, (17–23 Jan 70), Jan 24, 1970.

26. Richard R. Sexton, *et al*, *The Bolovens Campaign, 28 Jul–28 Dec 71* (Hq PACAF, Project
CHECO, May 8, 1974), pp xii, xiv, hereafter cited
as Sexton, *Bolovens Campaign*.

27. Msg, Vientiane to COMUSMACV,
260610Z May 70, subj: Arc Light-Headshed V;
hist, 7/13AF, Jul–Dec 70, I, pp 15–16.

28. Msg, Ofc USAIRA, Vientiane, to 7/13AF
and 7AF, 311130Z Aug 70, subj: Air Support for
Operation Gauntlet.

29. Msg, AOC Savannakhet to USAIRA Ops,
Vientiane, 290925Z Aug 70, subj: SGU Sweep
Operations.

30. Msgs, Ofc USAIRA, Vientiane, to 7/13AF
and 7AF, 311130Z Aug 70, subj: Air Support for
Operation Gauntlet; 7AF to Ofc USAIRA, Vientiane, 020325Z Sep 70, subj: none.

31. Hist data record, 21st SOSq, Sep 70.

32. Hist, USMACV, 1970, pp B:63, B:VIII:7–8;
ltr, Dep Chief of Fighters to DOC, subj: Resume of
Significant Events, Period 6 Sep 70 to 9 Oct 70,
Oct 10, 1970.

33. Hist, 56th SOWg, Oct–Dec 71, I, p 57–58.

34. Working Paper, 7AF, Gauntlet II, Jun 10, 1970.

35. Hist, 56th SOWg, Oct–Dec 71, I, p 56.

36. PACAF Summary of Air Ops, SEA, Sep 70,
p 2:7; ltr, Dep Chief of Fighters to DOC, subj:
Resume of Significant Events, Period 6 Sep 70 to
9 Oct 70, Oct 10, 1970.

Chapter 9

1. Memo, Gen W. W. Momyer for Gen Richard
H. Ellis, subj: Corona Harvest (USAF Operations
in Laos, 1 Jan 70–13 Jan 71), Jun 16, 1975, hereafter cited as memo, Momyer for Ellis.

2. Butcher End of Tour Rprt.

3. Commando Hunt III, p 162; Commando
Hunt V, p 206.

4. Hist data record, Infiltration Surveillance Div,
TFA, (Apr–Jun 71), Jul 23, 1971.

5. Shields, *Igloo White, 1970–1971*, p 37.

6. Msg, Maj Gen [William P.] McBride to Maj
Gen [Joseph G.] Wilson, subj: TFA, Feb 4, 1971.

7. Hist, 56th SOWg, Oct–Dec 70, I, p 107.

8. Msg, AFSSO 7AF to AFSSO 7/13 AF,
311225Z Dec 70, retransmitting msg, USAIRA,
Vientiane, to Maj Gen Triantfellu, Lt Gen Dough-
erty, and Gen Clay, 281200Z Dec 70.

9. Working Paper, 7AF, Silver Buckle, nd [ca.
Jun 10, 1971].

10. *Ibid.*

11. *Ibid.*; hist, 7/13AF, 1971, I, p 39.

12. Introduction to USAIRA, Vientiane, Desert
Rat Summaries; msgs, AOC, Intelligence, Savannakhet, to USAIRA, Intelligence, Vientiane,
161430Z Feb 71, AOC, Savannakhet, to USAIRA,
Ops, Vientiane, 150833Z Mar 71, subj: Air Package, Desert Rat; hist, 7/13AF, 1971, I, pp 39–40.

13. Annex D, Sep 22, 1971, to 7AF OPlan 715,
Northeast Monsoon Campaign.

14. Quoted in msg, JCS to CINCPAC, 242003Z
Dec 70.

15. Msg, DIA to AIG 925, 241623Z Dec 70,
subj: Watch Rprt of 24 Dec 70.

16. Msg, DOD/PRO to CINCPACAF, CINC-
PACFLT, *et al*, 292112Z Jan 71, subj: Viet Cong
MR–2 Efforts to Purchase Weapons and Ammu-
nition from GVN Personnel.

17. Nguyen Duy Hinh, *Indochina Monograph*:
Lam Son 719 (Washington, 1979), pp 65–73,
90–91, 96–97, 99–104, 117–21; Kissinger,
White House Years, p. 1004; Davidson, *Vietnam
at War*, pp 575–87; hist, USMACV, 1971, II, pp
E:15– E:33; Edward P. Brynn and Michael L.
Timhomhirov, *Air Power against Armor* (Hq
PACAF, Project CHECO, unpublished MS),
118.

18. Msg, COMUSMACV to CINCPAC, 220315Z Mar 71, subj: Assessment of Effects of Operations Lam Son 719 and Thoan Thang 01–71NS.

19. Msg, COMUSMACV to JCS and CINCPAC, 031015Z Apr 71, subj: Vietnamization; Clarke, *The Final Years*, pp 473–74.

20. Hist, USMACV, 1971, II, pp E:33–E:34.

21. *Public Papers of the Presidents of the United States: Richard Nixon, 1971* (Washington, 1972), pp 450–51; Kissinger, *White House Years*, pp 1004–8; Lewis Sorley, *Thunderbolt: General Creighton Abrams and the Army of His Times* (New York, 1992) pp 313–14.

22. Clarke, *The Final Years*, p 474.

23. Rprt, 7AF, Commando Hunt V, May 71, pp 82–85.

24. *Newsweek*, Apr 5, 1971, pp 25–29; *Time*, Mar 29, 1971, pp 22–23 and Apr 25, 1971, p 13.

25. *Public Papers of Richard Nixon, 1971*, pp 452–53.

26. *From Khe Sanh to Chepone* (Hanoi, 1971), pp 70–71.

27. Hist, USMACV, 1971, II, pp E:33–34.

28. Karnow, *Vietnam*, p 631.

29. Lester A. Sobol, with Hal Kosut, eds, *South Vietnam: U.S.-Communist Confrontation in South east Asia*, VI, *1971*, (New York, 1973), pp 173–86.

30. Col J. F. Loye, Jr., *et al*, *Lam Son 719, 30 January–24 March 1971: The South Vietnamese Incursion into Laos* (Hq PACAF, Project CHECO, Mar 24, 1971), p 18, hereafter cited as *Lam Son 719*; Commando Hunt V, pp 71–75.

31. Shields, *Igloo White, 1970–1971*, pp 41–42; msg, 7AF to CINCPACAF, 010400Z Mar 76, subj: Antipersonnel Sensor Concept; Defense Special Projects Gp Documentary Supplement II, Aug 70–Jun 72, Annex F, Systems.

32. Msg, Vientiane to 7AF, Vientiane 1068, 210455Z Feb 71; Commando Hunt V, pp 121–22.

33. End of Tour Rprt, Lt Col Roland P. Hight, Comdr, 16th SOSq, 1969–70, Feb 12, 71.

34. End of Tour Rprt, Lt Col Paul R. Pitt, Comdr, 13th Bomb Sq (Tactical), 1970–71, Feb 12, 1971.

35. Killpack End of Tour Rprt.

36. *Ibid.*; Msgs, 7AF to TFA, 180340Z Feb 71, subj: Sensor String Emplacement, 8th TFWg to 7AF, 230515Z Feb 71, subj: Sensor String Emplacement; Staff Summary Sheet, 7AF Dir/ Command and Control, subj: Sensor Emplacement, Mar 2, 1971.

37. Commando Hunt V, pp 180–82, 235–37; *Lam Son 719*, p 34.

38. Commando Hunt V, pp 100–2.

39. Hist, 56th SOWg, Apr–Jun 71, I, 86–95.

40. Msg, NPIC, Washington, D.C., to AIG 7840, 222342Z Jan 71.

41. Msg, 8th TFWg to AIG 7937, except CSAF and 131st Avn Co, 181300Z Jan 71, subj: 8th TFWg Wolf DISUM 043.

42. Msg, DIA to AIG 7010 and 7011, 190249Z Jan 71, subj: DIA Intelligence Bulletin, Far East Summary 18–71; DOD Intelligence Information Rprt, 1–516–003–73 (5800–05), Jan 22, 1973, subj: Infiltration Route in North Vietnam, Laos, and Cambodia.

43. Analysis Div, Intelligence Br, Dir/ Intelligence, TFA, The North Vietnamese Army Logistic System in Steel Tiger, 1971, pp 5–6, 8, 30.

44. DOD Intelligence Information Rprts, 1–516–0600–71 (5800–05–6), Dec 3, 1971, subj: Infiltration Route Utilized by the 3072d Infiltration Gp, 1–516–0577–71 (6800–05–6), Nov 12, 1971, subj: Formation, Training, and Infiltration of the 37th NVA Bn, 320th NVA Div, also known as 2189th Infiltration Gp, 1–516–003–73 (5800–05), cited above.

45. Memo, Momyer for Ellis.

46. Commando Hunt V, pp 129, 158–59.

47. *Ibid.*, p 54.

48. Memo, Momyer for Ellis.

49. End of Tour Rprt, Lt Col Wade R. Kilbride, Comdr, 22d SOSq and 602d SOSq, 1970–71, nd, hereafter cited as Kilbride End of Tour Rprt.

50. Commando Hunt V, pp 61, 261.

51. Intvw, Mildred Wiley with Lt Col Vaughn H. Gallacher, Dir, 7/13th Tactical Air Control Center, and Chief, Current Ops Div, 7/13th AF, 1970–71, Dec 16, 1971, pp 12–13.

52. Intvw, Martin J. Miller, Jr., and Joseph A. Ventolo, Jr., with Brig Gen William A. Fairbrother, Comdr, 14th SOWg, 1969–70, Jun 7, 1974, pp 14–15.

53. Hist, JCS: *The JCS and the War in Vietnam, 1971–1973* (Hist Div, Jt Secretariat, JCS, Sep 79), pt I, pp 249–50, hereafter cited as hist, JCS, *Vietnam, 1971–1973*.

54. 7AF Memo (Working Paper), Maj Ronald A. Cadieux, Surveillance Div, for Col [Reubin L.] Kingdon, [Jr.], subj: Acoustic vs Seismic Sensor for Personnel Detection, Sep 8, 1969.

Chapter 10

1. Notes, Melvin F. Porter, of discussions with Col Charles M. Morrison, Chief, Fighter Division, Hq, 7AF, Nov 18, 1970, hereafter cited as notes, Morrison intvw.

2. Melvin F. Porter, *Interdiction of Waterways and POL Pipelines, SEA* (Hq PACAF, Project CHECO, Dec 11, 1970), p 1, hereafter cited as Porter, *Waterways and Pipelines*; notes, Melvin F. Porter, of intvw with Capt Daniel A. Adair, JUSMAGTHAI J–2, Nov 2, 1970, hereafter cited as notes, Adair intvw.

3. TFA Waterways Briefing, nd [ca. fall 1970].

4. *Ibid.*; notes, Morrison intvw, Nov 18, 1970.

5. TFA Waterways Briefing, see note 3.

6. Notes, Adair intvw, Nov 2, 1970.

7. TFA Waterways Briefing, see note 3.

8. Porter, *Waterways and Pipelines*, p 3; Capt Stephen E. Wilson, Dir/Int, TFA, *The North Vietnamese Waterways System in Steel Tiger*, Jul 1. 1971, pp 12–15, hereafter cited as Wilson, *Waterways System*.

9. Ltr, Maj William B. Hill, Chief, Target Exploitation Br, to Dir/Int, TFA, subj: Waterway Targeting, Apr 11, 1970.

10. Hist, CINCPAC, 1970, II, pp 218–19.

11. *Ibid.*, p 219; ltr, Maj William B. Hill, see note 9.

12. Background paper, Hq 7AF, Waterway VII Complex, nd [ca. fall 1970].

13. Porter, *Waterways and Pipelines*, p 11.

14. Background paper, Hq 7AF, Waterway VII Complex, see note 12; background paper, TFA, Munitions Available, nd [ca. Nov 1970]; DOD Intelligence Information Rprt 6–856–0325–70, subj: Effect of Air Ops in SEA, Sep 14, 1970.

15. Porter, *Waterways and Pipelines*, p 10, fig 6; background paper, Hq 7AF, Waterway VII Complex, see note 12.

16. Wilson, *Waterways System*, pp 6–7.

17. Notes, Morrison intvw, Nov 18, 1970.

18. Wilson, *Waterways System*, p 11.

19. *Ibid.*, pp 16, 29.

20. *Ibid.*, pp 26–28.

21. Porter, *Waterways and Pipelines*, pp 28–29; 7AF, Commando Hunt VII, Jun 72, p 89.

22. Porter, *Waterways and Pipelines*, pp 14–15.

23. National Photographic Interpretation Center (NPIC), PI Memo R–53/69, Status of POL Pipeline in North Vietnam and Laos, Jun 69.

24. *Ibid.*; TFA POL Pipeline Study, nd [ca. Nov or Dec 70]; notes, Adair intvw, Nov 2, 1970; hist, 460th TRWg, Jul–Oct 69, I, p 21; NPIC, PI Memo R–108/69, POL Pipeline Developments in North Vietnam and Laos, Dec 69.

25. Notes, Adair intvw, Nov 2, 1970.

26. TFA POL Pipeline Study, see note 24.

27. Notes, Adair intvw, Nov 2, 1970.

28. TFA POL Pipeline Study, see note 24; TFA Dir/Int, *The North Vietnamese POL Logistics System in the Steel Tiger Operating Area of Southern Laos*, Feb 1, 1971, hereafter cited as TFA, *POL Logistics, 1971*.

29. Notes, Adair intvw, Nov 2, 1970.

30. *Ibid.*

31. TFA, *POL Logistics, 1971*, p 14.

32. Msg, 7AF to 366th TFWg, 8th TFWg, *et al*, 230500Z Apr 71, subj: Strafing POL Pipelines; notes, Morrison intvw, Nov 18, 1970.

33. TFA, *POL Logistics, 1971*, p 15.

34. Notes, Morrison intvw, Nov 18, 1970.

35. Hist data record, lst SOSq, Sep 69.

36. TFA, *POL Logistics, 1971*, p 15; hist, USMACV, 1971, p III:47.

37. Msg, CINCPAC to CJCS, 172233Z Jun 72, subj: New POL Pipeline.

38. 7AF, Commando Hunt VII, Jun 72, p 89.

Chapter 11

1. Annex EE, May 5, 1971, to 7AF OPlan 730, Southwest Monsoon Plan.

2. Annex D, Sep 22, 1971, to 7AF OPlan 715, Northeast Monsoon Campaign.

3. Kilbride end of tour rprt.

4. Intvw, Maj Donald J. Moore with Lt Col Robert E. Lambert, Dir/Int, 56th SOWg, 1969–1970, Jan 13, 1970.

5. Annex B, May 5, 1971, to 7AF OPlan 730, Southwest Monsoon Plan; Capt Bruce P. Layton, *Commando Hunt VI* (Hq PACAF, Project CHECO, Jul 7, 1972), p 4, hereafter cited as *Commando Hunt VI*.

6. Commando Hunt V, pp 40, 44–46.

7. TAB A to App VIII to Annex EE, May 5, 1971, to 7AF OPlan 730, Southwest Monsoon Plan;

msg, 7AF to AIG 8304, 180330Z Jun 71, subj: Steel Tiger VR Sectors.

8. Annex B, May 5, 1971, to 7AF OPlan 730, Southwest Monsoon Plan.

9. Hist, TFA, Jul–Sep 71, pp 37–40; *Commando Hunt VI*, p 6.

10. Hist, TFA, Jul–Sep 71, pp 14–16, 39.

11. *Ibid.*, p 4.

12. *Ibid.*, pp 45–46.

13. Hq PACAF, with the support of SAC, Project Corona Harvest Study: "USAF Operations in Defense of South Vietnam," Jul 1, 71–Jun 30, 72, pp 18–19, hereafter cited as Corona Harvest, "Operations in Defense of South Vietnam."

14. USAF Mgt Summary, Southeast Asia, Nov 1, 68, p 14; Jun 17, 71, p 5; Oct 19, 71, p 5.

15. Corona Harvest, "Operations in Defense of South Vietnam," pp 16–18, 20.

16. Sexton, *Bolovens Campaign*, pp 1–3, 5, 7–10, 19–20.

17. Msgs, 7AF to CSAF, PACAF, 7/13AF, 211825Z Nov 71, subj: Operation Thao La,

AFSSO Udorn to AFSSO 7AF, 211144Z Nov 71 and 171145Z Dec 71, subj: Operation Thao La; 7AF to CSAF, PACAF, 7/13AF, 250200Z Nov 71, subj: Operation Thao La, AFSSO Udorn to AFSSO 7AF, 251350Z Nov 71 and 291555Z Nov 71, subj: Operation Thao La.

18. Msgs, AFSSO Udorn to AFSSO 7AF, 261315Z Nov 71 and 291555Z Nov 71, subj: Operation Thao La; AFSSO Udorn to AFSSO 7AF, 111412Z Dec 71 and 122115Z Dec 71, subj: Operation Thao La; Memo for Record, 7/13AF, DO to CD, subj: Tank Activity, Dec 15, 1971; AFSSO Udorn to AFSSO 7AF, 171145Z Dec 71, subj: Operation Thao La.

19. Msgs, 7AF to CSAF, PACAF, 7/13AF, 070128Z Dec 71 and 080215Z Dec 71, subj: Operation Thao La.

20. Hists, 7/13AF, 1972, I, p 69, USMACV, Jan 72–Mar 73, pp I:A:67, 69.

21. Commando Hunt VII, p 89; CINCPAC OPlan, Island Tree, Aug 5, 1971.

Chapter 12

1. Minutes of Udorn Special Meeting (afternoon session), Sep 9, 1968.

2. Draft memo, with App, DDR&E for Dep SECDEF, subj: Igloo White/Duel Blade/Duck Blind Evaluation Committee Rprt, Nov 25, 1968.

3. Thayer, *Systems Analysis*, II, p 78.

4. Corona Harvest Project Ofc, Captured Document Summaries, Southeast Asia, 1967–68.

5. DOD Intelligence Information Rprt 1516–0663–69 (5800–05), May 21, 1969, subj: Infiltration of the 521st Bn, 42d Regt, 350th NVA Div.

6. Intvw, Maj Ralph A. Rowley with Capt David L. Shields, FAC, Sep 1967–May 1968, Jan 10, 1972.

7. Rowley, *FAC Operations*, p 73.

8. DOD Intelligence Information Rprt 1516–0603–69 (5800–05), subj: Infiltration of the 294th Infiltration Gp through Laos and Cambodia.

9. M. G. Weiner, J. R. Brom, and R. E. Koon, RAND Corporation Memo RM–5760–RR, Oct 68, Infiltration of Personnel from North Vietnam (1959–1967), pp 32–33.

10. Thayer, *Systems Analysis*, I, p 145; hist, USMACV, 1970, p III:70.

11. Text, 7AF Briefing, Igloo White Antipersonnel Evaluation, nd [ca. Apr 69].

12. Memo, Gen George S. Brown, Comdr 7AF, for Dir/Plans, Jan 7, 1969.

13. Msg, TFA to 7AF, subj: TFA Assessment of Proposed DCPG Antipersonnel Test, Jan 12, 1969.

14. DCPG Study, Antipersonnel Impact Review, Jan 31, 1969; memo for [Lt] Gen [David] Jones, Vice Comdr 7AF, subj: Igloo White Antipersonnel Evaluation, Feb 21, 1969; text, 7AF Briefing, Igloo White Antipersonnel Evaluation, nd [ca. Apr 69].

15. Msg, 7AF to TFA, subj: Antipersonnel Test of Igloo White, May 29, 1969.

16. Msg, TFA to 7AF, 090510Z Jun 69, subj: Antipersonnel Test of Igloo White.

17. Thayer, *Systems Analysis*, II, p 78.

18. Msg, TFA to 7AF, 090510Z Jun 69, subj: Antipersonnel Test of Igloo White.

19. Talking Paper, 7AF, subj: Igloo White Antipersonnel Evaluation, Jun 27, 1969.

20. Hq PACAF, Project Corona Harvest, *Hardware: Munitions*, pp 3, 7, 11.

21. *Ibid.*, pp 32–34, 41.

22. *Ibid.*, pp 20, 123–26.

23. Memo, Dir/Tactics and Combat Systems to Dir/Ops, 7AF, subj: Use of Black Spot (AC–123), May 20, 1970.

24. Interagency Interdiction Study, p 72.

25. DOD Intelligence Rprt 1516–0577–71 (5800–05–6), Nov 12, 1971, subj: Formation,

Training, and Infiltration of the 37th Bn, 320th NVA Div, also known as the 2189th Infiltration Gp, hereafter cited as Formation, Training, and Infiltration of the 37th Bn, 320th NVA Div.

26. Msg, COMUSMACV-CINCPAC to DIA, Dir/NSA, *et al*, 011022Z Sep 66, subj: Supplemental Knowledgeability Brief.

27. Encl to ltr, CINCPAC to CINCSAC, USAF-SS, *et al*, subj: CINCPAC Ops Security of Arc Light Missions in Route Packages 2 and 3, Dec 27, 1972.

28. Formation, Training, and Infiltration of the 37th Bn, 320th NVA Div.

29. Msg, Saigon to CINCPAC, 100635Z Dec 70, subj: SEACOORDS Meeting, Saigon, Dec 17, 1970; hist, USMACV, 1970, p III:70.

30. Msg, DOD/PRO to CINCPAC, CINCPACFLT, *et al*, 280342Z Dec 70, subj: Organization and Deployment of the NVA 26th Bn.

31. Formation, Training, and Infiltration of the 37th Bn, 320th NVA Div.

32. Hist, USMACV, 1971, pp I:45–56.

33. Formation, Training, and Infiltration of the 37th Bn, 320th NVA Div.

34. Hist, USMACV, 1971, p I:46–47.

35. Memo, Dep DDR&E (SEAM) for DDR&E, subj: Vietnamization of the Interdiction Campaign, Personnel vs Trucks, May 4, 1971.

36. Memo, SECDEF to CJCS, subj: Improvement and Modernization of the RVNAF, May 17, 1971.

37. Atch to 7AF Paper, RVNAF Interdiction Capability, May 20, 1971.

38. Msg, CINCPAC to JCS, 281050Z May 71, subj: RVNAF Interdiction Capabilities.

39. Memo, Dep DDR&E (SEAM) for DDR&E, subj: Service, Agency, and JCS Response to Proposed Laotian Interdiction Alternatives, Jun 30, 1971.

40. *Ibid.*

41. Ltr, Leonard Sullivan to Robert G. Gibson, Research and Engineering Consultant, CINCPAC Staff, Jul 2, 1971.

42. Memo, SECDEF for Secretaries of the Military Depts, CJCS, and Dir/DSPG [formerly DCPG], subj: RVNAF Interdiction Alternatives, Jul 2, 1971; CINCPAC OPlan, Island Tree, Aug 5, 1971.

43. CINCPAC OPlan, Island Tree, Aug 5, 1971.

44. Island Tree, encl to End of Tour Rprt, Brig Gen Ernest F. John, DCS/Int, 7AF, 1970–71, Nov 24, 1971.

45. Gindoff, *NVA Logistic System*, pp 76–78; msg, MACV SSO to CINCPAC SSO, 030611Z Oct 71, subj: Island Tree Data Base Progress Rprt no 3.

46. Island Tree, encl to End of Tour Rprt, Brig Gen John, cited above; Gindoff, *NVA Logistic System*, p 78.

47. Ltr, Leonard Sullivan to Gen John D. Lavelle, Sep 10, 1971.

48. Ltr, Leonard Sullivan to Georges Duval, MACV Science Adviser, Sep 8, 1971.

49. *Ibid.*

50. Ltr, Leonard Sullivan to Georges Duval, MACV Science Adviser, Oct 5, 1971.

51. *Ibid.*

52. Msgs, TFA to 7AF, 090650Z Oct 71, subj: Commo/Liaison Sensor Program, 7AF to TFA, 131055Z Oct 71, subj: Commo/Liaison Sensor Program.

53. Gindoff, *NVA Logistic System*, pp 78–79.

54. *Ibid.*, p 80.

55. Msg, 7AF SSO to Hq USAF SSO, 020945Z Feb 72, subj: Sensor Derived BDA.

56. Ltr, Leonard Sullivan to Georges Duval, MACV Science Adviser, Dec 23, 1971.

57. Gindoff, *NVA Logistic System*, pp 79–80.

58. Hist data record, TFA, Dir/Intelligence, Jan 1–Mar 31, 1972; Corona Harvest, "Air Operations in Defense of South Vietnam," p 46.

59. Extract from DOD Intelligence Information Rprt 1516–0148–72, subj: Air Strike against the D–7th Bn, E–64th Regt, 320th NVA Div, Apr 7, 1971.

60. Gindoff, *NVA Logistic System*, pp 80–81.

61. *Ibid.*, p 81.

62. Msg, 7AF to CSAF and CINCPACAF, 030100Z Mar 72, retransmitting COMUSMACV 021020Z Mar 72.

63. Extract from DOD Intelligence Rprt 1516–0207–72, subj: Infiltration of the 2287th Infiltration Gp from North Vietnam, Apr 20, 1972.

64. Hist data record, TFA, Dir/Intelligence, Jan 1–Mar 31, 1972.

65. Hist, TFA, Apr 1–Jun 30, 1972, p 35; Gindoff, *NVA Logistic System*, pp 76–82.

66. Msg, CINCPAC to COMUSMACV, 140210Z Mar 72, subj: Island Tree Bomb Damage Assessment; End of Tour Rprt, Maj Gen Alton D. Slay, Asst DCS/Ops and DCS/Ops, 7AF, 1971–72, nd, hereafter cited as Slay End of Tour Rprt.

67. Gindoff, *NVA Logistic System*, p 76.

Chapter 13

1. Hist, JCS, *Vietnam, 1971–1973*, pt I, pp 106–7.

2. End of Tour Rprt, Col D. L. Evans, Dir/Int, TFA, 1971–1972, Jul 6, 1972, pp 11–12, hereafter cited as Evans End of Tour Rprt; Commando Hunt VII, p 15.

3. Commando Hunt VII, p 19.

4. Ltrs, Dir/Ops, 7/13AF, to CD, subj: Gunship/ OV–1 Activities, Oct 15, 1971, and nd [ca. later Oct 1971]; msg, 7/13AF to 56th SOWg, 191056Z Oct 71, subj: Request for AC–119 [sic] Mission Results.

5. USAF Mgt Summary, Southeast Asia, Nov 29, 1968, p 14; Dec 9, 1969, p 2:16; Dec 17, 1970, p 4; Dec 21, 1971, p 4; DCS/Personnel, Combat Tour Policy, Corona Harvest Personnel Support Study: Phase I, pt I, vol 3, tab 5; John Schlight, *The War in South Vietnam: The Years of the Offensive, 1965–1968* [*The Air Force in Southeast Asia*] (Washington: Office of Air Force History, 1988), pp 307–8.

6. Corona Harvest, "Operations in Defense of South Vietnam."

7. Commando Hunt VII, p 50.

8. Gindoff, *NVA Logistic System*, pp 38–39; Evans End of Tour Rprt, pp 11–12, 44.

9. Linsenmeyer, "Interdiction Operations," p 20.

10. Evans End of Tour Rprt, pp 2–5; PACAF Commando Hunt Briefing, nd [ca. Dec 1971], Tab 10 to North Vietnamese Current Assessment.

11. Intvw, Lt Col Vaughn H. Gallacher and Maj Lyn H. Officer with Lt Col Loyd J. King, C–130E pilot and wing operations officer, Oct 1971–[ca. Oct] 1972, Feb 8, 1973, pp 16–17, hereafter cited as King intvw; DOD Intelligence Information Rprt 2–237–111–72, subj: NVA Reaction to US/RLAF Air Operations, Aug 24, 1972.

12. Gindoff, *NVA Logistic System*, pp 18–19; ltr, Maj Francis J. Twait, Special Operations Force Liaison Officer, to Comdr, Special Operations Forces, subj: SOFLO Activity Rprt 14–73 (16–31 Jan 72), Jan 29, 1972.

13. Gindoff, *NVA Logistic System*, p 17; Commando Hunt VII, pp 134–35; msg, Maj Francis J. Twait to Comdr, Special Operations Forces, subj: SOFLO Activity Rprt 16–72 (16–29 Feb 72), Feb 29, 1972.

14. Intvw, Maj Lyn R. Officer, Hugh Ahmann, and Lt Col V. H. Gallacher with Lt Col Kenneth D. Negus, AC–130 Comdr, Apr 1971–Apr 1972, Dec 15, 1972, pp 9–11, hereafter cited as Negus intvw.

15. Lt Col Kenneth D. Negus, Jr., Analysis of Aerial Campaign in Southeast Asia, Jun 1972, [text] p 3.

16. Negus intvw, Dec 15, 1972, pp 107–2.

17. End of Tour Rprt, Lt Col Kenneth G. Harris, Comdr, 16th SOSq, 1971–1972, Jan 30, 1972, p 33.

18. Commando Hunt VII, pp 140–41; Corona Harvest," Operations in Defense of South Vietnam," pp 33–34.

19. Commando Hunt VII, pp 50–51; quarterly hist rprt, Reconnaissance/ Electronic Warfare Br, Dir/Op Plans, 7AF, Jan–Mar 72; Negus intvw, Dec 15, 1972, pp 27–28; End of Tour Rprt, Lt Col Lachlan McClay, Comdr, 23d TASSq, 1971–1972, Sep 18, 1972, pp 5–6.

20. Corona Harvest, "Operations in Defense of South Vietnam," pp 34–35.

21. App II to Annex D, Sep 22, 1971, to 7AF OPlan 715, Northeast Monsoon Campaign.

22. Memo, Dep DDR&E (SEAM) for DDR &E, subj: Truck "Killing" in the U.S. Interdiction Campaign, Oct 7, 1971.

23. Commando Hunt VII, pp 79, 259.

24. Negus intvw, Dec 15, 1972, pp 81–82.

25. See Note 22.

26. Negus intvw, Dec 15, 1972, pp 81–82.

27. Memo, Dep DDR&E (SEAM) for DDR &E, subj: Predicted Commando Hunt VII Effectiveness, Sep 20, 1971.

28. Commando Hunt VII, p 14; Hartsook, *Vietnamization and Withdrawal*, pp 78–79.

29. Hist data record, Target Br, TFA, Apr–Jun 71, p 3; Annex C, Sep 22, 1971, to 7AF OPlan 715, Northeast Monsoon Plan.

30. Hist, TFA, Oct–Dec 71, pp 25–27.

31. *Ibid.*, pp 27–28.

32. Slay End of Tour Rprt, pp 21–22,; End of Tour Rprt; Col William A. Nugen, Dir/Command and Control, 7AF, and Asst Chief, Air Ops Div, MACV, 1972, Jan 5, 1973, pp 6–7; King intvw, pp 74–76.

33. End of Tour Rprt, Col Thomas J. Mathews, Dir/Int, Vice Comdr, and Comdr, TFA, 1972, Dec 31, 1972, p 2, hereafter cited as Mathews End of Tour Rprt.

34. Hist TFA, Oct–Dec 1971, pp 47–48.

35. Atch to ltr, TFA to 7AF, subj: Basic Sensor Field Plan, Commando Hunt VII, Dec 11, 1971.

36. Gindoff, *NVA Logistic System*, p 94.

37. Atch to ltr, TFA to 7AF, subj: Current TFA Operations, Mar 26, 1972.

38. Negus intvw, Dec 15, 1972, pp 71–72.

39. *Ibid.*, pp 74–75.

40. Slay End of Tour Rprt, pp 30–32; Corona Harvest, "Operations in Defense of South Vietnam," pp 37–38.

41. Hist, TFA, Jul–Sep 71, pp 37–38; Shields, *Igloo White, 1970–1971*, pp 58–60; msg, 7AF to TFA, 388th TFWg, 7ACC, subj: IMC Air Strikes in Acoustic Targeting Areas, Jul 13, 1971.

42. Capt Eugene A. Taylor, Analysis Br, Dir/Intelligence, TFA, Special Study Rprt, Double Counting of Vehicular Movement within a Sensor String Field in Steel Tiger, Jul 24, 1971.

43. Memo, INAI for TFA Historian, subj: Addendum to INAI History for the Period Jan–Mar 72, Apr 16, 1972.

44. Hist data record, Dir/Intelligence, TFA, Jan–Mar 72.

45. Gindoff, *NVA Logistic System*, pp 66–67.

46. *Ibid.*, pp 52–53, 60–63; hist data record, INAI, TFA, Jan–Mar 72; Secret Working Paper, Dir/Command and Control, 7AF, Orbit Info Summary, Oct 71.

47. Commando Hunt VII, pp 23–45.

48. Slay End of Tour Rprt, p 27.

49. Commando Hunt VII, pp 46–61.

50. Ltr, Lt Col Donald R. Grigsby, Chief, Electronic Warfare/Reconnaissance Div, 7AF, to Maj Taylor, subj: Commando Hunt VII Data Requirements (Your ltr, 21 Dec 71), Apr 24, 1972; quarterly hist rprt, Reconnaissance/Electronic Warfare Br, Dir/Op Plans, 7AF, Oct–Dec 71.

51. Commando Hunt VII, pp 61, 150, 206; quarterly hist rprt, Reconnaissance/Electronic Warfare Br, Dir/Op Plans, 7AF, Jan–Mar 72; msg, ASD to CINCPACAF, TAC, and MAC, 191616Z Jun 72, subj: Gunships, Sensors, and BDA Imagery.

52. Commando Hunt VII, p 7.

53. Memo, Dep DDR&E (SEAM) for DDR&E, subj: Vietnam Trip no 14 (11–22 Oct 71), Oct 26, 1971.

54. Melvin Porter, *Proud Deep Alpha* (Hq PACAF, Project CHECO, Jul 20, 1972), pp xii–xiii, 2–4, 12–21, 45; Commando Hunt VII, pp 144–49; Davidson, *Vietnam at War*, p 602.

55. Msg, CINCPAC to Adm Clary, Gen Clay, Gen Rosson, 210213Z Jan 72, retransmitting COMUSMACV 200945Z Jan 72.

56. Msg, TFA to 7AF, 291830Z Apr 72, subj: Contingency Plan for Steel Tiger East; Commando Hunt VII, p 61.

57. Msg, Gen Clay to Gen McNickle, 040015Z Apr 72, subj: Proposed SEA Operations.

58. Msg, TFA to 7AF, 140858Z Sep 72, subj: Sensor Field Status; hist, TFA, Apr–Jun 72, pp 2, 43.

59. Slay End of Tour Rprt, p 34.

60. App II to Annex D, Sep 22, 1971, to 7AF OPlan 715, Northeast Monsoon Campaign.

61. Slay End of Tour Rprt, pp 24–26, 32–34.

62. Mathews End of Tour Rprt, p 3.

Chapter 14

1. Clarke, *The Final Years*, pp 459–62; Davidson, *Vietnam at War*, pp 593–94.

2. Memo, SAF for SECDEF, subj: RVNAF Improvement and Modernization Program, Apr 6, 1971; see also: memo, SAF for SECDEF, subj: Military Vietnamization, atch to Air Staff Summary Sheet, Ofc of Special Asst for Vietnamization, subj: Military Vietnamization, Apr 10, 1971.

3. Ltr, Leonard Sullivan to John Kirk, COMUSMACV/ MACSA, Dec 17, 1969.

4. Ltr, Sullivan to Kirk, Jul 30, 1970.

5. *Ibid.*

6. Clarke, *The Final Years*, pp 418–20; Davidson, *Vietnam at War*, pp 585–88.

7. Memo, SECDEF for Service Secretaries and CJCS, subj: Military Vietnamization, Feb 19, 1971, atch to Air Staff Summary Sheet, Special Asst for Vietnamization, subj: same, Apr 10, 1971.

8. Msg, AFSSO 7AF to AFSSO CSAF, 030900Z Mar 71, subj: Military Vietnamization.

9. Memo, Dep DDR&E (SEAM) for DDR&E, subj: Preliminary Evaluation of Lam Son 719 and Proposed RVNAF Interdiction Alternatives, Apr 14, 1971.

10. Clarke, *The Final Years*, p 456.

11. Memo, Dep DDR&E (SEAM), for DDR&E, subj: Preliminary Evaluation of Lam Son 719 and Proposed RVNAF Interdiction Alternatives, Apr 14, 1971.

12. *Ibid.*

13. Hist, USMACV, 1969, pp F:III:4:8–9, 4:A:1.

14. *Ibid.*, pp F:III:4:5, 4:C:1.
15. *Ibid.*, pp F:III:4:2–3.
16. *Ibid.*, p F:III:4:9.
17. *Ibid.*, 1970, pp B:III:32–33.
18. *Ibid.*; hist, 56th SOWg, Jul–Sep 70, I, 49.
19. Hist, 56th SOWg, Jan–Mar 70, I, 52–53.
20. *Ibid.*, I, 51–52.
21. *Ibid.*, I, 49.
22. Hist, USMACV, 1970, p B:IX:3.
23. *Ibid.*, p B:IX:5.
24. Hist, CINCPAC, 1969, III, 155–56.
25. *Ibid.*, pp 156–58.
26. *Ibid.*, p 160.
27. *Public Papers of Richard Nixon, 1971*, pp 452–53.
28. Hist, CINCPAC, 1970, II, 215–16.
29. *Ibid.*, pp 216–17.
30. *Ibid.*, 1971, I, 185.
31. Msg, COMUSMACV to CINCPAC, 110920Z Jan 71, subj: Prairie Fire/Nickel Steel Progress Rprt 1464.
32. Command Hist, CINCPAC, 1969, III, 162.
33. Msg, COMUSMACV to CINCPAC, 311100Z Dec 71, subj: Prairie Fire/Nickel Steel Progress Rprt 1453.
34. Msg, COMUSMACV to CINCPAC, 220550Z Jan 71, subj: Footboy.
35. Hist, USMACV, 1971–1972, pp B:3:16–18, 26; DOD Rprt on Selected Air and Ground Operations in Cambodia and Laos, Sep 10, 1973.
36. Hist, USMACV, 1971–1972, p B:3:18.
37. *Ibid.*, pp B:3:26.
38. Hists, CINCPAC, 1968, III, 265–67, 1970, II, 222–24; msg, CINCPAC to COMUSMACV, 251247Z Dec 70, subj: Salem House Operating Authorities.
39. Hist, CINCPAC, 1970, II, 230; Shields, *Igloo White, 1970–1971*, pp 48–49.
40. Staff Summary Sheet, Dir/Ops Plans, 7AF, with atch, subj: Sensor Implants in Freedom Deal, Dec 18, 1970; Staff Summary Sheet, Dir/Command and Control, 7AF, subj: Cambodian Sensors Monitored by TACC-A, Feb 10, 1971.
41. Hist, CINCPAC, 1970, II, 226.
42. *Ibid.*, pp 228–29; hist, CINCPAC, 1971, I, 186–87; msg, CINCPAC to CINCPACFLT, CINCPACAF, *et al*, 260253Z Jan 72, retransmitting JCS to CINCPAC, 260032Z Jan 72, subj: Request for Standby Authorities.
43. Hist, USMACV, 1971–1972, p B:3:18; DOD Rprt on Selected Air and Ground Operations in Cambodia and Laos, Sep 10, 1973.
44. Credible Chase Study Rprt, Minigunship Concept for RVNAF Interdiction and Mobility Self-sufficiency, Ofc of Special Asst for Vietnamization, May 28, 1971.
45. Memo, Dep DDR&E (SEAM) for Brig Gen F. E. Karhohs, USA, Dir/Vietnam Task Force (ISA), subj: Vietnamization of Interdiction Ops, Feb 19, 1971.
46. Memo, Henry A. Kissinger to Under SECSTATE, Dep SECDEF, Dir/CIA, and CJCS, subj: Assessment of the Situation in South Vietnam, Apr 15, 1971.
47. Memo, SECDEF for Assst to the President for National Security Affairs, subj: Improvement and Modernization of the South Vietnamese Armed Forces, Apr 16, 1971.
48. Hist, JCS, *Vietnam, 1971–1973*, pt I, pp 327–31.

Chapter 15

1. Hist, JCS, *Vietnam, 1971–1973*, pt I, pp 333–34, 337.
2. Msgs, USAF SSO to PACAF SSO, 051955Z Mar 71, subj: Palletized Night Attack, USAF SSO to PACAF SSO, 100300Z Mar 71, subj: Palletized Night Attack.
3. Draft ltr, Leonard Sullivan to Georges Duval, MACSA, nd; James J. Haggerty, ed, *The 1970 Aerospace Yearbook* (Washington, 1970), p R:47; John W. R. Taylor, ed, *Jane's All the World Aircraft, 1973–1974* (London, 1973), pp 344–45.
4. Background Papers, Ofc of Special Asst for Vietnamization, Credible Chase Concept, Aug 5, 1971.
5. Tab A to memo, Dep DDR&E (SEAM) for DDR&E, subj: Preliminary Evaluation of Lam Son 719 and Proposed RVNAF Interdiction Alternatives, Apr 14, 1971; memo, SECDEF for Service Secretaries and Dir/DSPG, subj: Vietnamization of the Laotian Interdiction Campaign, Apr 20, 1971.
6. Ltr, Leonard Sullivan to Robert G. Gibson, CINCPAC Research and Engineering Consultant, Apr 27, 1971.
7. Atch to memo, Sully [Leonard Sullivan] for Mr. [Everett A.] Pyatt, May 17, 1971.
8. Msg, COMUSMACTHAI to CSAF, CINCPAC, *et al*, 161210Z Jul 71, subj: Pave Coin.

9. Credible Chase Study Rprt, Ofc of Special Asst for Vietnamization, Minigunship Concept for RVNAF Interdiction and Mobility Self-sufficiency, May 28, 1971.

10. Memo, Dep DDR&E (SEAM) for DDR&E, subj: Service, Agency, and JCS Responses to Proposed Laotian Interdiction Alternatives, Jun 30, 1971.

11. Memo, SECDEF for the Service Secretaries, CJCS, and Dir/DSPG, subj: RVNAF Interdiction Alternatives, Jul 2, 1971.

12. Memo, SECDEF for SAF, subj: Combat Evaluation of the Minigunship Concept, Jul 30, 1971; memo, SAF for SECDEF, subj: Combat Evaluation of the Minigunship Concept, Jul 12, 1971.

13. Msg, COMUSMACV to 7AF, 210635Z Aug 71, subj: Credible Chase, retransmitting CINCPAC to COMUSMACV and CINCPACAF, 210337 Aug 71.

14. Msgs, CSAF to AF Advisory Gp, Tan Son Nhut, 271937Z Aug 71, subj: Air Staff Briefing for Col Vo Dinh and Party, 7AF to CINCPACAF, 230201Z Sep 71, subj: Credible Chase.

15. Atch to ltr, Maj Gen James H. Watkins to MACV J–3, subj: Vietnamization of the Interdiction Effort, Oct 13, 1971.

16. Memo, SECDEF to CJCS, subj: Vietnamization of Interdiction Ops, Oct 8, 1971.

17. Memo, SAF for CSAF, subj: Credible Chase, Oct 21, 1971.

18. Msg, TAC to CINCPAC, 161615Z Oct 71, subj: Test of Credible Chase Concept.

19. Memo, Dep DDR&E (SEAM) for DDR&E, subj: Vietnam Trip (11–22 Oct 71), Oct 26, 1971.

20. Incl 2 to atch to ltr, MACV J–3 to Brig Gen W. H. Lanagan, USMC, and Col Van Kiem ARVN, subj: Minutes of CICC Meeting, Oct 19, 1971.

21. Ltr, CSAF to SAF, subj: Vietnamization of Interdiction, Nov 19, 1971.

22. Memo, SECDEF for CJCS, subj: Credible Chase Program, Nov 29, 1971.

23. Msgs, COMUSMACV to CJCS, 020115Z Dec 71, subj: Credible Chase, CINCPAC to CJCS, 020630Z Dec 71, subj: Credible Chase.

24. Msgs, MACV to CINCPAC, info JCS, 231135Z Dec 71, subj: Credible Chase Program, CINCPAC to JCS, 312245Z Dec 71, subj: Credible Chase Follow-on Program.

25. Memo, CJCS for SECDEF, subj: Credible Chase Program, Dec 10, 1971.

26. Hq TAC, OPlan XX, Jan 15, 1972; msgs, COMUSMACV to 7AF, 242129Z Jan 72, subj: Credible Chase Combat Evaluation, CINCPACAF to CSAF, 010331Z Feb 72, subj: Credible Chase Combat Evaluation; Memo for Record, Lt Col Russell D. Terpenning to Col [Raymond A.] Boyd, subj: Trip Rprt, Light Aircraft Conference, 4 Apr (PACAF), Apr 20, 1972; Hist, JCS, *Vietnam, 1971–1973*, pt I. pp 347–48.

27. Memo for Record, Frank Tapparo, Asia Div, Ofc of Asst SECDEF (Systems Analysis), subj: Visit to Credible Chase, May 23, 1972.

28. Hist, Ofc of Special Asst for Vietnamization, Jul–Dec 72, pp 15–17.

29. Briefing, Ofc of Special Asst for Vietnamization, Vietnamization of Interdiction, nd [ca. Oct 71].

30. Atch 3 to memo, Col Raymond A. Boyd for Chief AF Advisory Gp, Vietnam, subj: CRIMP Review, Nov 16, 1971.

31. *Ibid.*; msg, COMUSMACV to CINCPAC, 211625Z Jan 72, subj: Vietnamization of Interdiction Operations.

32. Msg, CINCPAC to JCS, 294036Z Jan 72, subj: Vietnamization of Interdiction Ops; hist, Ofc of Special Asst for Vietnamization, Jan–Apr 73, p 6.

33. Study Rprt, Ofc of Special Asst for Vietnamization, Evaluating CBU–55 Weapon for VNAF, Jun 2, 1971.

34. Ltr, Leonard Sullivan to John E. Kirk, MACSA, Mar 9, 1970.

35. Ltr, Dep DDR&E (SEAM) to COMUSMACV, Apr 10, 1971.

36. Msg, CINCPAC to JCS, 290436Z Jan 72, subj: Vietnamization of Interdiction Operations; App to memo, CJCS to SECDEF, JCSM 54–72, subj: Vietnamization of Interdiction Operations, Feb 14, 1972; study rprt, Evaluating CBU–55 Weapon System for the VNAF, Jun 2, 1971.

37. Annex B to Credible Chase Study Rprt on Minigunship Concept for RVNAF Interdiction and Mobility Self-sufficiency, May 28, 1971.

38. Ltr, Leonard Sullivan to Georges Duval, MACSA, Aug 9, 1971.

39. Memo, SECDEF for CJCS, subj: Improvement and Modernization of the RVNAF, May 17, 1971.

40. App to memo, CJCS for SECDEF, JCSM–274–71, subj: Improvement and Modernization of the Republic of Vietnam Armed Forces, Jun 15, 1971.

41. Memo, SECDEF for the Service Secretaries, CJCS, and Dir/DSPG, subj: RVNAF Interdiction Alternatives, Jul 2, 1971.

42. CINCPAC OPlan, Island Tree, Aug 5, 1971.

43. Memo for Record, Ofc of Asst SECDEF (ISA), Regional Programs, subj: Vietnamization Meeting with Secretary Laird, Sep 27, 1971.

44. Memo, SECDEF for CJCS, subj: Vietnamization of Interdiction Operations, Oct 8, 1971.

45. Msg, CINCPAC to CINCPACAF, 010003Z Sep 71, subj: Island Tree.

46. Memo, SECDEF for CJCS, subj: Vietnamization of Interdiction Operations, Oct 8, 1971.

47. Memo, Dep DDR&E (SEAM) for DDR&E, subj: Vietnam Trip no 14 (11–22 Oct 71), Oct 26, 1971.

48. *Ibid.*

49. Atch to ltr, Brig Gen Otis C. Moore to MACV J–3, subj: Vietnamization of the Interdiction Effort, Oct 13, 1971.

50. Msg, COMUSMACV to CINCPAC, 271106Z Oct 71, subj: Vietnamization of Interdiction Ops.

51. Memo, Dep DDR&E (SEAM) for DDR&E, subj: Vietnam Trip no 14 (11–22 Oct 71), Oct 26, 1971.

52. 7AF OPlan 732, Vietnamization of Interdiction, Nov 22, 1971.

53. Apps 3 and 5 to Annex C, 7AF OPlan 732, Nov 22, 1971; ltr, Maj Gen James H. Watkins to Lt Gen Tran Van Minh, Comdr, VNAF, Nov 13, 1971; msgs, 7AF to CINCPAC, 040830Z Dec 71, subj: After Visit Rprt, COMUSMACV to CINCPAC, 271106Z Oct 71, subj: Vietnamization of Interdiction Ops.

54. Atch to Staff Summary Sheet, 7AF Dir/Ops, subj: Vietnamization of Air Interdiction, Dec 7, 1971; memo, Lt Col Deafenbaugh for Dir/Ops, subj: VNAF Interdiction Record, Dec 14, 1971.

55. Msg, State to Vientiane, 161735Z Dec 71, subj: VNAF Interdiction Ops in Laos.

56. Msg, Vientiane to 7AF, 171120Z Dec 71, subj: none.

57. Msg, Vientiane to COMUSMACV, 081046Z Jan 72, subj: none.

58. Msg, AF Advisory Gp, Vietnam, to CINCPACAF, 260630Z Apr 72, subj: Progress of Vietnamization.

59. End of Tour Rprt, Maj Gen James H. Watkins, Chief, AF Advisory Gp, USMACV, 1971–1972, May 14, 1972.

60. Memo, Dep DDR&E (SEAM) for Brig Gen R. E. Pursley, subj: Plausible RVNAF Interdiction Program, Oct 27, 1971.

61. Msg, COMUSMACV to CINCPAC, 080921Z Nov 71, subj: Vietnamization of Interdiction.

62. Memo for Record, Dep DDR&E (SEAM), subj: Commentary on MACV Interdiction Strategy and Its Vietnamization Implications, Nov 18, 1971.

63. Memo, CJCS for SECDEF, JCSM–500–71, subj: Vietnamization of Interdiction Ops, Nov 12, 1971.

64. Memo, SECDEF for CJCS, subj: Vietnamization of Interdiction Ops, Dec 6, 1971.

65. Memo, SECDEF for CJCS, subj: Vietnamization of Interdiction, Mar 10, 1972.

66. Msg, JCS to CINCPAC, 062214Z Apr 72, subj: Progress of Vietnamization.

Chapter 16

1. Msg, COMUSMACV to CINCPAC, 201345Z Jun 71, subj: RVNAF Interdiction Capabilities.

2. 91st Cong, 2d Sess, *Investigation into the Electronic Battlefield Program*, p 147.

3. Msg, CINCUSARPAC to CINCPAC, 302300Z Jun 71, subj: RVNAF Interdiction Capabilities.

4. Msg, 7AF to CINCPACAF, 120015Z Jan 72, subj: U.S. Force Planning, SEA.

5. Hist, TFA, Jul–Sep 72, p 51.

6. Msg, CSAF to SAC, TAC, *et al*, 030020Z Feb 72, subj: Pave Onyx.

7. Msgs, Rome Air Development Center to 7AF, 072140Z Apr 72, subj: Pave Onyx; TFA to 7AF, 200215Z Apr 72, subj: Pave Onyx Activations in the Ban Dong Area; Gindoff, *NVA Logistic System*, p 75.

8. Msg, Rome Air Development Center to CSAF, 302030Z May 72, subj: Pave Onyx Cross Correlator.

9. Msg, TFA to 7AF, 191015A Apr 72, subj: Pave Onyx Acoustic Correlation.

10. Msg, TFA to 7AF, 110930Z May 72, subj: Pave Onyx Cross Correlation/Field Deployment.

11. Msg, CSAF to CINCPACAF, 011341Z May 72, subj: Pave Onyx Acoustic Cross Correlation.

12. Hist, TFA, Apr–Jun 72, p 34; Gindoff, *NVA Logistic System*, pp 85–88.

13. Msg, Rome Air Development Center to CSAF, 302030Z Mar 72, subj: Pave Onyx Cross Correlation.

14. Ltr, Lt Col Earl D. McClintock to TAWC, subj: TAWC Liaison Ofc Activity Rprt 7–72 (1–15 Apr 72), Apr 15, 1972.

15. Ltr, Lt Col Earl D. McClintock to TAWC, subj: TAWC Liaison Ofc Activity Rprt 9–72 (1–15 May 72), May 15, 1972.

16. Msg, TFA to 7AF, 191015Z Apr 72, subj: Pave Onyx Acoustic Correlation.

17. Msg, Rome Air Development Center to ASD Liaison Ofc, Tan Son Nhut, 131810Z May 72, subj: CORLOC.

18. Msgs, ASD Liaison Ofc, Tan Son Nhut, to Rome Air Development Center, 170150Z May 72 and 180730Z May 72, subj: Acoustic Gun Location; hist, TFA, Apr–Jun 72, pp 15–16.

19. Msg, 7AF to TFA, 190045Z May 72, subj: Development of Acoustic Gun Locating System.

20. Msg, AFSC to AFSC Liaison Ofc, Vietnam, and Rome Development Center, 192100Z May 72, subj: Acoustic Gun Detection.

21. Msg, TFA to 7AF, 220745Z Jun 72, subj: Acoustic Gun Locator System Limitations/Capabilities; hist, TFA, Apr–Jun 72, pp 23–24.

22. Hist, TFA, Jul–Sep 72, pp 17–18.

23. Hist, TFA, Apr–Jun 72, pp 22–30; msg, TFA to 7AF, 08 [illegible] Jun 72, subj: Gun Location System.

24. Msg, TFA to 7AF, 220745Z Jun 72, subj: Acoustic Gun Locator System Limitations/Capabilities; Memo for Record, Col Patrick H. Caulfield, Dir/Technical Ops, TFA, subj: Acugun Equipment Requirements, Jun 22, 1972.

25. Hist, TFA, Jul–Sep 72, pp 2, 25, 45; ltr, TAWC to TAC, subj: Quick Look Rprt on Artillery Locating System, Oct 31, 1972.

26. DSPG Documentary Supplement I, Jan 69–Aug 70, pp II:25–26.

27. Annex I to JCS Rprt, Vietnamization: RVNAF Improvement and Modernization (Phase III) and Related U.S. Planning, Jan 20, 1970; 91st Cong, 2d sess, *Investigation into the Electronic Battlefield Program*, p 13, 28; DSPG Documentary Supplement I, Jun 69–Aug 70. pp II:28.

28. Annex I to JCS Rprt, Vietnamization: RVNAF Improvement and Modernization (Phase III) and Related U.S. Planning, Jan 29, 1970.

29. Staff Paper, 7AF, VNAF Monitoring System in Pleiku Area, Dart II, Oct 12, 1971; 91st Cong, 2d sess, *Investigation into the Electonic Battlefield Program*, pp 124–25; ltr, Asst DCS/Ops, 7AF, to DCS/Plans, subj: 7AF OPlan 498–69, Combined Campaign Plan Quarterly Rprt (Your ltr, 26 Dec 69), Jan 7, 1970.

30. Atch to End of Tour Rprt, Significant VNAF Achievements from a Headquarters Point of View, Col William A. Lafferty, Dir/Plans and Programs, AF Advisory Gp, Vietnam, 1969–71, Jun 9, 1971.

31. Memo, SECDEF to SECARMY, SECNAV, SAF, Dir/DSPG, subj: Vietnamization of the Laotian Interdiction Campaign, Apr 20, 1971.

32. Credible Chase Study Rprt, Asst for Vietnamization, DCS/ Plans and Ops, Minigunship for RVNAF Interdiction and Mobility Self-sufficiency, May 28, 1971.

33. Memo, Dir/DSPG for Dep SECDEF, subj: Vietnamization of Interdiction Efforts, Jun 9, 1971.

34. Msg, CINCPAC to COMUSMACV, 040449Z Jun 71, subj: RVNAF Interdiction Capabilities.

35. Msg, CINCPACAF to CINCPAC, 222051Z Jun 71, subj: RVNAF Interdiction Capabilities.

36. Msg, CINCUSARPAC to CINCPAC, 302300Z Jun 71, subj: RVNAF Interdiction Capabilities.

37. Memo, SECDEF for CJCS, subj: Vietnamization of Interdiction Ops, Oct 8, 1971.

38. Position Paper, Ofc of Special Asst for Vietnamization, VNAF Sensor Readout/Delivery Capability, Oct 19, 1971.

39. Atch 6 to Tab F to Air Staff Summary Sheet, Ofc of Special Asst for Vietnamization, subj: Vietnamization of Interdiction, Nov 12, 1971.

40. Memo for Record, MACV J–3, subj: Rprt of MR I Sensor Conference (13–14 Jan 72), Jan 24, 1972.

41. Ltr, Capt Willie A. Robert, Jr., to Dir/Ops, AF Advisory Gp, Vietnam, subj: Memo for Record (Trip Rprt: Deployment of C–47 Aircraft from Tan Son Nhut to Da Nang for Sensor Orbit), nd [ca. Apr 72].

42. Atch to Staff Summary Sheet, Dir/Ops, AF Advisory Gp, Vietnam, subj: Status of VNAF Sensor Program, May 31, 1972; hist, TFA, Jul– Sep 72, p 40.

43. Msg, 7AF to CINCPACAF, 160630Z Oct 71, subj: Vietnamization of Interdiction Ops; Hq PACAF, Book of Talking and Background Papers, Vietnamization of the Interdiction Effort, Oct 17, 1971; Position Paper, Ofc of Special Assistant for Vietnamization, VNAF Sensor/Readout Capability, Oct 19, 1971.

44. Msgs, USAFTAWC to AF Advisory Gp, Vietnam, 072300Z Dec 71, subj: Sensor Program; COMUSMACV to CINCPAC, 171045Z Apr 72,

subj: Progress of Vietnamization; app to memo, CJCS for SECDEF, JCSM–54–72, subj: Vietnamization of Interdiction Ops, Feb 14, 1972; atch to Staff Summary Sheet, Dir/Ops, AF Advisory Gp, Vietnam, subj: Status of VNAF Sensor Program, May 31, 1972.

45. Msg, CINCPAC to CINCPACAF and CINCUSARPAC, 210213Z Jan 72, retransmitting COMUSMACV to CINCPAC, 200945Z Jan 72.

46. Msgs, CINCPAC to CJCS, 210149Z Jan 72, and JCS to CINCPAC, 260032Z Jan 72, subj: Request for Standby Authorities.

47. 91st Cong, 2d sess, *Investigation into the Electronic Battlefield Program*, p 3.

48. Hearings before a Subcommittee of the House Committee on Appropriations, 92d Cong, 2d sess, *Department of Defense Appropriations for 1973*, pt 8, p 1006.

49. *Ibid.*, pp 1007–8.

50. House Committee on Appropriations, Rprt no 92, *Department of Defense Appropriations Bill, 1973, Electronics and Telecommunications Equipment*, Sep 11, 1972, p 199.

51. Msg, 7AF to CINCPACF, 120015Z Jan 72, subj: U.S. Force Planning, SEA.

52. Msg, 13AF to 7AF, 100905Z Jul 72, subj: Task Force Alpha.

53. Msg, MACV Technical Assistance Coordinator to Dep DDR&E (SEAM), 250725Z Sep 72.

54. Staff Summary Sheet, 7AF Dir/Plans, subj: Phasedown of TFA, Aug 18, 1972; msgs, 13AF to PACAF, 120310Z Oct 72, subj: TFA Inactivation; JCS to CINCPAC, 182217Z Nov 72, subj: Igloo White System; memo, Dep Asst SECDEF (Resources and Management) for DDR &E, Asst SECDEF (ISA), and Asst SECDEF (Systems and Analysis), subj: Igloo White, Nov 14, 1972.

55. Minutes, Udorn Special Meeting (afternoon session), Sep 9, 1968.

56. Msg, JCS to CINCPAC, 182217Z Nov 72, subj: Igloo White System.

57. Msg, CINCPACAF to CINCPAC, 210225Z Nov 72, subj: Igloo White System.

58. Msg, COMUSMACV to CINCPAC, 210331Z Nov 72, subj: Post Hostilities Sensor Surveillance.

59. Msg, COMUSMACV to CINCPAC, 230345Z Nov 72, subj: Post Hostilities Sensor Surveillance System.

60. Msg, JCS to CINCPAC, 231942Z Nov 72, subj: Implantation of Sensors.

61. Msg, CINCPAC to JCS, 242230Z Nov 72, subj: Implantation of Sensors.

62. Memo, JCS for SECDEF, JCSM–449–72, subj: Post Hostilities Sensor Surveillance System, Nov 22, 1972.

63. Memo, JCS for SECDEF, JCSM–509–72, subj: Post Hostilities Surveillance System, Nov 29, 1972.

64. Msg, JCS to CINCPAC, 012352Z Dec 72, subj: Implantation of Sensors.

65. Msg, COMUSMACV to CINCPAC, 031020Z Dec 72, subj: Implantation of Sensors.

66. Disposition Form, MACV Dir/Ops, subj: Post Hostilities Sensor System, nd [ca. Dec 72]; msg, COMUSMACV to CINCPAC, subj: Post Hostilities Sensor Surveillance System, nd [ca. Dec 72].

67. Msgs, 7AF to CINCPACAF, nd [ca. Dec 72], subj: Post Hostilities Surveillance System; 7AF to CINCPACAF and 13AF, 110812Z Dec 72, subj: Dart Ops; TFA to CINCPACAF, 13AF, *et al*, 210630Z Dec 72, subj: Amendment to 13AF PAD 73–13–4 TFA.

68. Msg, CINCPACAF to 7AF, 13AF, *et al*, 230403Z Dec 72, subj: DART Requirements.

69. Msg, 5621 TCS/DART to MACV, 210240Z Jan 73, subj: Recap of DART Status/Capabilities.

70. Hists, USSAG, Feb 15–Mar 31, 1973, p 70, Apr–Jun 73, p 105; 91st Cong, 2d sess, *Investigation into the Electronic Battlefield Program*, pp 147–48.

Chapter 17

1. *Pentagon Papers: Gravel Edition*, IV, pp 115–16, 119–20, 126–31.

2. Hist, USMACV, 1967, III, pp 1090–1102; 1968, II, pp 911–19.

3. Van Staaveren, hist, Task Force Alpha, pp 34–43, 47–53.

4. Slay End of Tour Rprt, p 89.

5. Shaplen, *Bitter Victory*, p 160.

6. Slay End of Tour Rprt, pp 82–83, 85–89.

7. End of Tour Rprt, Col William L. Skliar, Chief, Tactical Air Control Center, 1970–71, nd, p 9.

8. Earl H. Tilford, Jr., *Setup: What the Air Force Did in Vietnam and Why* (Maxwell AFB, Alabama: Air University Press, 1991), pp 219–20

9. Slay End of Tour Rprt, p 34.

10. Killpack End of Tour Rprt, pp 13, 16.

Notes to pages 294–303

11. Slay End of Tour Rprt, p 32.
12. *Ibid.*, pp 32–34.
13. Shaplen, *Bitter Victory*, pp 158–59.
14. Hq PACAF, Summary of Air Ops in SEA, Feb 1973; Slay End of Tour Rprt, pp 20–21.
15. End of Tour Rprts, 1st Lt W. W. Working, Target Analysis Officer, TFA, 1968–69, nd, n.p.; Col James H. Radd, Dir/Tactics and Combat Systems, DCS/Ops, 7AF, 1969–70, nd, p 3.
16. Shaplen, *Bitter Victory*, p 160; Denis Warner, *Certain Victory: How Hanoi Won the War* (Kansas City: Sheed Andrews and McMeel, 1978), pp 114–15; Tad Szulc, *The Illusion of Peace: Foreign Policy in the Nixon Years* (New York: Viking Press, 1978), p 50.
17. Commando Hunt, p 81; Commando Hunt III, p 82; Commando Hunt V, p 57; Commando Hunt VII, p 82.
18. Evans End of Tour Rprt, pp 2–3, 5.
19. Truong Nhu T'ang, *A Vietcong Memoir*, pp 170–71.
20. Tran Van Tra, *History of the Bulwark B–2 Theater, V: Concluding the 30 Years War; Southeast Asia Crisis Report No. 1247* (Washington: Foreign Broadcast Information Service, Feb 2, 1983), p 49.
21. Thompson and Frizzell, *Vietnam*, pp 148–49.
22. *Ibid.*, p 141.
23. Briefing by Charles B. Liddell, Jr., Hq PACAF, Ops Analysis Ofc, Steel Tiger Output—Supply Limited or Demand Limited?, Jul 13, 1972.
24. Herman Gilster, 'Air Interdiction in a Protracted War: An Economic Evaluation," *Air University Review*, May–Jun 1977, p 16, cited hereafter as Gilster, 'Economic Evaluation"; oral comments by Lt Col Vance O. Mitchell, USAF, Ret., former AC–119K navigator and member of panel evaluating this manuscript, Dec 9, 1993.
25. William W. Momyer, *Air Power in Three Wars* (no publisher, nd, reprint, Office of Air Force History, 1985), p 207.
26. Gilster, 'Economic Evaluation," pp 16–17.
27. *Public Papers of the Presidents of the United States, Richard Nixon, 1970*, p 536; Karnow, *Vietnam*, pp 609–12.
28. Dir/Mgt Analysis, Hq USAF, USAF Mgt Analysis, Southeast Asia, Nov 1, 1968, pp SEA i, SEA 41; Commando Hunt, p 189; Commando Hunt III, p 125; Commando Hunt V, p 93; Commando Hunt VII, p 135.
29. Earl H. Tilford, Jr., *Search and Rescue in Southeast Asia, 1961–1975* (Washington: Office of Air Force History, 1980), pp 121, 133, 155.
30. *Report of the Electronic Battlefield Subcommittee of the Preparedness Investigating Subcommittee of the Senate Committee on Armed Services*, 92d Congress, 1st Session, pp 12–13.
31. Gilster, 'Economic Evaluation," pp 17–18; Thompson and Frizzell, *Vietnam*, pp 145–46.
32. Westmoreland, *A Soldier Reports*, pp 329–31.
33. Briefing notes by C. V. Sturdevant, Hq PACAF, Ops Analysis Ofc, Comments on Output Estimates, May 20, 1972.
34. Atch to ltr, DCS/Plans to Vice CSAF, subj: Contributions of the Igloo White System, Mar 12, 1971.

328

Glossary

A–1	The Douglas Skyraider, a piston-powered, single-engine attack plane built in one- or two-place versions. Because of its age—it saw service as the Navy's AD–1 during the Korean War—it was nicknamed the Spad, after the World War I fighter.
A–6	The Grumman Intruder, a two-place, twin-jet attack plane flown by the Navy and Marine Corps.
A–7	A single-place, single-jet attack plane built by Ling Temco Vought and flown by the Navy and Air Force.
A–26	A twin-engine, shoulder-wing attack plane, powered by piston engines and built by Douglas Aircraft, that served in World War II, the Korean War, and the Vietnam conflict.
A–37	An attack version of the T–37 trainer.
AAA	antiaircraft artillery.
ABCCC	Airborne battlefield command and control center, a C-130 fitted out to control air traffic and direct strikes.
AC–47	Gunship version of the C–47 transport.
AC–119G	Gunship version of the AC–119 transport.
AC–119K	An AC-119 with auxiliary jet engines.
AC–123A	C–123 transport fitted with sensors to locate targets at night and a bomb dispenser to attack them. (Black Spot)
AC–130	Gunship version of the C–130.
ACC	aircraft control center.
ACIC	Aeronautical Chart and Information Center.
Acoubuoy	An acoustic sensor designed to hang from trees by its parachute.
Acousid	An acoustic and seismic intrusion detector capable of reacting to sound or vibration in the ground.
Acoustic gun locating	The attempt to employ acoustic sensors to pinpoint North Vietnamese artillery pieces.
Acoustic targeting	An area monitored by acoustic sensors in an attempt to locate truck parks and similar installations.
ACRP	Airborne Communications Reconnaissance Program.
ACSq	air commando squadron.
Acugun	acoustic gun locating.
ACWg	air commando wing.
Adm.	Admiral.
Adsid	An air delivered seismic intrusion detector designed to be dropped from jet aircraft.
AFLC	Air Force Logistics Command.
AFSC	Air Force Systems Command.
AFSSO	Air Force Special Security Office.
AIG	address indicating group.
AMTI	airborne moving target indicator.
AOC	air operations center.
AP–2H	A Navy OP-2E fitted out for interdiction. See TRIM.

Glossary

Arc Light	B-52 operations in Southeast Asia.
ARPA	Advanced Research Projects Agency.
ARVN	Army of the Republic of Vietnam.
ASD	Aeronautical Systems Division.
ASI	Aerospace Studies Institute.
A Shau Valley	A terrain feature that served as a conduit for enemy supplies and reinforcements destined from the Ho Chi Minh Trail in southern Laos to northwestern South Vietnam.
AU–23	A single-engine Fairchild Turboporter light transport fitted out as a minigunship.
AU–24	A Helio Stallion single-engine light transport fitted out as a minigunship.
B–52	The Boeing Stratofortress, an eight-jet strategic bomber.
B–57	The Canberra, a British-designed, twin-jet medium bomber built in the United States by Martin.
Bat Cat	An EC–121 aircraft that relayed information from sensors to a control center.
BDA	bomb damage assessment.
Black Crow	An airborne sensor designed to detect the electronic emissions from the ignition systems of gasoline engines.
Black Spot	A Fairchild C-123 transport equipped to locate and destroy targets at night.
Blindbat	A C-130 modified to locate and illuminate targets at night.
blocking belt	A series of interdiction points covering all known roads and bypasses at a given chokepoint.
blocking point	An interdiction point.
BLU	bomb live unit.
BLU–24	An antipersonnel bomblet used with the CBU-24.
BLU–59	An antipersonnel bomblet fuzed for random detonation and used with the CBU-49.
BLU–66	An antipersonnel bomblet used with the CBU-46.
Blue Orbit	One of the locations from which relay aircraft retransmitted sensor signals.
Brown Beaver	An EC-47, operating out of Nakhon Phanom; in direct contact with forward air controllers, it tried to alert them to the location of radio transmitters it had pinpointed.
C–7	The twin-engine, piston-powered de Havilland Caribou; originally a U.S. Army transport, turned over to the Air Force in 1967.
C–47	A low-wing Douglas transport, designed in the 1930s and powered by two radial piston engines.
C–119	A twin-boom Fairchild transport; two radial engines powered the G model, but the K version also had two auxiliary jet engines.
C–123	A Fairchild transport originally powered by two piston engines; the K model also mounted a pair of auxiliary jets.
C–130	The Lockheed Hercules, a medium-range transport powered by four turboprop engines.
Candlestick	A C-123 modified to locate and illuminate targets at night.
Capt.	Captain.
CBU	Cluster bomb unit; a weapon featuring a dispenser that releases a large number of small bomblets; the dispenser may remain attached to the aircraft or open after release to scatter its contents.
CBU-24	A cluster bomb unit designed for flak suppression.

CBU–26	A cluster bomb unit dispensing antipersonnel munitions capable of penetrating a jungle canopy before exploding.
CBU–49	A cluster bomb unit dispensing delayed-action munitions.
CBU–52	A cluster bomb unit dispensing antipersonnel bomblets also employed against vehicles.
CBU–55	A cluster bomb dispensing canisters of an explosive gas similar to propane.
CBU–58	Replacement for the CBU-24.
CH–3	A twin-turbine, single-rotor helicopter built by Sikorsky for the Air Force and Navy.
CH–34	A single-engine, single-rotor Sikorsky helicopter, older and less powerful than the CH-3.
CH–53	A twin-turbine Sikorsky helicopter, with a six-bladed overhead rotor, flown by the Marine Corps and the Air Force.
CHECO	Contemporary Historical Evaluation (later Examination) of Counterinsurgency (later Combat and eventually Current) Operations.
Choke point	An area where the nature of the terrain limits the choice of transit routes and simplifies interdiction.
The "Chokes"	The area southwest of Ban Karai Pass where several highways converged.
CIA	Central Intelligence Agency.
CICC	Combined Interdiction Coordinating Committee; a coordinating group organized at Saigon to oversee regional interdiction operations.
CINCPAC	Commander in Chief, Pacific Command.
CINCPACAF	Commander in Chief, Pacific Air Forces.
CINCPACFLT	Commander in Chief, Pacific Fleet.
CINCSAC	Commander in Chief, Strategic Air Command.
CINCUSARPAC	Commander in Chief, United States Army, Pacific.
CINCUSAFE	Commander in Chief, United States Air Forces in Europe.
CJCS	The Chairman, Joint Chiefs of Staff.
Cluster bomb unit	See CBU.
CO	commanding officer.
Cobra	A draft plan for aerial interdiction in southern North Vietnam and the panhandle of Laos.
Col.	Colonel.
Combat King	Combat evaluation of the AC-119K gunship.
Combat Sierra	An attempt to use a radar transponder, dropped from a gunship, as an aiming point for B-52s.
Combined Interdiction Coordinating Committee	See CICC.
Combat Spyspot	A ground-based radar used to direct air strikes, especially by B–52s.
Cooper-Church Amendent	A rider to defense appropriations legislation for fiscal 1971 that forbade the introduction of American ground troops into Thailand, Laos, or Cambodia; sponsored by Senators John Sherman Cooper and Frank Church.
Comdr.	Commander.
commandable microphone	A type of acoustic sensor that could be turned on or off by remote control.
Commando Bolt	The use of sensor strings to determine the arrival of a convoy at a selected point of impact, the Loran coordinates of which were known

Glossary

	to strike aircraft.
Commando Hunt	One of a series of seven aerial interdiction operations conducted against the Ho Chi Minh Trail in southern Laos.
Commando Nail	Night and all-weather bombing by radar-equipped aircraft.
Commando Sabre	A project to test the F-100 as an aircraft for forward air controllers.
Commando Scarf	A project for dropping old stocks of gravel mines before the explosive became inert.
COMMIKE	Commandable microphone.
Commo	communication.
COMNAVFORV	Commander, Naval Forces, Vietnam.
Compass Flag	An attempt to use the QU-22 for communications reconnaissance.
COMUSMACTHAI	Commander, Unites States Military Assistance Command, Thailand.
COMUSMACV	Commander, United States Military Assistance Command, Vietnam.
Copperhead	Call sign of the Commando Bolt control team.
CORLOC	Correlation locating. See cross correlator.
Corona Harvest	An Air Force project to gather data on the Vietnam War.
Coronet Ink	An airborne camouflage detector.
Credible Chase	A program to convert a light utility transport into a minigunship.
CRIMP	Consolidated RVNAF Improvement and Modernization Plan.
cross correlator	The compass and overlay used with the Pave Onyx missile locating system in determining the point of origin of generator noise associated with surface-to-air missile sites.
CS	A type of tear gas.
CSAF	Chief of Staff, United States Air Force.
CY	calendar year.
DART	deployable automatic relay terminal.
DCPG	Defense Communications Planning Group.
DCS	Deputy Chief of Staff.
D/D	destroyed or damaged.
DDR&E	Director, Defense Research and Engineering.
Defense Communications Planning Group	The organization responsible for the equipment needed to translate Project Jason's recommendations into reality and establish an air-supported electronic barrier to infiltration. See Defense Special Projects Group.
Defense Special Projects Group	Successor to the Defense Communications Planning Group.
Demilitarized zone	A buffer established in 1954 between the territories that became North Vietnam and South Vietnam.
Dep	deputy.
Deployable automatic relay terminal	Portable equipment, originally mounted in a van, for receiving and interpreting sensor data.
Desert Rat	An operation, launched from southwestern Laos in conjunction with Lam Son 719 and designed to disrupt logistics activity around Muong Phine.
Destructor	A 500-pound magnetic-fuzed antivehicular mine.
Det	detachment.
DIA	Defense Intelligence Agency.
Diamond Arrow	A Lao operation in the fall of 1969 that cleared the area between Saravane and Ban Toumlan.
Dir	director, directorate.
DISUM	daily intelligence summary.

DIT	Director of Targets.
DITA	An element of the Directorate of Intelligence, Task Force Alpha.
DITT	Deputy Director of Targets.
DMPI	designated mean point of impact.
DMZ	demilitarized zone.
DO	Director of Operations.
DOC	Directorate of Combat Operations.
DOCO	An element of the Directorate of Combat Operations, Seventh Air Force.
DOD	Department of Defense.
Dragontooth	A mine weighing less than an ounce but capable of inflicting wounds or puncturing truck tires.
Dry season	The northeast monsoon, a period of dry weather in southern Laos, usually lasting from November into March.
DSPG	Defense Special Projects Group.
Duck Blind	The use of sensors by ground forces within South Vietnam.
Duel Blade	The line of sensor-supported outposts just south of the demilitarized zone.
Dump Truck	During the combat test of air-supported interdiction, that element of the electronic barrier in southern Laos dealing with troop infiltration.
EA-3	Navy version of the EB-66.
EA–6	A Grumman A–6 fitted out for electronic warfare.
EB–66	An Air Force twin-jet light bomber modified to intercept or jam enemy electronic signals; originally built by Douglas for the Navy.
EC–47	A C–47 transport modified to intercept enemy radio traffic and locate transmitters.
EC–121	A Lockheed Superconstellation transport fitted out to relay radio traffic or interpret or relay the radio signals from sensors planted to detect hostile movement.
Earth Angel	Reconnaissance patrols made up of three or four defectors from the North Vietnamese Army.
EDET	Engine detector. See ignition detector.
Electro-optically guided bomb	A bomb fitted with movable fins and a homing device sensitive to contrasts in reflected light.
Encl	enclosure.
F–4	The McDonnell Douglas Phantom, a twin-jet, two-place tactical fighter flown by the Navy, Air Force, and Marine Corps.
F–100	The North American Super Sabre, a single-jet tactical fighter built in single-seat and two-place models.
F–105	The Republic Thunderchief, a single-jet tactical fighter; a two-place model was armed with antiradiation missiles and used to suppress enemy radar.
FAC	Forward Air Controller.
Fadsid	The fighter air-delivered seismic intrusion detector, an unsuccessful type of sensor.
FCS	fire control system.
Ferret III	An EC-121 sensor relay aircraft carrying equipment for plotting sensor activations.
Fishhook	The portion of Cambodia east of Snuol and Mimot that juts into South Vietnam; a base area used by the North Vietnamese and Viet Cong.
559th Transportation Group	The North Vietnamese military organization that operated the Ho Chi Minh Trail.

Glossary

Flasher	A team of aircraft that, when alerted by a controller at the Infiltration Surveillance Center, relied upon Loran to bomb a specific Commando Bolt impact point.
Footboy	Covert operations against North Vietnam launched by the United States Military Assistance Command's Studies and Observations Group.
Fountain Pen	A plan for psychological operations in Laos.
470th Transportation Group	The North Vietnamese military organization that operated the extension of the Ho Chi Minh Trail from Laos into Cambodia.
Free-fire zone	An area where the unrestricted delivery or jettison of aerial munitions is permitted.
Free-strike zone	See free-fire zone.
Freedom Deal	The air interdiction zone established in Cambodia following the 1970 invasion.
Fuel-Air Munition	A bomb employing an explosive gas like propane; see CBU–55.
Funny bomb	See M36.
Gatling gun	Nickname for the multibarrel weapons used in Air Force gunships.
Gauntlet	A two-phase offensive conducted in southwestern Laos from early September until mid-November 1970.
GCI	ground-controlled intercept.
Gen.	General.
Gp	group.
Grand Slam	Aerial photography of the demilitarized zone conducted in the spring of 1969.
Gravel	pebble-sized explosive mines.
Green Orbit	One of the locations from which relay aircraft retransmitted sensor signals.
Green Weenie	A laser modified to give off visible light to illuminate targets.
Ground surveillance monitor	A technician at the Infiltration Surveillance Center who analyzed sensor data.
Gun location system	See acoustic gun locating.
Gunship II	The AC-130 prototype.
GVN	Government of Vietnam.
Hark	A type of radio used by roadwatch teams to report directly to airborne controllers.
Headshed	Call sign for the two cells, Headshed I and II, at the Task Force Alpha command and control center during Commando Hunt VII. See Termite.
Hist	history.
Ho Chi Minh Trail	A complex of roads, trails, and waterways that carried men and cargo from north Vietnam through southern Laos to South Vietnam and Cambodia.
Hq	headquarters.
Hunter-killer	A team of aircraft, one of which locates targets for another to attack.
Hz	Hertz, a measure of electro-magnetic frequency.
Iaw	in accordance with.
IBM 360/40	The original computer installed at the Infiltration Surveillance Center.
IBM 360/65	The type of computer used at the Infiltration Center during the Commando Hunt operations.
IBM 2250	A display console used at the Infiltration Surveillance Center, especially for Commando Bolt activity.

Igloo White	The air-supported, electronic, anti-infiltration system that resulted from Project Jason; covered the Ho Chi Minh Trail and monitored from a surveillance center at the Nakhon Phanom Royal Thai Air Base. Successor to Muscle Shoals.
Ignition detector	A sensor that reacted to the electromagnetic emissions from the ignition system of a gasoline engine. See Black Crow; EDET.
IMC	instrument meteorological conditions.
INAI	Analysis Division, Directorate of Intelligence, Task Force Alpha.
Infiltration surveillance center	The installation at Nakhon Phanom Air Base, Thailand, that received, stored, and interpreted sensor data in order to provide intelligence, issue target advisories, or direct air strikes.
Ink	An airborne camouflage detector.
Interdiction point	A road cut surrounded by antipersonnel and antivehicular mines.
Interstation	A subsector headquarters on the Ho Chi Minh Trail controlling both troop infiltration and truck traffic.
Invert	The call sign of the aircraft control and reporting post that functioned at Nakhon Phanom during the early weeks of Operation Commando Hunt.
ISA	International Security Affairs.
ISC	Infiltration Surveillance Center.
Island Tree	A combined interdiction plan drafted in the summer of 1970 but never formally adopted; an attempt to locate troop infiltration routes in southern Laos.
J–3	The operations section of a joint staff.
Jason	A study, launched by the Department of Defense, that resulted in a recommendation that the United States establish an air-supported electronic barrier to infiltration through Laos.
JCS	Joint Chiefs of Staff.
JCSM	Joint Chiefs of Staff Memorandum.
JTF	joint task force.
Junction City, Junior	A Lao operation that resulted in the temporary occupation of Muong Phine during September and October 1969.
JUSMAGTHAI	Joint United States Military Advisory Group, Thailand.
Karst	Pillar-shaped limestone formations common in southern Laos.
Khmer Rouge	The Cambodian communist movement and its armed forces.
Lam Son	A village where Le Loi, a Fifteenth Century Vietnamese leader, defeated the Chinese, a name frequently used for South Vietnamese operations like Lam Son 719, the invasion of southern Laos in 1971.
Laser-guided bomb	A bomb fitted with movable fins and a homing device sensitive to the reflected energy of a laser beam.
Left Jab	An operation, conducted in June 1969 by Lao forces, to relieve pressure on Attopeu and locate targets for air attack.
LGB	laser-guided bomb.
Liberation Route	The branch of the Ho Chi Minh Trail that carried men and supplies to Cambodia. See 470th Transportation Group.
Loran	Long-Range Radio Aids to Navigation, a system based upon the difference in time required for electronic signals to travel to an aircraft from two different transmitters on the ground.
Lt.	Lieutenant.
Lt. Col.	Lieutenant Colonel.
Lt. Gen.	Lieutenant General.

Glossary

M36	The so-called funny bomb, an incendiary weapon that scattered 182 thermite bomblets over an area the size of a football field.
MAC	Military Airlift Command.
MACSA	The studies and analysis section on the staff of the United States Military Assistance Command, Vietnam.
MACV	Military Assistance Command, Vietnam.
Maj.	Major.
Maj. Gen.	Major General.
Menu	The operation, March 1969–May 1970, during which B–52s secretly bombed North Vietnamese and Viet Cong bases in Cambodia; the targets bore the nicknames Lunch, Dinner, Breakfast, Snack, and Dessert.
MiG	An aircraft designed by the Mikoyan-Gurevich design bureau.
MiG–19	A twin-engine, Soviet-built, jet interceptor flown by the North Vietnamese.
MiG–21	A single-engine, Soviet-built, jet interceptor flown by the North Vietnamese.
Minigunship	A light aircraft mounting a side-firing multibarrel cannon.
Misch munitions	A variety of 40-mm rounds lined with a flint-like substance that shattered upon detonation and caused sparks when the shards struck a hard surface.
Mk 36	A 500-pound magnetic-fuzed antivehicular mine, nicknamed the Destructor.
Mk 82	A 500-pound high-explosive bomb.
MR	Military Region.
Msg	message.
Mud River	During combat testing of air-supported interdiction, that element of the electronic barrier in southern Laos dealing with vehicles.
Munitions package	A combination of laser-guided bombs, antipersonnel, and antivehicular mines used to establish an interdiction point.
Muscle Shoals	The air-supported antivehicular and antipersonnel interdiction of the Ho Chi Minh Trail, as deployed and tested between September 67 and June 68. In the latter month Muscle Shoals became Igloo White.
Nail	Call sign of forward air controllers operating out of Nakhon Phanom.
Napalm	The jellied petroleum used in fire bombs.
Nd	no date.
Neutralize	The aerial bombardment of enemy forces massing near Con Thien, South Vietnam, in late 1967.
Nickel Steel	Operations in the demilitarized zone launched by the Studies and Observations Group, United States Military Assistance Command, Vietnam.
Night observation device	A refinement of the starlight scope light intensifier.
Nite Owl	An attempt, in the fall of 1969, to employ forward air controllers in F–4s against chokepoints near Mu Gia and Ban Karai Passes.
Norden bombsight	Invented by Carl Norden, this optical device saw extensive service during World War II. The OP-2E used it when planting sensors in southern Laos.
northeast monsoon	A period of dry weather in southern Laos, usually lasting from November into March.
NPIC	National Photographic Interpretation Center.
NSA	National Security Agency.

NVA	North Vietnamese Army.
NVN	North Vietnam.
O–1	A single-engine, two-place, light monoplane built by Cessna and used by forward air controllers.
O–2	A two-place, twin-boom light monoplane, with piston engines mounted forward and aft of the cabin. The Air Force purchased the aircraft from Cessna for use by forward air controllers.
OP-2E	A Lockheed patrol plane, flown by Navy crews, modified for planting electronic sensors.
OV–1	The Grumman Mohawk, a two-place, twin-turboprop battlefield surveillance aircraft flown by the Army.
OV–10	The North American Rockwell Bronco, a two-place, twin-boom, twin turboprop counterinsurgency aircraft flown by the Air Force and Marine Corps.
OPlan	Operations Plan.
OpOrd	Operations Order.
Orgy	A B-52 operation conducted on March 6, 1972, against an apparently occupied bivouac site on the troop infiltration route through southern Laos.
PACAF	Pacific Air Forces.
PAD	program action directive.
Panther	A team of two strike aircraft and a forward air controller. When alerted by the Infiltration Surveillance Center, the forward air controller used a light intensification device to find trucks that had triggered a string of Commando Bolt sensors.
Partially validated Arc Light area	A previously cleared B-52 target that required only last-minute confirmation from the embassy at Vientiane before an attack could be launched.
Pathet Lao	Land of the Lao, the name chosen by the communist faction in Laos and applied to its armed forces.
Pave Aegis	An AC-130 mounting a 105-mm howitzer.
Pave Cap	A development project intended to produce a pallet-mounted multi-barrel cannon.
Pave Coin	The evaluation in Thailand of a light aircraft for general counterinsurgency missions, including gunship operations.
Pave Eagle	The attempt to employ the QU-22 as a sensor relay aircraft.
Pave Knife	A pod-mounted laser target designator fitted in an F-4.
Pave Nail	An OV-10 using a laser to mark targets for fighter-bombers carrying laser-guided bombs.
Pave Onyx	An Air Force effort to deploy a system for locating surface-to-air missile sites on the Ho Chi Minh Trail.
Pave Pronto	A series of AC-130 modifications based on the AC-130 Surprise Package gunship. See Surprise Package.
Pave Spectre	A longer-range model of the C-130 fitted out as a gunship.
Paveway (also Pave Way)	The overall name for the use of the F-4 to release laser-guided or electro-optically guided bombs.
Phu Dung	See Prairie Fire.
PI	photo interpretation.
POL	petroleum, oil, lubricants.
Post-hostilities sensor system	A sensor field planted to monitor a Vietnamese cease-fire.

Glossary

Pouncer	The use of an A-6, equipped with an airborne moving target indicator, to locate trucks that its accompanying F-4s or A-7s might then attack.
Prairie Fire	The use of ground reconnaissance or combat teams against supply and infiltration routes in Laos, just west of the South Vietnamese border.
Provost Priority Research and Development	Objectives for Vietnam Support, a research and development task force established within the Office of the Secretary of Defense.
PSR	Pacific Security Region.
Psy Ops	psychological warfare operations.
QU-22	A single-engine Beech Debonair low-wing light monoplane modified for sensor relay or communications monitoring.
Rabet	radio beacon transponder.
Ranch Hand	The aerial defoliation program conducted by the Air Force in Southeast Asia.
RAND	The name—an acronym for Research and Development—of a non-profit think tank established to conduct studies for the Air Force.
R&D	research and development.
Raven	Air Force forward air controllers assigned to the air attache in Laos; for much of the war, they posed as civilian employees of the embassy.
RC-135	Reconnaissance version of the Boeing KC-135 aerial tanker.
RF–4	Reconnaissance version of the F–4 fighter.
RLAF	Royal Laotian Air Force.
Road Rip	An attempt during Commando Hunt I to cut roads where sensors indicated heavy traffic.
Roadwatch team	A small team organized by representatives of the Central Intelligence Agency or the Military Assistance Command, Vietnam, and sent into southern Laos or northeastern Cambodia to report highway traffic.
Rockeye	A 500-pound cluster bomb unit that scattered small bomblets containing shaped explosive charges for penetrating armor.
ROE	rules of engagement.
Rolling Thunder	The air war against North Vietnam, 1965-68.
Route Package I	The southernmost armed reconnaissance area in North Vietnam.
RSq	reconnaissance squadron.
Russell Committee	The group, headed by Adm. James S. Russell, that reviewed sensor effectiveness in Southeast Asia, reporting in November 1968.
RVN	Republic of Vietnam.
RVNAF	Republic of Vietnam Armed Forces.
RWg	reconnaissance wing.
SAC	Strategic Air Command.
SAF	Secretary of the Air Force.
Salem House	The operating area for patrols dispatched into northeastern Cambodia by the Studies and Observations Group, U.S. Military Assistance Command, Vietnam.
SAM	surface-to-air missile.
SCAR	strike control and reconnaissance.
SEA or SEAsia	Southeast Asia.
SEACOORDS	Southeast Asia Coordinating Council.
SEAM	Southeast Asia Matters.
Search	An operation, conducted during Commando Hunt I, that provided prompt and intensive aerial reconnaissance of areas selected by forward air controllers.
SECARMY	Secretary of the Army.

SECDEF	Secretary of Defense.
SECNAV	Secretary of the Navy.
SECSTATE	Secretary of State.
Self-contained night attack system	Nighttime target acquisition and attack by the same aircraft.
Sensor strike zone	A segment of road kept under close electronic surveillance so that technicians at Nakhon Phanom could predict the arrival of a truck convoy at a specific point and issue appropriate instructions to strike aircraft.
Sentinel Suffix/Simplex	Loran correlation of aerial mapping.
SGU	Special Guerrilla Units.
Shed Light	An Air Force project to improve its ability to fight at night.
Shiloh III	A proposed operation that would have sent Prairie Fire teams to the mountain passes leading from North Vietnam into southern Laos.
Shock	A strike against the enemy transportation net in southern Laos based on intelligence from all sources and involving tactical aircraft from all the services.
short-term road-watch and target acquisition teams	Reconnaissance units dispatched into Laos and Cambodia by the Studies and Observations Group, United States Military Assistance Command, Vietnam.
Silver Buckle	A probe by Lao forces of the Muong Nong region of southern Laos conducted in January and February 1971.
Single manager concept	The placing of Air Force and Marine Corps tactical combat aircraft under the direction of an Air Force officer.
SLAM	Seek, Locate, Annihilate, Monitor; an attempt to use ground reconnaissance teams to locate targets for B-52s in southern Laos, just west of the South Vietnamese border.
SLAR	side-looking airborne radar.
SOA	special operating area.
SOF	special operations force.
SOFLO	Special Operations Force Liaison Office.
Sortie	A takeoff and landing by a single aircraft; any flight by a single aircraft against the enemy.
SOSq	special operations squadron.
Southwest Monsoon Planning Group	The organization that drafted the Seventh Air Force southwest monsoon season campaign plan for 1969.
Southwest monsoon season	A period of heavy rain in southern Laos, usually lasting from May through September.
SOWg	special operations wing.
Sparky FAC	Nickname for the Commando Bolt control team in the Infiltration Surveillance Center at Nakhon Phanom.
Special Arc Light operating areas	Regions in southern Laos submitted in advance to the United States Ambassador at Vientiane and cleared for B-52 attack during a specified time.
Spikebuoy	An air-delivered seismic sensor designed to bury its nose extension in the earth.
Sq	squadron.
SSO	special security office.
Starlight scope	A device that captures and intensifies existing light to enable an observer to locate targets at night.
Steel Tiger	The aerial interdiction zone in southeastern Laos.

Glossary

STOL	short takeoff and landing.
Strike box	A road segment that, on the basis of current sensor data, should provide targets for gunships.
Strike controller	The member of a Sparky FAC team who directed the strike upon a selected Commando Bolt impact point.
Strike module	The grouping of sensor strings used in Commando Bolt activity.
Strike nominator	The member of a Sparky FAC team who interpreted sensor data to select likely targets.
Strike technician	The member of a Sparky FAC team who advised the appropriate airborne battlefield command and control center of Commando Bolt strikes.
Studies and Observations Group	That element of the United States Military Assistance Command, Vietnam, responsible for directing raids, reconnaissance patrols, and clandestine activity in Laos, Cambodia, and North Vietnam.
Surprise Package	A number of modifications that improved the ability of the early AC-130s to find and destroy targets.
Surveillance technician	An individual at the Infiltration Surveillance Center who analyzed sensor data.
SVN	South Vietnam.
Sycamore	Call sign of the Task Force Alpha operations center during Commando Hunt I.
T-28	A two-place trainer, powered by a single radial engine, built by North American Aviation and used in Laos as an attack aircraft.
TAC	Tactical Air Command.
TACAIR	Tactical air.
TACC	Tactical Air Control Center.
TACCONSq	tactical air control squadron.
TACS	Tactical Air Control System.
Tactical air navigation system	A navigation aid utilizing a radio beacon broadcast from a ground station.
Tactical analysis officer	The individual who evaluated information transmitted from sensors to the Infiltration Surveillance Center. See ground surveillance monitor.
Tailwind	A Prairie Fire raid conducted southeast of Chavane, Laos, in support of Operation Gauntlet.
Target analyst	An individual assigned to the Infiltration Surveillance Center who evaluated intelligence on moving targets to determine whether an attack should be launched.
Target assessment officer	See ground surveillance monitor.
Targeteer	An individual assigned to the Infiltration Surveillance Center who evaluated intelligence on fixed targets to determine whether an attack should be launched.
TASGp	tactical air support group.
Task Force Alpha	The command that maintained and operated the Infiltration Surveillance Center at Nakhon Phanom Air Base, Thailand.
TASSq	tactical air support squadron.
TAWC	Tactical Air Warfare Center.
TCS	tactical control squadron.
Termite	The new designation of Headshed II when that control cell assumed responsibility for directing air strikes.
Tet	The lunar new year celebrated in South Vietnam.

TFA	Task Force Alpha.
TFSq	tactical fighter squadron.
TFWg	tactical fighter wing.
Thao La	An operation by Lao forces in the Ban Thateng region, November-December 1971.
Thot Not	See Salem House.
Tiger	Call sign of forward air controllers of the Thailand-based 388th Tactical Fighter Wing.
Tiger Hound	An operating area in southern Laos south of 17 degrees north latitude.
Tight Jaw	A program begun in 1969 to train South Vietnamese in the use of sensors.
TM	technical manual.
Toan Thang	Total Victory, a nickname used for South Vietnamese Operations against communist bases in Cambodia.
Toan Thang 01-71	South Vietnamese operations in Cambodia during the spring of 1971.
TOI	An element of the Directorate of Technical Operations, Task Force Alpha.
Traffic control point	See interdiction point.
Trail campaign	The dropping of propaganda leaflets to undermine the morale of troops using and operating the Ho Chi Minh Trail.
TRIM	Trail-Road Interdiction, Multi-sensor, a Navy project to develop a self-contained night attack system. See AP-2H.
Trolling	Flying within range of enemy radar to cause the operators to transmit, thus revealing the location and characteristics of their equipment.
Tropic Moon	An Air Force research and development effort that produced three types of self-contained night attack aircraft.
TRWg	tactical reconnaissance wing.
Turnpike	An aerial interdiction campaign that sought to make use of sorties that became available as a result of restrictions on bombing North Vietnam that went into effect on April 1, 1968.
UC–123	A Fairchild cargo plane, powered by two radial engines, modified to dispense herbicide. Beginning in 1969, only the UC-123K, with two auxiliary jet engines, dispensed defoliants.
UH–1	A single-rotor, single-turbine, helicopter developed by Bell as a troop carrier, gunship, and command craft for the Army.
USA	U.S. Army.
USAF	U.S. Air Force.
USAFSS	United States Air Force Security Service.
USAID	United States Agency for International Development.
USAIRA	United States Air attaché.
USMACV	U.S. Military Assistance Command, Vietnam.
USMC	U.S. Marine Corps.
USN	U.S. Navy.
USSAG	United States Special Activities Group.
VC	Viet Cong.
VC/NV.'.	Viet Cong/North Vietnamese Army.
Viet Cong	South Vietnamese communist forces.
Vietnamization	The program, foreshadowed by President Johnson and conducted by President Nixon, that sought to train and arm the South Vietnamese to take over the fighting and ultimately assume responsibility for the defense of their country.
VNAF	South Vietnamese Air Force.

Glossary

VO	United States Navy observation squadron.
Vol	volume.
VR	visual reconnaissance.
Wet season	See southwest monsoon season.
White Orbit	One of the locations from which relay aircraft retransmitted sensor signals.
Wide-area antipersonnel mine	Any of three mines, released by cluster bomb units, that utilized standard antipersonnel bomblets, weighed about one pound, and extended wire triggers for distances up to 25 feet.
Wolf	Call sign of Ubon-based forward air controllers flying F-4s.
XT plotter	A device capable of automatically monitoring a theoretical total of 99 sensors

Bibliographic Note

The Air Force Historical Studies Office, when it was still the Office of Air Force History, embarked upon three books that together cover Air Force operations in Laos during the Vietnam War. Lt. Col. Richard R. Sexton, USAF, and Maj. Victor B. Anthony, USAF, collaborated on an account of the air war in Northern Laos. The other two volumes deal with the war in southern Laos, principally the campaign to interdict the movement of men and cargo on the Ho Chi Minh Trail. In his book, Mr. Jacob Van Staaveren focused on the period before 1968. This volume begins where his ends and recounts the story of aerial interdiction until the North Vietnamese invasion of South Vietnam in March 1972 brought the campaign to an abrupt halt.

Over the years, a number of published works have appeared that mention the aerial interdiction of traffic on the Ho Chi Minh Trail, but as yet no single volume deals exclusively with the subject. A few Vietnamese have recently shared their memories of what it was like to be on the receiving end of the interdiction campaign, and some Americans have visited Vietnam and reported their conversations with persons who labored or traveled on the trail. The hope exists that a normalization of relations between the United States and the Socialist Republic of Vietnam will someday provide access to Vietnamese records, but no such breakthrough occurred in time for this volume. On the other hand, the body of official documentation on the American side seems as complete as it ever can be, given the closing of offices and destruction of files over the years. Perhaps this bibliographic note, along with the one in Mr. Van Staaveren's book, will encourage the writing of a single-volume synthesis of air operations in southern Laos intended for the general reader.

Government Collections

After 1968, when Mr. Van Staaveren's narrative ends, the microfilmed message files of the Commander in Chief, Pacific, so valuable to that earlier volume, yield progressively less information, probably because the more important or sensitive items were either filed separately—in which case they have vanished—or transmitted outside normal communication channels and never microfilmed.

Fortunately, the Air Force has microfilmed many of the files of the Seventh Air Force and the Seventh/Thirteenth Air Force for 1968 and subsequent years. When the task of documenting, reporting, and analyzing various aspects of the war in Southeast Asia began in 1962, a project bearing the title of Contemporary Historical Evaluation of Counterinsurgency Operations, or Project CHECO, assumed responsibility for the microfilming. Although both the nature of the war and the project's scope of interest changed, the acronym endured, but, the better to reflect its actual duties, CHECO came to stand for Contemporary Historical Evaluation of Combat Operations and ultimately for Contemporary Historical Examination of Current Operations.

As it moved from examining a counterinsurgency to evaluating an air war in Southeast Asia (or elsewhere when necessary), Project CHECO turned out more than twelve hundred cartridges of microfilmed documents dealing with the Air Force in almost

Bibliographic Note

every aspect of the Vietnam War. This collection enjoys a special importance because the bulk of the original files of the Seventh Air Force and Seventh/Thirteenth Air Force have perished. The quality of film is uneven, however, and a number of cartridges—most of them dating from early in the war—are illegible. Finding aids are available, mainly in the form of two microfilmed indices arranged by key word, one dealing with documents that were classified Top Secret at the time of filming and the other with those that were Secret or less. (A similar computer print-out exists of material located at the Air Force Historical Research Agency, Maxwell Air Force Base, Alabama, dealing specifically with air operations in southern Laos, but this index is so massive as to be almost useless.) Lists of the material in many of the individual Project CHECO microfilm cartridges have been compiled and are available at the Air Force Historical Studies Office, Bolling Air Force Base, Washington, DC.

Besides preserving records on microfilm, Project CHECO produced more than two hundred reports on various aspects of the war in Southeast Asia; these now form a part of the holdings of both the Air Force Historical Studies Office and the Air Force Historical Research Center. Either repository can provide a useful guide to the CHECO reports. Most of the reports have appeared in print, though a few survive only in draft form on microfilm. If the authors preserved their source materials, the documentation was either published in conjunction with the report or preserved in the CHECO microfilm collection. When issued, the reports, with rare exceptions, carried security classifications, but over the years most have been declassified.

The collections consulted for this book include the holdings of the Office of Assistant for Vietnamization, an element of the Office of Deputy Chief of Staff, Plans and Operations, from 1970 to the end of the war. These retired files, along with the histories of the same office now located at the Air Force Historical Studies Office, document the belated effort to prepare the South Vietnamese to conduct simplified aerial interdiction. Along with paperwork unique to Air Force headquarters, the office preserved copies of key memoranda reflecting decisions by the Secretary of Defense and recommendations from the Joint Chiefs of Staff.

Other source material came from outside the Air Force. Thanks to Ms. Mary C. Remmy, the central files of the Office of Director, Defense Research and Engineering, yielded helpful information. In addition, the Office of Deputy Director, Defense Research and Engineering (Policy and Planning), since disbanded, had preserved as late as 1977 many of the files of the Deputy Director, Defense Research and Engineering (Southeast Asia Matters), Mr. Leonard Sullivan, Jr., who played an active role in shaping the interdiction campaign. The collection dealing specifically with Southeast Asia contained not only correspondence, reports, and recommendations involving Mr. Sullivan, but also information on the Defense Communications Planning Group, redesignated the Defense Special Projects Group before its abolition. Although the position of Deputy Director, Defense Research and Engineering (Southeast Asia Matters), no longer existed at the time of my research, and Mr. Sullivan had left the government, Dr. Jeanne Mintz and Lt. Col. Robert W. Oliver, USMC (Ret.), provided insights into the material in his files.

Also a component of the Office of Secretary of Defense, the Office of Director of Planning and Evaluation, precursor of the Office of Assistant Secretary of Defense (Program Analysis and Evaluation), proved another fruitful source of documents. Mr. Charles Pugh of the Document Control Section made available a number of items, including Thomas C. Thayer's *A Systems Analysis View of the Vietnam War, 1965–1972*, in

344

twelve typescript volumes, which has since been greatly abridged and published as *War without Fronts: The American Experience in Vietnam*. The files of Mr. Frank Tapparo's Asia Division of the Office of Deputy Director for Regional Programs contained, among other useful documents, an interagency study, completed in June 1970, on the effectiveness of U.S. air operations in southern Laos. After many a reorganization, the Asia Division now forms a part of the Europe and Pacific Division, in the office of Deputy Assistant Secretary of Defense (Program Analysis and Evaluation) for Theater Assessment and Planning.

The intelligence documents used in the narrative came from various places. The microfilm collections amassed by the Commander in Chief, Pacific, proved disappointing, but the Project CHECO microfilm yielded a number of interrogation reports, summaries, and estimates. Surviac—a Department of Defense information analysis center located at Wright-Patterson Air Force Base, Ohio, and operated under contract from the Defense Logistics Agency—forwarded copies of the Seventh Air Force Weekly Air Intelligence Summaries covering the most intensive periods of the interdiction campaign. In an especially generous response to a request by Capt. William A. Buckingham, Jr., USAF, the library of the Defense Intelligence Agency sent a number of helpful items.

End of Tour Reports proved invaluable because Air Force policy required them of officers being reassigned or retiring after serving in most of the critical posts throughout Southeast Asia. Although the reporting officer may not have prepared the document himself, at the very least he read it and endorsed its conclusions. The End of Tour Reports used in this study have been microfilmed and indexed by name, though not by subject, and are now available at the Air Force Historical Studies Office, as well as at the Air Force Historical Research Agency.

The Oral History Interviews cited in the history contain unique insights into the aerial campaign fought against the Ho Chi Minh Trail. Indeed, the Air Force Oral History Program represents a coordinated effort by historians throughout the Air Force to preserve the observations and reflections of individuals who have held important assignments or participated in major operations. Transcripts of the Oral History Interviews used for this volume reside in typescript or on microfilm at the Air Force Historical Studies Office and the Air Force Historical Research Agency. Unfortunately, the catalogue of Oral History Interviews, in its latest edition (1989), lacks the topical index that made the earlier version so useful.

Air Force Historical Publications and Studies

Anthony, Victor B. *The Air Force in Southeast Asia: Tactics and Techniques of Night Operations, 1961–1970*. Washington: Office of Air Force History, March 1973.

Ballard, Jack S. *The U.S. Air Force in Southeast Asia: Development and Employment of Fixed-Wing Gunships, 1962–1971*. Washington: Office of Air Force History, January 1974.

———. *The U.S. Air Force in Southeast Asia: Development and Employment of Fixed-Wing Gunships, 1962–1972*. Washington: Office of Air Force History, 1982.

Berger, Carl, ed. *The United States Air Force in Southeast Asia, 1961–1973: An Illustrated Account*. Revised edition. Washington: Office of Air Force History, 1984.

Buckingham, William A. Jr. *Operation Ranch Hand: The Air Force and Herbicides in Southeast Asia, 1961–1971*. Washington: Office of Air Force History, 1982.

Bibliographic Note

Hartsook, Elizabeth H. *The Air Force in Southeast Asia: The Administration Emphasizes Air Power, 1969*. Washington: Office of Air Force History, November 1971.

———. *The Air Force in Southeast Asia: Shield for Vietnamization and Withdrawal*. Washington: Office of Air Force History, July 1976.

McGuire, James. *Development of All-Weather and Night Truck Kill Capability*. Maxwell AFB, Alabama: Aerospace Studies Institute, Project Corona Harvest, January 1970.

Momyer, William W. *Air Power in Three Wars*. No publisher, nd. Reprinted, Office of Air Force History, 1985.

Rowley, Ralph A. *The Air Force in Southeast Asia: FAC Operations, 1965–1970*. Washington: Office of Air Force History, May 1975.

Schlight, John. *The United States Air Force in Southeast Asia; The War in South Vietnam: The Years of the Offensive, 1968–1968*. Washington: Office of Air Force History, 1988.

Tilford, Earl H., Jr. *Search and Rescue in Southeast Asia, 1961–1965*. Washington: Office of Air Force History, 1980.

———. *Setup: What the Air Force Did in Vietnam and Why*. Maxwell AFB, Alabama: Air University Press, 1991.

Wolk, Herman S. *USAF Plans and Policies: R&D for Southeast Asia, 1968*. Washington: Office of Air Force History, July 1970.

Project CHECO Reports

Barnette, B. H., Jr. *"Ink" Development and Employment*. September 24, 1973.

Caine, Phillip D. *Igloo White, July 1968–December 1969*. January 10, 1970.

Colwell, Robert F. *USAF Tactical Reconnaissance in Southeast Asia, July 1969–June 1971*. November 23, 1971.

Elder, Paul W., and Melly, Peter J. *Rules of Engagement, November 1969–September 1972*. March 1, 1973.

Gatlin, Jesse C. *Igloo White (Initial Phase)*. July 31, 1968.

Layton, Bruce P. *Commando Hunt VI*. July 7, 1972.

Loye, J. F., Jr., St. Clair, G. K., *et al. Lam Son 719, 30 January–24 March 1971: The South Vietnamese Incursion into Laos*. March 24, 1971.

Porter, Melvin F. *The EC–47 in SEA, April 1968–July 1970*. September 12, 1970.

———. *Interdiction of Waterways and POL Pipelines, SEA*. December 11, 1970.

———. *Tactical Control Squadron Operations in SEAsia*. October 15, 1969.

Pralle, James B. *Arc Light, June 1967–December 1968*. August 15, 1969.

Schlight, John. *Rules of Engagement, 1 January 1966–1 November 1969*. 1969.

Sexton, Richard R., Porter, Melvin, *et al. The Bolovens Campaign, 28 July–28 December 1971*. May 8, 1974.

Shields, Henry S. *Igloo White, January 1970–September 1971*. November 1, 1971.

Thompson, A. W. *Strike Control and Reconnaissance (SCAR) in Southeast Asia*. January 22, 1969.

Thorndale, C. William. *Interdiction in Route Package I, 1968*. June 30, 1969.

Till, Jerald J., and Thomas, James C. *Pave Aegis Weapon System (AC–130E Gunship)*. February 16, 1973.

Valentiny, Edward. *USAF Operations from Thailand, 1 January to 1 July 1968*. November 20, 1968.

Other Reports

Central Intelligence Agency. Bruce Palmer, Jr. "U.S. Intelligence and Vietnam," *CIA Studies in Intelligence*, Special Issue, 1984.

Department of Defense, Department of State, *et al*. Effectiveness of U.S. Air Operations in Southern Laos: An Interagency Study, June 12, 1970.

Department of Defense. Selected Air and Ground Operations in Cambodia and Laos, September 10, 1973.

———. Assistant Secretary of Defense (Systems Analysis). Thomas C. Thayer, ed. *A Systems Analysis View of the Vietnam War, 1965–1972*, 12 vols, 1975.

Foreign Broadcast Information Service. Southeast Asia Report no 1247, Vietnam; *A History of the Bulwark B–2 Theater*, vol 5: *Concluding the 30-Years War*, February 2, 1983.

Joint Chiefs of Staff. Vietnamization: RVNAF Improvement and Modernization (Phase III) and Related U.S. Planning, January 20, 1970.

CINCPAC Scientific Advisory Group. R. F. Linsenmeyer, C. E. Thompson, E. L. Henry. Working Paper no 5–70: Interdiction Operations in Southeast Asia, May 26, 1970.

Sharp, U. S. Grant, CINCPAC, and Westmoreland, William C., COMUSMACV, *Report on the War in Vietnam (As of 30 June 1968)*. Washington: Government Printing Office, 1969.

Hq USAF. Deputy Chief of Staff, Plans and Operations. Contributions of the Igloo White System, March 12, 1971.

———. Office of Special Assistant for Vietnamization. Credible Chase Study Report, May 28, 1971.

———. Director of Operations. Trends, Indicators, and Analyses, a recurring report.

———. Director of Operations. Southwest [Monsoon] Forecast: Enemy Infiltration and Logistics Movement versus Air Interdiction (June–November 1969), April 10, 1969.

Hq PACAF. Deputy Chief of Staff, Intelligence. Truck Destruction in Southeast Asia, November 1968–June 1969, July 1969.

———. Operations Analysis Office. Briefing by Charles H. Liddell. Steel Tiger Output— Supply Limited or Demand Limited? July 13, 1972.

———. Project Corona Harvest. In-Country and Out-Country Strike Operations in Southeast Asia, 1 January 1965–31 December 1969, Vol III, Hardware: Munitions.

———. Summary of Air Operations, Southeast Asia, a recurring report.

———. (With the support of SAC) Project Corona Harvest Study. USAF Operations in Defense of South Vietnam, July 1, 1971–June 30, 1972.

Hq, Seventh Air Force. Commando Hunt, May 20, 1969.

———. Commando Hunt III, May 1970.

———. Commando Hunt V, May 1971.

———. Commando Hunt VII, June 1972

———. Study Guide: War of Interdiction versus Infiltration, May 1, 1968.

———. Dir/Tactical Analysis. Herman L. Gilster, Richard D. Duckworth, *et al*. An Economic Analysis of the Steel Tiger Interdiction Campaign, 1 November 1969–30 June 1970.

Bibliographic Note

Task Force Alpha. Commando Bolt Operations, November 20, 1969–April 30, 1970.
————. Double Counting within a Sensor String Field in Steel Tiger, July 24, 1971
————. Laos Exploitable Enemy Patterns, 1969.
————. Means and Methods of Truck Infiltration in Southern Laos, April 15, 1968.
————. North Vietnamese Army Logistic System in Steel Tiger, July 10, 1971.
————. North Vietnamese Army Logistic System in Steel Tiger, July 1, 1972.
————. The North Vietnamese POL Logistics System in the Steel Tiger Operating Area of Southern Laos, February 1, 1971.
————. The North Vietnamese Waterways System in Steel Tiger, July 1, 1971.
————. Truck Park Working Group Report, August 1968.
USAF Tactical Air Warfare Center. Draft final report, B–57G Combat Evaluation, February 1971.
————. Final report, Pave Knife Combat Evaluation, August 1971.
553d Reconnaissance Wing. Pave Eagle Study, June 15, 1969.
————. Pave Eagle II Evaluation, September 17, 1970.
RAND Corporation. M. G. Weiner, J. R. Brom, and R. E. Koon. Infiltration of Personnel from North Vietnam, 1959–1967, October 1968.
U. S. Marine Corps Historical Center. Vietnam Revisited: Conversation with William D. Broyles, Jr., December 11, 1984.

Recurring Official Histories

The Joint Chiefs of Staff and the War in Vietnam. Commander in Chief, Pacific.
U.S. Military Assistance Command, Vietnam.
U.S. Support Activities Group.
Defense Communications Planning Group (redesignated Defense Special Projects Group) documentation books.
Seventh Air Force.
Seventh/Thirteenth Air Force.
Special Assistant for Vietnamization, Deputy Chief of Staff, Plans and Operations.
Task Force Alpha.
14th Special Operations Wing.
56th Special Operations Wing.
8th Tactical Fighter Wing.
366th Tactical Fighter Wing.
432d Tactical Reconnaissance Wing.
460th Tactical Reconnaissance Wing.

Congressional Documents

Background Information Relating to Southeast Asia and Vietnam. Senate Committee on Foreign Relations, 83d Cong, 2d sess.
Department of Defense Appropriations for 1973. Hearings, Subcommittee of the House Committee on Appropriations, 92d Cong, 2d sess.
Department of Defense Appropriations Bill, Electronics and Telecommunications Equipment. Report, House Committee on Appropriations, 92d Cong, 2d sess.
Investigation into the Electronic Battlefield Program. Hearings, Electronic Battlefield

Subcommittee, Senate Committee on Armed Services, 91st Cong, 2d sess.

Investigation into the Electronic Battlefield Program. Report, Electronic Battlefield Subcommittee, Senate Committee on Armed Services, 92d Cong, 1st sess.

Weather Modification. Report, Subcommittee on Oceans and International Environment, Senate Committee on Foreign Relations, 93d Cong, 2d sess.

Oral History Interviews

Atchison, Maj. Richard M., OV–10 navigator, 1971–1972, July 16, 1975.

Breeze, Col. William A., Chief, Intelligence Division, and Chief, Technical Intelligence Division, Task Force Alpha, 1967–1968, January 15, 1970.

Brown, Gen. George S., Commander, Seventh Air Force, 1968–1970, March 30, 1970 (revised April 2, 1970); October 19–20, 1970.

Burcham, Col. Lee A., Chief of Targets, Task Force Alpha, 1968–1969, January 29, 1970.

Costin, Maj. James, 56th Special Operations Wing, 1969–1970, February 6, 1973.

Fairbrother, Brig. Gen. William H., Commander, 14th Special Operations Wing, 1969–1970, June 7, 1974.

Gallacher, Lt. Col. V. H., Director, and Chief, Current Operations Division, Joint Seventh/Thirteenth Air Force Tactical Air Control Center, 1970–1971, December 16, 1971.

Hall, Col. Robert E., Director of Operations, Seventh/Thirteenth Air Force, 1971–1972, January 26, 1973.

Hartley, Lt. Col. Howard K., Assistant Air Attaché, Laos, 1968–1969, July 19, 1974.

Hartman, Lt. Col. William B., 16th Special Operations Squadron, 1971–1972, December 11, 1972.

Jones, Lt. Gen. David C., Deputy Chief of Staff, Operations, and Vice Commander, Seventh Air Force, 1969, November 4–6, 1969.

King, Lt. Col. Loyd J, AC–130E Pilot and Operations Officer, 1971–1972, February 8, 1973.

Lambert, Lt. Col. Robert E., Director of Intelligence, 56th Special Operations Wing, 1969–1970, January 13, 1970.

Maddock, Capt. Mike, Target Officer, Task Force Alpha, 1969–1970, July 9, 1970.

McCoskrie, Col. Roland K., Commander, 56th Special Operations Wing, 1967–1968, July 14, 1975.

McCutchen, Col. Robert, Airborne Battlefield Command and Control Center and Director of Operations, Seventh/Thirteenth Air Force, 1970–1971, December 21, 1971.

Myers, Capt. Ron F., 56th Special Operations Wing Briefing Officer, February 1969–1970, July 15, 1970.

Negus, Lt. Col. Kenneth D., AC–130 Commander, 1971–1972, December 15, 1972.

Opitz, Lt. Col. Stephen J., AC–130 Sensor Operator and Navigator, 1971–1972, July 18, 1972.

Robinson, 1st. Lt. Harold R., Target Analyst, Task Force Alpha, 1967–1968, December 4, 1968.

Ryan, Gen. John D., CINCSAC, 1964–1967, CINCPACAF, 1967–1968, Vice Chief of Staff, 1968–1969, Chief of Staff, 1969–1971, May 20, 1971.

Shields, Capt. David L., Forward Air Controller, 1967–1968, January 10, 1972.

Smith, Col. Howard P., Director/Targets, Seventh Air Force, 1967–1968, July 10, 1970.

Bibliographic Note

Walker, Col. William L., Director/Intelligence, Task Force Alpha, 1967–1968, June 8, 1971.

Wehner, 1st. Lt. Clement E., Jr., Task Force Alpha, 1968–1969, July 15, 1979.

End of Tour Reports

Anderson, Col. Earl, Commander, 25th Tactical Fighter Squadron, 1971–1972, June 1971.

Butcher, Brig. Gen. Chester J., Commander, Task Force Alpha, 1969–1970, August 3, 1970.

Evans, Col. D. L., Director of Intelligence, Task Force Alpha, 1971–1972, July 6, 1972.

Harris, Lt. Col. Kenneth G., Commander, 16th Special Operations Squadron, 1971–1972, January 30, 1972.

Hight, Lt. Col. Roland P. Commander, 16th Special Operations Squadron, 1969–1970, February 12, 1971.

Humphries, Col. Francis A., Commander, 8th Tactical Fighter Wing, 1972–1974, January 17, 1974.

John, Brig. Gen. Ernest F, Deputy Chief of Staff, Intelligence, Seventh Air Force, 1970–1971, November 24, 1971.

Kilbride, Lt. Col. Wade R., Commander, 22d Special Operations Squadron and 602d Special Operations Squadron, 1970–1971, nd.

Killpack, Col. Larry M., Commander, 8th Tactical Fighter Wing, 1970–1971, nd.

Lafferty, Col. William A., Director, Plans and Program, Air Force Advisory Group, Vietnam, 1969–1971, June 9, 1971.

Mathews, Col.. Thomas J., Director of Intelligence, Vice Commander, and Commander, Task Force Alpha, 1972, December 31, 1972.

McClay, Lt. Col. Lachlan, Commander, 23d Tactical Air Support Squadron, 1971–1972, September 18, 1972.

Nugen, Col. William A., Director, Command and Control, Seventh Air Force, and Assistant Chief, Air Operations Division, Military Assistance Command, Vietnam, 1972, January 5, 1973.

Pitt, Lt. Col. Paul R., Commander, 13th Bomb Squadron (Tactical), 1970–1971, July 31, 1971.

Slay, Maj. Gen. Alton D., Assistant Deputy Chief of Staff, Operations, and Deputy Chief of Staff, Seventh Air Force, 1971–1972, nd.

Steger, Col. William E., Commander, 3d Combat Service Group and 6351st Combat Support Group, 1970–1971, nd.

Taylor, Lt. Col. Fred S., III, Air Force Systems Command Liaison Officer, Tan Son Nhut Air Base, South Vietnam, 1971, September 17, 1971.

Thompson, Col. Clair G., Commander, 432d Combat Support Group, 1971–1972, nd.

Walsh, Col. Edward J., Jr., Commander, 56th Special Operations Wing, 1970–1971, July 15, 1971.

Books

Boettcher, Thomas D. *Vietnam*: *The Valor and the Sorrow*; *From the Home Front to the Front Lines in Words and Pictures*. Boston-Toronto: Little, Brown and Co, 1985.

Chanoff, David, and Doan Van Toai. *Portrait of the Enemy*. New York: Random House, 1986.

Bibliographic Note

Clarke, Jeffrey J. *The United States Army in Vietnam*; *Advice and Support*: *The Final Years, 1965–1973*. Washington: Center of Military History, 1988.

Clodfelter, Mark. *The Limits of Air Power*: *The American Bombing of North Vietnam*. New York: The Free Press, 1989.

Cooper, Chester L. *The Lost Crusade*: *America in Vietnam*. New York: Dodd, Mead and Co, 1970.

Davidson, Phillip B. *Vietnam at War*: *The History, 1946–1975*. Novato, California: Presidio Press, 1988.

Hammond, William M. *The United States Army in Vietnam*; *Public Affairs*: *The Military and the Media, 1962–1968*. Washington: Center of Military History, 1988.

Hannah, Norman B. *The Key to Failure*: *Laos and the Vietnam War*. Lanham, Maryland, New York, and London: Madison Books, 1987.

Head, William, and Grinter, Lawrence E., eds. *Looking Back on the Vietnam War*: *A 1990s Perspective on the Decisions, Combat, and Legacies*. Westport, Connecticut: Greenwood Press, 1993.

Herring, George C. *America's Longest War*: *The United States and Vietnam, 1950–1975*. New York: Alfred A Knopf, 1986.

Karnow, Stanley. *Vietnam*: *A History*. New York: The Viking Press, 1983.

Kissinger, Henry. *White House Years*. Boston-Toronto: Little, Brown and Co., 1979.

Knappman, Edward W., ed. *South Vietnam*: *U.S.-Communist Confrontation in Southeast Asia, 1972–1973*. New York: Fact on File, 1973.

Lewy, Guenter. *America in Vietnam*. New York: Oxford University Press, 1978.

Maclear, Michael. *The Ten Thousand Day War*: *Vietnam, 1945–1975*. New York: St. Martin's Press, 198.

McGarvey, Patrick J., ed. *Visions of Victory*: *Selected Vietnamese Communist Military Writings, 1964–1968*. Stanford, California: Hoover Institute on War, Revolution, and Peace, 1970.

Millet, Stanley, ed. *South Vietnam*: *U.S.-Communist Confrontation in Southeast Asia, 1968*. New York: Facts on File, 1974.

———, ed. *South Vietnam*: *U.S.-Communist Confrontation in Southeast Asia, 1969*. New York: Facts on File, 1974.

Nguyen Duy Hinh. *Indochina Monographs*: *Lam Son 719*. Washington: Center of Military History, 1979.

Nolan, Keith William. *Into Laos*: *The Story of Dewey Canyon II/Lam Son 719*. Novato, California: Presidio Press, 1986.

North Vietnam, Government of. *From Khe Sanh to Chepone*. Hanoi: Foreign Language Publishing House, 1971.

Oberdorfer, Don. *Tet*. Garden City, New York: Doubleday and Co, 1971.

Palmer, Bruce, Jr. *The 25-Year War*: *America's Military Role in Vietnam*. Lexington: University of Kentucky Press, 1984.

Palmer, Dave Richard. *Summons of the Trumpet*: *U.S.-Vietnam in Perspective*. San Rafael, California: Presidio Press, 1978.

Shaplen, Robert. *Bitter Victory*. New York: Harper and Row, 1986.

Sharp, U. S. Grant. *Strategy for Defeat*: *Vietnam in Retrospect*. San Rafael, California: Presidio Press, 1978.

Sobel, Lester A, ed. *South Vietnam*: *U.S.-Communist Confrontation in Southeast Asia, 1970*. New York: Facts on File, 1973.

Bibliographic Note

————, ed. *South Vietnam: U.S.-Communist Confrontation in Southeast Asia, 1971*. New York: Facts on File, 1973.

Sorley, Lewis. *Thunderbolt: General Creighton Abrams and the Army of His Times*. New York: Simon and Schuster, 1992.

Sullivan, William H. *Obbligato, 1939–1979: Notes on a Foreign Service Career*. New York: W. W. Norton, 1984.

Thayer, Thomas C. *War without Fronts: The American Experience in Vietnam*. Boulder, Colorado, and London: Westview Press, 1985.

Thompson, W. Scott, and Frizzell, Donaldson W., eds. *The Lessons of Vietnam*. New York: Crane, Russak and Co, 1977.

Truong Nhu T'ang, with Chanoff, David, and Doan Van Toai. *A Viet Cong Memoir*. New York: Harcourt Brace Jovanovich, 1985.

Turley, William S. *The Second Indochina War: A Short Political and Military History*. Boulder, Colorado, and London: Westview Press, 1986.

United States, Government of. Department of Defense. *The Pentagon Papers: The Defense Department History of United States Decisionmaking on Vietnam,* 5 vols. Boston: Beacon Press, 1971.

————. National Archives and Records Service. *Public Papers of the Presidents of the United States: Richard Nixon, 1969*. Washington: Office of the *Federal Register*, 1970. *Richard Nixon, 1970*. Washington: Office of the *Federal Register*, 1971. *Richard Nixon, 1971*. Washington: Office of the *Federal Register*, 1972. *Richard Nixon, 1972*. Washington: Office of the *Federal Register*, 1974.

Warner, Denis A. *Certain Victory: How Hanoi Won the War*. Kansas City, Kansas: Sheed Andrew and McMeel, 1978.

Westmoreland, William C. *A Soldier Reports*. Garden City, New York: Doubleday and Co, 1976.

Articles

Berent, Mark E. "A Group Called Wolf." *Air Force Magazine*, August 1971, pp 88-91.

Brodie, Bernard. "Why Were We so (Strategically) Wrong?" *Military Review*, June 1972, pp 40–46.

Broyles, William, Jr. "The Road to Hill 10: A Veteran's Return to Vietnam." *The Atlantic Monthly*, April 1985, pp 91–118.

Frisbee, John L. "Igloo White," *Air Force Magazine*, June 1971, pp 48–53.

Gilster, Herman. "Air Interdiction in a Protracted War: An Economic Evaluation." *Air University Review*, May–June 1977, pp 2–18.

Gray, Colin S. "What Hath RAND Wrought?" *Military Review*, May 1972, pp 22–33.

Guilmartin, John F., Jr. "Bombing the Ho Chi Minh Trail: A Preliminary Analysis of the Effects of Air Interdiction," *Air Power History*, Winter 1991, pp 3–17.

Hamlin, Ross E. "Side-Firing Weapon Systems: A New Application of an Old Concept." *Air University Review*, January–February 1970, pp 76–88.

Messex, Curtis L. "Night on the Trail," *Air Force Magazine*, January 1972, pp 56–60.

Osur, Alan M. "Black-White Relations in the U. S. Military, 1940–1972." *Air University Review*, November–December 1981, pp 69–78.

Sesser, Stan. "A Reporter at Large: Forgotten Country." *The New Yorker*, August 20, 1990, pp 39–68.

Tilford, Earl H., Jr. "Setup: Why and How the U.S. Air Force Got Lost in Vietnam," *Armed Forces and Society*, Spring 1991, pp 327–42.

Weiss, George. "Laos Truck Kills Approach 25,000 Mark," *Armed Forces Journal*, May 3, 1971, p 15.

Yudkin, Richard A. "Vietnam: Policy, Strategy, and Air Power," *Air Force Magazine*, February 1973, pp 31–35.

Index

Numbers in ***bold italic*** indicate illustrations.

Index

Index

Index

Index

South Vietnam. *See* Vietnamization and withdrawal.
South Vietnamese military units
  1st Division: 273
  2d Regiment: 273
  3d Marine Division: 273
Souvanna Phouma: 25, 34, 44, 102, 117, 120, *163*, 181, 244, 263–64
Soviet Union
  intelligence ships: 137, *165*, 192
  provides support for North Vietnam: 3, 37, 99, 133, 173–74, 176, 195, 215, 296
  relations with China: 298
Sparky forward air controllers: 124–26. *See also* Forward air controllers.
Starbird, Lt. Gen. Alfred E., USA: 9, 29
Steel Tiger: 26, 43, 44, 49–50, 51–52, 123, 131
Stennis, Senator John C. (D-Mississippi): 11, 12, 14
Strategic Air Command: 95, 213
Studies and Observations Group: 31, 136, 241, 242, 244, 246
Stung Treng, Cambodia: 193
Sullivan, Leonard, Jr.: 21–22, 24, 68, 194–95, 196, 198–99, 200, 203, 221–23, 232, 234, 238, 240–41, 248–50, 252–54, 256, 259–60, 262, 264
Sullivan, William H.: 25, 30, 33, 34, 38, 42, 43–50, 51, 55, 102, 118, 167, 243–44, 279, 301
Sycamore: 104, 105, 107, 111, 113, 124. *See also* Task Force Alpha.

Tacan: 39
Tactical Air Command: 61, 85, 255–57, 256
Tailwind, Operation: 145
Tan Son Nhut Air Base, South Vietnam: 32, 37, 90, 124
Tapparo, Frank A.: 257
Task Force Alpha. *See also* Interdiction campaigns, Commando Hunt; Interdiction campaigns, Commando Bolt.
  concentrates on trucks: 23, 24, 147
  direct control of strikes: 103–5, 124–25, 226
  and embassy: 43, 132
  Igloo White 19, 31, 34, 36, 75, 103, 172, 176, 280, 282
  Infiltration Surveillance Center: *82*
    capabilities: 23, 188–89
    confirms targets: 37–38
    Headshed cell: 224, 225, 226

improvements: 107–8, 223
    intelligence value: 113, 148, 236
    staffing reductions: 143
    Termite cell: 224, 225, 226
  intelligence from more than sensor data: 37, 38, 105
  invasion impact: 234–35, 279, 302
  and Khe Sanh siege: 17, 19, 22
  missions and responsibilities: 24, 26, 27, 37, 43, 75, 84, 105, 106, 108, 115, 143, 147, 148, 155, 179, 197, 225, 228, 235, 268–73
  modifications: 84, 88, 103, 126, 147, 148, 179, 188, 223, 228–29
  operation direction: 20–21, 23–24, 37, 103–5, 113, 115, 123–25, 148, 170, 178, 179, 223–24, 225–26
  performance: 24, 112, 115, 131–32, 148, 220–23, 235–36
  personnel infiltration: 19–20, 22, 161, 185–86, 189–92, 197–203, 265
  phaseout: 249, 267, 268, 279–82
  and roadwatch teams: 30, 111–12
  Sycamore: 104, 105, 107, 111, 113, 124
Taylor, Maxwell D.: 15, 58, 228. *See also* Wise Men.
Tchepone, Laos: 116, 121, 144, 260
  aerial defenses near: 29, 58, 70, 72, 92, 98, 130, 157, 167, 169, 218–19
  blocking belt site: 230–31
  defoliation near: 33, 120
  fighting near: 121, 144, 145
  during Lam Son 719: 149–52, 153, 154, 155, 238
  pipelines near: 124
  storage area and transshipment point: 5, 89, 91, 102, 107, 119, 153, 168
  waterways near: 168, 169, 170
Terry, Maj. Roland W.: 54
Tet attacks: 13–15, 17–18, 22, 23, 56, 59, *76*, 99, 109, 187, 188, 234
Thanh Hoa, North Vietnam: 36
Thayer, Thomas C.: 297
Thompson, Lt. Col. Paul D.: 145
Thot Not patrols: 247, 248. *See also* Salem House patrols; Reconnaissance teams.
Tiger Hound: 26, 167
Toan Thang, Operation: 138
Tonkin Gulf: 87, 140, 213
Tonkin Gulf Resolution: 140, 141
Traffic control points. *See* Choke points; Interdiction points; Road cuts.

364